SOLUTI
MANUAL
FOR

JONATHAN BERK
Stanford University

PETER DEMARZO
Stanford University

Accuracy Editors

MARK SIMONSON
Arizona State University

TIMOTHY SULLIVAN
Bentley University

Pearson Prentice Hall

Boston San Francisco New York
London Toronto Sydney Tokyo Singapore Madrid
Mexico City Munich Paris Cape Town Hong Kong Montreal

Acquisitions Editor: Tessa O'Brien
Executive Developmental Editor: Rebecca Ferris-Caruso
Production Editor: Alison Eusden
Manufacturing Buyer: Linda Cox

This work is protected by United States copyright laws and is provided solely for the use of instructors in teaching their courses and assessing student learning. Dissemination or sale of any part of this work (including on the World Wide Web) will destroy the integrity of the work and is not permitted. The work and materials from it should never be made available to students except by instructors using the accompanying text in their classes. All recipients of this work are expected to abide by these restrictions and to honor the intended pedagogical purposes and the needs of other instructors who rely on these materials.

Prentice Hall
is an imprint of

www.pearsonhighered.com

1 2 3 4 5 6 BB 13 12 11 10

ISBN-13: 978-0-13-610399-8
ISBN-10: 0-13-610399-5

Contents

Chapter 1
The Corporation

1-1. **What is the most important difference between a corporation and *all* other organization forms?**
A corporation is a legal entity separate from its owners. This means ownership shares in the corporation can be freely traded. None of the other organizational forms share this characteristic.

1-2. **What does the phrase *limited liability* mean in a corporate context?**
Owners' liability is limited to the amount they invested in the firm. Stockholders are not responsible for any encumbrances of the firm; in particular, they cannot be required to pay back any debts incurred by the firm.

1-3. **Which organization forms give their owners limited liability?**
Corporations and limited liability companies give owners limited liability. Limited partnerships provide limited liability for the limited partners, but not for the general partners.

1-4. **What are the main advantages and disadvantages of organizing a firm as a corporation?**
Advantages: Limited liability, liquidity, infinite life
Disadvantages: Double taxation, separation of ownership and control

1-5. **Explain the difference between an S corporation and a C corporation.**
C corporations much pay corporate income taxes; S corporations do not pay corporate taxes but must pass through the income to shareholders to whom it is taxable. S corporations are also limited to 75 shareholders and cannot have corporate or foreign stockholders.

1-6. **You are a shareholder in a C corporation. The corporation earns $2 per share before taxes. Once it has paid taxes it will distribute the rest of its earnings to you as a dividend. The corporate tax rate is 40% and the personal tax rate on (both dividend and non-dividend) income is 30%. How much is left for you after all taxes are paid?**
First the corporation pays the taxes. After taxes, $\$2 \times (1-0.4) = \$1.20$ is left to pay dividends. Once the dividend is paid, personal tax on this must be paid, which leaves $\$1.20 \times (1-0.3) = \$0.84$. So after all the taxes are paid, you are left with 84¢.

1-7. **Repeat Problem 6 assuming the corporation is an S corporation.**
An S corporation does not pay corporate income tax. So it distributes $2 to its stockholders. These stockholders must then pay personal income tax on the distribution. So they are left with $\$2 \times (1-0.3) = \$1.40$.

1-8. You have decided to form a new start-up company developing applications for the iPhone. Give examples of the three distinct types of financial decisions you will need to make.

As the manager of an iPhone applications developer, you will make three types of financial decisions.

i. You will make investment decisions such as determining which type of iPhone application projects will offer your company a positive NPV and therefore your company should develop.

ii. You will make the decision on how to fund your iPhone application investments and what mix of debt and equity your company will have.

iii. You will be responsible for the cash management of your company, ensuring that your company has the necessary funds to make investments, pay interest on loans, and pay your employees.

1-9. Corporate managers work for the owners of the corporation. Consequently, they should make decisions that are in the interests of the owners, rather than their own. What strategies are available to shareholders to help ensure that managers are motivated to act this way?

Shareholders can do the following.

i. Ensure that employees are paid with company stock and/or stock options.

ii. Ensure that underperforming managers are fired.

iii. Write contracts that ensure that the interests of the managers and shareholders are closely aligned.

iv. Mount hostile takeovers.

1-10. Suppose you are considering renting an apartment. You, the renter, can be viewed as an agent while the company that owns the apartment can be viewed as the principal. What principal-agent conflicts do you anticipate? Suppose, instead, that you work for the apartment company. What features would you put into the lease agreement that would give the renter incentives to take good care of the apartment?

The agent (renter) will not take the same care of the apartment as the principal (owner), because the renter does not share in the costs of fixing damage to the apartment. To mitigate this problem, having the renter pay a deposit should motivate the renter to keep damages to a minimum. The deposit forces the renter to share in the costs of fixing any problems that are caused by the renter.

1-11. You are the CEO of a company and you are considering entering into an agreement to have your company buy another company. You think the price might be too high, but you will be the CEO of the combined, much larger company. You know that when the company gets bigger, your pay and prestige will increase. What is the nature of the agency conflict here and how is it related to ethical considerations?

There is an ethical dilemma when the CEO of a firm has opposite incentives to those of the shareholders. In this case, you (as the CEO) have an incentive to potentially overpay for another company (which would be damaging to your shareholders) because your pay and prestige will improve.

1-12. Are hostile takeovers necessarily bad for firms or their investors? Explain.

No. They are a way to discipline managers who are not working in the interests of shareholders.

1-13. What is the difference between a public and private corporation?

The shares of a public corporation are traded on an exchange (or "over the counter" in an electronic trading system) while the shares of a private corporation are not traded on a public exchange.

1-14. Explain why the bid-ask spread is a transaction cost.

Investors always buy at the ask and sell at the bid. Since ask prices always exceed bid prices, investors "lose" this difference. It is one of the costs of transacting. Since the market makers take the other side of the trade, they make this difference.

1-15. The following quote on Yahoo! Stock appeared on February 11, 2009, on Yahoo! Finance:

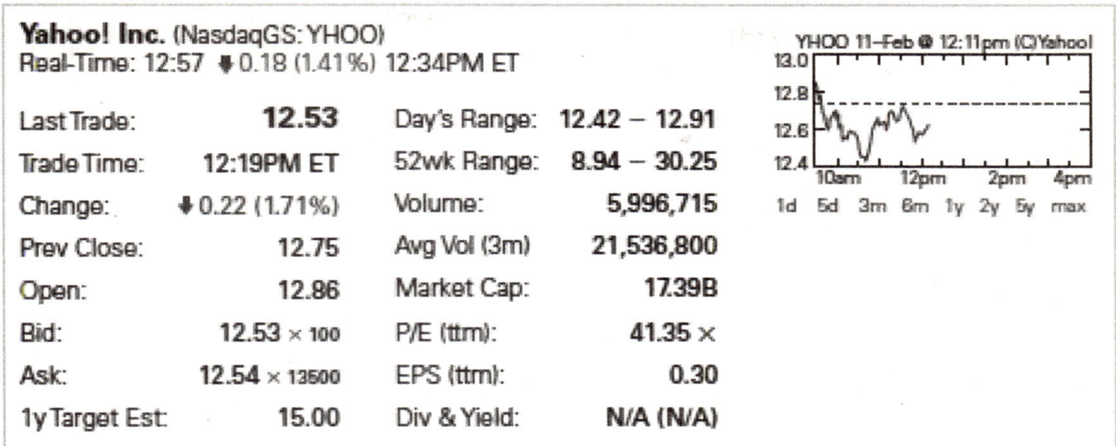

Yahoo! Inc. (NasdaqGS: YHOO)
Real-Time: 12:57 ⬇0.18 (1.41%) 12:34PM ET

Last Trade:	**12.53**	Day's Range:	12.42 – 12.91
Trade Time:	12:19PM ET	52wk Range:	8.94 – 30.25
Change:	⬇0.22 (1.71%)	Volume:	5,996,715
Prev Close:	12.75	Avg Vol (3m)	21,536,800
Open:	12.86	Market Cap:	17.39B
Bid:	12.53 × 100	P/E (ttm):	41.35 ×
Ask:	12.54 × 13500	EPS (ttm):	0.30
1y Target Est:	15.00	Div & Yield:	N/A (N/A)

If you wanted to buy Yahoo!, what price would you pay? How much would you receive if you wanted to sell Yahoo!?

You would buy at $12.54 and sell for $12.53.

Chapter 2

Introduction to Financial Statement Analysis

2-1. What four financial statements can be found in a firm's 10-K filing? What checks are there on the accuracy of these statements?

In a firm's 10-K filing, four financial statements can be found: the balance sheet, the income statement, the statement of cash flows, and the statement of stockholders' equity. Financial statements in form 10-K are required to be audited by a neutral third party, who checks and ensures that the financial statements are prepared according to GAAP and that the information contained is reliable.

2-2. Who reads financial statements? List at least three different categories of people. For each category, provide an example of the type of information they might be interested in and discuss why.

Users of financial statements include present and potential investors, financial analysts, and other interested outside parties (such as lenders, suppliers and other trade creditors, and customers). Financial managers within the firm also use the financial statements when making financial decisions.

Investors. Investors are concerned with the risk inherent in and return provided by their investments. Bondholders use the firm's financial statements to assess the ability of the company to make its debt payments. Stockholders use the statements to assess the firm's profitability and ability to make future dividend payments.

Financial analysts. Financial analysts gather financial information, analyze it, and make recommendations. They read financial statements to determine a firm's value and project future earnings, so that they can provide guidance to businesses and individuals to help them with their investment decisions.

Managers. Managers use financial statement to look at trends in their own business, and to compare their own results with that of competitors.

2-3. Find the most recent financial statements for Starbucks' corporation (SBUX) using the following sources:

a. From the company's Web site www.starbucks.com (*Hint*: Search for "investor relations.")

b. From the SEC Web site www.sec.gov. (*Hint*: Search for company filings in the EDGAR database.)

c. From the Yahoo! Finance Web site http://finance.yahoo.com.

d. From at least one other source. (*Hint*: Enter "SBUX 10K" at www.google.com.)

Each method will help find the same SEC filings. Yahoo! Finance also provides some analysis such as charts and key statistics.

2-4. Consider the following potential events that might have occurred to Global Conglomerate on December 30, 2009. For each one, indicate which line items in Global's balance sheet would be affected and by how much. Also indicate the change to Global's book value of equity.

a. Global used $20 million of its available cash to repay $20 million of its long-term debt.

b. A warehouse fire destroyed $5 million worth of uninsured inventory.

c. Global used $5 million in cash and $5 million in new long-term debt to purchase a $10 million building.

d. A large customer owing $3 million for products it already received declared bankruptcy, leaving no possibility that Global would ever receive payment.

e. Global's engineers discover a new manufacturing process that will cut the cost of its flagship product by over 50%.

f. A key competitor announces a radical new pricing policy that will drastically undercut Global's prices.

a. Long-term liabilities would decrease by $20 million, and cash would decrease by the same amount. The book value of equity would be unchanged.

b. Inventory would decrease by $5 million, as would the book value of equity.

c. Long-term assets would increase by $10 million, cash would decrease by $5 million, and long-term liabilities would increase by $5 million. There would be no change to the book value of equity.

d. Accounts receivable would decrease by $3 million, as would the book value of equity.

e. This event would not affect the balance sheet.

f. This event would not affect the balance sheet.

2-5. What was the change in Global Conglomerate's book value of equity from 2008 to 2009 according to Table 2.1? Does this imply that the market price of Global's shares increased in 2009? Explain.

Global Conglomerate's book value of equity increased by $1 million from 2008 to 2009. An increase in book value does not necessarily indicate an increase in Global's share price. The market value of a stock does not depend on the historical cost of the firm's assets, but on investors' expectation of the firm's future performance. There are many events that may affect Global's future profitability, and hence its share price, that do not show up on the balance sheet.

2-6. Use EDGAR to find Qualcomm's 10K filing for 2009. From the balance sheet, answer the following questions:

a. How much did Qualcomm have in cash and short-term investments?

b. What were Qualcomm's total accounts receivable?

c. What were Qualcomm's total assets?

d. What were Qualcomm's total liabilities? How much of this was long-term debt?

e. What was the book value of Qualcomm's equity?

a. $2,717 million (cash) and $8,352 million (short-term investments/marketable securities) for a total of $11,069 million

b. $700 million

c. $27,445 million

d. 7,129 million, nothing

e. $20,316 million

2-7. Find online the annual 10-K report for Peet's Coffee and Tea (PEET) for 2008. Answer the following questions from their balance sheet:

a. How much cash did Peet's have at the end of 2008?

b. What were Peet's total assets?

c. What were Peet's total liabilities? How much debt did Peet's have?

d. What was the book value of Peet's equity?

a. At the end of 2008, Peet's had cash and cash equivalents of $4.719 million.

b. Peet's total assets were $176.352 million.

c. Peet's total liabilities were $32.445 million, and it had no debt.

d. The book value of Peet's equity was $143.907 million.

2-8. In March 2005, General Electric (GE) had a book value of equity of $113 billion, 10.6 billion shares outstanding, and a market price of $36 per share. GE also had cash of $13 billion, and total debt of $370 billion. Four years later, in early 2009, GE had a book value of equity of $105 billion, 10.5 billion shares outstanding with a market price of $10.80 per share, cash of $48 billion, and total debt of $524 billion. Over this period, what was the change in GE's

a. market capitalization?

b. market-to-book ratio?

c. book debt-equity ratio?

d. market debt-equity ratio?

e. enterprise value?

a. 2005 Market Capitalization: 10.6 billion shares x $36.00/share = $381.6 billion. 2009 Market Capitalization: 10.5 billion shares x $10.80/share = $113.4. The change over the period is $113.4 - $381.6 = -$268.2 billion.

b. 2005 Market-to-Book $= \frac{381.6}{113} = 3.38$. 2009 Market-to-Book $= \frac{113.4}{105} = 1.08$. The change over the period is: 1.08 – 3.38 = -2.3.

c. 2005 Book Debt-to-Equity $= \frac{370}{113} = 3.27$. 2009 Book Debt-to-Equity $= \frac{524}{105} = 4.99$. The change over the period is: 4.99 – 3.27 = 1.72.

d. 2005 Market Debt-to-Equity $= \frac{370}{381.6} = 0.97$. 2009 Market Debt-to-Equity $= \frac{524}{113.4} = 4.62$. The change over the period is: 4.62 – 0.97 = 3.65.

e. 2005 Enterprise Value = $381.6 - 13 + 370 = $738.6 billion. 2009 Enterprise Value = $113.4 - 48 + 524 = $589.4 billion. The change over the period is: $589.4 – 738.6 = - $149.2 billion.

2-9. In July 2007, Apple had cash of $7.12 billion, current assets of $18.75 billion, current liabilities of $6.99 billion, and inventories of $0.25 billion.

a. What was Apple's current ratio?

b. What was Apple's quick ratio?

c. In July 2007, Dell had a quick ratio of 1.25 and a current ratio of 1.30. What can you say about the asset liquidity of Apple relative to Dell?

a. Apple's current ratio $= \dfrac{18.75}{6.99} = 2.68$

b. Apple's quick ratio $= \dfrac{18.75 - 0.25}{6.99} = 2.65$

c. Apple has significantly more liquid assets than Dell relative to current liabilities.

2-10. In November 2007, Abercrombie and Fitch (ANF) had a book equity of $1458 million, a price per share of $75.01, and 86.67 million shares outstanding. At the same time, The Gap (GPS) had a book equity of $5194 million, a share price of $20.09, and 798.22 million shares outstanding.

a. What is the market-to-book ratio of each of these clothing retailers?

b. What conclusions can you draw by comparing the two ratios?

a. ANF's market-to-book ratio $= \dfrac{75.01 \times 86.67}{1{,}458} = 4.59$

GPS's market-to-book ratio $= \dfrac{20.09 \times 798.22}{5{,}194} = 3.09$

b. The market values, in a relative sense, the outlook of Abercrombie and Fitch more favorably than it does The Gap. For every dollar of equity invested in ANF, the market values that dollar today at $4.59 versus $3.09 for a dollar invested in the GPS. Equity investors are willing to pay relatively more today for shares of ANF than for GPS because they expect ANF to produce superior performance in the future.

2-11. Find online the annual 10-K report for Peet's Coffee and Tea (PEET) for 2008. Answer the following questions from the income statement:

a. What were Peet's revenues for 2008? By what percentage did revenues grow from 2007?

b. What were Peet's operating and net profit margin in 2008? How do they compare with its margins in 2007?

c. What were Peet's diluted earnings per share in 2008? What number of shares is this EPS based on?

a. Increase in revenues $= \dfrac{284{,}822}{249{,}349} - 1 = 14.23\%$

b. Operating margin (2007) $= \dfrac{11{,}606}{249{,}349} = 4.66\%$

Operating margin (2008) $= \dfrac{17{,}001}{284{,}822} = 5.97\%$

Net profit margin (2007) $= \dfrac{8{,}377}{249{,}349} = 3.36\%$

Net profit margin (2008) $= \dfrac{11{,}165}{284{,}822} = 3.92\%$

Both margins increased compared with the year before.

c. The diluted earnings per share in 2008 was $0.80. The number of shares used in this calculation of diluted EPS was 13.997 million.

2-12. Suppose that in 2010, Global launches an aggressive marketing campaign that boosts sales by 15%. However, their operating margin falls from 5.57% to 4.50%. Suppose that they have no other income, interest expenses are unchanged, and taxes are the same percentage of pretax income as in 2009.

a. What is Global's EBIT in 2010?

b. What is Global's income in 2010?

c. If Global's P/E ratio and number of shares outstanding remains unchanged, what is Global's share price in 2010?

a. Revenues in 2009 = 1.15 × 186.7 = $214.705 million

EBIT = 4.50% × 214.705 = $9.66 million (there is no other income)

b. Net Income = EBIT – Interest Expenses – Taxes = (9.66 – 7.7) × (1 – 26%) = $1.45 million

c. Share price = (P/E Ratio in 2005) × (EPS in 2006) = $25.2 \times \left(\frac{1.45}{3.6}\right) = \$10.15$

2-13. Suppose a firm's tax rate is 35%.

a. What effect would a $10 million operating expense have on this year's earnings? What effect would it have on next year's earnings?

b. What effect would a $10 million capital expense have on this year's earnings if the capital is depreciated at a rate of $2 million per year for five years? What effect would it have on next year's earnings?

a. A $10 million operating expense would be immediately expensed, increasing operating expenses by $10 million. This would lead to a reduction in taxes of 35% × $10 million = $3.5 million. Thus, earnings would decline by 10 – 3.5 = $6.5 million. There would be no effect on next year's earnings.

b. Capital expenses do not affect earnings directly. However, the depreciation of $2 million would appear each year as an operating expense. With a reduction in taxes of 2 × 35% = $0.7 million, earnings would be lower by 2 – 0.7 = $1.3 million for each of the next 5 years.

2-14. You are analyzing the leverage of two firms and you note the following (all values in millions of dollars):

	Debt	Book Equity	Market Equity	Operating Income	Interest Expense
Firm A	500	300	400	100	50
Firm B	80	35	40	8	7

a. What is the market debt-to-equity ratio of each firm?

b. What is the book debt-to-equity ratio of each firm?

c. What is the interest coverage ratio of each firm?

d. Which firm may have more difficulty meeting its debt obligations? Explain.

a. **Firm A:** Market debt-equity ratio $= \frac{500}{400} = 1.25$

Firm B: Market debt-equity ratio $= \frac{80}{40} = 2.00$

b. **Firm A:** Book debt-equity ratio $= \frac{500}{300} = 1.67$

Firm B: Book debt-equity ratio $= \frac{80}{35} = 2.29$

c. **Firm A:** Interest coverage ratio $= \frac{100}{50} = 2.00$

Firm B: Interest coverage ratio $= \frac{8}{7} = 1.14$

d. Firm B has a lower coverage ratio and will have slightly more difficulty meeting its debt obligations than Firm A.

2-15. Quisco Systems has 6.5 billion shares outstanding and a share price of $18. Quisco is considering developing a new networking product in house at a cost of $500 million. Alternatively, Quisco can acquire a firm that already has the technology for $900 million worth (at the current price) of Quisco stock. Suppose that absent the expense of the new technology, Quisco will have EPS of $0.80.

a. Suppose Quisco develops the product in house. What impact would the development cost have on Quisco's EPS? Assume all costs are incurred this year and are treated as an R&D expense, Quisco's tax rate is 35%, and the number of shares outstanding is unchanged.

b. Suppose Quisco does not develop the product in house but instead acquires the technology. What effect would the acquisition have on Quisco's EPS this year? (Note that acquisition expenses do not appear directly on the income statement. Assume the firm was acquired at the start of the year and has no revenues or expenses of its own, so that the only effect on EPS is due to the change in the number of shares outstanding.)

c. Which method of acquiring the technology has a smaller impact on earnings? Is this method cheaper? Explain.

a. If Quisco develops the product in-house, its earnings would fall by $500 × (1 – 35%) = $325 million. With no change to the number of shares outstanding, its EPS would decrease by $\$0.05 = \frac{\$325}{6500}$ to $0.75. (Assume the new product would not change this year's revenues.)

b. If Quisco acquires the technology for $900 million worth of its stock, it will issue $900 / 18 = 50 million new shares. Since earnings without this transaction are $0.80 × 6.5 billion = $5.2 billion, its EPS with the purchase is $\frac{5.2}{6.55} = \$0.794$.

c. Acquiring the technology would have a smaller impact on earnings. But this method is not cheaper. Developing it in-house is less costly and provides an immediate tax benefit. The earnings impact is not a good measure of the expense. In addition, note that because the acquisition permanently increases the number of shares outstanding, it will reduce Quisco's earnings per share in future years as well.

2-16. In January 2009, American Airlines (AMR) had a market capitalization of $1.7 billion, debt of $11.1 billion, and cash of $4.6 billion. American Airlines had revenues of $23.8 billion. British

Airways (BABWF) had a market capitalization of $2.2 billion, debt of $4.7 billion, cash of $2.6 billion, and revenues of $13.1 billion.

a. **Compare the market capitalization-to-revenue ratio (also called the price-to-sales ratio) for American Airlines and British Airways.**

b. **Compare the enterprise value-to-revenue ratio for American Airlines and British Airways.**

c. **Which of these comparisons is more meaningful? Explain.**

a. Market capitalization-to-revenue ratio

$$= \frac{1.7}{23.8} = 0.07 \text{ for American Airlines}$$

$$= \frac{2.2}{13.1} = 0.17 \text{ for British Airways}$$

b. Enterprise value-to-revenue ratio

$$= \frac{(1.7 + 11.1 - 4.6)}{23.8} = 0.35 \text{ for American Airlines}$$

$$= \frac{(2.2 + 4.7 - 2.6)}{13.1} = 0.33 \text{ for British Airways}$$

c. The market capitalization to revenue ratio cannot be meaningfully compared when the firms have different amounts of leverage, as market capitalization measures only the value of the firm's equity. The enterprise value to revenue ratio is therefore more useful when firm's leverage is quite different, as it is here.

2-17. Find online the annual 10-K for Peet's Coffee and Tea (PEET) for 2008.

a. **Compute Peet's net profit margin, total asset turnover, and equity multiplier.**

b. **Use this data to compute Peet's ROE using the DuPont Identity.**

c. **If Peet's managers wanted to increase its ROE by one percentage point, how much higher would their asset turnover need to be?**

d. **If Peet's net profit margin fell by one percentage point, by how much would their asset turnover need to increase to maintain their ROE?**

a. $\text{Net profit margin} = \frac{11{,}165}{284{,}822} = 3.92\%$

$\text{Asset Turnover} = \frac{284{,}822}{176{,}352} = 1.62$

$\text{Asset Multiplier} = \frac{176{,}352}{143{,}907} = 1.23$

b. $\text{Peet's ROE (DuPont)} = 3.92\% \times 1.62 \times 1.23 = 7.81\%$

c. Peet's Revised ROE = 3.92% × 1.83 × 1.23 = 8.82%.

Peet's would need to increase asset turnover to 1.83 times.

d. Peet's Maintained ROE = 2.92% × 2.18 × 1.23 = 7.83%.

To maintain ROE at 7.81%, asset turnover would need to increase to 2.18 times (differences due to rounding).

2-18. Repeat the analysis of parts (a) and (b) in Problem 17 for Starbucks Coffee (SBUX). Use the DuPont Identity to understand the difference between the two firms' ROEs.

$$\text{Net profit margin} = \frac{315.5}{10,383.0} = 3.04\%$$

$$\text{Asset Turnover} = \frac{10,383}{5,672.6} = 1.83$$

$$\text{Asset Multiplier} = \frac{5,673.6}{2,490.9} = 2.28$$

Starbucks's ROE (DuPont) = 3.04% x 1.83% x 2.28% = 12.67%

The two firms' ROEs differ mainly because the firms have different asset multipliers, implying that the difference in the ROE might be due to leverage.

2-19. Consider a retailing firm with a net profit margin of 3.5%, a total asset turnover of 1.8, total assets of $44 million, and a book value of equity of $18 million.

a. What is the firm's current ROE?

b. If the firm increased its net profit margin to 4%, what would be its ROE?

c. If, in addition, the firm increased its revenues by 20% (while maintaining this higher profit margin and without changing its assets or liabilities), what would be its ROE?

a. 3.5 x 1.8 x 44/18 = 15.4%

b. 4 x 1.8 x 44/18 = 17.6%

c. 4 x (1.8*1.2) x 44/18 = 21.1%

2-20. Find online the annual 10-K report for Peet's Coffee and Tea (PEET) for 2008. Answer the following questions from their cash flow statement:

a. How much cash did Peet's generate from operating activities in 2008?

b. What was Peet's depreciation expense in 2008?

c. How much cash was invested in new property and equipment (net of any sales) in 2008?

d. How much did Peet's raise from the sale of shares of its stock (net of any purchases) in 2008?

a. Net cash provided by operating activities was $25.444 million in 2008.

b. Depreciation and amortization expenses were $15.113 million in 2008.

c. Net cash used in new property and equipment was $25.863 million in 2008.

d. Peet's raised $3.138 million from sale of shares of its stock, while it spent $20.627 million on the purchase of common stock. Net of purchases Peet's raised –$17.489 million from the sale of its shares of stock (net of any purchases).

2-21. Can a firm with positive net income run out of cash? Explain.

A firm can have positive net income but still run out of cash. For example, to expand its current production, a profitable company may spend more on investment activities than it generates from operating activities and financing activities. Net cash flow for that period would be negative, although its net income is positive. It could also run out of cash if it spends a lot on financing activities, perhaps by paying off other maturing long-term debt, repurchasing shares, or paying dividends.

2-22. See the cash flow statement here for H. J. Heinz (HNZ) (in $ thousands):

PERIOD ENDING	29-Oct-08	30-Jul-08	30-Apr-08	30-Jan-08
Net Income	**276,710**	**228,964**	**194,062**	**218,532**
Operating Activities, Cash Flows Provided By or Used In				
Depreciation	69,997	75,733	74,570	73,173
Adjustments to net income	14,359	(13,142)	48,826	(47,993)
Changes in accounts receivables	(38,869)	(53,218)	100,732	(84,711)
Changes in liabilities	82,816	(111,577)	201,725	39,949
Changes in inventories	(195,186)	(114,121)	85,028	57,681
Changes in other operating activities	17,675	(26,574)	12,692	(2,097)
Total Cash Flow from Operating Activities	**227,502**	**(13,935)**	**717,635**	**254,534**
Investing Activities, Cash Flows Provided By or Used In				
Capital expenditures	(82,584)	(41,634)	(100,109)	(69,170)
Investments	(5,465)	5,465	(93,153)	(48,330)
Other cash flows from investing activities	(108,903)	732	(58,069)	20,652
Total Cash Flows from Investing Activities	**(196,952)**	**(35,437)**	**(251,331)**	**(96,848)**
Financing Activities, Cash Flows Provided By or Used In				
Dividends paid	(131,483)	(131,333)	(119,452)	(121,404)
Sale purchase of stock	78,774	1,210	(76,807)	(79,288)
Net borrowings	515,709	114,766	(283,696)	64,885
Other cash flows from financing activities	(282)	2,000	(46,234)	39,763
Activities	**462,718**	**(13,357)**	**(526,189)**	**(96,044)**
Effect of exchange rate changes	(119,960)	(610)	32,807	6,890
Change in Cash and Cash Equivalents	**$373,308**	**(63,339)**	**(27,078)**	**$68,532**

a. **What were Heinz's cumulative earnings over these four quarters? What were its cumulative cash flows from operating activities?**

b. **What fraction of the cumulative cash flows from operating activities was used for investment over the four quarters?**

c. **What fraction of the cumulative cash flows from operating activities was used for financing activities over the four quarters?**

a. Heinz's cumulative earnings over these four quarters was $871 million. Its cumulative cash flows from operating activities was $1.19 billion

b. Fraction of cash from operating activities used for investment over the 4 quarters:

	29-Oct-08	30-Jul-08	30-Apr-08	30-Jan-08	4 quarters
Operating Activities	227,502	–13,935	717,635	254,534	1,185,736
Investing Activities	–196,952	–35,437	–251,331	–96,848	–580,568
CFI/CFO	86.57%	–254.30%	35.02%	38.05%	48.96%

c. Fraction of cash from operating activities used for financing over the 4 quarters:

	29-Oct-08	30-Jul-08	30-Apr-08	30-Jan-08	4 quarters
Operating Activities	227,502	–13,935	717,635	254,534	1,185,736
Financing Activities	462,718	–13,357	–526,189	–96,044	–1,050,885
CFF/CFO	–203.39%	–95.85%	79.32%	37.73%	14.58%

2-23. Suppose your firm receives a $5 million order on the last day of the year. You fill the order with $2 million worth of inventory. The customer picks up the entire order the same day and pays $1 million upfront in cash; you also issue a bill for the customer to pay the remaining balance of $4 million in 30 days. Suppose your firm's tax rate is 0% (i.e., ignore taxes). Determine the consequences of this transaction for each of the following:

a. Revenues

b. Earnings

c. Receivables

d. Inventory

e. Cash

a. Revenues: increase by $5 million

b. Earnings: increase by $3 million

c. Receivables: increase by $4 million

d. Inventory: decrease by $2 million

e. Cash: increase by $3 million (earnings) – $4 million (receivables) + $2 million (inventory) = $1 million (cash).

2-24. Nokela Industries purchases a $40 million cyclo-converter. The cyclo-converter will be depreciated by $10 million per year over four years, starting this year. Suppose Nokela's tax rate is 40%.

a. What impact will the cost of the purchase have on earnings for each of the next four years?

b. What impact will the cost of the purchase have on the firm's cash flow for the next four years?

a. Earnings for the next 4 years would have to deduct the depreciation expense. After taxes, this would lead to a decline of 10 × (1 – 40%) = $6 million each year for the next 4 years.

b. Cash flow for the next four years: less $36 million (–6 + 10 – 40) this year, and add $4 million (–6 + 10) for three following years.

2-25. The balance sheet information for Clorox Co. (CLX) in 2004–2005 is shown here, with data in $ thousands:

Balance Sheet:	31-Mar-05	31-Dec-04	30-Sep-04	30-Jun-04
Assets				
Current Assets				
Cash and cash equivalents	293,000	300,000	255,000	232,000
Net receivables	401,000	362,000	385,000	460,000
Inventory	374,000	342,000	437,000	306,000
Other current assets	60,000	43,000	53,000	45,000
Total Current Assets	**1,128,000**	**1,047,000**	**1,130,000**	**1,043,000**
Long-term investments	128,000	97,000	—	200,000
Property, plant, and equipment	979,000	991,000	995,000	1,052,000
Goodwill	744,000	748,000	736,000	742,000
Other assets	777,000	827,000	911,000	797,000
Total Assets	**3,756,000**	**3,710,000**	**3,772,000**	**3,834,000**
Liabilities				
Current Liabilities				
Accounts payable	876,000	1,467,000	922,000	980,000
Short/current long-term debt	410,000	2,000	173,000	288,000
Other current liabilities	—	—	—	—
Total Current Liabilities	**1,286,000**	**1,469,000**	**1,095,000**	**1,268,000**
Long-term debt	2,381,000	2,124,000	474,000	475,000
Other liabilities	435,000	574,000	559,000	551,000
Total Liabilities	**4,102,000**	**4,167,000**	**2,128,000**	**2,294,000**
Total Stockholder Equity	**–346,000**	**–457,000**	**1,644,000**	**1,540,000**
Total Liabilities & Stockholder Equity	**$3,756,000**	**$3,710,000**	**$3,772,000**	**$3,834,000**

a. **What change in the book value of Clorox's equity took place at the end of 2004?**

b. **Is Clorox's market-to-book ratio meaningful? Is its book debt-equity ratio meaningful? Explain.**

c. **Find online Clorox's other financial statements from that time. What was the cause of the change to Clorox's book value of equity at the end of 2004?**

d. **Does Clorox's book value of equity in 2005 imply that the firm is unprofitable? Explain.**

a. The book value of Clorox's equity decreased by $2.101 billion compared with that at the end of previous quarter, and was negative.

b. Because the book value of equity is negative in this case, Clorox's market-to-book ratio and its book debt-equity ratio are not meaningful. Its market debt-equity ratio may be used in comparison.

c. Information from the statement of cash flows helped explain that the decrease of book value of equity resulted from an increase in debt that was used to repurchase $2.110 billion worth of the firm's shares.

d. Negative book value of equity does not necessarily mean the firm is unprofitable. Loss in gross profit is only one possible cause. If a firm borrows to repurchase shares or invest in intangible assets (such as R&D), it can have a negative book value of equity.

2-26. Find online the annual 10-K report for Peet's Coffee and Tea (PEET) for 2008. Answer the following questions from the notes to their financial statements:

a. **What was Peet's inventory of green coffee at the end of 2008?**

b. **What property does Peet's lease? What are the minimum lease payments due in 2009?**

c. **What was the fair value of all stock-based compensation Peet's granted to employees in 2008? How many stock options did Peet's have outstanding at the end of 2008?**

d. What fraction of Peet's 2008 sales came from specialty sales rather than its retail stores? What fraction came from coffee and tea products?

a. Peet's coffee carried $17.732 million of green coffee beans in their inventory at the end of 2008.

b. Peet's leases its Emeryville, California, administrative offices and its retail stores and certain equipment under operating leases that expire from 2009 through 2019. The minimum lease payments due in 2009 are $15.222 million.

c. The fair value of all stock-based compensation Peet's granted to its employees in 2008 is $2.711 million. Peet's had 2,696,019 stock options outstanding at the end of 2008.

d. 34.1% of Peet's 2008 sales came from specialty sales rather than its retail stores. 53% of Peet's 2008 sales came from coffee and tea products.

2-27. Find online the annual 10-K report for Peet's Coffee and Tea (PEET) for 2008.

a. Which auditing firm certified these financial statements?

b. Which officers of Peet's certified the financial statements?

a. Deloitte & Touche LLP certified Peet's financial statements.

b. The CEO, Patrick J. O'Dea, and the CFO, Thomas P. Cawley certified Peet's financial statements.

2-28. WorldCom reclassified $3.85 billion of operating expenses as capital expenditures. Explain the effect this reclassification would have on WorldCom's cash flows. (*Hint:* Consider taxes.) WorldCom's actions were illegal and clearly designed to deceive investors. But if a firm could legitimately choose how to classify an expense for tax purposes, which choice is truly better for the firm's investors?

By reclassifying $3.85 billion operating expenses as capital expenditures, WorldCom increased its net income but lowered its cash flow for that period. If a firm could legitimately choose how to classify an expense, expensing as much as possible in a profitable period rather than capitalizing them will save more on taxes, which results in higher cash flows, and thus is better for the firm's investors.

Chapter 3

Arbitrage and Financial Decision Making

3-1. Honda Motor Company is considering offering a $2000 rebate on its minivan, lowering the vehicle's price from $30,000 to $28,000. The marketing group estimates that this rebate will increase sales over the next year from 40,000 to 55,000 vehicles. Suppose Honda's profit margin with the rebate is $6000 per vehicle. If the change in sales is the only consequence of this decision, what are its costs and benefits? Is it a good idea?

The benefit of the rebate is tat Honda will sell more vehicles and earn a profit on each additional vehicle sold:

Benefit = Profit of $6,000 per vehicle × 15,000 additional vehicles sold = $90 million.

The cost of the rebate is that Honda will make less on the vehicles it would have sold:

Cost = Loss of $2,000 per vehicle × 40,000 vehicles that would have sold without rebate = $80 million.

Thus, Benefit – Cost = $90 million – $80 million = $10 million, and offering the rebate looks attractive.

(Alternatively, we could view it in terms of total, rather than incremental, profits. The benefit as $6000/vehicle × 55,000 sold = $330 million, and the cost is $8,000/vehicle × 40,000 sold = $320 million.)

3-2. You are an international shrimp trader. A food producer in the Czech Republic offers to pay you 2 million Czech koruna today in exchange for a year's supply of frozen shrimp. Your Thai supplier will provide you with the same supply for 3 million Thai baht today. If the current competitive market exchange rates are 25.50 koruna per dollar and 41.25 baht per dollar, what is the value of this deal?

Czech buyer's offer = 2,000,000 CZK / (25.50 CZK/USD) = 78,431.37 USD

Thai supplier's offer = 3,000,000 THB / (41.25 THB/USD) = 72,727.27 USD

The value of the deal is $78,431 – 72,727 = $5704 today.

3-3. Suppose the current market price of corn is $3.75 per bushel. Your firm has a technology that can convert 1 bushel of corn to 3 gallons of ethanol. If the cost of conversion is $1.60 per bushel, at what market price of ethanol does conversion become attractive?

The price in which ethanol becomes attractive is ($3.75 + $1.60 / bushel of corn) / (3 gallons of ethanol / bushel of corn) = $1.78 per gallon of ethanol.

3-4. Suppose your employer offers you a choice between a $5000 bonus and 100 shares of the company stock. Whichever one you choose will be awarded today. The stock is currently trading for $63 per share.

a. Suppose that if you receive the stock bonus, you are free to trade it. Which form of the bonus should you choose? What is its value?

b. Suppose that if you receive the stock bonus, you are required to hold it for at least one year. What can you say about the value of the stock bonus now? What will your decision depend on?

a. Stock bonus = 100 × $63 = $6,300

Cash bonus = $5,000

Since you can sell (or buy) the stock for $6,300 in cash today, its value is $6,300 which is better than the cash bonus.

b. Because you could buy the stock today for $6,300 if you wanted to, the value of the stock bonus cannot be more than $6,300. But if you are not allowed to sell the company's stock for the next year, its value to you could be less than $6,300. Its value will depend on what you expect the stock to be worth in one year, as well as how you feel about the risk involved. You might decide that it is better to take the $5,000 in cash then wait for the uncertain value of the stock in one year.

3-5. You have decided to take your daughter skiing in Utah. The best price you have been able to find for a roundtrip air ticket is $359. You notice that you have 20,000 frequent flier miles that are about to expire, but you need 25,000 miles to get her a free ticket. The airline offers to sell you 5000 additional miles for $0.03 per mile.

a. Suppose that if you don't use the miles for your daughter's ticket they will become worthless. What should you do?

b. What additional information would your decision depend on if the miles were not expiring? Why?

a. The price of the ticket if you purchase it is $t. Price if you purchase the miles $p x 5000. So you should purchase the miles.

b. In part a, the existing miles are worthless if you don't use them. Now, they are not worthless, so you must add in the cost of using them. Because there is no competitive market price for these miles (you can purchase at 3¢ but not sell for that price) the decision will depend on how much you value the existing miles (which will depend on your likelihood of using them in the future).

3-6. Suppose the risk-free interest rate is 4%.

a. Having $200 today is equivalent to having what amount in one year?

b. Having $200 in one year is equivalent to having what amount today?

c. Which would you prefer, $200 today or $200 in one year? Does your answer depend on when you need the money? Why or why not?

a. Having $200 today is equivalent to having 200 × 1.04 = $208 in one year.

b. Having $200 in one year is equivalent to having 200 / 1.04 = $192.31 today.

c. Because money today is worth more than money in the future, $200 today is preferred to $200 in one year. This answer is correct even if you don't need the money today, because by investing the $200 you receive today at the current interest rate, you will have more than $200 in one year.

3-7. You have an investment opportunity in Japan. It requires an investment of $1 million today and will produce a cash flow of ¥ 114 million in one year with no risk. Suppose the risk-free interest rate in the United States is 4%, the risk-free interest rate in Japan is 2%, and the current competitive exchange rate is ¥ 110 per $1. What is the NPV of this investment? Is it a good opportunity?

Cost = $1 million today

Benefit = ¥114 million in one year

$$= ¥114 \text{ million in one year} \div \left(\frac{¥1.02 \text{ in one year}}{¥ \text{ today}}\right) = ¥111.76 \text{ million today}$$

$$= ¥111.76 \text{ million today} \div \left(\frac{110¥}{\$ \text{ today}}\right) = \$1.016 \text{ million today}$$

NPV = \$1.016 million – \$1 million = \$16,000

The NPV is positive, so it is a good investment opportunity.

3-8. Your firm has a risk-free investment opportunity where it can invest \$160,000 today and receive \$170,000 in one year. For what level of interest rates is this project attractive?

160,000 x (1+r) = 170,000 implies r = 170,000/160,000 – 1 = 6.25%

3-9. You run a construction firm. You have just won a contract to build a government office building. Building it will take one year and require an investment of \$10 million today and \$5 million in one year. The government will pay you \$20 million upon the building's completion. Suppose the cash flows and their times of payment are certain, and the risk-free interest rate is 10%.

a. What is the NPV of this opportunity?

b. How can your firm turn this NPV into cash today?

a. $NPV = PV_{Benefits} - PV_{Costs}$

$$PV_{Benefits} = \$20 \text{ million in one year} \div \left(\frac{\$1.10 \text{ in one year}}{\$ \text{ today}}\right)$$

$$= \$18.18 \text{ million}$$

$$PV_{\text{This year's cost}} = \$10 \text{ million today}$$

$$PV_{\text{Next year's cost}} = \$5 \text{ million in one year} \div \left(\frac{\$1.10 \text{ in one year}}{\$ \text{ today}}\right)$$

$$= \$4.55 \text{ million today}$$

$$NPV = 18.18 - 10 - 4.55 = \$3.63 \text{ million today}$$

b. The firm can borrow \$18.18 million today, and pay it back with 10% interest using the \$20 million it will receive from the government (18.18 × 1.10 = 20). The firm can use \$10 million of the 18.18 million to cover its costs today and save \$4.55 million in the bank to earn 10% interest to cover its cost of 4.55 × 1.10 = \$5 million next year.

This leaves 18.18 – 10 – 4.55 = \$3.63 million in cash for the firm today.

3-10. Your firm has identified three potential investment projects. The projects and their cash flows are shown here:

Project	Cash Flow Today (\$)	Cash Flow in One Year (\$)
A	–10	20
B	5	5
C	20	–10

Suppose all cash flows are certain and the risk-free interest rate is 10%.

a. What is the NPV of each project?

b. If the firm can choose only one of these projects, which should it choose?

c. If the firm can choose any two of these projects, which should it choose?

a. $$NPV_A = -10 + \frac{20}{1.1} = \$8.18$$

$$NPV_B = 5 + \frac{5}{1.1} = \$9.55$$

$$NPV_C = 20 - \frac{10}{1.1} = \$10.91$$

b. If only one of the projects can be chosen, project C is the best choice because it has the highest NPV.

c. If two of the projects can be chosen, projects B and C are the best choice because they offer a higher total NPV than any other combinations.

3-11. Your computer manufacturing firm must purchase 10,000 keyboards from a supplier. One supplier demands a payment of \$100,000 today plus \$10 per keyboard payable in one year. Another supplier will charge \$21 per keyboard, also payable in one year. The risk-free interest rate is 6%.

a. What is the difference in their offers in terms of dollars today? Which offer should your firm take?

b. Suppose your firm does not want to spend cash today. How can it take the first offer and not spend \$100,000 of its own cash today?

a. $$\text{Supplier 1: } PV_{\text{Costs}} = 100{,}000 + \$10 \times \frac{10{,}000}{1.06} = \$194{,}339.62$$

$$\text{Supplier 2: } PV_{\text{Costs}} = 21 \times \frac{10{,}000}{1.06} = \$198{,}113.21$$

Costs are lower under the first supplier's offer, so it is better choice.

b. The firm can borrow \$100,000 at 6% from a bank for one year to make the initial payment to the first supplier. One year later, the firm will pay back the bank \$106,000 (100,000 × 1.06) and the first supplier \$100,000 (10 × 10,000), for a total of \$206,000. This amount is less than the \$210,000 (21 × 10,000) the second supplier asked for.

3-12. Suppose Bank One offers a risk-free interest rate of 5.5% on both savings and loans, and Bank Enn offers a risk-free interest rate of 6% on both savings and loans.

a. What arbitrage opportunity is available?

b. Which bank would experience a surge in the demand for loans? Which bank would receive a surge in deposits?

c. What would you expect to happen to the interest rates the two banks are offering?

a. Take a loan from Bank One at 5.5% and save the money in Bank Enn at 6%.

b. Bank One would experience a surge in the demand for loans, while Bank Enn would receive a surge in deposits.

c. Bank One would increase the interest rate, and/or Bank Enn would decrease its rate.

3-13. Throughout the 1990s, interest rates in Japan were lower than interest rates in the United States. As a result, many Japanese investors were tempted to borrow in Japan and invest the proceeds in the United States. Explain why this strategy does not represent an arbitrage opportunity.

There is exchange rate risk. Engaging in such transactions may incur a loss if the value of the dollar falls relative to the yen. Because a profit is not guaranteed, this strategy is not an arbitrage opportunity.

3-14. An American Depositary Receipt (ADR) is security issued by a U.S. bank and traded on a U.S. stock exchange that represents a specific number of shares of a foreign stock. For example, Nokia Corporation trades as an ADR with symbol NOK on the NYSE. Each ADR represents one share of Nokia Corporation stock, which trades with symbol NOK1V on the Helsinki stock exchange. If the U.S. ADR for Nokia is trading for $17.96 per share, and Nokia stock is trading on the Helsinki exchange for 14.78 € per share, use the Law of One Price to determine the current $/€ exchange rate.

We can trade one share of Nokia stock for $17.96 per share in the U.S. and €14.78 per share in Helsinki. By the Law of One Price, these two competitive prices must be the same at the current exchange rate. Therefore, the exchange rate must be:

$$\frac{\$17.96/\text{share of Nokia}}{€14.78/\text{share of Nokia}} = \$1.215/€ \text{ today.}$$

3-15. The promised cash flows of three securities are listed here. If the cash flows are risk-free, and the risk-free interest rate is 5%, determine the no-arbitrage price of each security before the first cash flow is paid.

Security	Cash Flow Today ($)	Cash Flow in One Year ($)
A	500	500
B	0	1000
C	1000	0

$$PV_{\text{Cash Flows of A}} = 500 + \frac{500}{1.05} = \$976.19$$

$$PV_{\text{Cash Flows of B}} = \frac{1000}{1.05} = \$952.38$$

$$PV_{\text{Cash Flows of C}} = \$1{,}000$$

While the total cash flows paid by each security is the same ($1000), securities A and B are worth less than $1000 because some or all of the money is received in the future.

3-16. An Exchange-Traded Fund (ETF) is a security that represents a portfolio of individual stocks. Consider an ETF for which each share represents a portfolio of two shares of Hewlett-Packard (HPQ), one share of Sears (SHLD), and three shares of General Electric (GE). Suppose the current stock prices of each individual stock are as shown here:

Stock	Current Market Price
HPQ	$28
SHLD	$40
GE	$14

a. What is the price per share of the ETF in a normal market?

b. If the ETF currently trades for $120, what arbitrage opportunity is available? What trades would you make?

c. **If the ETF currently trades for $150, what arbitrage opportunity is available? What trades would you make?**

a. We can value the portfolio by summing the value of the securities in it:

Price per share of ETF = 2 × $28 + 1 × $40 + 3 × $14 = $138

b. If the ETF currently trades for $120, an arbitrage opportunity is available. To take advantage of it, one should buy ETF for $120, sell two shares of HPQ, sell one share of SHLD, and sell three shares of GE. Total profit for such transaction is $18.

c. If the ETF trades for $150, an arbitrage opportunity is also available. It can be realized by buying two shares of HPQ, one share of SHLD, and three shares of GE, and selling one share of the ETF for $150. Total profit would be $12.

3-17. Consider two securities that pay risk-free cash flows over the next two years and that have the current market prices shown here:

Security	Price Today ($)	Cash Flow in One Year ($)	Cash Flow in Two Years ($)
B1	94	100	0
B2	85	0	100

a. **What is the no-arbitrage price of a security that pays cash flows of $100 in one year and $100 in two years?**

b. **What is the no-arbitrage price of a security that pays cash flows of $100 in one year and $500 in two years?**

c. **Suppose a security with cash flows of $50 in one year and $100 in two years is trading for a price of $130. What arbitrage opportunity is available?**

a. This security has the same cash flows as a portfolio of one share of B1 and one share of B2. Therefore, its no-arbitrage price is 94 + 85 = $179.

b. This security has the same cash flows as a portfolio of one share of B1 and five shares of B2. Therefore, its no-arbitrage price is 94 + 5 × 85 = $519

c. There is an arbitrage opportunity because the no-arbitrage price should be $132 (94 / 2 + 85). One should buy two shares of the security at $130/share and sell one share of B1 and two shares of B2. Total profit would be $4 (94 + 85 × 2 – 130 × 2).

3-18. Suppose a security with a risk-free cash flow of $150 in one year trades for $140 today. If there are no arbitrage opportunities, what is the current risk-free interest rate?

The PV of the security's cash flow is ($150 in one year)/(1 + *r*), where *r* is the one-year risk-free interest rate. If there are no arbitrage opportunities, this PV equals the security's price of $140 today.

Therefore,

$$\$140 \text{ today} = \frac{(\$150 \text{ in one year})}{(1+r)}$$

Rearranging:

$$\frac{(\$150 \text{ in one year})}{\$140 \text{ today}} = (1+r) = \$1.0714 \text{ in one year / \$ today, so } r = 7.14\%$$

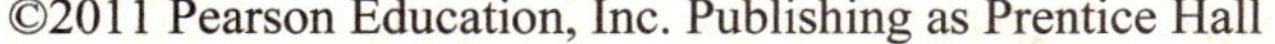

3-19. Xia Corporation is a company whose sole assets are $100,000 in cash and three projects that it will undertake. The projects are risk-free and have the following cash flows:

Project	Cash Flow Today ($)	Cash Flow in One Year ($)
A	–20,000	30,000
B	–10,000	25,000
C	–60,000	80,000

Xia plans to invest any unused cash today at the risk-free interest rate of 10%. In one year, all cash will be paid to investors and the company will be shut down.

a. What is the NPV of each project? Which projects should Xia undertake and how much cash should it retain?

b. What is the total value of Xia's assets (projects and cash) today?

c. What cash flows will the investors in Xia receive? Based on these cash flows, what is the value of Xia today?

d. Suppose Xia pays any unused cash to investors today, rather than investing it. What are the cash flows to the investors in this case? What is the value of Xia now?

e. Explain the relationship in your answers to parts (b), (c), and (d).

a. $$NPV_A = -20,000 + \frac{30,000}{1.1} = \$7,272.73$$

$$NPV_B = -10,000 + \frac{25,000}{1.1} = \$12,727.27$$

$$NPV_C = -60,000 + \frac{80,000}{1.1} = \$12,727.27$$

All projects have positive NPV, and Xia has enough cash, so Xia should take all of them.

b. Total value today = Cash + NPV(projects) = 100,000 + 7,272.73 + 12,727.27 + 12,727,27 = $132,727.27

c. After taking the projects, Xia will have 100,000 – 20,000 – 30,000 – 60,000 = $10,000 in cash left to invest at 10%. Thus, Xia's cash flows in one year = 30,000 + 25,000 + 80,000 + 10,000 × 1.1 = $146,000.

$$\text{Value of Xia today} = \frac{146,000}{1.1} = \$132,727.27$$

The same as calculated in b.

d. Unused cash = 100,000 – 20,000 – 30,000 – 60,000 = $10,000

Cash flows today = $10,000

Cash flows in one year = 30,000 + 25,000 + 80,000 = $135,000

$$\text{Value of Xia today} = 10,000 + \frac{135,000}{1.1} = \$132,727.27$$

e. Results from b, c, and d are the same because all methods value Xia's assets today. Whether Xia pays out cash now or invests it at the risk-free rate, investors get the same value today. The point is that a firm cannot increase its value by doing what investors can do by themselves (and is the essence of the separation principle).

A-1. **The table here shows the no-arbitrage prices of securities A and B that we calculated.**

		Cash Flow in One Year	
Security	**Market Price Today**	**Weak Economy**	**Strong Economy**
Security A	231	0	600
Security B	346	600	0

a. **What are the payoffs of a portfolio of one share of security A and one share of security B?**

b. **What is the market price of this portfolio? What expected return will you earn from holding this portfolio?**

a. $A+B$ pays \$600 in both cases (i.e., it its risk free).

b. Market price $= 231 + 346 = 577$. Expected return is $\dfrac{(600-577)}{577} = 4.0\%$ 3.98% risk-free interest rate.

A-2. **Suppose security C has a payoff of \$600 when the economy is weak and \$1800 when the economy is strong. The risk-free interest rate is 4%.**

a. **Security C has the same payoffs as what portfolio of the securities A and B in problem A.1?**

b. **What is the no-arbitrage price of security C?**

c. **What is the expected return of security C if both states are equally likely? What is its risk premium?**

d. **What is the difference between the return of security C when the economy is strong and when it is weak?**

e. **If security C had a risk premium of 10%, what arbitrage opportunity would be available?**

a. $C = 3A + B$

b. Price of $C = 3 \times 231 + 346 = 1039$

c. Expected payoff is $\dfrac{600}{2} + \dfrac{1,800}{2} = 1,200$. Expected return $= \dfrac{1,200 - 1,039}{1,039} = 15.5\%$

Risk premium $= 15.5 - 4 = 11.5\%$

d. Return when strong $= \dfrac{1,800 - 1,039}{1,039} = 73\%$, return when weak $= \dfrac{600 - 1039}{1039} = -42\%$

Difference $= 73 - (-42) = 115\%$

e. Price of C given 10% risk premium $= \dfrac{1,200}{1.14} = \$1,053$

Buy $3A + B$ for 1039, sell C for 1053, and earn a profit of $1,053 - 1,039 = \$14$.

A-3. **You work for Innovation Partners and are considering creating a new security. This security would pay out \$1000 in one year if the last digit in the closing value of the Dow Jones Industrial index in one year is an even number and zero if it is odd. The one-year risk-free interest rate is 5%. Assume that all investors are averse to risk.**

a. **What can you say about the price of this security if it were traded today?**

b. Say the security paid out $1000 if the last digit of the Dow is odd and zero otherwise. Would your answer to part (a) change?

c. Assume both securities (the one that paid out on even digits and the one that paid out on odd digits) trade in the market today. Would that affect your answers?

a. Whether the last digit in the Dow is odd or even has no correlation with the Dow index itself or anything else in the economy. Hence the payout of this security does not vary with anything else in the economy, so it will not have a risk premium. So the price of the security will be

$$\frac{\frac{1}{2}(1000)+\frac{1}{2}(0)}{1.05} = \$476.19.$$

b. No.

c. The answers would remain the same; however, in this case if the actual prices departed from $476.19, an arbitrage opportunity would result because by purchasing both securities you can create a riskless investment. The investment will only have a 5% return if the price of the basket of both securities is $476.19 x 2 =$952.38.

A-4. Suppose a risky security pays an expected cash flow of $80 in one year. The risk-free rate is 4%, and the expected return on the market index is 10%.

a. If the returns of this security are high when the economy is strong and low when the economy is weak, but the returns vary by only half as much as the market index, what risk premium is appropriate for this security?

b. What is the security's market price?

a. Half as variable $\Rightarrow$ half the risk premium of market $\Rightarrow$ risk premium is 3%

b. Market price $= \dfrac{\$80}{1+4\%+3\%} = \dfrac{\$80}{1.07} = \$74.77$

A-5. Suppose Hewlett-Packard (HPQ) stock is currently trading on the NYSE with a bid price of $28.00 and an ask price of $28.10. At the same time, a NASDAQ dealer posts a bid price for HPQ of $27.85 and an ask price of $27.95.

a. Is there an arbitrage opportunity in this case? If so, how would you exploit it?

b. Suppose the NASDAQ dealer revises his quotes to a bid price of $27.95 and an ask price of $28.05. Is there an arbitrage opportunity now? If so, how would you exploit it?

c. What must be true of the highest bid price and the lowest ask price for no arbitrage opportunity to exist?

a. There is an arbitrage opportunity. One would buy from the NASDAQ dealer at $27.95 and sell to NYSE dealer at $28.00, making profit of $0.05 per share.

b. There is no arbitrage opportunity.

c. To eliminate any arbitrage opportunity, the highest bid price should be lower then the lowest ask price.

A-6. Consider a portfolio of two securities: one share of Johnson and Johnson (JNJ) stock and a bond that pays $100 in one year. Suppose this portfolio is currently trading with a bid price of $141.65 and an ask price of $142.25, and the bond is trading with a bid price of $91.75 and an ask price of $91.95. In this case, what is the no-arbitrage price range for JNJ stock?

According to the law of one price, the price that portfolio of securities is trading is equal to the sum of the price of securities within the portfolio. If the portfolio, composed of a bond and JNJ stock is currently trading with a bid price of $141.65 and an ask price of $142.25, and the bond is trading at a bid price of \$91.75 and an ask price of \$91.95, then the no-arbitrage price of the stock should be between \$(141.65 – 91.95) and \$(142.25 – 91.75) or between \$49.70 and \$50.50.

At any price below \$49.90 or above \$50.30 an arbitrage opportunity would exist. For example, if the stock were currently trading at \$49, an investor could purchase the stock and the bond for \$49 + \$91.95 = \$140.95 and then immediately sell the portfolio for \$141.65 and have an arbitrage of \$141.65 – 140.95 = \$0.70. If the price of the stock was \$50.60, then an investor could purchase the portfolio for \$142.25 and sell the bond and stock individually for \$91.75 and \$50.60 respectively. The investor would gain an arbitrage of \$91.75 + \$50.60 – \$142.25 = \$0.10.

Chapter 4
The Time Value of Money

4-1. **You have just taken out a five-year loan from a bank to buy an engagement ring. The ring costs \$5000. You plan to put down \$1000 and borrow \$4000. You will need to make annual payments of \$1000 at the end of each year. Show the timeline of the loan from your perspective. How would the timeline differ if you created it from the bank's perspective?**

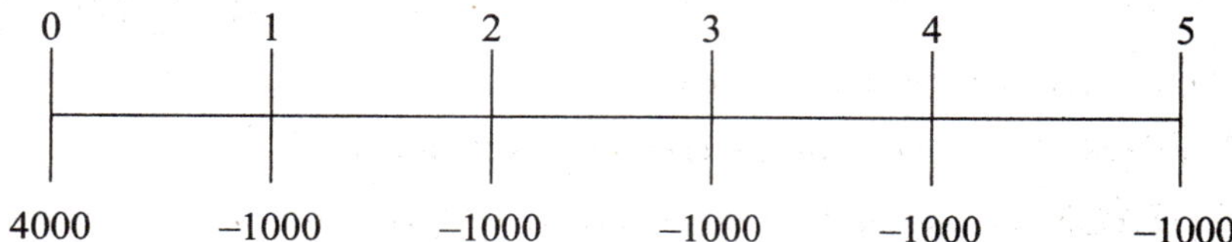

From the bank's perspective, the timeline is the same except all the signs are reversed.

4-2. **You currently have a four-year-old mortgage outstanding on your house. You make monthly payments of \$1500. You have just made a payment. The mortgage has 26 years to go (i.e., it had an original term of 30 years). Show the timeline from your perspective. How would the timeline differ if you created it from the bank's perspective?**

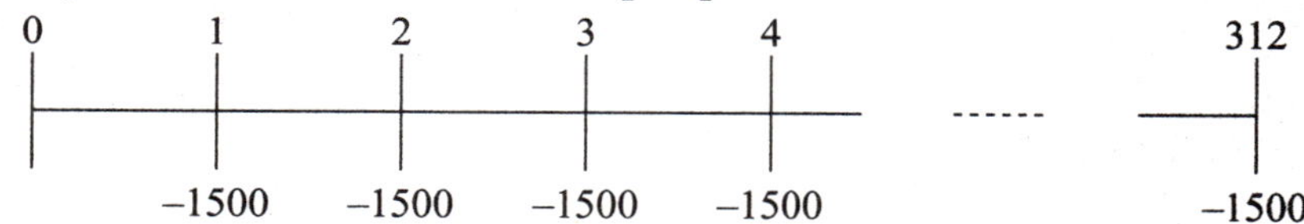

From the bank's perspective, the timeline would be identical except with opposite signs.

4-3. **Calculate the future value of \$2000 in**

a. **Five years at an interest rate of 5% per year.**

b. **Ten years at an interest rate of 5% per year.**

c. **Five years at an interest rate of 10% per year.**

d. **Why is the amount of interest earned in part (a) less than half the amount of interest earned in part (b)?**

a. Timeline:

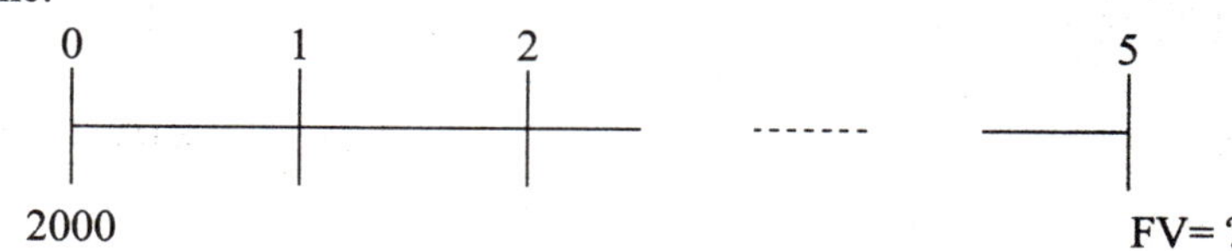

$FV_5 = 2,000 \times 1.05^5 = 2,552.56$

b. Timeline:

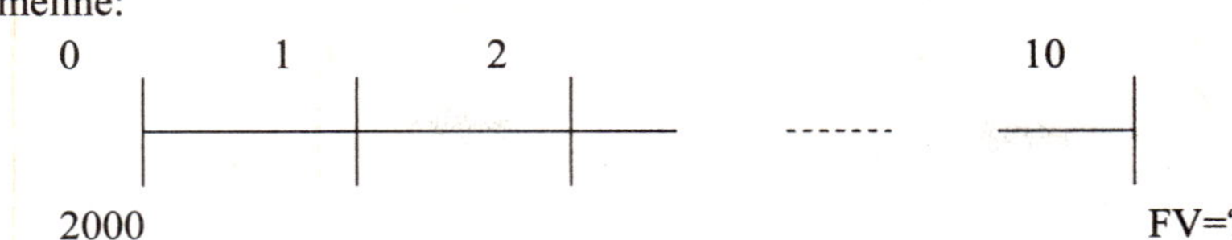

$$FV_{10} = 2,000 \times 1.05^{10} = 3,257.79$$

c. Timeline:

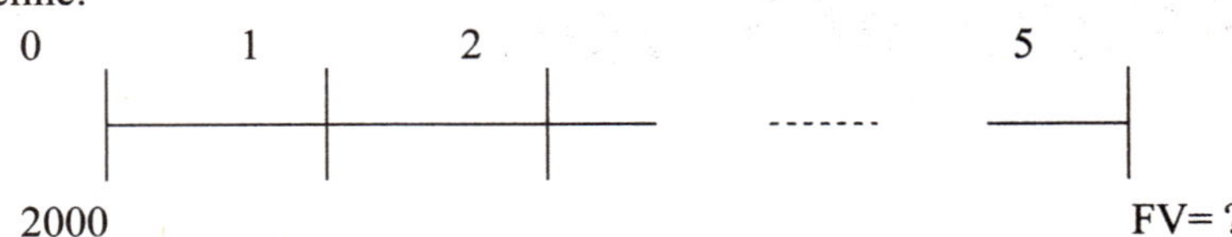

$$FV_5 = 2,000 \times 1.1^5 = 3,221.02$$

d. Because in the last 5 years you get interest on the interest earned in the first 5 years as well as interest on the original $2,000.

4-4. **What is the present value of $10,000 received**

a. Twelve years from today when the interest rate is 4% per year?

b. Twenty years from today when the interest rate is 8% per year?

c. Six years from today when the interest rate is 2% per year?

a. Timeline:

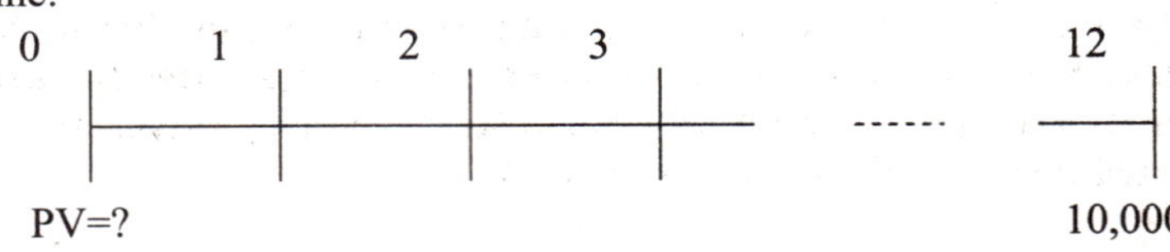

$$PV = \frac{10,000}{1.04^{12}} = 6,245.97$$

b. Timeline:

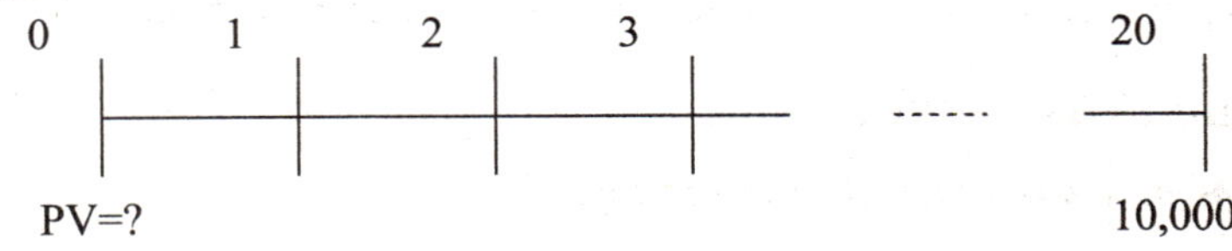

$$PV = \frac{10,000}{1.08^{20}} = 2,145.48$$

c. Timeline:

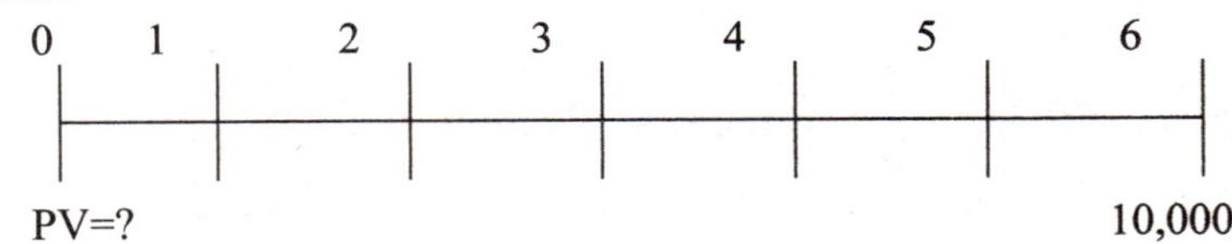

$$PV = \frac{10,000}{1.02^{6}} = 8,879.71$$

4-5. Your brother has offered to give you either $5000 today or $10,000 in 10 years. If the interest rate is 7% per year, which option is preferable?

Timeline:

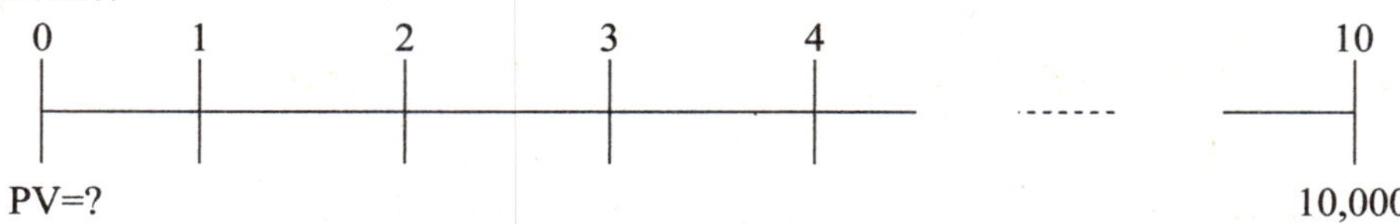

$$PV = \frac{10,000}{1.07^{10}} = 5,083.49$$

So the 10,000 in 10 years is preferable because it is worth more.

4-6. Consider the following alternatives:

i. $100 received in one year

ii. $200 received in five years

iii. $300 received in ten years

a. Rank the alternatives from most valuable to least valuable if the interest rate is 10% per year.

b. What is your ranking if the interest rate is only 5% per year?

c. What is your ranking if the interest rate is 20% per year?

a. Option ii > Option iii > Option i

rate		10%	
Amount	Years		PV
100		1	90.9090909
200		5	124.184265
300		10	115.662987

b. Option iii > Option ii > Option i

rate		5%	
Amount	Years		PV
100		1	95.2380952
200		5	156.705233
300		10	184.173976

c. Option i > Option ii > Option iii

rate	20%	
Amount	Years	PV
100	1	83.33333
200	5	80.37551
300	10	48.45167

4-7. Suppose you invest $1000 in an account paying 8% interest per year.

a. What is the balance in the account after 3 years? How much of this balance corresponds to "interest on interest"?

b. What is the balance in the account after 25 years? How much of this balance corresponds to interest on interest?

a. The balance after 3 years is $1259.71; interest on interest is $19.71.

b. The balance after 25 years is \$6848.48; interest on interest is \$3848.38.

rate	8%		
amt	1000		
years	1	3	25
balance	1080	1259.712	6848.475
simple interest	80	240	2000
interest on interest	0	19.712	3848.475

4-8. **Your daughter is currently eight years old. You anticipate that she will be going to college in 10 years. You would like to have \$100,000 in a savings account to fund her education at that time. If the account promises to pay a fixed interest rate of 3% per year, how much money do you need to put into the account today to ensure that you will have \$100,000 in 10 years?**

Timeline:

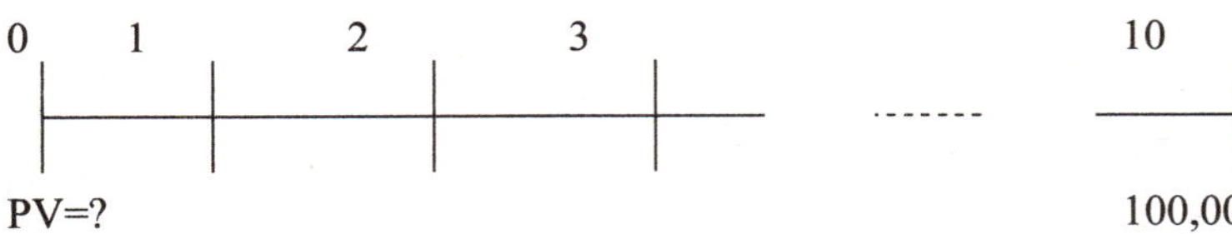

$$PV=\frac{100,000}{1.03^{10}}=74,409.39$$

4-9. **You are thinking of retiring. Your retirement plan will pay you either \$250,000 immediately on retirement or \$350,000 five years after the date of your retirement. Which alternative should you choose if the interest rate is**

a. 0% per year?

b. 8% per year?

c. 20% per year?

Timeline: Same for all parts

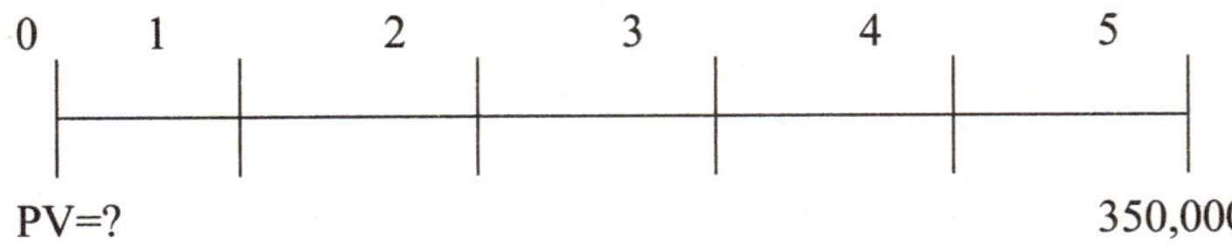

a. $$PV=\frac{350,000}{1.0^5}=350,000$$

So you should take the 350,000

b. $$PV=\frac{350,000}{1.08^5}=238,204$$

You should take the 250,000.

c. $$PV=\frac{350,000}{1.2^5}=140,657$$

You should take the 250,000.

4-10. Your grandfather put some money in an account for you on the day you were born. You are now 18 years old and are allowed to withdraw the money for the first time. The account currently has \$3996 in it and pays an 8% interest rate.

a. How much money would be in the account if you left the money there until your 25th birthday?

b. What if you left the money until your 65th birthday?

c. How much money did your grandfather originally put in the account?

a. Timeline:

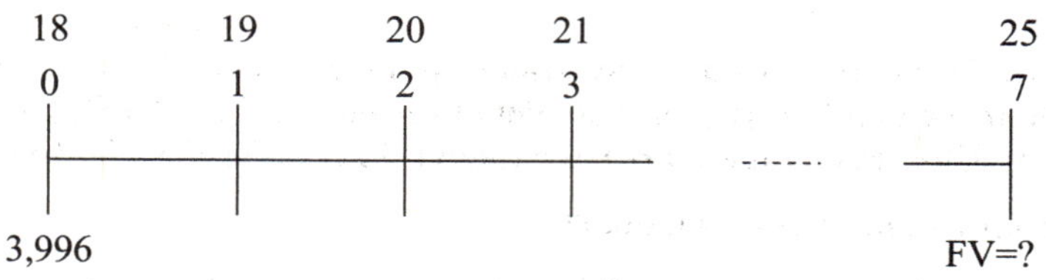

$$FV = 3,996(1.08)^7$$
$$= 6,848.44$$

b. Timeline:

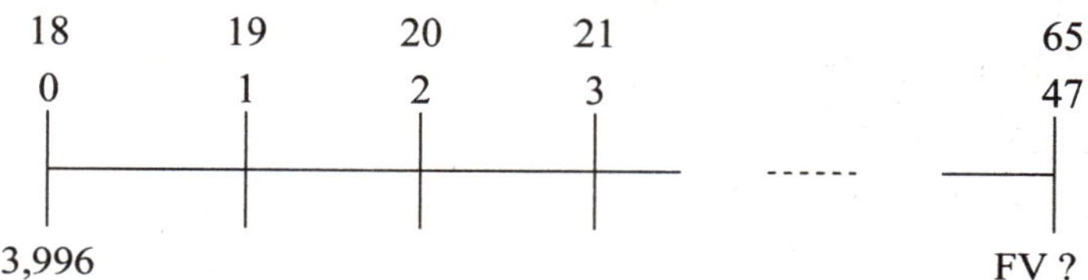

$$FV = 3,996(1.08)^{47} = 148,779$$

c. Timeline:

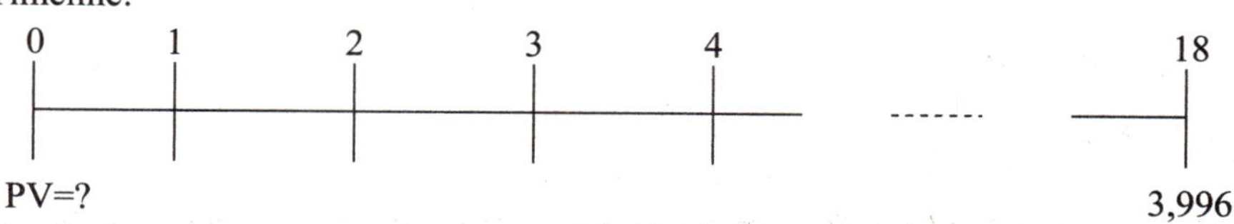

$$PV = \frac{3,996}{1.08^{18}} = 1,000$$

4-11. Suppose you receive \$100 at the end of each year for the next three years.

a. If the interest rate is 8%, what is the present value of these cash flows?

b. What is the future value in three years of the present value you computed in (a)?

c. Suppose you deposit the cash flows in a bank account that pays 8% interest per year. What is the balance in the account at the end of each of the next three years (after your deposit is made)? How does the final bank balance compare with your answer in (b)?

a. \$257.71

b. $324.64

c. $324.64

rate	8%			
year	0	1	2	3
cf		100	100	100
PV	$257.71			
FV				324.64
Bank Balance	0	100	208	324.64

4-12. You have just received a windfall from an investment you made in a friend's business. He will be paying you $10,000 at the end of this year, $20,000 at the end of the following year, and $30,000 at the end of the year after that (three years from today). The interest rate is 3.5% per year.

a. What is the present value of your windfall?

b. What is the future value of your windfall in three years (on the date of the last payment)?

a. Timeline:

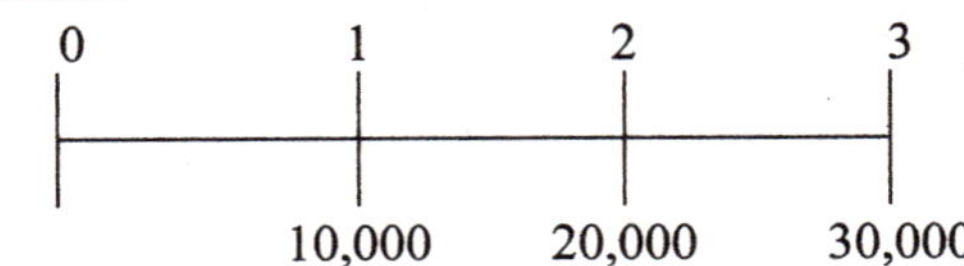

$$PV = \frac{10,000}{1.035} + \frac{20,000}{1.035^2} + \frac{30,000}{1.035^3}$$
$$= 9,662 + 18,670 + 27,058 = 55,390$$

b. Timeline:

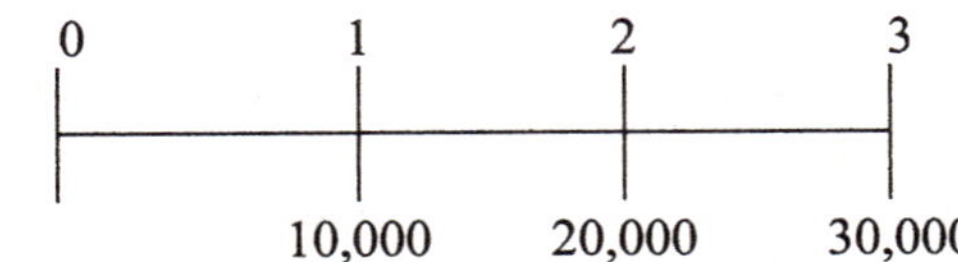

$$FV = 55,390 \times 1.035^3$$
$$= 61,412$$

4-13. You have a loan outstanding. It requires making three annual payments at the end of the next three years of $1000 each. Your bank has offered to allow you to skip making the next two payments in lieu of making one large payment at the end of the loan's term in three years. If the interest rate on the loan is 5%, what final payment will the bank require you to make so that it is indifferent between the two forms of payment?

Timeline:

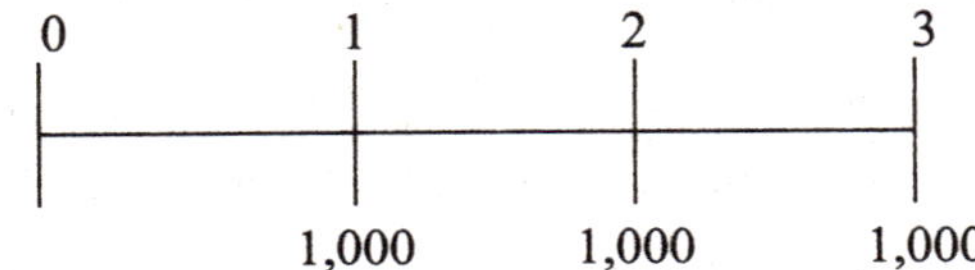

First, calculate the present value of the cash flows:

$$PV = \frac{1,000}{1.05} + \frac{1,000}{1.05^2} + \frac{1,000}{1.05^3} = 952 + 907 + 864 = 2,723$$

Once you know the present value of the cash flows, compute the future value (of this present value) at date 3.

$$FV_3 = 2,723 \times 1.05^3 = 3,152$$

4-14. You have been offered a unique investment opportunity. If you invest \$10,000 today, you will receive \$500 one year from now, \$1500 two years from now, and \$10,000 ten years from now.

a. What is the NPV of the opportunity if the interest rate is 6% per year? Should you take the opportunity?

b. What is the NPV of the opportunity if the interest rate is 2% per year? Should you take it now?

Timeline:

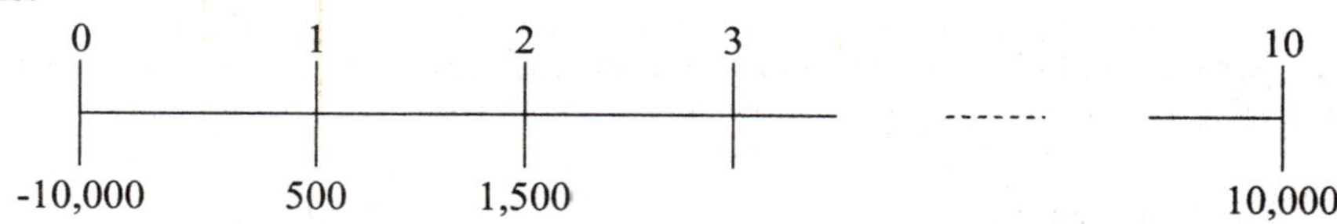

a. $$NPV = -10,000 + \frac{500}{1.06} + \frac{1,500}{1.06^2} + \frac{10,000}{1.06^{10}}$$

$$= -10,000 + 471.70 + 1,334.99 + 5,583.95 = -2,609.36$$

Since the NPV < 0, don't take it.

b. $$NPV = -10,000 + \frac{500}{1.02} + \frac{1,500}{1.02^2} + \frac{10,000}{1.02^{10}}$$

$$= -10,000 + 490.20 + 1,441.75 + 8,203.48 = 135.43$$

Since the NPV > 0, take it.

4-15. Marian Plunket owns her own business and is considering an investment. If she undertakes the investment, it will pay \$4000 at the end of each of the next three years. The opportunity requires an initial investment of \$1000 plus an additional investment at the end of the second year of \$5000. What is the NPV of this opportunity if the interest rate is 2% per year? Should Marian take it?

Timeline:

0	1	2	3
−1,000	4,000	−1,000	4,000

$$NPV = -1,000 + \frac{4,000}{(1.02)} - \frac{1,000}{(1.02)^2} + \frac{4,000}{(1.02)^3}$$

$$= -1,000 + 3,921.57 - 961.17 + 3,769.29 = 5,729.69$$

Yes, make the investment.

4-16. **Your buddy in mechanical engineering has invented a money machine. The main drawback of the machine is that it is slow. It takes one year to manufacture $100. However, once built, the machine will last forever and will require no maintenance. The machine can be built immediately, but it will cost $1000 to build. Your buddy wants to know if he should invest the money to construct it. If the interest rate is 9.5% per year, what should your buddy do?**

Timeline:

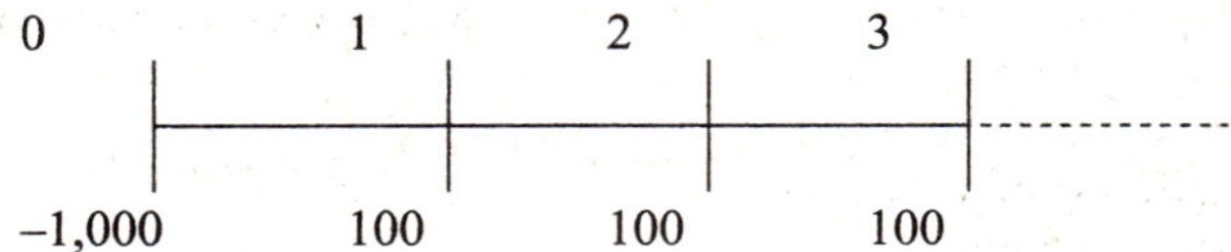

To decide whether to build the machine you need to calculate the NPV. The cash flows the machine generates are a perpetuity, so by the PV of a perpetuity formula:

$$PV = \frac{100}{0.095} = 1,052.63.$$

So the $NPV = 1,052.63 - 1,000 = 52.63$. He should build it.

4-17. **How would your answer to Problem 16 change if the machine takes one year to build?**

Timeline:

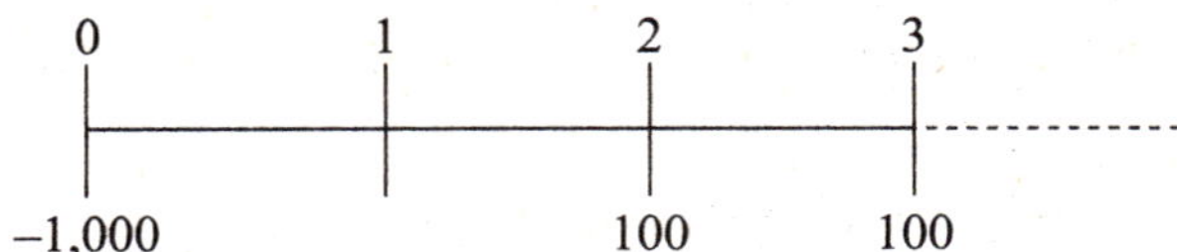

To decide whether to build the machine, you need to calculate the NPV: The cash flows the machine generates are a perpetuity with first payment at date 2. Computing the PV at date 1 gives

$$PV_1 = \frac{100}{0.095} = 1,052.63.$$

So the value today is

$$PV_0 = \frac{1,052.63}{1.095} = 961.31 \text{ So the } NPV = 961.31 - 1,000 = -38.69.$$

He should not build the machine.

4-18. **The British government has a consol bond outstanding paying £100 per year forever. Assume the current interest rate is 4% per year.**

a. **What is the value of the bond immediately after a payment is made?**

b. **What is the value of the bond immediately before a payment is made?**

Timeline:

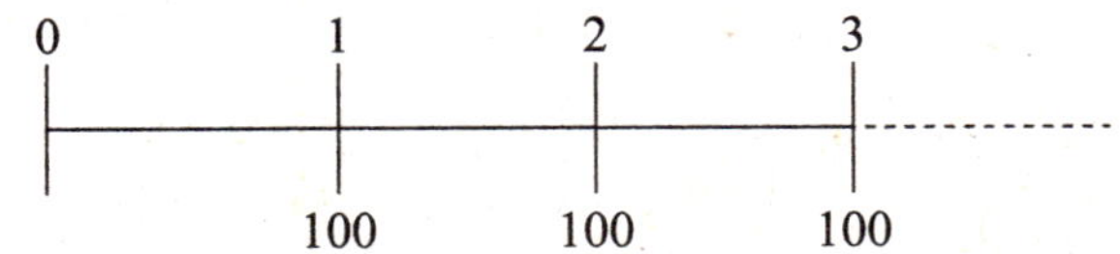

a. The value of the bond is equal to the present value of the cash flows. By the perpetuity formula:

$$PV = \frac{100}{0.04} = £2,500.$$

b. The value of the bond is equal to the present value of the cash flows. The cash flows are the perpetuity plus the payment that will be received immediately.

$PV = 100/0.04 + 100 = £2,600$

4-19. What is the present value of $1000 paid at the end of each of the next 100 years if the interest rate is 7% per year?

Timeline:

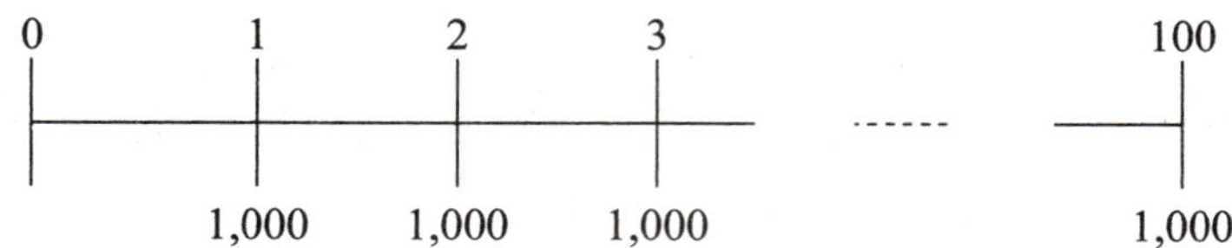

The cash flows are a 100 year annuity, so by the annuity formula:

$$PV = \frac{1,000}{0.07}\left(1 - \frac{1}{1.07^{100}}\right) = 14,269.25.$$

4-20. You are head of the Schwartz Family Endowment for the Arts. You have decided to fund an arts school in the San Francisco Bay area in perpetuity. Every five years, you will give the school $1 million. The first payment will occur five years from today. If the interest rate is 8% per year, what is the present value of your gift?

Timeline:

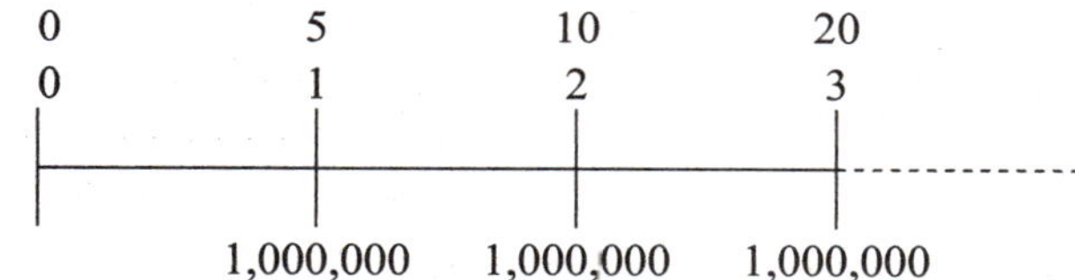

First we need the 5-year interest rate. If the annual interest rate is 8% per year and you invest $1 for 5 years you will have, by the 2nd rule of time travel, $(1.08)^5 = 1.4693\ 2808$. So the 5 year interest rate is 46.93%. The cash flows are a perpetuity, so:

$$PV = \frac{1,000,000}{0.46932808} = 2,130,833.$$

4-21. When you purchased your house, you took out a 30-year annual-payment mortgage with an interest rate of 6% per year. The annual payment on the mortgage is $12,000. You have just made a payment and have now decided to pay the mortgage off by repaying the outstanding balance. What is the payoff amount if

a. You have lived in the house for 12 years (so there are 18 years left on the mortgage)?

b. You have lived in the house for 20 years (so there are 10 years left on the mortgage)?

c. You have lived in the house for 12 years (so there are 18 years left on the mortgage) and you decide to pay off the mortgage immediately *before* the twelfth payment is due?

a. Timeline:

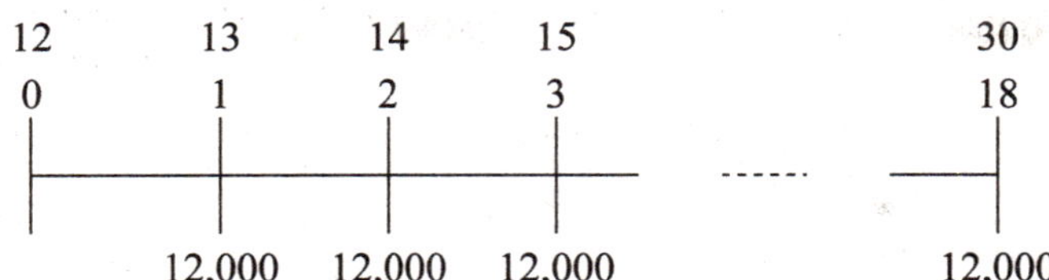

To pay off the mortgage you must repay the remaining balance. The remaining balance is equal to the present value of the remaining payments. The remaining payments are an 18-year annuity, so:

$$PV = \frac{12,000}{0.06}\left(1 - \frac{1}{1.06^{18}}\right)$$
$$= 129,931.24.$$

b. Timeline:

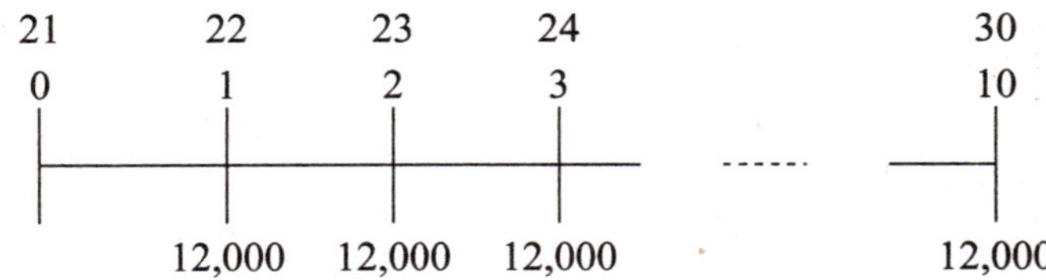

To pay off the mortgage you must repay the remaining balance. The remaining balance is equal to the present value of the remaining payments. The remaining payments are a 10 year annuity, so:

$$PV = \frac{12,000}{0.06}\left(1 - \frac{1}{1.06^{10}}\right) = 88,321.04.$$

c. Timeline:

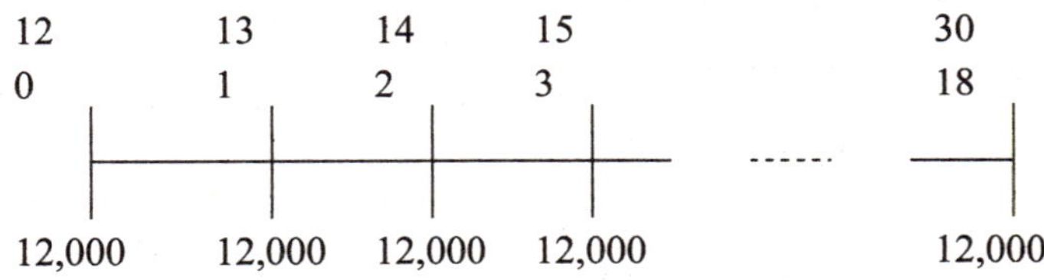

If you decide to pay off the mortgage immediately before the 12th payment, you will have to pay exactly what you paid in part (a) as well as the 12th payment itself:

$$129,931.24 + 12,000 = 141,931.24.$$

4-22. You are 25 years old and decide to start saving for your retirement. You plan to save $5000 at the end of each year (so the first deposit will be one year from now), and will make the last deposit when you retire at age 65. Suppose you earn 8% per year on your retirement savings.

a. How much will you have saved for retirement?

b. How much will you have saved if you wait until age 35 to start saving (again, with your first deposit at the end of the year)?

amount	$5,000	
rate	8%	
retirement age	65	
start age	25	35
Savings	1,295,282.59	566,416.06

4-23. Your grandmother has been putting \$1000 into a savings account on every birthday since your first (that is, when you turned 1). The account pays an interest rate of 3%. How much money will be in the account on your 18th birthday immediately after your grandmother makes the deposit on that birthday?

Timeline:

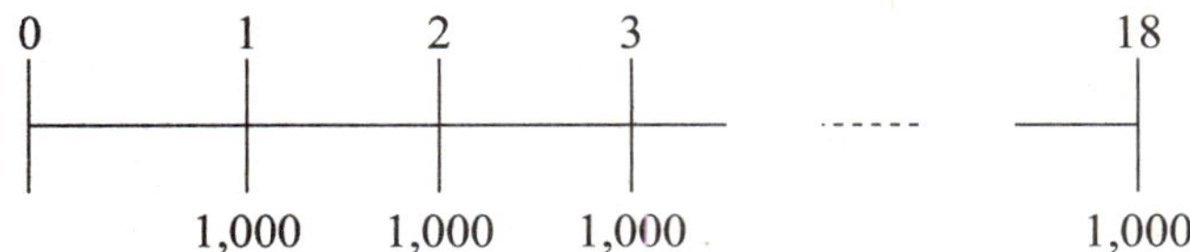

We first calculate the present value of the deposits at date 0. The deposits are an 18-year annuity:

$$\text{PV} = \frac{1,000}{0.03}\left(1 - \frac{1}{1.03^{18}}\right) = 13,753.51$$

Now, we calculate the future value of this amount:

$$\text{FV} = 13,753.51(1.03)^{18} = 23,414.43$$

4-24. A rich relative has bequeathed you a growing perpetuity. The first payment will occur in a year and will be \$1000. Each year after that, you will receive a payment on the anniversary of the last payment that is 8% larger than the last payment. This pattern of payments will go on forever. If the interest rate is 12% per year,

a. What is today's value of the bequest?

b. What is the value of the bequest immediately after the first payment is made?

a. Timeline:

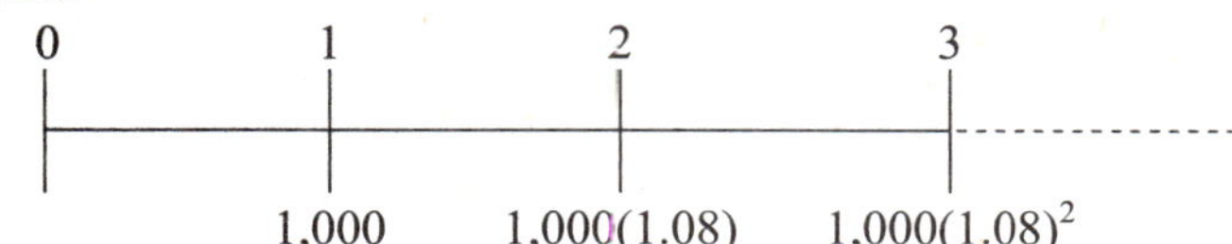

Using the formula for the PV of a growing perpetuity gives:

$$\text{PV} = \left(\frac{1,000}{0.12 - 0.08}\right) = 25,000.$$

b. Timeline:

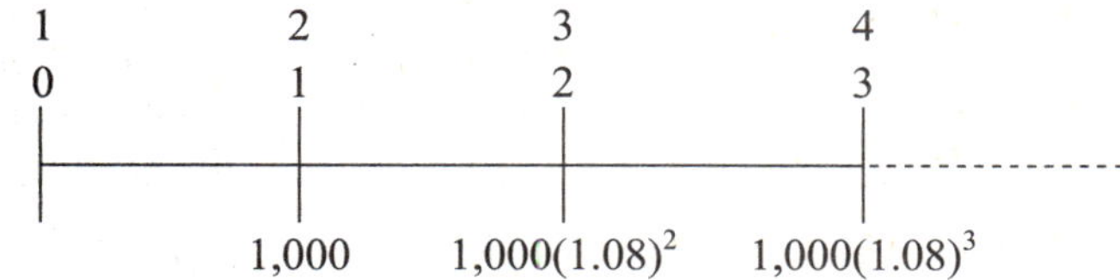

Using the formula for the PV of a growing perpetuity gives:

$$\text{PV} = \frac{1,000(1.08)}{0.12 - 0.08} = 27,000.$$

4-25. You are thinking of building a new machine that will save you \$1000 in the first year. The machine will then begin to wear out so that the savings *decline* at a rate of 2% per year forever. What is the present value of the savings if the interest rate is 5% per year?

Timeline:

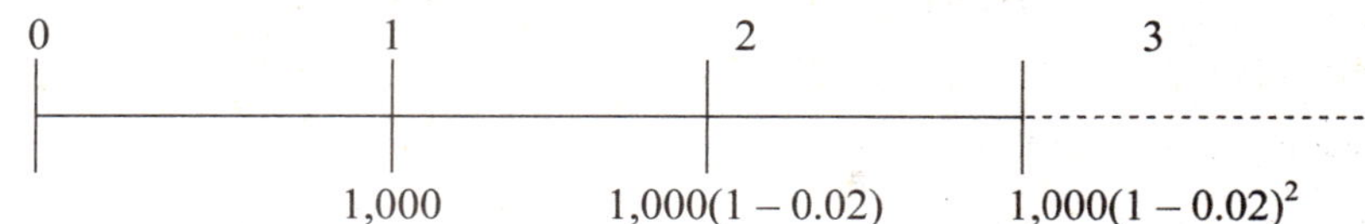

We must value a growing perpetuity with a negative growth rate of -0.02:

$$PV = \frac{1,000}{0.05 - -0.02} = \$14,285.71$$

4-26. **You work for a pharmaceutical company that has developed a new drug. The patent on the drug will last 17 years. You expect that the drug's profits will be \$2 million in its first year and that this amount will grow at a rate of 5% per year for the next 17 years. Once the patent expires, other pharmaceutical companies will be able to produce the same drug and competition will likely drive profits to zero. What is the present value of the new drug if the interest rate is 10% per year?**

Timeline:

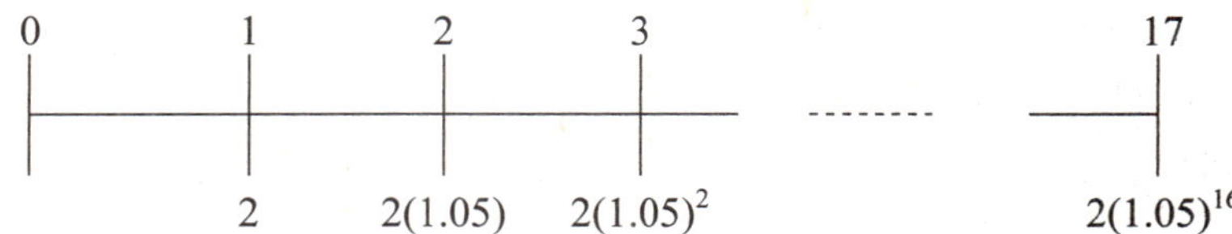

This is a 17-year growing annuity. By the growing annuity formula we have

$$PV = \frac{2,000,000}{0.1 - 0.05}\left(1 - \left(\frac{1.05}{1.1}\right)^{17}\right) = 21,861,455.80$$

4-27. **Your oldest daughter is about to start kindergarten at a private school. Tuition is \$10,000 per year, payable at the *beginning* of the school year. You expect to keep your daughter in private school through high school. You expect tuition to increase at a rate of 5% per year over the 13 years of her schooling. What is the present value of the tuition payments if the interest rate is 5% per year? How much would you need to have in the bank now to fund all 13 years of tuition?**

Timeline:

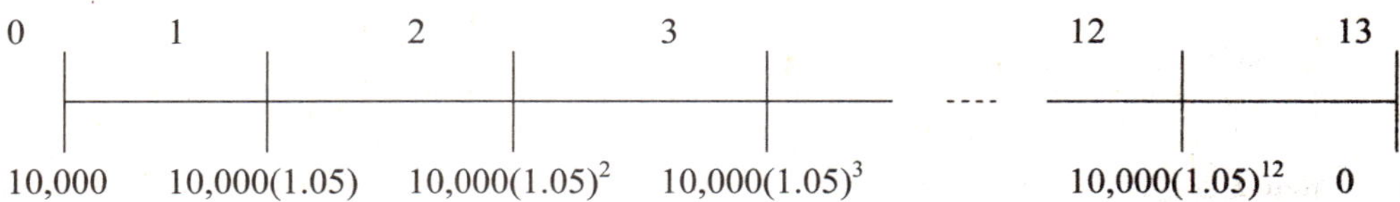

This problem consist of two parts: today's tuition payment of \$10,000 and a 12-year growing annuity with first payment of 10,000(1.05). However we cannot use the growing annuity formula because in this case r = g. We can just calculate the present values of the payments and add them up:

$$PV_{GA} = \frac{10,000(1.05)}{(1.05)} + \frac{10,000(1.05)^2}{(1.05)^2} + \frac{10,000(1.05)^3}{(1.05)^3} + \cdots + \frac{10,000(1.05)^{12}}{(1.05)^{12}}$$

$$= 10,000 + 10,000 + 10,000 + \cdots + 10,000 = 10,000 \times 12$$

$$= 120,000$$

Adding the initial tuition payment gives:

$120,000 + 10,000 = 130,000.$

4-28. A rich aunt has promised you $5000 one year from today. In addition, each year after that, she has promised you a payment (on the anniversary of the last payment) that is 5% larger than the last payment. She will continue to show this generosity for 20 years, giving a total of 20 payments. If the interest rate is 5%, what is her promise worth today?

Timeline:

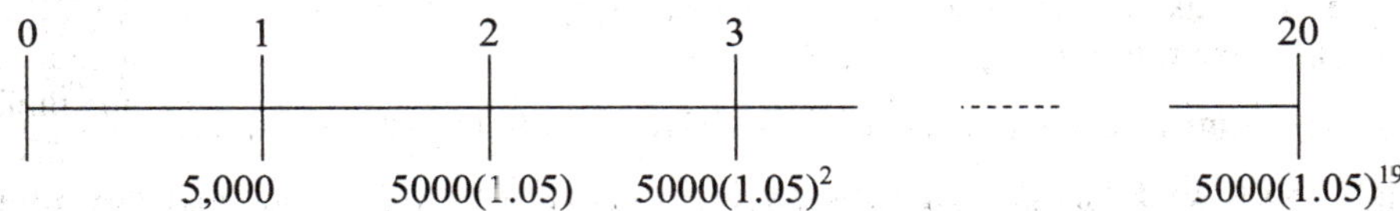

This value is equal to the PV of a 20-year annuity with a first payment of $5,000. However we cannot use the growing annuity formula because in this case r = g. So instead we can just find the present values of the payments and add them up:

$$PV_{GA} = \frac{5,000}{(1.05)} + \frac{5,000(1.05)}{(1.05)^2} + \frac{5,000(1.05)^2}{(1.05)^3} + \cdots + \frac{5,000(1.05)^{19}}{(1.05)^{20}}$$

$$= \frac{5,000}{1.05} + \frac{5,000}{1.05} + \frac{5,000}{1.05} + \cdots + \frac{5,000}{1.05} = \frac{5,000}{1.05} \times 20 = 95,238.$$

4-29. You are running a hot Internet company. Analysts predict that its earnings will grow at 30% per year for the next five years. After that, as competition increases, earnings growth is expected to slow to 2% per year and continue at that level forever. Your company has just announced earnings of $1,000,000. What is the present value of all future earnings if the interest rate is 8%? (Assume all cash flows occur at the end of the year.)

Timeline:

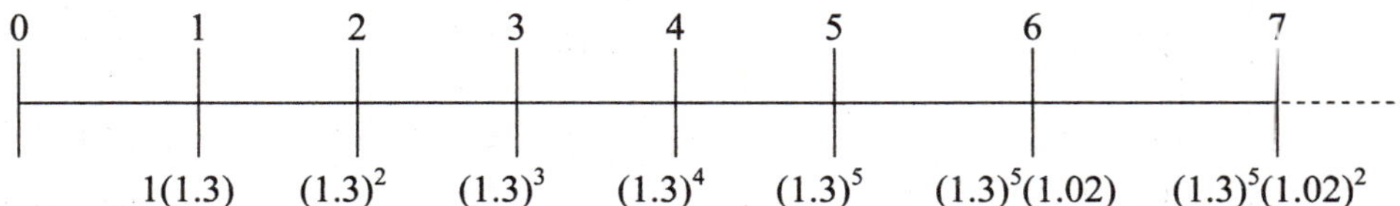

This problem consists of two parts:

(1) A growing annuity for 5 years;

(2) A growing perpetuity after 5 years.

First we find the PV of (1):

$$PV_{GA} = \frac{1.3}{0.08-0.3}\left(1-\left(\frac{1.3}{1.08}\right)^5\right) = \$9.02 \text{ million.}$$

Now we calculate the PV of (2). The value at date 5 of the growing perpetuity is

$$PV_5 = \frac{(1.3)^5(1.02)}{0.08-0.02} = \$63.12 \text{ million} \Rightarrow PV_0 = \frac{63.12}{(1.08)^5} = \$42.96 \text{ million.}$$

Adding the present value of (1) and (2) together gives the PV value of future earnings:

$\$9.02 + \$42.96 = \$51.98$ million.

4-30. Your brother has offered to give you \$100, starting next year, and after that growing at 3% for the next 20 years. You would like to calculate the value of this offer by calculating how much money you would need to deposit in the local bank so that the account will generate the same cash flows as he is offering you. Your local bank will guarantee a 6% annual interest rate so long as you have money in the account.

a. How much money will you need to deposit into the account today?

b. Using an Excel spreadsheet, show explicitly that you can deposit this amount of money into the account, and every year withdraw what your brother has promised, leaving the account with nothing after the last withdrawal.

a. The amount to be deposited in the account is \$1456.15.

Year	Cash flows of Brother's deal	PV of Brother's deal with 6% discount factor
0	-	-
1	\$ 100.00	\$ 94.34
2	\$ 103.00	\$ 91.67
3	\$ 106.09	\$ 89.08
4	\$ 109.27	\$ 86.55
5	\$ 112.55	\$ 84.10
6	\$ 115.93	\$ 81.72
7	\$ 119.41	\$ 79.41
8	\$ 122.99	\$ 77.16
9	\$ 126.68	\$ 74.98
10	\$ 130.48	\$ 72.86
11	\$ 134.39	\$ 70.80
12	\$ 138.42	\$ 68.79
13	\$ 142.58	\$ 66.85
14	\$ 146.85	\$ 64.95
15	\$ 151.26	\$ 63.12
16	\$ 155.80	\$ 61.33
17	\$ 160.47	\$ 59.59
18	\$ 165.28	\$ 57.91
19	\$ 170.24	\$ 56.27
20	\$ 175.35	\$ 54.68
	Sum of cash flows with 6% discount factor ->	\$ 1,456.15

b.

Year	Payout	Remaining Balance
0	$ -	$ 1,456.15
1	$ 100.00	$ 1,443.52
2	$ 103.00	$ 1,427.13
3	$ 106.09	$ 1,406.67
4	$ 109.27	$ 1,381.80
5	$ 112.55	$ 1,352.16
6	$ 115.93	$ 1,317.36
7	$ 119.41	$ 1,276.99
8	$ 122.99	$ 1,230.63
9	$ 126.68	$ 1,177.79
10	$ 130.48	$ 1,117.98
11	$ 134.39	$ 1,050.66
12	$ 138.42	$ 975.28
13	$ 142.58	$ 891.22
14	$ 146.85	$ 797.84
15	$ 151.26	$ 694.45
16	$ 155.80	$ 580.32
17	$ 160.47	$ 454.67
18	$ 165.28	$ 316.67
19	$ 170.24	$ 165.43
20	$ 175.35	$ (0.00)

4-31. You have decided to buy a perpetuity. The bond makes one payment at the end of every year forever and has an interest rate of 5%. If you initially put $1000 into the bond, what is the payment every year?

Timeline:

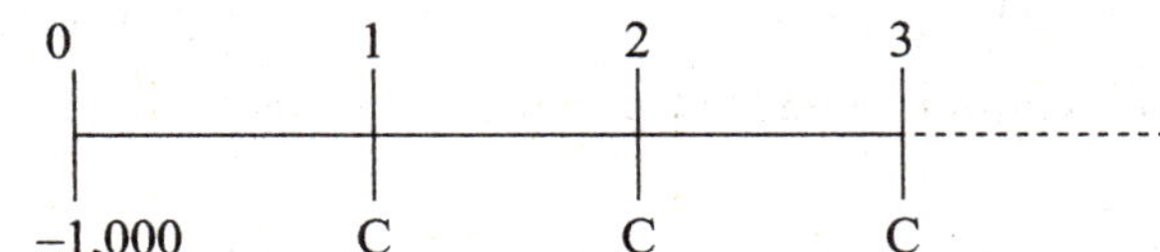

$$P = \frac{C}{r} \Rightarrow C = P \times r = 1{,}000 \times 0.05 = \$50$$

4-32. You are thinking of purchasing a house. The house costs $350,000. You have $50,000 in cash that you can use as a down payment on the house, but you need to borrow the rest of the purchase price. The bank is offering a 30-year mortgage that requires annual payments and has an interest rate of 7% per year. What will your annual payment be if you sign up for this mortgage?

Timeline: (From the perspective of the bank)

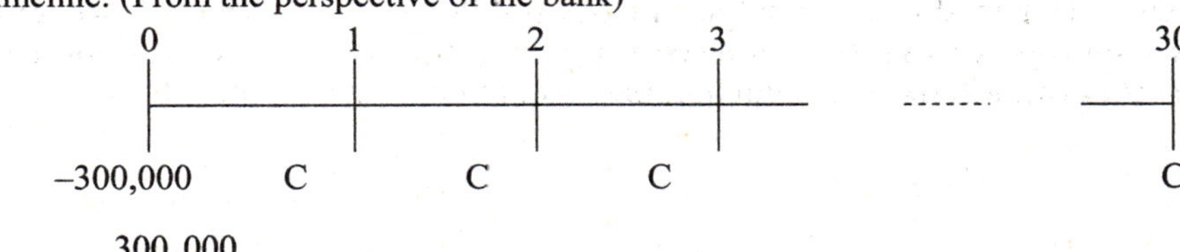

$$C = \frac{300{,}000}{\frac{1}{0.07}\left(1 - \frac{1}{1.07^{30}}\right)} = \$24{,}176$$

4-33. You are thinking about buying a piece of art that costs $50,000. The art dealer is proposing the following deal: He will lend you the money, and you will repay the loan by making the same payment every two years for the next 20 years (i.e., a total of 10 payments). If the interest rate is 4%, how much will you have to pay every two years?

Timeline:

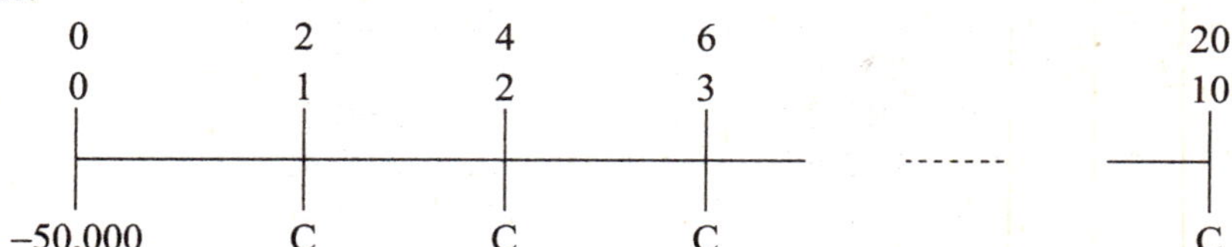

This cash flow stream is an annuity. First, calculate the 2-year interest rate: the 1-year rate is 4%, and $1 today will be worth $(1.04)^2 = 1.0816$ in 2 years, so the 2-year interest rate is 8.16%. Using the equation for an annuity payment:

$$C = \frac{50,000}{\frac{1}{0.0816}\left(1 - \frac{1}{(1.0816)^{10}}\right)} = \$7,505.34.$$

4-34. You would like to buy the house and take the mortgage described in Problem 32. You can afford to pay only $23,500 per year. The bank agrees to allow you to pay this amount each year, yet still borrow $300,000. At the end of the mortgage (in 30 years), you must make a *balloon* payment; that is, you must repay the remaining balance on the mortgage. How much will this balloon payment be?

Timeline: (where X is the balloon payment.)

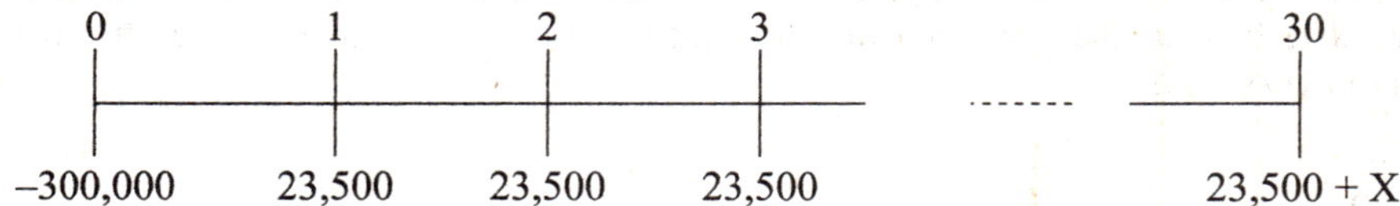

The present value of the loan payments must be equal to the amount borrowed:

$$300,000 = \frac{23,500}{0.07}\left(1 - \frac{1}{1.07^{30}}\right) + \frac{X}{(1.07)^{30}}.$$

Solving for X:

$$X = \left[300,000 - \frac{23,500}{0.07}\left(1 - \frac{1}{1.07^{30}}\right)\right](1.07)^{30} = \$63,848$$

4-35. You are saving for retirement. To live comfortably, you decide you will need to save $2 million by the time you are 65. Today is your 30th birthday, and you decide, starting today and continuing on every birthday up to and including your 65th birthday, that you will put the same amount into a savings account. If the interest rate is 5%, how much must you set aside each year to make sure that you will have $2 million in the account on your 65th birthday?

Timeline:

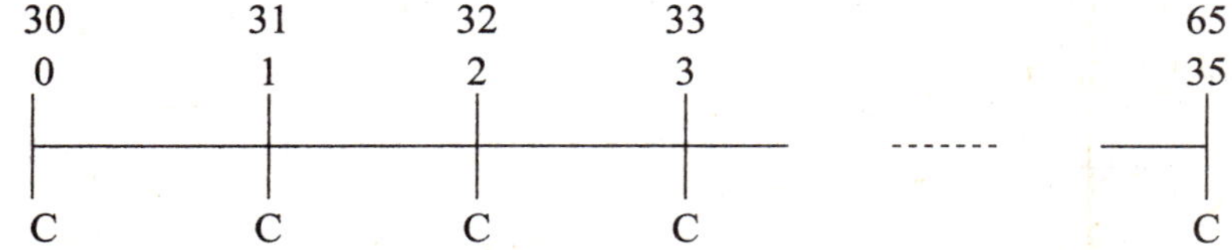

FV = $2 million

The PV of the cash flows must equal the PV of $2 million in 35 years. The cash flows consist of a 35-year annuity, plus the contribution today, so the PV is:

$$PV = \frac{C}{0.05}\left(1 - \frac{1}{(1.05)^{35}}\right) + C.$$

The PV of $2 million in 35 years is

$$\frac{2,000,000}{(1.05)^{35}} = \$362,580.57.$$

Setting these equal gives:

$$\frac{C}{0.05}\left(1 - \frac{1}{(1.05)^{35}}\right) + C = 362,580.57$$

$$\Rightarrow C = \frac{362,580.57}{\frac{1}{0.05}\left(1 - \frac{1}{(1.05)^{35}}\right) + 1} = \$20,868.91.$$

4-36. You realize that the plan in Problem 35 has a flaw. Because your income will increase over your lifetime, it would be more realistic to save less now and more later. Instead of putting the same amount aside each year, you decide to let the amount that you set aside grow by 3% per year. Under this plan, how much will you put into the account today? (Recall that you are planning to make the first contribution to the account today.)

Timeline:

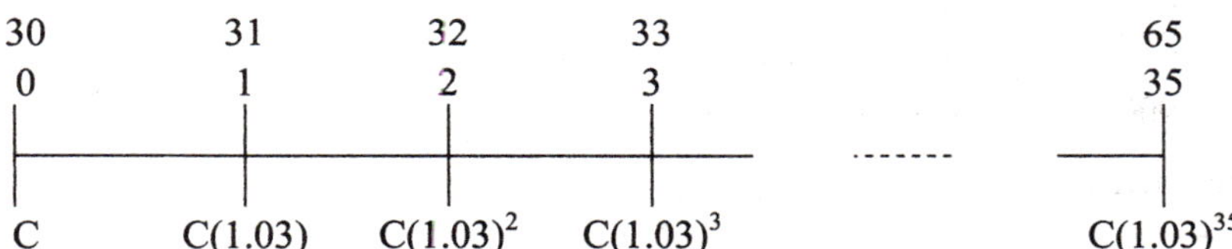

FV = 2 million

The PV of the cash flows must equal the PV of $2 million in 35 years. The cash flow consists of a 35 year growing annuity, plus the contribution today. So the PV is:

$$PV = \frac{C(1.03)}{0.05 - 0.03}\left(1 - \left(\frac{1.03}{1.05}\right)^{35}\right) + C.$$

The PV of $2 million in 35 years is:

$$\frac{2,000,000}{(1.05)^{35}} = \$362,580.57.$$

Setting these equal gives:

$$\frac{C(1.03)}{0.05 - 0.03}\left(1 - \left(\frac{1.03}{1.05}\right)^{35}\right) + C = 362,580.57.$$

Solving for C,

$$C = \frac{362,580.57}{\frac{1.03}{0.05-0.03}\left(1-\left(\frac{1.03}{1.05}\right)^{35}\right)+1} = \$13,823.91.$$

4-37. You are 35 years old, and decide to save $5000 each year (with the first deposit one year from now), in an account paying 8% interest per year. You will make your last deposit 30 years from now when you retire at age 65. During retirement, you plan to withdraw funds from the account at the end of each year (so your first withdrawal is at age 66). What constant amount will you be able to withdraw each year if you want the funds to last until you are 90?

$53,061

rate	8%	
Save amt	$5,000	
Years to retire	30	
Amt at retirement	566,416.06	
Years in retirement	25	
Amt to withdraw	53,061.16	

4-38. You have an investment opportunity that requires an initial investment of $5000 today and will pay $6000 in one year. What is the IRR of this opportunity?

Timeline:

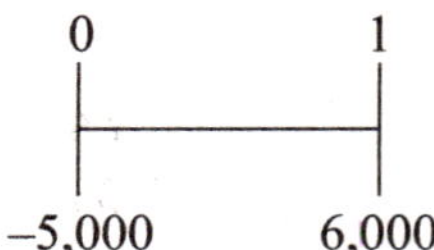

IRR is the r that solves:

$$\frac{6,000}{1+r} = 5,000 = \frac{6,000}{5,000} - 1 = 20\%.$$

4-39. Suppose you invest $2000 today and receive $10,000 in five years.

a. What is the IRR of this opportunity?

b. Suppose another investment opportunity also requires $2000 upfront, but pays an equal amount at the end of each year for the next five years. If this investment has the same IRR as the first one, what is the amount you will receive each year?

Timeline

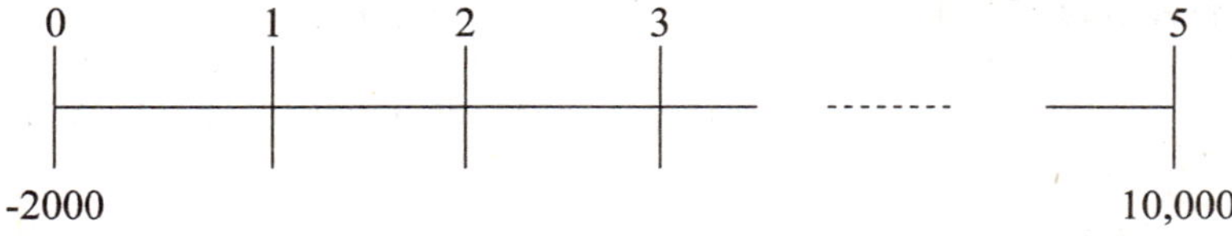

IRR solves $2000=10000/(1+r)^5$

So $\text{IRR} = \left(\frac{10000}{2000}\right)^{1/5} - 1 = 37.97\%$.

Solution part b

Timeline

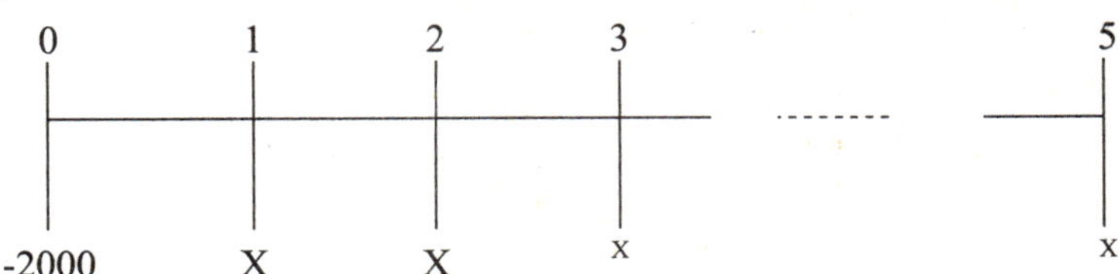

X solves

$$2000 = \frac{X}{IRR}$$

so

$$X = \frac{2000 \times IRR}{\left(1 - \frac{1}{(1+IRR)^5}\right)}$$

$= \$949.27$

4-40. **You are shopping for a car and read the following advertisement in the newspaper: "Own a new Spitfire! No money down. Four annual payments of just $10,000." You have shopped around and know that you can buy a Spitfire for cash for $32,500. What is the interest rate the dealer is advertising (what is the IRR of the loan in the advertisement)? Assume that you must make the annual payments at the end of each year.**

Timeline:

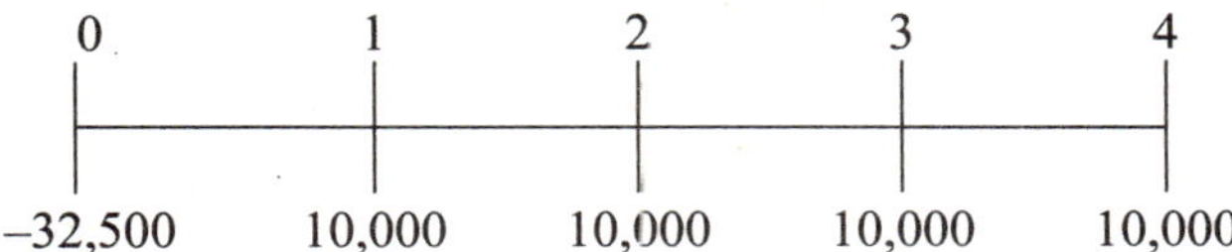

The PV of the car payments is a 4-year annuity:

$$\text{PV} = \frac{10,000}{\text{r}}\left(1 - \frac{1}{(1+\text{r})^4}\right)$$

Setting the NPV of the cash flow stream equal to zero and solving for r gives the IRR:

$$\text{NPV} = 0 = -32,500 + \frac{10,000}{\text{r}}\left(1 - \frac{1}{(1+\text{r})^4}\right) \Rightarrow \frac{10,000}{\text{r}}\left(1 - \frac{1}{(1+\text{r})^4}\right) = 32,500$$

To find r we either need to guess or use the annuity calculator. You can check and see that r = 8.85581% solves this equation. So the IRR is 8.86%.

4-41. **A local bank is running the following advertisement in the newspaper: "For just $1000 we will pay you $100 forever!" The fine print in the ad says that for a $1000 deposit, the bank will pay $100 every year in perpetuity, starting one year after the deposit is made. What interest rate is the bank advertising (what is the IRR of this investment)?**

Timeline:

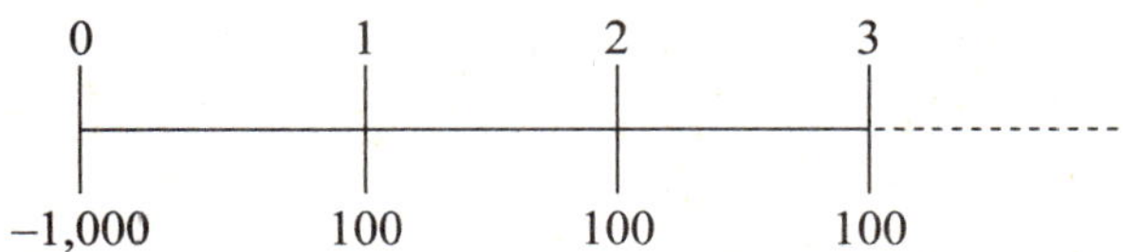

The payments are a perpetuity, so

$$PV = \frac{100}{r}.$$

Setting the NPV of the cash flow stream equal to zero and solving for r gives the IRR:

$$NPV = 0 = \frac{100}{r} - 1,000 \Rightarrow r = \frac{100}{1,000} = 10\%.$$

So the IRR is 10%.

4-42. The Tillamook County Creamery Association manufactures Tillamook Cheddar Cheese. It markets this cheese in four varieties: aged 2 months, 9 months, 15 months, and 2 years. At the shop in the dairy, it sells 2 pounds of each variety for the following prices: \$7.95, \$9.49, \$10.95, and \$11.95, respectively. Consider the cheese maker's decision whether to continue to age a particular 2-pound block of cheese. At 2 months, he can either sell the cheese immediately or let it age further. If he sells it now, he will receive \$7.95 immediately. If he ages the cheese, he must give up the \$7.95 today to receive a higher amount in the future. What is the IRR (expressed in percent per month) of the investment of giving up \$79.50 today by choosing to store 20 pounds of cheese that is currently 2 months old and instead selling 10 pounds of this cheese when it has aged 9 months, 6 pounds when it has aged 15 months, and the remaining 4 pounds when it has aged 2 years?

Timeline:

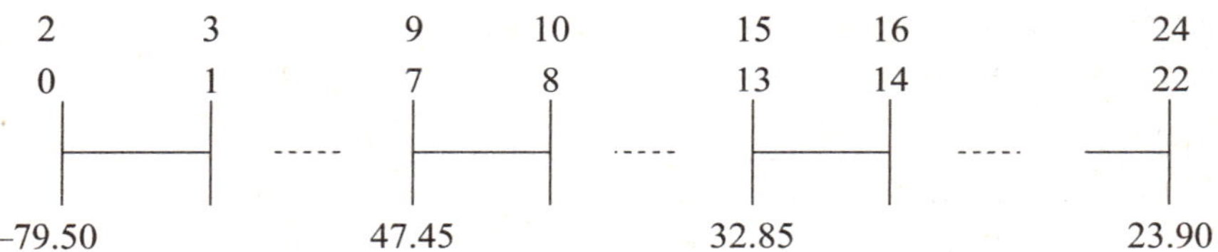

The PV of the cash flows generated by storing the cheese is:

$$PV = \frac{47.45}{(1+r)^7} + \frac{32.85}{(1+r)^{13}} + \frac{23.90}{(1+r)^{22}}.$$

The IRR is the r that sets the NPV equal to zero:

$$NPV = 0 = -79.50 + \frac{47.45}{(1+r)^7} + \frac{32.85}{(1+r)^{13}} + \frac{23.90}{(1+r)^{22}}.$$

By iteration or by using a spreadsheet (see 4.35.xls), the r that solves this equation is r = 2.28918% so the IRR is 2.29% per month.

4-43. Your grandmother bought an annuity from Rock Solid Life Insurance Company for \$200,000 when she retired. In exchange for the \$200,000, Rock Solid will pay her \$25,000 per year until she dies. The interest rate is 5%. How long must she live after the day she retired to come out ahead (that is, to get more in *value* than what she paid in)?

Timeline:

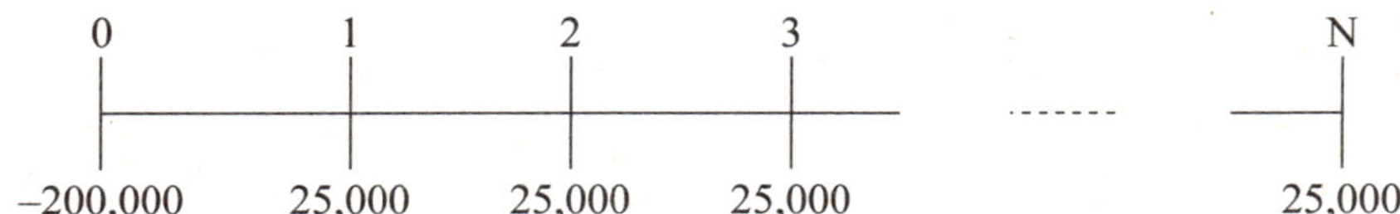

She breaks even when the NPV of the cash flows is zero. The value of N that solves this is:

$$NPV = -200,000 + \frac{25,000}{0.05}\left(1 - \frac{1}{(1.05)^N}\right) = 0$$

$$\Rightarrow 1 - \frac{1}{(1.05)^N} = \frac{200,000 \times 0.05}{25,000} = 0.4$$

$$\frac{1}{(1.05)^N} = 0.6 \Rightarrow (1.05)^N = \frac{1}{0.6}$$

$$\log(1.05)^N = \log\left(\frac{1}{0.6}\right)$$

$$N\log(1.05) = -\log(0.6)$$

$$N = \frac{-\log(0.6)}{\log(1.05)}$$

$$= 10.5.$$

So if she lives 10.5 or more years, she comes out ahead.

4-44. You are thinking of making an investment in a new plant. The plant will generate revenues of $1 million per year for as long as you maintain it. You expect that the maintenance cost will start at $50,000 per year and will increase 5% per year thereafter. Assume that all revenue and maintenance costs occur at the end of the year. You intend to run the plant as long as it continues to make a positive cash flow (as long as the cash generated by the plant exceeds the maintenance costs). The plant can be built and become operational immediately. If the plant costs $10 million to build, and the interest rate is 6% per year, should you invest in the plant?

Timeline:

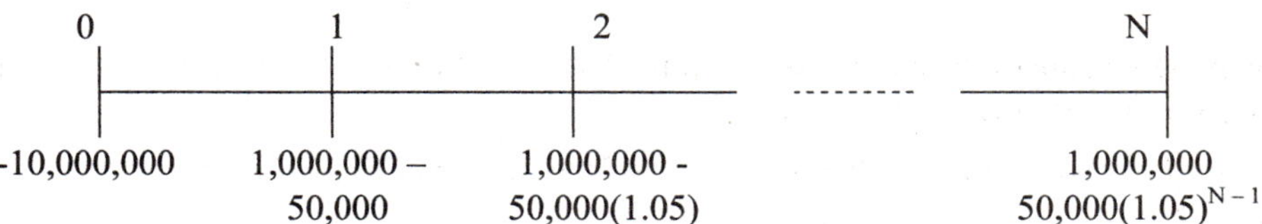

The plant will shut down when:

$$1,000,000 - 50,000(1.05)^{N-1} < 0$$

$$(1.05)^{N-1} > \frac{1,000,000}{50,000} = 20$$

$$(N-1)\log(1.05) > \log(20)$$

$$N > \frac{\log(20)}{\log(1.05)} + 1 = 62.4.$$

So the last year of production will be in year 62.

The cash flows consist of two pieces, the 62 year annuity of the $1,000,000 and the growing annuity.

The PV of the annuity is

$$PV_A = \frac{1,000,000}{0.06}\left(1 - \frac{1}{(1.06)^{62}}\right) = 16,217,006.$$

The PV of the growing annuity is

$$PV_{GA} = \frac{-50,000}{0.06 - 0.05}\left(1 - \left(\frac{1.05}{1.06}\right)^{62}\right) = -2,221,932.$$

So the PV of all the cash flows is

$$PV = 16,217,006 - 2,221,932 = \$13,995,074.$$

So the NPV $= 13,995,07 - 10,000,000 = \$3,995,074$, and you should build it.

4-45. **You have just turned 30 years old, have just received your MBA, and have accepted your first job. Now you must decide how much money to put into your retirement plan. The plan works as follows: Every dollar in the plan earns 7% per year. You cannot make withdrawals until you retire on your sixty-fifth birthday. After that point, you can make withdrawals as you see fit. You decide that you will plan to live to 100 and work until you turn 65. You estimate that to live comfortably in retirement, you will need $100,000 per year starting at the end of the first year of retirement and ending on your 100th birthday. You will contribute the same amount to the plan at the end of every year that you work. How much do you need to contribute each year to fund your retirement?**

Timeline:

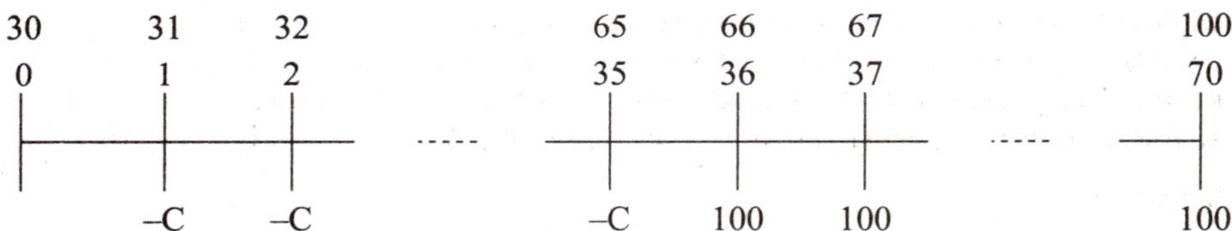

The present value of the costs must equal the PV of the benefits. So begin by dividing the problem into two parts, the costs and the benefits.

Costs: The costs are the contributions, a 35-year annuity with the first payment in one year:

$$PV_{costs} = \frac{C}{0.07}\left(1 - \frac{1}{(1.07)^{35}}\right).$$

Benefits: The benefits are the payouts after retirement, a 35-year annuity paying $100,000 per year with the first payment 36 years from today. The value of this annuity in year 35 is:

$$PV_{35} = \frac{100,000}{0.07}\left(1 - \frac{1}{(1.07)^{35}}\right).$$

The value today is just the discounted value in 35 years:

$$PV_{benefits} = \frac{PV_{35}}{(1.07)^{35}} = \frac{100,000}{0.07(1.07)^{35}}\left(1 - \frac{1}{(1.07)^{35}}\right) = 121,272.$$

Since the PV of the costs must equal the PV of the benefits (or equivalently the NPV of the cash flow must be zero):

$$121{,}272 = \frac{C}{0.07}\left(1 - \frac{1}{(1.07)^{35}}\right).$$

Solving for C gives:

$$C = \frac{121{,}272 \times 0.07}{\left(1 - \frac{1}{(1.07)^{35}}\right)} = 9{,}366.29.$$

4-46. Problem 45 is not very realistic because most retirement plans do not allow you to specify a fixed amount to contribute every year. Instead, you are required to specify a fixed percentage of your salary that you want to contribute. Assume that your starting salary is $75,000 per year and it will grow 2% per year until you retire. Assuming everything else stays the same as in Problem 45, what percentage of your income do you need to contribute to the plan every year to fund the same retirement income?

Timeline: (f = Fraction of your salary that you contribute)

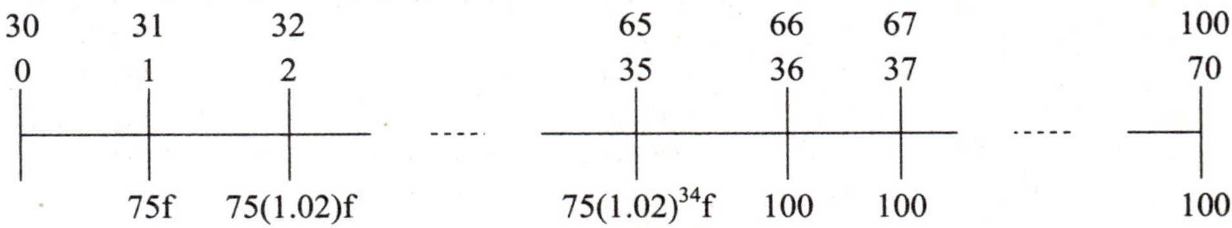

The present value of the costs must equal the PV of the benefits. So begin by dividing the problem into two parts, the costs and the benefits.

Costs: The costs are the contributions, a 35-year growing annuity with the first payment in one year. The PV of this is:

$$PV_{costs} = \frac{75{,}000f}{0.07 - 0.02}\left(1 - \left(\frac{1.02}{1.07}\right)^{35}\right).$$

Benefits: The benefits are the payouts after retirement, a 35-year annuity paying $100,000 per year with the first payment 36 years from today. The value of this annuity in year 35 is:

$$PV_{35} = \frac{100{,}000}{0.07}\left(1 - \frac{1}{(1.07)^{35}}\right).$$

The value today is just the discounted value in 35 years.

$$PV_{benefits} = \frac{PV_{35}}{(1.07)^{35}} = \frac{100{,}000}{0.07(1.07)^{35}}\left(1 - \frac{1}{(1.07)^{35}}\right) = 121{,}272$$

Since the PV of the costs must equal the PV of the benefits (or equivalently the NPV of the cash flows must be zero):

$$121{,}272 = \frac{75{,}000f}{0.07 - 0.02}\left(1 - \left(\frac{1.02}{1.07}\right)^{35}\right).$$

Solving for f, the fraction of your salary that you would like to contribute:

$$f = \frac{121,272 \times (0.07 - 0.02)}{75,000\left(1 - \left(\frac{1.02}{1.07}\right)^{35}\right)} = 9.948\%.$$

So you would contribute approximately 10% of your salary. This amounts to $7,500 in the first year, which is lower than the plan in the prior problem.

Chapter 5

Interest Rates

5-1. **Your bank is offering you an account that will pay 20% interest in total for a two-year deposit. Determine the equivalent discount rate for a period length of**

a. **Six months.**

b. **One year.**

c. **One month.**

a. Since 6 months is $\frac{6}{24}=\frac{1}{4}$ of 2 years, using our rule $(1+0.2)^{\frac{1}{4}}=1.0466$

So the equivalent 6 month rate is 4.66%.

b. Since one year is half of 2 years $(1.2)^{\frac{1}{2}}=1.0954$

So the equivalent 1 year rate is 9.54%.

c. Since one month is $\frac{1}{24}$ of 2 years, using our rule $(1+0.2)^{\frac{1}{24}}=1.00763$

So the equivalent 1 month rate is 0.763%.

5-2. **Which do you prefer: a bank account that pays 5% per year (EAR) for three years or**

a. **An account that pays $2\frac{1}{2}\%$ every six months for three years?**

b. **An account that pays $7\frac{1}{2}\%$ every 18 months for three years?**

c. **An account that pays $\frac{1}{2}\%$ per month for three years?**

If you deposit \$1 into a bank account that pays 5% per year for 3 years you will have $(1.05)^3=1.15763$ after 3 years.

a. If the account pays $2\frac{1}{2}\%$ per 6 months then you will have $(1.025)^6=1.15969$ after 3 years, so you prefer $2\frac{1}{2}\%$ every 6 months.

b. If the account pays $7\frac{1}{2}\%$ per 18 months then you will have $(1.075)^2=1.15563$ after 3 years, so you prefer 5% per year.

c. If the account pays $\frac{1}{2}\%$ per month then you will have $(1.005)^{36}=1.19668$ after 3 years, so you prefer $\frac{1}{2}\%$ every month.

5-3. Many academic institutions offer a sabbatical policy. Every seven years a professor is given a year free of teaching and other administrative responsibilities at full pay. For a professor earning $70,000 per year who works for a total of 42 years, what is the present value of the amount she will earn while on sabbatical if the interest rate is 6% (EAR)?

Timeline:

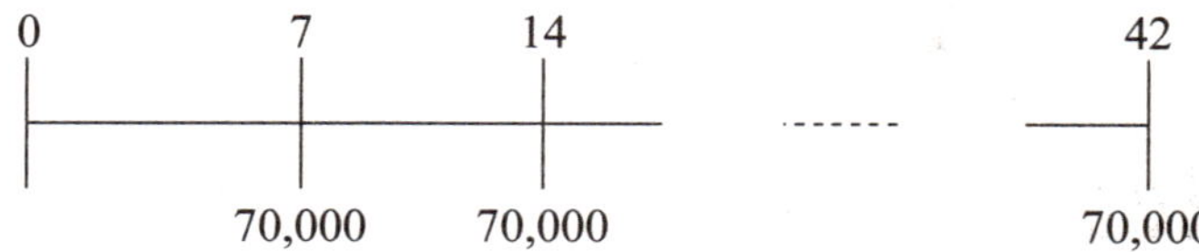

Because $(1.06)^7 = 1.50363$, the equivalent discount rate for a 7-year period is 50.363%.

Using the annuity formula

$$PV = \frac{70,000}{0.50363}\left(1 - \frac{1}{(1.50363)^6}\right) = \$126,964$$

5-4. You have found three investment choices for a one-year deposit: 10% APR compounded monthly, 10% APR compounded annually, and 9% APR compounded daily. Compute the EAR for each investment choice. (Assume that there are 365 days in the year.)

For a $1 invested in an account with 10% APR with monthly compounding you will have

$$\left(1 + \frac{0.1}{12}\right)^{12} = \$1.10471$$

So the EAR is 10.471%.

For a $1 invested in an account with 10% APR with annual compounding you will have

$$(1 + 0.1) = \$1.10$$

So the EAR is 10%.

For a $1 invested in an account with 9% APR with daily compounding you will have

$$\left(1 + \frac{0.09}{365}\right)^{365} = 1.09416$$

So the EAR is 9.416%.

5-5. You are considering moving your money to new bank offering a one-year CD that pays an 8% APR with monthly compounding. Your current bank's manager offers to match the rate you have been offered. The account at your current bank would pay interest every six months. How much interest will you need to earn every six months to match the CD?

With 8% APR, we can calculate the EAR as follows:

$$EAR = \left(1 + \frac{0.08}{12}\right)^{12} = 8.3\%$$

Over six months this works out to be $1.083^{\frac{1}{2}} - 1 = 0.040672$. Hence you need to earn 4.0672% interest rate to match the CD.

5-6. Your bank account pays interest with an EAR of 5%. What is the APR quote for this account based on semiannual compounding? What is the APR with monthly compounding?

Using the formula for converting from an EAR to an APR quote

$$\left(1+\frac{\text{APR}}{\text{k}}\right)^{\text{k}}=1.05$$

Solving for the APR

$$\text{APR}=\left((1.05)^{\frac{1}{\text{k}}}-1\right)\text{k}$$

With annual payments k = 1, so APR = 5%

With semiannual payments k = 2, so APR = 4.939%

With monthly payments k = 12, so APR = 4.889%

5-7. Suppose the interest rate is 8% APR with monthly compounding. What is the present value of an annuity that pays $100 every six months for five years?

Using the PV of an annuity formula with N = 10 payments and C = $100 with r = 4.067% per 6 month interval, since there is an 8% APR with monthly compounding: 8% / 12 = 0.6667% per month, or (1.006667)^6 – 1 = 4.067% per 6 months.

$$\text{PV}=100\times\frac{1}{.04067}\left(1-\frac{1}{1.04067^{10}}\right)=\$808.39$$

5-8. You can earn $50 in interest on a $1000 deposit for eight months. If the EAR is the same regardless of the length of the investment, how much interest will you earn on a $1000 deposit for

a. 6 months.

b. 1 year.

c. 1½ years.

$$EAR=1.05^{12/8}-1=7.593\%$$

a) $1000(1.07593^{1/2}-1)=37.27$

b) $1000(1.07593-1)=75.93$

c) $1000(1.07593^{3/2}-1)=116.03$

5-9. Suppose you invest $100 in a bank account, and five years later it has grown to $134.39.

a. What APR did you receive, if the interest was compounded semiannually?

b. What APR did you receive if the interest was compounded monthly?

The EAR can be calculated as follows:

$$\left(\frac{f}{p}\right)^{1/5}-1=(1.3439)^{1/5}-1=6.0897\%$$

a) Using the formula for EAR, we can calculate the APR for semi-annual compounding.

$$APR=2\times\left\{(EAR+1)^{1/2}-1\right\}=2\times\left\{(1.06897)^{1/2}-1\right\}=6\%$$

b) Similarly we can calculate the APR for monthly compounding

$$APR = 12\times\left\{(EAR+1)^{1/12}-1\right\} = 12\times\left\{(1.06897)^{1/12}-1\right\} = 5.926\%$$

5-10. Your son has been accepted into college. This college guarantees that your son's tuition will not increase for the four years he attends college. The first $10,000 tuition payment is due in six months. After that, the same payment is due every six months until you have made a total of eight payments. The college offers a bank account that allows you to withdraw money every six months and has a fixed APR of 4% (semiannual) guaranteed to remain the same over the next four years. How much money must you deposit today if you intend to make no further deposits and would like to make all the tuition payments from this account, leaving the account empty when the last payment is made?

Timeline:

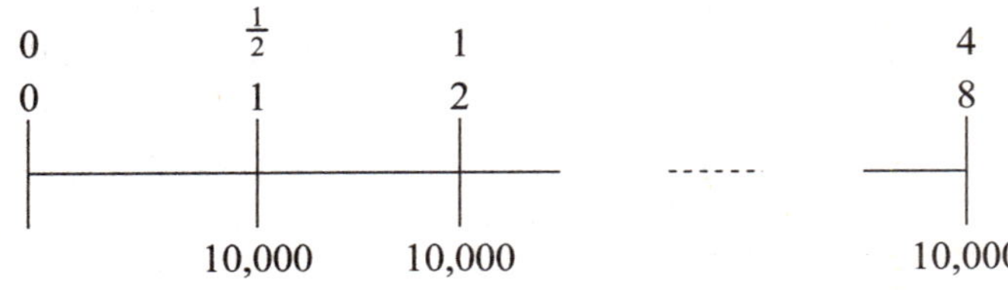

4% APR (semiannual) implies a semiannual discount rate of $\frac{4\%}{2} = 2\%$

So, $PV = \frac{10,000}{0.02}\left(1-\frac{1}{(1.02)^8}\right)$

$= \$73,254.81$

5-11. You make monthly payments on your mortgage. It has a quoted APR of 5% (monthly compounding). What percentage of the outstanding principal do you pay in interest each month?

Using the formula for computing the discount rate from an APR quote:

$$\text{Discount Rate} = \frac{5}{12} = 0.41667\%$$

5-12. Capital One is advertising a 60-month, 5.99% APR motorcycle loan. If you need to borrow $8000 to purchase your dream Harley Davidson, what will your monthly payment be?

Timeline:

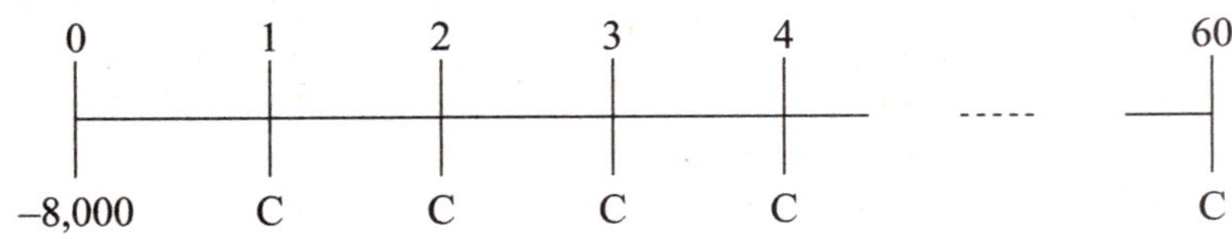

5.99 APR monthly implies a discount rate of

$$\frac{5.99}{12} = 0.499167\%$$

Using the formula for computing a loan payment

$$C = \frac{8,000}{\frac{1}{0.00499167}\left(1 - \frac{1}{(1.00499167)^{60}}\right)} = \$154.63$$

5-13. Oppenheimer Bank is offering a 30-year mortgage with an EAR of 5 ⅜%.. If you plan to borrow $150,000, what will your monthly payment be?

Timeline:

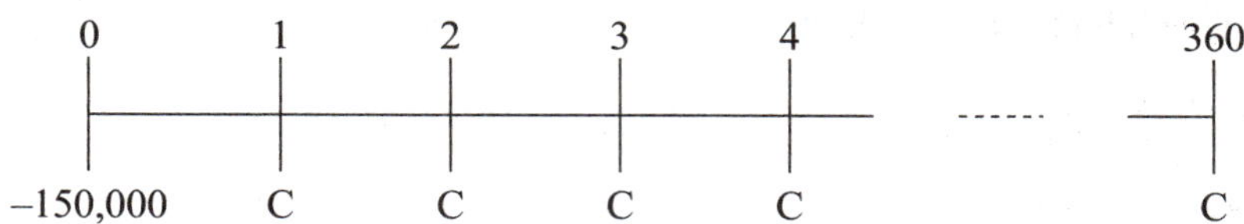

$$(1+0.05375)^{\frac{1}{12}} = 1.0043725$$

So $5\frac{3}{8}$% EAR implies a discount rate of 0.43725%

Using the formula for computing a loan payment

$$C = \frac{150,000}{\frac{1}{0.0043725}\left(1 - \frac{1}{(1.0043725)^{360}}\right)} = \$828.02$$

5-14. You have decided to refinance your mortgage. You plan to borrow whatever is outstanding on your current mortgage. The current monthly payment is $2356 and you have made every payment on time. The original term of the mortgage was 30 years, and the mortgage is exactly four years and eight months old. You have just made your monthly payment. The mortgage interest rate is 6⅜% (APR). How much do you owe on the mortgage today?

Timeline:

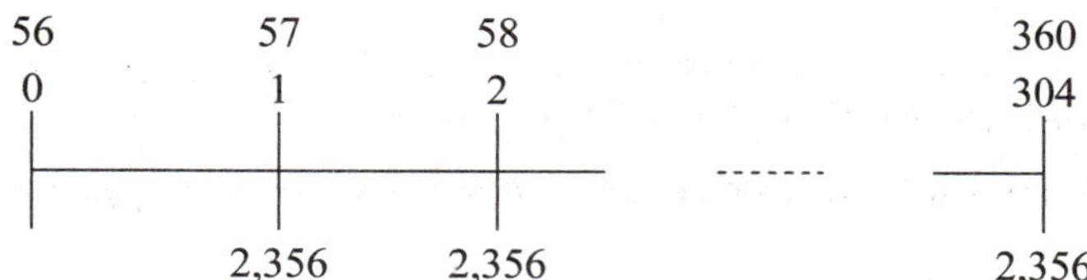

To find out what is owed compute the PV of the remaining payments using the loan interest rate to compute the discount rate:

$$\text{Discount Rate} = \frac{6.375}{12} = 0.53125\%$$

$$PV = \frac{2,356}{0.0053125}\left(1 - \frac{1}{(1.0053125)^{304}}\right) = \$354,900$$

5-15. You have just sold your house for $1,000,000 in cash. Your mortgage was originally a 30-year mortgage with monthly payments and an initial balance of $800,000. The mortgage is currently exactly 18½ years old, and you have just made a payment. If the interest rate on the mortgage is 5.25% (APR), how much cash will you have from the sale once you pay off the mortgage?

First we need to compute the original loan payment

Timeline #1:

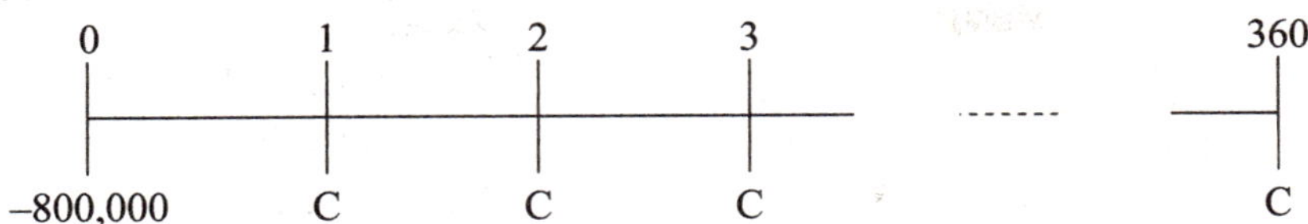

$5\frac{1}{4}\%$ APR (monthly) implies a discount rate of $\frac{5.25}{12} = 0.4375\%$

Using the formula for a loan payment

$$C = \frac{800,000 \times 0.004375}{\left(1 - \frac{1}{(1.004375)^{360}}\right)} = \$4,417.63$$

Now we can compute the PV of continuing to make these payments

The timeline is

Timeline #2:

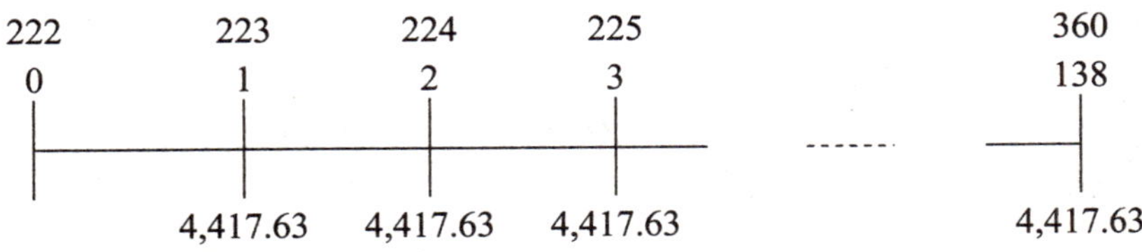

Using the formula for the PV of an annuity

$$PV = \frac{4,417.63}{0.004375}\left(1 - \frac{1}{(1.004375)^{138}}\right) = \$456,931.41$$

So, you would keep \$1,000,000 - \$456,931 = \$543,069.

5-16. You have just purchased a home and taken out a \$500,000 mortgage. The mortgage has a 30-year term with monthly payments and an APR of 6%.

a. How much will you pay in interest, and how much will you pay in principal, during the first year?

b. How much will you pay in interest, and how much will you pay in principal, during the 20th year (i.e., between 19 and 20 years from now)?

a. APR of 6% = 0.5% per month. Payment $= \frac{500,000}{\frac{1}{.005}\left(1 - \frac{1}{1.005^{360}}\right)} = \$2997.75$.

Total annual payments = 2997.75 × 12 = \$35,973.

Loan balance at the end of 1 year $= \$2997.75 \times \frac{1}{.005}\left(1 - \frac{1}{1.005^{348}}\right) = \$493,860$.

Therefore, 500,000 – 493,860 = \$6140 in principal repaid in first year, and 35,973 – 6140 = \$29833 in interest paid in first year.

b. Loan balance in 19 years (or 360 – 19×12 = 132 remaining pmts) is

$$\$2997.75\times\frac{1}{.005}\left(1-\frac{1}{1.005^{132}}\right)=\$289{,}162\,.$$

Loan balance in 20 years = $\$2997.75\times\frac{1}{.005}\left(1-\frac{1}{1.005^{120}}\right)=\$270{,}018\,.$

Therefore, 289,162 – 270,018 = \$19,144 in principal repaid, and \$35,973 – 19,144 = \$16,829 in interest repaid.

5-17. Your mortgage has 25 years left, and has an APR of 7.625% with monthly payments of \$1449.

a. What is the outstanding balance?

b. Suppose you cannot make the mortgage payment and you are in danger of losing your house to foreclosure. The bank has offered to renegotiate your loan. The bank expects to get \$150,000 for the house if it forecloses. They will lower your payment as long as they will receive at least this amount (in present value terms). If current 25-year mortgage interest rates have dropped to 5% (APR), what is the lowest monthly payment you could make for the remaining life of your loan that would be attractive to the bank?

a. The monthly discount rate is

$$\frac{0.07625}{12}=0.635\%$$

$$\text{Present Value}=\left(\frac{1449}{0.00635}\right)\times\left\{1-\left(\frac{1}{1.00635^{300}}\right)\right\}=194{,}024.13$$

b. Here the present value is \$150,000 and the monthly payment needs to be calculated.

$r = 5/1200 = 0.004167$

$$\textit{Payment}=\frac{150000\times 0.004167}{\left(1-\frac{1}{1.004167^{25\times 12}}\right)}=876.88$$

5-18. You have an outstanding student loan with required payments of \$500 per month for the next four years. The interest rate on the loan is 9% APR (monthly). You are considering making an extra payment of \$100 today (that is, you will pay an extra \$100 that you are not required to pay). If you are required to continue to make payments of \$500 per month until the loan is paid off, what is the amount of your final payment? What effective rate of return (expressed as an APR with monthly compounding) have you earned on the \$100?

We begin with the timeline of our required payments

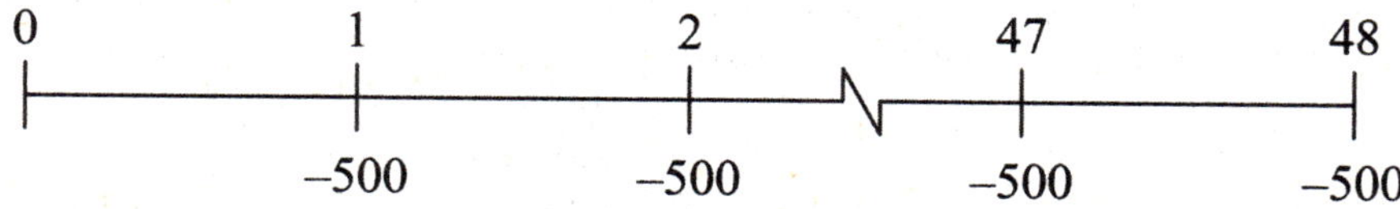

(1) Let's compute our remaining balance on the student loan. As we pointed out earlier, the remaining balance equals the present value of the remaining payments. The loan interest rate is 9% APR, or 9% / 12 = 0.75% per month, so the present value of the payments is

$$\text{PV}=\frac{500}{0.0075}\left(1-\frac{1}{1.0075^{48}}\right)=\$20{,}092.39$$

Using the annuity spreadsheet to compute the present value, we get the same number:

N	I	PV	PMT	FV
48	0.75 %	20,092.39	–500	0

Thus, your remaining balance is $20,092.39.

If you prepay an extra $100 today, your will lower your remaining balance to $20,092.39 – 100 = $19,992.39. Though your balance is reduced, your required monthly payment does not change. Instead, you will pay off the loan faster; that is, it will reduce the payments you need to make at the very end of the loan. How much smaller will the final payment be? With the extra payment, the timeline changes:

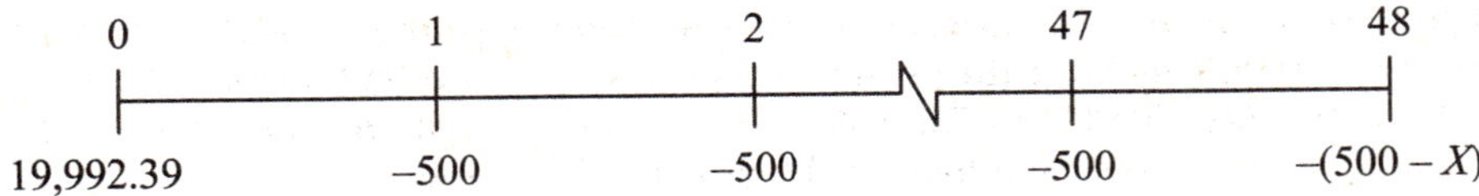

That is, we will pay off by paying $500 per month for 47 months, and some smaller amount, $500 – X, in the last month. To solve for X, recall that the PV of the remaining cash flows equals the outstanding balance when the loan interest rate is used as the discount rate:

$$19{,}992.39 = \frac{500}{0.0075}\left(1 - \frac{1}{(1+0.0075)^{48}}\right) - \frac{X}{1.0075^{48}}$$

Solving for X gives

$$19{,}992.39 = 20{,}092.39 - \frac{X}{1.0075^{48}}$$

$$X = \$143.14$$

So the final payment will be lower by $143.14.

You can also use the annuity spreadsheet to determine this solution. If you prepay $100 today, and make payments of $500 for 48 months, then your final balance at the end will be a credit of $143.14:

N	I	PV	PMT	FV
48	0.75 %	19,992.39	-500	143.14

(2) The extra payment effectively lets us exchange $100 today for $143.14 in four years. We claimed that the return on this investment should be the loan interest rate. Let's see if this is the case:

$\$100 \times (1.0075)^{48} = \$143.14$, so it is.

Thus, you earn a 9% APR (the rate on the loan).

5-19. Consider again the setting of Problem 18. Now that you realize your best investment is to prepay your student loan, you decide to prepay as much as you can each month. Looking at your budget, you can afford to pay an extra $250 per month in addition to your required monthly payments of $500, or $750 in total each month. How long will it take you to pay off the loan?

The timeline in this case is:

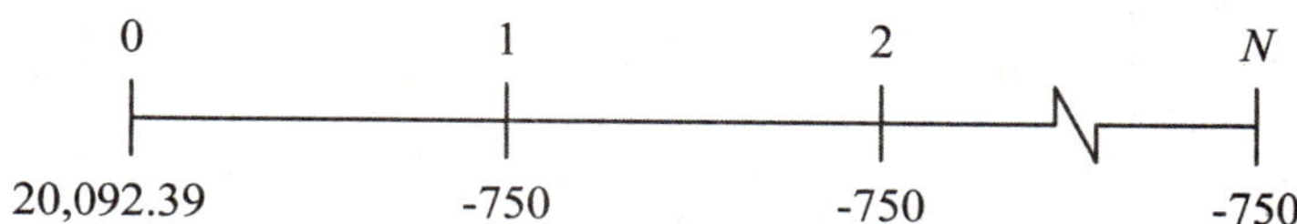

and we want to determine the number of monthly payments N that we will need to make. That is, we need to determine what length annuity with a monthly payment of $750 has the same present value as the loan balance, using the loan interest rate as the discount rate. As we did in Chapter 4, we set the outstanding balance equal to the present value of the loan payments and solve for N.

$$\frac{750}{0.0075}\left(1-\frac{1}{1.0075^N}\right)=20,092.39$$

$$\left(1-\frac{1}{1.0075^N}\right)=\frac{20,092.39\times 0.0075}{750}=0.200924$$

$$\frac{1}{1.0075^N}=1-0.200924=0.799076$$

$$1.0075^N=1.25145$$

$$N=\frac{\text{Log}(1.25145)}{\text{Log}(1.0075)}=30.02$$

We can also use the annuity spreadsheet to solve for N.

N	I	PV	PMT	FV
30.02	0.75 %	20,092.39	–750	0

So, by prepaying the loan, we will pay off the loan in about 30 months or 2 ½ years, rather than the four years originally scheduled. Because N of 30.02 is larger than 30, we could either increase the 30th payment by a small amount or make a very small 31st payment. We can use the annuity spreadsheet to determine the remaining balance after 30 payments.

N	I	PV	PMT	FV
30	0.75 %	20,092.39	–750	–13.86

If we make a final payment of $750.00 + $13.86 = $763.86, the loan will be paid off in 30 months.

5-20. Oppenheimer Bank is offering a 30-year mortgage with an APR of 5.25%. With this mortgage your monthly payments would be $2000 per month. In addition, Oppenheimer Bank offers you the following deal: Instead of making the monthly payment of $2000 every month, you can make half the payment every two weeks (so that you will make $52/2 = 26$ payments per year). With this plan, how long will it take to pay off the mortgage of $150,000 if the EAR of the loan is unchanged?

If we make $\frac{2,000}{2}=\$1,000$ every 2 weeks the timeline is as follows.

Timeline:

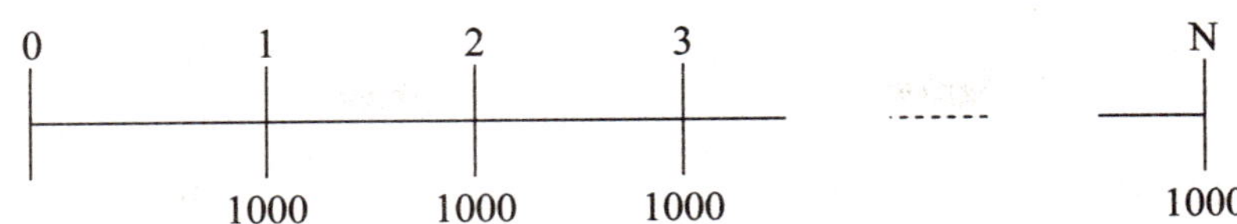

Now since there are 26 weeks in a year

$(1.0525)^{\frac{1}{26}} = 1.001970.$

So, the discount rate is 0.1970%.

To compute N we set the PV of the loan payments equal to the outstanding balance

$$150,000 = \frac{1000}{0.001970}\left(1 - \frac{1}{(1.001970)^N}\right)$$

and solve for N:

$$1 - \left(\frac{1}{1.001970}\right)^N = \frac{150,000 \times 0.001970}{1000} = 0.2955$$

$$\left(\frac{1}{1.001970}\right)^N = 0.7045$$

$$N = \frac{\log(0.7045)}{\log\left(\frac{1}{1.001970}\right)} = 177.98.$$

So it will take 178 payments to pay off the mortgage. Since the payments occur every two weeks, this will take $178 \times 2 = 356$ weeks or under 7 years. (It is shorter because there are approximately 2 extra payments every year.)

5-21. Your friend tells you he has a very simple trick for shortening the time it takes to repay your mortgage by one-third: Use your holiday bonus to make an extra payment on January 1 of each year (that is, pay your monthly payment due on that day twice). If you take out your mortgage on July 1, so your first monthly payment is due August 1, and you make an extra payment every January 1, how long will it take to pay off the mortgage? Assume that the mortgage has an original term of 30 years and an APR of 12%.

The principle balance does not matter, so just pick 100,000. Begin by computing the monthly payment. The discount rate is 12%/12 = 1%.

Timeline #1:

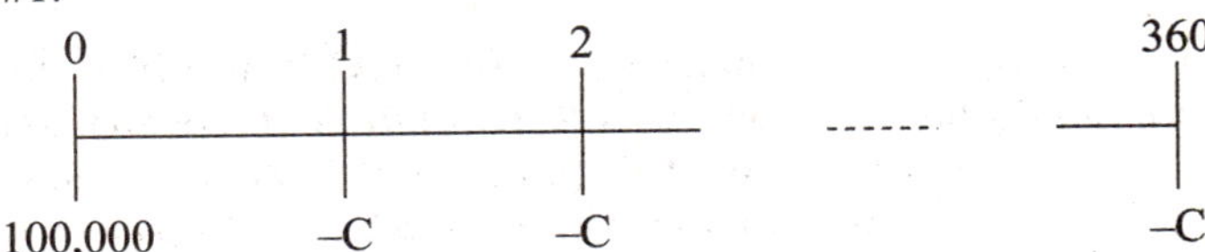

Using the formula for the loan payment,

$$C = \frac{100,000 \times 0.01}{\left(1 - \frac{1}{1.01^{360}}\right)} = \$1,028.61.$$

Next we write out the cash flows with the extra payment.

Timeline #2:

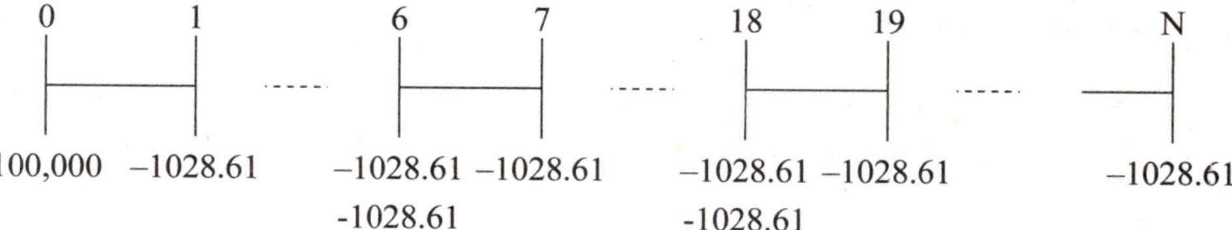

The cash flow consists of 2 annuities.

i. The original payments. The PV of these payments is

$$PV_{org} = \frac{1,028.61}{0.01}\left(1-\left(\frac{1}{1.01}\right)^{N}\right).$$

ii. The extra payment every Christmas. There are m such payments, where m is the number of *years* you keep the loan. (For the moment we will not worry about the possibility that m is not a whole number.) Since the time period between payments is 1 year, we first have to compute the discount rate.

$$(1.01)^{12} = 1.12683$$

So the discount rate is 12.683%.

Now the present value of the extra payments in month 6 consists of the remaining $m - 1$ payments (an annuity) and the payment in month 6. So the PV is:

$$PV_6 = \frac{1,028.61}{0.12683}\left(1-\frac{1}{(1.12683)^{m-1}}\right)+1,028.61.$$

To get the value today, we must discount these cash flows to month 0. Recall that the monthly discount rate is 1%. So the value today of the extra payment is:

$$PV_{extra} = \frac{PV_6}{(1.01)^6} = \frac{1,028.61}{0.12683(1.01)^6}\left(1-\frac{1}{(1.12683)^{m-1}}\right)+\frac{1,028.61}{(1.01)^6}.$$

To find out how long it will take to repay the loan, we need to determine the number of years until the value of our loan payments has a present value at the loan rate equal to the amount we borrowed. Because the number of monthly payments $N = 12 \times m$, we can write this as the following expression, which we need to solve for m:

$$100,000 = PV_{org} + PV_{extra}$$

$$100,000 = \frac{1,028.61}{0.01}\left(1-\left(\frac{1}{1.01}\right)^{12m}\right)+\frac{1,028.61}{0.12683(1.01)^6}\left(1-\frac{1}{(1.12683)^{m-1}}\right)+\frac{1,028.61}{(1.01)^6}.$$

The only way to find m is to iterate (guess). The answer is $m = 19.04$ years, or approximately 19 years.

In fact, after exactly 19 years the PV of the payments is:

$$PV = \frac{1,028.61}{0.01}\left(1-\left(\frac{1}{1.01}\right)^{228}\right)+\frac{1,028.61}{0.12683(1.01)^6}\left(1-\frac{1}{(1.12683)^{18}}\right)+\frac{1,028.61}{(1.01)^6} = \$99,939.$$

Since you initially borrowed \$100,000 the PV of what you still owe at the end of 19 years is \$100,000 – \$99,939 = \$61. The future value of this in 19 years and one month is:

$$61 \times (1.01)^{229} = \$596.$$

So, you will have a partial payment of \$596 in the first month of the 19th year. Because the mortgage will take about 19 years to pay off this way—which is close to $\frac{2}{3}$ of its life of 30 years—your friend is right.

5-22. You need a new car and the dealer has offered you a price of \$20,000, with the following payment options: (a) pay cash and receive a \$2000 rebate, or (b) pay a \$5000 down payment and finance the rest with a 0% APR loan over 30 months. But having just quit your job and started an MBA program, you are in debt and you expect to be in debt for at least the next 2 ½ years. You plan to use credit cards to pay your expenses; luckily you have one with a low (fixed) rate of 15% APR (monthly). Which payment option is best for you?

You can use any money that you don't spend on the car to pay down your credit card debt. Paying down the loan is equivalent to an investment earning the loan rate of 15% APR. Thus, your opportunity cost of capital is 15% APR (monthly) and so the discount rate is 15 / 12 = 1.25% per month. Computing the present value of option (ii) at this discount rate, we find

$$\text{PV(ii)} = -5000 + (-500) \times \frac{1}{.0125}\left(1 - \frac{1}{1.0125^{30}}\right) = -5000 - 12,444 = -\$17,444$$

You are better off taking the loan from the dealer and using any extra money to pay down your credit card debt.

5-23. The mortgage on your house is five years old. It required monthly payments of \$1402, had an original term of 30 years, and had an interest rate of 10% (APR). In the intervening five years, interest rates have fallen and so you have decided to refinance—that is, you will roll over the outstanding balance into a new mortgage. The new mortgage has a 30-year term, requires monthly payments, and has an interest rate of 6 5⁄8% (APR).

a. What monthly repayments will be required with the new loan?

b. If you still want to pay off the mortgage in 25 years, what monthly payment should you make after you refinance?

c. Suppose you are willing to continue making monthly payments of \$1402. How long will it take you to pay off the mortgage after refinancing?

d. Suppose you are willing to continue making monthly payments of \$1402, and want to pay off the mortgage in 25 years. How much additional cash can you borrow today as part of the refinancing?

a. First we calculate the outstanding balance of the mortgage. There are 25 × 12 = 300 months remaining on the loan, so the timeline is as follows.

Timeline #1:

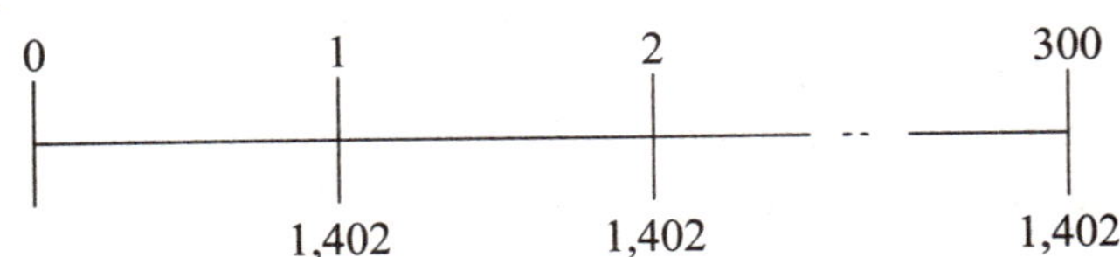

To determine the outstanding balance we discount at the original rate, i.e., $\frac{10}{12} = 0.8333\%$.

$$\text{PV} = \frac{1402}{0.008333}\left(1 - \frac{1}{(1.008333)^{300}}\right) = \$154,286.22$$

Next we calculate the loan payment on the new mortgage.

Timeline #2:

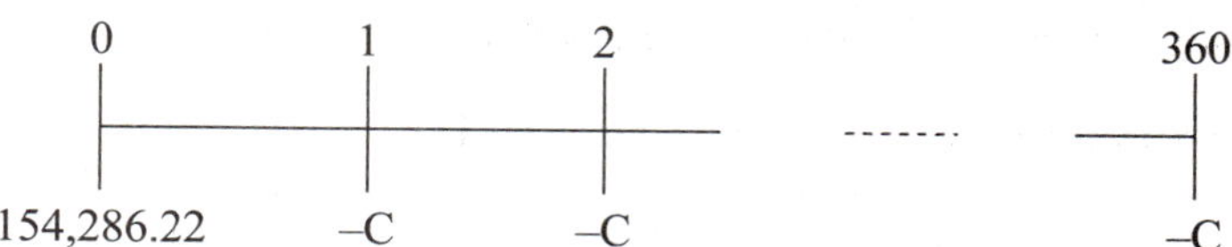

The discount rate on the new loan is the new loan rate: $\frac{6.625}{12} = 0.5521\%$.

Using the formula for the loan payment:

$$\text{C} = \frac{154,286.22 \times 0.005521}{\left(1 - \left(\frac{1}{1.005521}\right)^{360}\right)} = \$987.93.$$

b. $$\text{C} = \frac{154,286.22 \times 0.005521}{\left(1 - \left(\frac{1}{1.005521}\right)^{300}\right)} = \$1,053.85$$

c. $\text{PV} = \frac{1402}{0.005521}\left(1 - \frac{1}{(1.005521)^{N}}\right) = \$154,286.22 \Rightarrow N = 170$ months (You can use trial and error or the annuity calculator to solve for N.)

d. $$\text{PV} = \frac{1402}{0.005521}\left(1 - \frac{1}{(1.005521)^{300}}\right) = \$205,255$$

$\Rightarrow$ you can keep $205,259 - 154,286 = \$50,969$

(Note: results may differ slightly due to rounding.)

5-24. You have credit card debt of $25,000 that has an APR (monthly compounding) of 15%. Each month you pay the minimum monthly payment only. You are required to pay only the outstanding interest. You have received an offer in the mail for an otherwise identical credit card with an APR of 12%. After considering all your alternatives, you decide to switch cards, roll over the outstanding balance on the old card into the new card, and borrow additional money as well. How much can you borrow today on the new card without changing the minimum monthly payment you will be required to pay?

The discount rate on the original card is:

$$\frac{15}{12} = 1.25\%.$$

Assuming that your current monthly payment is the interest that accrues, it equals:

$$\$25,000 \times \frac{0.15}{12} = \$312.50.$$

Timeline:

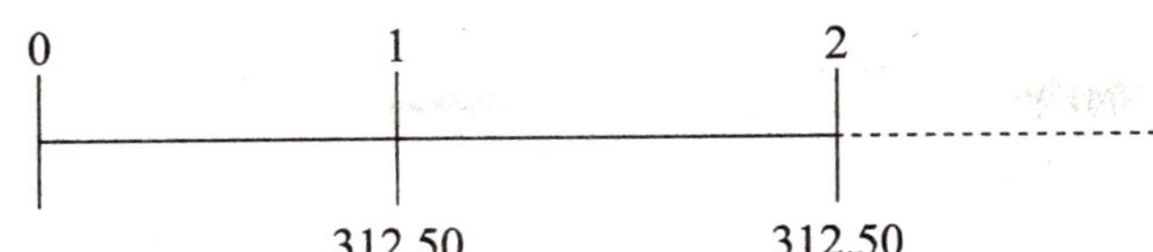

This is a perpetuity. So the amount you can borrow at the new interest rate is this cash flow discounted at the new discount rate. The new discount rate is $\frac{12}{12} = 1\%$.

So, $PV = \frac{312.50}{0.01} = \$31,250.$

So by switching credit cards you are able to spend an extra $31,250 - 25,000 = \$6,250$.

You do not have to pay taxes on this amount of new borrowing, so this is your after-tax benefit of switching cards.

5-25. In 1975, interest rates were 7.85% and the rate of inflation was 12.3% in the United States. What was the real interest rate in 1975? How would the purchasing power of your savings have changed over the year?

$$r_r = \frac{r-i}{1+i} = \frac{7.85\% - 12.3\%}{1.123} = -3.96\%$$

The purchasing power of your savings declined by 3.96% over the year.

5-26. If the rate of inflation is 5%, what nominal interest rate is necessary for you to earn a 3% real interest rate on your investment?

$1 + r_r = \frac{1+r}{1+i}$ implies $1 + r = (1 + r_r)(1 + i) = (1.03)(1.05) = 1.0815$.

Therefore, a nominal rate of 8.15% is required.

5-27. Can the nominal interest rate available to an investor be significantly negative? (*Hint*: Consider the interest rate earned from saving cash "under the mattress.") Can the real interest rate be negative? Explain.

By holding cash, an investor earns a nominal interest rate of 0%. Since an investor can always earn at least 0%, the nominal interest rate cannot be negative. The real interest rate can be negative, however. It is negative whenever the rate of inflation exceeds the nominal interest rate.

5-28. Consider a project that requires an initial investment of $100,000 and will produce a single cash flow of $150,000 in five years.

a. What is the NPV of this project if the five-year interest rate is 5% (EAR)?

b. What is the NPV of this project if the five-year interest rate is 10% (EAR)?

c. What is the highest five-year interest rate such that this project is still profitable?

a. $NPV = -100{,}000 + 150{,}000 / 1.05^5 = \$17{,}529.$

b. $NPV = -100{,}000 + 150{,}000 / 1.10^5 = -\$6862.$

c. The answer is the IRR of the investment: IRR = (150,000 / 100,000)1/5 – 1 = 8.45%.

5-29. Suppose the term structure of risk-free interest rates is as shown below:

Term	1 year	2 years	3 years	5 years	7 years	10 years	20 years
Rate (EAR, %)	1.99	2.41	2.74	3.32	3.76	4.13	4.93

a. **Calculate the present value of an investment that pays \$1000 in two years and \$2000 in five years for certain.**

b. **Calculate the present value of receiving \$500 per year, with certainty, at the end of the next five years. To find the rates for the missing years in the table, linearly interpolate between the years for which you do know the rates. (For example, the rate in year 4 would be the average of the rate in year 3 and year 5.)**

c. **Calculate the present value of receiving \$2300 per year, with certainty, for the next 20 years. Infer rates for the missing years using linear interpolation. (*Hint* : Use a spreadsheet.)**

a. Timeline:

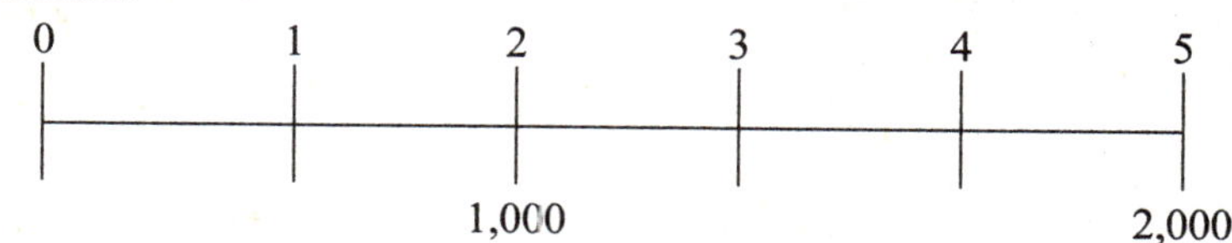

Since the opportunity cost of capital is different for investments of different maturities, we must use the cost of capital associated with each cash flow as the discount rate for that cash flow:

$$PV = \frac{1,000}{(1.0241)^2} + \frac{2,000}{(1.0332)^5} = \$2,652.15.$$

b. Timeline:

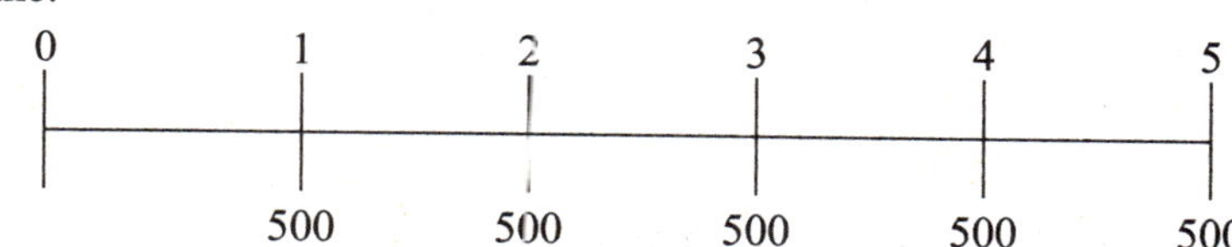

Since the opportunity cost of capital is different for investments of different maturities, we must use the cost of capital associated with each cash flow as the discount rate for that cash flow. Unfortunately, we do not have a rate for a 4-year cash flow, so we linearly interpolate.

$$r_4 = \frac{1}{2}(2.74) + \frac{1}{2}(3.32) = 3.03$$

$$PV = \frac{500}{1.0199} + \frac{500}{(1.0241)^2} + \frac{500}{(1.0274)^3} + \frac{500}{(1.0303)^4} + \frac{500}{(1.0332)^5} = \$2,296.43$$

c. Timeline:

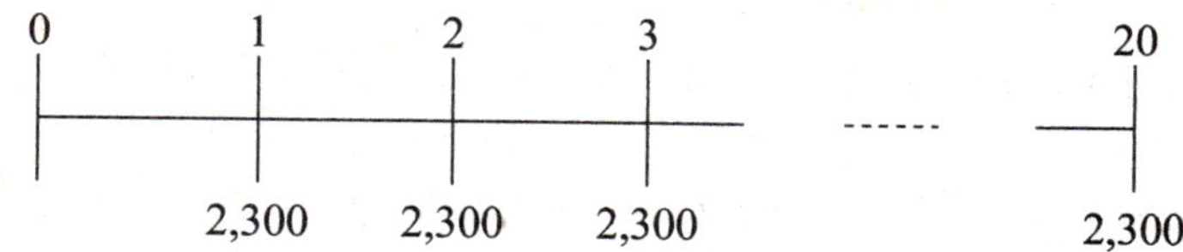

Since the opportunity cot of capital is different for investments of different maturities, we must use the cost of capital associated with each cash flow as the discount rate for that cash flow. Unfortunately, we do not have a rate for a number of years, so we linearly interpolate.

$$r_4 = \frac{1}{2}(2.74) + \frac{1}{2}(3.32)$$
$$= 3.03$$

$$r_6 = \frac{1}{2}(3.32) + \frac{1}{2}(3.76)$$
$$= 3.54$$

$$r_8 = \frac{2}{3}(3.76) + \frac{1}{3}(4.13)$$
$$= 3.883$$

$$r_9 = \frac{1}{3}(3.76) + \frac{2}{3}(4.13)$$
$$= 4.0067$$

$$r_{11} = \frac{9}{10}(4.13) + \frac{1}{10}(4.93)$$
$$= 4.21$$

$$r_{12} = \frac{8}{10}(4.13) + \frac{2}{10}(4.93)$$
$$= 4.29$$

$$r_{13} = 4.37$$
$$r_{14} = 4.45$$
$$r_{15} = 4.53$$
$$r_{16} = 4.61$$
$$r_{17} = 4.64$$
$$r_{18} = 4.77$$
$$r_{19} = 4.85$$

$$PV = \frac{2{,}300}{1+r_1} + \frac{2{,}300}{(1+r_2)^2} + \frac{2{,}300}{(1+r_3)^3} + \ldots + \frac{2{,}300}{(1+r_{20})^{20}}$$
$$= \frac{2{,}300}{1.0199} + \frac{2{,}300}{1.0241} + \frac{2{,}300}{1.0274} + \ldots + \frac{2{,}300}{(1.0493)^{20}}$$
$$= \$30{,}636.56$$

5-30. Using the term structure in Problem 29, what is the present value of an investment that pays $100 at the end of each of years 1, 2, and 3? If you wanted to value this investment correctly using the annuity formula, which discount rate should you use?

PV = 100 / 1.0199 + 100 / 1.0241^2 + 100 / 1.0274^3 =$285.61.

To determine the single discount rate that would compute the value correctly, we solve the following for r:

PV = 285.61 = 100/(1 + r) + 100 / $(1 + r)^2$ + 100/$(1 + r)^3$ = $285.61.

This is just an IRR calculation. Using trial and error or the annuity calculator, r = 2.50%. Note that this rate is between the 1, 2, and 3-yr rates given.

5-31. What is the shape of the yield curve given the term structure in Problem 29? What expectations are investors likely to have about future interest rates?

The yield curve is increasing. This is often a sign that investors expect interest rates to rise in the future.

5-32. Suppose the current one-year interest rate is 6%. One year from now, you believe the economy will start to slow and the one-year interest rate will fall to 5%. In two years, you expect the economy to be in the midst of a recession, causing the Federal Reserve to cut interest rates drastically and the one-year interest rate to fall to 2%. The one-year interest rate will then rise to 3% the following year, and continue to rise by 1% per year until it returns to 6%, where it will remain from then on.

a. If you were certain regarding these future interest rate changes, what two-year interest rate would be consistent with these expectations?

b. What current term structure of interest rates, for terms of 1 to 10 years, would be consistent with these expectations?

c. Plot the yield curve in this case. How does the one-year interest rate compare to the 10-year interest rate?

a. The one-year interest rate is 6%. If rates fall next year to 5%, then if you reinvest at this rate over two years you would earn (1.06)(1.05) = 1.113 per dollar invested. This amount corresponds to an EAR of $(1.113)^{1/2} - 1 = 5.50\%$ per year for two years. Thus, the two-year rate that is consistent with these expectations is 5.50%.

b. We can apply the same logic for future years:

Year	Future Interest Rates	FV from reinvesting	EAR
1	6%	1.0600	6.00%
2	5%	1.1130	5.50%
3	2%	1.1353	4.32%
4	3%	1.1693	3.99%
5	4%	1.2161	3.99%
6	5%	1.2769	4.16%
7	6%	1.3535	4.42%
8	6%	1.4347	4.62%
9	6%	1.5208	4.77%
10	6%	1.6121	4.89%

c. We can plot the yield curve using the EARs in (b); note that the 10-year rate is below the 1-year rate (yield curve is inverted).

5-33. Figure 5.4 shows that Wal-Mart's five-year borrowing rate is 3.1% and GE Capital's is 10%. Which would you prefer? $500 from Wal-Mart paid today or a promise that the firm will pay you $700 in five years? Which would you choose if GE Capital offered you the same alternatives?

We can use the interest rates each company must pay on a 5-year loan as the discount rate.

PV for GE Capital = $700 / 1.10^5 = \$434.64 < \$500$ today, so take the money now.

PV for Wal-Mart = $700 / 1.031^5 = \$600.90 > \$500$ today, so take the promise.

5-34. Your best taxable investment opportunity has an EAR of 4%. You best tax-free investment opportunity has an EAR of 3%. If your tax rate is 30%, which opportunity provides the higher after-tax interest rate?

After-tax rate = 4%(1 – .30) = 2.8%, which is less than your tax-free investment with pays 3%.

5-35. Your uncle Fred just purchased a new boat. He brags to you about the low 7% interest rate (APR, monthly compounding) he obtained from the dealer. The rate is even lower than the rate he could have obtained on his home equity loan (8% APR, monthly compounding). If his tax rate is 25% and the interest on the home equity loan is tax deductible, which loan is truly cheaper?

After-tax cost of home equity loan is 8%(1 – .25) = 6%, which is cheaper than the dealer's loan (for which interest is not tax-deductible). Thus, the home equity loan is cheaper. (Note that this could also be done in terms of EARs.)

5-36. You are enrolling in an MBA program. To pay your tuition, you can either take out a standard student loan (so the interest payments are not tax deductible) with an EAR of 5½% or you can use a tax-deductible home equity loan with an APR (monthly) of 6%. You anticipate being in a very low tax bracket, so your tax rate will be only 15%. Which loan should you use?

Using the formula to convert an APR to an EAR:

$$\left(1+\frac{0.06}{12}\right)^{12}=1.06168.$$

So the home equity loan has an EAR of 6.168%. Now since the rate on a tax deductible loan is a before-tax rate, we must convert this to an after-tax rate to compare it.

$$6.168\times(1-0.15)=5.243\%$$

Since the student loan has a larger after tax rate, you are better off using the home equity loan.

5-37. Your best friend consults you for investment advice. You learn that his tax rate is 35%, and he has the following current investments and debts:

- **A car loan with an outstanding balance of $5000 and a 4.8% APR (monthly compounding)**
- **Credit cards with an outstanding balance of $10,000 and a 14.9% APR (monthly compounding)**
- **A regular savings account with a $30,000 balance, paying a 5.50% EAR**
- **A money market savings account with a $100,000 balance, paying a 5.25% APR (daily compounding)**
- **A tax-deductible home equity loan with an outstanding balance of $25,000 and a 5.0%**

APR (monthly compounding)

a. Which savings account pays a higher after-tax interest rate?

b. Should your friend use his savings to pay off any of his outstanding debts? Explain.

a. The regular savings account pays 5.5% EAR, or 5.5%(1 – .35) = 3.575% after tax. The money-market account pays $(1 + 5.25\%/365)^{365} - 1$ = 5.39% or 5.39%(1 – .35) = 3.50% after tax. Therefore, the regular savings account pays a higher rate.

b. Your friend should pay off the credit card loans and the car loan, since they have after-tax costs of 14.9% APR and 4.8% APR respectively, which exceed the rate earned on savings. The home equity loan should not be repaid, as its EAR = $(1 + 5\%/12)^{12} - 1$ = 5.12%, for an after-tax rate of only 5.125(1 – .35) = 3.33%, which is below the rate earned on savings.

5-38. Suppose you have outstanding debt with an 8% interest rate that can be repaid anytime, and the interest rate on U.S. Treasuries is only 5%. You plan to repay your debt using any cash that you don't invest elsewhere. Until your debt is repaid, what cost of capital should you use when evaluating a new risk-free investment opportunity? Why?

The appropriate cost of capital for a new risk-free investment is 8%, since you could earn 8% without risk by paying off your existing loan and avoiding interest charges.

5-39. In the summer of 2008, at Heathrow Airport in London, Bestofthebest (BB), a private company, offered a lottery to win a Ferrari or 90,000 British pounds, equivalent at the time to about $180,000. Both the Ferrari and the money, in 100 pound notes, were on display. If the U.K. interest rate was 5% per year, and the dollar interest rate was 2% per year (EARs), how much did it cost the company in dollars each month to keep the cash on display? That is, what was the opportunity cost of keeping it on display rather than in a bank account? (Ignore taxes.)

Because the prize is in pounds, we should use the pound interest rate (comparable risk). $(1.05)^{(1/12)} - 1 = .4074\%$. 0.4074% x 90k = 366.7 pounds per month, or $733 per month at the current exchange rate.

5-40. You firm is considering the purchase of a new office phone system. You can either pay $32,000 now, or $1000 per month for 36 months.

a. Suppose your firm currently borrows at a rate of 6% per year (APR with monthly compounding). Which payment plan is more attractive?

b. Suppose your firm currently borrows at a rate of 18% per year (APR with monthly compounding). Which payment plan would be more attractive in this case?

a. The payments are as risky as the firm's other debt. So opportunity cost = debt rate. PV(36 month annuity of 1000 at 6%/12 per month) = $32,871. So pay cash.

b. PV(annuity at 18%/12 per mo) = $27,661. So pay over time.

Chapter 6

Investment Decision Rules

6-1. **Your brother wants to borrow $10,000 from you. He has offered to pay you back $12,000 in a year. If the cost of capital of this investment opportunity is 10%, what is its NPV? Should you undertake the investment opportunity? Calculate the IRR and use it to determine the maximum deviation allowable in the cost of capital estimate to leave the decision unchanged.**

NPV = 12000/1.1 – 10000=909.09. Take it!

IRR = 12000/10000 – 1 = 20%

The cost of capital can increase by up to 10% without changing the decision

6-2. **You are considering investing in a start-up company. The founder asked you for $200,000 today and you expect to get $1,000,000 in nine years. Given the riskiness of the investment opportunity, your cost of capital is 20%. What is the NPV of the investment opportunity? Should you undertake the investment opportunity? Calculate the IRR and use it to determine the maximum deviation allowable in the cost of capital estimate to leave the decision unchanged.**

$$NPV = \left(\frac{1000000}{1.2^9}\right) - 200000 = -6193$$

$$IRR = \left(\frac{1000000}{200000}\right)^{1/9} - 1 = 19.58\%$$

Do not take the project. A drop in the cost of capital of just 20 – 19.58 – 0.42% would change the decision.

6-3. **You are considering opening a new plant. The plant will cost $100 million upfront. After that, it is expected to produce profits of $30 million at the end of every year. The cash flows are expected to last forever. Calculate the NPV of this investment opportunity if your cost of capital is 8%. Should you make the investment? Calculate the IRR and use it to determine the maximum deviation allowable in the cost of capital estimate to leave the decision unchanged.**

Timeline:

NPV = –100 + 30/8% = $275 million. Yes, make the investment.

IRR: 0 = –100 + 30/IRR. IRR = 30/100 = 30%. Okay as long as cost of capital does not go above 30%.

6-4. Your firm is considering the launch of a new product, the XJ5. The upfront development cost is \$10 million, and you expect to earn a cash flow of \$3 million per year for the next five years. Plot the NPV profile for this project for discount rates ranging from 0% to 30%. For what range of discount rates is the project attractive?

r	NPV	IRR
0%	5.000	15.24%
5%	2.988	
10%	1.372	
15%	0.056	
20%	-1.028	
25%	-1.932	
30%	-2.693	

R	NPV	IRR
0%	5.000	15.24%
5%	2.846	
10%	1.248	
15% .	049	
20%	–.857	
30%	–1.546	

The project should be accepted as long as the discount rate is below 15.24%.

6-5. Bill Clinton reportedly was paid \$10 million to write his book *My Way*. The book took three years to write. In the time he spent writing, Clinton could have been paid to make speeches. Given his popularity, assume that he could earn \$8 million per year (paid at the end of the year) speaking instead of writing. Assume his cost of capital is 10% per year.

a. What is the NPV of agreeing to write the book (ignoring any royalty payments)?

b. Assume that, once the book is finished, it is expected to generate royalties of \$5 million in the first year (paid at the end of the year) and these royalties are expected to decrease at a rate of 30% per year in perpetuity. What is the NPV of the book with the royalty payments?

a. Timeline:

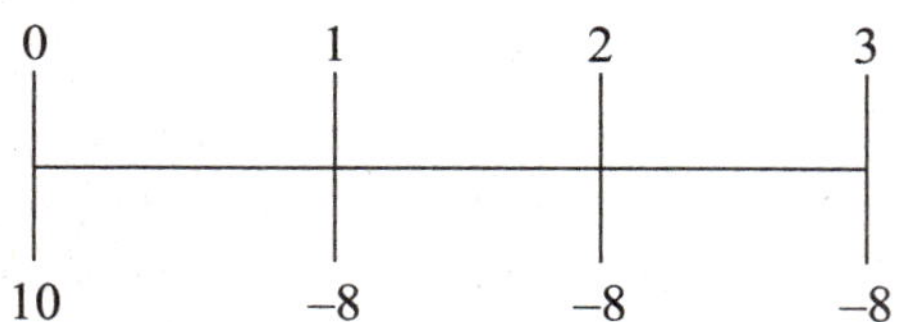

$$NPV = 10 - \frac{8}{0.1}\left(1 - \frac{1}{(1.1)^3}\right) = -\$9.895 \text{ million}$$

b. Timeline:

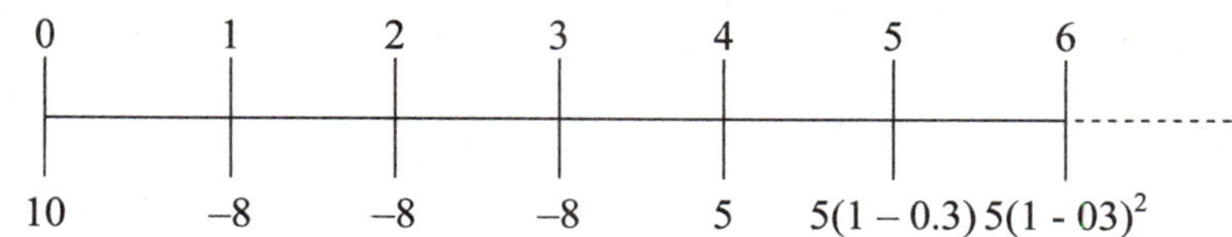

First calculate the PV of the royalties at year 3. The royalties are a declining perpetuity:

$$PV_5 = \frac{5}{0.1-(-0.3)} = \frac{5}{0.4} = 12.5 \text{ million}$$

So the value today is

$$PV_{royalties} = \frac{12.5}{(1.1)^3} = 9.391$$

Now add this to the NPV from part a), $NPV = -9.895 + 9.391 = -\$503{,}381$.

6-6. FastTrack Bikes, Inc. is thinking of developing a new composite road bike. Development will take six years and the cost is \$200,000 per year. Once in production, the bike is expected to make \$300,000 per year for 10 years. Assume the cost of capital is 10%.

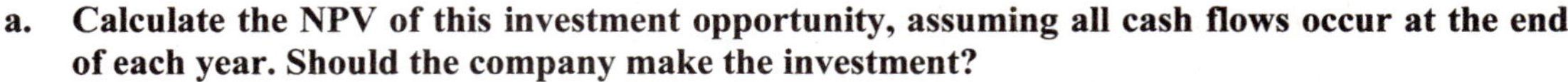

a. Calculate the NPV of this investment opportunity, assuming all cash flows occur at the end of each year. Should the company make the investment?

b. By how much must the cost of capital estimate deviate to change the decision? (*Hint*: Use Excel to calculate the IRR.)

c. What is the NPV of the investment if the cost of capital is 14%?

a. Timeline:

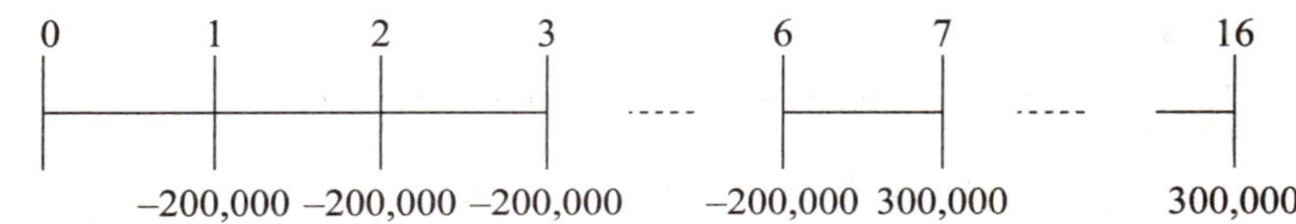

i. $$\text{NPV} = -\frac{200{,}000}{r}\left(1-\frac{1}{(1+r)^6}\right)+\left(\frac{1}{(1+r)^6}\right)\frac{300{,}000}{r}\left(1-\frac{1}{(1+r)^{10}}\right)$$

$$= -\frac{200{,}000}{0.1}\left(1-\frac{1}{(1.1)^6}\right)+\left(\frac{1}{(1.1)^6}\right)\frac{300{,}000}{0.1}\left(1-\frac{1}{(1.1)^{10}}\right)$$

=\$169,482

NPV > 0, so the company should take the project.

ii. Setting the NPV = 0 and solving for r (using a spreadsheet) the answer is IRR = 12.66%.

So if the estimate is too low by 2.66%, the decision will change from accept to reject.

	1	2	3	4	5	6	1	2	3	4	5	6	7	8	9	10
	-200	-200	-200	-200	-200	-200	300	300	300	300	300	300	300	300	300	300
IRR	12.66%															
NPV																
10%	\$169.482															
14%	(\$64.816)															

iii. Timeline:

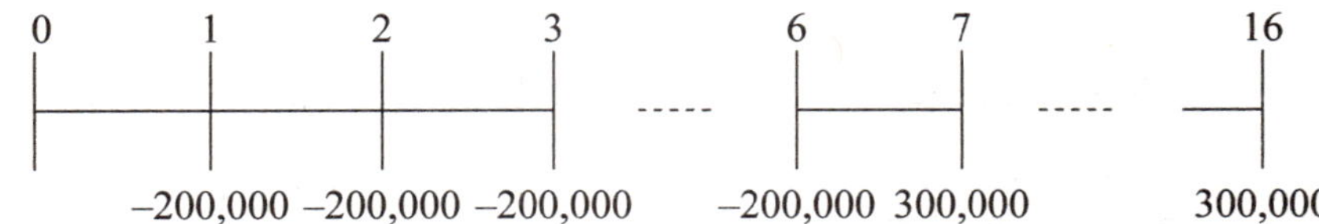

$$\text{NPV} = -\frac{200{,}000}{r}\left(1-\frac{1}{(1+r)^6}\right)+\left(\frac{1}{(1+r)^6}\right)\frac{300{,}000}{r}\left(1-\frac{1}{(1+r)^{10}}\right)$$

$$= -\frac{200{,}000}{0.14}\left(1-\frac{1}{(1.14)^6}\right)+\left(\frac{1}{(1.14)^6}\right)\frac{300{,}000}{0.14}\left(1-\frac{1}{(1.14)^{10}}\right)$$

$$= -\$64.816$$

6-7. OpenSeas, Inc. is evaluating the purchase of a new cruise ship. The ship would cost \$500 million, and would operate for 20 years. OpenSeas expects annual cash flows from operating the ship to be \$70 million (at the end of each year) and its cost of capital is 12%.

a. Prepare an NPV profile of the purchase.

b. Estimate the IRR (to the nearest 1%) from the graph.

c. Is the purchase attractive based on these estimates?

d. How far off could OpenSeas' cost of capital be (to the nearest 1%) before your purchase decision would change?

a.

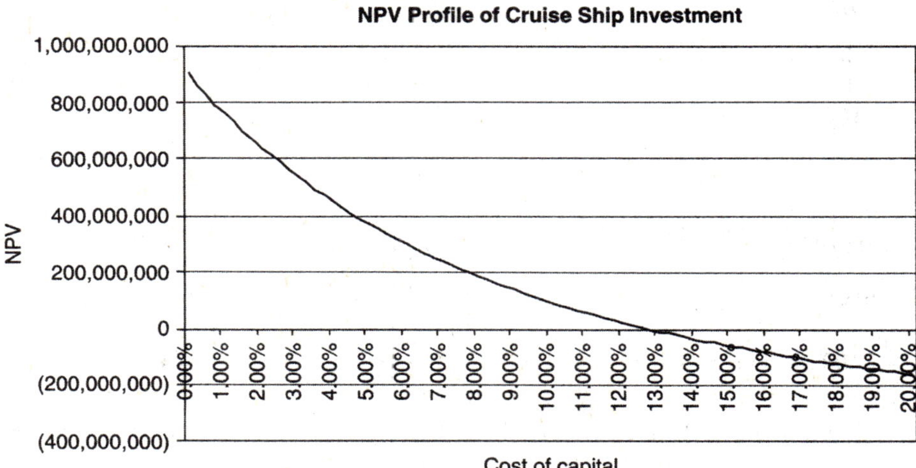

b. The IRR is the point at which the line crosses the *x*-axis. In this case, it falls very close to 13%. Using Excel, the IRR is 12.72%.

c. Yes, because the NPV is positive at the discount rate of 12%.

d. The discount rate could be off by 0.72% before the investment decision would change.

R	NPV (000s)
0%	\$900.00
5%	\$372.35
10%	\$95.95
12%	\$22.86
13%	(\$8.27)
15%	(\$61.85)
20%	(\$159.13)
25%	(\$223.23)

6-8. You are considering an investment in a clothes distributor. The company needs \$100,000 today and expects to repay you \$120,000 in a year from now. What is the IRR of this investment

opportunity? Given the riskiness of the investment opportunity, your cost of capital is 20%. What does the IRR rule say about whether you should invest?

IRR = 120000/100000 – 1 = 20%. You are indifferent

6-9. **You have been offered a very long term investment opportunity to increase your money one hundredfold. You can invest $1000 today and expect to receive $100,000 in 40 years. Your cost of capital for this (very risky) opportunity is 25%. What does the IRR rule say about whether the investment should be undertaken? What about the NPV rule? Do they agree?**

$$IRR = \left(\frac{100000}{1000}\right)^{1/40} - 1 = 12.2\%$$

$$NPV = \frac{100000}{1.25^{40}} - 1000 = -986.71$$

Both rules agree—do not undertake the investment.

6-10. **Does the IRR rule agree with the NPV rule in Problem 3? Explain.**

Timeline:

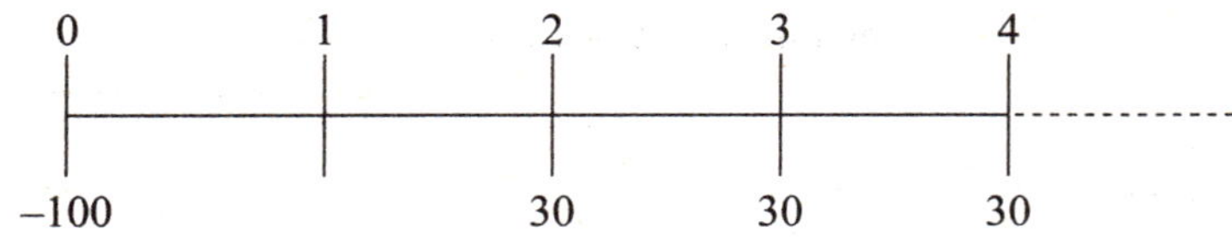

$$NPV = \left(\frac{1}{1.08}\right)\frac{30}{0.08} - 100 = \$247.22\ million$$

The IRR solves

$$\left(\frac{1}{1+r}\right)\frac{30}{r} - 100 = 0 \Rightarrow r = 24.16\%$$

Since the IRR exceeds the 8% discount rate, the IRR gives the same answer as the NPV rule.

6-11. **How many IRRs are there in part (a) of Problem 5? Does the IRR rule give the right answer in this case? How many IRRs are there in part (b) of Problem 5? Does the IRR rule work in this case?**

Timeline:

0	1	2	3
10	–8	–8	–8

IRR is the r that solves

$$NPV = 0 = 10 - \frac{8}{r}\left(1 - \frac{1}{(1+r)^3}\right)$$

To determine how many solutions this equation has, plot the NPV as a function of r

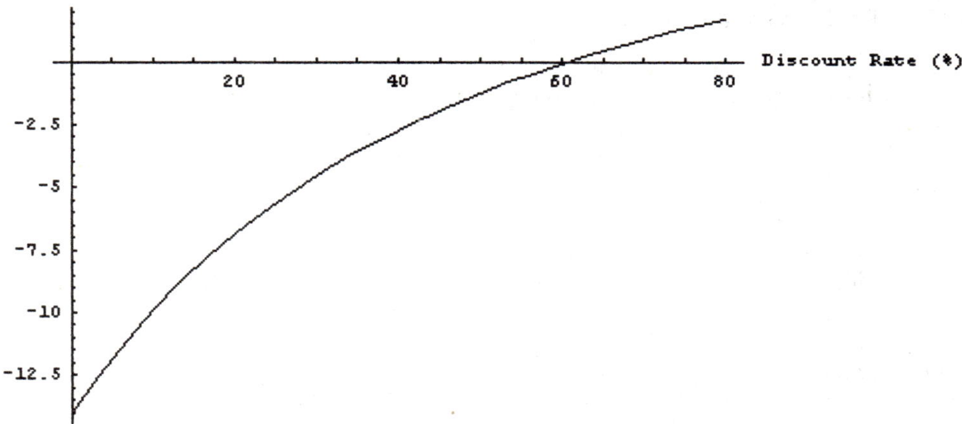

From the plot there is one IRR of 60.74%.

Since the IRR is much greater than the discount rate, the IRR rule says write the book. Since this is a negative NPV project (from 6.5a), the IRR gives the wrong answer.

Timeline:

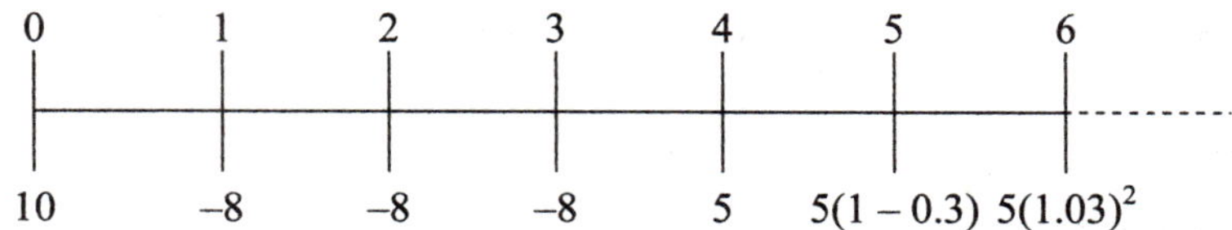

From 6.5(b) the NPV of these cash flows is

$$NPV = 10 - \frac{8}{r}\left(1 - \frac{1}{(1+r)^3}\right) + \frac{1}{(1+r)^3}\left(\frac{5}{r+0.3}\right)$$

Plotting the NPV as a function of the discount rate gives

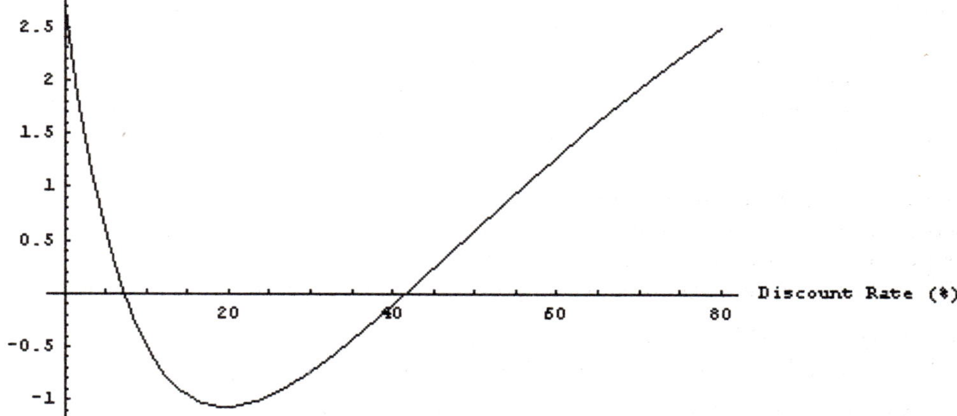

The plot shows that there are 2 IRRs – 7.165% and 41.568%. The IRR does give an answer in this case, so it does not work

6-12. Professor Wendy Smith has been offered the following deal: A law firm would like to retain her for an upfront payment of $50,000. In return, for the next year the firm would have access to 8 hours of her time every month. Smith's rate is $550 per hour and her opportunity cost of capital is 15% (EAR). What does the IRR rule advise regarding this opportunity? What about the NPV rule?

The timeline of this investment opportunity is:

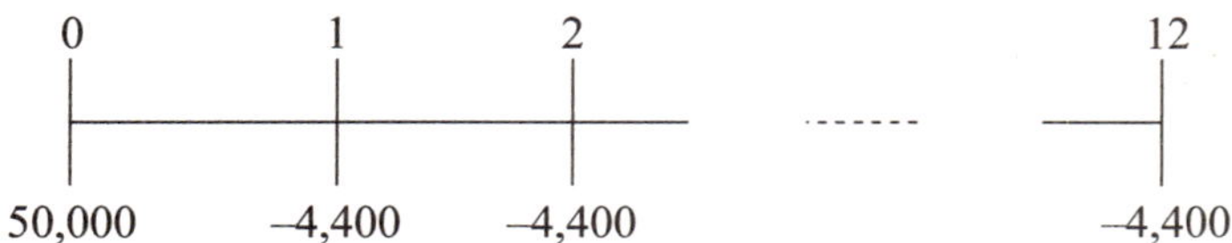

Computing the NPV of the cash flow stream

$$NPV = 50,000 - \frac{4,400}{r}\left(1 - \frac{1}{(1+r)^{12}}\right)$$

To compute the IRR, we set the NPV equal to zero and solve for r. Using the annuity spreadsheet gives

N	I	PV	PMT	FV
12	0.8484%	50,000	–4,400	0

The monthly IRR is 0.8484, so since

$$(1.008484)^{12} = 1.106696$$

then 0.8484% monthly corresponds to an EAR of 10.67%. Smith's cost of capital is 15%, so according to the IRR rule, she should turn down this opportunity.

Let's see what the NPV rule says. If you invest at an EAR of 15%, then after one month you will have

$$(1.15)^{1/12} = 1.011715$$

so the monthly discount rate is 1.1715%. Computing the NPV using this discount rate gives

$$NPV = 50,000 - \frac{4,400}{0.011715}\left(1 - \frac{1}{(1.011715)^{12}}\right) = \$1010.06,$$

which is positive, so the correct decision is to accept the deal. Smith can also be relatively confident in this decision. Based on the difference between the IRR and the cost of capital, her cost of capital would have to be 15 – 10.67 = 4.33% *lower* to reverse the decision

6-13. Innovation Company is thinking about marketing a new software product. Upfront costs to market and develop the product are $5 million. The product is expected to generate profits of $1 million per year for 10 years. The company will have to provide product support expected to cost $100,000 per year in perpetuity. Assume all profits and expenses occur at the end of the year.

a. What is the NPV of this investment if the cost of capital is 6%? Should the firm undertake the project? Repeat the analysis for discount rates of 2% and 12%.

b. How many IRRs does this investment opportunity have?

c. Can the IRR rule be used to evaluate this investment? Explain.

a. Timeline:

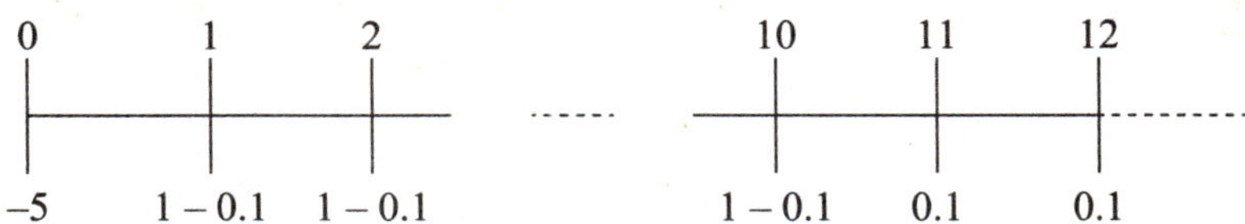

The PV of the profits is

$$PV_{profits} = \frac{1}{r}\left(1 - \frac{1}{(1+r)^{10}}\right)$$

The PV of the support costs is

$$PV_{\text{support}} = \frac{0.1}{r}$$

$$NPV = -5 + PV_{\text{profits}} + PV_{\text{support}} = -5 + \frac{1}{r}\left(1 - \left(\frac{1}{(1+r)^{10}}\right)\right) - \frac{0.1}{r}$$

r = 6% then NPV = $693,420.38

r = 2% then NPV = –$1,017,414.99

r = 12% then NPV = –$183,110.30

b. From the answer to part (a) there are 2 IRRs: 2.745784% and 10.879183%

c. The IRR rule says nothing in this case because there are 2 IRRs, therefore the IRR rule cannot be used to evaluate this investment

6-14. You own a coal mining company and are considering opening a new mine. The mine itself will cost $120 million to open. If this money is spent immediately, the mine will generate $20 million for the next 10 years. After that, the coal will run out and the site must be cleaned and maintained at environmental standards. The cleaning and maintenance are expected to cost $2 million per year in perpetuity. What does the IRR rule say about whether you should accept this opportunity? If the cost of capital is 8%, what does the NPV rule say?

The timeline of this investment opportunity is:

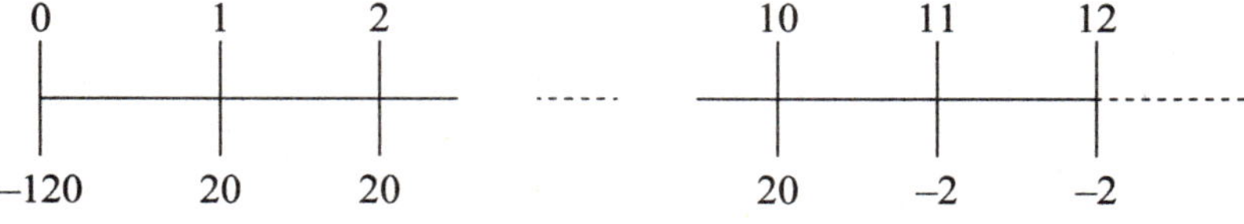

Computing the NPV of the cash flow stream:

$$NPV = -120 + \frac{20}{r}\left(1 - \frac{1}{(1+r)^{10}}\right) - \frac{2}{r(1+r)^{10}}.$$

You can verify that r = 0.02924 or 0.08723 gives an NPV of zero. There are two IRRs, so you cannot apply the IRR rule. Let's see what the NPV rule says. Using the cost of capital of 8% gives

$$NPV = -120 + \frac{20}{r}\left(1 - \frac{1}{(1+r)^{10}}\right) - \frac{2}{r(1+r)^{10}} = 2.621791$$

So the investment has a positive NPV of $2,621,791. In this case the NPV as a function of the discount rate is n shaped.

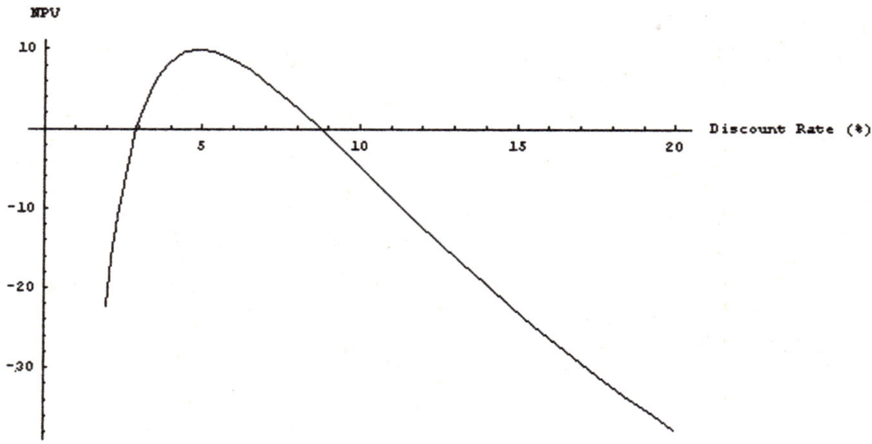

If the opportunity cost of capital is *between* 2.93% and 8.72%, the investment should be undertaken.

6-15. Your firm spends $500,000 per year in regular maintenance of its equipment. Due to the economic downturn, the firm considers forgoing these maintenance expenses for the next three years. If it does so, it expects it will need to spend $2 million in year 4 replacing failed equipment.

a. What is the IRR of the decision to forgo maintenance of the equipment?

b. Does the IRR rule work for this decision?

c. For what costs of capital is forgoing maintenance a good decision?

a. IRR = 15.091

b. No

c. COC > IRR = 15.091%

	1	2	3	4	
	500	500	500	-2000	
IRR =	15.09%				
NPV at 10% =		($122.60)			
IRR rule does not work, Positive NPV only if r > 15.09%					

6-16. You are considering investing in a new gold mine in South Africa. Gold in South Africa is buried very deep, so the mine will require an initial investment of \$250 million. Once this investment is made, the mine is expected to produce revenues of \$30 million per year for the next 20 years. It will cost \$10 million per year to operate the mine. After 20 years, the gold will be depleted. The mine must then be stabilized on an ongoing basis, which will cost \$5 million per year in perpetuity. Calculate the IRR of this investment. (*Hint*: Plot the NPV as a function of the discount rate.)

Timeline:

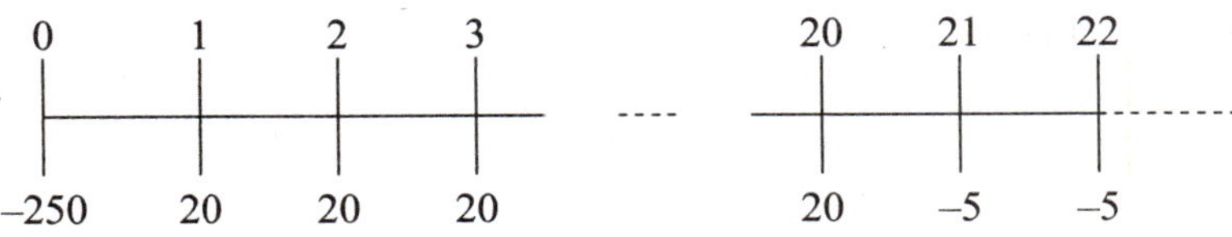

$$PV_{operating\ profits} = \frac{20}{r}\left(1 - \frac{1}{(1+r)^{20}}\right)$$

In year 20, the PV of the stabilizations costs are $PV_{20} = \frac{5}{r}$

So the PV today is $PV_{\text{stabilization costs}} = \frac{1}{(1+r)^{20}}\left(\frac{5}{r}\right)$

$$NPV = -250 + \frac{20}{r}\left(1 - \frac{1}{(1+r)^{20}}\right) - \frac{1}{(1+r)^{20}}\left(\frac{5}{r}\right)$$

Plotting this out gives

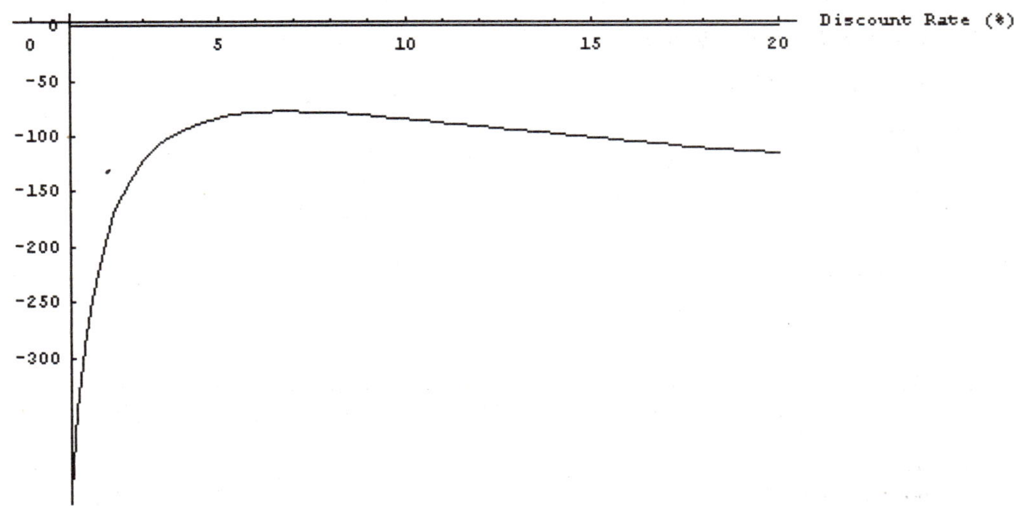

So no IRR exists.

6-17. Your firm has been hired to develop new software for the university's class registration system. Under the contract, you will receive \$500,000 as an upfront payment. You expect the

development costs to be $450,000 per year for the next three years. Once the new system is in place, you will receive a final payment of $900,000 from the university four years from now.

a. **What are the IRRs of this opportunity?**

b. **If your cost of capital is 10%, is the opportunity attractive?**

Suppose you are able to renegotiate the terms of the contract so that your final payment in year 4 will be $1 million.

c. **What is the IRR of the opportunity now?**

d. **Is it attractive at these terms?**

a.

	0	1	2	3	4
	500	-450	-450	-450	900
IRR =	8.53%				
IRR =	31.16%				
NPV at 10% =		$ (4.37)			

b. No

c.

	0	1	2	3	4
	500	-450	-450	-450	1000
IRR =	#NUM!	(does not exist)			
IRR =	#NUM!				
NPV at 10% =		$ 63.93			

d. Yes

6-18. **You are considering constructing a new plant in a remote wilderness area to process the ore from a planned mining operation. You anticipate that the plant will take a year to build and cost $100 million upfront. Once built, it will generate cash flows of $15 million at the end of every year over the life of the plant. The plant will be useless 20 years after its completion once the mine runs out of ore. At that point you expect to pay $200 million to shut the plant down and restore the area to its pristine state. Using a cost of capital of 12%,**

a. **What is the NPV of the project?**

b. **Is using the IRR rule reliable for this project? Explain.**

c. **What are the IRR's of this project?**

Timeline:

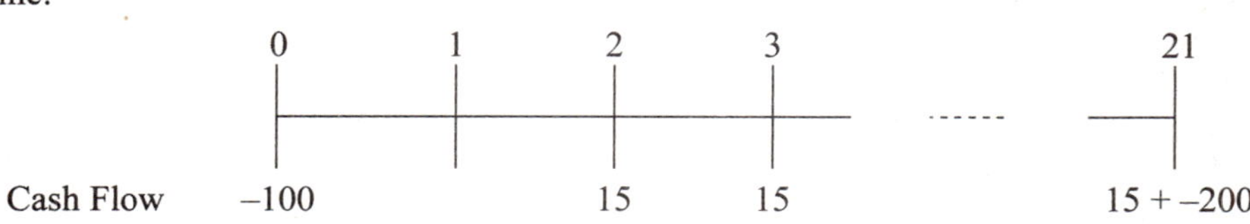

a. $NPV = -100 + \dfrac{15\frac{1}{r}\left(1-\frac{1}{(1+r)^{20}}\right)}{(1+r)} - \dfrac{200}{(1+r)^{21}}$ with r = 12%, NPV = -18.5 million

b. No, IRR rule is not reliable, because the project has a negative cash flow that comes after the positive ones.

c. Because the total cash flows are equal to zero (–100 + 15 x 20 – 200 = 0), one IRR must be 0%. Because the cash flows change sign more than once, we can have a second IRR. This IRR solves

$\frac{15\frac{1}{r}\left(1-\frac{1}{(1+r)^{20}}\right)}{(1+r)}-\frac{200}{(1+r)^{21}}-100=0$. Using trial and error, Excel, or plotting the NPV profile, we can find a second IRR of 7.06%. Because there are two IRRs the rule does not apply.

6-19. You are a real estate agent thinking of placing a sign advertising your services at a local bus stop. The sign will cost $5000 and will be posted for one year. You expect that it will generate additional revenue of $500 per month. What is the payback period?

5000 / 500 = 10 months.

6-20. You are considering making a movie. The movie is expected to cost $10 million upfront and take a year to make. After that, it is expected to make $5 million when it is released in one year and $2 million per year for the following four years. What is the payback period of this investment? If you require a payback period of two years, will you make the movie? Does the movie have positive NPV if the cost of capital is 10%?

Timeline:

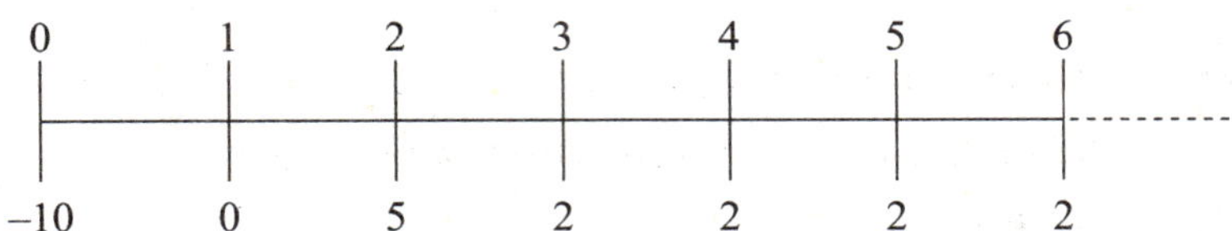

It will take 5 years to pay back the initial investment, so the payback period is 5 years. You will not make the movie.

$$NPV=-10+\frac{5}{(1+r)^2}+\frac{2}{r}\left(1-\frac{1}{(1+r)^4}\right)\frac{1}{(1+r)^2}=-10+\frac{5}{(1.1)^2}+\frac{2}{0.1(1.1)^2}\left(1-\frac{1}{(1.1)^4}\right)=-\$628,322$$

So the NPV agrees with the payback rule in this case

0	1	2	3	4	5
-10	5	2	2	2	2
Payback =	4 years				
NPV at 10% =		$0.31	million		

6-21. You are deciding between two mutually exclusive investment opportunities. Both require the same initial investment of $10 million. Investment A will generate $2 million per year (starting at the end of the first year) in perpetuity. Investment B will generate $1.5 million at the end of the first year and its revenues will grow at 2% per year for every year after that.

a. Which investment has the higher IRR?

b. Which investment has the higher NPV when the cost of capital is 7%?

c. In this case, for what values of the cost of capital does picking the higher IRR give the correct answer as to which investment is the best opportunity?

a. Timeline:

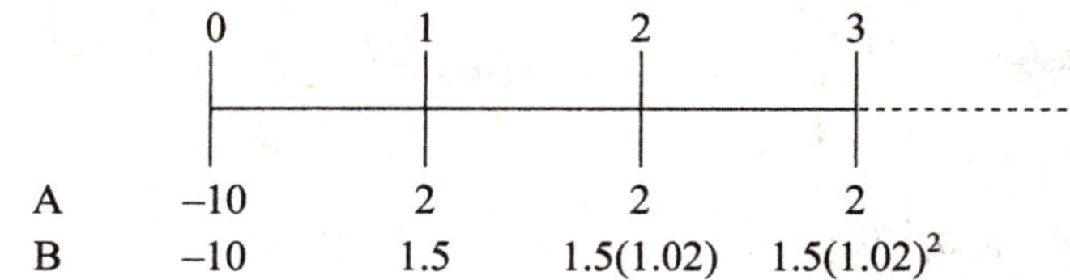

$$NPV_A = \frac{2}{r} - 10$$

Setting $NPV_A = 0$ and solving for r

$IRR_A = 20\%$

$$NPV_B = \frac{1.5}{r - 0.02} - 10$$

Setting $NPV_B = 0$ and solving for r

$$\frac{1.5}{r - 0.02} = 10 \Rightarrow r - 0.02 = 0.15 \Rightarrow r = 17\%. \text{ So, } IRR_B = 17\%$$

Based on the IRR, you always pick project A.

b. Substituting r = 0.07 into the NPV formulas derived in part (a) gives

NPV_A = \$18.5714 million,

NPV_B = \$20 million.

So the NPV says take B.

c. Here is a plot of NPV of both projects as a function of the discount rate. The NPV rule selects A (and so agrees with the IRR rule) for all discount rates to the right of the point where the curves cross.

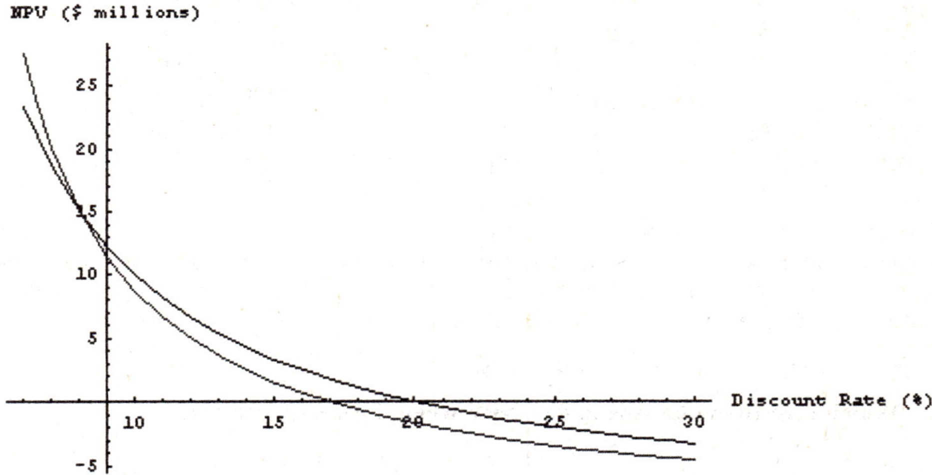

$$NPV_A = NPV_B$$

$$\frac{2}{r} = \frac{1.5}{r-0.02}$$

$$\frac{r}{2} = \frac{r-0.02}{1.5}$$

$$1.5r = 2r - 0.04$$

$$0.5r = 0.04$$

$$r = 0.08$$

So the IRR rule will give the correct answer for discount rates greater than 8%

6-22. You have just started your summer internship, and your boss asks you to review a recent analysis that was done to compare three alternative proposals to enhance the firm's manufacturing facility. You find that the prior analysis ranked the proposals according to their IRR, and recommended the highest IRR option, Proposal A. You are concerned and decide to redo the analysis using NPV to determine whether this recommendation was appropriate. But while you are confident the IRRs were computed correctly, it seems that some of the underlying data regarding the cash flows that were estimated for each proposal was not included in the report. For Proposal B, you cannot find information regarding the total initial investment that was required in year 0. And for Proposal C, you cannot find the data regarding additional salvage value that will be recovered in year 3. Here is the information you have:

Proposal	IRR	Year 0	Year 1	Year 2	Year 3
A	60.0%	–100	30	153	88
B	55.0%	?	0	206	95
C	50.0%	–100	37	0	204 + ?

Suppose the appropriate cost of capital for each alternative is 10%. Using this information, determine the NPV of each project. Which project should the firm choose?

Why is ranking the projects by their IRR not valid in this situation?

a. Project A: $NPV(A) = -100 + 30/1.10 + 153/1.10^2 + 88/1.10^3 = \$119.83$

Project B: We can use the IRR to determine the initial cash flow:

$CF_0(B) = -(206/1.55^2 + 95/1.55^3) = -\$111.25.$

Thus, $NPV(B) = -111.25 + 0/1.10 + 206/1.10^2 + 95/1.10^3 = \$130.37$

Project C: We can use the IRR to determine the final cash flow:

$CF_3(C) = 100 \times 1.50^3 - 37 \times 1.50^2 = \$254.25.$

Thus, $NPV(C) = -100 + 37/1.10 + 0/1.10^2 + 254.25/1.10^3 = \$124.65$

b. Ranking the projects by their IRR is not valid in this situation because the projects have different scale and different pattern of cash flows over time.

6-23. Use the incremental IRR rule to correctly choose between the investments in Problem 21 when the cost of capital is 7%. At what cost of capital would your decision change?

Timeline:

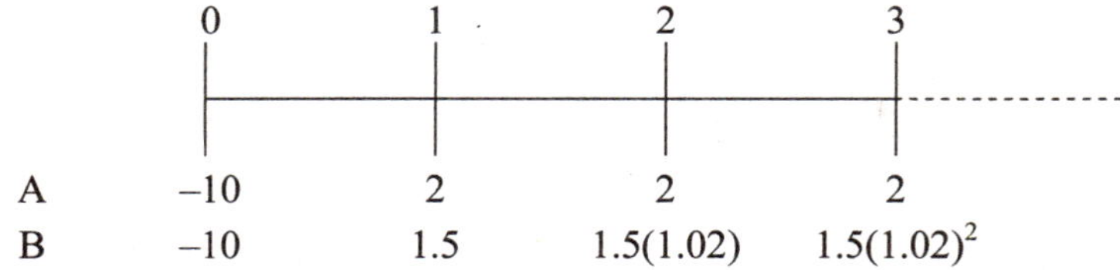

	0	1	2	3
A	–10	2	2	2
B	–10	1.5	1.5(1.02)	$1.5(1.02)^2$

To calculate the incremental IRR subtract A from B

0   1.5 – 2   1.5(1.02)–2 $1.5(1.02)^2–2$ …

$$NPV = \frac{1.5}{r-0.02} - \frac{2}{r} = 0$$

$$\frac{2}{r} = \frac{1.5}{r-0.02}$$

$$\frac{r}{2} = \frac{r-0.02}{1.5}$$

$$1.5r = 2r - 0.04$$

$$0.5r = 0.04$$

$$r = 0.08$$

So the incremental IRR is 8%. This rate is above the cost of capital, so we should take B.

6-24. You work for an outdoor play structure manufacturing company and are trying to decide between two projects:

	Year-End Cash Flows ($ thousands)			
Project	**0**	**1**	**2**	**IRR**
Playhouse	–30	15	20	10.4%
Fort	–80	39	52	8.6%

You can undertake only one project. If your cost of capital is 8%, use the incremental IRR rule to make the correct decision.

Timeline:

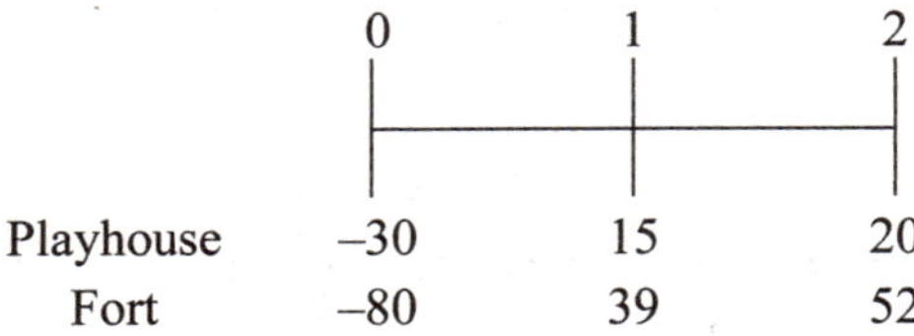

	0	1	2
Playhouse	–30	15	20
Fort	–80	39	52

Subtract the Playhouse cash flows from the Fort

–50   24   32

$$NPV = -50 + \frac{24}{1+r} + \frac{32}{(1+r)^2}$$

Solving for r

$$r = \frac{-2(50) + 24 + \sqrt{24^2 + 4(50)(32)}}{2(50)}$$

$= 7.522\%$

Since the incremental IRR of 7.522% is less than the cost of capital of 8%, you should take the Playhouse.

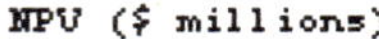

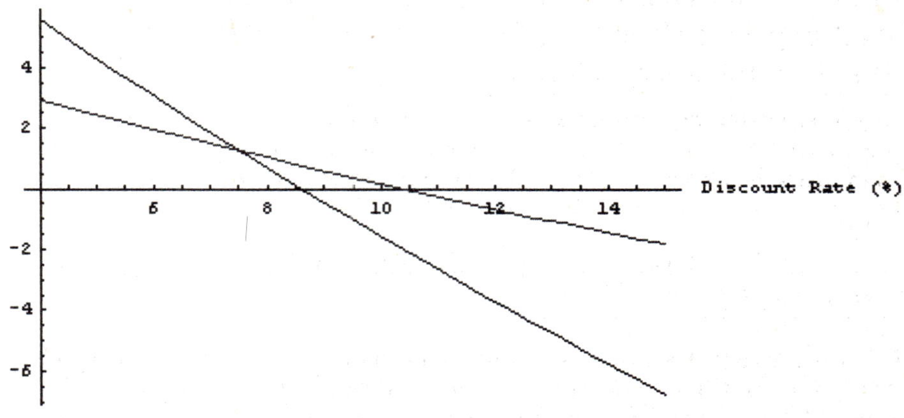

6-25. **You are evaluating the following two projects:**

Project	Year-End Cash Flows ($ thousands) 0	1	2
X	–30	20	20
Y	–80	40	60

Use the incremental IRR to determine the range of discount rates for which each project is optimal to undertake. Note that you should also include the range in which it does not make sense to take either project.

To compute the incremental IRR, we first need to compute the difference between the cash flows. Compute Y-X to make sure the incremental net investment is negative and the other cash flows are positive:

Project	Year-End Cash Flows ($ thousands) 0	1	2	IRR
X	–30	20	20	21.53%
Y	–80	40	60	15.14%
Y-X	–50	20	40	11.65%

Because all three projects have a negative cash flow followed by positive cash flows, the IRR rule can be used to decide whether to invest. The incremental IRR rule says Y is preferred to X for all discount rates less than 11.65%. The IRR rule says X should be undertaken for discount rates less than 21.53%, so combining this information, Y should be taken on for rates up to 11.65%, for rates between 11.65% and 21.53% X should be undertaken, and neither project should be undertaken for rates above 21.53%.

6-26. **Consider two investment projects, which both require an upfront investment of $10 million, and both of which pay a constant positive amount each year for the next 10 years. Under what conditions can you rank these projects by comparing their IRRs?**

They have the same scale, and the same timing (10-year annuities). Thus, as long as they have the same risk (and therefore, cost of capital), we can compare them based on their IRRs.

6-27. **You are considering a safe investment opportunity that requires a $1000 investment today, and will pay $500 two years from now and another $750 five years from now.**

a. What is the IRR of this investment?

b. If you are choosing between this investment and putting your money in a safe bank account that pays an EAR of 5% per year for any horizon, can you make the decision by simply comparing this EAR with the IRR of the investment? Explain.

a. 6.16%

b. Yes – because they have the same timing, scale, and risk (safe), you can choose the investment with the higher IRR.

6-28. **AOL is considering two proposals to overhaul its network infrastructure. They have received two bids. The first bid, from Huawei, will require a $20 million upfront investment and will generate $20 million in savings for AOL each year for the next three years. The second bid, from Cisco, requires a $100 million upfront investment and will generate $60 million in savings each year for the next three years.**

a. What is the IRR for AOL associated with each bid?

b. If the cost of capital for this investment is 12%, what is the NPV for AOL of each bid? Suppose Cisco modifies its bid by offering a lease contract instead. Under the terms of the lease, AOL will pay $20 million upfront, and $35 million per year for the next three years. AOL's savings will be the same as with Cisco's original bid.

c. Including its savings, what are AOL's net cash flows under the lease contract? What is the IRR of the Cisco bid now?

d. Is this new bid a better deal for AOL than Cisco's original bid? Explain.

a. Huawei 83.9%, Cisco 36.3%

b. Huawei $28.0 m, Cisco $44.1m

c. CF = –20, 25,25,25,

IRR = 111.9%

d. No! Despite a higher IRR, it actually involves borrowing 80 upfront and pay 35 per year, which is a borrowing cost of 14.9%, which is higher than AOL's borrowing cost.

6-29. **Natasha's Flowers, a local florist, purchases fresh flowers each day at the local flower market. The buyer has a budget of $1000 per day to spend. Different flowers have different profit margins, and also a maximum amount the shop can sell. Based on past experience, the shop has estimated the following NPV of purchasing each type:**

	NPV per bunch	Cost per bunch	Max. Bunches
Roses	$ 3	$20	25
Lilies	8	30	10
Pansies	4	30	10
Orchids	20	80	5

What combination of flowers should the shop purchase each day?

	NPV per bunch	Cost per bunch	Max. Bunches		Profitability Index (per bunch)	Max Investment
Roses	$3	$20	25		0.150	$500
Lilies	$8	$30	10		0.267	$300
Pansies	$4	$30	10		0.133	$300
Orchids	$20	$80	5		0.250	$400

Buy $300 of lilies, $400 of orchids, and $300 of roses

6-30. **You own a car dealership and are trying to decide how to configure the showroom floor. The floor has 2000 square feet of usable space. You have hired an analyst and asked her to estimate the NPV of putting a particular model on the floor and how much space each model requires:**

Model	NPV	Space Requirement (sq. ft.)
MB345	$3000	200
MC237	5000	250
MY456	4000	240
MG231	1000	150
MT347	6000	450
MF302	4000	200
MG201	1500	150

In addition, the showroom also requires office space. The analyst has estimated that office space generates an NPV of $14 per square foot. What models should be displayed on the floor and how many square feet should be devoted to office space?

Model	NPV	Space Requirement (sq. ft.)	NPV/sqft		
MB345	$3,000	200	$15.0		
MC237	$5,000	250	$20.0		
MY456	$4,000	240	$16.7		
MG231	$1,000	150	$6.7		
MT347	$6,000	450	$13.3		
MF302	$4,000	200	$20.0		
MG201	$1,500	150	$10.0		
Take the MC237, MF302, MY456, and MB345 (890 sqft)					
Use remaining 1,110 sqft for office space.					

6-31. Kaimalino Properties (KP) is evaluating six real estate investments. Management plans to buy the properties today and sell them five years from today. The following table summarizes the initial cost and the expected sale price for each property, as well as the appropriate discount rate based on the risk of each venture.

Project	Cost Today	Discount Rate	Expected Sale Price in Year 5
Mountain Ridge	$ 3,000,000	15%	$18,000,000
Ocean Park Estates	15,000,000	15%	75,500,000
Lakeview	9,000,000	15%	50,000,000
Seabreeze	6,000,000	8%	35,500,000
Green Hills	3,000,000	8%	10,000,000
West Ranch	9,000,000	8%	46,500,000

KP has a total capital budget of $18,000,000 to invest in properties.

a. What is the IRR of each investment?

b. What is the NPV of each investment?

c. Given its budget of $18,000,000, which properties should KP choose?

d. Explain why the profitably index method could not be used if KP's budget were $12,000,000 instead. Which properties should KP choose in this case?

a. We can compute the IRR for each as IRR = $(\text{Sale Price/Cost})^{1/5} - 1$. See spreadsheet below.

b. We can compute the NPV for each as NPV = Sale Price/$(1+r)^5$ – Cost. See spreadsheet below.

Project	Cost Today	Discount Rate	Expected Sale Price in Year 5	IRR	NPV	Profitability Index
Mountain Ridge	$ 3,000,000	15%	$ 18,000,000	43.1%	$ 5,949,181	1.98
Ocean Park Estates	15,000,000	15%	$ 75,500,000	38.2%	22,536,844	1.50
Lakeview	9,000,000	15%	$ 50,000,000	40.9%	15,858,837	1.76
Seabreeze	6,000,000	8%	$ 35,500,000	42.7%	18,160,703	3.03
Green Hills	3,000,000	8%	$ 10,000,000	27.2%	3,805,832	1.27
West Ranch	9,000,000	8%	$ 46,500,000	38.9%	22,647,119	2.52

c. We can rank projects according to their profitability index = NPV/Cost, as shown below. Thus, KP should invest in Seabreeze, West Ranch, and Mountain Ridge. (Note that ranking projects according to their IRR would not maximize KP's total NPV, and so would not lead to the correct selection.)

d. The profitability index fails because the top-ranked projects do not completely use up the budget. In this case, you should take Mountain Ridge and West Ranch.

6-32. Orchid Biotech Company is evaluating several development projects for experimental drugs. Although the cash flows are difficult to forecast, the company has come up with the following estimates of the initial capital requirements and NPVs for the projects. Given a wide variety of staffing needs, the company has also estimated the number of research scientists required for each development project (all cost values are given in millions of dollars).

Project Number	Initial Capital	Number of Research Scientists	NPV
I	$10	2	$10.1
II	15	3	19.0
III	15	4	22.0
IV	20	3	25.0
V	30	12	60.2

a. Suppose that Orchid has a total capital budget of $60 million. How should it prioritize these projects?

b. Suppose in addition that Orchid currently has only 12 research scientists and does not anticipate being able to hire any more in the near future. How should Orchid prioritize these projects?

c. If instead, Orchid had 15 research scientists available, explain why the profitability index ranking cannot be used to prioritize projects. Which projects should it choose now?

Project	PI	NPV/Headcount
I	1.01	5.1
II	1.27	6.3
III	1.47	5.5
IV	1.25	8.3
V	2.01	5.0

a. The PI rule selects projects V, III, II. These are also the optimal projects to undertake (as the budget is used up fully taking the projects in order).

b. Need Update from Jonathan. The PI rule selects IV and II alone, because the project with the next highest PI (that is NPV/Headcount), V, cannot be undertaken without violating the resource constraint. However, this choice of projects does not maximize NPV. Orchid should also take on III and I. This solution is better than taking V and I (which is also affordable), and shows that it may be optimal to skip some projects in the PI ranking if they will not fit within the budget (and there is unused budget remaining).

c. Can't use it because (i) you don't hit the constraint exactly. Now choose V and IV.

Chapter 7
Fundamentals of Capital Budgeting

7-1. Pisa Pizza, a seller of frozen pizza, is considering introducing a healthier version of its pizza that will be low in cholesterol and contain no trans fats. The firm expects that sales of the new pizza will be $20 million per year. While many of these sales will be to new customers, Pisa Pizza estimates that 40% will come from customers who switch to the new, healthier pizza instead of buying the original version.

a. Assume customers will spend the same amount on either version. What level of incremental sales is associated with introducing the new pizza?

b. Suppose that 50% of the customers who will switch from Pisa Pizza's original pizza to its healthier pizza will switch to another brand if Pisa Pizza does not introduce a healthier pizza. What level of incremental sales is associated with introducing the new pizza in this case?

a. Sales of new pizza – lost sales of original = 20 – 0.40(20) = $12 million

b. Sales of new pizza – lost sales of original pizza from customers who would not have switched brands = 20 – 0.50(0.40)(20) = $16 million

7-2. Kokomochi is considering the launch of an advertising campaign for its latest dessert product, the Mini Mochi Munch. Kokomochi plans to spend $5 million on TV, radio, and print advertising this year for the campaign. The ads are expected to boost sales of the Mini Mochi Munch by $9 million this year and by $7 million next year. In addition, the company expects that new consumers who try the Mini Mochi Munch will be more likely to try Kokomochi's other products. As a result, sales of other products are expected to rise by $2 million each year.

Kokomochi's gross profit margin for the Mini Mochi Munch is 35%, and its gross profit margin averages 25% for all other products. The company's marginal corporate tax rate is 35% both this year and next year. What are the incremental earnings associated with the advertising campaign?

	A	B	C	D	E
1			Year	1	2
2	**Incremental Earnings Forecast ($000s)**				
3	1	Sales of Mini Mochi Munch		9,000	7,000
4	2	Other Sales		2,000	2,000
5	3	Cost of Goods Sold		(7,350)	(6,050)
6	4	**Gross Profit**		3,650	2,950
7	5	Selling, General & Admin.		(5,000)	-
8	6	Depreciation		-	-
9	7	**EBIT**		(1,350)	2,950
10	8	Income tax at 35%		473	(1,033)
11	9	**Unlevered Net Income**		**(878)**	**1,918**

7-3. Home Builder Supply, a retailer in the home improvement industry, currently operates seven retail outlets in Georgia and South Carolina. Management is contemplating building an eighth retail store across town from its most successful retail outlet. The company already owns the land for this store, which currently has an abandoned warehouse located on it. Last month, the marketing department spent $10,000 on market research to determine the extent of customer demand for the new store. Now Home Builder Supply must decide whether to build and open the new store.

Which of the following should be included as part of the incremental earnings for the proposed new retail store?

a. The cost of the land where the store will be located.

b. The cost of demolishing the abandoned warehouse and clearing the lot.

c. The loss of sales in the existing retail outlet, if customers who previously drove across town to shop at the existing outlet become customers of the new store instead.

d. The $10,000 in market research spent to evaluate customer demand.

e. Construction costs for the new store.

f. The value of the land if sold.

g. Interest expense on the debt borrowed to pay the construction costs.

a. No, this is a sunk cost and will not be included directly. (But see (f) below.)

b. Yes, this is a cost of opening the new store.

c. Yes, this loss of sales at the existing store should be deducted from the sales at the new store to determine the incremental increase in sales that opening the new store will generate for HBS.

d. No, this is a sunk cost.

e. This is a capital expenditure associated with opening the new store. These costs will, therefore, increase HBS's depreciation expenses.

f. Yes, this is an opportunity cost of opening the new store. (By opening the new store, HBS forgoes the after-tax proceeds it could have earned by selling the property. This loss is equal to the sale price less the taxes owed on the capital gain from the sale, which is the difference between the sale price and the book value of the property. The book value equals the initial cost of the property less accumulated depreciation.)

g. While these financing costs will affect HBS's actual earnings, for capital budgeting purposes we calculate the incremental earnings without including financing costs to determine the project's unlevered net income.

7-4. Hyperion, Inc. currently sells its latest high-speed color printer, the Hyper 500, for $350. It plans to lower the price to $300 next year. Its cost of goods sold for the Hyper 500 is $200 per unit, and this year's sales are expected to be 20,000 units.

a. Suppose that if Hyperion drops the price to $300 immediately, it can increase this year's sales by 25% to 25,000 units. What would be the incremental impact on this year's EBIT of such a price drop?

b. Suppose that for each printer sold, Hyperion expects additional sales of $75 per year on ink cartridges for the next three years, and Hyperion has a gross profit margin of 70% on ink cartridges. What is the incremental impact on EBIT for the next three years of a price drop this year?

a. Change in EBIT = Gross profit with price drop – Gross profit without price drop

= 25,000 × (300 – 200) – 20,000 ×(350 – 200)

= – $500,000

b. Change in EBIT from Ink Cartridge sales = 25,000 × $75 × 0.70 – 20,000 × $75 × 0.70 = $262,500

Therefore, incremental change in EBIT for the next 3 years is

Year 1: $262,500 – 500,000 = -$237,500

Year 2: $262,500

Year 3: $262,500

7-5.  **After looking at the projections of the HomeNet project, you decide that they are not realistic. It is unlikely that sales will be constant over the four-year life of the project. Furthermore, other companies are likely to offer competing products, so the assumption that the sales price will remain constant is also likely to be optimistic. Finally, as production ramps up, you anticipate lower per unit production costs resulting from economies of scale. Therefore,you decide to redo the projections under the following assumptions: Sales of 50,000 units in year 1 increasing by 50,000 units per year over the life of the project, a year 1 sales price of $260/unit, decreasing by 10% annually and a year 1 cost of $120/unit decreasing by 20% annually. In addition, new tax laws allow you to depreciate the equipment over three rather than five years using straightline depreciation.**

a. **Keeping the other assumptions that underlie Table 7.1 the same, recalculate unlevered net income (that is, reproduce Table 7.1 under the new assumptions, and note that we are ignoring cannibalization and lost rent).**

b. **Recalculate unlevered net income assuming, in addition, that each year 20% of sales comes from customers who would have purchased an existing Linksys router for $100/unit and that this router costs $60/unit to manufacture.**

a.

		Year	0	1	2	3	4	5
Incremental Earnings Forecast ($000s)								
1	Sales		-	13,000	23,400	31,590	37,908	-
2	Cost of Goods Sold			(6,000)	(9,600)	(11,520)	(12,288)	-
3	**Gross Profit**		-	7,000	13,800	20,070	25,620	-
4	Selling, General & Admin.		-	(2,800)	(2,800)	(2,800)	(2,800)	-
5	Research & Development		(15,000)	-	-	-	-	-
6	Depreciation		-	(2,500)	(2,500)	(2,500)	-	-
7	**EBIT**		(15,000)	1,700	8,500	14,770	22,820	-
8	Income tax at 40%		6,000	(680)	(3,400)	(5,908)	(9,128)	-
9	**Unlevered Net Income**		**(9,000)**	**1,020**	**5,100**	**8,862**	**13,692**	-

b.

		Year	0	1	2	3	4	5
Incremental Earnings Forecast ($000s)								
1	Sales		-	12,000	21,400	28,590	33,908	-
2	Cost of Goods Sold			(5,400)	(8,400)	(9,720)	(9,888)	-
3	**Gross Profit**		-	6,600	13,000	18,870	24,020	-
4	Selling, General & Admin.		-	(2,800)	(2,800)	(2,800)	(2,800)	-
5	Research & Development		(15,000)	-	-	-	-	-
6	Depreciation		-	(2,500)	(2,500)	(2,500)	-	-
7	**EBIT**		(15,000)	1,300	7,700	13,570	21,220	-
8	Income tax at 40%		6,000	(520)	(3,080)	(5,428)	(8,488)	-
9	**Unlevered Net Income**		**(9,000)**	**780**	**4,620**	**8,142**	**12,732**	-

7-6. **Cellular Access, Inc. is a cellular telephone service provider that reported net income of $250 million for the most recent fiscal year. The firm had depreciation expenses of $100 million, capital expenditures of $200 million, and no interest expenses. Working capital increased by $10 million. Calculate the free cash flow for Cellular Access for the most recent fiscal year.**

FCF = Unlevered Net Income + Depreciation – CapEx – Increase in NWC= 250 + 100 – 200 – 10 = $140 million.

7-7. **Castle View Games would like to invest in a division to develop software for video games. To evaluate this decision, the firm first attempts to project the working capital needs for this operation. Its chief financial officer has developed the following estimates (in millions of dollars):**

	Year 1	Year 2	Year 3	Year 4	Year 5
Cash	6	12	15	15	15
Accounts Receivable	21	22	24	24	24
Inventory	5	7	10	12	13
Accounts Payable	18	22	24	25	30

Assuming that Castle View currently does not have any working capital invested in this division, calculate the cash flows associated with changes in working capital for the first five years of this investment.

		Year0	Year1	Year2	Year3	Year4	Year5
1	Cash		6	12	15	15	15
2	Accounts Receivable		21	22	24	24	24
3	Inventory		5	7	10	12	13
4	Accounts Payable		18	22	24	25	30
5	Net working capital (1+2+3-4)	0	14	19	25	26	22
6	Increase in NWC		14	5	6	1	-4

7-8. Mersey Chemicals manufactures polypropylene that it ships to its customers via tank car. Currently, it plans to add two additional tank cars to its fleet four years from now. However, a proposed plant expansion will require Mersey's transport division to add these two additional tank cars in two years' time rather than in four years. The current cost of a tank car is $2 million, and this cost is expected to remain constant. Also, while tank cars will last indefinitely, they will be depreciated straight-line over a five-year life for tax purposes. Suppose Mersey's tax rate is 40%. When evaluating the proposed expansion, what incremental free cash flows should be included to account for the need to accelerate the purchase of the tank cars?

initial tank car cost	4	replace date without expansion	4
inflation rate	0%	replace date with expansion	2
depreciable life	5	tax rate	40%

Year:	0	1	2	3	4	5	6	7	8	9	10
with expansion											
CapEx			-4								
Depreciation Tax Shield				0.32	0.32	0.32	0.32	0.32			
FCF	0	0	-4	0.32	0.32	0.32	0.32	0.32	0	0	0
without expansion											
CapEx					-4						
Depreciation Tax Shield						0.32	0.32	0.32	0.32	0.32	
FCF	0	0	0	0	-4	0.32	0.32	0.32	0.32	0.32	0
Incremental FCF (with-without)	0	0	-4	0.32	4.32	0	0	0	-0.32	-0.32	0

7-9. Elmdale Enterprises is deciding whether to expand its production facilities. Although long-term cash flows are difficult to estimate, management has projected the following cash flows for the first two years (in millions of dollars):

	Year 1	Year 2
Revenues	125	160
Costs of goods sold and operating expenses other than depreciation	40	60
Depreciation	25	36
Increase in net working capital	5	8
Capital expenditures	30	40
Marginal corporate tax rate	35%	35%

a. **What are the incremental earnings for this project for years 1 and 2?**

b. **What are the free cash flows for this project for the first two years?**

a.

		Year 1	2
Incremental Earnings Forecast ($000s)			
1	Sales	125.0	160.0
2	Costs of good sold and operating expenses other than depreciation	(40.0)	(60.0)
3	Depreciation	(25.0)	(36.0)
4	**EBIT**	60.0	64.0
5	Income tax at 35%	(21.0)	(22.4)
6	**Unlevered Net Income**	**39.0**	**41.6**

b.

Free Cash Flow ($000s)		1	2
7	Plus: Depreciation	25.0	36.0
8	Less: Capital Expenditures	(30.0)	(40.0)
9	Less: Increases in NWC	(5.0)	(8.0)
10	**Free Cash Flow**	**29.0**	**29.6**

7-10. **You are a manager at Percolated Fiber, which is considering expanding its operations in synthetic fiber manufacturing. Your boss comes into your office, drops a consultant's report on your desk, and complains, "We owe these consultants $1 million for this report, and I am not sure their analysis makes sense. Before we spend the $25 million on new equipment needed for this project, look it over and give me your opinion." You open the report and find the following estimates (in thousands of dollars):**

	Project Year				
	1	2	...	9	10
Sales revenue	30,000	30,000		30,000	30,000
− Cost of goods sold	18,000	18,000		18,000	18,000
= Gross profit	12,000	12,000		12,000	12,000
− General, sales, and administrative expenses	2,000	2,000		2,000	2,000
− Depreciation	2,500	2,500		2,500	2,500
= Net operating income	7,500	7,500		7,500	7,500
− Income tax	2,625	2,625		2,625	2,625
Net Income	4,875	4,875		4,875	4,875

All of the estimates in the report seem correct. You note that the consultants used straight-line depreciation for the new equipment that will be purchased today (year 0), which is what the accounting department recommended. The report concludes that because the project will increase earnings by $4.875 million per year for 10 years, the project is worth $48.75 million. You think back to your halcyon days in finance class and realize there is more work to be done!

First, you note that the consultants have not factored in the fact that the project will require $10 million in working capital upfront (year 0), which will be fully recovered in year 10. Next, you see they have attributed $2 million of selling, general and administrative expenses to the project, but you know that $1 million of this amount is overhead that will be incurred even if the project is not accepted. Finally, you know that accounting earnings are not the right thing to focus on!

a. Given the available information, what are the free cash flows in years 0 through 10 that should be used to evaluate the proposed project?

b. If the cost of capital for this project is 14%, what is your estimate of the value of the new project?

a. Free Cash Flows are:

	0	1	2	...	9	10
= Net income		4,875	4,875		4,875	4,875
+ Overhead (after tax at 35%)		650	650		650	650
+ Depreciation		2,500	2,500		2,500	2,500
− Capex	25,000					
− Inc. in NWC	10,000					−10000
FCF	−35,000	8,025	8,025	...	8,025	18,025

b. $NPV = -35 + 8.025 \times \frac{1}{.14}\left(1 - \frac{1}{1.14^9}\right) + \frac{18.025}{1.14^{10}} = 9.56$

7-11. Using the assumptions in part a of Problem 5 (assuming there is no cannibalization),

a. Calculate HomeNet's net working capital requirements (that is, reproduce Table 7.4 under the assumptions in Problem 5(a)).

b. Calculate HomeNet's FCF (that is, reproduce Table 7.3 under the same assumptions as in (a)).

a.

		Year	0	1	2	3	4	5
Net Working Capital Forecast ($000s)								
1	Cash requirements		-	-	-	-	-	-
2	Inventory		-	-	-	-	-	-
3	Receivables (15% of Sales)		-	1,950	3,510	4,739	5,686	-
4	Payables (15% of COGS)		-	(900)	(1,440)	(1,728)	(1,843)	-
5	**Net Working Capital**		-	**1,050**	**2,070**	**3,011**	**3,843**	-

b.

		Year	0	1	2	3	4	5
Incremental Earnings Forecast ($000s)								
1	Sales		-	13,000	23,400	31,590	37,908	-
2	Cost of Goods Sold			(6,000)	(9,600)	(11,520)	(12,288)	-
3	**Gross Profit**		-	7,000	13,800	20,070	25,620	-
4	Selling, General & Admin.		-	(2,800)	(2,800)	(2,800)	(2,800)	-
5	Research & Development		(15,000)	-	-	-	-	-
6	Depreciation		-	(2,500)	(2,500)	(2,500)	-	-
7	**EBIT**		(15,000)	1,700	8,500	14,770	22,820	-
8	Incometaxat40%		6,000	(680)	(3,400)	(5,908)	(9,128)	-
9	**Unlevered Net Income**		(9,000)	1,020	5,100	8,862	13,692	-
Free Cash Flow ($000s)								
10	Plus: Depreciation		-	2,500	2,500	2,500	-	-
11	Less: Capital Expenditures		(7,500)	-	-	-	-	-
12	Less: Increases in NWC		-	(1,050)	(1,020)	(941)	(833)	3,843
13	**Free Cash Flow**		**(16,500)**	**2,470**	**6,580**	**10,421**	**12,860**	**3,843**

7-12. A bicycle manufacturer currently produces 300,000 units a year and expects output levels to remain steady in the future. It buys chains from an outside supplier at a price of $2 a chain. The plant manager believes that it would be cheaper to make these chains rather than buy them. Direct in-house production costs are estimated to be only $1.50 per chain. The necessary machinery would cost $250,000 and would be obsolete after 10 years. This investment could be depreciated to zero for tax purposes using a 10-year straight-line depreciation schedule. The plant manager estimates that the operation would require additional working capital of $50,000 but argues that this sum can be ignored since it is recoverable at the end of the 10 years. Expected proceeds from scrapping the machinery after 10 years are $20,000.

If the company pays tax at a rate of 35% and the opportunity cost of capital is 15%, what is the net present value of the decision to produce the chains in-house instead of purchasing them from the supplier?

Solution: FCF=EBIT (1-t) + depreciation – CAPX – ΔNWC

FCF from outside supplier = -$2x300,000 x (1 – .35) = -$390k per year.

$$\text{NPV(outside)} = -\$390{,}000\frac{1}{0.15}\left(1-\frac{1}{1.15^{10}}\right)$$
$$= -\$1.9573M$$

FCF in house:

in year 0: – 250 CAPX – 50 NWC= – 300K

FCF in years 1-9:	–\$1.50 x 300,000	cost
	–\$25,000	–depreciation
	-\$475,000	= incremental EBIT
	+\$166,250	– tax
	-\$308,750	= (1-t) x EBIT
	+\$25,000	+ depreciation
	-\$283,750	= FCF

FCF in year 10: –\$283,750 + (1 – 0.35) x \$20,000 + \$50,000 = –\$220,750 FCF

Note that the book value of the machinery is zero; hence, its scrap proceeds (\$20,000) are fully taxed.

The NWC (\$50,000) is recovered at book value and hence not taxed.

NPV (in house): –\$300k

+ annuity of –\$283,750 for 9 years

$$+\frac{-\$220{,}750}{1.15^{10}}$$

$$= -\$300k - \frac{\$283{,}750}{0.15}\left(1-\frac{1}{1.15^{9}}\right) - \frac{\$220{,}750}{1.15^{10}}$$
$$= -\$1.7085M$$

Thus, in-house is cheaper, with a cost savings of (\$1.9573M - \$1.7085M) = \$248.8K in present value terms.

7-13. One year ago, your company purchased a machine used in manufacturing for \$110,000. You have learned that a new machine is available that offers many advantages; you can purchase it for \$150,000 today. It will be depreciated on a straight-line basis over 10 years, after which it has no salvage value. You expect that the new machine will produce EBITDA (earning before interest, taxes, depreciation, and amortization) of \$40,000 per year for the next 10 years. The current machine is expected to produce EBITDA of \$20,000 per year. The current machine is being depreciated on a straight-line basis over a useful life of 11 years, after which it will have no salvage value, so depreciation expense for the current machine is \$10,000 per year. All other expenses of the two machines are identical. The market value today of the current machine is \$50,000. Your company's tax rate is 45%, and the opportunity cost of capital for this type of equipment is 10%. Is it profitable to replace the year-old machine?

Replacing the machine increases EBITDA by 40,000 – 20,000 = 20,000. Depreciation expenses rises by \$15,000 – \$10,000 = \$5,000. Therefore, FCF will increase by (20,000) × (1-0.45) + (0.45)(5,000) = \$13,250 in years 1 through 10.

In year 0, the initial cost of the machine is \$150,000. Because the current machine has a book value of \$110,000 – 10,000 (one year of depreciation) = \$100,000, selling it for \$50,000 generates a capital gain of 50,000 – 100,000 = –50,000. This loss produces tax savings of 0.45 × 50,000 = \$22,500, so that the after-tax proceeds from the sales including this tax savings is \$72,500. Thus, the FCF in year 0 from replacement is

–150,000 + 72,500 = –\$77,500.

NPV of replacement = –77,500 + 13,250 × (1 / .10)(1 – 1 / 1.10^{10}) = \$3916. There is a small profit from replacing the machine.

7-14. Beryl's Iced Tea currently rents a bottling machine for \$50,000 per year, including all maintenance expenses. It is considering purchasing a machine instead, and is comparing two options:

a. Purchase the machine it is currently renting for \$150,000. This machine will require \$20,000 per year in ongoing maintenance expenses.

b. Purchase a new, more advanced machine for \$250,000. This machine will require \$15,000 per year in ongoing maintenance expenses and will lower bottling costs by \$10,000 per year. Also, \$35,000 will be spent upfront in training the new operators of the machine.

Suppose the appropriate discount rate is 8% per year and the machine is purchased today. Maintenance and bottling costs are paid at the end of each year, as is the rental of the machine. Assume also that the machines will be depreciated via the straight-line method over seven years and that they have a 10-year life with a negligible salvage value. The marginal corporate tax rate is 35%. Should Beryl's Iced Tea continue to rent, purchase its current machine, or purchase the advanced machine?

We can use Eq. 7.5 to evaluate the free cash flows associated with each alternative. Note that we only need to include the components of free cash flows that vary across each alternative. For example, since NWC is the same for each alternative, we can ignore it.

The spreadsheet below computes the relevant FCF from each alternative. Note that each alternative has a negative NPV—this represents the PV of the costs of each alternative. We should choose the one with the highest NPV (lowest cost), which in this case is purchasing the existing machine.

a. See spreadsheet

b. See spreadsheet

	A	B	D	E	F	G	H	I	J	K	L	M	N
5			0	1	2	3	4	5	6	7	8	9	10
6	**Rent Machine**												
7	1	Rent		(50,000)	(50,000)	(50,000)	(50,000)	(50,000)	(50,000)	(50,000)	(50,000)	(50,000)	(50,000)
8	2	**FCF(rent)**		(32,500)	(32,500)	(32,500)	(32,500)	(32,500)	(32,500)	(32,500)	(32,500)	(32,500)	(32,500)
9	3	**NPV at 8%**	**(218,078)**										
10	**Purchase Current Machine**												
11	4	Maintenance		(20,000)	(20,000)	(20,000)	(20,000)	(20,000)	(20,000)	(20,000)	(20,000)	(20,000)	(20,000)
12	5	Depreciation		21,429	21,429	21,429	21,429	21,429	21,429	21,429	-	-	-
13	6	Capital Expenditures	(150,000)										
14	7	**FCF(purchase current)**	(150,000)	(5,500)	(5,500)	(5,500)	(5,500)	(5,500)	(5,500)	(5,500)	(13,000)	(13,000)	(13,000)
15	8	**NPV at 8%**	**(198,183)**										
16	**Purchase Advanced Machine**												
17	9	Maintenance		(15,000)	(15,000)	(15,000)	(15,000)	(15,000)	(15,000)	(15,000)	(15,000)	(15,000)	(15,000)
18	10	Other Costs	(35,000)	10,000	10,000	10,000	10,000	10,000	10,000	10,000	10,000	10,000	10,000
19	11	Depreciation		35,714	35,714	35,714	35,714	35,714	35,714	35,714	-	-	-
20	12	Capital Expenditures	(250,000)										
21	13	**FCF(purchase advanced)**	(272,750)	9,250	9,250	9,250	9,250	9,250	9,250	9,250	(3,250)	(3,250)	(3,250)
22	14	**NPV at 8%**	**(229,478)**										

7-15. Markov Manufacturing recently spent \$15 million to purchase some equipment used in the manufacture of disk drives. The firm expects that this equipment will have a useful life of five years, and its marginal corporate tax rate is 35%. The company plans to use straight-line depreciation.

a. What is the annual depreciation expense associated with this equipment?

b. What is the annual depreciation tax shield?

c. **Rather than straight-line depreciation, suppose Markov will use the MACRS depreciation method for five-year property. Calculate the depreciation tax shield each year for this equipment under this accelerated depreciation schedule.**

d. **If Markov has a choice between straight-line and MACRS depreciation schedules, and its marginal corporate tax rate is expected to remain constant, which should it choose? Why?**

e. **How might your answer to part (d) change if Markov anticipates that its marginal corporate tax rate will increase substantially over the next five years?**

a. $15 million / 5 years = $3 million per year

b. $3 million × 35% = $1.05 million per year

c.

Year	0	1	2	3	4	5
MACRS Depreciation						
Equipment Cost	15,000					
MACRS Depreciation Rate	20.00%	32.00%	19.20%	11.52%	11.52%	5.76%
Depreciation Expense	3,000	4,800	2,880	1,728	1,728	864
Depreciation Tax Shield (at 35% tax rate)	1,050	1,680	1,008	605	605	302

d. In both cases, its total depreciation tax shield is the same. But with MACRS, it receives the depreciation tax shields sooner—thus, MACRS depreciation leads to a higher NPV of Markov's FCF.

e. If the tax rate will increase substantially, than Markov may be better off claiming higher depreciation expenses in later years, since the tax benefit at that time will be greater.

7-16. **Your firm is considering a project that would require purchasing $7.5 million worth of new equipment. Determine the present value of the depreciation tax shield associated with this equipment if the firm's tax rate is 40%, the appropriate cost of capital is 8%, and the equipment can be depreciated**

a. **Straight-line over a 10-year period, with the first deduction starting in one year.**

b. **Straight-line over a five-year period, with the first deduction starting in one year.**

c. **Using MACRS depreciation with a five-year recovery period and starting immediately.**

d. **Fully as an immediate deduction.**

		Equipment Cost	7.5									
		Tax Rate	40.00%									
		Cost of capital	8.00%									
						Depreciation Tax Shield (Tc*Dep)						
	PV(DTS)	Year 0	Year 1	Year 2	Year 3	Year 4	Year 5	Year 6	Year 7	Year 8	Year 9	Year 10
a	**2.013**		0.3	0.3	0.3	0.3	0.3	0.3	0.3	0.3	0.3	0.3
b	**2.396**		0.6	0.6	0.6	0.6	0.6					
MACRS table		20%	32%	19.20%	11.52%	11.52%	5.76%					
c	**2.629**	0.6	0.96	0.576	0.3456	0.3456	0.1728					
d	**3.000**	3										

7-17. **Arnold Inc. is considering a proposal to manufacture high-end protein bars used as food supplements by body builders. The project requires use of an existing warehouse, which the firm acquired three years ago for $1m and which it currently rents out for $120,000. Rental rates are not expected to change going forward. In addition to using the warehouse, the project requires an up-front investment into machines and other equipment of $1.4m. This investment can be fully depreciated straight-line over the next 10 years for tax purposes. However, Arnold Inc. expects to terminate the project at the end of eight years and to sell the machines and equipment for $500,000. Finally, the project requires an initial investment into net working capital equal to**

10% of predicted first-year sales. Subsequently, net working capital is 10% of the predicted sales over the following year. Sales of protein bars are expected to be $4.8m in the first year and to stay constant for eight years. Total manufacturing costs and operating expenses (excluding depreciation) are 80% of sales, and profits are taxed at 30%.

a. What are the free cash flows of the project?

b. If the cost of capital is 15%, what is the NPV of the project?

a. Assumptions:

(1) The warehouse can be rented out again for $120,000 after 8 years.

(2) The NWC is fully recovered at book value after 8 years.

FCF = EBIT (1 – t) + Depreciation – CAPX – Change in NWC

FCF in year 0: – 1.4m CAPX – 0.48m Change in NWC = –1.88m

FCF in years 1-7:

$4.8m	Sales
–$3.84m	–Cost (80%)
$0.96m	=Gross Profit
–$0.12m	–Lost Rent
–$0.14m	–Depreciation
$0.70m	=EBIT
–$0.21m	–Tax (30%)
$0.49m	= (1 – t) x EBIT
$0.14m	+Depreciation
$0.63m	= FCF

Note that there is no more CAPX nor investment into NWC in years 1–7.

FCF in year 8: $0.63m + [$0.5m – 0.30 x ($0.5m – $0.28m)] + $0.48m = $1.544m

Note that the book value of the machinery is still $0.28m when sold, and only the difference between the sale price ($0.5m) and the book value is taxed.

The NWC ($0.48m) is recovered at book value and hence its sale is not taxed at all.

b. The NPV is the present value of the FCFs in years 0 to 8:

NPV= -$1.88m

+ an annuity of $0.63m for 7 years

$$+\frac{\$1.544m}{1.15^8}$$

$$= -\$1.88m + \frac{\$0.63m}{0.15}\left(1-\frac{1}{1.15^7}\right)+\frac{\$1.544m}{1.15^8}$$

$$= \$1.2458m$$

7-18. Bay Properties is considering starting a commercial real estate division. It has prepared the following four-year forecast of free cash flows for this division:

	Year 1	Year 2	Year 3	Year 4
Free Cash Flow	–$185,000	$12,000	$99,000	$240,000

Assume cash flows after year 4 will grow at 3% per year, forever. If the cost of capital for this division is 14%, what is the continuation value in year 4 for cash flows after year 4? What is the value today of this division?

The expected cash flow in year 5 is 240,000 × 1.03 = 247,200. We can value the cash flows in year 5 and beyond as a growing perpetuity:

Continuation Value in Year 4 = 247,200/(0.14 – 0.03) = $2,247,273

We can then compute the value of the division by discounting the FCF in years 1 through 4, together with the continuation value:

$$NPV = \frac{-185{,}000}{1.14} + \frac{-12{,}000}{1.14^2} + \frac{99{,}000}{1.14^3} + \frac{240{,}000 + 2{,}247{,}273}{1.14^4} = \$1{,}367{,}973$$

7-19. Your firm would like to evaluate a proposed new operating division. You have forecasted cash flows for this division for the next five years, and have estimated that the cost of capital is 12%. You would like to estimate a continuation value. You have made the following forecasts for the last year of your five-year forecasting horizon (in millions of dollars):

	Year 5
Revenues	1200
Operating income	100
Net income	50
Free cash flows	110
Book value of equity	400

a. **You forecast that future free cash flows after year 5 will grow at 2% per year, forever. Estimate the continuation value in year 5, using the perpetuity with growth formula.**

b. **You have identified several firms in the same industry as your operating division. The average P/E ratio for these firms is 30. Estimate the continuation value assuming the P/E ratio for your division in year 5 will be the same as the average P/E ratio for the comparable firms today.**

c. **The average market/book ratio for the comparable firms is 4.0. Estimate the continuation value using the market/book ratio.**

a. FCF in year 6 = 110 × 1.02 = 112.2

Continuation Value in year 5 = 112.2 / (12% – 2%) = $1,122.

b. We can estimate the continuation value as follows:

Continuation Value in year 5 = (Earnings in year 5) × (P/E ratio in year 5)

= $50 × 30 = $1500.

c. We can estimate the continuation value as follows:

Continuation Value in year 5 = (Book value in year 5) × (M/B ratio in year 5)

= $400 × 4 = $1600.

7-20. In September 2008, the IRS changed tax laws to allow banks to utilize the tax loss carryforwards of banks they acquire to shield their future income from taxes (prior law restricted the ability of acquirers to use these credits). Suppose Fargo Bank acquires Covia Bank and with it acquires $74 billion in tax loss carryforwards. If Fargo Bank is expected to generate taxable income of 10 billion per year in the future, and its tax rate is 30%, what is the present value of these acquired tax loss carryforwards given a cost of capital of 8%?

We can shield $10 billion per year for the next 7 years, and $4 billion in year 8. Given a tax rate of 30%, this represents of tax savings of $3 billion in years 1–7, and $1.2 billion in year 8.

$$\text{PV} = 3\times\frac{1}{.08}\left(1-\frac{1}{1.08^7}\right)+\frac{1.2}{1.08^8}=\$16.27B$$

7-21. Using the FCF projections in part b of Problem 11, calculate the NPV of the HomeNet project assuming a cost of capital of

a. 10%.

b. 12%.

c. 14%.

What is the IRR of the project in this case?

a.

		Year	0	1	2	3	4	5
Net Present Value ($000s)								
1	**Free Cash Flow**		(16,500)	2,470	6,580	10,421	12,860	3,843
2	Project Cost of Capital	10%						
3	Discount Factor		1.000	0.909	0.826	0.751	0.683	0.621

		Year	0	1	2	3	4	5
1	**PV of Free Cash Flow**		(16,500)	2,245	5,438	7,830	8,783	2,386
2	**NPV**		**10,182**					
3	**IRR**		28.8%					

b.

		Year	0	1	2	3	4	5
Net Present Value ($000s)								
1	**Free Cash Flow**		(16,500)	2,470	6,580	10,421	12,860	3,843
2	Project Cost of Capital	12%						
3	Discount Factor		1.000	0.893	0.797	0.712	0.636	0.567

		Year	0	1	2	3	4	5
1	**PV of Free Cash Flow**		(16,500)	2,205	5,246	7,418	8,172	2,181
2	**NPV**		**8,722**					
3	**IRR**		28.8%					

c.

		Year	0	1	2	3	4	5
Net Present Value ($000s)								
1	**Free Cash Flow**		(16,500)	2,470	6,580	10,421	12,860	3,843
2	Project Cost of Capital	14%						
3	Discount Factor		1.000	0.877	0.769	0.675	0.592	0.519

		Year	0	1	2	3	4	5
1	**PV of Free Cash Flow**		(16,500)	2,167	5,063	7,034	7,614	1,996
2	**NPV**		**7,374**					
3	**IRR**		28.8%					

7-22. For the assumptions in part (a) of Problem 5, assuming a cost of capital of 12%, calculate the following:

a. The break-even annual sales price decline.

b. The break-even annual unit sales increase.

a. 28.5%

b. 25350

7-23. Bauer Industries is an automobile manufacturer. Management is currently evaluating a proposal to build a plant that will manufacture lightweight trucks. Bauer plans to use a cost of capital of 12% to evaluate this project. Based on extensive research, it has prepared the following incremental free cash flow projections (in millions of dollars):

	Year 0	Years 1–9	Year 10
Revenues		100.0	100.0
– Manufacturing expenses (other than depreciation)		–35.0	–35.0
– Marketing expenses		–10.0	–10.0
– Depreciation		–15.0	–15.0
= EBIT		40.0	40.0
– Taxes (35%)		–14.0	–14.0
= Unlevered net income		26.0	26.0
+ Depreciation		+15.0	+15.0
– Increases in net working capital		–5.0	–5.0
– Capital expenditures	–150.0		
+ Continuation value			+12.0
= Free cash flow	–150.0	36.0	48.0

a. For this base-case scenario, what is the NPV of the plant to manufacture lightweight trucks?

b. Based on input from the marketing department, Bauer is uncertain about its revenue forecast. In particular, management would like to examine the sensitivity of the NPV to the revenue assumptions. What is the NPV of this project if revenues are 10% higher than forecast? What is the NPV if revenues are 10% lower than forecast?

c. Rather than assuming that cash flows for this project are constant, management would like to explore the sensitivity of its analysis to possible growth in revenues and operating expenses. Specifically, management would like to assume that revenues, manufacturing expenses, and marketing expenses are as given in the table for year 1 and grow by 2% per

year every year starting in year 2. Management also plans to assume that the initial capital expenditures (and therefore depreciation), additions to working capital, and continuation value remain as initially specified in the table. What is the NPV of this project under these alternative assumptions? How does the NPV change if the revenues and operating expenses grow by 5% per year rather than by 2%?

d. To examine the sensitivity of this project to the discount rate, management would like to compute the NPV for different discount rates. Create a graph, with the discount rate on the *x*-axis and the NPV on the *y*-axis, for discount rates ranging from 5% to 30%. For what ranges of discount rates does the project have a positive NPV?

	Year	0	1	2	3	4	5	6	7	8	9	10
Free Cash Flow Forecast ($ millions)												
1	Sales	—	100.0	100.0	100.0	100.0	100.0	100.0	100.0	100.0	100.0	100.0
2	Manufacturing	—	(35.0)	(35.0)	(35.0)	(35.0)	(35.0)	(35.0)	(35.0)	(35.0)	(35.0)	(35.0)
3	Marketing Expenses	—	(10.0)	(10.0)	(10.0)	(10.0)	(10.0)	(10.0)	(10.0)	(10.0)	(10.0)	(10.0)
4	Depreciation	—	(15.0)	(15.0)	(15.0)	(15.0)	(15.0)	(15.0)	(15.0)	(15.0)	(15.0)	(15.0)
5	EBIT	—	40.0	40.0	40.0	40.0	40.0	40.0	40.0	40.0	40.0	40.0
6	Income tax at 35%	—	(14.0)	(14.0)	(14.0)	(14.0)	(14.0)	(14.0)	(14.0)	(14.0)	(14.0)	(14.0)
7	**Unlevered Net Income**	—	26.0	26.0	26.0	26.0	26.0	26.0	26.0	26.0	26.0	26.0
8	Depreciation	—	15.0	15.0	15.0	15.0	15.0	15.0	15.0	15.0	15.0	15.0
9	Inc. in NWC	—	(5.0)	(5.0)	(5.0)	(5.0)	(5.0)	(5.0)	(5.0)	(5.0)	(5.0)	(5.0)
10	Capital Expenditures	(150.0)	—	—	—	—	—	—	—	—	—	—
11	Continuation value	—	—	—	—	—	—	—	—	—	—	12.0
12	**Free Cash Flow**	(150.0)	36.0	36.0	36.0	36.0	36.0	36.0	36.0	36.0	36.0	48.0
13	**NPV at 12%**	**57.3**	—	—	—	—	—	—	—	—	—	—

a. The NPV of the estimate free cash flow is

$$\text{NPV} = -150 + 36 \times \frac{1}{0.12}\left(1 - \frac{1}{1.12^9}\right) + \frac{48}{1.12^{10}} = \$57.3 \text{ million.}$$

b.

Initial Sales	90	100	110
NPV	20.5	57.3	94.0

c.

Growth Rate	0%	2%	5%
NPV	57.3	72.5	98.1

d. NPV is positive for discount rates below the IRR of 20.6%.

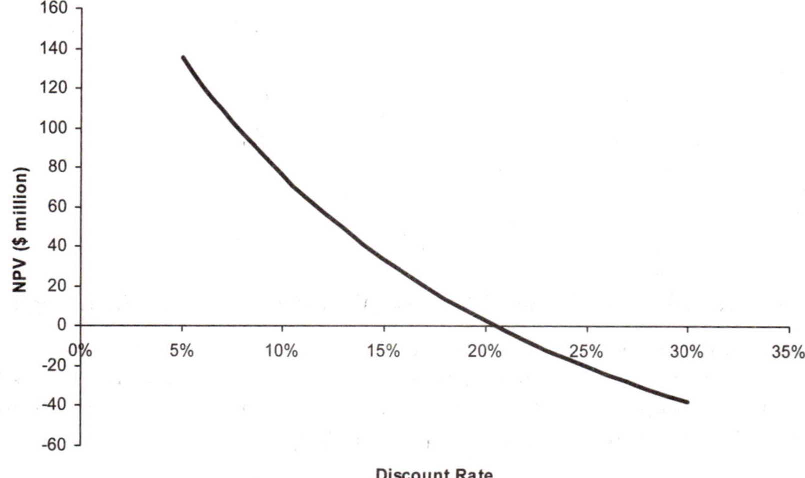

7-24. Billingham Packaging is considering expanding its production capacity by purchasing a new machine, the XC-750. The cost of the XC-750 is $2.75 million. Unfortunately, installing this machine will take several months and will partially disrupt production. The firm has just completed a $50,000 feasibility study to analyze the decision to buy the XC-750, resulting in the following estimates:

- ***Marketing*: Once the XC-750 is operating next year, the extra capacity is expected to generate $10 million per year in additional sales, which will continue for the 10-year life of the machine.**
- ***Operations*: The disruption caused by the installation will decrease sales by $5 million this year. Once the machine is operating next year, the cost of goods for the products produced by the XC-750 is expected to be 70% of their sale price. The increased production will require additional inventory on hand of $1 million to be added in year 0 and depleted in year 10.**
- ***Human Resources*: The expansion will require additional sales and administrative personnel at a cost of $2 million per year.**
- ***Accounting*: The XC-750 will be depreciated via the straight-line method over the 10-year life of the machine. The firm expects receivables from the new sales to be 15% of revenues and payables to be 10% of the cost of goods sold. Billingham's marginal corporate tax rate is 35%.**

a. Determine the incremental earnings from the purchase of the XC-750.

b. Determine the free cash flow from the purchase of the XC-750.

c. If the appropriate cost of capital for the expansion is 10%, compute the NPV of the purchase.

d. While the expected new sales will be $10 million per year from the expansion, estimates range from $8 million to $12 million. What is the NPV in the worst case? In the best case?

e. What is the break-even level of new sales from the expansion? What is the break-even level for the cost of goods sold?

f. Billingham could instead purchase the XC-900, which offers even greater capacity. The cost of the XC-900 is $4 million. The extra capacity would not be useful in the first two years of operation, but would allow for additional sales in years 3–10. What level of additional sales (above the $10 million expected for the XC-750) per year in those years would justify purchasing the larger machine?

a. See spreadsheet on next page.

b. See spreadsheet on next page.

c. See spreadsheet on next page.

d. See data tables in spreadsheet on next page.

e. See data tables in spreadsheet on next page.

f. See spreadsheet on next page—need additional sales of $11.384 million in years 3–10 for larger machine to have a higher NPV than XC-750.

Incremental Effects
(with vs. without XC-750)

Year	0	1	2	3	4	5	6	7	8	9	10
Sales Revenues	-5,000	10,000	10,000	10,000	10,000	10,000	10,000	10,000	10,000	10,000	10,000
Cost of Goods Sold	3,500	-7,000	-7,000	-7,000	-7,000	-7,000	-7,000	-7,000	-7,000	-7,000	-7,000
S, G & A Expenses		-2,000	-2,000	-2,000	-2,000	-2,000	-2,000	-2,000	-2,000	-2,000	-2,000
Depreciation		-275	-275	-275	-275	-275	-275	-275	-275	-275	-275
EBIT	-1,500	725	725	725	725	725	725	725	725	725	725
Taxes at 35%	525	-254	-254	-254	-254	-254	-254	-254	-254	-254	-254
Unlevered Net Income	-975	471	471	471	471	471	471	471	471	471	471
Depreciation		275	275	275	275	275	275	275	275	275	275
Capital Expenditures	-2,750										
Add. To Net Work. Cap.	-600	-1,200	0	0	0	0	0	0	0	0	1,000
FCF	-4,325	-454	746	746	746	746	746	746	746	746	1,746
Cost of Capital	10.00%										
PV(FCF)	-4,325	-413	617	561	510	463	421	383	348	316	673
NPV	-164.6										

Net Working Capital Calculation

Year	0	1	2	3	4	5	6	7	8	9	10
Receivables at 15%	-750	1500	1500	1500	1500	1500	1500	1500	1500	1500	1500
Payables at 10%	350	-700	-700	-700	-700	-700	-700	-700	-700	-700	-700
Inventory	1000	1000	1000	1000	1000	1000	1000	1000	1000	1000	0
NWC	600	1800	1800	1800	1800	1800	1800	1800	1800	1800	800

Sensitivity Analysis: New Sales

New Sales (000s)	8	9	10	10.143	11	12
NPV	-2472	-1318	-165	0	989	2142

Sensitivity Analysis: Cost of Goods Sold

COGS	67%	68%	69.545%	69%	70%	71%

Incremental Effects
(with vs. without XC-900)

Year	0	1	2	3	4	5	6	7	8	9	10
Sales Revenues	-5,000	10,000	10,000	11,384	11,384	11,384	11,384	11,384	11,384	11,384	11,384
Cost of Goods Sold	3,500	-7,000	-7,000	-7,969	-7,969	-7,969	-7,969	-7,969	-7,969	-7,969	-7,969
S, G & A Expenses		-2,000	-2,000	-2,000	-2,000	-2,000	-2,000	-2,000	-2,000	-2,000	-2,000
Depreciation		-400	-400	-400	-400	-400	-400	-400	-400	-400	-400
EBIT	-1,500	600	600	1,015	1,015	1,015	1,015	1,015	1,015	1,015	1,015
Taxes at 35%	525	-210	-210	-355	-355	-355	-355	-355	-355	-355	-355
Unlevered Net Income	-975	390	390	660	660	660	660	660	660	660	660
Depreciation		400	400	400	400	400	400	400	400	400	400
Capital Expenditures	-4,000										
Add. To Net Work. Cap.	-600	-1,200	0	-111	0	0	0	0	0	0	1,000
FCF	-5,575	-410	790	949	1,060	1,060	1,060	1,060	1,060	1,060	2,060
Cost of Capital	10.00%										
PV(FCF)	-5,575	-373	653	713	724	658	598	544	494	450	794
NPV	0.0										

Net Working Capital Calculation

Year	0	1	2	3	4	5	6	7	8	9	10
Receivables at 15%	-750	1500	1500	1708	1708	1708	1708	1708	1708	1708	1708
Payables at 10%	350	-700	-700	-797	-797	-797	-797	-797	-797	-797	-797
Inventory	1000	1000	1000	1000	1000	1000	1000	1000	1000	1000	0
NWC	600	1800	1800	1911	1911	1911	1911	1911	1911	1911	911

s

Chapter 8
Valuing Bonds

8-1. A 30-year bond with a face value of $1000 has a coupon rate of 5.5%, with semiannual payments.

a. What is the coupon payment for this bond?

b. Draw the cash flows for the bond on a timeline.

a. The coupon payment is:

$$CPN = \frac{\text{Coupon Rate} \times \text{Face Value}}{\text{Number of Coupons per Year}} = \frac{0.055 \times \$1000}{2} = \$27.50.$$

b. The timeline for the cash flows for this bond is (the unit of time on this timeline is six-month periods):

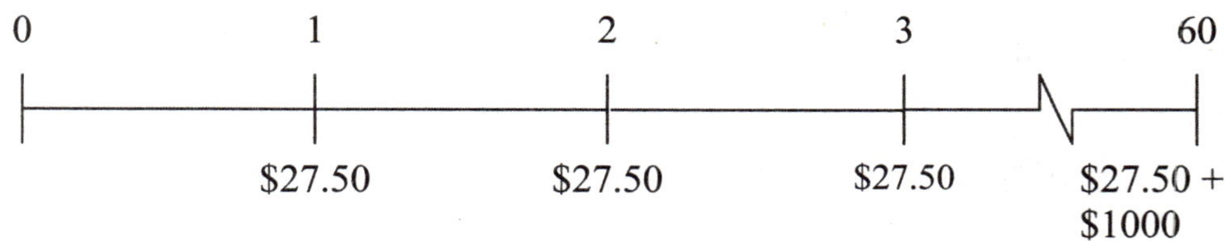

$P = 100/(1.055)^2 = \$89.85$

8-2. Assume that a bond will make payments every six months as shown on the following timeline (using six-month periods):

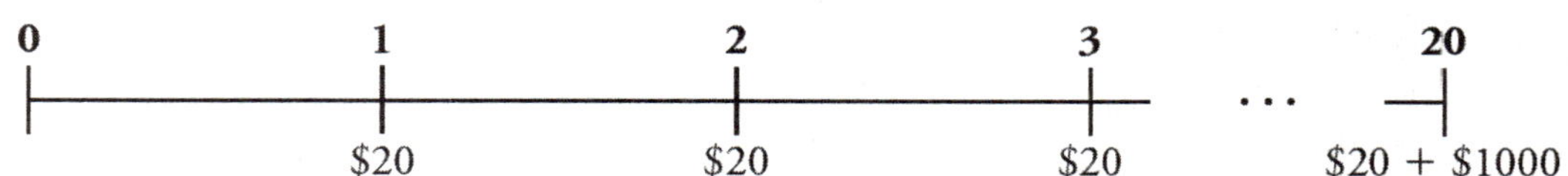

a. What is the maturity of the bond (in years)?

b. What is the coupon rate (in percent)?

c. What is the face value?

a. The maturity is 10 years.

b. (20/1000) x 2 = 4%, so the coupon rate is 4%.

c. The face value is $1000.

8-3. The following table summarizes prices of various default-free, zero-coupon bonds (expressed as a percentage of face value):

Maturity (years)	1	2	3	4	5
Price (per $100 face value)	$95.51	$91.05	$86.38	$81.65	$76.51

a. Compute the yield to maturity for each bond.

b. Plot the zero-coupon yield curve (for the first five years).

c. Is the yield curve upward sloping, downward sloping, or flat?

a. Use the following equation.

$$1+\text{YTM}_n = \left(\frac{\text{FV}_n}{\text{P}}\right)^{1/n}$$

$$1+\text{YTM}_1 = \left(\frac{100}{95.51}\right)^{1/1} \Rightarrow \text{YTM}_1 = 4.70\%$$

$$1+\text{YTM}_1 = \left(\frac{100}{91.05}\right)^{1/2} \Rightarrow \text{YTM}_1 = 4.80\%$$

$$1+\text{YTM}_3 = \left(\frac{100}{86.38}\right)^{1/3} \Rightarrow \text{YTM}_3 = 5.00\%$$

$$1+\text{YTM}_4 = \left(\frac{100}{81.65}\right)^{1/4} \Rightarrow \text{YTM}_4 = 5.20\%$$

$$1+\text{YTM}_5 = \left(\frac{100}{76.51}\right)^{1/5} \Rightarrow \text{YTM}_5 = 5.50\%$$

b. The yield curve is as shown below.

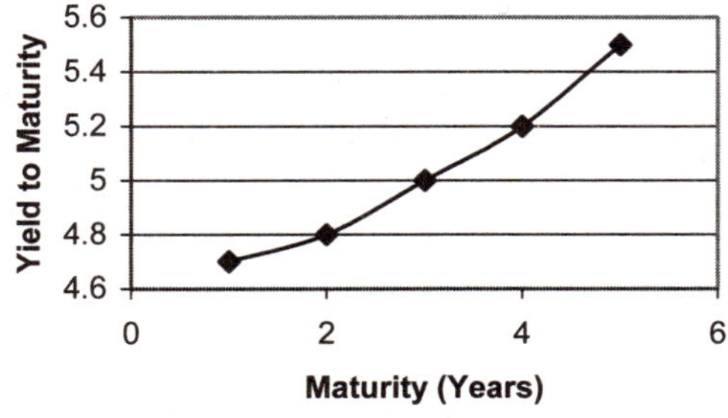

c. The yield curve is upward sloping.

8-4. Suppose the current zero-coupon yield curve for risk-free bonds is as follows:

Maturity (years)	1	2	3	4	5
YTM	5.00%	5.50%	5.75%	5.95%	6.05%

a. What is the price per \$100 face value of a two-year, zero-coupon, risk-free bond?

b. What is the price per \$100 face value of a four-year, zero-coupon, risk-free bond?

c. What is the risk-free interest rate for a five-year maturity?

a. $P = 100(1.055)^2 = \$89.85$

b. $P = 100/(1.0595)^4 = \$79.36$

c. 6.05%

8-5. In the box in Section 8.1, Bloomberg.com reported that the three-month Treasury bill sold for a price of \$100.002556 per \$100 face value. What is the yield to maturity of this bond, expressed as an EAR?

$$\left(\frac{100}{100.002556}\right)^4 - 1 = -0.01022\%$$

8-6. Suppose a 10-year, \$1000 bond with an 8% coupon rate and semiannual coupons is trading for a price of \$1034.74.

a. What is the bond's yield to maturity (expressed as an APR with semiannual compounding)?

b. If the bond's yield to maturity changes to 9% APR, what will the bond's price be?

a. $$\$1,034.74 = \frac{40}{(1+\frac{YTM}{2})} + \frac{40}{(1+\frac{YTM}{2})^2} + \cdots + \frac{40+1000}{(1+\frac{YTM}{2})^{20}} \Rightarrow YTM = 7.5\%$$

Using the annuity spreadsheet:

	NPER	Rate	PV	PMT	FV	Excel Formula
Given:	20		-1,034.74	40	1,000	
Solve For Rate:		3.75%				=RATE(20,40,-1034.74,1000)

Therefore, YTM = 3.75% × 2 = 7.50%

b. $$PV = \frac{40}{(1+\frac{.09}{2})} + \frac{40}{(1+\frac{.09}{2})^2} + L + \frac{40+1000}{(1+\frac{.09}{2})^{20}} = \$934.96.$$

Using the spreadsheet

With a 9% YTM = 4.5% per 6 months, the new price is \$934.96

	NPER	Rate	PV	PMT	FV	Excel Formula
Given:	20	4.50%		40	1,000	
Solve For PV:			(934.96)			=PV(0.045,20,40,1000)

8-7. Suppose a five-year, $1000 bond with annual coupons has a price of $900 and a yield to maturity of 6%. What is the bond's coupon rate?

$$900 = \frac{C}{(1+.06)} + \frac{C}{(1+.06)^2} + \cdots + \frac{C+1000}{(1+.06)^5} \Rightarrow C = \$36.26, \text{ so the coupon rate is 3.626\%.}$$

We can use the annuity spreadsheet to solve for the payment.

	NPER	Rate	PV	PMT	FV	Excel Formula
Given:	5	6.00%	-900.00		1,000	
Solve For PMT:				36.26		=PMT(0.06,5,-900,1000)

Therefore, the coupon rate is 3.626%.

8-8. The prices of several bonds with face values of $1000 are summarized in the following table:

Bond	A	B	C	D
Price	$972.50	$1040.75	$1150.00	$1000.00

For each bond, state whether it trades at a discount, at par, or at a premium.

Bond A trades at a discount. Bond D trades at par. Bonds B and C trade at a premium.

8-9. Explain why the yield of a bond that trades at a discount exceeds the bond's coupon rate.

Bonds trading at a discount generate a return both from receiving the coupons and from receiving a face value that exceeds the price paid for the bond. As a result, the yield to maturity of discount bonds exceeds the coupon rate.

8-10. Suppose a seven-year, $1000 bond with an 8% coupon rate and semiannual coupons is trading with a yield to maturity of 6.75%.

a. Is this bond currently trading at a discount, at par, or at a premium? Explain.

b. If the yield to maturity of the bond rises to 7% (APR with semiannual compounding), what price will the bond trade for?

a. Because the yield to maturity is less than the coupon rate, the bond is trading at a premium.

b. $$\frac{40}{(1+.035)} + \frac{40}{(1+.035)^2} + \cdots + \frac{40+1000}{(1+.035)^{14}} = \$1,054.60$$

	NPER	Rate	PV	PMT	FV	Excel Formula
Given:	14	3.50%		40	1,000	
Solve For PV:			(1,054.60)			=PV(0.035,14,40,1000)

8-11. Suppose that General Motors Acceptance Corporation issued a bond with 10 years until maturity, a face value of $1000, and a coupon rate of 7% (annual payments). The yield to maturity on this bond when it was issued was 6%.

a. What was the price of this bond when it was issued?

b. Assuming the yield to maturity remains constant, what is the price of the bond immediately before it makes its first coupon payment?

c. Assuming the yield to maturity remains constant, what is the price of the bond immediately after it makes its first coupon payment?

a. When it was issued, the price of the bond was

$$P = \frac{70}{(1+.06)} + ... + \frac{70+1000}{(1+.06)^{10}} = \$1073.60.$$

b. Before the first coupon payment, the price of the bond is

$$P = 70 + \frac{70}{(1+.06)} ... + \frac{70+1000}{(1+.06)^{9}} = \$1138.02.$$

c. After the first coupon payment, the price of the bond will be

$$P = \frac{70}{(1+.06)} ... + \frac{70+1000}{(1+.06)^{9}} = \$1068.02.$$

8-12. Suppose you purchase a 10-year bond with 6% annual coupons. You hold the bond for four years, and sell it immediately after receiving the fourth coupon. If the bond's yield to maturity was 5% when you purchased and sold the bond,

a. What cash flows will you pay and receive from your investment in the bond per $100 face value?

b. What is the internal rate of return of your investment?

a. First, we compute the initial price of the bond by discounting its 10 annual coupons of $6 and final face value of $100 at the 5% yield to maturity.

	NPER	Rate	PV	PMT	FV	Excel Formula
Given:	10	5.00%		6	100	
Solve For PV:			(107.72)			= PV(0.05,10,6,100)

Thus, the initial price of the bond = $107.72. (Note that the bond trades above par, as its coupon rate exceeds its yield.)

Next we compute the price at which the bond is sold, which is the present value of the bonds cash flows when only 6 years remain until maturity.

	NPER	Rate	PV	PMT	FV	Excel Formula
Given:	6	5.00%		6	100	
Solve For PV:			(105.08)			= PV(0.05,6,6,100)

Therefore, the bond was sold for a price of $105.08. The cash flows from the investment are therefore as shown in the following timeline.

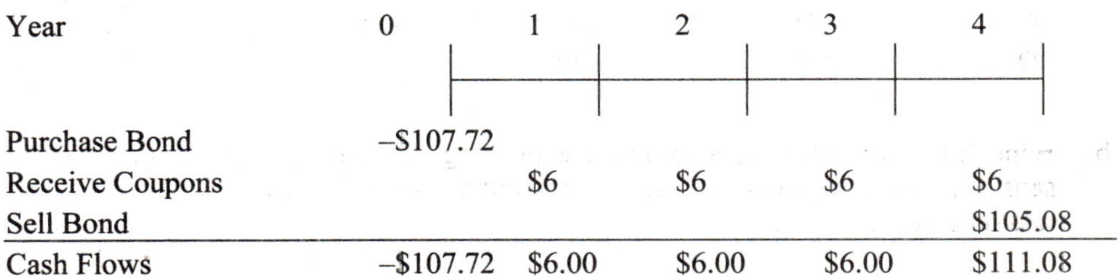

Year	0	1	2	3	4
Purchase Bond	–$107.72				
Receive Coupons		$6	$6	$6	$6
Sell Bond					$105.08
Cash Flows	–$107.72	$6.00	$6.00	$6.00	$111.08

b. We can compute the IRR of the investment using the annuity spreadsheet. The PV is the purchase price, the PMT is the coupon amount, and the FV is the sale price. The length of the investment N = 4 years. We then calculate the IRR of investment = 5%. Because the YTM was the same at the time of purchase and sale, the IRR of the investment matches the YTM.

	NPER	Rate	PV	PMT	FV	Excel Formula
Given:	4		–107.72	6	105.08	
Solve For Rate:		5.00%				= RATE(4,6,-107.72,105.08)

8-13. Consider the following bonds:

Bond	Coupon Rate (annual payments)	Maturity (years)
A	0%	15
B	0%	10
C	4%	15
D	8%	10

a. What is the percentage change in the price of each bond if its yield to maturity falls from 6% to 5%?

b. Which of the bonds A–D is most sensitive to a 1% drop in interest rates from 6% to 5% and why? Which bond is least sensitive? Provide an intuitive explanation for your answer.

a. We can compute the price of each bond at each YTM using Eq. 8.5. For example, with a 6% YTM, the price of bond A per $100 face value is

$$P(\text{bond A, 6\% YTM}) = \frac{100}{1.06^{15}} = \$41.73.$$

The price of bond D is

$$P(\text{bond D, 6\% YTM}) = 8 \times \frac{1}{.06}\left(1 - \frac{1}{1.06^{10}}\right) + \frac{100}{1.06^{10}} = \$114.72.$$

One can also use the Excel formula to compute the price: –PV(YTM, NPER, PMT, FV).

Once we compute the price of each bond for each YTM, we can compute the % price change as

$$\text{Percent change} = \frac{(\text{Price at 5\% YTM}) - (\text{Price at 6\% YTM})}{(\text{Price at 6\% YTM})}.$$

The results are shown in the table below.

Bond	Coupon Rate (annual payments)	Maturity (years)	Price at 6% YTM	Price at 5% YTM	Percentage Change
A	0%	15	$41.73	$48.10	15.3%
B	0%	10	$55.84	$61.39	9.9%
C	4%	15	$80.58	$89.62	11.2%
D	8%	10	$114.72	$123.17	7.4%

b. Bond A is most sensitive, because it has the longest maturity and no coupons. Bond D is the least sensitive. Intuitively, higher coupon rates and a shorter maturity typically lower a bond's interest rate sensitivity.

8-14. Suppose you purchase a 30-year, zero-coupon bond with a yield to maturity of 6%. You hold the bond for five years before selling it.

a. **If the bond's yield to maturity is 6% when you sell it, what is the internal rate of return of your investment?**

b. **If the bond's yield to maturity is 7% when you sell it, what is the internal rate of return of your investment?**

c. **If the bond's yield to maturity is 5% when you sell it, what is the internal rate of return of your investment?**

d. **Even if a bond has no chance of default, is your investment risk free if you plan to sell it before it matures? Explain.**

a. Purchase price = $100 / 1.06^{30}$ = 17.41. Sale price = $100 / 1.06^{25}$ = 23.30. Return = $(23.30 / 17.41)^{1/5} - 1$ = 6.00%. I.e., since YTM is the same at purchase and sale, IRR = YTM.

b. Purchase price = $100 / 1.06^{30}$ = 17.41. Sale price = $100 / 1.07^{25}$ = 18.42. Return = $(18.42 / 17.41)^{1/5} - 1$ = 1.13%. I.e., since YTM rises, IRR < initial YTM.

c. Purchase price = $100 / 1.06^{30}$ = 17.41. Sale price = $100 / 1.05^{25}$ = 29.53. Return = $(29.53 / 17.41)^{1/5} - 1$ = 11.15%. I.e., since YTM falls, IRR > initial YTM.

d. Even without default, if you sell prior to maturity, you are exposed to the risk that the YTM may change.

8-15. Suppose you purchase a 30-year Treasury bond with a 5% annual coupon, initially trading at par. In 10 years' time, the bond's yield to maturity has risen to 7% (EAR).

a. **If you sell the bond now, what internal rate of return will you have earned on your investment in the bond?**

b. **If instead you hold the bond to maturity, what internal rate of return will you earn on your investment in the bond?**

c. **Is comparing the IRRs in (a) versus (b) a useful way to evaluate the decision to sell the bond? Explain.**

a. 3.17%

b. 5%

c. We can't simply compare IRRs. By not selling the bond for its current price of $78.81, we will earn the current market return of 7% on that amount going forward.

8-16. Suppose the current yield on a one-year, zero coupon bond is 3%, while the yield on a five-year, zero coupon bond is 5%. Neither bond has any risk of default. Suppose you plan to invest for one year. You will earn more over the year by investing in the five-year bond as long as its yield does not rise above what level?

The return from investing in the 1 year is the yield. The return for investing in the 5 year for initial price p_0 and selling after one year at price p1 is $\frac{p_1}{p_0} - 1$. We have

$$p_0 = \frac{1}{(1.05)^5},$$

$$p_1 = \frac{1}{(1+y)^5}.$$

So you break even when

$$\frac{p_1}{p_0} - 1 = \frac{\frac{1}{(1+y)^4}}{\frac{1}{(1.05)^5}} - 1 = y_1 = 0.03$$

$$\frac{(1.05)^5}{(1+y)^4} = 1.03$$

$$y = \frac{(1.05)^{5/4}}{(1.03)^{1/4}} - 1 = 5.51\%.$$

For Problems 17–22, assume zero-coupon yields on default-free securities are as summarized in the following table:

Maturity (years)	1	2	3	4	5
Zero-coupon YTM	4.00%	4.30%	4.50%	4.70%	4.80%

8-17. What is the price today of a two-year, default-free security with a face value of $1000 and an annual coupon rate of 6%? Does this bond trade at a discount, at par, or at a premium?

$$P = \frac{CPN}{1+YTM_1} + \frac{CPN}{(1+YTM_2)^2} + \ldots + \frac{CPN+FV}{(1+YTM_N)^N} = \frac{60}{(1+.04)} + \frac{60+1000}{(1+.043)^2} = \$1032.09$$

This bond trades at a premium. The coupon of the bond is greater than each of the zero coupon yields, so the coupon will also be greater than the yield to maturity on this bond. Therefore it trades at a premium

8-18. What is the price of a five-year, zero-coupon, default-free security with a face value of $1000?

The price of the zero-coupon bond is

$$P = \frac{FV}{(1+YTM_N)^N} = \frac{1000}{(1+0.048)^5} = \$791.03$$

8-19. What is the price of a three-year, default-free security with a face value of $1000 and an annual coupon rate of 4%? What is the yield to maturity for this bond?

The price of the bond is

$$P = \frac{CPN}{1+YTM_1} + \frac{CPN}{(1+YTM_2)^2} + \ldots + \frac{CPN+FV}{(1+YTM_N)^N} = \frac{40}{(1+.04)} + \frac{40}{(1+.043)^2} + \frac{40+1000}{(1+.045)^3} = \$986.58.$$

The yield to maturity is

$$P = \frac{CPN}{1+YTM} + \frac{CPN}{(1+YTM)^2} + \ldots + \frac{CPN+FV}{(1+YTM)^N}$$

$$\$986.58 = \frac{40}{(1+YTM)} + \frac{40}{(1+YTM)^2} + \frac{40+1000}{(1+YTM)^3} \Rightarrow YTM = 4.488\%$$

8-20. What is the maturity of a default-free security with annual coupon payments and a yield to maturity of 4%? Why?

The maturity must be one year. If the maturity were longer than one year, there would be an arbitrage opportunity.

8-21. Consider a four-year, default-free security with annual coupon payments and a face value of $1000 that is issued at par. What is the coupon rate of this bond?

Solve the following equation:

$$1000 = CPN\left(\frac{1}{(1+.04)}+\frac{1}{(1+.043)^2}+\frac{1}{(1+.045)^3}+\frac{1}{(1+.047)^4}\right)+\frac{1000}{(1+.047)^4}$$

$CPN = \$46.76.$

Therefore, the par coupon rate is 4.676%.

8-22. Consider a five-year, default-free bond with annual coupons of 5% and a face value of $1000.

a. Without doing any calculations, determine whether this bond is trading at a premium or at a discount. Explain.

b. What is the yield to maturity on this bond?

c. If the yield to maturity on this bond increased to 5.2%, what would the new price be?

a. The bond is trading at a premium because its yield to maturity is a weighted average of the yields of the zero coupon bonds. This implied that its yield is below 5%, the coupon rate.

b. To compute the yield, first compute the price.

$$P = \frac{CPN}{1+YTM_1}+\frac{CPN}{(1+YTM_2)^2}+\ldots+\frac{CPN+FV}{(1+YTM_N)^N}$$

$$= \frac{50}{(1+.04)}+\frac{50}{(1+.043)^2}+\frac{50}{(1+.045)^3}+\frac{50}{(1+.047)^4}+\frac{50+1000}{(1+.048)^5} = \$1010.05$$

The yield to maturity is:

$$P = \frac{CPN}{1+YTM}+\frac{CPN}{(1+YTM)^2}+\ldots+\frac{CPN+FV}{(1+YTM)^N}$$

$$1010.05 = \frac{50}{(1+YTM)}+\ldots+\frac{50+1000}{(1+YTM)^N} \Rightarrow YTM = 4.77\%.$$

c. If the yield increased to 5.2%, the new price would be:

$$P = \frac{CPN}{1+YTM}+\frac{CPN}{(1+YTM)^2}+\ldots+\frac{CPN+FV}{(1+YTM)^N}$$

$$= \frac{50}{(1+.052)}+\ldots+\frac{50+1000}{(1+.052)^N} = \$991.39.$$

8-23. Prices of zero-coupon, default-free securities with face values of $1000 are summarized in the following table:

Maturity (years)	1	2	3
Price (per $1000 face value)	$970.87	$938.95	$904.56

Suppose you observe that a three-year, default-free security with an annual coupon rate of 10% and a face value of $1000 has a price today of $1183.50. Is there an arbitrage opportunity? If so, show specifically how you would take advantage of this opportunity. If not, why not?

First, figure out if the price of the coupon bond is consistent with the zero coupon yields implied by the other securities.

$$970.87 = \frac{1000}{(1+YTM_1)} \quad \rightarrow \quad YTM_1 = 3.0\%$$

$$938.95 = \frac{1000}{(1+YTM_2)^2} \quad \rightarrow \quad YTM_2 = 3.2\%$$

$$904.56 = \frac{1000}{(1+YTM_3)^3} \quad \rightarrow \quad YTM_3 = 3.4\%$$

According to these zero coupon yields, the price of the coupon bond should be:

$$\frac{100}{(1+.03)} + \frac{100}{(1+.032)^2} + \frac{100+1000}{(1+.034)^3} = \$1186.00.$$

The price of the coupon bond is too low, so there is an arbitrage opportunity. To take advantage of it:

	Today	1 Year	2 Years	3 Years
Buy 10 Coupon Bonds	−11835.00	+1000	+1000	+11,000
Short Sell 1 One-Year Zero	+970.87	−1000		
Short Sell 1 Two-Year Zero	+938.95		−1000	
Short Sell 11 Three-Year Zeros	+9950.16			−11,000
Net Cash Flow	24.98	0	0	0

8-24. Assume there are four default-free bonds with the following prices and future cash flows:

Bond	Price Today	Cash Flows Year 1	Year 2	Year 3
A	$934.58	1000	0	0
B	881.66	0	1000	0
C	1,118.21	100	100	1100
D	839.62	0	0	1000

Do these bonds present an arbitrage opportunity? If so, how would you take advantage of this opportunity? If not, why not?

To determine whether these bonds present an arbitrage opportunity, check whether the pricing is internally consistent. Calculate the spot rates implied by Bonds A, B, and D (the zero coupon bonds), and use this to check Bond C. (You may alternatively compute the spot rates from Bonds A, B, and C, and check Bond D, or some other combination.)

$$934.58 = \frac{1000}{(1+YTM_1)} \Rightarrow YTM_1 = 7.0\%$$

$$881.66 = \frac{1000}{(1+YTM_2)^2} \Rightarrow YTM_2 = 6.5\%$$

$$839.62 = \frac{1000}{(1+YTM_3)^3} \Rightarrow YTM_3 = 6.0\%$$

Given the spot rates implied by Bonds A, B, and D, the price of Bond C should be $1,105.21. Its price really is $1,118.21, so it is overpriced by $13 per bond. Yes, there is an arbitrage opportunity.

To take advantage of this opportunity, you want to (short) Sell Bond C (since it is overpriced). To match future cash flows, one strategy is to sell 10 Bond Cs (it is not the only effective strategy; any multiple of this strategy is also arbitrage). This complete strategy is summarized in the table below.

	Today	1 Year	2Years	3Years
Sell Bond C	11,182.10	–1,000	–1,000	–11,000
Buy Bond A	–934.58	1,000	0	0
Buy Bond B	–881.66	0	1,000	0
Buy 11 Bond D	–9,235.82	0	0	11,000
Net Cash Flow	130.04	0	0	0

Notice that your arbitrage profit equals 10 times the mispricing on each bond (subject to rounding error).

8-25. Suppose you are given the following information about the default-free, coupon-paying yield curve:

Maturity (years)	**1**	**2**	**3**	**4**
Coupon rate (annual payments)	0.00%	10.00%	6.00%	12.00%
YTM	2.000%	3.908%	5.840%	5.783%

a. Use arbitrage to determine the yield to maturity of a two-year, zero-coupon bond.

b. What is the zero-coupon yield curve for years 1 through 4?

a. We can construct a two-year zero coupon bond using the one and two-year coupon bonds as follows.

	Cash Flow in Year: 1	2	3	4
Two-year coupon bond ($1000 Face Value)	100	1,100		
Less: One-year bond ($100 Face Value)	(100)			
Two-year zero ($1100 Face Value)	-	1,100		

$$\text{Now, Price(2-year coupon bond)} = \frac{100}{1.03908} + \frac{1100}{1.03908^2} = \$1115.05$$

$$\text{Price(1-year bond)} = \frac{100}{1.02} = \$98.04.$$

By the Law of One Price:

Price(2 year zero) = Price(2 year coupon bond) – Price(One-year bond)

= 1115.05 – 98.04 = $1017.01

Given this price per $1100 face value, the YTM for the 2-year zero is (Eq. 8.3)

$$YTM(2) = \left(\frac{1100}{1017.01}\right)^{1/2} - 1 = 4.000\%.$$

b. We already know YTM(1) = 2%, YTM(2) = 4%. We can construct a 3-year zero as follows:

	Cash Flow in Year:			
	1	2	3	4
Three-year coupon bond ($1000 face value)	60	60	1,060	
Less: one-year zero ($60 face value)	(60)			
Less: two-year zero ($60 face value)	-	(60)		
Three-year zero ($1060 face value)	-	-	1,060	

Now, Price(3-year coupon bond) $= \dfrac{60}{1.0584} + \dfrac{60}{1.0584^2} + \dfrac{1060}{1.0584^3} = \$1004.29.$

By the Law of One Price:

Price(3-year zero) = Price(3-year coupon bond) – Price(One-year zero) – Price(Two-year zero)

= Price(3-year coupon bond) – PV(coupons in years 1 and 2)

$= 1004.29 - 60 / 1.02 - 60 / 1.04^2 = \$889.99.$

Solving for the YTM:

$$YTM(3) = \left(\frac{1060}{889.99}\right)^{1/3} - 1 = 6.000\%.$$

Finally, we can do the same for the 4-year zero:

	Cash Flow in Year:			
	1	2	3	4
Four-year coupon bond ($1000 face value)	120	120	120	1,120
Less: one-year zero ($120 face value)	(120)			
Less: two-year zero ($120 face value)	—	(120)		
Less: three-year zero ($120 face value)	—	—	(120)	
Four-year zero ($1120 face value)	—	—	—	1,120

Now, Price(4-year coupon bond) $= \dfrac{120}{1.05783} + \dfrac{120}{1.05783^2} + \dfrac{120}{1.05783^3} + \dfrac{1120}{1.05783^4} = \$1216.50.$

By the Law of One Price:

Price(4-year zero) = Price(4-year coupon bond) – PV(coupons in years 1–3)

$= 1216.50 - 120 / 1.02 - 120 / 1.04^2 - 120 / 1.06^3 = \$887.15.$

Solving for the YTM:

$$YTM(4) = \left(\frac{1120}{887.15}\right)^{1/4} - 1 = 6.000\%.$$

Thus, we have computed the zero coupon yield curve as shown.

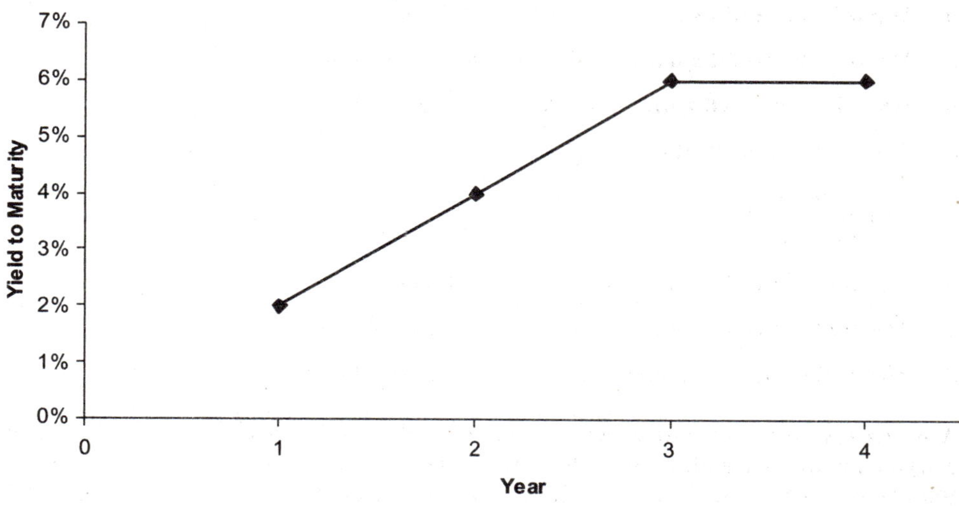

8-26. Explain why the expected return of a corporate bond does not equal its yield to maturity.

The yield to maturity of a corporate bond is based on the promised payments of the bond. But there is some chance the corporation will default and pay less. Thus, the bond's expected return is typically less than its YTM.

Corporate bonds have credit risk, which is the risk that the borrower will default and not pay all specified payments. As a result, investors pay less for bonds with credit risk than they would for an otherwise identical default-free bond. Because the YTM for a bond is calculated using the promised cash flows, the yields of bonds with credit risk will be higher than that of otherwise identical default-free bonds. However, the YTM of a defaultable bond is always higher than the expected return of investing in the bond because it is calculated using the promised cash flows rather than the expected cash flows.

8-27. Grummon Corporation has issued zero-coupon corporate bonds with a five-year maturity. Investors believe there is a 20% chance that Grummon will default on these bonds. If Grummon does default, investors expect to receive only 50 cents per dollar they are owed. If investors require a 6% expected return on their investment in these bonds, what will be the price and yield to maturity on these bonds?

$$\text{Price} = \frac{100((1-d)+d(r))}{1.06^5} = 67.25$$

$$\text{Yield}=\left(\frac{100}{67.25}\right)^{1/5} - 1 = 8.26\%$$

8-28. The following table summarizes the yields to maturity on several one-year, zero-coupon securities:

Security	Yield (%)
Treasury	3.1
AAA corporate	3.2
BBB corporate	4.2
B corporate	4.9

a. What is the price (expressed as a percentage of the face value) of a one-year, zero-coupon corporate bond with a AAA rating?

b. What is the credit spread on AAA-rated corporate bonds?

c. What is the credit spread on B-rated corporate bonds?

d. How does the credit spread change with the bond rating? Why?

a. The price of this bond will be

$$P = \frac{100}{1+.032} = 96.899.$$

b. The credit spread on AAA-rated corporate bonds is 0.032 – 0.031 = 0.1%.

c. The credit spread on B-rated corporate bonds is 0.049 – 0.031 = 1.8%.

d. The credit spread increases as the bond rating falls, because lower rated bonds are riskier.

8-29. Andrew Industries is contemplating issuing a 30-year bond with a coupon rate of 7% (annual coupon payments) and a face value of $1000. Andrew believes it can get a rating of A from Standard and Poor's. However, due to recent financial difficulties at the company, Standard and Poor's is warning that it may downgrade Andrew Industries bonds to BBB. Yields on A-rated, long-term bonds are currently 6.5%, and yields on BBB-rated bonds are 6.9%.

a. What is the price of the bond if Andrew maintains the A rating for the bond issue?

b. What will the price of the bond be if it is downgraded?

a. When originally issued, the price of the bonds was

$$P = \frac{70}{(1+0.065)} + \ldots + \frac{70+1000}{(1+.065)^{30}} = \$1065.29.$$

b. If the bond is downgraded, its price will fall to

$$P = \frac{70}{(1+0.069)} + \ldots + \frac{70+1000}{(1+.069)^{30}} = \$1012.53.$$

8-30. HMK Enterprises would like to raise $10 million to invest in capital expenditures. The company plans to issue five-year bonds with a face value of $1000 and a coupon rate of 6.5% (annual payments). The following table summarizes the yield to maturity for five-year (annualpay) coupon corporate bonds of various ratings:

Rating	AAA	AA	A	BBB	BB
YTM	6.20%	6.30%	6.50%	6.90%	7.50%

a. Assuming the bonds will be rated AA, what will the price of the bonds be?

b. How much total principal amount of these bonds must HMK issue to raise $10 million today, assuming the bonds are AA rated? (Because HMK cannot issue a fraction of a bond, assume that all fractions are rounded to the nearest whole number.)

c. What must the rating of the bonds be for them to sell at par?

d. Suppose that when the bonds are issued, the price of each bond is $959.54. What is the likely rating of the bonds? Are they junk bonds?

a. The price will be

$$P = \frac{65}{(1+.063)} + ... + \frac{65+1000}{(1+.063)^5} = \$1008.36.$$

b. Each bond will raise \$1008.36, so the firm must issue: $\frac{\$10,000,000}{\$1008.36} = 9917.13 \Rightarrow 9918$ bonds.

This will correspond to a principle amount of $9918 \times \$1000 = \$9,918,000$.

c. For the bonds to sell at par, the coupon must equal the yield. Since the coupon is 6.5%, the yield must also be 6.5%, or A-rated.

d. First, compute the yield on these bonds:

$$959.54 = \frac{65}{(1+YTM)} + ... + \frac{65+1000}{(1+YTM)^5} \Rightarrow YTM = 7.5\%.$$

Given a yield of 7.5%, it is likely these bonds are BB rated. Yes, BB-rated bonds are junk bonds.

8-31. A BBB-rated corporate bond has a yield to maturity of 8.2%. A U.S. Treasury security has a yield to maturity of 6.5%. These yields are quoted as APRs with semiannual compounding. Both bonds pay semiannual coupons at a rate of 7% and have five years to maturity.

a. What is the price (expressed as a percentage of the face value) of the Treasury bond?

b. What is the price (expressed as a percentage of the face value) of the BBB-rated corporate bond?

c. What is the credit spread on the BBB bonds?

a. $P = \frac{35}{(1+.0325)} + ... + \frac{35 + 1000}{(1+.0325)^{10}} = \$1,021.06 = 102.1\%$

b. $P = \frac{35}{(1+.041)} + ... + \frac{35 + 1000}{(1+.041)^{10}} = \$951.58 = 95.2\%$

c. 0. 17

8-32. The Isabelle Corporation rents prom dresses in its stores across the southern United States. It has just issued a five-year, zero-coupon corporate bond at a price of \$74. You have purchased this bond and intend to hold it until maturity.

a. What is the yield to maturity of the bond?

b. What is the expected return on your investment (expressed as an EAR) if there is no chance of default?

c. What is the expected return (expressed as an EAR) if there is a 100% probability of default and you will recover 90% of the face value?

d. What is the expected return (expressed as an EAR) if the probability of default is 50%, the likelihood of default is higher in bad times than good times, and, in the case of default, you will recover 90% of the face value?

e. For parts (b–d), what can you say about the five-year, risk-free interest rate in each case?

a. $\left(\frac{100}{74}\right)^{1/5} - 1 = 6.21\%$

b. In this case, the expected return equals the yield to maturity.

c. $\left(\dfrac{100\times 0.9}{74}\right)^{1/5} - 1 = 3.99\%$

d. $\left(\dfrac{100\times 0.9\times 0.5 + 100\times 0.5}{74}\right)^{1/5} - 1 = 5.12\%$

e. Risk-free rate is 6.21% in b, 3.99% in c, and less than 5.12% in d.

Appendix

Problems A.1–A.4 refer to the following table:

Maturity (years)	1	2	3	4	5
Zero-coupon YTM	4.0%	5.5%	5.5%	5.0%	4.5%

A.1. **What is the forward rate for year 2 (the forward rate quoted today for an investment that begins in one year and matures in two years)?**

From Eq 8A.2,

$$f_2 = \frac{(1+YTM_2)^2}{(1+YTM_1)} - 1 = \frac{1.055^2}{1.04} - 1 = 7.02\%$$

A.2. **What is the forward rate for year 3 (the forward rate quoted today for an investment that begins in two years and matures in three years)? What can you conclude about forward rates when the yield curve is flat?**

From Eq 8A.2,

$$f_3 = \frac{(1+YTM_3)^3}{(1+YTM_2)^2} - 1 = \frac{1.055^3}{1.055^2} - 1 = 5.50\%$$

When the yield curve is flat (spot rates are equal), the forward rate is equal to the spot rate.

A.3. **What is the forward rate for year 5 (the forward rate quoted today for an investment that begins in four years and matures in five years)?**

From Eq 8A.2,

$$f_5 = \frac{(1+YTM_5)^5}{(1+YTM_4)^4} - 1 = \frac{1.045^5}{1.050^4} - 1 = 2.52\%$$

When the yield curve is flat (spot rates are equal), the forward rate is equal to the spot rate.

A.4. **Suppose you wanted to lock in an interest rate for an investment that begins in one year and matures in five years. What rate would you obtain if there are no arbitrage opportunities?**

Call this rate $f_{1,5}$. If we invest for one-year at YTM1, and then for the 4 years from year 1 to 5 at rate $f_{1,5}$, after five years we would earn

$.1\ YTM_1 1\ f_{1,5}{}^4$

with no risk. No arbitrage means this must equal that amount we would earn investing at the current five year spot rate:

$(1 + YTM_1)(1 + f_{1,5})^4 + (1 + YTM_5)^5$.

Therefore, $$(1+f_{1,5})^4 = \frac{(1+YTM_5)^5}{1+YTM_1} = \frac{1.045^5}{1.04} = 1.19825$$

and so: $f_{1,5} = 1.19825^{1/4} - 1 = 4.625\%$.

A.5. **Suppose the yield on a one-year, zero-coupon bond is 5%. The forward rate for year 2 is 4%, and the forward rate for year 3 is 3%. What is the yield to maturity of a zero-coupon bond that matures in three years?**

We can invest for three years with risk by investing for one year at 5%, and then locking in a rate of 4% for the second year and 3% for the third year. The return from this strategy must equal the return from investing in a 3-year, zero-coupon bond (see Eq 8A.3):

$(1 + YTM_3)^3 = (1.05)(1.04)(1.03) = 1.12476$

Therefore: $YTM_3 = 1.12476^{1/3} - 1 = 3.997\%$.

Chapter 9
Valuing Stocks

9-1. Assume Evco, Inc., has a current price of \$50 and will pay a \$2 dividend in one year, and its equity cost of capital is 15%. What price must you expect it to sell for right after paying the dividend in one year in order to justify its current price?

We can use Eq. (9.1) to solve for the price of the stock in one year given the current price of \$50.00, the \$2 dividend, and the 15% cost of capital.

$$50 = \frac{2+X}{1.15}$$
$$X = 55.50$$

At a current price of \$50, we can expect Evco stock to sell for \$55.50 immediately after the firm pays the dividend in one year.

9-2. Anle Corporation has a current price of \$20, is expected to pay a dividend of \$1 in one year, and its expected price right after paying that dividend is \$22.

a. What is Anle's expected dividend yield?

b. What is Anle's expected capital gain rate?

c. What is Anle's equity cost of capital?

a. Div yld = 1/20 = 5%

b. Cap gain rate = (22-20)/20 = 10%

c. Equity cost of capital = 5% + 10% = 15%

9-3. Suppose Acap Corporation will pay a dividend of \$2.80 per share at the end of this year and \$3 per share next year. You expect Acap's stock price to be \$52 in two years. If Acap's equity cost of capital is 10%:

a. What price would you be willing to pay for a share of Acap stock today, if you planned to hold the stock for two years?

b. Suppose instead you plan to hold the stock for one year. What price would you expect to be able to sell a share of Acap stock for in one year?

c. Given your answer in part (b), what price would you be willing to pay for a share of Acap stock today, if you planned to hold the stock for one year? How does this compare to you answer in part (a)?

a. $P(0) = 2.80 / 1.10 + (3.00 + 52.00) / 1.10^2 = \$48.00$

b. $P(1) = (3.00 + 52.00) / 1.10 = \$50.00$

c. $P(0) = (2.80 + 50.00) / 1.10 = \$48.00$

9-4. **Krell Industries has a share price of $22 today. If Krell is expected to pay a dividend of $0.88 this year, and its stock price is expected to grow to $23.54 at the end of the year, what is Krell's dividend yield and equity cost of capital?**

Dividend Yield = 0.88 / 22.00 = 4%

Capital gain rate = (23.54 – 22.00) / 22.00 = 7%

Total expected return = r_E = 4% + 7% = 11%

9-5. **NoGrowth Corporation currently pays a dividend of $2 per year, and it will continue to pay this dividend forever. What is the price per share if its equity cost of capital is 15% per year?**

With simplifying assumption (as was made in the chapter) that dividends are paid at the end of the year, then the stock pays a total of $2.00 in dividends per year. Valuing this dividend as a perpetuity, we have, $P = \$2.00/0.15 = \$13.33$.

Alternatively, if the dividends are paid quarterly, we can value them as a perpetuity using a quarterly discount rate of $(1.15)^{\frac{1}{4}} - 1 = 3.556\%$ (see Eq. 5.1) then $P = \$0.5010.03556 = \$14.06$.

9-6. **Summit Systems will pay a dividend of $1.50 this year. If you expect Summit's dividend to grow by 6% per year, what is its price per share if its equity cost of capital is 11%?**

P = 1.50 / (11% – 6%) = $30

9-7. **Dorpac Corporation has a dividend yield of 1.5%. Dorpac's equity cost of capital is 8%, and its dividends are expected to grow at a constant rate.**

a. **What is the expected growth rate of Dorpac's dividends?**

b. **What is the expected growth rate of Dorpac's share price?**

a. Eq 9.7 implies r_E = Div Yld + g, so 8% – 1.5% = g = 6.5%.

b. With constant dividend growth, share price is also expected to grow at rate g = 6.5% (or we can solve this from Eq 9.2).

9-8. **Kenneth Cole Productions (KCP), suspended its dividend at the start of 2009. Suppose you do not expect KCP to resume paying dividends until 2011.You expect KCP's dividend in 2011 to be $0.40 per year (paid at the end of the year), and you expect it to grow by 5% per year thereafter. If KCP's equity cost of capital is 11%, what is the value of a share of KCP at the start of 2009?**

P(2010) = Div(2011)/(r – g) = 0.40/(.11 – .05) = 6.67

P(2009) = $6.67/1.11^2$ = $5.41

9-9. **DFB, Inc., expects earnings this year of $5 per share, and it plans to pay a $3 dividend to shareholders. DFB will retain $2 per share of its earnings to reinvest in new projects with an expected return of 15% per year. Suppose DFB will maintain the same dividend payout rate, retention rate, and return on new investments in the future and will not change its number of outstanding shares.**

a. **What growth rate of earnings would you forecast for DFB?**

b. **If DFB's equity cost of capital is 12%, what price would you estimate for DFB stock?**

c. **Suppose DFB instead paid a dividend of $4 per share this year and retained only $1 per share in earnings. If DFB maintains this higher payout rate in the future, what stock price would you estimate now? Should DFB raise its dividend?**

a. Eq 9.12: g = retention rate × return on new invest = (2/5) × 15% = 6%

b. P = 3 / (12% – 6%) = $50

c. $g = (1/5) \times 15\% = 3\%$, $P = 4 / (12\% - 3\%) = \$44.44$. No, projects are positive NPV (return exceeds cost of capital), so don't raise dividend.

9-10. Cooperton Mining just announced it will cut its dividend from $4 to $2.50 per share and use the extra funds to expand. Prior to the announcement, Cooperton's dividends were expected to grow at a 3% rate, and its share price was $50. With the new expansion, Cooperton's dividends are expected to grow at a 5% rate. What share price would you expect after the announcement? (Assume Cooperton's risk is unchanged by the new expansion.) Is the expansion a positive NPV investment?

Estimate r_E: $r_E = \text{Div Yield} + g = 4 / 50 + 3\% = 11\%$

New Price: $P = 2.50/(11\% - 5\%) = \$41.67$

In this case, cutting the dividend to expand is not a positive NPV investment.

9-11. Gillette Corporation will pay an annual dividend of $0.65 one year from now. Analysts expect this dividend to grow at 12% per year thereafter until the fifth year. After then, growth will level off at 2% per year. According to the dividend-discount model, what is the value of a share of Gillette stock if the firm's equity cost of capital is 8%?

Value of the first 5 dividend payments:

$$PV_{1-5} = \frac{0.65}{(0.08-0.12)}\left(1-\left(\frac{1.12}{1.08}\right)^5\right) = \$3.24.$$

Value on date 5 of the rest of the dividend payments:

$$PV_5 = \frac{0.65(1.12)^4 1.02}{0.08-0.02} = 17.39.$$

Discounting this value to the present gives

$$PV_0 = \frac{17.39}{(1.08)^5} = \$11.83.$$

So the value of Gillette is: $P = PV_{1-5} + PV_0 = 3.24 + 11.83 = \$15.07.$

9-12. Colgate-Palmolive Company has just paid an annual dividend of $0.96. Analysts are predicting an 11% per year growth rate in earnings over the next five years. After then, Colgate's earnings are expected to grow at the current industry average of 5.2% per year. If Colgate's equity cost of capital is 8.5% per year and its dividend payout ratio remains constant, what price does the dividend-discount model predict Colgate stock should sell for?

PV of the first 5 dividends:

$$PV_{first\ 5} = \frac{0.96(1.11)}{0.085-0.11}\left(1-\left(\frac{1.11}{1.085}\right)^5\right) = 5.14217.$$

PV of the remaining dividends in year 5:

$$PV_{\text{remaining in year 5}} = \frac{0.96(1.11)^5(1.052)}{0.085-0.052} = 51.5689.$$

Discounting back to the present

$$PV_{remaining} = \frac{51.5689}{(1.085)^5} = 34.2957.$$

Thus the price of Colgate is

$$P = PV_{first\ 5} + PV_{remaining} = 39.4378.$$

9-13. What is the value of a firm with initial dividend *Div*, growing for *n* years (i.e., until year *n* + 1) at rate g_1 and after that at rate g_2 forever, when the equity cost of capital is *r*?

$$P_0 = \overbrace{\frac{Div_1}{r-g_1}\left(1-\left(\frac{1+g_1}{1+r}\right)^n\right)}^{n\text{-year, constant growth annuity}} + \overbrace{\left(\frac{1+g_1}{1+r}\right)^n \frac{Div_1}{r-g_2}}^{PV\text{ of terminal value}}$$

$$= \underbrace{\frac{Div_1}{r-g_1}}_{\text{constant growth perpetuity}} + \underbrace{\left(\frac{1+g_1}{1+r}\right)^n \left(\frac{Div_1}{r-g_2} - \frac{Div_1}{r-g_1}\right)}_{\text{present value of difference of perpetuities in year } n}$$

9-14. Halliford Corporation expects to have earnings this coming year of $3 per share. Halliford plans to retain all of its earnings for the next two years. For the subsequent two years, the firm will retain 50% of its earnings. It will then retain 20% of its earnings from that point onward. Each year, retained earnings will be invested in new projects with an expected return of 25% per year. Any earnings that are not retained will be paid out as dividends. Assume Halliford's share count remains constant and all earnings growth comes from the investment of retained earnings. If Halliford's equity cost of capital is 10%, what price would you estimate for Halliford stock?

See the spreadsheet for Halliford's dividend forecast:

	Year	0	1	2	3	4	5	6
Earnings								
1	EPS Growth Rate (vs. prior yr)			25%	25%	12.5%	12.5%	5%
2	EPS		$3.00	$3.75	$4.69	$5.27	$5.93	$6.23
Dividends								
3	Retention Ratio		100%	100%	50%	50%	20%	20%
4	Dividend Payout Ratio		0%	0%	50%	50%	80%	80%
5	Div (2 × 4)		—	—	$2.34	$2.64	$4.75	$4.98

From year 5 on, dividends grow at constant rate of 5%. Therefore,

P(4) = 4.75/(10% – 5%) =$95.

Then P(0) = 2.34 / 1.10^3 + (2.64 + 95) / 1.10^4 = $68.45.

9-15. Suppose Cisco Systems pays no dividends but spent $5 billion on share repurchases last year. If Cisco's equity cost of capital is 12%, and if the amount spent on repurchases is expected to grow by 8% per year, estimate Cisco's market capitalization. If Cisco has 6 billion shares outstanding, what stock price does this correspond to?

Total payout next year = 5 billion × 1.08 = $5.4 billion

Equity Value = 5.4 / (12% – 8%) = $135 billion

Share price = 135 / 6 = $22.50

9-16. Maynard Steel plans to pay a dividend of \$3 this year. The company has an expected earnings growth rate of 4% per year and an equity cost of capital of 10%.

a. Assuming Maynard's dividend payout rate and expected growth rate remains constant, and Maynard does not issue or repurchase shares, estimate Maynard's share price.

b. Suppose Maynard decides to pay a dividend of \$1 this year and use the remaining \$2 per share to repurchase shares. If Maynard's total payout rate remains constant, estimate Maynard's share price.

c. If Maynard maintains the dividend and total payout rate given in part (b), at what rate are Maynard's dividends and earnings per share expected to grow?

a. Earnings growth = EPS growth = dividend growth = 4%. Thus, P = 3 / (10% – 4%) = \$50.

b. Using the total payout model, P = 3/(10% – 4%) = \$50.

c. $g = r_E$ – Div Yield = 10% – 1/50 = 8%

9-17. Benchmark Metrics, Inc. (BMI), an all-equity financed firm, just reported EPS of \$5.00 per share for 2008. Despite the economic downturn, BMI is confident regarding its current investment opportunities. But due to the financial crisis, BMI does not wish to fund these investments externally. The Board has therefore decided to suspend its stock repurchase plan and cut its dividend to \$1 per share (vs. almost \$2 per share in 2007), and retain these funds instead. The firm has just paid the 2008 dividend, and BMI plans to keep its dividend at \$1 per share in 2009 as well. In subsequent years, it expects its growth opportunities to slow, and it will still be able to fund its growth internally with a target 40% dividend payout ratio, and reinitiating its stock repurchase plan for a total payout rate of 60%. (All dividends and repurchases occur at the end of each year.)

Suppose BMI's existing operations will continue to generate the current level of earnings per share in the future. Assume further that the return on new investment is 15%, and that reinvestments will account for all future earnings growth (if any). Finally, assume BMI's equity cost of capital is 10%.

a. Estimate BMI's EPS in 2009 and 2010 (before any share repurchases).

b. What is the value of a share of BMI at the start of 2009?

a. To calculate earnings growth, we can use the formula: g = (retention rate) × RONI.

In 2008, BMI retains \$4 of its \$5 in EPS, for a retention rate of 80%, and an earnings growth rate of 80% × 15% = 12%. Thus, EPS2009 = \$5.00 × (1.12) = \$5.60.

In 2009, BMI retains \$4.60 of its \$5.60 in EPS, for a retention rate of 82.14% and an earnings growth rate of 82.14% × 15% = 12.32%. So, EPS2010 = \$5.60 × (1.1232) = \$6.29.

b. From 2010 on, the firm plans to retain 40% of EPS, for a growth rate of 40% × 15% = 6%.

Total Payouts in 2010 are 60% of EPS, or 60% × \$6.29 = \$3.774.

Thus, the value of the stock at the end of 2009 is, given the 6% future growth rate,

P2009 = \$3.77/(10% - 6%) = \$94.35.

Given the \$1 dividend in 2009, we get a share price in 2008 of

P2008 = (\$1 + 94.35)/1.10 = \$86.68.

9-18. Heavy Metal Corporation is expected to generate the following free cash flows over the next five years:

Year	1	2	3	4	5
FCF ($ millions)	53	68	78	75	82

After then, the free cash flows are expected to grow at the industry average of 4% per year. Using the discounted free cash flow model and a weighted average cost of capital of 14%:

a. Estimate the enterprise value of Heavy Metal.

b. If Heavy Metal has no excess cash, debt of $300 million, and 40 million shares outstanding, estimate its share price.

a. V(4) = 82 / (14% – 4%) = $820

$V(0) = 53 / 1.14 + 68/1.14^2 + 78 / 1.14^3 + (75 + 820) / 1.14^4 = \$681$

b. P = (681 + 0 – 300)/40 = $9.53

9-19. IDX Technologies is a privately held developer of advanced security systems based in Chicago. As part of your business development strategy, in late 2008 you initiate discussions with IDX's founder about the possibility of acquiring the business at the end of 2008. Estimate the value of IDX per share using a discounted FCF approach and the following data:

- **Debt: $30 million**
- **Excess cash: $110 million**
- **Shares outstanding: 50 million**
- **Expected FCF in 2009: $45 million**
- **Expected FCF in 2010: $50 million**
- **Future FCF growth rate beyond 2010: 5%**
- **Weighted-average cost of capital: 9.4%**

From 2010 on, we expect FCF to grow at a 5% rate. Thus, using the growing perpetuity formula, we can estimate IDX's Terminal Enterprise Value in 2009 = $50/(9.4% – 5%) = $1136.

Adding the 2009 cash flow and discounting, we have

Enterprise Value in 2008 = ($45 + $1136)/(1.094) = $1080.

Adjusting for Cash and Debt (net debt), we estimate an equity value of

Equity Value = $1080 + 110 – 30 = $1160.

Dividing by number of shares:

Value per share = $1160/50 = $23.20.

9-20. Sora Industries has 60 million outstanding shares, $120 million in debt, $40 million in cash, and the following projected free cash flow for the next four years:

	Year	0	1	2	3	4
Earnings and FCF Forecast ($ millions)						
1	Sales	433.0	468.0	516.0	547.0	574.3
2	*Growth versus Prior Year*		*8.1%*	*10.3%*	*6.0%*	*5.0%*
3	Cost of Goods Sold		(313.6)	(345.7)	(366.5)	(384.8)
4	**Gross Profit**		154.4	170.3	180.5	189.5
5	Selling, General, and Administrative		(93.6)	(103.2)	(109.4)	(114.9)
6	Depreciation		(7.0)	(7.5)	(9.0)	(9.5)
7	**EBIT**		53.8	59.6	62.1	65.2
8	Less: Income Tax at 40%		(21.5)	(23.8)	(24.8)	(26.1)
9	Plus: Depreciation		7.0	7.5	9.0	9.5
10	Less: Capital Expenditures		(7.7)	(10.0)	(9.9)	(10.4)
11	Less: Increase in NWC		(6.3)	(8.6)	(5.6)	(4.9)
12	**Free Cash Flow**		**25.3**	**24.6**	**30.8**	**33.3**

a. **Suppose Sora's revenue and free cash flow are expected to grow at a 5% rate beyond year 4. If Sora's weighted average cost of capital is 10%, what is the value of Sora's stock based on this information?**

b. **Sora's cost of goods sold was assumed to be 67% of sales. If its cost of goods sold is actually 70% of sales, how would the estimate of the stock's value change?**

c. **Let's return to the assumptions of part (a) and suppose Sora can maintain its cost of goods sold at 67% of sales. However, now suppose Sora reduces its selling, general, and administrative expenses from 20% of sales to 16% of sales. What stock price would you estimate now? (Assume no other expenses, except taxes, are affected.)**

*d. **Sora's net working capital needs were estimated to be 18% of sales (which is their current level in year 0). If Sora can reduce this requirement to 12% of sales starting in year 1, but all other assumptions remain as in part (a), what stock price do you estimate for Sora? (*Hint*: This change will have the largest impact on Sora's free cash flow in year 1.)**

a. $V(3) = 33.3 / (10\% - 5\%) = 666$

$V(0) = 25.3 / 1.10 + 24.6 / 1.10^2 + (30.8 + 666) / 1.10^3 = 567$

$P(0) = (567 + 40 - 120) / 60 = \$8.11$

	Year	0	1	2	3	4	5
Earnings Forecast ($000s)			8%	10%	6%	5%	5%
1	Sales	433.00	468.00	516.00	546.96	574.31	603.02
2	Cost of Goods Sold		(327.60)	(361.20)	(382.87)	(402.02)	(422.12)
3	**Gross Profit**		140.40	154.80	164.09	172.29	180.91
4	Selling, General & Admin.		(93.60)	(103.20)	(109.39)	(114.86)	(120.60)
6	Depreciation		(7.00)	(7.50)	(9.00)	(9.45)	(9.92)
7	**EBIT**		39.80	44.10	45.70	47.98	50.38
8	Income tax at 40%		(15.92)	(17.64)	(18.28)	(19.19)	(20.15)
9	**Unlevered Net Income**		23.88	26.46	27.42	28.79	30.23
Free Cash Flow ($000s)							
10	Plus: Depreciation		7.00	7.50	9.00	9.45	9.92
11	Less: Capital Expenditures		(7.70)	(10.00)	(9.90)	(10.40)	(10.91)
12	Less: Increases in NWC		(6.30)	(8.64)	(5.57)	(4.92)	(5.17)
13	**Free Cash Flow**		**16.88**	**15.32**	**20.94**	**22.92**	**24.07**

b. Free cash flows change as follows:

Hence V(3) = 458, and V(0) = 388. Thus, P(0) = $5.13.

	Year	0	1	2	3	4	5
Earnings Forecast ($000s)			8%	10%	6%	5%	5%
1	Sales	433.00	468.00	516.00	546.96	574.31	603.02
2	Cost of Goods Sold		(313.56)	(345.72)	(366.46)	(384.79)	(404.03)
3	**Gross Profit**		154.44	170.28	180.50	189.52	199.00
4	Selling, General & Admin.		(74.88)	(82.56)	(87.51)	(91.89)	(96.48)
6	Depreciation		(7.00)	(7.50)	(9.00)	(9.45)	(9.92)
7	**EBIT**		72.56	80.22	83.98	88.18	92.59
8	Income tax at 40%		(29.02)	(32.09)	(33.59)	(35.27)	(37.04)
9	**Unlevered Net Income**		43.54	48.13	50.39	52.91	55.55
Free Cash Flow ($000s)							
10	Plus: Depreciation		7.00	7.50	9.00	9.45	9.92
11	Less: Capital Expenditures		(7.70)	(10.00)	(9.90)	(10.40)	(10.91)
12	Less: Increases in NWC		(6.30)	(8.64)	(5.57)	(4.92)	(5.17)
13	**Free Cash Flow**		**36.54**	**36.99**	**43.92**	**47.04**	**49.39**

c. New FCF:

Now V(3) = 941, V(0) = 804, P(0) = $12.07

d. Inc. in NWC in yr1 = 12% Sales(1) – 18% Sales(0)

Inc in NWC in later years = 12% × change in sales

	Year	0	1	2	3	4	5
Earnings Forecast ($000s)			8%	10%	6%	5%	5%
1	Sales	433.00	468.00	516.00	546.96	574.31	603.02
2	Cost of Goods Sold		(313.56)	(345.72)	(366.46)	(384.79)	(404.03)
3	**Gross Profit**		154.44	170.28	180.50	189.52	199.00
4	Selling, General & Admin.		(93.60)	(103.20)	(109.39)	(114.86)	(120.60)
6	Depreciation		(7.00)	(7.50)	(9.00)	(9.45)	(9.92)
7	**EBIT**		53.84	59.58	62.10	65.21	68.47
8	Income tax at 40%		(21.54)	(23.83)	(24.84)	(26.08)	(27.39)
9	**Unlevered Net Income**		32.30	35.75	37.26	39.13	41.08
Free Cash Flow ($000s)							
10	Plus: Depreciation		7.00	7.50	9.00	9.45	9.92
11	Less: Capital Expenditures		(7.70)	(10.00)	(9.90)	(10.40)	(10.91)
12	Less: Increases in NWC		21.78	(5.76)	(3.72)	(3.28)	(3.45)
13	**Free Cash Flow**		**53.38**	**27.49**	**32.65**	**34.90**	**36.64**

New FCF:

Now V(3) = 698, V(0) = 620, P(0) = $9.00

9-21. Consider the valuation of Kenneth Cole Productions in Example 9.7.

a. Suppose you believe KCP's initial revenue growth rate will be between 4% and 11% (with growth slowing in equal steps to 4% by year 2011). What range of share prices for KCP is consistent with these forecasts?

b. Suppose you believe KCP's EBIT margin will be between 7% and 10% of sales. What range of share prices for KCP is consistent with these forecasts (keeping KCP's initial revenue growth at 9%)?

c. Suppose you believe KCP's weighted average cost of capital is between 10% and 12%. What range of share prices for KCP is consistent with these forecasts (keeping KCP's initial revenue growth and EBIT margin at 9%)?

d. What range of share prices is consistent if you vary the estimates as in parts (a), (b), and (c) simultaneously?

a. \$22.85 - \$25.68

b. \$19.60 - \$27.50

c. \$22.24 --- \$28.34

d. \$16.55 --- \$32.64

9-22. You notice that PepsiCo has a stock price of \$52.66 and EPS of \$3.20. Its competitor, the Coca-Cola Company, has EPS of \$2.49. Estimate the value of a share of Coca-Cola stock using only this data.

PepsiCo P/E = 52.66/3.20 = 16.46x. Apply to Coca-Cola: \$2.49 ×16.46 = \$40.98.

9-23. Suppose that in January 2006, Kenneth Cole Productions had EPS of \$1.65 and a book value of equity of \$12.05 per share.

a. Using the average P/E multiple in Table 9.1, estimate KCP's share price.

b. What range of share prices do you estimate based on the highest and lowest P/E multiples in Table 9.1?

c. Using the average price to book value multiple in Table 9.1, estimate KCP's share price.

d. What range of share prices do you estimate based on the highest and lowest price to book value multiples in Table 9.1?

a. Share price = Average P/E × KCP EPS = 15.01 × \$1.65 = \$24.77

b. Minimum = 8.66 × \$1.65 = \$14.29, Maximum = 22.62 × \$1.65 = \$37.32

c. 2.84 × \$12.05 = \$34.22

d. 1.12 × \$12.05 = \$13.50, 8.11 × \$12.05 = \$97.73

9-24. Suppose that in January 2006, Kenneth Cole Productions had sales of \$518 million, EBITDA of \$55.6 million, excess cash of \$100 million, \$3 million of debt, and 21 million shares outstanding.

a. Using the average enterprise value to sales multiple in Table 9.1, estimate KCP's share price.

b. What range of share prices do you estimate based on the highest and lowest enterprise value to sales multiples in Table 9.1?

c. Using the average enterprise value to EBITDA multiple in Table 9.1, estimate KCP's share price.

d. What range of share prices do you estimate based on the highest and lowest enterprise value to EBITDA multiples in Table 9.1?

a. Estimated enterprise value for KCP = Average EV/Sales × KCP Sales = 1.06 × \$518 million = \$549 million. Equity Value = EV – Debt + Cash = \$549 – 3 + 100 = \$646 million. Share price = Equity Value / Shares = \$646/ 21 = \$30.77

b. \$16.21 – \$58.64

c. Est. enterprise value for KCP = Average EV/EBITDA × KCP EBITDA = 8.49 × \$55.6 million = \$472 million. Share Price = (\$472 – 3 + 100)/21 = \$27.10

d. \$22.25 – \$33.08

9-25. **In addition to footwear, Kenneth Cole Productions designs and sells handbags, apparel, and other accessories. You decide, therefore, to consider comparables for KCP outside the footwear industry.**

- a. **Suppose that Fossil, Inc., has an enterprise value to EBITDA multiple of 9.73 and a P/E multiple of 18.4. What share price would you estimate for KCP using each of these multiples, based on the data for KCP in Problems 23 and 24?**
- b. **Suppose that Tommy Hilfiger Corporation has an enterprise value to EBITDA multiple of 7.19 and a P/E multiple of 17.2. What share price would you estimate for KCP using each of these multiples, based on the data for KCP in Problems 23 and 24?**

a. Using EV/EBITDA: EV = 55.6 × 9.73 = 541 million, P = (541 + 100 – 3) / 21 = $30.38

Using P/E: P = 1.65 × 18.4 = $30.36

Thus, KCP appears to be trading at a "discount" relative to Fossil.

b. Using EV/EBITDA: EV = 55.6 × 7.19 = 400 million, P = (400 + 100 – 3) / 21 = $23.67

Using P/E: P = 1.65 × 17.2 = $28.38

Thus, KCP appears to be trading at a "premium" relative to Tommy Hilfiger using EV/EBITDA, but at a slight discount using P/E.

9-26. **Consider the following data for the airline industry in early 2009 (EV = enterprise value, BV = book value, NM = not meaningful because divisor is negative). Discuss the challenges of using multiples to value an airline.**

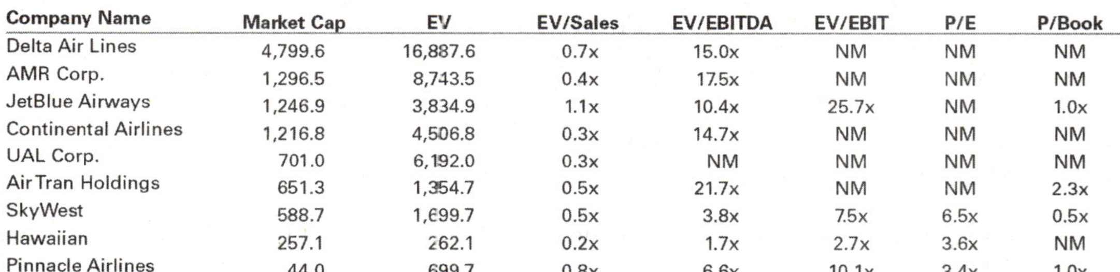

Company Name	Market Cap	EV	EV/Sales	EV/EBITDA	EV/EBIT	P/E	P/Book
Delta Air Lines	4,799.6	16,887.6	0.7x	15.0x	NM	NM	NM
AMR Corp.	1,296.5	8,743.5	0.4x	17.5x	NM	NM	NM
JetBlue Airways	1,246.9	3,834.9	1.1x	10.4x	25.7x	NM	1.0x
Continental Airlines	1,216.8	4,506.8	0.3x	14.7x	NM	NM	NM
UAL Corp.	701.0	6,192.0	0.3x	NM	NM	NM	NM
AirTran Holdings	651.3	1,354.7	0.5x	21.7x	NM	NM	2.3x
SkyWest	588.7	1,699.7	0.5x	3.8x	7.5x	6.5x	0.5x
Hawaiian	257.1	262.1	0.2x	1.7x	2.7x	3.6x	NM
Pinnacle Airlines	44.0	699.7	0.8x	6.6x	10.1x	3.4x	1.0x

Source: Capital IQ

All the multiples show a great deal of variation across firms. This makes the use of multiples problematic because there is clearly more to valuation than the multiples reveal. Without a clear understanding of what drives the differences in multiples across airlines, it is unclear what the "correct" multiple to use is when trying to value a new airline.

9-27. **You read in the paper that Summit Systems from Problem 6 has revised its growth prospects and now expects its dividends to grow at 3% per year forever.**

- a. **What is the new value of a share of Summit Systems stock based on this information?**
- b. **If you tried to sell your Summit Systems stock after reading this news, what price would you be likely to get and why?**

a. $P = 1.50/(11\% - 3\%) = \$18.75$.

b. Given that markets are efficient, the new growth rate of dividends will already be incorporated into the stock price, and you would receive $18.75 per share. Once the information about the revised growth rate for Summit Systems reaches the capital market, it will be quickly and efficiently reflected in the stock price.

9-28. In early 2009, Coca-Cola Company had a share price of $46. Its dividend was $1.52, and you expect Coca-Cola to raise this dividend by approximately 7% per year in perpetuity.

a. If Coca-Cola's equity cost of capital is 8%, what share price would you expect based on your estimate of the dividend growth rate?

b. Given Coca-Cola's share price, what would you conclude about your assessment of Coca-Cola's future dividend growth?

a. P = 1.52 / (8% – 7%) = $152

b. Based on the market price, our growth forecast is probably too high. Growth rate consistent with market price is g = r_E – div yield = 8% – 1.52 / 46 = 4.70%, which is more reasonable.

9-29. Roybus, Inc., a manufacturer of flash memory, just reported that its main production facility in Taiwan was destroyed in a fire. While the plant was fully insured, the loss of production will decrease Roybus' free cash flow by $180 million at the end of this year and by $60 million at the end of next year.

a. If Roybus has 35 million shares outstanding and a weighted average cost of capital of 13%, what change in Roybus' stock price would you expect upon this announcement? (Assume the value of Roybus' debt is not affected by the event.)

b. Would you expect to be able to sell Roybus' stock on hearing this announcement and make a profit? Explain.

a. PV(change in FCF) = $-180 / 1.13 - 60 / 1.13^2 = -206$

Change in V = –206, so if debt value does not change, P drops by 206 / 35 =$5.89 per share.

b. If this is public information in an efficient market, share price will drop immediately to reflect the news, and no trading profit is possible.

9-30. Apnex, Inc., is a biotechnology firm that is about to announce the results of its clinical trials of a potential new cancer drug. If the trials were successful, Apnex stock will be worth $70 per share. If the trials were unsuccessful, Apnex stock will be worth $18 per share. Suppose that the morning before the announcement is scheduled, Apnex shares are trading for $55 per share.

a. Based on the current share price, what sort of expectations do investors seem to have about the success of the trials?

b. Suppose hedge fund manager Paul Kliner has hired several prominent research scientists to examine the public data on the drug and make their own assessment of the drug's promise. Would Kliner's fund be likely to profit by trading the stock in the hours prior to the announcement?

c. What would limit the fund's ability to profit on its information?

a. Market seems to assess a somewhat greater than 50% chance of success.

b. Yes, if they have better information than other investors.

c. Market may be illiquid; no one wants to trade if they know Kliner has better info. Kliner's trades will move prices significantly, limiting profits.

Chapter 10
Capital Markets and the Pricing of Risk

10-1. The figure below shows the one-year return distribution for RCS stock. Calculate

a. The expected return.

b. The standard deviation of the return.

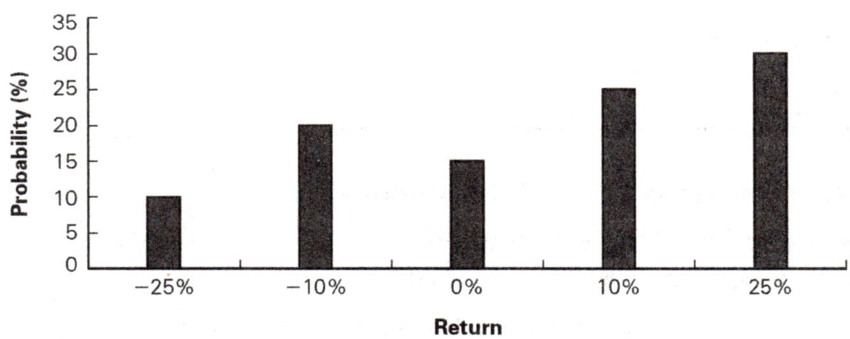

a. $E[R] = -0.25(0.1) - 0.1(0.2) + 0.1(0.25) + 0.25(0.3) = 5.5\%$

b. $$\begin{aligned}\text{Variance}[R] &= (-0.25 - 0.055)^2 \times 0.1 + (-0.1 - 0.055)^2 \times 0.2 \\ &\quad + (0.1 - 0.055)^2 \times 0.25 + (0.25 - 0.055)^2 \times 0.3 \\ &= 2.6\%\end{aligned}$$

Standard Deviation $= \sqrt{0.026} = 16.13\%$

10-2. The following table shows the one-year return distribution of Startup, Inc. Calculate

a. The expected return.

b. The standard deviation of the return.

Probability	40%	20%	20%	10%	10%
Return	–100%	–75%	–50%	–25%	1000%

a. $E[R] = -1(0.4) - 0.75(0.2) - 0.5(0.2) - 0.25(0.1) + 10(0.1) = 32.5\%$

b. $$\begin{aligned}\text{Variance}[R] &= (-1 - 0.325)^2\, 0.4 + (-0.75 - 0.325)^2\, 0.2 + (-0.5 - 0.325)^2\, 0.2 \\ &\quad + (-0.25 - 0.325)^2\, 0.1 + (10 - 0.325)^2\, 0.1 \\ &= 10.46\end{aligned}$$

Standard Deviation $= \sqrt{10.46} = 3.235 = 323.5\%$

10-3. Characterize the difference between the two stocks in Problems 1 and 2. What trade-offs would you face in choosing one to hold?

Startup has a higher expected return, but is riskier. It is impossible to say which stock I would prefer. It depends on risk performances and what other stocks I'm holding.

10-4. You bought a stock one year ago for \$50 per share and sold it today for \$55 per share. It paid a \$1 per share dividend today.

a. What was your realized return?

b. How much of the return came from dividend yield and how much came from capital gain?

Compute the realized return and dividend yield on this equity investment.

a. $R = \dfrac{1+(55-50)}{50} = 0.12 = 12\%$

b. $R_{\text{div}} = \dfrac{1}{50} = 2\%$

$R_{\text{capital gain}} = \dfrac{55-50}{50} = 10\%$

The realized return on the equity investment is 12%. The dividend yield is 10%.

10-5. Repeat Problem 4 assuming that the stock fell \$5 to \$45 instead.

a. Is your capital gain different? Why or why not?

b. Is your dividend yield different? Why or why not?

Compute the capital gain and dividend yield under the assumption the stock price has fallen to \$45.

a. $R_{\text{capital gain}} = 45 - 50/50 = -10\%$. Yes, the capital gain is different, because the difference between the current price and the purchase price is different than in Problem 1.

b. The dividend yield does not change, because the dividend is the same as in Problem 1.

The capital gain changes with the new lower price; the dividend yield does not change.

10-6. Using the data in the following table, calculate the return for investing in Boeing stock from January 2, 2003, to January 2, 2004, and also from January 2, 2008, to January 2, 2009, assuming all dividends are reinvested in the stock immediately.

Historical Stock and Dividend Data for Boeing

Date	Price	Dividend	Date	Price	Dividend
1/2/03	33.88		1/2/08	86.62	
2/5/03	30.67	0.17	2/6/08	79.91	0.40
5/14/03	29.49	0.17	5/7/08	84.55	0.40
8/13/03	32.38	0.17	8/6/08	65.40	0.40
11/12/03	39.07	0.17	11/5/08	49.55	0.40
1/2/04	41.99		1/2/09	45.25	

Date	Price	Dividend	R	1+R
1/2/2003	33.88			
2/5/2003	30.67	0.17	-8.97%	0.910272
5/14/2003	29.49	0.17	-3.29%	0.967069
8/13/2003	32.38	0.17	10.38%	1.103764
11/12/2003	39.07	0.17	21.19%	1.211859
1/2/2004	41.99		7.47%	1.074738
			26.55%	1.265491

Date	Price	Dividend	R	1+R
1/2/2008	86.62			
2/6/2008	79.91	0.4	-7.28%	0.927153
5/7/2008	84.55	0.4	6.31%	1.063071
8/6/2008	65.4	0.4	-22.18%	0.778238
11/5/2008	49.55	0.4	-23.62%	0.763761
1/2/2009	45.25		-8.68%	0.913219
			-46.50%	0.535006

10-7. The last four years of returns for a stock are as follows:

1	2	3	4
–4%	+28%	+12%	+4%

a. What is the average annual return?

b. What is the variance of the stock's returns?

c. What is the standard deviation of the stock's returns?

Given the data presented, make the calculations requested in the question.

a. $\text{Average annual return} = \dfrac{-4\% + 28\% + 12\% + 4\%}{4} = 10\%$

b. $\text{Variance of returns} = \dfrac{(-4\% - 10\%)^2 + (28\% - 10\%)^2 + (12\% - 10\%)^2 + (4\% - 10\%)^2}{3}$

$= 0.01867$

c. $\text{Standard deviation of returns} = \sqrt{\text{variance}} = \sqrt{0.01867} = 13.66\%$

The average annual return is 10%. The variance of return is 0.01867. The standard deviation of returns is 13.66%.

10-8. Assume that historical returns and future returns are independently and identically distributed and drawn from the same distribution.

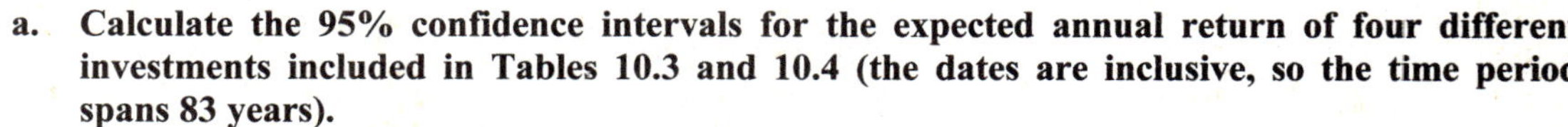

a. Calculate the 95% confidence intervals for the expected annual return of four different investments included in Tables 10.3 and 10.4 (the dates are inclusive, so the time period spans 83 years).

b. Assume that the values in Tables 10.3 and 10.4 are the true expected return and volatility (i.e., estimated without error) and that these returns are normally distributed. For each

investment, calculate the probability that an investor will not lose more than 5% in the next year? (*Hint*: you can use the function normdist(*x*,mean,volatility,1) in Excel to compute the probability that a normally distributed variable with a given mean and volatility will fall below *x*.)

c. **Do all the probabilities you calculated in part (b) make sense? If so, explain. If not, can you identify the reason?**

Investment	Return Volatility (Standard Deviation)	Average Annual Return	Standard Error	Lower Bound Confidence Interval	Upper Bound Confidence Interval		Part b answer
Small stocks	41.50%	20.90%	4.56%	11.79%	30.01%	26.63%	73.37%
S&P 500	20.60%	11.60%	2.26%	7.08%	16.12%	21.02%	78.98%
Corporate bonds	7.00%	6.60%	0.77%	5.06%	8.14%	4.87%	95.13%
Treasury bills	3.10%	3.90%	0.34%	3.22%	4.58%	0.20%	99.80%

c. No. You cannot lose money on Treasury Bills. The problem is that the returns to Treasuries are not normally distributed.

10-9. Consider an investment with the following returns over four years:

1	2	3	4
10%	20%	–5%	15%

a. **What is the compound annual growth rate (CAGR) for this investment over the four years?**

b. **What is the average annual return of the investment over the four years?**

c. **Which is a better measure of the investment's past performance?**

d. **If the investment's returns are independent and identically distributed, which is a better measure of the investment's expected return next year?**

a.

1	2	3	4	Ave
10%	20%	-5%	15%	10.00%
				CAGR
1.10	1.20	0.95	1.15	9.58%

b. see table above

c. CAGR

d. Arithmetic average

10-10. Download the spreadsheet from MyFinanceLab that contains historical monthly prices and dividends (paid at the end of the month) for Ford Motor Company stock (Ticker: F) from August 1994 to August 1998. Calculate the realized return over this period, expressing your answer in percent per month.

Ford Motor Co (F)

Month	Stock Price	Dividend	Return	1+R
Aug-97	43.000		0.05199	1.05199
Jul-97	40.875	0.420	0.08671	1.08671
Jun-97	38.000		0.01333	1.01333
May-97	37.500		0.07914	1.07914
Apr-97	34.750	0.420	0.12096	1.12096
Mar-97	31.375		-0.04563	0.95437
Feb-97	32.875		0.02335	1.02335
Jan-97	32.125	0.385	0.00806	1.00806
Dec-96	32.250		-0.01527	0.98473
Nov-96	32.750		0.04800	1.04800
Oct-96	31.250	0.385	0.01232	1.01232
Sep-96	31.250		-0.06716	0.93284
Aug-96	33.500		0.03475	1.03475
Jul-96	32.375	0.385	0.01189	1.01189
Jun-96	32.375		-0.11301	0.88699
May-96	36.500		0.01742	1.01742
Apr-96	35.875	0.350	0.05382	1.05382
Mar-96	34.375		0.10000	1.10000
Feb-96	31.250		0.05932	1.05932
Jan-96	29.500	0.350	0.03377	1.03377
Dec-95	28.875		0.02212	1.02212
Nov-95	28.250		-0.01739	0.98261
Oct-95	28.750	0.350	-0.06506	0.93494
Sep-95	31.125		0.01220	1.01220
Aug-95	30.750		0.06034	1.06034
Jul-95	29.000	0.310	-0.01479	0.98521
Jun-95	29.750		0.01709	1.01709
May-95	29.250		0.07834	1.07834
Apr-95	27.125	0.310	0.02084	1.02084
Mar-95	26.875		0.02871	1.02871
Feb-95	26.125		0.03465	1.03465
Jan-95	25.250	0.260	-0.08484	0.91516
Dec-94	27.875		0.02765	1.02765
Nov-94	27.125		-0.08051	0.91949
Oct-94	29.500	0.260	0.07243	1.07243
Sep-94	27.750		-0.05128	0.94872
Aug-94	29.250			

TotalReturn (product of 1+R's)	1.67893
Equivalent Monthly return = (TotalReturn)^(1/36)-1 =	1.45%

10-11. Using the same data as in Problem 10, compute the

a. Average monthly return over this period.

b. Monthly volatility (or standard deviation) over this period.

Ford Motor Co (F)

Month	Stock Price	Dividend	Return
Aug-97	43.000		0.05199
Jul-97	40.875	0.420	0.08671
Jun-97	38.000		0.01333
May-97	37.500		0.07914
Apr-97	34.750	0.420	0.12096
Mar-97	31.375		-0.04563
Feb-97	32.875		0.02335
Jan-97	32.125	0.385	0.00806
Dec-96	32.250		-0.01527
Nov-96	32.750		0.04800
Oct-96	31.250	0.385	0.01232
Sep-96	31.250		-0.06716
Aug-96	33.500		0.03475
Jul-96	32.375	0.385	0.01189
Jun-96	32.375		-0.11301
May-96	36.500		0.01742
Apr-96	35.875	0.350	0.05382
Mar-96	34.375		0.10000
Feb-96	31.250		0.05932
Jan-96	29.500	0.350	0.03377
Dec-95	28.875		0.02212
Nov-95	28.250		-0.01739
Oct-95	28.750	0.350	-0.06506
Sep-95	31.125		0.01220
Aug-95	30.750		0.06034
Jul-95	29.000	0.310	-0.01479
Jun-95	29.750		0.01709
May-95	29.250		0.07834
Apr-95	27.125	0.310	0.02084
Mar-95	26.875		0.02871
Feb-95	26.125		0.03465
Jan-95	25.250	0.260	-0.08484
Dec-94	27.875		0.02765
Nov-94	27.125		-0.08051
Oct-94	29.500	0.260	0.07243
Sep-94	27.750		-0.05128
Aug-94	29.250		

Average Monthly Return	1.60%
Std Dev of Monthly Return	5.46%

a. Average Return over this period: 1.60%

b. Standard Deviation over the Period: 5.46%

10-12. Explain the difference between the average return you calculated in Problem 11(a) and the realized return you calculated in Problem 10. Are both numbers useful? If so, explain why.

Both numbers are useful. The realized return (in problem 10.5) tells you what you actually made if you hold the stock over this period. The average return (problem 10.6) over the period can be used as an estimate of the monthly expected return. If you use this estimate, then this is what you expect to make on the stock in the next month.

10-13. Compute the 95% confidence interval of the estimate of the average monthly return you calculated in Problem 11(a).

Month	Stock Price	Dividend	Return
Aug-98	44.625		-0.21711
Jul-98	57.000	0.420	-0.02678
Jun-98	59.000		0.13735
May-98	51.875		0.13233
Apr-98	45.813	23.680	0.07221
Mar-98	64.813		0.14586
Feb-98	56.563		0.10907
Jan-98	51.000	0.420	0.05884
Dec-97	48.563		0.12936
Nov-97	43.000		-0.01574
Oct-97	43.688	0.420	-0.02255
Sep-97	45.125		0.04942
Aug-97	43.000		0.05199
Jul-97	40.875	0.420	0.08671
Jun-97	38.000		0.01333
May-97	37.500		0.07914
Apr-97	34.750	0.420	0.12096
Mar-97	31.375		-0.04563
Feb-97	32.875		0.02335
Jan-97	32.125	0.385	0.00806
Dec-96	32.250		-0.01527
Nov-96	32.750		0.04800
Oct-96	31.250	0.385	0.01232
Sep-96	31.250		-0.06716
Aug-96	33.500		0.03475
Jul-96	32.375	0.385	0.01189
Jun-96	32.375		-0.11301
May-96	36.500		0.01742
Apr-96	35.875	0.350	0.05382
Mar-96	34.375		0.10000
Feb-96	31.250		0.05932
Jan-96	29.500	0.350	0.03377
Dec-95	28.875		0.02212
Nov-95	28.250		-0.01739
Oct-95	28.750	0.350	-0.06506
Sep-95	31.125		0.01220
Aug-95	30.750		0.06034
Jul-95	29.000	0.310	-0.01479
Jun-95	29.750		0.01709
May-95	29.250		0.07834

Month	Stock Price	Dividend	Return
Apr-95	27.125	0.310	0.02084
Mar-95	26.875		0.02871
Feb-95	26.125		0.03465
Jan-95	25.250	0.260	-0.08484
Dec-94	27.875		0.02765
Nov-94	27.125		-0.08051
Oct-94	29.500	0.260	0.07243
Sep-94	27.750		-0.05128
Aug-94	29.250		

Average Monthly Return	2.35%	
Std Dev of Monthly Return	7.04%	
Std Error of Estimate = (Std Dev)/sqrt(36) =	1.02%	
95% Confidence Interval of average monthly return	0.31%	4.38%

10-14. How does the relationship between the average return and the historical volatility of individual stocks differ from the relationship between the average return and the historical volatility of large, well-diversified portfolios?

For large portfolios there is a relationship between returns and volatility—portfolios with higher returns have higher volatilities. For stocks, no clear relation exists.

10-15. Download the spreadsheet from MyFinanceLab containing the data for Figure 10.1.

a. Compute the average return for each of the assets from 1929 to 1940 (The Great Depression).

b. Compute the variance and standard deviation for each of the assets from 1929 to 1940.

c. Which asset was riskiest during the Great Depression? How does that fit with your intuition?

a/b.

	S&P 500	Small Stocks	Corp Bonds	World Portfolio	Treasury Bills	CPI
Average	2.553%	16.550%	5.351%	2.940%	0.859%	1.491%
Variance:	0.1018	0.6115	0.0013	0.0697	0.0002	0.0022
Standard deviation:	31.904%	78.195%	3.589%	26.398%	1.310%	4.644%

Evaluate:

c. The riskiest assets were the small stocks. Intuition tells us that this asset class would be the riskiest.

10-16. Using the data from Problem 15, repeat your analysis over the 1990s.

a. Which asset was riskiest?

b. Compare the standard deviations of the assets in the 1990s to their standard deviations in the Great Depression. Which had the greatest difference between the two periods?

c. If you only had information about the 1990s, what would you conclude about the relative risk of investing in small stocks?

a. Using Excel:

	S&P 500	Small Stocks	Corp Bonds	World Portfolio	Treasury Bills	CPI
Average	18.990%	14.482%	9.229%	12.819%	4.961%	2.935%
Variance:	0.0201	0.0460	0.0062	0.0194	0.0002	0.0002
Standard deviation:	14.161%	21.451%	7.858%	13.938%	1.267%	1.239%

The riskiest asset class was small stocks.

b. The greatest absolute difference in standard deviation is in the small stocks asset class, which saw standard deviation fall 56.7%. But in relative terms, the riskiness of corporate bonds rose 118% (relative to 1940), while the riskiness of small stocks fell only 72.6% (relative to 1940 levels). Inflation is now much less risky as well, falling in relative riskiness by 73.3%.

c. If you were only looking at the 1990s, you would conclude that small stocks are relatively less risky than they actually are.

The results that one can derive from analyzing data from a particular time period can change depending on the time period analyzed. These differences can be large if the time periods being analyzed are short.

10-17. What if the last two decades had been "normal"? Download the spreadsheet from MyFinanceLab containing the data for Figure 10.1.

a. Calculate the arithmetic average return on the S&P 500 from 1926 to 1989.

b. Assuming that the S&P 500 had simply continued to earn the average return from (a), calculate the amount that $100 invested at the end of 1925 would have grown to by the end of 2008.

c. Do the same for small stocks.

a. The arithmetic average return of the S&P 500 from 1926–1989 is 12.257%.

b. Using 12.257% as the annual return during the period 1990-2008, $100 invested in the S&P 500 in 1926 would have grown to $442,618 by 2008.

c. The arithmetic average return for small stocks from 1926–1989 is 23.186%. Using 23.186% as the annual return during the period 1990–2008, $100 invested in small stocks in 1926 would have grown to $51,412,602 by 2008.

10-18. Consider two local banks. Bank A has 100 loans outstanding, each for $1 million, that it expects will be repaid today. Each loan has a 5% probability of default, in which case the bank is not repaid anything. The chance of default is independent across all the loans. Bank B has only one loan of $100 million outstanding, which it also expects will be repaid today. It also has a 5% probability of not being repaid. Explain the difference between the type of risk each bank faces. Which bank faces less risk? Why?

The expected payoffs are the same, but bank A is less risky.

10-19. Using the data in Problem 18, calculate

a. The expected overall payoff of each bank.

b. The standard deviation of the overall payoff of each bank.

a. Expected payoff is the same for both banks

$$\text{Bank B} = \$100 \text{ million} \times 0.95 = \$95 \text{ million}$$

$$\text{Bank A} = (\$1 \text{ million} \times 0.95) \times 100 = \$95 \text{ million}$$

b. Bank B

$$\text{Variance} = (100-95)^2\, 0.95 + (0-95)^2\, 0.05 = 475$$

$$\text{Standard Deviation} = \sqrt{475} = 21.79$$

Bank A

$$\text{Variance of each loan} = (1-0.95)^2\, 0.95 (0-0.95)^2\, 0.05 = 0.0475$$

$$\text{Standard Deviation of each loan} = \sqrt{0.0475} = 0.2179$$

Now the bank has 100 loans that are all independent of each other so the standard deviation of the average loan is

$$\frac{0.2179}{\sqrt{100}} = 0.02179.$$

But the bank has 100 such loans so the standard deviation of the portfolio is

$$100 \times 0.02179 = 2.179,$$

which is much lower than Bank B.

10-20. Consider the following two, completely separate, economies. The expected return and volatility of all stocks in both economies is the same. In the first economy, all stocks move together—in good times all prices rise together and in bad times they all fall together. In the second economy, stock returns are independent—one stock increasing in price has no effect on the prices of other stocks. Assuming you are risk-averse and you could choose one of the two economies in which to invest, which one would you choose? Explain.

A risk-averse investor would choose the economy in which stock returns are independent because this risk can be diversified away in a large portfolio.

10-21. Consider an economy with two types of firms, S and I. S firms all move together. I firms move independently. For both types of firms, there is a 60% probability that the firms will have a 15% return and a 40% probability that the firms will have a −10% return. What is the volatility (standard deviation) of a portfolio that consists of an equal investment in 20 firms of (a) type S, and (b) type I?

a. $E[R] = 0.15(0.6) - 0.1(0.4) = 0.05$

$$\text{Standard Deviation} = \sqrt{(0.15-0.05)^2\, 0.6 + (-0.1-0.05)^2\, 0.4} = 0.12247$$

Because all S firms in the portfolio move together there is no diversification benefit. So the standard deviation of the portfolio is the same as the standard deviation of the stocks—12.25%.

b. $E[R] = 0.15(0.6) - 0.1(0.4) = 0.05$

$$\text{Standard Deviation} = \sqrt{(0.15-0.05)^2\, 0.6 + (-0.1-0.05)^2\, 0.4} = 0.12247$$

Type I stocks move independently. Hence the standard deviation of the portfolio is

$$\text{SD(Portfolio of 20 Type I stocks)} = \frac{0.12247}{\sqrt{20}} = 2.74\%.$$

10-22. Using the data in Problem 21, plot the volatility as a function of the number of firms in the two portfolios.

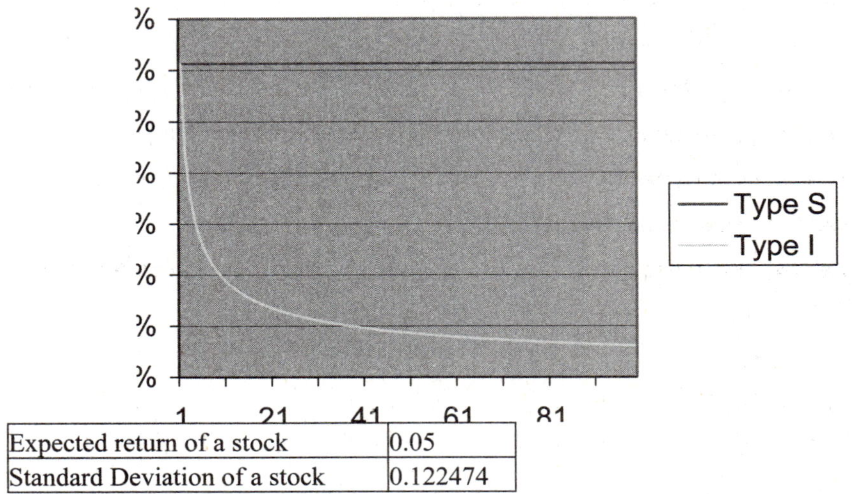

Expected return of a stock	0.05
Standard Deviation of a stock	0.122474

Number of Stocks	Type S	Type I	Number of Stocks	Type S	Type I	Number of Stocks	Type S	Type I	Number of Stocks	Type S	Type I
1	12.25%	12.25%	29	12.25%	2.27%	57	12.25%	1.62%	85	12.25%	1.33%
2	12.25%	8.66%	30	12.25%	2.24%	58	12.25%	1.61%	86	12.25%	1.32%
3	12.25%	7.07%	31	12.25%	2.20%	59	12.25%	1.59%	87	12.25%	1.31%
4	12.25%	6.12%	32	12.25%	2.17%	60	12.25%	1.58%	88	12.25%	1.31%
5	12.25%	5.48%	33	12.25%	2.13%	61	12.25%	1.57%	89	12.25%	1.30%
6	12.25%	5.00%	34	12.25%	2.10%	62	12.25%	1.56%	90	12.25%	1.29%
7	12.25%	4.63%	35	12.25%	2.07%	63	12.25%	1.54%	91	12.25%	1.28%
8	12.25%	4.33%	36	12.25%	2.04%	64	12.25%	1.53%	92	12.25%	1.28%
9	12.25%	4.08%	37	12.25%	2.01%	65	12.25%	1.52%	93	12.25%	1.27%
10	12.25%	3.87%	38	12.25%	1.99%	66	12.25%	1.51%	94	12.25%	1.26%
11	12.25%	3.69%	39	12.25%	1.96%	67	12.25%	1.50%	95	12.25%	1.26%
12	12.25%	3.54%	40	12.25%	1.94%	68	12.25%	1.49%	96	12.25%	1.25%
13	12.25%	3.40%	41	12.25%	1.91%	69	12.25%	1.47%	97	12.25%	1.24%
14	12.25%	3.27%	42	12.25%	1.89%	70	12.25%	1.46%	98	12.25%	1.24%
15	12.25%	3.16%	43	12.25%	1.87%	71	12.25%	1.45%	99	12.25%	1.23%
16	12.25%	3.06%	44	12.25%	1.85%	72	12.25%	1.44%			
17	12.25%	2.97%	45	12.25%	1.83%	73	12.25%	1.43%			
18	12.25%	2.89%	46	12.25%	1.81%	74	12.25%	1.42%			
19	12.25%	2.81%	47	12.25%	1.79%	75	12.25%	1.41%			
20	12.25%	2.74%	48	12.25%	1.77%	76	12.25%	1.40%			
21	12.25%	2.67%	49	12.25%	1.75%	77	12.25%	1.40%			
22	12.25%	2.61%	50	12.25%	1.73%	78	12.25%	1.39%			
23	12.25%	2.55%	51	12.25%	1.71%	79	12.25%	1.38%			
24	12.25%	2.50%	52	12.25%	1.70%	80	12.25%	1.37%			
25	12.25%	2.45%	53	12.25%	1.68%	81	12.25%	1.36%			
26	12.25%	2.40%	54	12.25%	1.67%	82	12.25%	1.35%			
27	12.25%	2.36%	55	12.25%	1.65%	83	12.25%	1.34%			
28	12.25%	2.31%	56	12.25%	1.64%	84	12.25%	1.34%			

10-23. Explain why the risk premium of a stock does not depend on its diversifiable risk.

Investors can costlessly remove diversifiable risk from their portfolio by diversifying. They, therefore, do not demand a risk premium for it.

10-24. Identify each of the following risks as most likely to be systematic risk or diversifiable risk:

a. The risk that your main production plant is shut down due to a tornado.

b. The risk that the economy slows, decreasing demand for your firm's products.

c. The risk that your best employees will be hired away.

d. The risk that the new product you expect your R&D division to produce will not materialize.

a. diversifiable risk

b. systematic risk

c. diversifiable risk

d. diversifiable risk

10-25. Suppose the risk-free interest rate is 5%, and the stock market will return either 40% or −20% each year, with each outcome equally likely. Compare the following two investment strategies: (1) invest for one year in the risk-free investment, and one year in the market, or (2) invest for both years in the market.

a. Which strategy has the highest expected final payoff?

b. Which strategy has the highest standard deviation for the final payoff?

c. Does holding stocks for a longer period decrease your risk?

R(i) : (1.05)(1.40)-1 = 47% or (1.05)(0.80) −1 = −16%

R(ii) : 1.4^2 -1 = 96%, 1.4 × 0.8 − 1 = 12%, 0.8 × 1.4 − 1=12%, .8 × .8 − 1 = −36%

a. ER(i) = (47% − 16%)/2 = 15.5%

ER(ii) = (96% + 12% + 12% − 36%)/4 = 21%

b. Vol(i) =sqrt(1/2 $(47\% - 15.5\%)^2$ + 1/2$(-16\% - 15.5\%)^2$) = 31.5%

Vol(ii)=sqrt(1/4 $(96\%\text{-}21\%)^2$ + ½$(12\% - 21\%)^2$ + 1/4$(-36\% - 21\%)^2$) = 47.5%

c. No

10-26. Download the spreadsheet from MyFinanceLab containing the realized return of the S&P 500 from 1929–2008. Starting in 1929, divide the sample into four periods of 20 years each. For each 20-year period, calculate the final amount an investor would have earned given a $1000 initial investment. Also express your answer as an annualized return. If risk were eliminated by holding stocks for 20 years, what would you expect to find? What can you conclude about long-run diversification?

Amount after 1929–1948 Period	$1,741.26	2.81%
Amount after 1949–1968 Period	$15,848.17	14.82%
Amount after 1969–1988 Period	$6,198.78	9.55%
Amount after 1989–2008 Period	$5,043.04	8.43%

If risk were eliminated by holding stocks for 20 years, you would expect to find similar returns for all four periods, which you do not.

10-27. What is an efficient portfolio?

An efficient portfolio is any portfolio that only contains systemic risk; it contains no diversifiable risk.

10-28. What does the beta of a stock measure?

Beta measures the amount of systemic risk in a stock

10-29. You turn on the news and find out the stock market has gone up 10%. Based on the data in Table 10.6, by how much do you expect each of the following stocks to have gone up or down: (1) Starbucks, (2) Tiffany & Co., (3) Hershey, and (4) Exxon Mobil.

Beta*10%

Starbucks 10.4%

Tiffany & Co. 16.4%

Hershey 1.9%

Exxon Mobil 5.6%

10-30. Based on the data in Table 10.6, estimate which of the following investments do you expect to lose the most in the event of a severe market down turn: (1) A \$1000 investment in eBay, (2) a \$5000 investment in Abbott Laboratories, or (3) a \$2500 investment in Walt Disney.

For each 10% market decline,

eBay down 10%*1.93 = 19.3%,

19.3% × 1000 = \$193 loss;

Abbott down 10%*.18 = 1.8%,

1.8% × 5000 = \$90 loss;

Disney down 10%*.96 = 9.6%,

9.6% × 2500 = \$240 loss;

Disney investment will lose most.

10-31. Suppose the market portfolio is equally likely to increase by 30% or decrease by 10%.

a. Calculate the beta of a firm that goes up on average by 43% when the market goes *up* and goes down by 17% when the market goes *down*.

b. Calculate the beta of a firm that goes up on average by 18% when the market goes *down* and goes down by 22% when the market goes *up*.

c. Calculate the beta of a firm that is expected to go up by 4% *independently* of the market.

a. $$\text{Beta} = \frac{\Delta \text{ Stock}}{\Delta \text{ Market}} = \frac{43-(-17)}{30-(-10)} = \frac{60}{40} = 1.5$$

b. $$\text{Beta} = \frac{\Delta \text{ Stock}}{\Delta \text{ Market}} = \frac{-18-22}{30-(-10)} = \frac{-40}{40} = -1$$

c. A firm that moves independently has no systemic risk so Beta = 0

10-32. Suppose the risk-free interest rate is 4%.

a. i. Use the beta you calculated for the stock in Problem 31(a) to estimate its expected return.

ii. How does this compare with the stock's actual expected return?

b. i. Use the beta you calculated for the stock in Problem 31(b) to estimate its expected return.

ii. How does this compare with the stock's actual expected return?

a. $E[R_M] = ½ (30\%) + ½ (–10\%) = 10\%$

i.. $E[R] = 4\% + 1.5 (10\% – 4\%) = 13\%$

ii. Actual Expected return =

(43% – 17%) / 2 = 13%

b. i. . $E[R] = 4\% – 1(10\% – 4\%) = -2\%$

ii. Actual l expected Return =

(–22% + 18%) / 2 = –2%

10-33. Suppose the market risk premium is 5% and the risk-free interest rate is 4%. Using the data in Table 10.6, calculate the expected return of investing in

a. Starbucks' stock.

b. Hershey's stock.

c. Autodesk's stock.

a. $4\%+1.04 \times 5\% = 9.2\%$

b. $4\% + 0.19 \times 5\% = 4.95\%$

c. $4\% + 2.31 \times 5\% = 15.55\%$

10-34. Given the results to Problem 33, why don't all investors hold Autodesk's stock rather than Hershey's stock?

Hershey's stock has less market risk, so investors don't need as high an expected return to hold it. Hershey's stock will perform much better in a market downturn.

10-35. Suppose the market risk premium is 6.5% and the risk-free interest rate is 5%. Calculate the cost of capital of investing in a project with a beta of 1.2.

$$\text{Cost of Capital} = r_f + \beta\left(E[R_m] - r_f\right) = 5 + 1.2(6.5) = 12.8\%$$

10-36. State whether each of the following is inconsistent with an efficient capital market, the CAPM, or both:

a. A security with only diversifiable risk has an expected return that exceeds the risk-free interest rate.

b. A security with a beta of 1 had a return last year of 15% when the market had a return of 9%.

c. Small stocks with a beta of 1.5 tend to have higher returns on average than large stocks with a beta of 1.5.

a. This statement is inconsistent with both.

b. This statement is consistent with both.

c. This statement is inconsistent with the CAPM but not necessarily with efficient capital markets.

Chapter 11

Optimal Portfolio Choice and the Capital Asset Pricing Model

11-1. You are considering how to invest part of your retirement savings. You have decided to put $200,000 into three stocks: 50% of the money in GoldFinger (currently $25/share), 25% of the money in Moosehead (currently $80/share), and the remainder in Venture Associates (currently $2/share). If GoldFinger stock goes up to $30/share, Moosehead stock drops to $60/share, and Venture Associates stock rises to $3 per share,

a. What is the new value of the portfolio?

b. What return did the portfolio earn?

c. If you don't buy or sell shares after the price change, what are your new portfolio weights?

a. Let n_i be the number of share in stock I, then

$$n_G = \frac{200{,}000 \times 0.5}{25} = 4{,}000$$

$$n_M = \frac{200{,}000 \times 0.25}{80} = 625$$

$$n_V = \frac{200{,}000 \times 0.25}{2} = 25{,}000.$$

The new value of the portfolio is

$$p = 30n_G + 60n_M + 3n_v$$

$$= \$232{,}500.$$

b. $\text{Return} = \dfrac{232{,}500}{200{,}000} - 1 = 16.25\%$

c. The portfolio weights are the fraction of value invested in each stock.

GoldFinger: $\dfrac{n_G \times 30}{232{,}500} = 51.61\%$

Moosehead: $\dfrac{n_M \times 60}{232{,}500} = 16.13\%$

Venture: $\dfrac{n_V \times 3}{232{,}500} = 32.26\%$

11-2. You own three stocks: 1000 shares of Apple Computer, 10,000 shares of Cisco Systems, and 5000 shares of Goldman Sachs Group. The current share prices and expected returns of Apple, Cisco, and Goldman are, respectively, $125, $19, $120 and 12%, 10%, 10.5%.

a. What are the portfolio weights of the three stocks in your portfolio?

b. What is the expected return of your portfolio?

c. Assume that both Apple and Cisco go up by $5 and Goldman goes down by $10. What are the new portfolio weights?

d. Assuming the stocks' expected returns remain the same, what is the expected return of the portfolio at the new prices?

				Value	a.	b.	New Price	New Value	c.	d.
Apple	1000	125	12	125000	0.136612022	1.639344262	130	130000	0.142076503	1.704918033
Cisco	10000	19	10	190000	0.207650273	2.076502732	24	240000	0.262295082	2.62295082
Goldman	5000	120	10.5	600000	0.655737705	6.885245902	110	550000	0.601092896	6.31147541
		Total		915000		10.6010929				10.63934426

11-3. Consider a world that only consists of the three stocks shown in the following table:

Stock	Total Number of Shares Outstanding	Current Price per Share	Expected Return
First Bank	100 Million	$100	18%
Fast Mover	50 Million	$120	12%
Funny Bone	200 Million	$30	15%

a. Calculate the total value of all shares outstanding currently.

b. What fraction of the total value outstanding does each stock make up?

c. You hold the market portfolio, that is, you have picked portfolio weights equal to the answer to part b (that is, each stock's weight is equal to its contribution to the fraction of the total value of all stocks). What is the expected return of your portfolio?

Stock	Total Number of Shares Outstanding	Current Price per Share	Expected Return	Value	b.	
First Bank	100.00	$100	18%	$10,000.00	0.454545455	8.18%
Fast Mover	50.00	$120	12%	$6,000.00	0.272727273	3.27%
Funny Bone	200.00	$30	15%	$6,000.00	0.272727273	4.09%
			a. (in mill)	$22,000.00	c.	15.55%

11-4. There are two ways to calculate the expected return of a portfolio: either calculate the expected return using the value and dividend stream of the portfolio as a whole, or calculate the weighted average of the expected returns of the individual stocks that make up the portfolio. Which return is higher?

Both calculations of expected return of a portfolio give the same answer.

11-5. Using the data in the following table, estimate (a) the average return and volatility for each stock, (b) the covariance between the stocks, and (c) the correlation between these two stocks.

Year	2004	2005	2006	2007	2008	2009
Stock A	–10%	20%	5%	–5%	2%	9%
Stock B	21%	7%	30%	–3%	–8%	25%

a. $\overline{R}_A = \dfrac{-10+20+5-5+2+9}{6} = 3.5\%$

$\overline{R}_B = \dfrac{21+30+7-3-8+25}{6}$

$= 12\%$

$$\text{Variance of A} = \frac{1}{5}\begin{bmatrix}(-0.1-0.035)^2 + \\ (0.2-0.08)^2 + (0.05-0.035)^2 + \\ (-0.05-0.035)^2 + (0.02-0.035)^2 \\ +(0.09-0.035)^2\end{bmatrix}$$

$= 0.01123$

Volatility of A $= SD(R_A) = \sqrt{\text{Variance of A}} = \sqrt{.01123} = 10.60\%$

$$\text{Variance of B} = \frac{1}{5}\begin{bmatrix}(0.21-0.12)^2 + (0.3-0.12)^2 + \\ (0.07-0.12)^2 + (-0.03-0.12)^2 + \\ (-0.08-0.12)^2 + (0.25-0.12)^2\end{bmatrix}$$

$= 0.02448$

Volatility of B $= SD(R_B) = \sqrt{\text{Variance of B}} = \sqrt{.02448} = 15.65\%$

b. $$\text{Covariance} = \frac{1}{5}\begin{bmatrix}(-0.1-0.035)(0.21-0.12) + \\ (0.2-0.035)(0.3-0.12) + \\ (0.05-0.035)(0.07-0.12) + \\ (-0.05-0.035)(-0.03-0.12) + \\ (0.02-0.035)(-0.08-0.12) + \\ (0.09-0.035)(0.25-0.12)\end{bmatrix}$$

$= 0.104\%$

c. $$\text{Correlation} = \frac{\text{Covariance}}{SD(R_A)SD(R_B)}$$

$= 6.27\%$

11-6. Use the data in Problem 5, consider a portfolio that maintains a 50% weight on stock A and a 50% weight on stock B.

a. What is the return each year of this portfolio?

b. Based on your results from part a, compute the average return and volatility of the portfolio.

c. **Show that (i) the average return of the portfolio is equal to the average of the average returns of the two stocks, and (ii) the volatility of the portfolio equals the same result as from the calculation in Eq. 11.9.**

d. **Explain why the portfolio has a lower volatility than the average volatility of the two stocks.**

a, b, and c. See table below.

Year	2004	2005	2006	2007	2008	2009
A&B	5.5%	13.5%	17.5%	-4.0%	-3.0%	17.0%
Ave	7.75%					
Vol	9.72%					

d. The portfolio has a lower volatility than the average volatility of the two stocks because some of the idiosyncratic risk of the stocks in the portfolio is diversified away.

11-7. **Using your estimates from Problem 5, calculate the volatility (standard deviation) of a portfolio that is 70% invested in stock A and 30% invested in stock B.**

$\text{Variance} = (0.7)^2\, 0.106^2 + (0.3)^2\, 0.1565^2 + 2(0.7)(0.3)(0.0627)(0.106)(0.1565)^{.5} =$

$\text{Standard Deviation} = \sqrt{} = 9.02\%$

11-8. **Using the data from Table 11.3, what is the covariance between the stocks of Alaska Air Lines and Southwest Air Lines?**

$\text{covariance} = \text{con} \times SD(R_D) \times SD(R_{AA}) = 0.30 \times 0.38 \times 0.31 = 0.03534$

11-9. **Suppose two stocks have a correlation of 1. If the first stock has an above average return this year, what is the probability that the second stock will have an above average return?**

Because the correlation is perfect, they move together (always) and so the probability is 1.

11-10. **Arbor Systems and Gencore stocks both have a volatility of 40%. Compute the volatility of a portfolio with 50% invested in each stock if the correlation between the stocks is (a) + 1, (b) 0.50, (c) 0, (d) −0.50, and (e) −1.0. In which cases is the volatility lower than that of the original stocks?**

stock vol	40%
corr	50-50 Port
1	40.0%
0.5	34.6%
0	28.3%
-0.5	20.0%
-1	0.0%

Volatility of portfolio is less if the correlation is < 1.

11-11. Suppose Wesley Publishing's stock has a volatility of 60%, while Addison Printing's stock has a volatility of 30%. If the correlation between these stocks is 25%, what is the volatility of the following portfolios of Addison and Wesley: (a) 100% Addison, (b) 75% Addison and 25% Wesley, and (c) 50% Addison and 50% Wesley.

	Vol	Corr
Wesley	60%	25%
Addison	30%	
Portfolio		
x_A	x_W	Vol
100%	0%	30.00%
75%	25%	30.00%
50%	50%	36.74%

11-12. Suppose Avon and Nova stocks have volatilities of 50% and 25%, respectively, and they are perfectly negatively correlated. What portfolio of these two stocks has zero risk?

Avon has twice the risk, so the portfolio needs twice as much weight on Nova => 2/3 Avon, 1/3 Nova.

11-13. Suppose Tex stock has a volatility of 40%, and Mex stock has a volatility of 20%. If Tex and Mex are uncorrelated,

a. What portfolio of the two stocks has the same volatility as Mex alone?

b. What portfolio of the two stocks has the smallest possible volatility?

	Vol	Corr
Tex	40%	0%
Mex	20%	
Portfolio		
x_tex	x_mex	Vol
0%	100%	20.00%
10%	90%	18.44%
20%	80%	17.89%
30%	70%	18.44%
40%	60%	20.00%
50%	50%	22.36%
60%	40%	25.30%
70%	30%	28.64%
80%	20%	32.25%
90%	10%	36.06%
100%	0%	40.00%

11-14. Using the data from Table 11.3, what is volatility of an equally weighted portfolio of Microsoft, Alaska Air, and Ford Motor stock?

27.1%

var-cov			
MSFT	0.1369	0.03515	0.040404
AA	0.03515	0.1444	0.025536
Ford	0.040404	0.025536	0.1764
	ave var	0.152567	
	ave cov	0.033697	
	volatility	0.270777	
		0.270777	

11-15. Suppose that the average stock has a volatility of 50%, and that the correlation between pairs of stocks is 20%. Estimate the volatility of an equally weighted portfolio with (a) 1 stock, (b) 30 stocks, (c) 1000 stocks.

Vol	50%
Var	0.25
Corr	20%
Covar	0.05
N	Vol
1	50.0%
30	23.8%
1000	22.4%

11-16. What is the volatility (standard deviation) of an equally weighted portfolio of stocks within an industry in which the stocks have a volatility of 50% and a correlation of 40% as the portfolio becomes arbitrarily large?

$\sqrt{\text{ave cov}} = (0.5 \times 0.5 \times 0.4)^{0.5} = 31.62\%$

11-17. Consider an equally weighted portfolio of stocks in which each stock has a volatility of 40%, and the correlation between each pair of stocks 20%.

a. What is the volatility of the portfolio as the number of stocks becomes arbitrarily large?

b. What is the average correlation of each stock with this large portfolio?

a. Ave Covar = 40% × 40% × 20%=0.032

Limit Vol = $(.032)^{0.5}$ = 17.89%

b. From Eq. 11.13

Corr = SD(Rp)/SD(Ri) = 17.89%/40% = 44.72%

11-18. Stock A has a volatility of 65% and a correlation of 10% with your current portfolio. Stock B has a volatility of 30% and a correlation of 25% with your current portfolio. You currently hold both stocks. Which will increase the volatility of your portfolio: (i) selling a small amount of stock B and investing the proceeds in stock A, or (ii) selling a small amount of stock A and investing the proceeds in stock B?

From Eq. 11.13, marginal contribution to risk is SD(Ri) × Corr(Ri,Rp)

For A: 65% × 10% = 6.5%;

For B: 30% × 25% = 7.5%.

So, volatility increases if we sell A and add B.

11-19. You currently hold a portfolio of three stocks, Delta, Gamma, and Omega. Delta has a volatility of 60%, Gamma has a volatility of 30%, and Omega has a volatility of 20%. Suppose you invest 50% of your money in Delta, and 25% each in Gamma and Omega.

a. What is the highest possible volatility of your portfolio?

b. If your portfolio has the volatility in (a), what can you conclude about the correlation between Delta and Omega?

a. Max vol = weighted average = .5(60%) + .25(30%) + .25(20%) = 42.5%

b. Correlation = 1 (otherwise there would be some diversification)

11-20. Suppose Ford Motor stock has an expected return of 20% and a volatility of 40%, and Molson Coors Brewing has an expected return of 10% and a volatility of 30%. If the two stocks are uncorrelated,

a. What is the expected return and volatility of an equally weighted portfolio of the two stocks?

b. Given your answer to (a), is investing all of your money in Molson Coors stock an efficient portfolio of these two stocks?

c. Is investing all of your money in Ford Motor an efficient portfolio of these two stocks?

a.

	A	B	Corr
ER	20%	10%	
Vol	40%	30%	0%
XA	XB	Vol	ER
50%	50%	25.0%	15.0%

b. No, dominated by 50-50 portfolio.

c. Yes, not dominated.

11-21. Suppose Intel's stock has an expected return of 26% and a volatility of 50%, while Coca-Cola's has an expected return of 6% and volatility of 25%. If these two stocks were perfectly negatively correlated (i.e., their correlation coefficient is −1),

a. Calculate the portfolio weights that remove all risk.

b. If there are no arbitrage opportunities, what is the risk-free rate of interest in this economy?

a. If the two stocks are perfectly correlated negatively, they fluctuate due to the same risks, but in opposite directions. Because Intel is twice as volatile as Coke, we will need to hold twice as much Coke stock as Intel in order to offset Intel's risk. That is, our portfolio should be 2/3 Coke and 1/3 Intel.

We can check this using Eq. 11.9.

$$\begin{aligned}Var(R_P) &= (2/3)^2 SD(R_{Coke})^2 + (1/3)^2 SD(R_{Intel})^2 + 2(2/3)(1/3)\text{Corr}(R_{Coke}, R_{Intel}) SD(R_{Coke}) SD(R_{Intel}) \\ &= (2/3)^2(0.25^2) + (1/3)^2(0.50^2) + 2(2/3)(1/3)(-1)(.25)(.50) \\ &= 0\end{aligned}$$

b. From Eq. 11.3, the expect return of the portfolio is

$$\begin{aligned}E[R_P] &= (2/3)E[R_{Coke}] + (1/3)E[R_{Intel}] \\ &= (2/3)6\% + (1/3)26\% \\ &= 12.67\%.\end{aligned}$$

Because this portfolio has no risk, the risk-free interest rate must also be 12.67%.

For Problems 22–25, suppose Johnson & Johnson and the Walgreen Company have expected returns and volatilities shown below, with a correlation of 22%.

	E[R]	**SD[R]**
Johnson & Johnson	7%	16%
Walgreen Company	10%	20%

11-22. Calculate (a) the expected return and (b) the volatility (standard deviation) of a portfolio that is equally invested in Johnson & Johnson's and Walgreen's stock.

In this case, the portfolio weights are $x_j = x_w = 0.50$. From Eq. 11.3,

$$\begin{aligned} E[R_P] &= x_j E[R_j] + x_w E[R_w] \\ &= 0.50(7\%) + 0.50(10\%) \\ &= 8.5\%. \end{aligned}$$

We can use Eq. 11.9.

$$\begin{aligned} SD(R_P) &= \sqrt{x_j^{\,2} SD(R_j)^2 + x_w^{\,2} SD(R_w)^2 + 2x_j x_w Corr(R_j, R_w) SD(R_j) SD(R_w)} \\ &= \sqrt{.50^2(.16^2) + .50^2(.20)^2 + 2(.50)(.50)(.22)(.16)(.20)} \\ &= 14.1\% \end{aligned}$$

11-23. For the portfolio in Problem 22, if the correlation between Johnson & Johnson's and Walgreen's stock were to increase,

a. Would the expected return of the portfolio rise or fall?

b. Would the volatility of the portfolio rise or fall?

a. The expected return would remain constant, assuming only the correlation changes, $0.5 \times 0.07 + 0.5 \times 0.10 = 0.085$.

b. The volatility of the portfolio would increase (due to the correlation term in the equation for the volatility of a portfolio).

11-24. Calculate (a) the expected return and (b) the volatility (standard deviation) of a portfolio that consists of a long position of $10,000 in Johnson & Johnson and a short position of $2000 in Walgreen's.

In this case, the total investment is $10,000 – 2,000 = $8,000, so the portfolio weights are x_j = 10,000/8,000 = 1.25, x_w = –2,000/8,000 = –0.25. From Eq. 11.3,

$$\begin{aligned} E[R_P] &= x_j E[R_j] + x_w E[R_w] \\ &= 1.25(7\%) - 0.25(10\%) \\ &= 6.25\%. \end{aligned}$$

We can use Eq. 11.9,

$$\begin{aligned} SD(R_P) &= \sqrt{x_j^{\,2} SD(R_j)^2 + x_w^{\,2} SD(R_w)^2 + 2x_j x_w Corr(R_j, R_w) SD(R_j) SD(R_w)} \\ &= \sqrt{1.25^2(.16^2) + (-0.25)^2(.20)^2 + 2(1.25)(-0.25)(.22)(.16)(.20)} \\ &= 19.5\%. \end{aligned}$$

11-25. Using the same data as for Problem 22, calculate the expected return and the volatility (standard deviation) of a portfolio consisting of Johnson & Johnson's and Walgreen's stocks using a wide range of portfolio weights. Plot the expected return as a function of the portfolio volatility. Using

your graph, identify the range of Johnson & Johnson's portfolio weights that yield efficient combinations of the two stocks, rounded to the nearest percentage point.

The set of efficient portfolios is approximately those portfolios with no more than 65% invested in J&J (this is the portfolio with the lowest possible volatility).

x(J&J)	x(Walgreen)	SD	ER
-50%	150%	29.30%	11.50%
-40%	140%	27.32%	11.20%
-30%	130%	25.38%	10.90%
-20%	120%	23.50%	10.60%
-10%	110%	21.70%	10.30%
0%	100%	20.00%	10.00%
10%	90%	18.42%	9.70%
20%	80%	16.99%	9.40%
30%	70%	15.77%	9.10%
40%	60%	14.79%	8.80%
50%	50%	14.11%	8.50%
60%	40%	13.78%	8.20%
65%	**35%**	**13.75%**	**8.05%**
70%	30%	13.82%	7.90%
80%	20%	14.23%	7.60%
90%	10%	14.97%	7.30%
100%	0%	16.00%	7.00%
110%	-10%	17.27%	6.70%
120%	-20%	18.73%	6.40%
130%	-30%	20.34%	6.10%
140%	-40%	22.07%	5.80%
150%	-50%	23.88%	5.50%

11-26. A hedge fund has created a portfolio using just two stocks. It has shorted $35,000,000 worth of Oracle stock and has purchased $85,000,000 of Intel stock. The correlation between Oracle's and Intel's returns is 0.65. The expected returns and standard deviations of the two stocks are given in the table below:

	Expected Return	Standard Deviation
Oracle	12.00%	45.00%
Intel	14.50%	40.00%

a. **What is the expected return of the hedge fund's portfolio?**

b. **What is the standard deviation of the hedge fund's portfolio?**

a. The total value of the portfolio is $50m (=-$35+$85). This means that the weight on Oracle is –70% and the weight on Intel is 170%. The expected return is

$$\text{Expected return} = -0.7 \times 12\% + 1.7 \times 14.5\%$$
$$= 16.25\%.$$

b.

$$\text{Variance} = (-0.7)^2 \times (0.45)^2 + (1.7)^2 \times (0.40)^2$$
$$+ 2 \times (-0.7) \times (1.7) \times 0.65 \times 0.45 \times 0.40$$
$$= 0.283165$$

Std dev = (.283165)^.5 = 53.2%

11-27. Consider the portfolio in Problem 26. Suppose the correlation between Intel and Oracle's stock increases, but nothing else changes. Would the portfolio be more or less risky with this change?

An increase in the correlation would increase the variance of the portfolio; meanwhile, the expected return of the portfolio would remain constant. The riskiness of the portfolio would increase.

11-28. Fred holds a portfolio with a 30% volatility. He decides to short sell a small amount of stock with a 40% volatility and use the proceeds to invest more in his portfolio. If this transaction reduces the risk of his portfolio, what is the minimum possible correlation between the stock he shorted and his original portfolio?

From Eq. 11.13, for a small transaction size, short selling A and investing in P changes risk according to SD(Rp) – SD(Ra)Corr(Ra,Rp).

We gain the risk of the portfolio and lose the risk A has in common with the portfolio. For this to be negative, we must have

SD(Rp)/SD(Ra) < Corr(Ra,Rp)

or

Corr > 30%/40% = 75%.

11-29. Suppose Target's stock has an expected return of 20% and a volatility of 40%, Hershey's stock has an expected return of 12% and a volatility of 30%, and these two stocks are uncorrelated.

a. What is the expected return and volatility of an equally weighted portfolio of the two stocks?

Consider a new stock with an expected return of 16% and a volatility of 30%. Suppose this new stock is uncorrelated with Target's and Hershey's stock.

b. Is holding this stock alone attractive compared to holding the portfolio in (a)?

c. Can you improve upon your portfolio in (a) by adding this new stock to your portfolio? Explain.

a.

	A	B	Corr
ER	20%	12%	
Vol	40%	30%	0%
XA	XB	Vol	ER
50%	50%	25.0%	16.0%

b. No, it has the same expected return with higher volatility.

c. Yes, adding this stock and reducing weight on the others will reduce risk while leaving expected return unchanged.

11-30. You have $10,000 to invest. You decide to invest $20,000 in Google and short sell $10,000 worth of Yahoo! Google's expected return is 15% with a volatility of 30% and Yahoo!'s expected return is 12% with a volatility of 25%. The stocks have a correlation of 0.9. What is the expected return and volatility of the portfolio?

Expected return = 18%

Volatility= $\sqrt{x^2 0.3^2 + y^2 0.25^2 + 2xy0.9 \times 0.3 \times 0.25} = 39.05\%$

11-31. You expect HGH stock to have a 20% return next year and a 30% volatility. You have $25,000 to invest, but plan to invest a total of $50,000 in HGH, raising the additional $25,000 by shorting *either* KBH or LWI stock. Both KBH and LWI have an expected return of 10% and a volatility

of 20%. If KBH has a correlation of +0.5 with HGH, and LWI has a correlation of −0.50 with HGH, which stock should you short?

Either strategy has expected return of 2(20%) – 1(10%) = 30%.

But the portfolio has lower volatility if correlation is +0.5; because you are shorting a POSITIVE correlation, it leads to lower risk.

+2 HGH – KBH volatility = 52.9%

+2 HGH – LWI volatility = 72.1%

11-32. Suppose you have $100,000 in cash, and you decide to borrow another $15,000 at a 4% interest rate to invest in the stock market. You invest the entire $115,000 in a portfolio J with a 15% expected return and a 25% volatility.

a. What is the expected return and volatility (standard deviation) of your investment?

b. What is your realized return if J goes up 25% over the year?

c. What return do you realize if J falls by 20% over the year?

a. $x = \frac{115,000}{100,000} = 1.15$

$$E[R] = r_f + x(E[R_j] - r) = 4\% + 1.15(11\%) = 16.65\%$$

$$\text{Volatility} = x\ SD[R_j] = 1.15\ 25\% = 28.75\%$$

b. $R = \frac{115,000(1.25) - 15,000(1.04)}{100,000} - 1 = 28.15\%$

c. $R = \frac{115,000(0.80) - 15,000(1.04)}{100,000} - 1 = -23.6\%$

11-33. You have $100,000 to invest. You choose to put $150,000 into the market by borrowing $50,000.

a. If the risk-free interest rate is 5% and the market expected return is 10%, what is the expected return of your investment?

b. If the market volatility is 15%, what is the volatility of your investment?

a. Er = 5% + 1.5 × (10% – 5%) = 12.5%

b. Vol = 1.5 × 15% = 22.5%

11-34. You currently have $100,000 invested in a portfolio that has an expected return of 12% and a volatility of 8%. Suppose the risk-free rate is 5%, and there is another portfolio that has an expected return of 20% and a volatility of 12%.

a. What portfolio has a higher expected return than your portfolio but with the same volatility?

b. What portfolio has a lower volatility than your portfolio but with the same expected return?

Invest an amount x in the other portfolio and the expected return and volatility are

$$E[R_x] = r_f + x(E[R_O] - r_f) = 5\% + x(20\% - 5\%)$$

$$SD(R_x) = x\ SD(R_O) = x(12\%).$$

a. So to maintain the volatility at 8%, $x = 8\%/12\% = 2/3$, you should invest $66,667 in the other portfolio and the remaining $33,333 in the risk-free investment. Your expected return will then be 15%.

b. Alternatively, to keep the expected return equal to the current value of 12%, x must satisfy 5% + x(15%) = 12%, so x = 46.667%. Now you should invest $46,667 in the other portfolio and $53,333 in the risk-free investment, lowering your volatility to 5.6%

11-35. Assume the risk-free rate is 4%. You are a financial advisor, and must choose *one* of the funds below to recommend to each of your clients. Whichever fund you recommend, your clients will then combine it with risk-free borrowing and lending depending on their desired level of risk.

	Expected Return	Volatility
Fund A	10%	10%
Fund B	15%	22%
Fund C	6%	2%

Which fund would you recommend without knowing your client's risk preference?

Sharpe ratios of A,B and C are .6,.5 and 1, so you would choose C; it is the best choice no matter what your clients' risk preferences.

11-36. Assume all investors want to hold a portfolio that, for a given level of volatility, has the maximum possible expected return. Explain why, when a risk-free asset exists, all investors will choose to hold the same portfolio of risky stocks.

Investors who want to maximize their expected return for a given level of volatility will pick portfolios that maximize their Sharpe ratio. The set of portfolios that do this is a combination of a risk free asset—a single portfolio of risk assets—the tangential portfolio.

11-37. In addition to risk-free securities, you are currently invested in the Tanglewood Fund, a broadbased fund of stocks and other securities with an expected return of 12% and a volatility of 25%. Currently, the risk-free rate of interest is 4%. Your broker suggests that you add a venture capital fund to your current portfolio. The venture capital fund has an expected return of 20%, a volatility of 80%, and a correlation of 0.2 with the Tanglewood Fund. Calculate the required return and use it to decide whether you should add the venture capital fund to your portfolio.

$$\text{Required Return} = 4\% + 80\%(.2) \times \frac{(21\% - 14\%)}{20\%} = 10.4\%$$

You should add some of the venture fund to your portfolio because it has an expected return that exceeds the required return.

11-38. You have noticed a market investment opportunity that, given your current portfolio, has an expected return that exceeds your required return. What can you conclude about your current portfolio?

Your current portfolio is not efficient.

11-39. You are currently only invested in the Natasha Fund (aside from risk-free securities). It has an expected return of 14% with a volatility of 20%. Currently, the risk-free rate of interest is 3.8%. Your broker suggests that you add Hannah Corporation to your portfolio. Hannah Corporation has an expected return of 20%, a volatility of 60%, and a correlation of 0 with the Natasha Fund.

a. Is your broker right?

b. You follow your broker's advice and make a substantial investment in Hannah stock so that, considering only your risky investments, 60% is in the Natasha Fund and 40% is in Hannah stock. When you tell your finance professor about your investment, he says that you made a mistake and should reduce your investment in Hannah. Is your finance professor right?

c. **You decide to follow your finance professor's advice and reduce your exposure to Hannah. Now Hannah represents 15% of your risky portfolio, with the rest in the Natasha fund. Is this the correct amount of Hannah stock to hold?**

	Initial Portfolio	60-40 Portfolio	85-15 Portfolio
Natasha Fund			
Expected Return	0.14	0.14	0.14
Volatility	0.2	0.2	0.2
Hannah Stock			
Expected Return	0.2	0.2	0.2
Volatilty	0.6	0.6	0.6
Risk Free Rate	0.038	0.038	0.038
Portfolio weight in Hannah	0	0.4	0.15
Expected Return of Portfolio	0.14	0.164	0.149
Volatility of Portfolio	0.2	0.268328157	0.192353841
Beta	0	2	1.459459459
Required Return	0.038	0.29	0.2

a) Yes, because the expected return of Hannah stock exceeds the required return.
b) Yes, because the expected return of Hannah stock is less than the required return.
c) Yes, because now the required and expected return are the same.

11-40. Calculate the Sharpe ratio of each of the three portfolios in Problem 39. What portfolio weight in Hannah stock maximizes the Sharpe ratio?

	Initial Portfolio	60-40 Portfolio	85-15 Portfolio
Natasha Fund			
Expected Return	0.14	0.14	0.14
Volatility	0.2	0.2	0.2
Hannah Stock			
Expected Return	0.2	0.2	0.2
Volatilty	0.6	0.6	0.6
Risk Free Rate	0.038	0.038	0.038
Portfolio weight in Hannah	0	0.4	0.15
Expected Return of Portfolio	0.14	0.164	0.149
Volatility of Portfolio	0.2	0.268328157	0.192353841
Sharpe Ratio	0.51	0.469574275	0.577061522
	0.09002	0.097166359	0.102053829

The Sharpe Ratio is maximized at 15% in Hannah Stock.

11-41. Returning to Problem 37, assume you follow your broker's advice and put 50% of your money in the venture fund.

a. What is the Sharpe ratio of the Tanglewood Fund?

b. What is the Sharpe ratio of your new portfolio?

c. What is the optimal fraction of your wealth to invest in the venture fund? (*Hint*:Use Excel and round your answer to two decimal places.)

a. 0.32 b. 0.271 c. 13%

	Initial Portfolio	50-50 Split	
Tanglewood Fund			
Expected Return	0.12	0.12	
Volatility	0.25	0.25	0.25
Venture Fund			
Expected Return	0.2	0.2	
Volatilty	0.8	0.8	
Risk Free Rate	0.04	0.04	
Portfolio weight in Hannah	0	0.5	
Expected Return of Portfolio	0.12	0.16	
Volatility of Portfolio	0.25	0.44229515	0.25
Sharpe Ratio	0.32	0.271312041	
	0.0656	0.072557445	

The Sharpe Ratio is maximized at 12% in the venture fund.

Weight in venture fund	Expected Return	Volatility	Sharpe Ratio	
0	0.12	0.25	0.32	Part a
0.01	0.1208	0.249223293	0.324207256	
0.02	0.1216	0.248694592	0.328113287	
0.03	0.1224	0.248415479	0.331702358	
0.04	0.1232	0.248386795	0.334961446	
0.05	0.124	0.248608628	0.337880469	
0.06	0.1248	0.249080308	0.340452445	
0.07	0.1256	0.24980042	0.342673563	
0.08	0.1264	0.250766824	0.344543184	
0.09	0.1272	0.251976685	0.346063763	
0.1	0.128	0.253426518	0.347240694	
0.11	0.1288	0.25511223	0.348082097	
0.12	0.1296	0.257029181	0.34859855	
0.13	0.1304	0.25917224	0.348802788	Part c
0.14	0.1312	0.261535848	0.348709366	
0.15	0.132	0.264114085	0.348334319	
0.16	0.1328	0.266900731	0.347694814	
0.17	0.1336	0.269889329	0.346808821	
0.18	0.1344	0.27307325	0.34569479	
0.19	0.1352	0.276445745	0.34437137	
0.2	0.136	0.28	0.342857143	
0.21	0.1368	0.283729184	0.341170403	

Weight in venture fund	Expected Return	Volatility	Sharpe Ratio	
0.22	0.1376	0.287626494	0.339328963	
0.23	0.1384	0.29168519	0.337350004	
0.24	0.1392	0.295898631	0.335249945	
0.25	0.14	0.300260304	0.333044358	
0.26	0.1408	0.304763843	0.330747896	
0.27	0.1416	0.309403054	0.328374263	
0.28	0.1424	0.314171927	0.325936187	
0.29	0.1432	0.319064649	0.323445422	
0.3	0.144	0.324075608	0.320912766	
0.31	0.1448	0.329199408	0.318348082	
0.32	0.1456	0.33443086	0.315760334	
0.33	0.1464	0.339764992	0.313157631	
0.34	0.1472	0.345197045	0.31054727	
0.35	0.148	0.350722469	0.307935789	
0.36	0.1488	0.356336919	0.305329013	
0.37	0.1496	0.362036255	0.302732112	
0.38	0.1504	0.36781653	0.300149642	
0.39	0.1512	0.373673989	0.297585605	
0.4	0.152	0.379605058	0.295043487	
0.41	0.1528	0.385606341	0.29252631	
0.42	0.1536	0.39167461	0.290036671	
0.43	0.1544	0.3978068	0.287576784	
0.44	0.1552	0.404	0.285148515	
0.45	0.156	0.410251447	0.282753421	
0.46	0.1568	0.416558519	0.280392777	
0.47	0.1576	0.422918727	0.278067611	
0.48	0.1584	0.42932971	0.275778725	
0.49	0.1592	0.435789227	0.273526725	
0.5	0.16	0.44229515	0.271312041	Part b
0.51	0.1608	0.448845463	0.269134947	
0.52	0.1616	0.45543825	0.26699558	
0.53	0.1624	0.462071694	0.264893958	
0.54	0.1632	0.468744067	0.262829994	
0.55	0.164	0.475453731	0.260803506	
0.56	0.1648	0.482199129	0.258814238	
0.57	0.1656	0.488978783	0.256861861	
0.58	0.1664	0.495791287	0.254945989	
0.59	0.1672	0.502635305	0.253066187	
0.6	0.168	0.509509568	0.251221975	
0.61	0.1688	0.516412868	0.24941284	
0.62	0.1696	0.523344055	0.247638239	
0.63	0.1704	0.530302037	0.245897604	
0.64	0.1712	0.537285771	0.244190349	
0.65	0.172	0.544294268	0.242515874	
0.66	0.1728	0.551326582	0.240873566	
0.67	0.1736	0.558381814	0.239262807	
0.68	0.1744	0.565459106	0.237682971	
0.69	0.1752	0.572557639	0.236133431	

11-42. When the CAPM correctly prices risk, the market portfolio is an efficient portfolio. Explain why.

All investors will want to maximize their Sharpe ratios by picking efficient portfolios. When a riskless asset exists this means that all investors will pick the same efficient portfolio, and because the sum of all investors' portfolios is the market portfolio this efficient portfolio must be the market portfolio.

11-43. A big pharmaceutical company, DRIg, has just announced a potential cure for cancer. The stock price increased from \$5 to \$100 in one day. A friend calls to tell you that he owns DRIg. You proudly reply that you do too. Since you have been friends for some time, you know that he holds the market, as do you, and so you both are invested in this stock. Both of you care only about expected return and volatility. The risk-free rate is 3%, quoted as an APR based on a 365-day year. DRIg made up 0.2% of the market portfolio before the news announcement.

a. **On the announcement your overall wealth went up by 1% (assume all other price changes canceled out so that without DRIg, the market return would have been zero). How is your wealth invested?**

b. **Your friend's wealth went up by 2%. How is he invested?**

a. 26.16% is in the market; the rest in the risk-free asset.

b. 52.53% is in the market; the rest in the risk-free asset.

11-44. Your investment portfolio consists of \$15,000 invested in only one stock—Microsoft. Suppose the risk-free rate is 5%, Microsoft stock has an expected return of 12% and a volatility of 40%, and the market portfolio has an expected return of 10% and a volatility of 18%. Under the CAPM assumptions,

a. **What alternative investment has the lowest possible volatility while having the same expected return as Microsoft? What is the volatility of this investment?**

b. **What investment has the highest possible expected return while having the same volatility as Microsoft? What is the expected return of this investment?**

a. Under the CAPM assumptions, the market is efficient; that is, a leveraged position in the market has the highest expected return of any portfolio for a given volatility and the lowest volatility for a given expected return. By holding a leveraged position in the market portfolio, you can achieve an expected return of

$$E[R_P] = r_f + x(E[R_m] - r_f) = 5\% + x \times 5\%.$$

Setting this equal to 12% gives $12 = 5 + 5x \Rightarrow x = 1.4$.

So the portfolio with the lowest volatility and that has the same return as Microsoft has $\$15{,}000 \times 1.4 = \$21{,}000$ in the market portfolio and borrows $\$21{,}000 - \$15{,}000 = \$6{,}000$; that is, –\$6,000 in the force asset.

$$SD(R_p) = xSD[R_m] = 1.4 \times 18 = 25.2\%$$

Note that this is considerably lower than Microsoft's volatility.

b. A leveraged portion in the market has volatility η

$$SD(R_p) = xSD(R_m) = x \times 18\%.$$

Setting this equal to the volatility of Microsoft gives

$$40\% = x \times 18\%$$

$$x = \frac{40}{18} = 2.222.$$

So the portfolio with the highest expected return that has the same volatility as Microsoft has $\$15{,}000 \times 2.2 = \$33{,}000$ in the market portfolio and borrows $33{,}000 - 15{,}000 = \$18{,}333.33$, that is –\$18,333.33 in the in force asset.

$$E\left[R_p\right] = r_f + x\left(E\left[R_m\right] - r_f\right) = 5\% + 2.222 \times 5\% = 16.11\%$$

Note that this is considerably higher than Microsoft's expected return.

11-45. Suppose you group all the stocks in the world into two mutually exclusive portfolios (each stock is in only one portfolio): growth stocks and value stocks. Suppose the two portfolios have equal size (in terms of total value), a correlation of 0.5, and the following characteristics:

	Expected Return	Volatility
Value Stocks	13%	12%
Growth Stocks	17%	25%

The risk free rate is 2%.

a. **What is the expected return and volatility of the market portfolio (which is a 50–50 combination of the two portfolios)?**

b. **Does the CAPM hold in this economy? (*Hint* : Is the market portfolio efficient?)**

a. Erm = 15%, vol = 16.3%

b. Value stocks have a higher sharpe ratio than the market, so mkt is not efficient.

11-46. Suppose the risk-free return is 4% and the market portfolio has an expected return of 10% and a volatility of 16%. Johnson and Johnson Corporation (Ticker: JNJ) stock has a 20% volatility and a correlation with the market of 0.06.

a. **What is Johnson and Johnson's beta with respect to the market?**

b. **Under the CAPM assumptions, what is its expected return?**

a. $\beta_{JJ} = 0.06 \times \dfrac{0.2}{0.16} = 0.075$

b. $\mathrm{E}[\mathrm{R}_{JJ}] = 0.04 + 0.075(0.1 - 0.04) = 4.45\%$

11-47. Consider a portfolio consisting of the following three stocks:

	Portfolio Weight	Volatility	Correlation with the Market Portfolio
HEC Corp	0.25	12%	0.4
Green Midget	0.35	25%	0.6
AliveAndWell	0.4	13%	0.5

The volatility of the market portfolio is 10% and it has an expected return of 8%. The risk-free rate is 3%.

a. **Compute the beta and expected return of each stock.**

b. **Using your answer from part a, calculate the expected return of the portfolio.**

c. **What is the beta of the portfolio?**

d. **Using your answer from part c, calculate the expected return of the portfolio and verify that it matches your answer to part b.**

	Portfolio Weight	Volatility	Correlation with the Market Portfolio	Beta (Part a answer)	Expected Return (Part a answer)
HEC Corp	0.25	12%	0.4	0.48	5.4
Green Midget	0.35	25%	0.6	1.5	10.5
AliveAndWell	0.4	13%	0.5	0.65	6.25
				Part c answer:	Part b answer
			Porfolio	0.905	7.525
					Part d answer
		Expected Return calculated from porfolio bet			7.525

11-48. Suppose Intel stock has a beta of 2.16, whereas Boeing stock has a beta of 0.69. If the risk-free interest rate is 4% and the expected return of the market portfolio is 10%, what is the expected return of a portfolio that consists of 60% Intel stock and 40% Boeing stock, according to the CAPM?

$\beta = (0.6)(2.16) + (0.4)(0.69) = 1.572$

$E[R] = 4 + (1.572)(10 - 4) \;\; = 13.432\%$

11-49. What is the risk premium of a zero-beta stock? Does this mean you can lower the volatility of a portfolio without changing the expected return by substituting out any zero-beta stock in a portfolio and replacing it with the risk-free asset?

Risk premium = 0. It is uncorrelated with the market, so there is no incremental risk from adding it to your portfolio.

Note also that since the stock is positively correlated with itself (which is part of the market), to have zero beta it must be negatively correlated with the other stocks. Thus, it offsets risk that other stocks have. Thus, taking it out will not reduce risk.

Chapter 12

Estimating the Cost of Capital

12-1. Suppose Pepsico's stock has a beta of 0.57. If the risk-free rate is 3% and the expected return of the market portfolio is 8%, what is Pepsico's equity cost of capital?

3% + 0.57 × (8%-3%) = 5.85%

12-2. Suppose the market portfolio has an expected return of 10% and a volatility of 20%, while Microsoft's stock has a volatility of 30%.

a. Given its higher volatility, should we expect Microsoft to have an equity cost of capital that is higher than 10%?

b. What would have to be true for Microsoft's equity cost of capital to be equal to 10%?

a. No, volatility includes diversifiable risk, and so it cannot be used to assess the equity cost of capital.

b. Microsoft stock would need to have a beta of 1.

12-3. Aluminum maker Alcoa has a beta of about 2.0, whereas Hormel Foods has a beta of 0.45. If the expected excess return of the marker portfolio is 5%, which of these firms has a higher equity cost of capital, and how much higher is it?

Alcoa is 5% × (2-0.45) = 7.75% higher.

12-4. Suppose all possible investment opportunities in the world are limited to the five stocks listed in the table below. What does the market portfolio consist of (what are the portfolio weights)?

Stock	Price/Share ($)	Number of Shares Outstanding (millions)
A	10	10
B	20	12
C	8	3
D	50	1
E	45	20

Total value of the market $= 10 \times 10 + 20 \times 12 + 8 \times 3 + 50 \times 1 + 45 \times 20 = \$1.314$ billion

Stock	Portfolio Weight
A	$\frac{10\times10}{1314}=7.61\%$
B	$\frac{20\times12}{1314}=18.26\%$
C	$\frac{8\times3}{1314}=1.83\%$
D	$\frac{50}{1314}=3.81\%$
E	$\frac{45\times20}{1314}=68.49\%$

12-5. Using the data in Problem 4, suppose you are holding a market portfolio, and have invested $12,000 in Stock C.

a. How much have you invested in Stock A?

b. How many shares of Stock B do you hold?

c. If the price of Stock C suddenly drops to $4 per share, what trades would you need to make to maintain a market portfolio?

a. 12,000 × (MC A / MC C) = 12,000 × (10 × 10)/(8 × 3) = $50,000

b. 12,000/8 = 1,500 shares of B,

1,500 × (shrs B/shrs C) = 1500 × 12/3 = 6000 shares of B

c. No trades are needed; it is a passive portfolio.

12-6. Suppose Best Buy stock is trading for $40 per share for a total market cap of $16 billion, and Walt Disney has 1.8 billion shares outstanding. If you hold the market portfolio, and as part of it hold 100 shares of Best Buy, how many shares of Walt Disney do you hold?

Best Buy has 16/40 = 0.4 billion shares outstanding.

Therefore, you hold 100 × (1.8/.4) = 450 shares of Disney.

12-7. Standard and Poor's also publishes the S&P Equal Weight Index, which is an equally weighted version of the S&P 500.

a. To maintain a portfolio that tracks this index, what trades would need to be made in response to daily price changes?

b. Is this index suitable as a market proxy?

a. Sell winners, buy losers, to maintain an equal investment in each.

b. No. The market portfolio should represent the aggregate portfolio of all investors. However, in aggregate, investors must hold more of larger market cap stocks; the aggregate portfolio is value weighted, not equally weighted.

12-8. Suppose that in place of the S&P 500, you wanted to use a broader market portfolio of all U.S. stocks and bonds as the market proxy. Could you use the same estimate for the market risk premium when applying the CAPM? If not, how would you estimate the correct risk premium to use?

No, expected return of this portfolio would be lower due to bonds. Compute the historical excess return of this new index.

12-9. From the start of 1999 to the start of 2009, the S&P 500 had a negative return. Does this mean the market risk premium we should use in the CAPM is negative?

No! Investors were not expecting a negative return. To estimate an expected return, we need much more data.

12-10. You need to estimate the equity cost of capital for XYZ Corp. You have the following data available regarding past returns:

Year	Risk-free Return	Market Return	XYZ Return
2007	3%	6%	10%
2008	1%	–37%	–45%

a. What was XYZ's average historical return?

b. Compute the market's and XYZ's excess returns for each year. Estimate XYZ's beta.

c. Estimate XYZ's historical alpha.

d. Suppose the current risk-free rate is 3%, and you expect the market's return to be 8%. Use the CAPM to estimate an expected return for XYZ Corp.'s stock.

e. Would you base your estimate of XYZ's equity cost of capital on your answer in part (a) or in part (d)? How does your answer to part (c) affect your estimate? Explain.

a. (10% – 45%)/2 = -17.5%

b. Excess returns:

MKT 3%, –38%

XYZ 7%, –46%

Beta = (7 – (–46))/(3 – (–38)) = 1.29

c. Alpha = intercept =

E[Rs-rf] – beta × (E[Rm -rf]) =

(7%-46%)/2 – 1.29 × (3%-38%)/2 = 3.1%

d. E[R] = 3% + 1.29 × (8% - 3%) = 9.45%

e. Use (d) – CAPM is more reliable than average past returns, which would imply a negative cost of capital in this case!

Ignore (c), as alpha is not persistent.

12-11. Go to Chapter Resources on MyFinanceLab and use the data in the spreadsheet provided to estimate the beta of Nike and Dell stock based on their monthly returns from 2004–2008. (*Hint*: You can use the slope() function in Excel.)

NKE 0.63

Dell 1.35

12-12. Using the same data as in Problem 11, estimate the alpha of Nike and Dell stock, expressed as % per month. (*Hint*: You can use the intercept() function in Excel.)

NKE = 0.86%/month

Dell = -1.4% per month

12-13. Using the same data as in Problem 11, estimate the 95% confidence interval for the alpha and beta of Nike and Dell stock using Excel's regression tool (from the data analysis menu).

	Coefficients	*Standard Error*	*t Stat*	*P-value*	*Lower 95%*	*Upper 95%*	*Lower 95.0%*	*Upper 95.0%*
Intercept	-0.01445	0.009175	-1.57447	0.120819	-0.03281	0.00392	-0.03281	0.00392
VW	1.352638	0.229004	5.906622	1.94E-07	0.894237	1.811038	0.894237	1.811038

	Coefficients	*Standard Error*	*t Stat*	*P-value*	*Lower 95%*	*Upper 95%*	*Lower 95.0%*	*Upper 95.0%*
Intercept	0.008592	0.006462	1.329547	0.188873	-0.00434	0.021528	-0.00434	0.021528
VW	0.632996	0.161298	3.924397	0.000233	0.310124	0.955869	0.310124	0.955869

12-14. In mid-2009, Ralston Purina had AA-rated, 6-year bonds outstanding with a yield to maturity of 3.75%.

a. What is the highest expected return these bonds could have?

b. At the time, similar maturity Treasuries has a yield of 3%. Could these bonds actually have an expected return equal to your answer in part (a)?

c. If you believe Ralston Purina's bonds have 1% chance of default per year, and that expected loss rate in the event of default is 40%, what is your estimate of the expected return for these bonds?

a. Risk-free => y = 3.75%

b. no

c. y-d × l= 3.75% – 1%(.40) = 3.35%

12-15. In mid-2009, Rite Aid had CCC-rated, 6-year bonds outstanding with a yield to maturity of 17.3%. At the time, similar maturity Treasuries had a yield of 3%. Suppose the market risk premium is 5% and you believe Rite Aid's bonds have a beta of 0.31. If the expected loss rate of these bonds in the event of default is 60%, what annual probability of default would be consistent with the yield to maturity of these bonds?

Rd = 3% + .31(5%) = 4.55%

= y – pL = 17.3% – p(.60)

p = (17.3% – 4.55%)/.60 = 21.25%

12-16. The Dunley Corp. plans to issue 5-year bonds. It believes the bonds will have a BBB rating. Suppose AAA bonds with the same maturity have a 4% yield. Assume the market risk premium is 5% and use the data in Table 12.2 and Table 12.3.

a. Estimate the yield Dunley will have to pay, assuming an expected 60% loss rate in the event of default during average economic times. What spread over AAA bonds will it have to pay?

b. Estimate the yield Dunley would have to pay if it were a recession, assuming the expected loss rate is 80% at that time, but the beta of debt and market risk premium are the same as in average economic times. What is Dunley's spread over AAA now?

c. **In fact, one might expect risk premia and betas to increase in recessions. Redo part (b) assuming that the market risk premium and the beta of debt both increase by 20%; that is, they equal 1.2 times their value in recessions.**

a. Use CAPM to estimate expected return, using AAA rate as rf rate: r+.1 × rp=4% + .10(5%) = 4.5%

So, y – p × l = 4.5%

y = 4.5% + p(60%) = 4.5% + .4%(60%) = 4.74%

Spread = 0.74%

b. Use CAPM to estimate expected return, using AAA rate as rf rate: r+.1 × rp=4% + .10(5%) = 4.5%

y= 4.5% + 3%(80%) = 6.90%

Spread = 2.9%

c. Use CAPM to estimate expected return, using AAA rate as rf rate: r+.1 × 1.2 × rp × 1.2=4% + .10(5%)1.2^2 = 4.72%

So, y – p × l = 4.5%

y = 4.72% + p(80%) = 4.72% + 3%(80%) = 7.12%

Spread = 3.12%

12-17. Your firm is planning to invest in an automated packaging plant. Harburtin Industries is an allequity firm that specializes in this business. Suppose Harburtin's equity beta is 0.85, the riskfree rate is 4%, and the market risk premium is 5%. If your firm's project is all equity financed, estimate its cost of capital.

Project beta = 0.85 (using all equity comp)

Thus, rp = 4% + 0.85(5%) = 8.25%

12-18. Consider the setting of Problem 17. You decided to look for other comparables to reduce estimation error in your cost of capital estimate. You find a second firm, Thurbinar Design, which is also engaged in a similar line of business. Thurbinar has a stock price of $20 per share, with 15 million shares outstanding. It also has $100 million in outstanding debt, with a yield on the debt of 4.5%. Thurbinar's equity beta is 1.00.

a. **Assume Thurbinar's debt has a beta of zero. Estimate Thurbinar's unlevered beta. Use the unlevered beta and the CAPM to estimate Thurbinar's unlevered cost of capital.**

b. **Estimate Thurbinar's equity cost of capital using the CAPM. Then assume its debt cost of capital equals its yield, and using these results, estimate Thurbinar's unlevered cost of capital.**

c. **Explain the difference between your estimate in part (a) and part (b).**

d. **You decide to average your results in part (a) and part (b), and then average this result with your estimate from Problem 17. What is your estimate for the cost of capital of your firm's project?**

a. E = 20 × 15 = 300

E+D = 400

Bu = 300/400 × 1.00 + 100/400 × 0 = 0.75

Ru = 4% + .75(5%) = 7.75%

b. Re = 4% + 1.0 × 5% = 9%

Ru = 300/400 × 9% + 100/400 × 4.5% = 7.875%

c. In the first case, we assumed the debt had a beta of zero, so rd = rf = 4%

In the second case, we assumed rd = ytm = 4.5%

d. Thurbinar Ru = (7.75 + 7.875)/2 = 7.8125%

Harburtin Ru = 8.25%

Estimate = (8.25% + 7.8125%)/2 = 8.03%

12-19. IDX Tech is looking to expand its investment in advanced security systems. The project will be financed with equity. You are trying to assess the value of the investment, and must estimate its cost of capital. You find the following data for a publicly traded firm in the same line of business:

Debt Outstanding (book value, AA-rated)	$400 million
Number of shares of common stock	80 million
Stock price per share	$15.00
Book value of Equity per share	$6.00
Beta of equity	1.20

What is your estimate of the project's beta? What assumptions do you need to make?

Assume debt is risk-free and market value = book value. Assume comparable assets have same risk as project.

Be = 1.20, Bd = 0

E = 15 × 80 = 1200

D = 400

Bu = (1200/1600) × 1.20 + (400/1600) × 0 = 0.90

12-20. In June 2009, Cisco Systems had a market capitalization of $115 billion. It had A-rated debt of $10 billion as well as cash and short-term investments of $34 billion, and its estimated equity beta at the time was 1.27.

a. What is Cisco's enterprise value?

b. Assuming Cisco's debt has a beta of zero, estimate the beta of Cisco's underlying business enterprise.

a. EV = E + D – C = 115 + 10 – 34 = $91 billion

b. Net Debt = 10 – 34 = -24

Ru = (115/91) × 1.27 + (-24/91) × 0 = 1.60

12-21. Consider the following airline industry data from mid-2009:

Company Name	Market Capitalization ($mm)	Total Enterprise Value ($mm)	Equity Beta	Debt Ratings
Delta Air Lines (DAL)	4,938.5	17,026.5	2.04	BB
Southwest Airlines (LUV)	4,896.8	6,372.8	0.966	A/BBB
JetBlue Airways (JBLU)	1,245.5	3,833.5	1.91	B/CCC
Continental Airlines (CAL)	1,124.0	4,414.0	1.99	B

a. **Use the estimates in Table 12.3 to estimate the debt beta for each firm (use an average if multiple ratings are listed).**

b. **Estimate the asset beta for each firm.**

c. **What is the average asset beta for the industry, based on these firms?**

Company Name	Market Capitalization ($mm)	Total Enterprise Value ($mm)	2 Year Beta	Debt Ratings	Debt beta	asset beta
Delta Air Lines (DAL)	4,938.5	17,026.5	2.04	BB	0.17	0.712
Southwest Airlines (LUV)	4,896.8	6,372.8	0.966	A/BBB	0.075	0.760
JetBlue Airways (JBLU)	1,245.5	3,833.5	1.91	B/CCC	0.285	0.813
Continental Airlines (CAL)	1,124.0	4,414.0	1.99	B	0.26	0.701
					Average	0.746

12-22. Weston Enterprises is an all-equity firm with three divisions. The soft drink division has an asset beta of 0.60, expects to generate free cash flow of $50 million this year, and anticipates a 3% perpetual growth rate. The industrial chemicals division has an asset beta of 1.20, expects to generate free cash flow of $70 million this year, and anticipates a 2% perpetual growth rate. Suppose the risk-free rate is 4% and the market risk premium is 5%.

a. **Estimate the value of each division.**

b. **Estimate Weston's current equity beta and cost of capital. Is this cost of capital useful for valuing Weston's projects? How is Weston's equity beta likely to change over time?**

a. Soft drink

Ru = 4% + .6 × 5% = 7%

V = 50/(7% - 3%) = 1250

Chemical

Ru = 4% + 1.20 × 5% = 10%

V = 70/(10% - 2%) = 875

Total = 1250 + 875 = $2.125 billion

b. Weston Beta (portfolio)

1250/2125 × .6 + 875/2125 × 1.2 = 0.85

Re = 4% + 0.85 × 5% = 8.25%

Not useful! Individual divisions are either less risky or more risky. Over time, Weston's equity beta will decline towards 0.6 as the soft drink division has a higher growth rate and so will represent a larger fraction of the firm.

12-23. Harrison Holdings, Inc. (HHI) is publicly traded, with a current share price of $32 per share. HHI has 20 million shares outstanding, as well as $64 million in debt. The founder of HHI, Harry Harrison, made his fortune in the fast food business. He sold off part of his fast food empire, and purchased a professional hockey team. HHI's only assets are the hockey team, together with 50% of the outstanding shares of Harry's Hotdogs restaurant chain. Harry's Hotdogs (HDG) has a market capitalization of $850 million, and an enterprise value of $1.05 billion. After a little research, you find that the average asset beta of other fast food restaurant chains is 0.75. You also find that the debt of HHI and HDG is highly rated, and so you decide to estimate the beta of both firms' debt as zero. Finally, you do a regression analysis on HHI's historical stock returns in comparison to the S&P 500, and estimate an equity beta of 1.33. Given this information, estimate the beta of HHI's investment in the hockey team.

HHI Equity = 32 × 20 = $640

HHI debt = $64

HHI asset beta = (640/(640+64)) 1.33 + (64/(640+64)) 0 = 1.21

Holdings of Hotdogs = 850/2 = 425

Value of Hockey Team = (640+64)-425 = $279

Hotdog equity beta : (850/1050) × Be + (200/1050) × 0 = 0.75

Be = 0.75 × 1050/850 = 0.93 for hotdog equity

So, if B = hockey team beta,

(425/(425+279)) 0.93 + (279/(425+279)) × B = 1.21

B = 1.64

Beta of hockey team = 1.64

12-24. Your company operates a steel plant. On average, revenues from the plant are $30 million per year. All of the plants costs are variable costs and are consistently 80% of revenues, including energy costs associated with powering the plant, which represent one quarter of the plant's costs, or an average of $6 million per year. Suppose the plant has an asset beta of 1.25, the riskfree rate is 4%, and the market risk premium is 5%. The tax rate is 40%, and there are no other costs.

a. Estimate the value of the plant today assuming no growth.

b. Suppose you enter a long-term contract which will supply all of the plant's energy needs for a fixed cost of $3 million per year (before tax). What is the value of the plant if you take this contract?

c. How would taking the contract in (b) change the plant's cost of capital? Explain.

a. FCF = (30 – .8(30))(1-.40) = 3.6 million

Ru = 4% + 1.25 × 5% = 10.25%

V= 3.6/.1025 = 35.12 million

b. FCF without energy = (30 – 18)(1 – .40) = 7.2

Cost of capital = 10.25%

Energy cost after tax = 3(1 – .40) = 1.8

Cost of capital = 4%

V = 7.2/.1025 – 1.8/.04 = 70.24 – 45 = 25.24 million

c. FCF = 7.2 – 1.8 = 5.4

5.4/25.24 = 21.4%

Risk is increased because now energy costs are fixed. Thus a higher cost of capital is appropriate.

12-25. Unida Systems has 40 million shares outstanding trading for $10 per share. In addition, Unida has $100 million in outstanding debt. Suppose Unida's equity cost of capital is 15%, its debt cost of capital is 8%, and the corporate tax rate is 40%.

a. What is Unida's unlevered cost of capital?

b. What is Unida's after-tax debt cost of capital?

c. What is Unida's weighted average cost of capital?

a. E = 40 × $10 = $400

D = $100

Ru = 400/500 × 15% + 100/500 × 8% = 13.6%

b. Rd=8% × (1-40%) = 4.8%

c. Rwacc = 400/500 × 15% + 100/500 × 4.8% = 12.96%

12-26. You would like to estimate the weighted average cost of capital for a new airline business. Based on its industry asset beta, you have already estimated an unlevered cost of capital for the firm of 9%. However, the new business will be 25% debt financed, and you anticipate its debt cost of capital will be 6%. If its corporate tax rate is 40%, what is your estimate of its WACC?

Ru = 9% = 75% Re + 25% Rd = 75% Re + 25%(6%)

Re = (9% – 25%(6%))/75% = 10%

Rwacc = 75%(10%) – 25%(6%)(1 – 40%) = 8.4%

Chapter 13

Investor Behavior and Capital Market Efficiency

13-1. Assume that all investors have the same information and care only about expected return and volatility. If new information arrives about one stock, can this information affect the price and return of other stocks? If so, explain why?

Yes. When the new information arrives, it will change the attractiveness of this stock. If other stock prices do not change, then investors would want to increase their weight in this stock, implying they would not be holding the market portfolio.

13-2. Assume that the CAPM is a good description of stock price returns. The market expected return is 7% with 10% volatility and the risk-free rate is 3%. New news arrives that does not change any of these numbers but it does change the expected return of the following stocks:

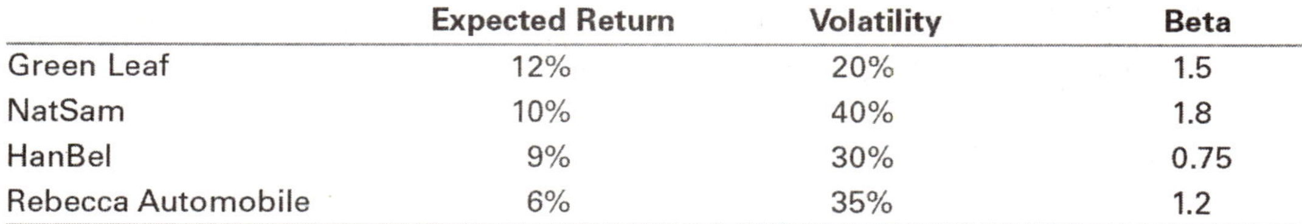

	Expected Return	Volatility	Beta
Green Leaf	12%	20%	1.5
NatSam	10%	40%	1.8
HanBel	9%	30%	0.75
Rebecca Automobile	6%	35%	1.2

a. At current market prices, which stocks represent buying opportunities?

b. On which stocks should you put a sell order in?

According to the CAPM, we should hold the market portfolio. But once new news arrives and we update our expectations, we may find profitable trading opportunities if we can trade before prices fully adjust to the news. Assuming we initially hold the market portfolio, we can improve gain by investing more in stocks with positive alphas and less in stocks with negative alphas.

	Expected Return	Volatility	Beta	Required Return (CAPM)	Alpha
Green Leaf	12%	20%	1.5	9.0%	3.0%
NatSam	10%	40%	1.8	10.2%	-0.2%
HanBel	9%	30%	0.75	6.0%	3.0%
Rebecca Automobile	6%	35%	1.2	7.8%	-1.8%

a. Green Leaf, HanBel

b. Rebecca Automobile and possibly NatSam (although its alpha is close enough to zero that we might regard it as insignificant).

13-3. **Suppose the CAPM equilibrium holds perfectly. Then the risk-free interest rate increases, *and nothing else changes.***

a. **Is the market portfolio still efficient?**

b. **If your answer to a is yes, explain why. If not, describe which stocks would be buying opportunities and which stocks would be selling opportunities.**

a. No

b. Stocks with betas (calculated using the market portfolio prior to the interest rate change) greater than one will have positive alphas and so would be buying opportunities. Similarly stocks with betas less than one will be selling opportunities.

13-4. **You know that there are informed traders in the stock market, but you are uninformed. Describe an investment strategy that guarantees that you will not lose money to the informed traders and explain why it works.**

Invest in the market portfolio. Because the average investor must hold the market, by investing in the market you guarantee the average investor return. If the informed traders make higher returns than the average investor, somebody must make lower returns, so by holding the market you can guarantee that it is not you.

13-5. **What are the only conditions under which the market portfolio might not be an efficient portfolio?**

The market portfolio can be inefficient (so it is possible to beat the market) only if a significant number of investors either

1. Do not have rational expectations so that they misinterpret information and believe they are earning a positive alpha when they are actually earning a negative alpha, or
2. Care about aspects of their portfolios other than expected return and volatility, and so are willing to hold inefficient portfolios of securities.

13-6. **Explain what the following sentence means: The market portfolio is a fence that protects the sheep from the wolves, but nothing can protect the sheep from themselves.**

By investing in the market portfolio investors can protect themselves from being exploited by investors with better information than they have themselves. By choosing not to invest in the market portfolio, investors expose themselves to being exploited. If they do this because of overconfidence, they will lose money.

13-7. **You are trading in a market in which you know there are a few highly skilled traders who are better informed than you are. There are no transaction costs. Each day you randomly choose five stocks to buy and five stocks to sell (by, perhaps, throwing darts at a dartboard).**

a. **Over the long run will your strategy outperform, underperform, or have the same return as a buy and hold strategy of investing in the market portfolio?**

b. **Would your answer to part (a) change if all traders in the market were equally well informed and were equally skilled?**

a. You will underperform for two reasons: 1) transaction costs and 2) you will lose every time you trade with an informed investor. Of course in this problem only (2) will cause underperformance

b. This time the only source of losses are transaction costs. In this case, your trades should break even so you should earn the same return

13-8. Why does the CAPM imply that investors should trade very rarely?

Because they should hold the market portfolio which is a value weighted portfolio and thus requires no retrading when prices change to maintain the value weights.

13-9. Your brother Joe is a surgeon who suffers badly from the overconfidence bias. He loves to trade stocks and believes his predictions with 100% confidence. In fact, he is uninformed like most investors. Rumors are that Vital Signs (a startup that makes warning labels in the medical industry) will receive a takeover offer at $20 per share. Absent the takeover offer, the stock will trade at $15 per share. The uncertainty will be resolved in the next few hours. Your brother believes that the takeover will occur with certainty and has instructed his broker to buy the stock at any price less than $20. In fact, the true probability of a takeover is 50%, but a few people are informed and know whether the takeover will actually occur. They also have submitted orders. Nobody else is trading in the stock.

a. Describe what will happen to the market price once these orders are submitted if in fact the takeover will occur in a few hours. What will your brother's profits be: positive, negative or zero?

b. What range of possible prices could result once these orders are submitted if the takeover will not occur. What will your brother's profits be: positive, negative or zero?

c. What are your brother's expected profits?

a. In this case the informed traders and your brother will both submit buy orders for any price less than 20, so the only market clearing price is $20, and nobody trades. Zero profits.

b. In this case the informed traders will submit sell orders for any price above $15 and your brother will submit his buy order for any price below $20. Trade will occur at some price in between and your brother will make negative profits.

c. Negative

13-10. To put the turnover of Figure 13.3 into perspective, let's do a back of the envelope calculation of what an investor's average turnover per stock would be were he to follow a policy of investing in the S&P 500 portfolio. Because the portfolio is value weighted, the trading would be required when Standard and Poor's changes the constituent stocks. (Let's ignore additional, but less important reasons like new share issuances and repurchases.) Assuming they change 23 stocks a year (the historical average since 1962) what would you estimate the investor's per stock share turnover to be? Assume that the average total number of shares outstanding for the stocks that are added or deleted from the index is the same as the average number of shares outstanding for S&P 500 stocks.

46/523 = 8.8%.

13-11. How does the disposition effect impact investors' tax obligations?

The disposition effect causes investors to sell stocks that have appreciated and hold onto stocks that have depreciated. Thus investors are paying capital gains taxes that they could defer and deferring tax deductions they could take immediately. Because of the time value of money, these investors are therefore increasing their required tax obligations.

13-12. Consider the price paths of the following two stocks over six time periods:

	1	2	3	4	5	6
Stock 1	10	12	14	12	13	16
Stock 2	15	11	8	16	15	18

Neither stock pays dividends. Assume you are an investor with the disposition effect and you bought at time 1 and right now it is time 3. Assume throughout this question that you do no trading (other than what is specified) in these stocks.

a. Which stock(s) would you be inclined to sell? Which would you be inclined to hold onto?

b. How would your answer change if right now is time 6?

c. What if you bought at time 3 instead of 1 and today is time 6?

d. What if you bought at time 3 instead of 1 and today is time 5?

a. sell 1, hold 2

b. sell both

c. sell both

d. sell 2, hold 1

13-13. Suppose that all investors have the disposition effect. A new stock has just been issued at a price of $50, so all investors in this stock purchased the stock today. A year from now the stock will be taken over, for a price of $60 or $40 depending on the news that comes out over the year. The stock will pay no dividends. Investors will sell the stock whenever the price goes up by more than 10%.

a. Suppose good news comes out in 6 months (implying the takeover offer will be $60). What equilibrium price will the stock trade for after the news comes out, that is, the price that equates supply and demand?

b. Assume that you are the only investor who does not suffer from the disposition effect and your trades are small enough to not affect prices. Without knowing what will actually transpire, what trading strategy would you instruct your broker to follow?

a. $55.

b. Buy if the price goes up by 10% cr more.

13-14. Davita Spencer is a manager at Half Dome Asset Management. She can generate an alpha of 2% a year up to $100 million. After that her skills are spread too thin, so cannot add value and her alpha is zero. Half Dome charges a fee of 1% per year on the total amount of money under management (at the beginning of each year). Assume that there are always investors looking for positive alpha and no investor would invest in a fund with a negative alpha. In equilibrium, that is, when no investor either takes out money or wishes to invest new money,

a. What alpha do investors in Davita's fund expect to receive?

b. How much money will Davita have under management?

c. How much money will Half Dome generate in fee income?

a. Zero

b. $200 mil

c. $2 million

13-15. Assume the economy consisted of three types of people. 50% are fad followers, 45% are passive investors, they have read this book and so hold the market portfolio, and 5% are informed traders. The portfolio consisting of all the informed traders has a beta of 1.5 and an expected return of 15%. The market expected return is 11%. The risk-free rate is 5%.

a. What alpha do the informed traders make?

b. What is the alpha of the passive investors?

c. What is the expected return of the fad followers?

d. What alpha do the fad followers make?

a. 1%

b. 0

c. 10.6%

d. –0.1%

13-16. Explain what the size effect is.

The size effect is the empirical observation that firms with lower market capitalizations on average have higher average returns.

13-17. Assume all firms have the same expected dividends. If they have different expected returns, how will their market values and expected returns be related? What about the relation between their dividend yields and expected returns?

Firms with higher expected returns will have lower market values, and firms with high dividend yields will have high expected returns.

13-18. Each of the six firms in the table below is expected to pay the listed dividend payment every year in perpetuity.

Firm	Dividend ($ million)	Cost of Capital (%/Year)
S1	10	8
S2	10	12
S3	10	14
B1	100	8
B2	100	12
B3	100	14

a. Using the cost of capital in the table, calculate the market value of each firm.

b. Rank the three S firms by their market values and look at how their cost of capital is ordered. What would be the expected return for a self-financing portfolio that went long on the firm with the largest market value and shorted the firm with the lowest market value? (The expected return of a self-financing portfolio is the weighted average return of the constituent securities.) Repeat using the B firms.

c. Rank all six firms by their market values. How does this ranking order the cost of capital? What would be the expected return for a self-financing portfolio that went long on the firm with the largest market value and shorted the firm with the lowest market value?

d. Repeat part (c) but rank the firms by the dividend yield instead of the market value. What can you conclude about the dividend yield ranking compared to the market value ranking?

a.

Firm	Dividend	Cost of Capital	Market value
S1	10	8%	$125.00
S2	10	12%	$83.33
S3	10	14%	$71.43
B1	100	8%	$1,250.00
B2	100	12%	$833.33
B3	100	14%	$714.29

b.

Firm	Market Value	Cost of Capital	Self financing weights
S1	$125.00	8%	1
S2	$83.33	12%	
S3	$71.43	14%	(1.00)
B1	$1,250.00	8%	1
B2	$833.33	12%	
B3	$714.29	14%	(1.00)
	E[R] (S firms)	–6.00%	
	E[R] (B firms)	–6.00%	

c.

Firm	Market Value	Cost of Capital	Self financing weights
B1	$1,250.00	8%	1
B2	$833.33	12%	
B3	$714.29	14%	
S1	$125.00	8%	
S2	$83.33	12%	
S3	$71.43	14%	(1.00)
	E[R] (All firms)	-6.00%	

Firms will lower costs of capital tend to be higher in this sort, but the ranking is not perfect.

d.

Firm	Market Value	Dividend yield/Cost of Capital	Self financing weights
S1	$125.00	8%	(1.00)
B1	$1,250.00	8%	
S2	$83.33	12%	
B2	$833.33	12%	
S3	$71.43	14%	
B3	$714.29	14%	1.00
	E[R] (All firms)	6.00%	

Because the dividend yield equals the cost of capital, the sort ranks firms perfectly (in contrast to parts b and c) —firms with higher dividend yields have higher costs of capital.

13-19. Consider the following stocks, all of which will pay a liquidating dividend in a year and nothing in the interim:

	Market Capitalization ($ million)	Expected Liquidating Dividend ($ million)	Beta
Stock A	800	1000	0.77
Stock B	750	1000	1.46
Stock C	950	1000	1.25
Stock D	900	1000	1.07

a. **Calculate the expected return of each stock.**

b. **What is the sign of correlation between the expected return and market capitalization of the stocks?**

	Market Capitalization ($ million)	Total Liquidating Dividend ($ million)	Beta	Expected Return
Stock A	800	1000	0.77	0.25
Stock B	750	1000	1.46	0.33333333
Stock C	950	1000	1.25	0.05263158
Stock D	900	1000	1.07	0.11111111
				Correlation
				-0.9984206

13-20. In Problem 19, assume the risk-free rate is 3% and the market risk premium is 7%.

a. What does the CAPM predict the expected return for each stock should be?

b. Clearly, the CAPM predictions are not equal to the actual expected returns so the CAPM does not hold. You decide to investigate this further. To see what kind of mistakes the CAPM is making, you decide to regress the actual expected return onto the expected return predicted by the CAPM. What is the intercept and slope coefficient of this regression?

c. What are the residuals of the regression in (d)? That is, for each stock compute the difference between the actual expected return and the best fitting line given by the intercept and slope coefficient in (b).

d. What is the sign of the correlation between the residuals you calculated in (e) and market capitalization?

e. What can you conclude from your answers to part (b) of the previous problem and part (d) of this problem about the relation between firm size (market capitalization) and returns? (The results do not depend on the particular numbers in this problem. You are welcome to verify this for yourself by redoing the problems with another value for the market risk premium, and by picking the stock betas and market capitalizations randomly.)

	Market Capitalization ($ million)	Total Liquidating Dividend ($ million)	Beta	Expected Return	CAPM	Error	Residual + Intercept	Just Residual
Stock A	800	1000	0.77	0.25	0.0839	0.1661	0.18430808	0.08337312
Stock B	750	1000	1.46	0.33333333	0.1322	0.20113333	0.22982353	0.12888858
Stock C	950	1000	1.25	0.05263158	0.1175	-0.0648684	-0.0393684	-0.1403034
Stock D	900	1000	1.07	0.11111111	0.1049	0.00621111	0.02897663	-0.0719583

Risk Free rate	Market Risk Premium	Correlation	Slope	Intercept	Intercept	Correlation
3%	7.00%	-0.9984206	0.78297881	0.10093495	0.10093495	-0.9968741

13-21. Explain how to construct a positive-alpha trading strategy if stocks that have had relatively high returns in the past tend to have positive alphas and stocks that have had relatively low returns in the past tend to have negative alphas.

You buy stocks that have done well in the past and sell stocks that have done poorly.

13-22. If you can use past returns to construct a trading strategy that makes money (has a positive alpha), it is evidence that market portfolio is not efficient. Explain why.

If the market portfolio is efficient, then all stocks have zero alphas, and you could not construct any strategy that has a positive alpha.

13-23. Explain why you might expect stocks to have nonzero alphas if the market proxy portfolio is not highly correlated with the true market portfolio, even if the true market portfolio is efficient.

Because the proxy portfolio is not highly correlated with the market portfolio, it will not capture some components of systematic risk. The alphas reflect the risk components that the proxy portfolio is not capturing.

13-24. Explain why if some investors are subject to systematic behavioral biases, while others pick efficient portfolios, the market portfolio will not be efficient.

The market portfolio consists of the combination of all investors' portfolios. Because some investors hold inefficient portfolios that depart form efficient in systematic ways, the sum of all these investors' portfolios is not efficient. Since the rest of investors hold efficient portfolios, the sum of all investors' portfolios will not be efficient.

13-25. Explain why an employee who cares only about expected return and volatility will likely underweight the amount of money he invests in his own company's stock relative to an investor who does not work for his company.

Employees are already partially invested in their company due to their human capital. Their optimal diversification strategy should take this into account, and thus should underweight their own company's stock.

For Problems 26–28, refer to the following table of estimated factor betas.

Factor	MSFT	XOM	GE
MKT	1.068	0.243	0.747
SMB	–0.374	0.125	–0.478
HML	–0.814	0.144	–0.232
PR1YR	–0.226	–0.185	–0.147

13-26. Using the factor beta estimates in the table shown here and the expected return estimates in Table 13.1, calculate the risk premium of General Electric stock (ticker: GE) using the FFC factor specification.

	Factor	GE
MKT	0.59	0.747
SMB	0.23	–0.478
HML	0.41	–0.232
PR1YR	0.77	–0.147

Risk Premium (monthly)	0.12%
RP annual	1.48%

1.47% Annual Risk Premium

13-27. **You are currently considering an investment in a project in the energy sector. The investment has the same riskiness as Exxon Mobil stock (ticker: XOM). Using the data in Table 13.1 and the table above, calculate the cost of capital using the FFC factor specification if the current risk-free rate is 6% per year.**

	Factor	XOM
MKT	0.59	0.243
SMB	0.23	0.125
HML	0.41	0.144
PR1YR	0.77	–0.185

Risk Premium (monthly)	0.09%
RP annual	1.07%
R_f	6.00%
Cost of capital	7.07%
Annual Cost of Capital of	7.07%

13-28. **You work for Microsoft Corporation (ticker: MSFT), and you are considering whether to develop a new software product. The risk of the investment is the same as the risk of the company. Using the data in Table 13.1 and in the table above, calculate the cost of capital using the FFC factor specification if the current risk-free rate is 5.5% per year.**

	Factor	MSFT
MKT	0.59	1.068
SMB	0.23	–0.374
HML	0.41	–0.814
PR1YR	0.77	–0.226

Risk Premium (monthly)	0.04%
RP annual	0.44%
R_f	5.50%
Cost of capital	5.94%
Annual cost of capital of	5.94%

Chapter 14
Capital Structure in a Perfect Market

14-1. Consider a project with free cash flows in one year of $130,000 or $180,000, with each outcome being equally likely. The initial investment required for the project is $100,000, and the project's cost of capital is 20%. The risk-free interest rate is 10%.

a. What is the NPV of this project?

b. Suppose that to raise the funds for the initial investment, the project is sold to investors as an all-equity firm. The equity holders will receive the cash flows of the project in one year. How much money can be raised in this way—that is, what is the initial market value of the unlevered equity?

c. Suppose the initial $100,000 is instead raised by borrowing at the risk-free interest rate. What are the cash flows of the levered equity, and what is its initial value according to MM?

a. $E\left[C(1)\right]=\frac{1}{2}(130{,}000+180{,}000)=155{,}000,$

$$NPV=\frac{155{,}000}{1.20}-100{,}000=129{,}167-100{,}000=\$29{,}167$$

b. Equity value $=PV\left(C(1)\right)=\dfrac{155{,}000}{1.20}=129{,}167$

c. Debt payments $=100{,}000$, equity receives 20,000 or 70,000.

Initial value, by MM, is $129{,}167-100{,}000=\$29{,}167$.

14-2. You are an entrepreneur starting a biotechnology firm. If your research is successful, the technology can be sold for $30 million. If your research is unsuccessful, it will be worth nothing. To fund your research, you need to raise $2 million. Investors are willing to provide you with $2 million in initial capital in exchange for 50% of the unlevered equity in the firm.

a. What is the total market value of the firm without leverage?

b. Suppose you borrow $1 million. According to MM, what fraction of the firm's equity will you need to sell to raise the additional $1 million you need?

c. What is the value of your share of the firm's equity in cases (a) and (b)?

a. Total value of equity $=2\times\$2\text{m}=\$4\text{m}$

b. MM says total value of firm is still $4 million. $1 million of debt implies total value of equity is $3 million. Therefore, 33% of equity must be sold to raise $1 million.

c. In (a), 50% × $4m = $2m. In (b), 2/3 × $3m = $2m. Thus, in a perfect market the choice of capital structure does not affect the value to the entrepreneur.

14-3. Acort Industries owns assets that will have an 80% probability of having a market value of $50 million in one year. There is a 20% chance that the assets will be worth only $20 million. The current risk-free rate is 5%, and Acort's assets have a cost of capital of 10%.

a. If Acort is unlevered, what is the current market value of its equity?

b. Suppose instead that Acort has debt with a face value of $20 million due in one year. According to MM, what is the value of Acort's equity in this case?

c. What is the expected return of Acort's equity without leverage? What is the expected return of Acort's equity with leverage?

d. What is the lowest possible realized return of Acort's equity with and without leverage?

a. $\text{E[Value in one year]} = 0.8(50) + 0.2(20) = 44$. $\text{E} = \dfrac{44}{1.10} = \$40\text{m}.$

b. $\text{D} = \dfrac{20}{1.05} = 19.048$. Therefore, $E = 40 - 19.048 = \$20.952\text{m}.$

c. Without leverage, $\text{r} = \dfrac{44}{40} - 1 = 10\%$, with leverage, $\text{r} = \dfrac{44-20}{20.952} - 1 = 14.55\%.$

d. Without leverage, $\text{r} = \dfrac{20}{40} - 1 = -50\%$, with leverage, $\text{r} = \dfrac{0}{20.952} - 1 = -100\%.$

14-4. Wolfrum Technology (WT) has no debt. Its assets will be worth $450 million in one year if the economy is strong, but only $200 million in one year if the economy is weak. Both events are equally likely. The market value today of its assets is $250 million.

a. What is the expected return of WT stock without leverage?

b. Suppose the risk-free interest rate is 5%. If WT borrows $100 million today at this rate and uses the proceeds to pay an immediate cash dividend, what will be the market value of its equity just after the dividend is paid, according to MM?

c. What is the expected return of MM stock after the dividend is paid in part (b)?

a. $(.5 \times 450 + .5 \times 200)/250 = 1.30 \Rightarrow 30\%$

b. $\text{E} + \text{D} = 250, \text{D} = 100 \Rightarrow \text{E} = 150$

c. $(.5 \times (450-105) + .5 \times (200-105))/150 = 1.4667 \Rightarrow 46.67\%$

14-5. Suppose there are no taxes. Firm ABC has no debt, and firm XYZ has debt of $5000 on which it pays interest of 10% each year. Both companies have identical projects that generate free cash flows of $800 or $1000 each year. After paying any interest on debt, both companies use all remaining free cash flows to pay dividends each year.

a. Fill in the table below showing the payments debt and equity holders of each firm will receive given each of the two possible levels of free cash flows.

	ABC		XYZ	
FCF	Debt Payments	Equity Dividends	Debt Payments	Equity Dividends
$ 800				
$1000				

b. Suppose you hold 10% of the equity of ABC. What is another portfolio you could hold that would provide the same cash flows?

c. **Suppose you hold 10% of the equity of XYZ. If you can borrow at 10%, what is an alternative strategy that would provide the same cash flows?**

a.

	ABC		XYZ	
FCF	**Debt Payments**	**Equity Dividends**	**Debt Payments**	**Equity Dividends**
$800	0	800	500	300
$1,000	0	1000	500	500

b. Unlevered Equity = Debt + Levered Equity. Buy 10% of XYZ debt and 10% of XYZ Equity, get 50 + (30,50) = (80,100)

c. Levered Equity = Unlevered Equity + Borrowing. Borrow $500, buy 10% of ABC, receive (80,100) – 50 = (30, 50)

14-6. Suppose Alpha Industries and Omega Technology have identical assets that generate identical cash flows. Alpha Industries is an all-equity firm, with 10 million shares outstanding that trade for a price of $22 per share. Omega Technology has 20 million shares outstanding as well as debt of $60 million.

a. **According to MM Proposition I, what is the stock price for Omega Technology?**

b. **Suppose Omega Technology stock currently trades for $11 per share. What arbitrage opportunity is available? What assumptions are necessary to exploit this opportunity?**

a. $V(\text{alpha}) = 10 \times 22 = 220\text{m} = V(\text{omega}) = D + E \Rightarrow E = 220 - 60 = 160\text{m} \Rightarrow p = \$8$ per share.

b. Omega is overpriced. Sell 20 Omega, buy 10 alpha, and borrow 60. Initial = 220 – 220 + 60 = 60. Assumes we can trade shares at current prices and that we can borrow at the same terms as Omega (or own Omega debt and can sell at same price).

14-7. Cisoft is a highly profitable technology firm that currently has $5 billion in cash. The firm has decided to use this cash to repurchase shares from investors, and it has already announced these plans to investors. Currently, Cisoft is an all-equity firm with 5 billion shares outstanding. These shares currently trade for $12 per share. Cisoft has issued no other securities except for stock options given to its employees. The current market value of these options is $8 billion.

a. **What is the market value of Cisoft's non-cash assets?**

b. **With perfect capital markets, what is the market value of Cisoft's equity after the share repurchase? What is the value per share?**

a. Assets = cash + non-cash, Liabilities = equity + options, Non-cash assets = equity + options – cash $= 12 \times 5 + 8 - 5 = 63$ billion.

b. Equity = 60 – 5 =55. Repurchase $\frac{5\text{b}}{12} = 0.417\text{b}$ shares $\Rightarrow$ 4.583 b shares remain.

Per share value $= \frac{55}{4.583} = \$12$.

14-8. Schwartz Industry is an industrial company with 100 million shares outstanding and a market capitalization (equity value) of $4 billion. It has $2 billion of debt outstanding. Management have decided to delever the firm by issuing new equity to repay all outstanding debt.

a. **How many new shares must the firm issue?**

b. **Suppose you are a shareholder holding 100 shares, and you disagree with this decision. Assuming a perfect capital market, describe what you can do to undo the effect of this decision.**

a. Share price = 4b/100m = $40, Issue 2b/40 = 50 million shares

b. You can undo the effect of the decision by borrowing to buy additional shares, in the same proportion as the firm's actions, thus relevering your own portfolio. In this case you should buy 50 new shares and borrow $2000.

14-9. Zetatron is an all-equity firm with 100 million shares outstanding, which are currently trading for $7.50 per share. A month ago, Zetatron announced it will change its capital structure by borrowing $100 million in short-term debt, borrowing $100 million in long-term debt, and issuing $100 million of preferred stock. The $300 million raised by these issues, plus another $50 million in cash that Zetatron already has, will be used to repurchase existing shares of stock. The transaction is scheduled to occur today. Assume perfect capital markets.

a. What is the market value balance sheet for Zetatron

i. Before this transaction?

ii. After the new securities are issued but before the share repurchase?

iii. After the share repurchase?

b. At the conclusion of this transaction, how many shares outstanding will Zetatron have, and what will the value of those shares be?

a. i. A = 50 cash + 700 non-cash

L = 750 equity

ii. A = 350 cash + 700 non-cash

L = 750 equity + 100 short-term debt + 100 long-term debt + 100 preferred stock

iii. A = 700 non-cash

L = 400 equity + 100 short-term debt + 100 long-term debt + 100 preferred stock

b. Repurchase $\frac{350}{7.50} = 46.67$ shares $\Rightarrow$ 53.33 remain. Value is $\frac{400}{53.33} = 7.50$.

14-10. Explain what is wrong with the following argument: "If a firm issues debt that is risk free, because there is no possibility of default, the risk of the firm's equity does not change. Therefore, risk-free debt allows the firm to get the benefit of a low cost of capital of debt without raising its cost of capital of equity."

Any leverage raises the equity cost of capital. In fact, risk-free leverage raises it the most (because it does not share any of the risk).

14-11. Consider the entrepreneur described in Section 14.1 (and referenced in Tables 14.1–14.3). Suppose she funds the project by borrowing $750 rather than $500.

a. According to MM Proposition I, what is the value of the equity? What are its cash flows if the economy is strong? What are its cash flows if the economy is weak?

b. What is the return of the equity in each case? What is its expected return?

c. What is the risk premium of equity in each case? What is the sensitivity of the levered equity return to systematic risk? How does its sensitivity compare to that of unlevered equity? How does its risk premium compare to that of unlevered equity?

d. What is the debt-equity ratio of the firm in this case?

e. What is the firm's WACC in this case?

a. E = 1000 – 750 = 250. CF = (1400,900) – 500 (1.05) = (612.5,112.5)

b. R_e = (145%, – 55%), E[Re] = 45%, Risk premium = 45% – 5% = 40%

c. Return sensitivity = 145% – (-55%) = 200%. This sensitivity is 4x the sensitivity of unlevered equity (50%). Its risk premium is also 4x that of unlevered equity (40% vs. 10%).

d. $\frac{750}{250} = 3\text{x}$

e. 25%(45%)+75%(5%) = 15%

14-12. Hardmon Enterprises is currently an all-equity firm with an expected return of 12%. It is considering a leveraged recapitalization in which it would borrow and repurchase existing shares.

a. Suppose Hardmon borrows to the point that its debt-equity ratio is 0.50. With this amount of debt, the debt cost of capital is 6%. What will the expected return of equity be after this transaction?

b. Suppose instead Hardmon borrows to the point that its debt-equity ratio is 1.50. With this amount of debt, Hardmon's debt will be much riskier. As a result, the debt cost of capital will be 8%. What will the expected return of equity be in this case?

c. A senior manager argues that it is in the best interest of the shareholders to choose the capital structure that leads to the highest expected return for the stock. How would you respond to this argument?

a. $r_e = r_u + d/e(r_u - r_d) = 12\% + 0.50(12\% - 6\%) = 15\%$

b. $r_e = 12\% + 1.50(12\% - 8\%) = 18\%$

c. Returns are higher because risk is higher—the return fairly compensates for the risk. There is no free lunch.

14-13. Suppose Microsoft has no debt and an equity cost of capital of 9.2%. The average debt-to-value ratio for the software industry is 13%. What would its cost of equity be if it took on the average amount of debt for its industry at a cost of debt of 6%?

At a cost of debt of 6%:

$$r_E = r_U + \frac{D}{E}(r_U - r_D)$$

$$\begin{aligned} r_E &= 0.092 + \frac{0.13}{0.87}(0.092 - 0.06) \\ &= 0.0968 \\ &= 9.68\%. \end{aligned}$$

14-14. Global Pistons (GP) has common stock with a market value of \$200 million and debt with a value of \$100 million. Investors expect a 15% return on the stock and a 6% return on the debt. Assume perfect capital markets.

a. Suppose GP issues \$100 million of new stock to buy back the debt. What is the expected return of the stock after this transaction?

b. Suppose instead GP issues \$50 million of new debt to repurchase stock.

i. If the risk of the debt does not change, what is the expected return of the stock after this transaction?

ii. If the risk of the debt increases, would the expected return of the stock be higher or lower than in part (i)?

a. $wacc = \frac{2(15\%)}{3} + \frac{6\%}{3} = 12\% = r_u$.

b. i. $r_e = r_u + d/e(r_u - r_d) = 12 + \frac{150(12-6)}{150} = 18\%$

ii. if r_d is higher, r_e is lower. The debt will share some of the risk.

14-15. Hubbard Industries is an all-equity firm whose shares have an expected return of 10%. Hubbard does a leveraged recapitalization, issuing debt and repurchasing stock, until its debt-equity ratio is 0.60. Due to the increased risk, shareholders now expect a return of 13%. Assuming there are no taxes and Hubbard's debt is risk free, what is the interest rate on the debt?

$$wacc = r_u = 10\% = \frac{1}{1.6}13\% + \frac{0.6}{1.6}x \Rightarrow 1.6(10) - 13 = 3 = 0.6x \Rightarrow x = 5\%$$

14-16. Hartford Mining has 50 million shares that are currently trading for \$4 per share and \$200 million worth of debt. The debt is risk free and has an interest rate of 5%, and the expected return of Hartford stock is 11%. Suppose a mining strike causes the price of Hartford stock to fall 25% to \$3 per share. The value of the risk-free debt is unchanged. Assuming there are no taxes and the risk (unlevered beta) of Hartford's assets is unchanged, what happens to Hartford's equity cost of capital?

$$r_u = wacc = \frac{1}{2}(11) + \frac{1}{2}(5) = 8\%. \; r_e = 8\% + \frac{200}{150}(8\% - 5\%) = 12\%$$

14-17. Mercer Corp. is an all equity firm with 10 million shares outstanding and \$100 million worth of debt outstanding. Its current share price is \$75. Mercer's equity cost of capital is 8.5%. Mercer has just announced that it will issue \$350 million worth of debt. It will use the proceeds from this debt to pay off its existing debt, and use the remaining \$250 million to pay an immediate dividend. Assume perfect capital markets.

a. Estimate Mercer's share price just after the recapitalization is announced, but before the transaction occurs.

b. Estimate Mercer's share price at the conclusion of the transaction. (*Hint*: use the market value balance sheet.)

c. Suppose Mercer's existing debt was risk-free with a 4.25% expected return, and its new debt is risky with a 5% expected return. Estimate Mercer's equity cost of capital after the transaction.

a. MM => no change, \$75

b. Initial enterprise value = 75 × 10 + 100 = 850 million

New debt = 350 million

E = 850 – 350 = 500

Share price = 500/10 = \$50

c. Ru = (750/850) × 8.5% + (100/850) × 4.25% = 8%

Re = 8% + 350/500(8% – 5%) = 10.1%

14-18. In June 2009, Apple Computer had no debt, total equity capitalization of \$128 billion, and a (equity) beta of 1.7 (as reported on Google Finance). Included in Apple's assets was \$25 billion in cash and risk-free securities. Assume that the risk-free rate of interest is 5% and the market risk premium is 4%.

a. What is Apple's enterprise value?

b. What is the beta of Apple's business assets?

c. What is Apple's WACC?

a. 128-25=103 million

b. Because the debt is risk free, $\beta_U = \frac{E}{E+D}\beta_E$

$$= \frac{128}{103}(1.7)$$
$$= 2.11$$

c. $r_{WACC} = r_f + \beta\left(E[R_{Mkt}] - r_f\right) = 5 + 2.11 \times 4 = 13.4\%$

alternatively

$$r_E = r_f + \beta_E\left(E[R_{Mkt}] - r_f\right) = 5 + 1.7 \times 4 = 11.8\%$$

$$r_{wacc} = \frac{E}{E+D} r_E + \frac{D}{E+D} r_D = \frac{\$128}{\$103}(11.8\%) - \frac{\$25}{\$103}(5\%) = 13.4\%$$

14-19. Indell stock has a current market value of \$120 million and a beta of 1.50. Indell currently has risk-free debt as well. The firm decides to change its capital structure by issuing \$30 million in additional risk-free debt, and then using this \$30 million plus another \$10 million in cash to repurchase stock. With perfect capital markets, what will be the beta of Indell stock after this transaction?

Indell increases its net debt by \$40 million (\$30 million in new debt + \$10 million in cash paid out). Therefore, the value of its equity decreases to 120 – 40 = \$80 million.

If the debt is risk-free:

$$\beta_e = \beta_u\left(1 + \frac{D}{E}\right) = \frac{\beta_u(E+D)}{E} = \beta_u \times \frac{EV}{E},$$

where D is net debt, and EV is enterprise value . The only change in the equation is the value of equity. Therefore

$$\beta_e^{'} = \beta_e \frac{E}{E'} = 1.50\frac{120}{80} = 2.25.$$

14-20. Yerba Industries is an all-equity firm whose stock has a beta of 1.2 and an expected return of 12.5%. Suppose it issues new risk-free debt with a 5% yield and repurchases 40% of its stock. Assume perfect capital markets.

a. What is the beta of Yerba stock after this transaction?

b. What is the expected return of Yerba stock after this transaction?

Suppose that prior to this transaction, Yerba expected earnings per share this coming year of \$1.50, with a forward P/E ratio (that is, the share price divided by the expected earnings for the coming year) of 14.

c. **What is Yerba's expected earnings per share after this transaction? Does this change benefit shareholders? Explain.**

d. **What is Yerba's forward P/E ratio after this transaction? Is this change in the P/E ratio reasonable? Explain.**

a. $\beta_e = \beta_u(1+d/e) = 1.2\left(1+\frac{40}{60}\right) = 2$

b. $r_e = r_f + b\left(r_m - r_f\right) \Rightarrow r_m - r_f = \frac{12.5-5}{1.2} = 6.25 \Rightarrow r_e = 5 + 2(6.25) = 17.5\%$ from the CAPM, or

$r_e = r_u + d/e\left(r_u - r_d\right) = 12.5 + \frac{40(12.5-5)}{60} = 17.5$

c. $p = 14(1.50) = \$21$. Borrow 40%(21) = 8.4, interest = 5%(8.4) = 0.42. Earnings = 1.50 – 0.42 = 1.08, per share $= \frac{1.08}{0.60} = 1.80$.

No benefit; risk is higher. The stock price does not change.

d. $PE = \frac{21}{1.80} = 11.67$. It falls due to higher risk.

14-21. You are CEO of a high-growth technology firm. You plan to raise \$180 million to fund an expansion by issuing either new shares or new debt. With the expansion, you expect earnings next year of \$24 million. The firm currently has 10 million shares outstanding, with a price of \$90 per share. Assume perfect capital markets.

a. **If you raise the \$180 million by selling new shares, what will the forecast for next year's earnings per share be?**

b. **If you raise the \$180 million by issuing new debt with an interest rate of 5%, what will the forecast for next year's earnings per share be?**

c. **What is the firm's forward P/E ratio (that is, the share price divided by the expected earnings for the coming year) if it issues equity? What is the firm's forward P/E ratio if it issues debt? How can you explain the difference?**

a. Issue $\frac{180}{90} = 2$ million new shares $\Rightarrow$ 12 million shares outstanding.

New EPS $= \frac{24}{12} = \$2.00$ per share.

b. Interest on new debt $= 180 \times 5\% = \$9$ million. The interest expense will reduce earnings to 24 – 9 = \$15 million. With 10 million shares outstanding, $EPS = \frac{15}{10} = \$1.50$ per share.

c. By MM, share price is \$90 in either case. PE ratio with equity issue is $\frac{90}{2} = 45$.

PE ratio with debt is $\frac{\$90}{1.50} = 60$.

The higher PE ratio is justified because with leverage, EPS will grow at a faster rate.

14-22. Zelnor, Inc., is an all-equity firm with 100 million shares outstanding currently trading for \$8.50 per share. Suppose Zelnor decides to grant a total of 10 million new shares to employees as part of a new compensation plan. The firm argues that this new compensation plan will motivate employees and is a better strategy than giving salary bonuses because it will not cost the firm anything.

a. If the new compensation plan has no effect on the value of Zelnor's assets, what will be the share price of the stock once this plan is implemented?

b. What is the cost of this plan for Zelnor's investors? Why is issuing equity costly in this case?

a. Assets = 850m. New shares = 110. $\Rightarrow$ price $= \frac{850}{110} = \$7.73$

b. Cost = 100(8.50 – 7.73) = 77 m = 10(7.73). Issuing equity at below market price is costly.

Chapter 15
Debt and Taxes

15-1. Pelamed Pharmaceuticals has EBIT of $325 million in 2006. In addition, Pelamed has interest expenses of $125 million and a corporate tax rate of 40%.

a. What is Pelamed's 2006 net income?

b. What is the total of Pelamed's 2006 net income and interest payments?

c. If Pelamed had no interest expenses, what would its 2006 net income be? How does it compare to your answer in part (b)?

d. What is the amount of Pelamed's interest tax shield in 2006?

a. $\text{Net Income} = \text{EBIT} - \text{Interest} - \text{Taxes} = (325 - 125) \times (1 - 0.40) = \$120$ million.

b. Net income + Interest = 120 + 125 = $245 million

c. $\text{Net income} = \text{EBIT} - \text{Taxes} = 325 \times (1 - 0.40) = \$195$ million. This is $245 - 195 = \$50$ million lower than part (b).

d. Interest tax shield $= 125 \times 40\% = \$50$ million

15-2. Grommit Engineering expects to have net income next year of $20.75 million and free cash flow of $22.15 million. Grommit's marginal corporate tax rate is 35%.

a. If Grommit increases leverage so that its interest expense rises by $1 million, how will its net income change?

b. For the same increase in interest expense, how will free cash flow change?

a. Net income will fall by the after-tax interest expense to $\$20.750 - 1 \times (1 - 0.35) = \$20.10$ million.

b. Free cash flow is not affected by interest expenses.

15-3. Suppose the corporate tax rate is 40%. Consider a firm that earns $1000 before interest and taxes each year with no risk. The firm's capital expenditures equal its depreciation expenses each year, and it will have no changes to its net working capital. The risk-free interest rate is 5%.

a. Suppose the firm has no debt and pays out its net income as a dividend each year. What is the value of the firm's equity?

b. Suppose instead the firm makes interest payments of $500 per year. What is the value of equity? What is the value of debt?

c. What is the difference between the total value of the firm with leverage and without leverage?

d. The difference in part (c) is equal to what percentage of the value of the debt?

a. Net income $= 1000 \times (1 - 40\%) = \$600$. Thus, equity holders receive dividends of \$600 per year with no risk. $E = \frac{600}{5\%} = \$12,000$

b. Net income $= (1000 - 500) \times (1 - 0.40) = \$300 \Rightarrow E = \frac{300}{5\%} = \$6000$. Debt holders receive interest of \$500 per year $\Rightarrow$ D = \$10,000

c. With leverage = 6,000 + 10,000 = \$16,000

Without leverage = \$12,000

Difference = 16,000 – 12,000 = \$4000

d. $\frac{4,000}{10,000} = 40\% =$ corporate tax rate

15-4. Braxton Enterprises currently has debt outstanding of \$35 million and an interest rate of 8%. Braxton plans to reduce its debt by repaying \$7 million in principal at the end of each year for the next five years. If Braxton's marginal corporate tax rate is 40%, what is the interest tax shield from Braxton's debt in each of the next five years?

Year	0	1	2	3	4	5
Debt	35	28	21	14	7	0
Interest		2.8	2.24	1.68	1.12	0.56
Tax Shield		1.12	0.896	0.672	0.448	0.224

15-5. Your firm currently has \$100 million in debt outstanding with a 10% interest rate. The terms of the loan require the firm to repay \$25 million of the balance each year. Suppose that the marginal corporate tax rate is 40%, and that the interest tax shields have the same risk as the loan. What is the present value of the interest tax shields from this debt?

Year	0	1	2	3	4	5
Debt	100	75	50	25	0	0
Interest		10	7.5	5	2.5	0
Tax Shield		4	3	2	1	0
PV	\$8.30					

15-6. Arnell Industries has just issued \$10 million in debt (at par). The firm will pay interest only on this debt. Arnell's marginal tax rate is expected to be 35% for the foreseeable future.

a. Suppose Arnell pays interest of 6% per year on its debt. What is its annual interest tax shield?

b. What is the present value of the interest tax shield, assuming its risk is the same as the loan?

c. Suppose instead that the interest rate on the debt is 5%. What is the present value of the interest tax shield in this case?

a. Interest tax shield $= \$10 \times 6\% \times 35\% = \$0.21$ million

b. PV(Interest tax shield) $= \frac{\$0.21}{0.06} = \$3.5$ million

c. Interest tax shield = \$10 × 5% × 35% = \$0.175 million. $PV = \dfrac{\$0.175}{0.05} = \$3.5$ million.

15-7. Ten years have passed since Arnell issued \$10 million in perpetual interest only debt with a 6% annual coupon, as in Problem 6. Tax rates have remained the same at 35% but interest rates have dropped so Arnell's current cost of debt capital is 4%.

a. What is Arnell's annual interest tax shield?

b. What is the present value of the interest tax shield today?

a. Solution Interest tax shield $= \$10 \times 6\% \times 35\% = \$0.21$ million

b. Solution PV(Interest tax shield) $= \dfrac{\$0.21}{0.04} = \$5.25$ million.

Alternatively, new market value of debt is D = (10 ×.06)/.04 = \$15 million. Tc × D = 35% × 15 = \$5.25 million.

15-8. Bay Transport Systems (BTS) currently has \$30 million in debt outstanding. In addition to 6.5% interest, it plans to repay 5% of the remaining balance each year. If BTS has a marginal corporate tax rate of 40%, and if the interest tax shields have the same risk as the loan, what is the present value of the interest tax shield from the debt?

Interest tax shield in year 1 = \$30 × 6.5% × 40% = \$0.78 million. As the outstanding balance declines, so will the interest tax shield. Therefore, we can value the interest tax shield as a growing perpetuity with a growth rate of g = -5% and r = 6.5%:

$$PV = \frac{\$0.78}{6.5\% + 5\%} = \$6.78 \text{ million}$$

15-9. Safeco Inc. has no debt, and maintains a policy of holding \$10 million in excess cash reserves, invested in risk-free Treasury securities. If Safeco pays a corporate tax rate of 35%, what is the cost of permanently maintaining this \$10 million reserve? (*Hint*: what is the present value of the additional taxes that Safeco will pay?)

D = -\$10 million (negative debt)

So PV(Interest tax shield) = Tc × D = -\$3.5 million.

This is the present value of the future taxes Safeco will pay on the interest earned on its reserves.

15-10. Rogot Instruments makes fine Violins and Cellos. It has \$1 million in debt outstanding, equity valued at \$2 million, and pays corporate income tax at rate 35%. Its cost of equity is 12% and its cost of debt is 7%.

a. What is Rogot's pretax WACC?

b. What is Rogot's (effective after-tax) WACC?

a. $r_{wacc} = \dfrac{E}{E+D} r_E + \dfrac{D}{E+D} r_D(1-\tau_c) = \dfrac{2}{3}12 + \dfrac{1}{3}7 = 10.33\%$

b. $r_{wacc} = \dfrac{E}{E+D} r_E + \dfrac{D}{E+D} r_D(1-\tau_c) = \dfrac{2}{3}12 + \dfrac{1}{3}7(.65) = 9.52\%$

15-11. Rumolt Motors has 30 million shares outstanding with a price of $15 per share. In addition, Rumolt has issued bonds with a total current market value of $150 million. Suppose Rumolt's equity cost of capital is 10%, and its debt cost of capital is 5%.

a. What is Rumolt's pretax weighted average cost of capital?

b. If Rumolt's corporate tax rate is 35%, what is its after-tax weighted average cost of capital?

a. $E = \$15 \times 30 = \$450$ million. $D = \$150$ million.

$$\text{Pretax WACC} = \frac{450}{600}10\% + \frac{150}{600}5\% = 8.75\%$$

b. $$\text{WACC} = \frac{450}{600}10\% + \frac{150}{600}5\%(1-35\%) = 8.3125\%$$

15-12. Summit Builders has a market debt-equity ratio of 0.65 and a corporate tax rate of 40%, and it pays 7% interest on its debt. The interest tax shield from its debt lowers Summit's WACC by what amount?

$$\frac{D}{E+D} = \frac{0.65}{1.65} = 0.394\,.$$

Therefore, WACC = Pretax WACC – .394(7%)(.40) = Pretax WACC – 1.10%

So, it lowers it by 1.1%.

15-13. NatNah, a builder of acoustic accessories, has no debt and an equity cost of capital of 15%. Suppose NatNah decides to increase its leverage and maintain a market debt-to-value ratio of 0.5. Suppose its debt cost of capital is 9% and its corporate tax rate is 35%. If NatNah's pretax WACC remains constant, what will its (effective after-tax) WACC be with the increase in leverage?

$$\text{Pretax Wacc} - \frac{D}{E+D} r_D \tau = 15\% - 0.5 \times 0.09 \times 0.35 = 13.425\%$$

15-14. Restex maintains a debt-equity ratio of 0.85, and has an equity cost of capital of 12% and a debt cost of capital of 7%. Restex's corporate tax rate is 40%, and its market capitalization is $220 million.

a. If Restex's free cash flow is expected to be $10 million in one year, what constant expected future growth rate is consistent with the firm's current market value?

b. Estimate the value of Restex's interest tax shield.

a. $$WACC = \frac{1}{1.85}12\% + \frac{0.85}{1.85}7\%(1-0.40) = 8.42\%$$

$$V^L = E + D = 220 \times 1.85 = 407 = \frac{FCF}{WACC - g} = \frac{10}{0.0842 - g}$$

$$g = 0.0842 - \frac{10}{407} = 5.96\%$$

b. $$\text{pretax WACC} = \frac{1}{1.85}12\% + \frac{0.85}{1.85}7\% = 9.70\%$$

$$V^U = \frac{\text{FCF}}{\text{pretax WACC} - g} = \frac{10}{0.0970 - 0.0596} = \$267 \text{ million}$$

$$\text{PV}(\text{Interest Tax Shield}) = 407 - 267 = \$140 \text{ million}$$

15-15. Acme Storage has a market capitalization of $100 million and debt outstanding of $40 million. Acme plans to maintain this same debt-equity ratio in the future. The firm pays an interest rate of 7.5% on its debt and has a corporate tax rate of 35%.

a. If Acme's free cash flow is expected to be $7 million next year and is expected to grow at a rate of 3% per year, what is Acme's WACC?

b. What is the value of Acme's interest tax shield?

a. $V^L = E + D = 140 = \dfrac{FCF}{WACC - g} = \dfrac{7}{WACC - 3\%}$. Therefore WACC = 8%.

b. $\text{Pre-tax WACC} = \text{WACC} + \dfrac{D}{E+D} r_D \tau_C = 8\% + \dfrac{40}{140}(7.5\%)(0.35) = 8.75\%$

$$V^U = \frac{FCF}{\text{pretax WACC} - g} = \frac{7}{0.0875 - 0.03} = \$122 \text{ million}$$

$$\text{PV}(\text{Interest Tax Shield}) = V^L - V^U = 140 - 122 = \$18 \text{ million}$$

15-16. Milton Industries expects free cash flow of $5 million each year. Milton's corporate tax rate is 35%, and its unlevered cost of capital is 15%. The firm also has outstanding debt of $19.05 million, and it expects to maintain this level of debt permanently.

a. What is the value of Milton Industries without leverage?

b. What is the value of Milton Industries with leverage?

a. $V^U = \dfrac{5}{0.15} = \$33.33 \text{ million}$

b. $V^L = V^U + \tau_C D = 33.33 + 0.35 \times 19.05 = \$40 \text{ million}$

15-17. Suppose Microsoft has 8.75 billion shares outstanding and pays a marginal corporate tax rate of 35%. If Microsoft announces that it will payout $50 billion in cash to investors through a combination of a special dividend and a share repurchase, and if investors had previously assumed Microsoft would retain this excess cash permanently, by how much will Microsoft's share price change upon the announcement?

Reducing cash is equivalent to increasing leverage by $50 billion. PV of tax savings = 35% × 50 = $17.5 billion, or 17.5/ 8.75 = $2.00 per share price increase.

15-18. Kurz Manufacturing is currently an all-equity firm with 20 million shares outstanding and a stock price of $7.50 per share. Although investors currently expect Kurz to remain an all-equity firm, Kurz plans to announce that it will borrow $50 million and use the funds to repurchase shares. Kurz will pay interest only on this debt, and it has no further plans to increase or decrease the amount of debt. Kurz is subject to a 40% corporate tax rate.

a. What is the market value of Kurz's existing assets before the announcement?

b. What is the market value of Kurz's assets (including any tax shields) just after the debt is issued, but before the shares are repurchased?

c. What is Kurz's share price just before the share repurchase? How many shares will Kurz repurchase?

d. What are Kurz's market value balance sheet and share price after the share repurchase?

a. Assets = Equity = $7.50 × 20 = $150 million

b. Assets = 150 (existing) + 50 (cash) + 40% × 50 (tax shield) = $220 million

c. $E = \text{Assets} - \text{Debt} = 220 - 50 = \$170$ million. Share price $= \dfrac{\$170 \text{ million}}{20} = \$8.50$.

Kurz will repurchase $\dfrac{50}{8.50} = 5.882$ million shares.

d. Assets = 150 (existing) + 40% × 50 (tax shield) = \$170 million

Debt = \$50 million

E = A – D = 170 – 50 = \$120 million

$\text{Share price} = \dfrac{\$120}{20 - 5.882} = \$8.50/\text{share}$.

15-19. Rally, Inc., is an all-equity firm with assets worth \$25 billion and 10 billion shares outstanding. Rally plans to borrow \$10 billion and use these funds to repurchase shares. The firm's corporate tax rate is 35%, and Rally plans to keep its outstanding debt equal to \$10 billion permanently.

a. Without the increase in leverage, what would Rally's share price be?

b. Suppose Rally offers \$2.75 per share to repurchase its shares. Would shareholders sell for this price?

c. Suppose Rally offers \$3.00 per share, and shareholders tender their shares at this price. What will Rally's share price be after the repurchase?

d. What is the lowest price Rally can offer and have shareholders tender their shares? What will its stock price be after the share repurchase in that case?

a. Share price $= \dfrac{25}{10} = \$2.50$ per share

b. Just before the share repurchase:

$Assets = 25(\text{existing}) + 10(\text{cash}) + 35\% \times 10(\text{tax shield}) = \$38.5 \text{ billion}$

$E = 38.5 - 10 = 28.5 \Rightarrow \text{share price} = \dfrac{28.5}{10} = \$2.85/\text{share}.$

Therefore, shareholders will not sell for \$2.75 per share.

c. Assets = 25 (existing) + 35% × 10 (tax shield) = \$28.5 billion

E = 28.5 – 10 = 18.5 billion

$\text{Shares} = 10 - \dfrac{10}{3} = 6.667$ billion. Share price $= \dfrac{18.5}{6.667} = \$2.775$ share.

d. From (b), fair value of the shares prior to repurchase is \$2.85. At this price, Rally will have $10 - \dfrac{10}{2.85} = 6.49$ million shares outstanding, which will be worth $\dfrac{18.5}{6.49} = \$2.85$ after the repurchase. Therefore, shares will be willing to sell at this price.

15-20. Suppose the corporate tax rate is 40%, and investors pay a tax rate of 15% on income from dividends or capital gains and a tax rate of 33.3% on interest income. Your firm decides to add debt so it will pay an additional \$15 million in interest each year. It will pay this interest expense by cutting its dividend.

a. How much will debt holders receive after paying taxes on the interest they earn?

b. By how much will the firm need to cut its dividend each year to pay this interest expense?

c. By how much will this cut in the dividend reduce equity holders' annual after-tax income?

d. How much less will the government receive in total tax revenues each year?

e. What is the effective tax advantage of debt τ^*?

a. $15 × (1 – .333) = $10 million each year

b. Given a corporate tax rate of 40%, an interest expense of $15 million per year reduces net income by 15(1 – .4) = $9 million after corporate taxes.

c. $9 million dividend cut ⇒ $9 × (1 – .15) = $7.65 million per year.

d. Interest taxes = .333 × 15 = $5 million

Less corporate taxes = .40 × 15 = $6 million

Less dividend taxes = .15 × 9 = $1.35 million

⇒ Govt tax revenues change by 5 – 6 – 1.35 = $2.35 million

(Note this equals (a) – (c)).

e. $$\tau^* = 1 - \frac{(1-0.40)(1-0.15)}{1-0.333} = 23.5\%$$

15-21. Apple Corporation had no debt on its balance sheet in 2008, but paid $2 billion in taxes. Suppose Apple were to issue sufficient debt to reduce its taxes by $1 billion per year permanently. Assume Apple's marginal corporate tax rate is 35% and its borrowing cost is 7.5%.

a. If Apple's investors do not pay personal taxes (because they hold their Apple stock in tax-free retirement accounts), how much value would be created (what is the value of the tax shield)?

b. How does your answer change if instead you assume that Apple's investors pay a 15% tax rate on income from equity and a 35% tax rate on interest income?

a. $1 billion / 7.5% = $13.33 billion.

b. To reduce taxes by $1 billion, Apple will need to make interest payments of 1/.35 = $2.857 billion, or issue 2.857/.075 = $38.1 billion in debt.

T × = 1 – (1 – tc)(1 – te)/(1 – ti) = 1 – (.65)(.85)/.65 = 15%

T × D = 15% × $38.1 = $5.71 billion

15-22. Markum Enterprises is considering permanently adding $100 million of debt to its capital structure. Markum's corporate tax rate is 35%.

a. Absent personal taxes, what is the value of the interest tax shield from the new debt?

b. If investors pay a tax rate of 40% on interest income, and a tax rate of 20% on income from dividends and capital gains, what is the value of the interest tax shield from the new debt?

a. PV = τ_C D = 35% × 100 = $35 million.

b. $$\tau^* = 1 - \frac{(1-0.35)(1-0.20)}{1-0.40} = 13.33\%$$

PV = τ_C D = 13.33% × 100 = $13.33 million

15-23. Garnet Corporation is considering issuing risk-free debt or risk-free preferred stock. The tax rate on interest income is 35%, and the tax rate on dividends or capital gains from preferred

stock is 15%. However, the dividends on preferred stock are not deductible for corporate tax purposes, and the corporate tax rate is 40%.

a. **If the risk-free interest rate for debt is 6%, what is cost of capital for risk-free preferred stock?**

b. **What is the after-tax debt cost of capital for the firm? Which security is cheaper for the firm?**

c. **Show that the after-tax debt cost of capital is equal to the preferred stock cost of capital multiplied by (1 − τ^*).**

a. Investors receive 6% × (1 – .35) = 3.9% after-tax from risk-free debt. They must earn the same after-tax return from risk-free preferred stock. Therefore, the cost of capital for preferred stock is $\frac{3.9\%}{1-0.15\%} = 4.59\%$.

b. After-tax debt cost of capital = 6% × (1 – .40) = 3.60% is cheaper than the 4.59% cost of capital for preferred stock.

c. $\tau^* = 1 - \frac{(1-0.40)(1-0.15)}{1-0.35} = 21.54\%$

4.59% × (1 – .2154) = 3.60%

15-24. Suppose the tax rate on interest income is 35%, and the average tax rate on capital gains and dividend income is 10%. How high must the marginal corporate tax rate be for debt to offer a tax advantage?

$\tau^* = 1 - \frac{(1-\tau_C)(1-\tau_e)}{1-\tau_i} > 0$ if and only if $1-\tau_C < \frac{1-\tau_i}{1-\tau_e}$ or equivalently:

$\tau_C > 1 - \frac{1-\tau_i}{1-\tau_e} = 1 - \frac{0.65}{0.90} = 27.8\%$.

Thus, there is a tax advantage of debt as long as the marginal corporate tax rate is above 27.8%.

15-25. With its current leverage, Impi Corporation will have net income next year of $4.5 million. If Impi's corporate tax rate is 35% and it pays 8% interest on its debt, how much additional debt can Impi issue this year and still receive the benefit of the interest tax shield next year?

Net income of \$4.5 million $\Rightarrow \frac{4.5}{1-0.35} = \$6.923$ million in taxable income.

Therefore, Arundel can increase its interest expenses by $6.923 million, which corresponds to debt of:

$\frac{6.923}{0.08} = \$86.5$ million.

15-26. Colt Systems will have EBIT this coming year of $15 million. It will also spend $6 million on total capital expenditures and increases in net working capital, and have $3 million in depreciation expenses. Colt is currently an all-equity firm with a corporate tax rate of 35% and a cost of capital of 10%.

a. **If Colt is expected to grow by 8.5% per year, what is the market value of its equity today?**

b. **If the interest rate on its debt is 8%, how much can Colt borrow now and still have nonnegative net income this coming year?**

c. **Is there a tax incentive for Colt to choose a debt-to-value ratio that exceeds 50%? Explain.**

a. $FCF = EBIT \times (1-\tau) + Dep - Capex - \Delta NWC = 15 \times (1-0.35) + 3 - 6 = 6.75$

$E = \dfrac{6.75}{10\% - 8.5\%} = \$450$ million

b. Interest expense of \$15 million ⇒ debt of $\dfrac{15}{0.08} = \$187.5$ million.

c. No. The most they should borrow is 187.5 million; there is no interest tax shield from borrowing more.

15-27. PMF, Inc., is equally likely to have EBIT this coming year of \$10 million, \$15 million, or \$20 million. Its corporate tax rate is 35%, and investors pay a 15% tax rate on income from equity and a 35% tax rate on interest income.

a. What is the effective tax advantage of debt if PMF has interest expenses of \$8 million this coming year?

b. What is the effective tax advantage of debt for interest expenses in excess of \$20 million? (Ignore carryforwards.)

c. What is the expected effective tax advantage of debt for interest expenses between \$10 million and \$15 million? (Ignore carryforwards.)

d. What level of interest expense provides PMF with the greatest tax benefit?

a. $\tau^* = 1 - \dfrac{(1-\tau_C)(1-\tau_e)}{1-\tau_i} = 1 - \dfrac{(1-0.35)(1-0.15)}{1-0.35} = 15\%$

b. For interest expenses over \$20 million, net income is negative so $\tau_C = 0$.

Therefore, $\tau^* = 1 - \dfrac{(1-\tau_C)(1-\tau_e)}{1-\tau_i} = 1 - \dfrac{(1-0)(1-0.15)}{1-0.35} = -31\%$

c. For interest expenses between \$10 million and \$15 million, there is a $\frac{2}{3}$ chance that net income will be positive. Therefore, the expected corporate tax savings is $\frac{2}{3} \times 35\% = 23.3\%$. Thus,

$\tau^* = 1 - \dfrac{(1-\tau_C)(1-\tau_e)}{1-\tau_i} = 1 - \dfrac{(1-0.23)(1-0.15)}{1-0.35} = -0.3\%$.

d. There is a tax advantage up to an interest expense of \$10 million.

Chapter 16

Financial Distress, Managerial Incentives, and Information

16-1. **Gladstone Corporation is about to launch a new product. Depending on the success of the new product, Gladstone may have one of four values next year: \$150 million, \$135 million, \$95 million, and \$80 million. These outcomes are all equally likely, and this risk is diversifiable. Gladstone will not make any payouts to investors during the year. Suppose the risk-free interest rate is 5% and assume perfect capital markets.**

a. What is the initial value of Gladstone's equity without leverage?

Now suppose Gladstone has zero-coupon debt with a \$100 million face value due next year.

b. What is the initial value of Gladstone's debt?

c. What is the yield-to-maturity of the debt? What is its expected return?

d. What is the initial value of Gladstone's equity? What is Gladstone's total value with leverage?

a. $0.25 \times \dfrac{150+135+95+80}{1.05} = \$109.52 \text{ million}$

b. $0.25 \times \dfrac{100+100+95+80}{1.05} = \$89.28 \text{ million}$

c. $\text{YTM} = \dfrac{100}{89.29} - 1 = 12\%$

expected return = 5%

d. equity $= 0.25 \times \dfrac{50+35+0+0}{1.05} = \$20.24$ million total value = 89.28 +20.24 = \$109.52 million

16-2. **Baruk Industries has no cash and a debt obligation of \$36 million that is now due. The market value of Baruk's assets is \$81 million, and the firm has no other liabilities. Assume perfect capital markets.**

a. Suppose Baruk has 10 million shares outstanding. What is Baruk's current share price?

b. How many new shares must Baruk issue to raise the capital needed to pay its debt obligation?

c. After repaying the debt, what will Baruk's share price be?

a. $\dfrac{81-36}{10} = \$4.5 \,/\, \text{share}$

b. $\frac{36}{4.5} = 8$ million shares

c. $\frac{81}{18} = \$4.5 / \text{share}$

16-3. When a firm defaults on its debt, debt holders often receive less than 50% of the amount they are owed. Is the difference between the amount debt holders are owed and the amount they receive a *cost* of bankruptcy?

No. Some of these losses are due to declines in the value of the assets that would have occurred whether or not the firm defaulted. Only the incremental losses that arise from the bankruptcy process are bankruptcy costs.

16-4. Which type of firm is more likely to experience a loss of customers in the event of financial distress:

a. Campbell Soup Company or Intuit, Inc. (a maker of accounting software)?

b. Allstate Corporation (an insurance company) or Reebok International (a footwear and clothing firm)?

a. Intuit Inc.—its customers will care about their ability to receive upgrades to their software.

b. Allstate Corporation—its customers rely on the firm being able to pay future claims.

16-5. Which type of asset is more likely to be liquidated for close to its full market value in the event of financial distress:

a. An office building or a brand name?

b. Product inventory or raw materials?

c. Patent rights or engineering "know-how"?

a. Office building—there are many alternate users who would be likely to value the property similarly.

b. Raw materials—they are easier to reuse.

c. Patent rights—they would be easier to sell to another firm.

16-6. Suppose Tefco Corp. has a value of $100 million if it continues to operate, but has outstanding debt of $120 million that is now due. If the firm declares bankruptcy, bankruptcy costs will equal $20 million, and the remaining $80 million will go to creditors. Instead of declaring bankruptcy, management proposes to exchange the firm's debt for a fraction of its equity in a workout. What is the minimum fraction of the firm's equity that management would need to offer to creditors for the workout to be successful?

Creditors receive 80 million in bankruptcy, so they need to receive at least this much. Therefore, Tefco could offer its creditors 80% of the firm in a workout.

16-7. You have received two job offers. Firm A offers to pay you $85,000 per year for two years. Firm B offers to pay you $90,000 for two years. Both jobs are equivalent. Suppose that firm A's contract is certain, but that firm B has a 50% chance of going bankrupt at the end of the year. In that event, it will cancel your contract and pay you the lowest amount possible for you to not quit. If you did quit, you expect you could find a new job paying $85,000 per year, but you would be unemployed for 3 months while you search for it.

a. Say you took the job at firm B, what is the least firm B can pay you next year in order to match what you would earn if you quit?

b. Given your answer to part (b), and assuming your cost of capital is 5%, which offer pays you a higher present value of your expected wage?

c. Based on this example, discuss one reason why firms with a higher risk of bankruptcy may need to offer higher wages to attract employees.

a. If you quit, you would earn \$85k for ¾ of a year, or \$63.75k.

b. A = 85 + 85/1.05 = \$165.95k

B = 90 + ½ (90 + 63.75)/1.05 = \$163.21 k

c. The risk of bankruptcy decreases the expected wage an employee is set to receive, therefore the firm must pay a higher wage to incentivize the employee not to quit

16-8. As in Problem 1, Gladstone Corporation is about to launch a new product. Depending on the success of the new product, Gladstone may have one of four values next year: \$150 million, \$135 million, \$95 million, and \$80 million. These outcomes are all equally likely, and this risk is diversifiable. Suppose the risk-free interest rate is 5% and that, in the event of default, 25% of the value of Gladstone's assets will be lost to bankruptcy costs. (Ignore all other market imperfections, such as taxes.)

a. What is the initial value of Gladstone's equity without leverage?

Now suppose Gladstone has zero-coupon debt with a \$100 million face value due next year.

b. What is the initial value of Gladstone's debt?

c. What is the yield-to-maturity of the debt? What is its expected return?

d. What is the initial value of Gladstone's equity? What is Gladstone's total value with leverage?

Suppose Gladstone has 10 million shares outstanding and no debt at the start of the year.

e. If Gladstone does not issue debt, what is its share price?

f. If Gladstone issues debt of \$100 million due next year and uses the proceeds to repurchase shares, what will its share price be? Why does your answer differ from that in part (e)?

a. $0.25\times\frac{150+135+95+80}{1.05}=\$109.52\text{ million}$

b. $0.25\times\frac{100+100+95\times0.75+80\times0.75}{1.05}=\$78.87\text{ million}$

c. $\text{YTM}=\frac{100}{78.87}-1=26.79\%$

expected return = 5%

d. $\text{equity}=0.25\times\frac{50+35+0+0}{1.05}=\$20.24\text{ million total value}$

$=0.25\times\frac{150+135+95\times0.75+80\times0.75}{1.05}=\$99.11\text{ million}$

(or 78.87 + 20.24 = \$99.11 million)

e. $\frac{109.52}{10}=\$10.95\,/\,\text{share}$

f. $\frac{99.11}{10} = \$9.91/\text{share}$ Bankruptcy cost lowers share price.

Note that Gladstone will raise $78.87 million from the debt, and repurchase $\frac{78.87}{9.91} = 7.96 \text{ million shares}$. Its equity will be worth $20.24 million, for a share price of $\frac{20.24}{10-7.96} = \$9.91$ after the transaction is completed.

16-9. Kohwe Corporation plans to issue equity to raise $50 million to finance a new investment. After making the investment, Kohwe expects to earn free cash flows of $10 million each year. Kohwe currently has 5 million shares outstanding, and it has no other assets or opportunities. Suppose the appropriate discount rate for Kohwe's future free cash flows is 8%, and the only capital market imperfections are corporate taxes and financial distress costs.

a. What is the NPV of Kohwe's investment?

b. What is Kohwe's share price today?

Suppose Kohwe borrows the $50 million instead. The firm will pay interest only on this loan each year, and it will maintain an outstanding balance of $50 million on the loan. Suppose that Kohwe's corporate tax rate is 40%, and expected free cash flows are still $10 million each year.

c. What is Kohwe's share price today if the investment is financed with debt?

Now suppose that with leverage, Kohwe's expected free cash flows will decline to $9 million per year due to reduced sales and other financial distress costs. Assume that the appropriate discount rate for Kohwe's future free cash flows is still 8%.

d. What is Kohwe's share price today given the financial distress costs of leverage?

a. $\frac{10}{0.08} - 50 = \$75 \text{ million}$

b. $\frac{75}{5} = \$15/\text{share}$

c. $\frac{75 + 0.4 \times 50}{5} = \$19/\text{share}$

d. $\frac{\frac{9}{0.08} - 50 + 0.4 \times 50}{5} = \$16/\text{share}$

16-10. You work for a large car manufacturer that is currently financially healthy. Your manager feels that the firm should take on more debt because it can thereby reduce the expense of car warranties. To quote your manager, "If we go bankrupt, we don't have to service the warranties. We therefore have lower bankruptcy costs than most corporations, so we should use more debt." Is he right?

No, not necessarily. He has neglected the effect on customers. Customers will be less willing to buy the company's cars because the warranty is not as solid as the company's competitors. Since the warranty is presumably offered to entice customers to buy more cars, the overall effect could easily be to reduce value.

16-11. Apple Computer has no debt. As Problem 21 in Chapter 15 makes clear, by issuing debt Apple can generate a very large tax shield potentially worth over $10 billion. Given Apple's success, one would be hard pressed to argue that Apple's management are naïve and unaware of this huge potential to create value. A more likely explanation is that issuing debt would entail other costs. What might these costs be?

Apple has volatile cash flows, a high beta (around 2), and is a human-capital intensive firm. All of these things imply that Apple has relatively high distress costs.

16-12. Hawar International is a shipping firm with a current share price of $5.50 and 10 million shares outstanding. Suppose Hawar announces plans to lower its corporate taxes by borrowing $20 million and repurchasing shares.

a. With perfect capital markets, what will the share price be after this announcement?

Suppose that Hawar pays a corporate tax rate of 30%, and that shareholders expect the change in debt to be permanent.

b. If the only imperfection is corporate taxes, what will the share price be after this announcement?

c. Suppose the only imperfections are corporate taxes and financial distress costs. If the share price rises to $5.75 after this announcement, what is the PV of financial distress costs Hawar will incur as the result of this new debt?

a. The same price, $5.50/share, because financial transactions do not create value.

b. $0.3 \times \frac{20}{10} + 5.5 = \$6.10\,/\,\text{share}$

c. $(6.1 - 5.75) \times 10 = \$3.5$ million

16-13. Your firm is considering issuing one-year debt, and has come up with the following estimates of the value of the interest tax shield and the probability of distress for different levels of debt:

	Debt Level ($ million)						
	0	40	50	60	70	80	90
PV (interest tax shield, $ million)	0.00	0.76	0.95	1.14	1.33	1.52	1.71
Probability of Financial Distress	0%	0%	1%	2%	7%	16%	31%

Suppose the firm has a beta of zero, so that the appropriate discount rate for financial distress costs is the risk-free rate of 5%. Which level of debt above is optimal if, in the event of distress,the firm will have distress costs equal to

a. $2 million?

b. $5 million?

c. $25 million?

a. 80

b. 60

c. 40

	Debt Level ($ million)							Tax
	0	40	50	60	70	80	90	40%
PV(interest tax shield)	0.00	0.76	0.95	1.14	1.33	1.52	1.71	Vol
Prob(Financial Distress)	0%	0%	1%	2%	7%	16%	31%	20%
Distress Cost	5	5	5	5	5	5	5	Rf
PV(distress cost)	0.00	0.00	0.05	0.10	0.33	0.76	1.48	5%
Gain	0.00	0.76	0.90	1.05	1.00	0.76	0.24	
Optimal Debt		60						

16-14. Marpor Industries has no debt and expects to generate free cash flows of $16 million each year. Marpor believes that if it permanently increases its level of debt to $40 million, the risk of financial distress may cause it to lose some customers and receive less favorable terms from its suppliers. As a result, Marpor's expected free cash flows with debt will be only $15 million per year. Suppose Marpor's tax rate is 35%, the risk-free rate is 5%, the expected return of the market is 15%, and the beta of Marpor's free cash flows is 1.10 (with or without leverage).

a. Estimate Marpor's value without leverage.

b. Estimate Marpor's value with the new leverage.

a. $r = 5\% + 1.1 \times (15\% - 5\%) = 16\%$

$$V = \frac{16}{0.16} = \$100 \text{ million}$$

b. $r = 5\% + 1.1 \times (15\% - 5\%) = 16\%$

$$V = \frac{15}{0.16} + 0.35 \times 40 = \$107.75 \text{ million}$$

16-15. Real estate purchases are often financed with at least 80% debt. Most corporations, however, have less than 50% debt financing. Provide an explanation for this difference using the tradeoff theory.

According to trade-off theory, tax shield adds value while financial distress costs reduce a firm's value. The financial distress costs for a real estate investment are likely to be low, because the property can generally be easily resold for its full market value. In contrast, corporations generally face much higher costs of financial distress. As a result, corporations choose to have lower leverage.

16-16. On May 14, 2008, General Motors paid a dividend of $0.25 per share. During the same quarter GM lost a staggering $15.5 billion or $27.33 *per share*. Seven months later the company asked for billions of dollars of government aid and ultimately declared bankruptcy just over a year later, on June 1, 2009. At that point a share of GM was worth only a little more than a dollar.

a. If you ignore the possibility of a government bailout, the decision to pay a dividend given how close the company was to financial distress is an example of what kind of cost?

b. What would your answer be if GM executives anticipated that there was a possibility of a government bailout should the firm be forced to declare bankruptcy?

a. Agency cost—cashing out

b. By paying a dividend, executives increased the probability of bankruptcy and therefore the probability of receiving government funds. Since these government funds are funds that investors would not otherwise be entitled to, the payment of a dividend could actually *raise* firm value in this case.

16-17. Dynron Corporation's primary business is natural gas transportation using its vast gas pipeline network. Dynron's assets currently have a market value of $150 million. The firm is exploring the possibility of raising $50 million by selling part of its pipeline network and investing the $50 million in a fiber-optic network to generate revenues by selling high-speed network bandwidth. While this new investment is expected to increase profits, it will also substantially increase Dynron's risk. If Dynron is levered, would this investment be more or less attractive to equity holders than if Dynron had no debt?

If Dynron has no debt or if in all scenarios Dynron can pay the debt in full, equity holders will only consider the project's NPV in making the decision. If Dynron is heavily leveraged, equity holders will also gain from the increased risk of the new investment.

16-18. Consider a firm whose only asset is a plot of vacant land, and whose only liability is debt of $15 million due in one year. If left vacant, the land will be worth $10 million in one year. Alternatively, the firm can develop the land at an upfront cost of $20 million. The developed land will be worth $35 million in one year. Suppose the risk-free interest rate is 10%, assume all cash flows are risk-free, and assume there are no taxes.

a. If the firm chooses not to develop the land, what is the value of the firm's equity today? What is the value of the debt today?

b. What is the NPV of developing the land?

c. Suppose the firm raises $20 million from equity holders to develop the land. If the firm develops the land, what is the value of the firm's equity today? What is the value of the firm's debt today?

d. Given your answer to part (c), would equity holders be willing to provide the $20 million needed to develop the land?

a. $\text{equity} = 0$

$$\text{debt} = \frac{10}{1.1} = \$9.09 \text{ million}$$

b. $\text{NPV} = \dfrac{25}{1.1} - 20 = \$2.73 \text{ million}$

c. $\text{debt} = \dfrac{15}{1.1} = \$13.64 \text{ million}$

$$\text{equity} = \frac{35-15}{1.1} = \$18.18 \text{ million}$$

d. Equity holders will not be willing to accept the deal, because for them it is a negative NPV investment ($18.18 - 20 < 0$).

16-19. Sarvon Systems has a debt-equity ratio of 1.2, an equity beta of 2.0, and a debt beta of 0.30. It currently is evaluating the following projects, none of which would change the firm's volatility (amounts in $ millions):

Project	A	B	C	D	E
Investment	100	50	85	30	75
NPV	20	6	10	15	18

a. Which project will equity holders agree to fund?

b. What is the cost to the firm of the debt overhang?

a. A+D+E

b. Don't take B&C = loss of 6+10 = 16 million

d/e	1.20				
equity beta	2.00				
debt beta	0.30				
Cutoff	0.000				
Project	A	B	C	D	E
Investment	100	50	85	30	75
NPV	20	6	10	15	18
NPV/I	0.200	0.120	0.118	0.500	0.240

16-20. Zymase is a biotechnology start-up firm. Researchers at Zymase must choose one of three different research strategies. The payoffs (after-tax) and their likelihood for each strategy are shown below. The risk of each project is diversifiable.

Strategy	Probability	Payoff ($ million)
A	100%	75
B	50%	140
	50%	0
C	10%	300
	90%	40

a. Which project has the highest expected payoff?

b. Suppose Zymase has debt of $40 million due at the time of the project's payoff. Which project has the highest expected payoff for equity holders?

c. Suppose Zymase has debt of $110 million due at the time of the project's payoff. Which project has the highest expected payoff for equity holders?

d. If management chooses the strategy that maximizes the payoff to equity holders, what is the expected agency cost to the firm from having $40 million in debt due? What is the expected agency cost to the firm from having $110 million in debt due?

a. E(A) = $75 million

E(B) = 0.5 × 140 = $70 million

E(C) = 0.1 × 300 + 0.9 × 40 = $66 million

Project A has the highest expected payoff.

b. E(A) = 75 – 40 = $35 million

E(B) = 0.5 × (140 – 40) = $50 million

E(C) = 0.1 × (300 –40) + 0.9 × (40 – 40) = $26 million

Project B has the highest expected payoff for equity holders.

c. E(A) =$0 million

E(B) = 0.5 × (140 – 110) = $15 million

E(C) = 0.1 × (300 –110) = $19 million

Project C has the highest expected payoff for equity holders.

d. With \$40 million in debt, management will choose project B, which has an expected payoff for the firm that is 75 – 70 = \$5 million less than project A. Thus, the expected agency cost is \$5 million.

With \$110 million in debt, management will choose project C, resulting in an expected agency cost of 75 – 66 = \$9 million.

16-21. You own your own firm, and you want to raise \$30 million to fund an expansion. Currently, you own 100% of the firm's equity, and the firm has no debt. To raise the \$30 million solely through equity, you will need to sell two-thirds of the firm. However, you would prefer to maintain at least a 50% equity stake in the firm to retain control.

a. If you borrow \$20 million, what fraction of the equity will you need to sell to raise the remaining \$10 million? (Assume perfect capital markets.)

b. What is the smallest amount you can borrow to raise the \$30 million without giving up control? (Assume perfect capital markets.)

a. Market value of firm Assets $= 30/(2/3) = \$45$ million. With debt of \$20 million, equity is worth $45 - 20 = 25$, so you will need to sell $\frac{10}{25} = 40\%$ of the equity.

b. Given debt D, equity is worth 45 – D. Selling 50% of equity, together with debt must raise \$30 million: $5 \times (45 - D) + D = 30$. Solve for D = \$15 million.

16-22. Empire Industries forecasts net income this coming year as shown below (in thousands of dollars):

EBIT	\$1000
Interest expense	0
Income before tax	1000
Taxes	–350
Net income	**\$650**

Approximately \$200,000 of Empire's earnings will be needed to make new, positive-NPV investments. Unfortunately, Empire's managers are expected to waste 10% of its net income on needless perks, pet projects, and other expenditures that do not contribute to the firm. All remaining income will be returned to shareholders through dividends and share repurchases.

a. What are the two benefits of debt financing for Empire?

b. By how much would each \$1 of interest expense reduce Empire's dividend and share repurchases?

c. What is the increase in the *total* funds Empire will pay to investors for each \$1 of interest expense?

a. In addition to tax benefits of leverage, debt financing can benefit Empire by reducing wasteful investment.

b. Net income will fall by \$1 × 0.65 = \$0.65.

Because 10% of net income will be wasted, dividends and share repurchases will fall by \$0.65 × (1 – .10) = \$0.585.

c. Pay \$1 in interest, give up \$0.585 in dividends and share repurchases ⇒ Increase of 1 – 0.585 = \$0.415 per \$1 of interest.

16-23. Ralston Enterprises has assets that will have a market value in one year as follows:

Probability	1%	6%	24%	38%	24%	6%	1%
Value ($ million)	70	80	90	100	110	120	130

That is, there is a 1% chance the assets will be worth $70 million, a 6% chance the assets will be worth $80 million, and so on. Suppose the CEO is contemplating a decision that will benefit her personally but will reduce the value of the firm's assets by $10 million. The CEO is likely to proceed with this decision unless it substantially increases the firm's risk of bankruptcy.

a. **If Ralston has debt due of $75 million in one year, the CEO's decision will increase the probability of bankruptcy by what percentage?**

b. **What level of debt provides the CEO with the biggest incentive not to proceed with the decision?**

a. Without personal spending, there is a1% chance of bankruptcy.

With $10 million personal spending, there is a 7% chance—so the probability of bankruptcy, increased by 6%.

b. Debt between $90 and $100 million will provide the CEO with the biggest incentive not to proceed with personal spending because by doing so the chance of bankruptcy would increase by 38%.

16-24. Although the major benefit of debt financing is easy to observe—the tax shield—many of the indirect costs of debt financing can be quite subtle and difficult to observe. Describe some of these costs.

Overinvestment: Investing in negative NPV projects: underinvestment: Not investing in positive NPV projects; cashing out: paying out dividends instead of investing in positive NPV projects; employee job security: highly leveraged firms run the risk of bankruptcy and so cannot write long-term employment contracts and offer job security.

16-25. If it is managed efficiently, Remel Inc. will have assets with a market value of $50 million, $100 million, or $150 million next year, with each outcome being equally likely. However, managers may engage in wasteful empire building, which will reduce the firm's market value by $5 million in all cases. Managers may also increase the risk of the firm, changing the probability of each outcome to 50%, 10%, and 40%, respectively.

a. **What is the expected value of Remel's assets if it is run efficiently?**

Suppose managers will engage in empire building unless that behavior increases the likelihood of bankruptcy. They will choose the risk of the firm to maximize the expected payoff to equity holders.

b. **Suppose Remel has debt due in one year as shown below. For each case, indicate whether managers will engage in empire building, and whether they will increase risk. What is the expected value of Remel's assets in each case?**

i. **$44 million**

ii. **$49 million**

iii. **$90 million**

iv. **$99 million**

c. **Suppose the tax savings from the debt, after including investor taxes, is equal to 10% of the expected payoff of the debt. The proceeds from the debt, as well as the value of any tax savings, will be paid out to shareholders immediately as a dividend when the debt is issued. Which debt level in part (b) is optimal for Remel?**

a. $\frac{50+100+150}{3} = \$100 \text{ million}$

b. i. Empire building: value = 100 – 5 = $95 million

ii. Value = $100 million

iii. Empire building and increased risk: value = .5(50) + .1(100) + .4(150) – 5 = $90 million

iv. Increased risk: value = $95 million

c. Because the tax benefits are paid as a dividend, the manager will empire build or increase risk as determined in part (b). We can therefore determine the expected value with leverage by adding the expected tax benefit to the value calculated in part (b).

i. $95 + 10%(44) = $99.4 million

ii. $100 + 10%(49) = $104.9 million

iii. $\$90 + 10\%(0.5 \times 45 + 0.5 \times 90) = \$96.75$ million

iv. $95 + 10%(.5 × 50 + .5 × 99) = $102.45 million

Therefore, $49 million in debt is optimal; even though there is a tax benefit, the firm's optimal leverage is limited due to agency costs.

16-26. Which of the following industries have low optimal debt levels according to the trade-off theory? Which have high optimal levels of debt?

a. Tobacco firms

b. Accounting firms

c. Mature restaurant chains

d. Lumber companies

e. Cell phone manufacturers

a. Tobacco firms high optimal debt level—high free cash flow, low growth opportunities

b. Accounting firms low optimal debt level—high distress costs

c. Mature restaurant chains high optimal debt level—stable cash flows, low growth, low distress costs

d. Lumber companies high optimal debt level—stable cash flows, low growth, low distress costs

e. Cell phone manufacturers low optimal debt level—high growth opportunities, high distress costs

16-27. According to the managerial entrenchment theory, managers choose capital structure so as to preserve their control of the firm. On the one hand, debt is costly for managers because they risk losing control in the event of default. On the other hand, if they do not take advantage of the tax shield provided by debt, they risk losing control through a hostile takeover.

Suppose a firm expects to generate free cash flows of $90 million per year, and the discount rate for these cash flows is 10%. The firm pays a tax rate of 40%. A raider is poised to take over the firm and finance it with $750 million in permanent debt. The raider will generate the same free cash flows, and the takeover attempt will be successful if the raider can offer a premium of 20% over the current value of the firm. What level of permanent debt will the firm choose, according to the managerial entrenchment hypothesis?

$\text{Unlevered Value} = \frac{90}{0.10} = \$900.$

Levered Value with Raider = 900 + 40%(750) = $1.2 billion

To prevent successful raid, current management must have a levered value of at least $\frac{\$1.2 \text{ billion}}{1.20} = \$1 \text{ billion}$.

Thus, the minimum tax shield is $1 billion – 900 million = $100 million, which requires $\frac{100}{0.40} = \$250$ million in debt.

16-28. Info Systems Technology (IST) manufactures microprocessor chips for use in appliances and other applications. IST has no debt and 100 million shares outstanding. The correct price for these shares is either $14.50 or $12.50 per share. Investors view both possibilities as equally likely, so the shares currently trade for $13.50.

IST must raise $500 million to build a new production facility. Because the firm would suffer a large loss of both customers and engineering talent in the event of financial distress, managers believe that if IST borrows the $500 million, the present value of financial distress costs will exceed any tax benefits by $20 million. At the same time, because investors believe that managers know the correct share price, IST faces a lemons problem if it attempts to raise the $500 million by issuing equity.

a. Suppose that if IST issues equity, the share price will remain $13.50. To maximize the long term share price of the firm once its true value is known, would managers choose to issue equity or borrow the $500 million if

i. they know the correct value of the shares is $12.50?

ii. they know the correct value of the shares is $14.50?

b. Given your answer to part (a), what should investors conclude if IST issues equity? What will happen to the share price?

c. Given your answer to part (a), what should investors conclude if IST issues debt? What will happen to the share price in that case?

d. How would your answers change if there were no distress costs, but only tax benefits of leverage?

a. i. Borrowing has a net cost of $20 million, or $\frac{\$20}{100} = \$0.20$ per share. Selling $\frac{500}{13.50} = 37$ million shares at a premium of $1 per share has a benefit of $37 million, or $\frac{37}{137} = \$0.27$ per share (i.e., $\frac{12.50 \times 100 + 500}{100 + \frac{500}{13.50}} = 12.77 = 12.50 + 0.27$). Therefore, issue equity.

ii. Borrowing has a net cost of $20 million, or $\frac{\$20}{100} = \$0.20$ per share. Selling $\frac{500}{13.50} = 37$ million shares at a discount of $1 per share has a cost of $37 million, or $\frac{37}{137} = \$0.27$ per share. Therefore, issue debt.

b. If IST issues equity, investors would conclude IST is overpriced, and the share price would decline to $12.50.

c. If IST issues debt, investors would conclude IST is undervalued, and the share price would rise to $14.50.

d. If there are no costs from issuing debt, then equity is only issued if it is over-priced. But knowing this, investors would only buy equity at the lowest possible value for the firm. Because there would be no benefit to issuing equity, all firms would issue debt.

16-29. During the Internet boom of the late 1990s, the stock prices of many Internet firms soared to extreme heights. As CEO of such a firm, if you believed your stock was significantly overvalued, would using your stock to acquire non-Internet stocks be a wise idea, even if you had to pay a small premium over their fair market value to make the acquisition?

If the firm must pay 10% more than the target firm was worth, but can do the purchase using shares that were overvalued by more than 10%, in the long run the firm will gain from the acquisition.

16-30. "We R Toys" (WRT) is considering expanding into new geographic markets. The expansion will have the same business risk as WRT's existing assets. The expansion will require an initial investment of $50 million and is expected to generate perpetual EBIT of $20 million per year. After the initial investment, future capital expenditures are expected to equal depreciation, and no further additions to net working capital are anticipated.

WRT's existing capital structure is composed of $500 million in equity and $300 million in debt (market values), with 10 million equity shares outstanding. The unlevered cost of capital is 10%, and WRT's debt is risk free with an interest rate of 4%. The corporate tax rate is 35%, and there are no personal taxes.

a. WRT initially proposes to fund the expansion by issuing equity. If investors were not expecting this expansion, and if they share WRT's view of the expansion's profitability, what will the share price be once the firm announces the expansion plan?

b. Suppose investors think that the EBIT from WRT's expansion will be only $4 million. What will the share price be in this case? How many shares will the firm need to issue?

c. Suppose WRT issues equity as in part (b). Shortly after the issue, new information emerges that convinces investors that management was, in fact, correct regarding the cash flows from the expansion. What will the share price be now? Why does it differ from that found in part (a)?

d. Suppose WRT instead finances the expansion with a $50 million issue of permanent riskfree debt. If WRT undertakes the expansion using debt, what is its new share price once the new information comes out? Comparing your answer with that in part (c), what are the two advantages of debt financing in this case?

a. $\text{NPV of expansion } = 20 \times \frac{0.65}{0.1} - 50 = \$80 \text{ million}$

$\text{Equity value } = \frac{500+80}{10} = \$58/\text{share}$

b. $\text{NPV of expansion } = 4 \times \frac{0.65}{0.1} - 50 = -\$24 \text{ million share price } = \frac{500-24}{10} = \$47.6/\text{share}$

$\text{New shares } = \frac{50}{47.6} = 1.05 \text{ million shares}$

c. $\text{Share price } = \frac{500+50+80}{11.05} = \$57/\text{share}$

The share price is now lower than the answer from part (a), because in part (a), share price is fairly valued, while here shares issued in part (b) are undervalued. New shareholders' gain of $(57-47.6) \times 1.05 = \$10$ million = old shareholders' loss of (58 – 57) × 10.

d. Tax shield = 35%(50) = \$17.5 million

$$\text{Share price} = \frac{500+50+80+17.50-50}{10} = \$59.75 \text{ per share.}$$

Gain of \$2.75 per share compared to case (c). \$1 = avoid issuing undervalued equity, and \$1.75 from interest tax shield.

Chapter 17
Payout Policy

17-1. What options does a firm have to spend its free cash flow (after it has satisfied all interest obligations)?

It can retain them and use them to make investment, or hold them in cash. It can pay them out to equity holders, either by issuing a dividend or by repurchasing shares.

17-2. ABC Corporation announced that it will pay a dividend to all shareholders of record as of Monday, April 3, 2006. It takes three business days of a purchase for the new owners of a share of stock to be registered.

a. When is the last day an investor can purchase ABC stock and still get the dividend payment?

b. When is the ex-dividend day?

a. March 29

b. March 30

17-3. Describe the different mechanisms available to a firm to use to repurchase shares

There are three mechanisms. 1) In an open-market repurchase, the firm repurchases the shares in the open market. This is the most common mechanism in the United States. 2) In a tender offer the firm announces the intention to all shareholders to repurchase a fixed number of shares for a fixed price, conditional on shareholders agreeing to tender their shares. If not enough shares are tendered, the deal can be cancelled. 3) A targeted repurchase is similar to a tender offer except it is not open to all shareholders; only specific shareholder can tender their shares in a targeted repurchase.

17-4. RFC Corp. has announced a $1 dividend. If RFC's price last price cum-dividend is $50, what should its first ex-dividend price be (assuming perfect capital markets)?

Assuming perfect markets, the first ex-dividend price should drop by exactly the dividend payment. Thus, the first ex-dividend price should be $49 per share. In a perfect capital market, the first price of the stock on the ex-dividend day should be the closing price on the previous day less the amount of the dividend.

17-5. EJH Company has a market capitalization of $1 billion and 20 million shares outstanding. It plans to distribute $100 million through an open market repurchase. Assuming perfect capital markets:

a. What will the price per share of EJH be right before the repurchase?

b. How many shares will be repurchased?

c. What will the price per share of EJH be right after the repurchase?

a. $1 billion/20 million shares = $50 per share.

b. $100 million/$50 per share = 2 million shares.

c. If markets are perfect, then the price right after the repurchase should be the same as the price immediately before the repurchase. Thus, the price will be $50 per share.

17-6. KMS Corporation has assets with a market value of $500 million, $50 million of which are cash. It has debt of $200 million, and 10 million shares outstanding. Assume perfect capital markets.

a. What is its current stock price?

b. If KMS distributes $50 million as a dividend, what will its share price be after the dividend is paid?

c. If instead, KMS distributes $50 million as a share repurchase, what will its share price be once the shares are repurchased?

d. What will its new market debt-equity ratio be after either transaction?

a. (500 – 200)/10 = 30

b. (450 – 200)/10 = 25

c. (450 – 200)/(10 – 1.667) = 30

d. 200/250 = 0.8

17-7. Natsam Corporation has $250 million of excess cash. The firm has no debt and 500 million shares outstanding with a current market price of $15 per share. Natsam's board has decided to pay out this cash as a one-time dividend.

a. What is the ex-dividend price of a share in a perfect capital market?

b. If the board instead decided to use the cash to do a one-time share repurchase, in a perfect capital market what is the price of the shares once the repurchase is complete?

c. In a perfect capital market, which policy, in part (a) or (b), makes investors in the firm better off?

a. The dividend payoff is $250/$500 = $0.50 on a per share basis. In a perfect capital market the price of the shares will drop by this amount to $14.50.

b. $15

c. Both are the same.

17-8. Suppose the board of Natsam Corporation decided to do the share repurchase in Problem 7(b), but you, as an investor, would have preferred to receive a dividend payment. How can you leave yourself in the same position as if the board had elected to make the dividend payment instead?

If you sell 0.5/15 of one share you receive $0.50 and your remaining shares will be worth $14.50, leaving you in the same position as if the firm had paid a dividend.

17-9. Suppose you work for Oracle Corporation, and part of your compensation takes the form of stock options. The value of the stock option is equal to the difference between Oracle's stock price and an exercise price of $10 per share at the time that you exercise the option. As an option holder, would you prefer that Oracle use dividends or share repurchases to pay out cash to shareholders? Explain.

Because the payoff of the option depends upon Oracle's future stock price, you would prefer that Oracle use share repurchases, as it avoids the price drop that occurs when the stock price goes ex-dividend.

17-10. The HNH Corporation will pay a constant dividend of $2 per share, per year, in perpetuity. Assume all investors pay a 20% tax on dividends and that there is no capital gains tax. Suppose that other investments with equivalent risk to HNH stock offer an after-tax return of 12%.

a. What is the price of a share of HNH stock?

b. Assume that management makes a surprise announcement that HNH will no longer pay dividends but will use the cash to repurchase stock instead. What is the price of a share of HNH stock now?

a. P = $1.60/0.12 = $13.33

b. P = $2/0.12 = $16.67

17-11. Using Table 17.2, for each of the following years, state whether dividends were tax disadvantaged or not for individual investors with a one-year investment horizon:

a. 1985

b. 1989

c. 1995

d. 1999

e. 2005

Check table to see which years dividends are taxed at a higher rate. Dividends are tax disadvantaged for all years except 1988–1990, and 2003–2009.

17-12. What was the effective dividend tax rate for a U.S. investor in the highest tax bracket who planned to hold a stock for one year in 1981? How did the effective dividend tax rate change in 1982 when the Reagan tax cuts took effect? (Ignore state taxes.)

58.33% in 1981 and 37.5% in 1982

17-13. The dividend tax cut passed in 2003 lowered the effective dividend tax rate for a U.S. investor in the highest tax bracket to a historic low. During which other periods in the last 35 years was the effective dividend tax rate as low?

1988, 1989, or 1990

17-14. Suppose that all capital gains are taxed at a 25% rate, and that the dividend tax rate is 50%. Arbuckle Corp. is currently trading for $30, and is about to pay a $6 special dividend.

a. Absent any other trading frictions or news, what will its share price be just after the dividend is paid?

Suppose Arbuckle made a surprise announcement that it would do a share repurchase rather than pay a special dividend.

b. What net tax savings per share for an investor would result from this decision?

c. What would happen to Arbuckle's stock price upon the announcement of this change?

a. t*_d = (50% – 25%)/(1 – 25%) = 33.3%, P_ex = 30 – 6(1 – t*) = $26

b. With dividend, tax would be 6 × 50% = $3 for dividend, with a tax savings of 4 × 25% = $1 for capital loss, for a net tax from the dividend of $2 per share. This amount would be saved if Arbuckle does a share repurchase instead.

c. Stock price rises to by $2 to $32 to reflect the tax savings.

17-15. You purchased CSH stock for $40 one year ago and it is now selling for $50. The company has announced that it plans a $10 special dividend. You are considering whether to sell the stock now, or wait to receive the dividend and then sell.

a. Assuming 2008 tax rates, what ex-dividend price of CSH will make you indifferent between selling now and waiting?

b. Suppose the capital gains tax rate is 20% and the dividend tax rate is 40%, what ex-dividend price would make you indifferent now?

a. In 2008, the capital gains tax rate is 15%, and the dividend tax rate is 15%. The tax on a \$10 capital gain is \$1.50, and the tax on a \$10 special dividend is \$1.50. The after-tax income for both will be \$8.50.

b. If the capital gains tax rate is 20%, the tax on a \$10 capital gain is \$2.00, and the after-tax income is \$8.00. If the dividends tax rate is 40%, then the tax on a \$10 special dividend is \$4.00, and the after-tax income is \$6.00. The difference in after-tax income is \$2.00.

17-16. On Monday, November 15, 2004, TheStreet.com reported: "An experiment in the efficiency of financial markets will play out Monday following the expiration of a \$3.08 dividend privilege for holders of Microsoft." The story went on: "The stock is currently trading ex-dividend both the special \$3 payout and Microsoft's regular \$0.08 quarterly dividend, meaning a buyer doesn't receive the money if he acquires the shares now." Microsoft stock ultimately opened for trade at \$27.34 on the ex-dividend date (November 15), down \$2.63 from its previous close.

a. Assuming that this price drop resulted only from the dividend payment (no other information affected the stock price that day), what does this decline in price imply about the effective dividend tax rate for Microsoft?

b. Based on this information, which of the following investors are most likely to be the marginal investors (the ones who determine the price) in Microsoft stock:

i. Long-term individual investors?

ii. One-year individual investors?

iii. Pension funds?

iv. Corporations?

a. The price drop was \$2.63/\$\$3.08 = 85.39% of the dividend amount, implying an effective tax rate of 14.61%.

b. i. long-term individual investors

17-17. At current tax rates, which of the following investors are most likely to hold a stock that has a high dividend yield:

a. Individual investors?

b. Pension funds?

c. Mutual funds?

d. Corporations?

d. Corporations

17-18. Que Corporation pays a regular dividend of \$1 per share. Typically, the stock price drops by \$0.80 per share when the stock goes ex-dividend. Suppose the capital gains tax rate is 20%, but investors pay different tax rates on dividends. Absent transactions costs, what is the highest dividend tax rate of an investor who could gain from trading to capture the dividend?

Because the stock price drops by 80% of the dividend amount, shareholders are indifferent if t*_d = 20%. From Eq. 17.3, (td – tg)/(1 – tg) = t*, so td = tg + t* (1 – tg) = 36%. Investors who pay a lower tax rate than 36% could gain from a dividend capture strategy.

17-19. A stock that you know is held by long-term individual investors paid a large one-time dividend. You notice that the price drop on the ex-dividend date is about the size of the dividend payment.

You find this relationship puzzling given the tax disadvantage of dividends. Explain how the dividend-capture theory might account for this behavior.

Dividend capture theory states that investors with high effective dividend tax rates sell to investors with low effective dividend tax rates just before the dividend payment. The price drop therefore reflects the tax rate of the low effective dividend tax rate individuals.

17-20. Clovix Corporation has $50 million in cash, 10 million shares outstanding, and a current share price of $30. Clovix is deciding whether to use the $50 million to pay an immediate special dividend of $5 per share, or to retain and invest it at the risk-free rate of 10% and use the $5 million in interest earned to increase its regular annual dividend of $0.50 per share. Assume perfect capital markets.

a. Suppose Clovix pays the special dividend. How can a shareholder who would prefer an increase in the regular dividend create it on her own?

b. Suppose Clovix increases its regular dividend. How can a shareholder who would prefer the special dividend create it on her own?

a. Invest the $5 special dividend, and earn interest of $0.50 per year.

b. Borrow $5 today, and use the increase in the regular dividend to pay the interest of $0.50 per year on the loan.

17-21. Assume capital markets are perfect. Kay Industries currently has $100 million invested in short term Treasury securities paying 7%, and it pays out the interest payments on these securities each year as a dividend. The board is considering selling the Treasury securities and paying out the proceeds as a one-time dividend payment.

a. If the board went ahead with this plan, what would happen to the value of Kay stock upon the announcement of a change in policy?

b. What would happen to the value of Kay stock on the ex-dividend date of the one-time dividend?

c. Given these price reactions, will this decision benefit investors?

a. The value of Kay will remain the same.

b. The value of Kay will fall by $100 million.

c. It will neither benefit nor hurt investors.

17-22. Redo Problem 21, but assume that Kay must pay a corporate tax rate of 35%, and investors pay no taxes.

a. The value of Kay will rise by $35 million.

b. The value of Kay will fall by $100 million.

c. It will benefit investors.

17-23. Harris Corporation has $250 million in cash, and 100 million shares outstanding. Suppose the corporate tax rate is 35%, and investors pay no taxes on dividends, capital gains, or interest income. Investors had expected Harris to pay out the $250 million through a share repurchase. Suppose instead that Harris announces it will permanently retain the cash, and use the interest on the cash to pay a regular dividend. If there are no other benefits of retaining the cash, how will Harris' stock price change upon this announcement?

Effective tax disadvantage of retention is $t^* = 35\%$. (The reason is that Harris will pay 35% tax on the interest income it earns.) Thus, stock price falls by 35%*$250m/100m shares = $0.875 per share.

17-24. Redo Problem 21, but assume the following:

a. Investors pay a 15% tax on dividends but no capital gains taxes or taxes on interest income, and Kay does not pay corporate taxes.

b. Investors pay a 15% tax on dividends and capital gains, and a 35% tax on interest income, while Kay pays a 35% corporate tax rate.

a. Assuming investors pay a 15% tax on dividends but no capital gains taxes nor taxes on interest income, and Kay does not pay corporate taxes:

  a. The value of Kay will remain the same (dividend taxes don't affect cost of retaining cash, as they will be paid either way).

  b. The value of Kay will fall by \$85 million (100 × (1 – 15%)) to reflect after-tax dividend value.

  c. It will neither benefit nor hurt investors.

b. Assuming investors pay a 15% tax on dividends and capital gains, and a 35% tax on interest income, while Kay pays a 35% corporate tax rate

  a. Effective tax disadvantage of cash is 1 – (1 – tc)(1 – tg)/(1 – ti) = 1 – (1 – 35%)(1 – 15%)/(1 – 35%) = 15%, the equity value of Kay would go up by 15%*100 = 15 million on announcement.

  b. The value of Kay will fall by \$100 million on ex-div date (since tg = td, t*_d = 0).

  c. Given these price reactions, this decision will benefit investors by \$15 million

17-25. Raviv Industries has \$100 million in cash that it can use for a share repurchase. Suppose instead Raviv invests the funds in an account paying 10% interest for one year.

a. If the corporate tax rate is 40%, how much additional cash will Raviv have at the end of the year net of corporate taxes?

b. If investors pay a 20% tax rate on capital gains, by how much will the value of their shares have increased, net of capital gains taxes?

c. If investors pay a 30% tax rate on interest income, how much would they have had if they invested the \$100 million on their own?

d. Suppose Raviv retained the cash so that it would not need to raise new funds from outside investors for an expansion it has planned for next year. If it did raise new funds, it would have to pay issuance fees. How much does Raviv need to save in issuance fees to make retaining the cash beneficial for its investors? (Assume fees can be expensed for corporate tax purposes.)

a. 100 × 10% × (1 – 40%) = \$6 m

b. \$6 × (1 – 0.20) = \$4.8 million

c. 100*10% × (1 – 0.30) = \$7 million

d. \$1 spent on fees = \$1 × (1 – 0.40) × (1 – 0.20) = \$0.48 to investors after corporate and cap gain tax. To make up the shortfall, fees = (7 – 4.8)/0.48 = \$4.583 million.

17-26. Use the data in Table 15.3 to calculate the tax disadvantage of retained cash in the following:

a. 1998

b. 1976

a. 13.33%

b. −12.667%

17-27. Explain under which conditions an increase in the dividend payment can be interpreted as a signal of the following:

a. Good news

b. Bad news

a. By increasing dividends managers signal that they believe that future earnings will be high enough to maintain the new dividend payment.

b. Raising dividends signals that the firm does not have any positive NPV investment opportunities, which is bad news.

17-28. Why is an announcement of a share repurchase considered a positive signal?

By choosing to do a share repurchase, management credibly signals that they believe the stock is undervalued.

17-29. AMC Corporation currently has an enterprise value of $400 million and $100 million in excess cash. The firm has 10 million shares outstanding and no debt. Suppose AMC uses its excess cash to repurchase shares. After the share repurchase, news will come out that will change AMC's enterprise value to either $600 million or $200 million.

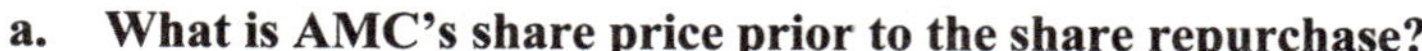

a. What is AMC's share price prior to the share repurchase?

b. What is AMC's share price after the repurchase if its enterprise value goes up? What is AMC's share price after the repurchase if its enterprise value declines?

c. Suppose AMC waits until after the news comes out to do the share repurchase. What is AMC's share price after the repurchase if its enterprise value goes up? What is AMC's share price after the repurchase if its enterprise value declines?

d. Suppose AMC management expects good news to come out. Based on your answers to parts (b) and (c), if management desires to maximize AMC's ultimate share price, will they undertake the repurchase before or after the news comes out? When would management undertake the repurchase if they expect bad news to come out?

e. Given your answer to part (d), what effect would you expect an announcement of a share repurchase to have on the stock price? Why?

a. Because Enterprise Value = Equity + Debt – Cash, AMC's equity value is

Equity = EV + Cash = $500 million.

Therefore,

Share price = ($500 million) / (10 million shares) = $50 per share.

b. AMC repurchases $100 million / ($50 per share) = 2 million shares. With 8 million remaining share outstanding (and no excess cash) its share price if its EV goes up to $600 million is

Share price = $600 / 8 = $75 per share.

And if EV goes down to $200 million:

Share price = $200 / 8 = $25 per share.

c. If EV rises to $600 million prior to repurchase, given its $100 million in cash and 10 million shares outstanding, AMC's share price will rise to:

Share price = (600 + 100) / 10 = $70 per share.

If EV falls to $200 million:

Share price = (200 + 100) / 10 = $30 per share.

The share price after the repurchase will be also be $70 or $30, since the share repurchase itself does not change the stock price.

Note: the difference in the outcomes for (a) vs (b) arises because by holding cash (a risk-free asset) AMC reduces the volatility of its share price.

d. If management expects good news to come out, they would prefer to do the repurchase first, so that the stock price would rise to $75 rather than $70. On the other hand, if they expect bad news to come out, they would prefer to do the repurchase after the news comes out, for a stock price of $30 rather than $25. (Intuitively, management prefers to do a repurchase if the stock is undervalued—they expect good news to come out —but not when it is overvalued because they expect bad news to come out.)

e. Based on (d), we expect managers to do a share repurchase before good news comes out and after any bad news has already come out. Therefore, if investors believe managers are better informed about the firm's future prospects, and that they are timing their share repurchases accordingly, a share repurchase announcement would lead to an increase in the stock price.

17-30. Berkshire Hathaway's A shares are trading at $120,000. What split ratio would it need to bring its stock price down to $50?

$120,000 per old share / $50 per new share = 2400 new shares / old share. A 2400:1 split would be required.

17-31. Suppose the stock of Host Hotels & Resorts is currently trading for $20 per share.

a. If Host issued a 20% stock dividend, what will its new share price be?

b. If Host does a 3:2 stock split, what will its new share price be?

c. If Host does a 1:3 reverse split, what will its new share price be?

a. With a 20% stock dividend, an investor holding 100 shares receives 20 additional shares. However, since the total value of the firm's shares is unchanged, the stock price should fall to:

Share price = $20 × 100 / 120 = $20 / 1.20 = $16.67 per share.

b. A 3:2 stock split means for every two shares currently held, the investor receives a third share. This split is therefore equivalent to a 50% stock dividend. The share price will fall to:

Share price = $20 × 2/3 = $20/ 1.50 = $13.33 per share.

c. A 1:3 reverse split implies that every three shares will turn into one share. Therefore, the stock price will rise to:

Share price = $20 × 3 / 1 = $60 per share.

17-32. Explain why most companies choose to pay stock dividends (split their stock).

Companies use stock splits to keep their stock prices in a range that reduces investor transaction costs.

17-33. When might it be advantageous to undertake a reverse stock split?

To avoid being delisted from an exchange because the price of the stock has fallen below the minimum required to stay listed.

17-34. After the market close on May 11, 2001, Adaptec, Inc., distributed a dividend of shares of the stock of its software division, Roxio, Inc. Each Adaptec shareholder received 0.1646 share of Roxio stock per share of Adaptec stock owned. At the time, Adaptec stock was trading at a price

of $10.55 per share (cum-dividend), and Roxio's share price was $14.23 per share. In a perfect market, what would Adaptec's ex-dividend share price be after this transaction?

The value of the dividend paid per Adaptec share was (0.1646 shares of Roxio) × ($14.23 per share of Roxio) = $2.34 per share. Therefore, ignoring tax effects or other news that might come out, we would expect Adaptec's stock price to fall to $10.55 – 2.34 = $8.21 per share once it goes ex-dividend. (Note: In fact, Adaptec stock opened on Monday May 14, 2001—the next trading day—at a price of $8.45 per share.)

Chapter 18

Capital Budgeting and Valuation with Leverage

18-1. Explain whether each of the following projects is likely to have risk similar to the average risk of the firm.

a. The Clorox Company considers launching a new version of Armor All designed to clean and protect notebook computers.

b. Google, Inc., plans to purchase real estate to expand its headquarters.

c. Target Corporation decides to expand the number of stores it has in the southeastern United States.

d. GE decides to open a new Universal Studios theme park in China.

a. While there may be some differences, the market risk of the cash flows from this new product is likely to be similar to Clorox's other household products. Therefore, it is reasonable to assume it has the same risk as the average risk of the firm.

b. A real estate investment likely has very different market risk than Google's other investments in Internet search technology and advertising. It would not be appropriate to assume this investment as risk equal to the average risk of the firm.

c. An expansion in the same line of business is likely to have risk equal to the average risk of the business.

d. The theme park will likely be sensitive to the growth of the Chinese economy. Its market risk may be very different from GE's other division, and from the company as a whole. It would not be appropriate to assume this investment as risk equal to the average risk of the firm.

18-2. Suppose Caterpillar, Inc., has 665 million shares outstanding with a share price of $74.77, and $25 billion in debt. If in three years, Caterpillar has 700 million shares outstanding trading for $83 per share, how much debt will Caterpillar have if it maintains a constant debt-equity ratio?

E = 665 million × $74.77 = $49.7 billion, D = $25 billion, D/E = 25/49.722 = 0.503.

E = 700 million × $83.00 = $58.1 billion. Constant D/E implies D = 58.1 × 0.503 = $29.2 billion.

18-3. In 2006, Intel Corporation had a market capitalization of $112 billion, debt of $2.2 billion, cash of $9.1 billion, and EBIT of more than $11 billion. If Intel were to increase its debt by $1 billion and use the cash for a share repurchase, which market imperfections would be most relevant for understanding the consequence for Intel's value? Why?

Intel's debt is a tiny fraction of its total value. Indeed, Intel has more cash than debt, so its net debt is negative. Intel is also very profitable; at an interest rate of 6%, interest on Intel's debt is only $132 million per year, which is less than 1.5% of its EBIT. Thus, the risk that Intel will default on its debt is extremely small. This risk will remain extremely small even if Intel borrows an additional $1 billion.

Thus, adding debt will not really change the likelihood of financial distress for Intel (which is nearly zero), and thus will also not lead to agency conflicts. As a result, the most important financial friction for such a debt increase is the tax savings Intel would receive from the interest tax shield. A secondary issue may be the signaling impact of the transaction—borrowing to do a share repurchase is usually interpreted as a positive signal that management may view the shares to be underpriced.

18-4. **Suppose Goodyear Tire and Rubber Company is considering divesting one of its manufacturing plants. The plant is expected to generate free cash flows of \$1.5 million per year, growing at a rate of 2.5% per year. Goodyear has an equity cost of capital of 8.5%, a debt cost of capital of 7%, a marginal corporate tax rate of 35%, and a debt-equity ratio of 2.6. If the plant has average risk and Goodyear plans to maintain a constant debt-equity ratio, what after-tax amount must it receive for the plant for the divestiture to be profitable?**

We can compute the levered value of the plant using the WACC method. Goodyear's WACC is

$$r_{wacc} = \frac{1}{1+2.6}8.5\% + \frac{2.6}{1+2.6}7\%(1-0.35) = 5.65\%.$$

Therefore, $V^L = \frac{1.5}{0.0565-0.025} = \$47.6$ million

A divestiture would be profitable if Goodyear received more than \$47.6 million after tax.

18-5. **Suppose Lucent Technologies has an equity cost of capital of 10%, market capitalization of \$10.8 billion, and an enterprise value of \$14.4 billion. Suppose Lucent's debt cost of capital is 6.1% and its marginal tax rate is 35%.**

a. What is Lucent's WACC?

b. If Lucent maintains a constant debt-equity ratio, what is the value of a project with average risk and the following expected free cash flows?

Year	0	1	2	3
FCF	−100	50	100	70

c. If Lucent maintains its debt-equity ratio, what is the debt capacity of the project in part (b)?

a. $r_{wacc} = \frac{10.8}{14.4}10\% + \frac{14.4-10.8}{14.4}6.1\%(1-0.35) = 8.49\%$

b. Using the WACC method, the levered value of the project at date 0 is

$$V^L = \frac{50}{1.0849} + \frac{100}{1.0849^2} + \frac{70}{1.0849^3} = 185.86.$$

Given a cost of 100 to initiate, the project's NPV is 185.86 – 100 = 85.86.

c. Lucent's debt-to-value ratio is d = (14.4 – 10.8) / 14.4 = 0.25. The project's debt capacity is equal to d times the levered value of its remaining cash flows at each date.

Year	0	1	2	3
FCF	–100	50	100	70
VL	185.86	151.64	64.52	0
D = d*VL	46.47	37.91	16.13	0.00

18-6. **Acort Industries has 10 million shares outstanding and a current share price of \$40 per share. It also has long-term debt outstanding. This debt is risk free, is four years away from maturity, has annual coupons with a coupon rate of 10%, and has a \$100 million face value. The first of the remaining coupon payments will be due in exactly one year. The riskless interest rates for all**

maturities are constant at 6%. Acort has EBIT of $106 million, which is expected to remain constant each year. New capital expenditures are expected to equal depreciation and equal $13 million per year, while no changes to net working capital are expected in the future. The corporate tax rate is 40%, and Acort is expected to keep its debt-equity ratio constant in the future (by either issuing additional new debt or buying back some debt as time goes on).

a. Based on this information, estimate Acort's WACC.

b. What is Acort's equity cost of capital?

a. We don't know Acort's equity cost of capital, so we cannot calculate WACC directly. However, we can compute it indirectly by estimating the discount rate that is consistent with Acort's market value. First, E = 10 × 40 = $400 million. The market value of Acort's debt is

$$D = 10 \times \frac{1}{0.06}\left(1 - \frac{1}{1.06^4}\right) + \frac{100}{1.06^4} = \$113.86 \text{ million.}$$

Therefore, Acort's enterprise value is E + D = 400 + 113.86 = 513.86.

Acort's $\quad FCF = EBIT \times (1 - \tau_C) + Dep - Capex - Inc\ in\ NWC$

FCF = 106 × (1 – 0.40) = 63.6

Because Acort is not expected to grow,

$$V^L = 513.86 = \frac{63.6}{r_{wacc}} \text{ and so } r_{wacc} = \frac{63.6}{513.86} = 12.38\%.$$

b. Using $r_{wacc} = \frac{E}{E+D} r_E + \frac{D}{D+E} r_D (1 - \tau_c)$,

$$12.38\% = \frac{400}{513.86} r_E + \frac{113.86}{513.86} 6\%(1 - 0.40)$$

solving for r_E:

$$r_E = \frac{513.86}{400}\left[12.38\% - \frac{113.86}{513.86} 6\%(1 - 0.40)\right] = 14.88\%.$$

18-7. Suppose Goodyear Tire and Rubber Company has an equity cost of capital of 8.5%, a debt cost of capital of 7%, a marginal corporate tax rate of 35%, and a debt-equity ratio of 2.6. Suppose Goodyear maintains a constant debt-equity ratio.

a. What is Goodyear's WACC?

b. What is Goodyear's unlevered cost of capital?

c. Explain, intuitively, why Goodyear's unlevered cost of capital is less than its equity cost of capital and higher than its WACC.

a. $r_{wacc} = \frac{1}{1+2.6} 8.5\% + \frac{2.6}{1+2.6} 7\%(1 - 0.35) = 5.65\%$

b. Because Goodyear maintains a target leverage ratio, we can use Eq. 18.6:

$$r_U = \frac{1}{1+2.6} 8.5\% + \frac{2.6}{1+2.6} 7\% = 7.42\%.$$

c. Goodyear's equity cost of capital exceeds its unlevered cost of capital because leverage makes equity riskier than the overall firm. Goodyear's WACC is less than its unlevered cost of capital because the WACC includes the benefit of the interest tax shield.

18-8. You are a consultant who was hired to evaluate a new product line for Markum Enterprises. The upfront investment required to launch the product line is $10 million. The product will generate free cash flow of $750,000 the first year, and this free cash flow is expected to grow at a rate of 4% per year. Markum has an equity cost of capital of 11.3%, a debt cost of capital of 5%, and a tax rate of 35%. Markum maintains a debt-equity ratio of 0.40.

a. What is the NPV of the new product line (including any tax shields from leverage)?

b. How much debt will Markum initially take on as a result of launching this product line?

c. How much of the product line's value is attributable to the present value of interest tax shields?

a. WACC = (1 / 1.4)(11.3%) + (.4 / 1.4)(5%)(1 – .35) = 9%

V^L = 0.75 / (9% – 4%) = $15 million

NPV = -10 + 15 = $5 million

b. Debt-to-Value ratio is (0.4) / (1.4) = 28.57%.

Therefore Debt is 28.57% × $15 million = $4.29 million.

c. Discounting at r_u gives unlevered value. r_u = (1 / 1.4)11.3% + (.4 / 1.4)5% = 9.5%

V^u = 0.75 / (9.5% – 4%) = $13.64 million

Tax shield value is therefore 15 – 13.64 = 1.36 million.

Alternatively, initial debt is $4.29 million, for a tax shield in the first year of 4.29 × 5% × 0.35 = 0.075 million. Then PV(ITS) = 0.075 / (9.5% – 4%) = 1.36 million.

Alternatively, initial debt is $4.29 million, for a tax shield in the first year of 4.29 × 5% × 0.35 = 0.075 million. Then PV(ITS) = 0.075 / (9.5% – 4%) = 1.36 million.

18-9. Consider Lucent's project in Problem 5.

a. What is Lucent's unlevered cost of capital?

b. What is the unlevered value of the project?

c. What are the interest tax shields from the project? What is their present value?

d. Show that the APV of Lucent's project matches the value computed using the WACC method.

a. $$r_U = \frac{10.8}{14.4}10\% + \frac{14.4-10.8}{14.4}6.1\% = 9.025\%$$

b. $$V^U = \frac{50}{1.09025} + \frac{100}{1.09025^2} + \frac{70}{1.09025^3} = 184.01$$

c. Using the results from problem 5(c):

Year	0	1	2	3
FCF	–100	50	100	70
VL	185.86	151.64	64.52	0
D = d*VL	46.47	37.91	16.13	0.00
Interest		2.83	2.31	0.98
Tax Shield		0.99	0.81	0.34

The present value of the interest tax shield is

$$PV(ITS) = \frac{0.99}{1.09025} + \frac{0.81}{1.09025^2} + \frac{0.34}{1.09025^3} = 1.85$$

d. $V^L = APV = 184.01 + 1.85 = 185.86$

This matches the answer in problem 5.

18-10. Consider Lucent's project in Problem 5.

a. What is the free cash flow to equity for this project?

b. What is its NPV computed using the FTE method? How does it compare with the NPV based on the WACC method?

a. Using the debt capacity calculated in problem 5, we can compute FCFE by adjusting FCF for after-tax interest expense ($D \times r_D \times (1 - tc)$) and net increases in debt ($D_t - D_{t-1}$).

Year	0	1	2	3
D	46.47	37.91	16.13	0.00
FCF	-$100.00	$50.00	$100.00	$70.00
After-tax Interest Exp.	$0.00	-$1.84	-$1.50	-$0.64
Inc. in Debt	$46.47	-$8.55	-$21.78	-$16.13
FCFE	-$53.53	$39.60	$76.72	$53.23

b. $$NPV = -53.53 + \frac{39.60}{1.10} + \frac{76.72}{1.10^2} + \frac{53.23}{1.10^3} = \$85.86$$

18-11. In year 1, AMC will earn $2000 before interest and taxes. The market expects these earnings to grow at a rate of 3% per year. The firm will make no net investments (i.e., capital expenditures will equal depreciation) or changes to net working capital. Assume that the corporate tax rate equals 40%. Right now, the firm has $5000 in risk-free debt. It plans to keep a constant ratio of debt to equity every year, so that on average the debt will also grow by 3% per year. Suppose the risk-free rate equals 5%, and the expected return on the market equals 11%. The asset beta for this industry is 1.11.

a. If AMC were an all-equity (unlevered) firm, what would its market value be?

b. Assuming the debt is fairly priced, what is the amount of interest AMC will pay next year? If AMC's debt is expected to grow by 3% per year, at what rate are its interest payments expected to grow?

c. Even though AMC's debt is *riskless* (the firm will not default), the future growth of AMC's debt is uncertain, so the exact amount of the future interest payments is risky. Assuming the future interest payments have the same beta as AMC's assets, what is the present value of AMC's interest tax shield?

d. Using the APV method, what is AMC's total market value, *V L*? What is the market value of AMC's equity?

e. What is AMC's WACC? (*Hint*: Work backward from the FCF and *V L*.)

f. Using the WACC method, what is the expected return for AMC equity?

g. Show that the following holds for AMC: .[SHERYL: there's an equation that should be set here, but I can't get it out of the PDF in correct for. It's on page 631].

h. Assuming that the proceeds from any increases in debt are paid out to equity holders, what cash flows do the equity holders expect to receive in one year? At what rate are those cash flows expected to grow? Use that information plus your answer to part (f) to derive the market value of equity using the FTE method. How does that compare to your answer in part (d)?

a. AMC has unlevered FCF of $\$2,000 \times 0.6 = \$1,200$.

From the CAPM, AMC's unlevered cost of capital is $5\% + 1.11 \times (11\% - 5\%) = 11.66\%$.

Discounting the FCF as a growing perpetuity tells us that the value of the firm, assuming growth of 3%, is:

$$V(\text{All Equity}) = \frac{\$1,200}{0.1166 - 0.03} = \$13,857.$$

b. Since the debt is risk-free, the interest rate paid on it must equal the risk-free rate of 5% (or else there would be an arbitrage opportunity). The firm has $5,000 of debt next year. The interest payment will be 5% of that, or $250. If the debt grows by 3% per year, so will the interest payments.

c. The expected value of next year's tax shield will be $250 × 40% = $100, and it will grow (with the growth of the debt) at a rate of 3%. But the exact amount of the tax shield is uncertain, since AMC may add new debt or repay some debt during the year, depending on their cash flows. This makes the actual amount of the tax shield risky (even though the debt itself is not). Since the beta of the tax shield due to debt is 1.11, the appropriate discount rate is 5% + 1.11 (11% – 5%) = 11.67%. We can now use the growing perpetuity formula and conclude that

$$PV(\text{Interest Tax Shields}) = \frac{\$100}{0.1166 - 0.03} = \$1,155.$$

d. The APV tells us that the value of a firm with debt equals the sum of the value of an all equity firm and the tax shield. From previous work (parts (a) and (c)), we get:

V(AMC) = $13,857 + $1,155 = $15,012.

The market value of the equity is therefore V – D = $15,012 - $5000 = $10,012.

e. Next year's FCF is $\$2,000 \times 0.6 = \$1,200$. It is expected to grow at 3%, so the WACC must satisfy:

$$V(\text{AMC}) = \frac{\$1,200}{r_{wacc} - 0.03} = \$15,000.$$

Solving for the WACC, we get WACC = 11 %.

f. By definition, $r_{wacc} = \frac{E}{V} \times r_E + \frac{D}{V} \times r_D \times (1 - \tau_c)$.

The return on the debt is 5%; the value of the debt is $5,000, the value of the firm is $15,000 and therefore the value of the equity is $15,000 – $5,000 = $10,000. Plugging into the above expression, we get:

$$11\% = \frac{\$10,000}{\$15,000} \times r_E + \frac{\$5,000}{\$15,000} \times 5\% \times (1 - 0.4) \Rightarrow r_E = 15\%.$$

g. From the CAPM, β_E must satisfy $15\% = 5\% + \beta_E (11\% - 5\%)$, so we conclude $\beta_E = 1.66$.

The relationship holds since ($10,000/$15,000) × 1.66 = 1.11, and the beta of the debt equals 0.

h. The debt is expected to increase to $\$5,000 \times (1 + 0.03) = \$5,150$, so the equity holders will get $150 due to the increase in debt. These proceeds will increase by 3% annually. (The second-year debt will be $\$5,000 \times (1 + 0.03)^2 = \$5,304.5$, with an increase in debt of $154.5, 3% higher than the $150 proceeds of year 1.) The expected FCF to equity at the end of the first year is therefore EBIT – Interest – Taxes + Debt proceeds, or FCFE = (2000 – 250) × (1 – .40) + 150 = $1200.

This cash flow is expected to grow at 3% per year. Thus, another way to compute the value of equity is to discount these cash flows directly at the MCR for the equity of 15% (from (f)):

$$E = \frac{FCFE}{r_E - g} = \frac{1200}{15\% - 3\%} = 10{,}000.$$

This is the same value we computed in (d), using the APV.

18-12. Prokter and Gramble (PG) has historically maintained a debt-equity ratio of approximately 0.20. Its current stock price is $50 per share, with 2.5 billion shares outstanding. The firm enjoys very stable demand for its products, and consequently it has a low equity beta of 0.50 and can borrow at 4.20%, just 20 basis points over the risk-free rate of 4%. The expected return of the market is 10%, and PG's tax rate is 35%.

a. This year, PG is expected to have free cash flows of $6.0 billion. What constant expected growth rate of free cash flow is consistent with its current stock price?

b. PG believes it can increase debt without any serious risk of distress or other costs. With a higher debt-equity ratio of 0.50, it believes its borrowing costs will rise only slightly to 4.50%. If PG announces that it will raise its debt-equity ratio to 0.5 through a leveraged recap, determine the increase in the stock price that would result from the anticipated tax savings.

a. $E = \$50 \times 2.5\text{ B} = \$125\text{ B}$

$D = 0.20 \times 125\text{ B} = \$25\text{ B}$

$V^L = E + D = \$150\text{ B}$

From CAPM: Equity Cost of Capital = 4% + 0.5(10% – 4%) = 7%

WACC = (125 / 150) 7% + (25 / 150) 4.2% (1 – 35%) = 6.29%

$V^L = FCF/(r_{wacc} - g) \Rightarrow g = r_{wacc} - FCF/V = 6.29\% - 6/150 = 2.29\%$

b. Initial Unlevered cost of capital (Eq. 18.6) = (125 / 150) 7% + (25 / 150) 4.2% = 6.53%

New Equity cost of capital (Eq. 18.10) = 6.53% + (.5)(6.53% – 4.5%) = 7.55%

New WACC = (1 / 1.5) 7.55% + (.5 / 1.5) 4.5% (1 – 35%) = 6.01%

$V^L = FCF / (r_{wacc} - g) = 6.0 / (6.01\% - 2.29\%) = 161.29$

This is a gain of 161.29 – 150 = $11.29 B or 11.29/2.5 = $4.52 per share.

Thus, share price rises to $54.52/share.

18-13. Amarindo, Inc. (AMR), is a newly public firm with 10 million shares outstanding. You are doing a valuation analysis of AMR. You estimate its free cash flow in the coming year to be $15 million, and you expect the firm's free cash flows to grow by 4% per year in subsequent years. Because the firm has only been listed on the stock exchange for a short time, you do not have an accurate assessment of AMR's equity beta. However, you do have beta data for UAL, another firm in the same industry:

	Equity Beta	Debt Beta	Debt-Equity Ratio
UAL	1.5	0.30	1

AMR has a much lower debt-equity ratio of 0.30, which is expected to remain stable, and its debt is risk free. AMR's corporate tax rate is 40%, the risk-free rate is 5%, and the expected return on the market portfolio is 11%.

a. Estimate AMR's equity cost of capital.

b. Estimate AMR's share price.

a. From Eq. 14.9, UAL Asset beta = (1/2) 1.5 + (1/2) 0.3 = 0.90

We can use this for AMR's asset beta.

To derive the equity beta, since AMR's debt is risk free we have (Eq. 14.10):

Equity Beta = Asset Beta × (1 + D/E) = 0.9 × 1.30 = 1.17.

From the SML

$r_e = 5\% + 1.17(11\% - 5\%) = 12.02\%$.

Alternatively, given an asset or unlevered beta of 0.90 for AMR, we have (from SML):

$r_u = 5\% + 0.90(11\% - 5\%) = 10.4\%$.

Then we can solve for r_e using Eq. 18.10:

$r_e = 10.4\% + 0.30\ (10.4\% - 5\%) = 12.02\%$.

b. Since D/E ratio is stable, we can value AMR using the WACC approach.

WACC = (1/1.3) 12.02% + (.3/1.3) 5% (1 – 40%) = 9.94%

Levered value of AMR (as a constant growth perpetuity):

$D + E = V^L = FCF/(r_{wacc} - g) = 15 / (9.94\% - 4\%) = \$252.52$ million

$E = (E / (D + E)) \times V^L = 252.52 / 1.3 = \$194.25$ million

Share price = 194.25 / 10 = $19.43

18-14. Remex (RMX) currently has no debt in its capital structure. The beta of its equity is 1.50. For each year into the indefinite future, Remex's free cash flow is expected to equal $25 million. Remex is considering changing its capital structure by issuing debt and using the proceeds to buy back stock. It will do so in such a way that it will have a 30% debt-equity ratio after the change, and it will maintain this debt-equity ratio forever. Assume that Remex's debt cost of capital will be 6.5%. Remex faces a corporate tax rate of 35%. Except for the corporate tax rate of 35%, there are no market imperfections. Assume that the CAPM holds, the risk-free rate of interest is 5%, and the expected return on the market is 11%.

a. Using the information provided, complete the following table:

	Debt-Equity Ratio	Debt Cost of Capital	Equity Cost of Capital	Weighted Average Cost of Capital
Before change in capital structure	0	N/A		
After change in capital structure	0.30	6.5%		

b. Using the information provided and your calculations in part (a), determine the value of the tax shield acquired by Remex if it changes its capital structure in the way it is considering.

a. Before Change: From the SML, $r_E = 5\% + 1.50 \times 6\% = 14\%$

Since the firm has no leverage, $r_{wacc} = r_U = r_E = 14\%$.

After the change, from Eq. 18.10:

$r_E = 14\% + 0.30(14\% - 6.5\%) = 16.25\%$.

Since the firm has D/E of 0.30, the WACC formula is

$$r_{wacc} = \frac{E}{D+E}R_E + \frac{D}{D+E}R_D(1-T_C)$$
$$= \frac{1}{1.3}16.25 + \frac{.3}{1.3}6.5(1-.35)$$
$$= 13.475\%.$$

We can also use Eq. 18.11: rwacc = 14% – (.3 / 1.3)(.35)(6.5%) = 13.475%.

b. We can compare Remex's value with and without leverage. Without leverage (and no expected growth),

$$V^U = \frac{FCF}{r_U} = \frac{25}{14\%} = \$178.57 \text{ million.}$$

With leverage (and no expected growth):

$$V^L = \frac{FCF}{r_{wacc}} = \frac{25}{13.475\%} = \$185.53 \text{ million}$$

Therefore, PV(ITS) = $V^L - V^U$ = 185.53 – 178.57 = $6.96 million.

18-15. You are evaluating a project that requires an investment of $90 today and provides a single cash flow of $115 for sure one year from now. You decide to use 100% debt financing, that is, you will borrow $90. The risk-free rate is 5% and the tax rate is 40%. Assume that the investment is fully depreciated at the end of the year, so without leverage you would owe taxes on the difference between the project cash flow and the investment, that is, $15.

a. Calculate the NPV of this investment opportunity using the APV method.

b. Using your answer to part (a), calculate the WACC of the project.

c. Verify that you get the same answer using the WACC method to calculate NPV.

d. Finally, show that flow-to-equity also correctly gives the NPV of this investment opportunity.

a. FCF at year end (after tax) = 115 – .40 × 25 = 105

Vu = 105/1.05 = 100

PV(its) = 40% × 5% × 90/1.05 = 1.71

VL = 100 + 1.71 = 101.71

NPV = 101.71 – 90 = 11.71

b. ru = rd = 5%, d = 90/101.71

tc = 40%,

WACC = 5% – (90/101.71)(40%)(5%) = 3.23%

NOTE: if ru = rd, must use techniques in section 18.8 to calculate WACC.

c. VL = 105/1.0323 = 101.71

NPV = 101.71 – 90 = 11.71

d. FCFE0 = 0

FCFE1 = 105 – 5%(90)(1-40%)-90 = 12.3

R_e = 5% (since no risk)

Value to equity = 12.3/1.05 = 11.71

18-16. Tybo Corporation adjusts its debt so that its interest expenses are 20% of its free cash flow. Tybo is considering an expansion that will generate free cash flows of $2.5 million this year and is expected to grow at a rate of 4% per year from then on. Suppose Tybo's marginal corporate tax rate is 40%.

a. If the unlevered cost of capital for this expansion is 10%, what is its unlevered value?

b. What is the levered value of the expansion?

c. If Tybo pays 5% interest on its debt, what amount of debt will it take on initially for the expansion?

d. What is the debt-to-value ratio for this expansion? What is its WACC?

e. What is the levered value of the expansion using the WACC method?

a. Unlevered value $V^U = FCF / (r_U - g) = 2.5 / (10\% - 4\%) = \$41.67$ million

b. From Eq. 18.14, $V^L = (1 + \tau_c k)\, V^U = (1 + 0.40 \times 0.20)\, 41.67 = \$45$ million

c. Interest = 20%(FCF) = 20%(2.5) = \$0.5 million = $r_D\, D = 0.05\, D$

Therefore, D = 0.5 / 0.05 = \$10 million

d. Debt-to-value $d = D / V^L = 10 / 45 = 0.2222$.

From Eq. 18.11, $r_{wacc} = 10\% - (0.2222)(0.40)5\% = 9.556\%$

e. Using the WACC method, $V^L = 2.5 / (9.556\% - 4\%) = \$45$ million

18-17. You are on your way to an important budget meeting. In the elevator, you review the project valuation analysis you had your summer associate prepare for one of the projects to be discussed:

	0	1	2	3	4
EBIT		10.0	10.0	10.0	10.0
Interest (5%)		–4.0	–4.0	–3.0	–2.0
Earnings Before Taxes		6.0	6.0	7.0	8.0
Taxes		–2.4	–2.4	–2.8	–3.2
Depreciation		25.0	25.0	25.0	25.0
Cap Ex	–100.0				
Additions to NWC	–20.0				20.0
Net New Debt	80.0	0.0	–20.0	–20.0	–40.0
FCFE	–40.0	28.6	8.6	9.2	9.8
NPV at 11% Equity Cost of Capital	5.9				

Looking over the spreadsheet, you realize that while all of the cash flow estimates are correct, your associate used the flow-to-equity valuation method and discounted the cash flows using the *company's* equity cost of capital of 11%. However, the project's incremental leverage is very different from the company's historical debt-equity ratio of 0.20: For this project, the company will instead borrow \$80 million upfront and repay \$20 million in year 2, \$20 million in year 3, and \$40 million in year 4. Thus, the *project's* equity cost of capital is likely to be higher than the firm's, not constant over time—invalidating your associate's calculation.

Clearly, the FTE approach is not the best way to analyze this project. Fortunately, you have your calculator with you, and with any luck you can use a better method before the meeting starts.

a. What is the present value of the interest tax shield associated with this project?

b. What are the free cash flows of the project?

c. What is the best estimate of the project's value from the information given?

a. First,

Interest Payment = Interest Rate (5%) × Prior period debt

From the tax calculation in the spreadsheet, we can see that the tax rate is 2.4/6 = 40%. Therefore,

Interest Tax shield = Interest Payment × Tax Rate (40%)

Because the tax shields are predetermined, we can discount them using the 5% debt cost of capital.

$$\text{PV(ITS)} = \frac{0.40(0.05)(80)}{1.05} + \frac{0.40(0.05)(80)}{1.05^2} + \frac{0.40(0.05)(60)}{1.05^3} + \frac{0.40(0.05)(40)}{1.05^4}$$
$$= \$4.67 \text{ million}$$

	Year 0	Year 1	Year 2	Year 3	Year 4
Debt	80	80	60	40	0
Interest at 5.0%		4	4	3	2
Tax shield 40.0%		1.6	1.6	1.2	0.8
PV 5.0%	$4.67				

b. We can use Eq. 7.5:

	0	1	2	3	4
EBIT		10	10	10	10
Taxes		-4	-4	-4	-4
Unlevered Net Income		6	6	6	6
Depreciation		25	25	25	25
Cap Ex	-100				
Additions to NWC	-20				20
FCF	-120	31	31	31	51

FCF = EBIT × (1 – T_c) + Depreciation – CapEx – ΔNWC

Alternatively, we can use Eq. 18.9:

FCF = FCFE + Int×(1 – T_C) – Net New Debt

	Year 0	Year 1	Year 2	Year 3	Year 4
FCFE	-40	28.6	8.6	9.2	9.8
+ After-tax Interest		2.4	2.4	1.8	1.2
- Net New Debt	-80	0	20	20	40
FCF	-120	31	31	31	51

c. With predetermined debt levels, the APV method is easiest.

Step 1: Determine r_U. Assuming the company has maintained a historical D/E ratio of 0.20, we can approximate its unlevered cost of capital using Eq. 18.6:

$$r_U = (1 / 1.2)\ 11\% + (.2 / 1.2)\ 5\% = 10\%$$

Step 2: Compute NPV of FCF without leverage

$$\text{NPV} = -120 + \frac{31}{1.10} + \frac{31}{1.10^2} + \frac{31}{1.10^3} + \frac{51}{1.10^4} = -8.1$$

Step 3: Compute APV

$$APV = NPV + PV(ITS) = -8.1 + 4.7 = -3.4$$

So the project actually has negative value.

18-18. Your firm is considering building a $600 million plant to manufacture HDTV circuitry. You expect operating profits (EBITDA) of $145 million per year for the next 10 years. The plant will be depreciated on a straight-line basis over 10 years (assuming no salvage value for tax purposes). After 10 years, the plant will have a salvage value of $300 million (which, since it will be fully depreciated, is then taxable). The project requires $50 million in working capital at the start, which will be recovered in year 10 when the project shuts down. The corporate tax rate is 35%. All cash flows occur at the end of the year.

a. If the risk-free rate is 5%, the expected return of the market is 11%, and the asset beta for the consumer electronics industry is 1.67, what is the NPV of the project?

b. Suppose that you can finance $400 million of the cost of the plant using 10-year, 9% coupon bonds sold at par. This amount is incremental new debt associated specifically with this project and will not alter other aspects of the firm's capital structure. What is the value of the project, including the tax shield of the debt?

a. First we compute the FCF:

$FCF_0 = -600$ (Capex) – 50 (Inc in NWC) = –650

Using Eq. 7.6:

$FCF_{1-9} = 145 \times (1 - 0.35) + 0.35 \times 60 = 115.25$

After-tax Salvage Value = $300 \times (1 - 0.35) = 195$

$FCF_{10} = 145 \times (1 - 0.35) + 0.35 \times 60 + 50$ (Inc in NWC) + 195 (salvage)

= 360.25

From the CAPM, $r_U = 5\% + 1.67(11\% - 5\%) = 15\%$

Therefore,

$$NPV = -650 + 115.25 \times \frac{1}{.15}\left(1 - \frac{1}{1.15^9}\right) + \frac{360.25}{1.15^{10}} = -11.0$$

Without leverage, project NPV is –$11 million.

b. Because the debt level is predetermined, we can use the APV approach. Because the bonds initially trade at par, the interest payments are the 9% coupon payments of the bond. Assuming annual coupons:

$$PV(ITS) = 400 \times 0.09 \times 0.35 \times \frac{1}{.09}\left(1 - \frac{1}{1.09^{10}}\right) = \$80.9 \text{ million.}$$

Therefore,

APV = NPV + PV(ITS) = –11 + 81 = $70 million.

Note that this project is only profitable as a result of the tax benefits of leverage.

18-19. DFS Corporation is currently an all-equity firm, with assets with a market value of $100 million and 4 million shares outstanding. DFS is considering a leveraged recapitalization to boost its share price. The firm plans to raise a fixed amount of permanent debt (i.e., the outstanding principal will remain constant) and use the proceeds to repurchase shares. DFS pays a 35% corporate tax rate, so one motivation for taking on the debt is to reduce the firm's tax liability. However, the upfront investment banking fees associated with the recapitalization will be 5% of the amount of debt raised. Adding leverage will also create the possibility of future financial distress or agency costs; shown below are DFS's estimates for different levels of debt:

Debt amount ($ million):	0	10	20	30	40	50
Present value of expected distress and agency costs ($ million):	0.0	–0.3	–1.8	–4.3	–7.5	–11.3

a. Based on this information, which level of debt is the best choice for DFS?

b. Estimate the stock price once this transaction is announced.

a. Because the debt is permanent, the value of the tax shield is 35% × D. From that we must deduct the 5% issuance cost, and the PV of distress and agency costs to determine the net benefit of leverage.

Debt Amount ($M):	0	10	20	30	40	50
PV of Expected Distress and Agency Costs ($M):	0.0	–0.3	–1.8	–4.3	–7.5	–11.3
Tax Benefit less Issuance Cost (30%):	0.0	+3.0	+6.0	+9.0	+12.0	+15.0
Net Benefit:	0.0	+2.7	+4.2	+4.7	+4.5	+3.7

Based on this information, the greatest net benefit occurs for debt = $30 million.

b. Value of assets goes up from $100M to $104.7M. Thus, the share price should rise to $26.175.

18-20. Your firm is considering a $150 million investment to launch a new product line. The project is expected to generate a free cash flow of $20 million per year, and its unlevered cost of capital is 10%. To fund the investment, your firm will take on $100 million in permanent debt.

a. Suppose the marginal corporate tax rate is 35%. Ignoring issuance costs, what is the NPV of the investment?

b. Suppose your firm will pay a 2% underwriting fee when issuing the debt. It will raise the remaining $50 million by issuing equity. In addition to the 5% underwriting fee for the equity issue, you believe that your firm's current share price of $40 is $5 per share less than its true value. What is the NPV of the investment including any tax benefits of leverage? (Assume all fees are on an after-tax basis.)

a. With permanent debt the APV method is simplest. NPV(unlevered) = –150 + 20 / 0.10 = $50 million. PV(ITS) = $\tau_c \times D$ = 35% × 100 = $35 million. Thus, the NPV with leverage is APV = NPV + PV(ITS) = 50 + 35 = $85 million.

b. Financing costs = 2% × 100 + 5% × 50 = $4.5 million. (We assume these amounts are after-tax.)

Underpricing cost = (5 / 40) × 50 = $6.25 million

APV = 85 – 4.5 – 6.25 = 74.25 million

18-21. Consider Avco's RFX project from Section 18.3. Suppose that Avco is receiving government loan guarantees that allow it to borrow at the 6% rate. Without these guarantees, Avco would pay 6.5% on its debt.

a. What is Avco's unlevered cost of capital given its true debt cost of capital of 6.5%?

b. **What is the unlevered value of the RFX project in this case? What is the present value of the interest tax shield?**

c. **What is the NPV of the loan guarantees? (*Hint* : Because the actual loan amounts will fluctuate with the value of the project, discount the expected interest savings at the unlevered cost of capital.)**

d. **What is the levered value of the RFX project, including the interest tax shield and the NPV of the loan guarantees?**

a. We use Eq. 18.6 with the true debt cost:

$$r_u = \frac{E}{E+D} r_E + \frac{D}{E+D} r_D = 0.50 \times 10\% + 0.50 \times 6.50\% = 8.25\%$$

b. The unlevered value is the PV of the FCF discounted at r_U:

$$V^U = 18 \times \frac{1}{.0825}\left(1 - \frac{1}{1.0825^4}\right) = \$59.29 \text{ million}$$

The amount of the interest tax shield each period is that same as computed in Table 18.5 in the text, but now we discount at $r_u = 8.25\%$:

$$PV(ITS) = \frac{0.73}{1.0825} + \frac{0.57}{1.0825^2} + \frac{0.39}{1.0825^3} + \frac{0.20}{1.0825^4} = \$1.62 \text{ million}$$

c. The loan guarantee reduces the interest paid from 6.5% to 6% each year. Thus, the savings in year t is 0.5% × D_{t-1}. The value of the loan guarantee is the present value of this savings. Because the debt amount D will vary with the value of the project over time, we discount the savings at rate r_U.

$$NPV(Loan) = \frac{.005 \times 30.62}{1.0825} + \frac{.005 \times 23.71}{1.0825^2} + \frac{.005 \times 16.32}{1.0825^3} + \frac{.005 \times 8.43}{1.0825^4} = \$0.34 \text{ million}$$

d. APV = V^U + PV(ITS) + NPV(Loan) = 59.29 + 1.62 + 0.34 = \$61.25 million

Note that this is the same value we originally computed using the WACC method, where we used the firm's actual borrowing cost rather than the true rate it would have received.

18-22. Arden Corporation is considering an investment in a new project with an unlevered cost of capital of 9%. Arden's marginal corporate tax rate is 40%, and its debt cost of capital is 5%.

a. **Suppose Arden adjusts its debt continuously to maintain a constant debt-equity ratio of 50%. What is the appropriate WACC for the new project?**

b. **Suppose Arden adjusts its debt once per year to maintain a constant debt-equity ratio of 50%. What is the appropriate WACC for the new project now?**

c. **Suppose the project has free cash flows of \$10 million per year, which are expected to decline by 2% per year. What is the value of the project in parts (a) and (b) now?**

a. $r_{wacc} = r_u - d\tau_c(r_D) = 9\% - (.5/1.5)(0.40)5\% = 8.333\%$

b. $r_{wacc} = r_u - d\tau_c(r_D + \phi(r_u - r_D))$

$$= 9\% - (.5/1.5)(0.40)\left(5\% + \frac{.05}{1.05}(9\% - 5\%)\right) = 8.308\%$$

Alternatively, from Eq. 18.17:

$$r_{wacc} = r_u - d\tau_c r_D \frac{1+r_u}{1+r_D}$$

$$= 9\% - (.5/1.5)(0.40)5\% \frac{1.09}{1.05} = 8.308\%$$

c. In case (a), $V^L = 10/(.08333 + .02) = \$96.78$ million.

In case (b), $V^L = 10/(.08308 + .02) = \$97.01$ million.

Note the minor difference in the two cases. Case (b) is higher because the tax shields are less risky when debt is fixed over the year.

18-23. XL Sports is expected to generate free cash flows of $10.9 million per year. XL has permanent debt of $40 million, a tax rate of 40%, and an unlevered cost of capital of 10%.

a. What is the value of XL's equity using the APV method?

b. What is XL's WACC? What is XL's equity value using the WACC method?

c. If XL's debt cost of capital is 5%, what is XL's equity cost of capital?

d. What is XL's equity value using the FTE method?

a. $V^U = 10.9 / 10\% = \$109$ million. PV(ITS) = 0.40 × $40 million = $16 million.

V^L = APV = 109 + 16 = $125 million, so E = 125 – 40 = $85 million.

b. $$r_{wacc} = r_u - d\tau_c(r_D + \phi(r_u - r_D)) = r_u - d\tau_c(r_D + r_u - r_D)$$
$$= r_u - d\tau_c r_u$$
$$= 10\% - (40/125)(0.40)10\% = 8.72\%$$

Using the WACC method, $V^L = 10.9 / 8.72\% = \$125$ million, so E = 125 – 40 = $85 million.

c. If XL's debt cost of capital is 5%, what is XL's equity cost of capital?

From Eq. 18.20:

$$r_E = r_u + \frac{D^s}{E}(r_u - r_D)$$

$$= 10\% + \frac{40-16}{125-40}(10\% - 5\%) = 11.412\%$$

d. FCFE = FCF – After-tax Interest + Net new debt = 10.9 – 5%(1 – 0.40)40 = 9.7

E = 9.7 / 0.11412 = $85 million.

18-24. Propel Corporation plans to make a $50 million investment, initially funded completely with debt. The free cash flows of the investment and Propel's incremental debt from the project follow:

Year	0	1	2	3
Free cash flows	–50	40	20	25
Debt	50	30	15	0

Propel's incremental debt for the project will be paid off according to the predetermined schedule shown. Propel's debt cost of capital is 8%, and its tax rate is 40%. Propel also estimates an unlevered cost of capital for the project of 12%.

a. **Use the APV method to determine the levered value of the project at each date and its initial NPV.**

b. **Calculate the WACC for this project at each date. How does the WACC change over time? Why?**

c. **Compute the project's NPV using the WACC method.**

d. **Compute the equity cost of capital for this project at each date. How does the equity cost of capital change over time? Why?**

e. **Compute the project's equity value using the FTE method. How does the initial equity value compare with the NPV calculated in parts (a) and (c)?**

a. Note that this answer actually uses the APV method instead of the WACC method.

We compute V^U at each date by discounting the project's <u>future</u> FCF at rate $r_U = 12\%$.

$(V_t^U = NPV(r_U, FCF_{t+1} : FCF_T))$:

Year	**0**	**1**	**2**	**3**
FCF	-50	40	20	25
V^u	\$69.45	\$37.79	\$22.32	

Then we compute the value of the future interest tax shields at each date by discounting at rate rD = 8%:

Year	**0**	**1**	**2**	**3**
D	50	30	15	0
interest at 8%		4	2.4	1.2
tax shield at 40%		1.6	0.96	0.48
PV(ITS)	\$2.69	\$1.30	\$0.44	

Finally, we compute $V^L = APV = V^U + PV(ITS)$:

Year	**0**	**1**	**2**	**3**
V^u	\$69.45	\$37.79	\$22.32	
PV(ITS)	\$2.69	\$1.30	\$0.44	
V^L	\$72.14	\$39.09	\$22.77	

Given the initial investment of \$50, the project's NPV is 72.14 – 50 = \$22.14.

b. We can compute the WACC at each date using Eq. 18.21. The debt-to-value ratio, d, is given by D/V^L. The debt persistence ϕ is given by $T^s/(\tau_c D)$, where T^s =PV(ITS) (since all tax shields are predetermined):

Year	<u>0</u>	<u>1</u>	<u>2</u>	<u>3</u>
D	50	30	15	0
V^L	\$72.14	\$39.09	\$22.77	
$d = D/V^L$	69%	77%	66%	
$T^s = PV(ITS)$	\$2.69	\$1.30	\$0.44	
T^s/t_cD	13.4%	10.8%	7.4%	
r_{wacc}	9.63%	9.41%	9.81%	

Note that the WACC changes over time, decreasing from date 0 to 1, and increasing from date 1 to 2. The WACC fluctuates because the leverage ratio of the project changes over time (as does the persistence of the debt).

c. We can compute the levered value of the project by discounting the FCF using the WACC at each date:

$$V_2^L = \frac{FCF_3}{1+r_{wacc}(2)} = \frac{25}{1.0981} = \$22.77$$

$$V_1^L = \frac{FCF_2 + V_2^L}{1+r_{wacc}(1)} = \frac{20+22.77}{1.0941} = \$39.09$$

$$V_0^L = \frac{FCF_1 + V_1^L}{1+r_{wacc}(0)} = \frac{40+39.09}{1.0963} = \$72.14.$$

Note that these results coincide with part (a).

d. We can compute the project's equity cost of capital using Eq. 18.20. Note that $D^s = D - T^s = D - PV(ITS)$:

Year	0	1	2	3
$D^s = D - T^s$	\$47.31	\$28.70	\$14.56	
$E = V^L - D$	\$22.14	\$9.09	\$7.77	
D^s/E	2.14	3.16	1.87	
r_E	20.55%	24.63%	19.50%	

Note the equity cost of capital rises and then falls with the project's effective debt-equity ratio, D^s/E.

e. We first compute FCFE at each date by deducting the after-tax interest expenses (equivalently, deducting interest and adding back the tax shield) and adding net increases in debt:

Year	0	1	2	3
FCF	-50	40	20	25
- Interest		-4	-2.4	-1.2
+ Tax shield		1.6	0.96	0.48
+ Inc. in Debt	50	-20	-15	-15
FCFE	0	17.6	3.56	9.28
E	22.14	9.09	7.77	

Then, we compute the equity value of the project by discounting FCFE using r_E at each date:

$$E_2 = \frac{FCFE_3}{1+r_E(2)} = \frac{9.28}{1.1950} = \$7.77$$

$$E_1 = \frac{FCFE_2 + E_2}{1+r_E(1)} = \frac{3.56+7.77}{1.2463} = \$9.09$$

$$E_0 = \frac{FCFE_1 + E_1}{1+r_E(0)} = \frac{17.60+9.09}{1.2055} = \$22.14$$

These values for equity match those computed earlier, and match the project's initial NPV.

Note that to use the WACC or FTE methods here, we relied on V^L computed in the APV method. We could also solve for the value using the WACC or FTE methods directly using the techniques in appendix 18A.3.

18-25. Gartner Systems has no debt and an equity cost of capital of 10%. Gartner's current market capitalization is $100 million, and its free cash flows are expected to grow at 3% per year. Gartner's corporate tax rate is 35%. Investors pay tax rates of 40% on interest income and 20% on equity income.

a. Suppose Gartner adds $50 million in permanent debt and uses the proceeds to repurchase shares. What will Gartner's levered value be in this case?

b. Suppose instead Gartner decides to maintain a 50% debt-to-value ratio going forward. If Gartner's debt cost of capital is 6.67%, what will Gartner's levered value be in this case?

a. From Eq. 18.25, $\tau^* = 1 - (1 - 0.35)(1 - 0.20) / (1 - 0.40) = 13.333\%$.

Using the APV method, $V^L = V^U + \tau_c D = 100 + 0.1333 \times 50 = \$106.67$ million

b. With a constant debt-to-value ratio, the WACC approach is easiest. We need to determine Gartner's WACC with this new leverage policy. To compute the WACC, we need to determine the new equity cost of capital using Eq. 18.24:

$$r_U = \frac{E}{E + D^s} r_E + \frac{D^s}{E + D^s} r_D^*.$$

Because Gartner initially has no leverage, $r_U = r_E = 10\%$. Next, $r_D^* = r_D\,(1 - \tau i)/(1 - \tau e) = 6.67\%(1 - 0.40) / (1 - 0.20) = 5.00\%$. With a constant debt-to-value ratio, $T^s = 0$ and $D^s / (E + D^s) = D / (E + D) = 50\%$. Thus,

$$10\% = 0.50 r_E + 0.50(5\%)$$

implying that r_E rises to 15%. Therefore, Gartner's WACC is

$$r_{wacc} = \frac{E}{E + D} r_E + \frac{D}{E + D} r_D (1 - \tau_c) = 0.50(15\%) + 0.50(6.67\%)(1 - 0.35) = 9.67\%.$$

We also need to estimate Gartner's FCF. Based on its current market cap,

$100 = FCF / (10\% - 3\%)$ implies $FCF = \$7$ million.

Therefore, with the new leverage,

$V^L = 7 / (9.67\% - 3\%) = \$\,104.95$ million.

18-26. Revtek, Inc., has an equity cost of capital of 12% and a debt cost of capital of 6%. Revtek maintains a constant debt-equity ratio of 0.5, and its tax rate is 35%.

a. What is Revtek's WACC given its current debt-equity ratio?

b. Assuming no personal taxes, how will Revtek's WACC change if it increases its debt-equity ratio to 2 and its debt cost of capital remains at 6%?

c. Now suppose investors pay tax rates of 40% on interest income and 15% on income from equity. How will Revtek's WACC change if it increases its debt-equity ratio to 2 in this case?

d. Provide an intuitive explanation for the difference in your answers to parts (b) and (c).

a. $$r_{wacc} = \frac{E}{E + D} r_E + \frac{D}{E + D} r_D (1 - \tau_c) = (1/1.5)(12\%) + (.5/1.5)(6\%)(1 - 0.35) = 9.3\%$$

b. From Eq. 18.6:

$$r_U = \frac{E}{E + D} r_E + \frac{D}{E + D} r_D = (1/1.5)(12\%) + (.5/1.5)(6\%) = 10\%$$

From Eq. 18.11:

$$r_{wacc} = r_U - d\tau_c r_D = 10\% - (2/3)(.35)6\% = 8.6\%$$

c. Given their initial capital structure, we would estimate Revtek's unlevered cost of capital as (using Eq. 18.24):

$$r_U = \frac{E}{E+D} r_E + \frac{D}{E+D} r_D^* = (1/1.5)(12\%) + (.5/1.5)(4.235\%) = 9.41\%.$$

We can also use Eq. 18.24 to calculate r_E with higher leverage:

$9.41\% = (1/3)r_E + (2/3)4.235\%$ so that $r_E = 19.76$.

Then,

$$r_{wacc} = \frac{E}{E+D} r_E + \frac{D}{E+D} r_D(1-\tau_c) = (1/3)(19.76\%) + (2/3)(6\%)(1-0.35) = 9.19\%.$$

d. When investors pay higher taxes on interest income than equity income, the tax benefit of leverage is reduced. Thus, for the same increase in leverage, the decline in the WACC is smaller in the presence of investor taxes.

Chapter 19
Valuation and Financial Modeling: A Case Study

19-1. **You would like to compare Ideko's profitability to its competitors' profitability using the EBITDA/sales multiple. Given Ideko's current sales of $75 million, use the information in Table 19.2 to compute a range of EBITDA for Ideko assuming it is run as profitably as its competitors.**

Ideko's 2005 sales are $75 million.

Find the highest and lowest EBITDA values across all three firms and the industry as a whole:

	EBITDA/Sales (%)	EBITDA ($ mil)
Oakley	17.0	12.75
Luxcottica	18.5	13.875
Nike	15.9	11.925
Industry	12.1	9.075

This implies an EBITDA range of $9.075 to $13.875 million.

19-2. **Assume that Ideko's market share will increase by 0.5% per year rather than the 1% used in the chapter. What production capacity will Ideko require each year? When will an expansion become necessary (when production volume will exceed the current level by 50%)?**

First compute the projected annual market share:

		Growth/Yr	2005	2006	2007	2008	2009	2010
Sales Data								
1	Market Size (000 units)	5.0%	10,000	10,500	11,025	11,576	12,155	12,763
2	Market Share	0.5%	10.0%	10.5%	11.0%	11.5%	12.0%	12.5%
3	Ave. Sales Price ($/unit)	2.0%	75.00	76.50	78.03	79.59	81.18	82.81

Using these projections, calculate the projected annual production volume:

		2005	2006	2007	2008	2009	2010
Production Volume (000 units)							
1	Market Size	10,000	10,500	11,025	11,576	12,155	12,763
2	Market Share	10.0%	10.5%	11.0%	11.5%	12.0%	12.5%
3	Production Volume (1x2)	1,000	1,103	1,213	1,331	1,459	1,595

Based on these estimates, it will be 2010 before current capacity is exceeded and an expansion becomes necessary.

19-3. **Under the assumption that Ideko market share will increase by 0.5% per year, you determine that the plant will require an expansion in 2010. The cost of this expansion will be $15 million. Assuming the financing of the expansion will be delayed accordingly, calculate the projected interest payments and the amount of the projected interest tax shields (assuming that the interest rates on the term loans remain the same as in the chapter) through 2010.**

			2005	2006	2007	2008	2009	2010
Debt & Interest Table ($000s)								
1	Outstanding Debt		100,000	100,000	100,000	100,000	100,000	115,000
2	Interest on Term Loan	6.80%		(6,800)	(6,800)	(6,800)	(6,800)	(6,800)
3	Interest Tax Shield			2,380	2,380	2,380	2,380	2,380

19-4. **Under the assumption that Ideko's market share will increase by 0.5% per year (and the investment and financing will be adjusted as described in Problem 3), you project the following depreciation:**

	Year	2005	2006	2007	2008	2009	2010
Fixed Assets and Capital Investment ($ 000)							
2	New Investment	5,000	5,000	5,000	5,000	5,000	20,000
3	Depreciation	(5,500)	(5,450)	(5,405)	(5,365)	(5,328)	(6,795)

Using this information, project net income through 2010 (that is, reproduce Table 19.7 under the new assumptions).

	Year	2005	2006	2007	2008	2009	2010
INCOME STATEMENT ($000s)							
1	Sales	75,000	84,341	94,631	105,956	118,413	132,105
2	Cost of Goods Sold						
3	Raw Materials	(16,000)	(17,816)	(19,794)	(21,946)	(24,285)	(26,828)
4	Direct Labor Costs	(18,000)	(20,639)	(23,611)	(26,955)	(30,715)	(34,938)
5	**Gross Profit**	41,000	45,886	51,226	57,056	63,413	70,339
6	Sales & Marketing	(11,250)	(13,916)	(17,034)	(20,662)	(23,683)	(26,421)
7	Administration	(13,500)	(12,651)	(14,195)	(14,834)	(15,394)	(17,174)
8	**EBITDA**	16,250	19,319	19,998	21,560	24,337	26,745
9	Depreciation	(5,500)	(5,450)	(5,405)	(5,365)	(5,328)	(6,795)
10	**EBIT**	10,750	13,869	14,593	16,196	19,009	19,949
11	Interest Expense (net)	(75)	(6,800)	(6,800)	(6,800)	(6,800)	(6,800)
12	**Pretax Income**	10,675	7,069	7,793	9,396	12,209	13,149
13	Income Tax	(3,736)	(2,474)	(2,728)	(3,289)	(4,273)	(4,602)
14	**Net Income**	**6,939**	**4,595**	**5,065**	**6,107**	**7,936**	**8,547**

19-5. Under the assumptions that Ideko's market share will increase by 0.5% per year (implying that the investment, financing, and depreciation will be adjusted as described in Problems 3 and 4) and that the forecasts in Table 19.8 remain the same, calculate Ideko's working capital requirements though 2010 (that is, reproduce Table 19.9 under the new assumptions).

	Year	2005	2006	2007	2008	2009	2010
Working Capital ($000s)							
Assets							
1	Accounts Receivable	18,493	13,864	15,556	17,418	19,465	21,716
2	Raw Materials	1,973	1,464	1,627	1,804	1,996	2,205
3	Finished Goods	4,192	4,741	5,351	6,029	6,781	7,615
4	Minimum Cash Balance	6,164	6,932	7,778	8,709	9,733	10,858
5	Total Current Assets	30,822	27,002	30,312	33,959	37,975	42,394
Liabilities							
6	Wages Payable	1,295	1,368	1,554	1,717	1,895	2,142
7	Other Accounts Payable	3,360	3,912	4,540	5,253	5,914	6,565
8	Total Current Liabilities	4,654	5,280	6,094	6,970	7,809	8,706
Net Working Capital		26,168	21,722	24,218	26,989	30,166	33,687
9	Increase in Net Working Capital		(4,446)	2,496	2,771	3,177	3,521

19-6. Under the assumptions that Ideko's market share will increase by 0.5% per year (implying that the investment, financing, and depreciation will be adjusted as described in Problems 3 and 4) but that the projected improvements in net working capital do not transpire (so the numbers in Table 19.8 remain at their 2005 levels through 2010), calculate Ideko's working capital requirements though 2010 (that is, reproduce Table 19.9 under these assumptions).

	Year	2005	2006	2007	2008	2009	2010
Working Capital ($000s)							
Assets							
1	Accounts Receivable	18,493	20,796	23,334	26,126	29,198	32,574
2	Raw Materials	1,973	2,197	2,440	2,706	2,994	3,308
3	Finished Goods	4,192	4,741	5,351	6,029	6,781	7,615
4	Minimum Cash Balance	6,164	6,932	7,778	8,709	9,733	10,858
5	Total Current Assets	30,822	34,666	38,903	43,569	48,705	54,354
Liabilities							
6	Wages Payable	1,295	1,368	1,554	1,717	1,895	2,142
7	Other Accounts Payable	3,360	3,912	4,540	5,253	5,914	6,565
8	Total Current Liabilities	4,654	5,280	6,094	6,970	7,809	8,706
Net Working Capital		26,168	29,386	32,809	36,599	40,897	45,648
9	Increase in Net Working Capital		3,218	3,423	3,790	4,297	4,751

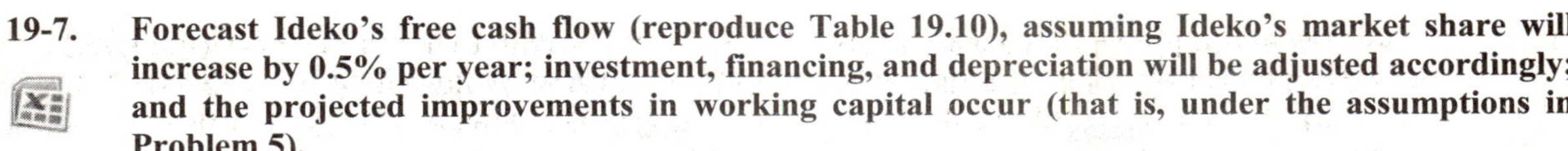

19-7. **Forecast Ideko's free cash flow (reproduce Table 19.10), assuming Ideko's market share will increase by 0.5% per year; investment, financing, and depreciation will be adjusted accordingly; and the projected improvements in working capital occur (that is, under the assumptions in Problem 5).**

	Year	2005	2006	2007	2008	2009	2010
	Free Cash Flow ($000s)						
1	**Net Income**		4,595	5,065	6,107	7,936	8,547
2	Plus: After-Tax Interest Expense		4,420	4,420	4,420	4,420	4,420
3	**Unlevered Net Income**		9,015	9,485	10,527	12,356	12,967
4	Plus: Depreciation		5,450	5,405	5,365	5,328	6,795
5	Less: Increases in NWC		4,446	(2,496)	(2,771)	(3,177)	(3,521)
6	Less: Capital Expenditures		(5,000)	(5,000)	(5,000)	(5,000)	(20,000)
7	**Free Cash Flow of Firm**		13,911	7,394	8,121	9,507	(3,759)
8	Plus: Net Borrowing		-	-	-	-	15,000
9	Less: After-Tax Interest Expense		(4,420)	(4,420)	(4,420)	(4,420)	(4,420)
10	**Free Cash Flow to Equity**		9,491	2,974	3,701	5,087	6,821

19-8. **Forecast Ideko's free cash flow (reproduce Table 19.10), assuming Ideko's market share will increase by 0.5% per year; investment, financing, and depreciation will be adjusted accordingly; and the projected improvements in working capital do *not* occur (that is, under the assumptions in Problem 6).**

	Year	2005	2006	2007	2008	2009	2010
	Free Cash Flow ($000s)						
1	**Net Income**		4,595	5,065	6,107	7,936	8,547
2	Plus: After-Tax Interest Expense		4,420	4,420	4,420	4,420	4,420
3	**Unlevered Net Income**		9,015	9,485	10,527	12,356	12,967
4	Plus: Depreciation		5,450	5,405	5,365	5,328	6,795
5	Less: Increases in NWC		(3,218)	(3,423)	(3,790)	(4,297)	(4,751)
6	Less: Capital Expenditures		(5,000)	(5,000)	(5,000)	(5,000)	(20,000)
7	**Free Cash Flow of Firm**		6,246	6,467	7,102	8,387	(4,989)
8	Plus: Net Borrowing		-	-	-	-	15,000
9	Less: After-Tax Interest Expense		(4,420)	(4,420)	(4,420)	(4,420)	(4,420)
10	**Free Cash Flow to Equity**		1,826	2,047	2,682	3,967	5,591

19-9. Reproduce Ideko's balance sheet and statement of cash flows, assuming Ideko's market share will increase by 0.5% per year; investment, financing, and depreciation will be adjusted accordingly; and the projected improvements in working capital occur (that is, under the assumptions in Problem 5).

	Year	2005	2006	2007	2008	2009	2010
BALANCE SHEET ($000s)							
Assets							
1	Cash & Cash Equivalents	6,164	6,932	7,778	8,709	9,733	10,858
2	Accounts Receivable	18,493	13,864	15,556	17,418	19,465	21,716
3	Inventories	6,164	6,205	6,978	7,833	8,777	9,820
4	**Total Current Assets**	30,822	27,002	30,312	33,959	37,975	42,394
5	Property, Plant and Equipment	49,500	49,050	48,645	48,281	47,952	61,157
6	Goodwill	72,332	72,332	72,332	72,332	72,332	72,332
7	**Total Assets**	152,654	148,384	151,289	154,572	158,259	175,883
Liabilities							
8	Accounts Payable	4,654	5,280	6,094	6,970	7,809	8,706
9	Debt	100,000	100,000	100,000	100,000	100,000	115,000
10	**Total Liabilities**	104,654	105,280	106,094	106,970	107,809	123,706
Stockholders' Equity							
11	Starting Stockholders' Equity		48,000	43,104	45,195	47,601	50,451
12	Net Income		4,595	5,065	6,107	7,936	8,547
13	Dividends	(2,000)	(9,491)	(2,974)	(3,701)	(5,087)	(6,821)
14	Capital Contributions	50,000	-	-	-	-	-
15	**Stockholders' Equity**	48,000	43,104	45,195	47,601	50,451	52,177
16	**Total Liabilities & Equity**	152,654	148,384	151,289	154,572	158,259	175,883

	Year	2005	2006	2007	2008	2009	2010
STATEMENT OF CASH FLOWS ($000s)							
1	**Net Income**		4,595	5,065	6,107	7,936	8,547
2	Depreciation		5,450	5,405	5,365	5,328	6,795
3	Changes in Working Capital						
4	Accounts Receivable		4,629	(1,691)	(1,862)	(2,048)	(2,251)
5	Inventory		(41)	(773)	(854)	(944)	(1,043)
6	Accounts Payable		626	814	876	838	898
7	**Cash from Operating Activities**		15,259	8,820	9,632	11,110	12,946
8	Capital Expenditures		(5,000)	(5,000)	(5,000)	(5,000)	(20,000)
9	Other Investment		-	-	-	-	-
10	**Cash from Investing Activities**		(5,000)	(5,000)	(5,000)	(5,000)	(20,000)
11	Net Borrowing		-	-	-	-	15,000
12	Dividends		(9,491)	(2,974)	(3,701)	(5,087)	(6,821)
13	Capital Contributions		-	-	-	-	-
14	**Cash from Financing Activities**		(9,491)	(2,974)	(3,701)	(5,087)	8,179
15	**Change in Cash & Cash Equivalents**		768	846	931	1,024	1,125

19-10. Reproduce Ideko's balance sheet and statement of cash flows, assuming Ideko's market share will increase by 0.5% per year; investment, financing, and depreciation will be adjusted accordingly; and the projected improvements in working capital do *not* occur (that is, under the assumptions in Problem 6).

	Year	2005	2006	2007	2008	2009	2010
BALANCE SHEET ($000s)							
Assets							
1	Cash & Cash Equivalents	6,164	6,932	7,778	8,709	9,733	10,858
2	Accounts Receivable	18,493	20,796	23,334	26,126	29,198	32,574
3	Inventories	6,164	6,938	7,792	8,734	9,775	10,922
4	**Total Current Assets**	30,822	34,666	38,903	43,569	48,705	54,354
5	Property, Plant and Equipment	49,500	49,050	48,645	48,281	47,952	61,157
6	Goodwill	72,332	72,332	72,332	72,332	72,332	72,332
7	**Total Assets**	152,654	156,048	159,880	164,182	168,990	187,844
Liabilities							
8	Accounts Payable	4,654	5,280	6,094	6,970	7,809	8,706
9	Debt	100,000	100,000	100,000	100,000	100,000	115,000
10	**Total Liabilities**	104,654	105,280	106,094	106,970	107,809	123,706
Stockholders' Equity							
11	Starting Stockholders' Equity		48,000	50,768	53,786	57,212	61,181
12	Net Income		4,595	5,065	6,107	7,936	8,547
13	Dividends	(2,000)	(1,826)	(2,047)	(2,682)	(3,967)	(5,591)
14	Capital Contributions	50,000	-	-	-	-	-
15	**Stockholders' Equity**	48,000	50,768	53,786	57,212	61,181	64,137
16	**Total Liabilities & Equity**	152,654	156,048	159,880	164,182	168,990	187,844

	Year	2005	2006	2007	2008	2009	2010
STATEMENT OF CASH FLOWS ($000s)							
1	**Net Income**		4,595	5,065	6,107	7,936	8,547
2	Depreciation		5,450	5,405	5,365	5,328	6,795
3	Changes in Working Capital						
4	Accounts Receivable		(2,303)	(2,537)	(2,793)	(3,072)	(3,376)
5	Inventory		(773)	(854)	(943)	(1,040)	(1,148)
6	Accounts Payable		626	814	876	838	898
7	**Cash from Operating Activities**		7,594	7,893	8,613	9,990	11,717
8	Capital Expenditures		(5,000)	(5,000)	(5,000)	(5,000)	(20,000)
9	Other Investment		-	-	-	-	-
10	**Cash from Investing Activities**		(5,000)	(5,000)	(5,000)	(5,000)	(20,000)
11	Net Borrowing		-	-	-	-	15,000
12	Dividends		(1,826)	(2,047)	(2,682)	(3,967)	(5,591)
13	Capital Contributions		-	-	-	-	-
14	**Cash from Financing Activities**		(1,826)	(2,047)	(2,682)	(3,967)	9,409
15	**Change in Cash & Cash Equivalents**		768	846	931	1,024	1,125

19-11. Calculate Ideko's unlevered cost of capital when Ideko's unlevered beta is 1.1 rather than 1.2, and all other required estimates are the same as in the chapter.

$$r_u = r_f + \beta_u \left(E\left[R_{mkt}\right] - r_f\right) = 4\% + 1.1(5\%) = 9.5\%$$

19-12. Calculate Ideko's unlevered cost of capital when the market risk premium is 6% rather than 5%, the risk-free rate is 5% rather than 4%, and all other required estimates are the same as in the chapter.

$$r_u = r_f + \beta_u\left(E\left[R_{mkt}\right] - r_f\right) = 5\% + 1.2(6\%) = 12.2\%$$

19-13. Using the information produced in the income statement in Problem 4, use EBITDA as a multiple to estimate the continuation value in 2010, assuming the current value remains unchanged (reproduce Table 19.15). Infer the EV/sales and the unlevered and levered P/E ratios implied by the continuation value you calculated.

Continuation Value: Multiples Approach ($000s)				
1	EBITDA in 2010	26,745	**Common Multiples**	
2	EBITDA multiple	9.1x	EV/Sales	1.8x
3	**Cont. Enterprise Value**	**243,377**	P/E (levered)	15.0x
4	Debt	(115,000)	P/E (unlevered)	18.8x
5	**Cont. Equity Value**	**128,377**		

19-14. How does the assumption on future improvements in working capital affect your answer to Problem 13?

It does not affect the answer because the working capital savings do not affect EBITDA or debt levels.

Continuation Value: Multiples Approach ($000s)				
1	EBITDA in 2010	26,745	**Common Multiples**	
2	EBITDA multiple	9.1x	EV/Sales	1.8x
3	**Cont. Enterprise Value**	**243,377**	P/E (levered)	15.0x
4	Debt	(115,000)	P/E (unlevered)	18.8x
5	**Cont. Equity Value**	**128,377**		

19-15. Approximately what expected future long-run growth rate would provide the same EBITDA multiple in 2010 as Ideko has today (i.e., 9.1)? Assume that the future debt-to-value ratio is held constant at 40%; the debt cost of capital is 6.8%; Ideko's market share will increase by 0.5% per year until 2010; investment, financing, and depreciation will be adjusted accordingly; and the projected improvements in working capital occur (i.e., the assumptions in Problem 5).

Approximately 5.6%.

Continuation Value: DCF and EBITDA Multiple ($000s)				
1	Long-term growth rate	5.60%	Target D/(E+D)	40.0%
2			Projected WACC	9.05%
Free Cash Flow in 2011				
3	Unlevered Net Income	13,693	**Cont. Enterprise Value**	**243,098**
4	Less: Inc. in NWC	(1,886)		
5	Less: Inc. in Fixed Assets	(3,425)	**Implied EBITDA Multiple**	**9.1x**
6	Free Cash Flow	8,382		

19-16. Approximately what expected future long-run growth rate would provide the same EBITDA multiple in 2010 as Ideko has today (i.e., 9.1). Assume that the future debt-to-value ratio is held constant at 40%; the debt cost of capital is 6.8%; Ideko's market share will increase by 0.5% per year; investment, financing, and depreciation will be adjusted accordingly; and the projected improvements in working capital do *not* occur (i.e., the assumptions in Problem 6).

Approximately 6.05%.

Continuation Value: DCF and EBITDA Multiple ($000s)				
1	Long-term growth rate	6.05%	Target D/(E+D)	40.0%
2			Projected WACC	9.05%
Free Cash Flow in 2011				
3	Unlevered Net Income	13,752	**Cont. Enterprise Value**	**243,161**
4	Less: Inc. in NWC	(2,762)		
5	Less: Inc. in Fixed Assets	(3,700)	**Implied EBITDA Multiple**	**9.1x**
6	Free Cash Flow	7,290		

19-17. Using the APV method, estimate the value of Ideko and the NPV of the deal using the continuation value you calculated in Problem 13 and the unlevered cost of capital estimate in Section 19.4. Assume that the debt cost of capital is 6.8%; Ideko's market share will increase by 0.5% per year until 2010; investment, financing, and depreciation will be adjusted accordingly; and the projected improvements in working capital occur (i.e., the assumptions in Problem 5).

The equity value is $90 million so the NPV of the deal is 90 – 53 = $37 million.

	Year	2005	2006	2007	2008	2009	2010
APV Method ($ millions)							
1	Free Cash Flow		13,911	7,394	8,121	9,507	(3,759)
2	**Unlevered Value V^u**	**180,136**	**184,238**	**195,268**	**206,674**	**217,835**	**243,377**
3	Interest Tax Shield		2,380	2,380	2,380	2,380	2,380
4	**Tax Shield Value T^s**	**9,811**	**8,098**	**6,269**	**4,315**	**2,228**	-
5	**APV: $V^L = V^u + T^s$**	**189,946**	**192,336**	**201,537**	**210,989**	**220,063**	**243,377**
6	Debt	(100,000)	(100,000)	(100,000)	(100,000)	(100,000)	(115,000)
7	**Equity Value**	**89,946**	**92,336**	**101,537**	**110,989**	**120,063**	**128,377**

19-18. Using the APV method, estimate the value of Ideko and the NPV of the deal using the continuation value you calculated in Problem 13 and the unlevered cost of capital estimate in Section 19.4. Assume that the debt cost of capital is 6.8%; Ideko's market share will increase by 0.5% per year; investment, financing, and depreciation will be adjusted accordingly; and the projected improvements in working capital do *not* occur (i.e., the assumptions in Problem 6).

The equity value is $80 million so the NPV of the deal is 90 – 53 = $27 million.

	Year	2005	2006	2007	2008	2009	2010
APV Method ($ millions)							
1	Free Cash Flow		6,246	6,467	7,102	8,387	(4,989)
2	**Unlevered Value V^u**	**170,107**	**180,872**	**192,492**	**204,639**	**216,717**	**243,377**
3	Interest Tax Shield		2,380	2,380	2,380	2,380	2,380
4	**Tax Shield Value T^s**	**9,811**	**8,098**	**6,269**	**4,315**	**2,228**	-
5	**APV: $V^L = V^u + T^s$**	**179,918**	**188,970**	**198,760**	**208,954**	**218,945**	**243,377**
6	Debt	(100,000)	(100,000)	(100,000)	(100,000)	(100,000)	(115,000)
7	**Equity Value**	**79,918**	**88,970**	**98,760**	**108,954**	**118,945**	**128,377**

19-19. Use your answers from Problems 17 and 18 to infer the value today of the projected improvements in working capital under the assumptions that Ideko's market share will increase by 0.5% per year and that investment, financing, and depreciation will be adjusted accordingly.

The value of the savings in working capital management is the difference between the value with and without the savings—approximately $10 million.

Chapter 20
Financial Options

20-1. Explain the meanings of the following financial terms:

a. Option

b. Expiration date

c. Strike price

d. Call

e. Put

a. Option: An option is a contract that gives one party the right, but not the obligation, to buy or sell an asset at some point in the future.

b. Expiration date: The last date on which the holder still has the right to exercise the option. If the option is American, the right can be exercised until the exercise date; if it is European, the option can be exercised only on the exercise date.

c. Strike price: the price at which the holder of the option has the right to buy or sell the asset.

d. Call: An option that gives its holder the right to buy an asset.

e. Put: An option that gives its holder the right to sell an asset.

20-2. What is the difference between a European option and an American option? Are European options available exclusively in Europe and American options available exclusively in America?

European options can be exercised *only* on the exercise date, while American options can be exercised on any date *prior* to the exercise date. Both types of options are traded in both Europe and America.

20-3. Below is an option quote on IBM from the CBOE Web site.

a. Which option contract had the most trades today?

b. Which option contract is being held the most overall?

c. Suppose you purchase one option with symbol IBM GA-E. How much will you need to pay your broker for the option (ignoring commissions)?

d. Explain why the last sale price is not always between the bid and ask prices.

e. Suppose you sell one option with symbol IBM GA-E. How much will you receive for the option (ignoring commissions)?

f. The calls with which strike prices are currently in-the-money? Which puts are in-the-money?

g. What is the difference between the option with symbol IBM GS-E and the option with symbol IBM HS-E?

IBM **102.22** +1.39

Jul 13 2009 @ 13:26 ET **Bid** 102.2 **Ask** 102.22 **Size** 6 × 6 **Vol** 5683797

Calls	Last Sale	Net	Bid	Ask	Vol	Open Int	Puts	Last Sale	Net	Bid	Ask	Vol	Open Int
09 Jul 95.00 (IBM GS-E)	7.50	0.95	7.40	7.60	26	8159	09 Jul 95.00 (IBM SS-E)	0.31	−0.24	0.25	0.35	2039	11452
09 Jul 100.00 (IBM GT-E)	3.50	0.72	3.40	3.50	1764	14436	09 Jul 100.00 (IBM ST-E)	1.25	−0.65	1.20	1.25	2262	19401
09 Jul 105.00 (IBM GA-E)	0.91	0.26	0.90	1.00	1945	23210	09 Jul 105.00 (IBM SA-E)	3.79	−1.56	3.60	3.80	379	8000
09 Jul 110.00 (IBM GB-E)	0.15	0.07	0.10	0.15	632	20808	09 Jul 110.00 (IBM SB-E)	7.57	−1.53	7.80	8.00	35	6536
09 Aug 95.00 (IBM HS-E)	8.75	1.35	8.40	8.60	32	1532	09 Aug 95.00 (IBM TS-E)	1.51	−0.49	1.50	1.60	1076	2766
09 Aug 100.00 (IBM HT-E)	5.11	0.91	4.80	5.00	122	2754	09 Aug 100.00 (IBM TT-E)	2.90	−0.86	3.00	3.20	513	5322
09 Aug 105.00 (IBM HA-E)	2.40	0.44	2.35	2.40	456	6091	09 Aug 105.00 (IBM TA-E)	5.99	−0.81	5.50	5.70	52	1586
09 Aug 110.00 (IBM HB-E)	0.95	0.25	0.90	0.95	207	3429	09 Aug 110.00 (IBM TB-E)	10.60	−0.40	9.10	9.30	10	751

Source: Chicago Board Options Exchange at www.cboe.com

a. 09 Jul 100 Put

b. 09 Jul 105 call

c. $\$1.00 \times 100 = \$100$

d. Last sale may have happened earlier in the day, whereas bid/ask are current quotes.

e. $\$0.90 \times 100 = \$90$

f. Calls : 95, 100

Puts : 105, 110

Identical except that the second expires one month later than the first.

20-4. Explain the difference between a long position in a put and a short position in a call.

When a party has a long position in a put, it has the right to sell the underlying asset at the strike price; when it has a short position in a call, it has the obligation to sell the underlying asset at the strike price if exercised. These are clearly different positions.

20-5. Which of the following positions benefit if the stock price increases?

a. Long position in a call

b. Short position in a call

c. Long position in a put

d. Short position in a put

Long call & short put

20-6. You own a call option on Intuit stock with a strike price of $40. The option will expire in exactly three months' time.

a. If the stock is trading at $55 in three months, what will be the payoff of the call?

b. If the stock is trading at $35 in three months, what will be the payoff of the call?

c. Draw a payoff diagram showing the value of the call at expiration as a function of the stock price at expiration.

Long call option: value at expiration:

a. $15

b. 0$

c. Draw graph:

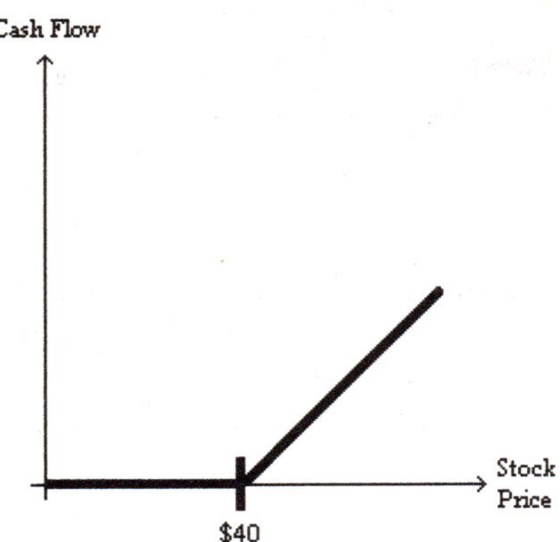

20-7. Assume that you have shorted the call option in Problem 6.

a. If the stock is trading at $55 in three months, what will you owe?

b. If the stock is trading at $35 in three months, what will you owe?

c. Draw a payoff diagram showing the amount you owe at expiration as a function of the stock price at expiration.

Short call: value at expiration date:

a. You owe $15.

b. You owe nothing.

c. Draw the payoff diagram:

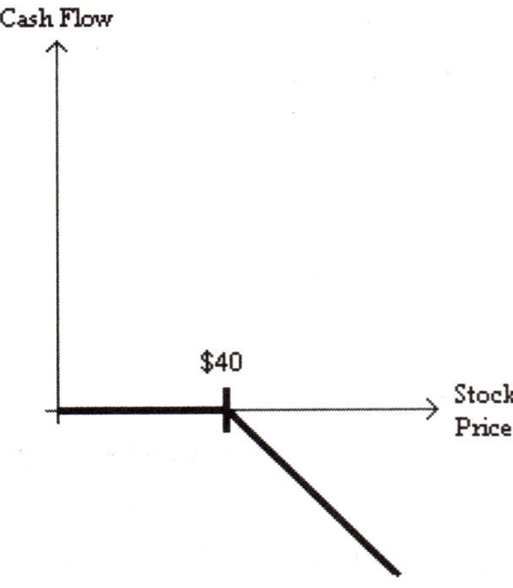

20-8. You own a put option on Ford stock with a strike price of $10. The option will expire in exactly six months' time.

a. If the stock is trading at $8 in six months, what will be the payoff of the put?

b. If the stock is trading at $23 in six months, what will be the payoff of the put?

c. Draw a payoff diagram showing the value of the put at expiration as a function of the stock price at expiration.

Long put value at expiration:

a. $2

b. $0

c. Draw payoff diagram:

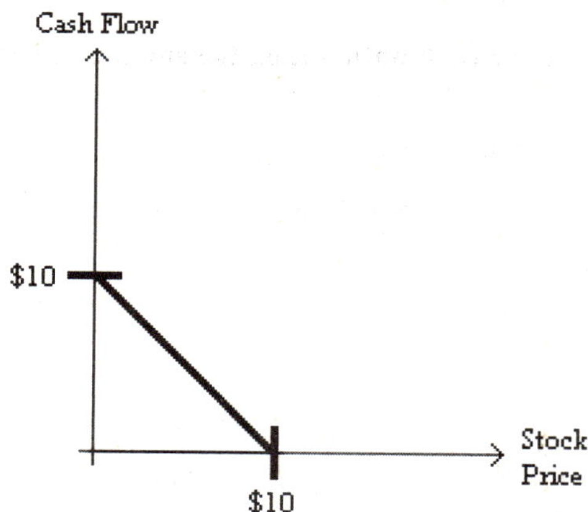

20-9. Assume that you have shorted the put option in Problem 8.

a. If the stock is trading at $8 in three months, what will you owe?

b. If the stock is trading at $23 in three months, what will you owe?

c. Draw a payoff diagram showing the amount you owe at expiration as a function of the stock price at expiration.

Short put: value at expiration:

a. You owe $2.

b. You owe nothing.

c. Draw payoff diagram:

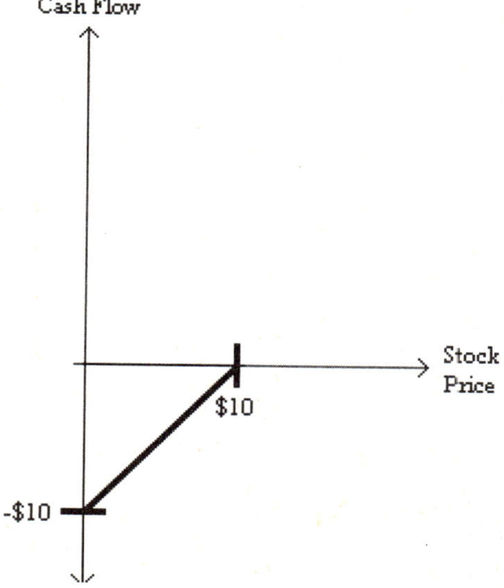

20-10. What position has more downside exposure: a short position in a call or a short position in a put? That is, in the worst case, in which of these two positions would your losses be greater?

Downside exposure is larger with a short call (the downside is unlimited) than with a short put (the downside cannot be larger than the strike price).

20-11. Consider the July 2009 IBM call and put options in Problem 3. Ignoring any interest you might earn over the remaining few days' life of the options:

a. Compute the break-even IBM stock price for each option (i.e., the stock price at which your total profit from buying and then exercising the option would be zero).

b. Which call option is most likely to have a return of −100%?

c. If IBM's stock price is $111 on the expiration day, which option will have the highest return?

a. For calls, strike + ask. For puts, strike – ask.

b. 110 call option is worthless if IBM is below 110.

c. 110 call option has return of 1/.15 – 1 = 567%.

20-12. You are long both a call and a put on the same share of stock with the same exercise date. The exercise price of the call is $40 and the exercise price of the put is $45. Plot the value of this combination as a function of the stock price on the exercise date.

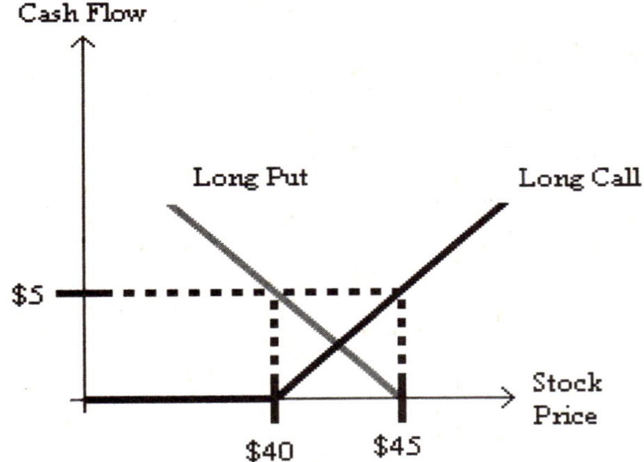

⇓

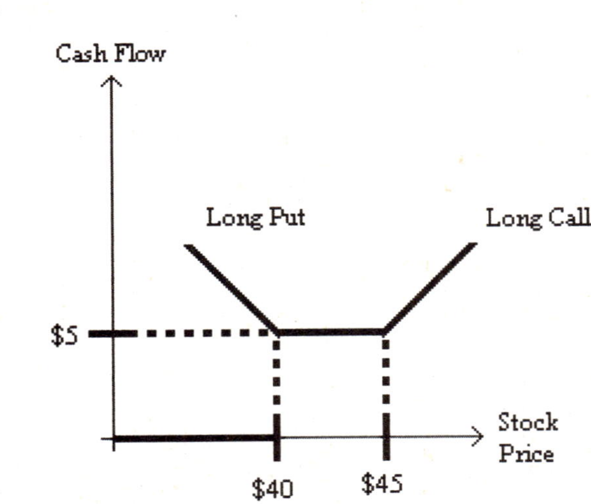

20-13. You are long two calls on the same share of stock with the same exercise date. The exercise price of the first call is \$40 and the exercise price of the second call is \$60. In addition, you are short two otherwise identical calls, both with an exercise price of \$50. Plot the value of this combination as a function of the stock price on the exercise date. What is the name of this combination of options?

The top curve is the \$40 Call, the middle curve is the \$60 Call, the bottom curve is the short position in two \$50 calls and the up then down curve is the combination.

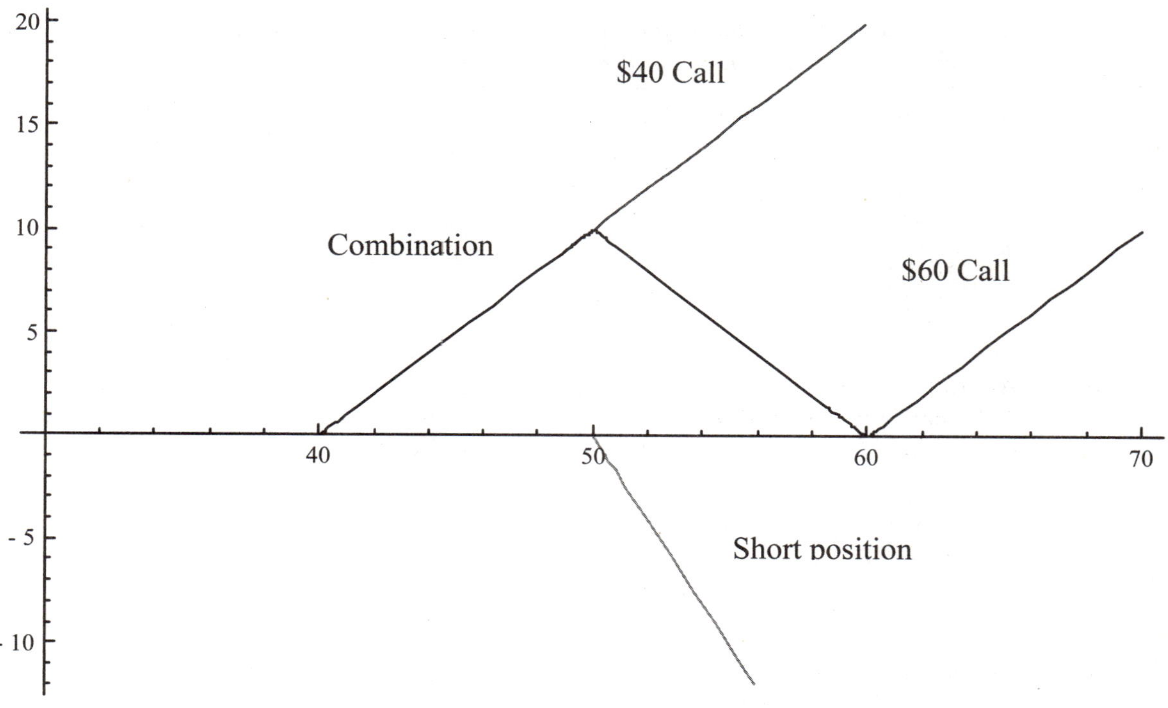

⇓

This is called a Butterfly Spread.

20-14. A forward contract is a contract to purchase an asset at a fixed price on a particular date in the future. Both parties are obligated to fulfill the contract. Explain how to construct a forward contract on a share of stock from a position in options.

A forward with price p can be constructed longing a call and shorting a put with strike p.

20-15. You own a share of Costco stock. You are worried that its price will fall and would like to insure yourself against this possibility. How can you purchase insurance against this possibility?

To protect against a fall in the price of Costco, you can buy a put with Costco as the underlying asset. By doing this, over the life of the option you are guaranteed to get at least the strike price from selling the stock you already have.

20-16. It is July 13, 2009, and you own IBM stock. You would like to insure that the value of your holdings will not fall significantly. Using the data in Problem 3, and expressing your answer in terms of a percentage of the current value of your portfolio:

a. **What will it cost to insure that the value of your holdings will not fall below $95 per share between now and the third Friday in July?**

b. **What will it cost to insure that the value of your holdings will not fall below $95 per share between now and the third Friday in August?**

c. **What will it cost to insure that the value of your holdings will not fall below $100 per share between now and the third Friday in August?**

a. To ensure that the value of your IBM does not fall significantly, you would purchase a protective put. The current ask price for a protective put with a strike price of $95 that expires the third Friday of July is $0.35 per share. As a percentage of your portfolio this cost to insure is $0.35/$102.22 = .0034 or 0.34% of the value of your portfolio.

b. The ask price of a protective put with a strike price of $95 that expires on the third Friday of August is $1.60. The cost to insure the value of your holdings will not fall is $1.60/$102.22 = 0.0157 or 1.57%.

c. The ask price of a protective put with a strike price of $100 that expires on the third Friday of August is $3.20. The cost to insure the value of your holdings will not fall is $3.20/$102.22 = 0.0313 or 3.13%.

20-17. Dynamic Energy Systems stock is currently trading for $33 per share. The stock pays no dividends. A one-year European put option on Dynamic with a strike price of $35 is currently trading for $2.10. If the risk-free interest rate is 10% per year, what is the price of a one-year European call option on Dynamic with a strike price of $35?

Put-call parity:

$$C = P + S - \frac{K}{1+r} = 2.10 + 33 - \frac{35}{1.1} = 3.282$$

20-18. You happen to be checking the newspaper and notice an arbitrage opportunity. The current stock price of Intrawest is $20 per share and the one-year risk-free interest rate is 8%. A one year put on Intrawest with a strike price of $18 sells for $3.33, while the identical call sells for $7. Explain what you must do to exploit this arbitrage opportunity.

The arbitrage opportunity exists because:

$$\$7 > \$3.33 + \$20 - \frac{\$18}{(1+0.08)} = \$6.66.$$

So the call is overpriced compared to the portfolio of a put, the stock, and risk-free borrowing.

As a result, the strategy would be to sell the call option, buy the put, buy the stock, and borrow $16.67 (the present value of $18).

The net amount left after doing this is $.34, with no cash flows when the options expire.

20-19. Consider the July 2009 IBM call and put options in Problem 3. Ignoring the negligible interest you might earn on TBills over the remaining few days' life of the options, show that there is no arbitrage opportunity using put-call parity for the options with a $100 strike price. Specifically:

a. **What is your profit/loss if you buy a call and TBills, and sell IBM stock and a put option?**

b. **What is your profit/loss if you buy IBM stock and a put option, and sell a call and TBills?**

c. **Explain why your answers to (a) and (b) are not both zero.**

a. Consider : Buy call & TBills, sell stock & put –3.50 – 100 + 102.2 + 1.20 = –0.10

b. Sell call & tBills, buy stock & put +3.40 +100 – 102.22 – 1.25 = –.07

c. Both negative due to transactions costs: call spread (0.10) + put spread (0.05) + stock spread (0.02) = 0.17 in total loss in (a) & (b)

20-20. Suppose Amazon stock is trading for $70 per share, and Amazon pays no dividends.

a. What is the maximum possible price of a call option on Amazon?

b. What is the maximum possible price of a put option on Amazon with a strike price of $100?

c. What is the minimum possible value of a call option on Amazon stock with a strike price of $50?

d. What is the minimum possible value of an American put option on Amazon stock with a strike price of $100?

a. $70 (Stock price)

b. $100 (strike price)

c. Intrinsic value = $20

d. Intrinsic value = $30

20-21. Consider the data for IBM options in Problem 3. Suppose a new American-style put option on IBM is issued with a strike price of $110 and an expiration date of August 1st.

a. What is the maximum possible price for this option?

b. What is the minimum possible price for this option?

a. No one will pay more than the price of the Aug option (which expires later), so $9.30.

b. No one would sell for less than the sale price of the July option: $7.80.

20-22. You are watching the option quotes for your favorite stock, when suddenly there is a news announcement. Explain what type of news would lead to the following effects:

a. Call prices increase, and put prices fall.

b. Call prices fall, and put prices increase.

c. Both call and put prices increase.

a. Good news about the stock, which raises its stock price

b. Bad news, which lowers the stock's price

c. News that increases the volatility of the stock

20-23. Explain why an American call option on a non-dividend-paying stock always has the same price as its European counterpart.

Because the option to exercise early is worthless, the American option provides no more benefits than its European counterpart.

20-24. Consider an American put option on XAL stock with a strike price of $55 and one year to expiration. Assume XAL pays no dividends, XAL is currently trading for $10 per share, and the one-year interest rate is 10%. If it is optimal to exercise this option early:

a. What is the price of a one-year American put option on XAL stock with a strike price of $60 per share?

b. What is the maximum price of a one-year American call option on XAL stock with a strike price of $55 per share?

a. It is optimal to exercise early puts with higher strikes, so value = intrinsic value of 60 – 10 = $50.

b. Because put has no time value, call value must be less than dis(55) = 55 – 55/1.10 = $5.

20-25. The stock of Harford Inc. is about to pay a $0.30 dividend. It will pay no more dividends for the next month. Consider call options that expire in one month. If the interest rate is 6% APR (monthly compounding), what is the maximum strike price where it could be possible that early exercise of the call option is optimal? (Round to the nearest dollar.)

$$0 > \underbrace{dis(K) + P - PV(Div)}_{\text{Time value}} > dis(K) - PV(Div)$$

so

$$PV(Div) > dis(K)$$

i.e., the discount on strike must be smaller than dividend. Given 6%/12 = 0.5% interest over the month,

K – K/1.005 < 0.30

so

K < 0.30 × 1.005/.005 = $60.30.

So, strikes at or below $60 per share could be exercised early.

20-26. Suppose the S&P 500 is at 900, and a one-year European call option with a strike price of $400 has a negative time value. If the interest rate is 5%, what can you conclude about the dividend yield of the S&P 500? (Assume all dividends are paid at the end of the year.)

Call has negative time value implies

$$dis(K) + P - PV(Div) < 0$$

which means that

$$dis(K) - PV(Div) < 0$$

or PV(div) > dis(K), or FV(divs) > interest on K = 5% × 400 = 20. So dividend yield must be at least 20/900 = 2.22%.

20-27. Suppose the S&P 500 is at 900, and it will pay a dividend of $30 at the end of the year. Suppose the interest rate is 2%. If a one-year European put option has a negative time value, what is the lowest possible strike price it could have?

$$-dis(K) + C + PV(div) < 0$$

implies that

$$-dis(K) + PV(div) < 0$$

or

$$dis(K) > PV(div)$$

$$\frac{Kr}{1+r} > \frac{div}{1+r}$$

$$Kr > div$$

so interest on strike must exceed the dividend: (.02 × K) > $30, so K > 1500.

20-28. Wesley Corp. stock is trading for $25/share. Wesley has 20 million shares outstanding and a market debt-equity ratio of 0.5. Wesley's debt is zero coupon debt with a 5-year maturity and a yield to maturity of 10%.

a. Describe Wesley's equity as a call option. What is the maturity of the call option? What is the market value of the asset underlying this call option? What is the strike price of this call option?

b. Describe Wesley's debt using a call option.

c. Describe Wesley's debt using a put option.

a. Maturity = 5 years

Assets = E + D = $25 × 20 + .5($25 × 20) = $500 + 250 = $750 million

Strike price = D = $250 million

b. Long the firm's assets and short the equity call option above

c. Long risk-free debt and short a put option on Wesley's assets with a 5-yr maturity and $250 million face value

20-29. Express the position of an equity holder in terms of put options.

An equity holder is long a put on a share of the value of the firm assets with the per share value of debt as the strike price, long a share on the assets of the firm and short a loan worth the value per share of the debt.

20-30. Use the option data in Figure 20.10 to determine the rate Google would pay if it issued $128 billion in zero-coupon debt due in January 2011. Suppose Google currently has 320 million shares outstanding, implying a market value of $135.1 billion. (Assume perfect capital markets.)

Issuing $128 billion in debt is equivalent to a claim on $400 of Google's assets per share. From Table 20.5, the average of the Bid-Ask spread of the 11 Jan 400 Call is $86.05. This gives a market value of the remaining equity of 86.05 × 320 = $27.54 billion. Subtracting from the total value of $135.1 billion gives the estimated value of the debt: 135.1 – 27.54 = 107.56 billion. The yield to maturity is then $\left(\frac{128}{107.56}\right)^{12/18} - 1 = 12.3\%$. The credit spread is therefore 12.3% – 1% = 11.1 %.

20-31. Suppose Google were to issue $96 billion in zero-coupon senior debt, and another $32 billion in zero-coupon junior debt, both due in January 2011. Use the option data in Figure 20.10 to determine the rate Google would pay on the junior debt issue. (Assume perfect capital markets.)

We can compute the rate on the senior debt as in Example 20.10. The debt value is $87.4 billion, and the rate is 6.46%.

Next, we can determine the value of equity. Because the firm has $96 + 32 = $128 billion in total debt, or 128b/320m = $400 per share, from Figure 20.10, the average of the Bid-Ask spread of the 11 Jan 400 Call is $86.05. This gives a market value of the remaining equity of 86.05 x320 = $27.54 bil.

Because Senior Debt + Junior Debt + Equity must equal the total value of $135.1 billion,

Junior debt has a value of 135.1 – 87.4 – 27.54 = $20.16 billion.

Therefore, the yield on the junior debt is

$$\left(\frac{32}{20.16}\right)^{12/18} - 1 = 36.1\%.$$

Chapter 21

Option Valuation

21-1. The current price of Estelle Corporation stock is \$25. In each of the next two years, this stock price will either go up by 20% or go down by 20%. The stock pays no dividends. The one-year risk-free interest rate is 6% and will remain constant. Using the Binomial Model, calculate the price of a one-year call option on Estelle stock with a strike price of \$25.

In this case, the stock price either rises to $S_u = 25\times1.20 = 30$ or falls to $S_d = 25\times0.80 = 20$. The option payoff is therefore either $C_u = 5$ or $C_d = 0$. The replicating portfolio is $\Delta = (5 - 0)/(30 - 20) = 0.5$ and

$B = (0 - 20\times0.5)/1.06 = -9.43$.

Therefore, $C = 0.5\times25 - 9.43 = \$3.07$.

21-2. Using the information in Problem 1, use the Binomial Model to calculate the price of a one year put option on Estelle stock with a strike price of \$25.

The parameters are the same as in 21-1, but the payoff of the put is 0 if the stock goes up and 5 if the stock goes down. Therefore, the replicating portfolio is

$\Delta = (0 - 5)/(30 - 20) = -0.5$ and $B = (5 - 20\times(-0.5))/1.06 = 14.15$.

Therefore, $P = -0.5 \times 25 + 14.15 = \$1.65$.

21-3. The current price of Natasha Corporation stock is \$6. In each of the next two years, this stock price can either go up by \$2.50 or go down by \$2. The stock pays no dividends. The one-year risk-free interest rate is 3% and will remain constant. Using the Binomial Model, calculate the price of a two-year call option on Natasha stock with a strike price of \$7.

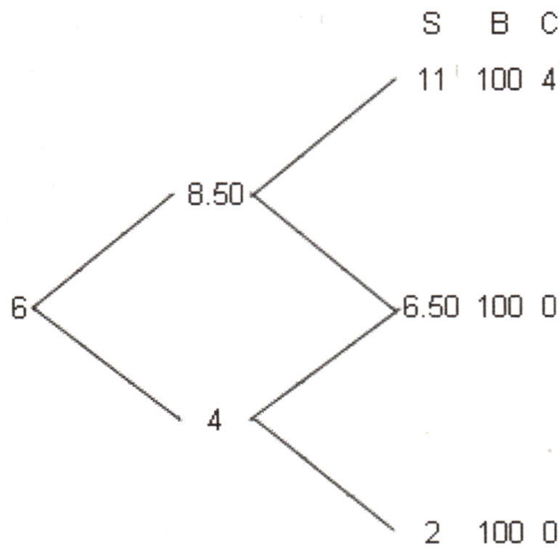

Up state at time 1: $\Delta = (4 - 0)/(11 - 6.50) = 0.889$, $B = (0 - 6.50{\times}0.889)/1.03 = -5.61$, therefore $C_u = 0.889{\times}8.50 - 5.61 = \$1.95$.

In the down state at time 1 the option is worth nothing. The call option at time 0 is therefore equivalent to the replicating portfolio $\Delta = (1.95 - 0)/(8.50 - 4) = 0.433$, $B = (0 - 4{\times}0.433)/1.03 = -1.68$ and so, by the Law of One Price, the initial option price is $0.433 \times 6 - 1.68 = \$0.92$.

21-4. **Using the information in Problem 3, use the Binomial Model to calculate the price of a two-year European put option on Natasha stock with a strike price of $7.**

If the stock goes up twice, the put is worth zero. If the stock ends up at $6.50, the put is worth $0.50; if the stock goes down twice, the put is worth $5. Given these final values, we can calculate the value of the put at earlier dates using the binomial model.

Up state at time 1: $\Delta = (0 - 0.50)/(11 - 6.50) = -0.111$ and $B = (0.50 - 6.50 \times (-0.111))/1.03 = 1.19$.

Therefore, $P_u = -0.111 \times 8.50 + 1.19 = \$0.25$.

Down state at time 1: $\Delta = (0.50 - 5)/(6.50 - 2) = -1$ and $B = (5 - 2{\times}(-1))/1.03 = 6.80$

Therefore, $P_d = -1{\times}4 + 6.80 = \$2.80$.

Time 0: $\Delta = (0.25 - 2.80)/(8.50 - 4) = -0.567$ and $B = (2.80 - 4{\times}(-0.567))/1.03 = 4.92$

Therefore, $P_d = -0.567{\times}6 + 4.92 = \$1.52$.

21-5. **Suppose the option in Example 21.1 actually sold in the market for $8. Describe a trading strategy that yields arbitrage profits.**

In Example 21.1, the theoretical put price is $3.30. If it actually sells for a higher price, it is overvalued, and we can sell it and buy the replicating portfolio to earn an arbitrage profit. This means that at t = 0, you will sell the put, short 0.3333 shares of stock, and invest $23.30 in Treasury Bills.

Following this strategy, you will earn the put price less $(60 \times (-0.3333) + 23.30) = \$3.30$ upfront.

Then, if the stock goes up, our portfolio of the put, shares, and borrowing is worth $\$0 - 0.3333 \times 72 + 23.30 \times 1.03 = \$0$. If it goes down, our portfolio is worth $-\$6 - 0.3333 \times \$54 + 23.30 \times 1.03 = \$0$, so that at maturity, the payoff of the option and the value of the replicating portfolio cancel out.

(Note that this is not the only arbitrage strategy one can follow—e.g., we could invest more in TBills initially—but it is the one that generates the most cash upfront without any risk of loss in the future.)

21-6. **Suppose the option in Example 21.2 actually sold today for $5. You do not know what the option will trade for next period. Describe a trading strategy that will yield arbitrage profits.**

In Example 21.2, the theoretical put price is $8.68. If it actually sells for $5, it is underpriced, which means we buy it and sell the replicating portfolio to earn an arbitrage profit. This means that at t = 0, you will buy the $5 put, buy 0.6633 shares of stock, and borrow $41.84.

Following this strategy, you will end up with $\$41.84 - 0.6633 \times 50 - 5 = \$3.68$ upfront.

At t = 1, you rebalance that portfolio according to the new Δ and B:

> If the stock goes up at date 1: we reduce our stock holdings to 0.3333 shares, using the proceeds to reduce our debt to $41.84 \times 1.03 - (0.6633 - 0.3333) \times \$60 = \$23.30$. Then, if the stock goes up again, our portfolio of the put, shares, and borrowing is worth $\$0 + 0.3333 \times 72 - 23.30 \times 1.03 = \$0$. If it goes down, our portfolio is worth $\$6 + 0.3333{\times}\$54 - 23.30{\times}1.03 = \$0$.
>
> If the stock goes down at date 1: we increase our stock holdings to 1 share, and increase our debt to $41.84 \times 1.03 + (1 - 0.6633) \times \$45 = \$58.25$. Then, if the stock goes up, our portfolio of the put, shares, and borrowing is worth $\$6 + 1 \times 54 - 58.25 \times 1.03 = \$0$. If it goes down, our portfolio is worth $\$19.50 + 1 \times 40.50 - 58.25 \times 1.03 = \$0$.

Thus, we have made a profit of $3.68 upfront, with a zero payoff no matter what happens in the future.

21-7. Eagletron's current stock price is $10. Suppose that over the current year, the stock price will either increase by 100% or decrease by 50%. Also, the risk-free rate is 25% (EAR).

a. What is the value today of a one-year at-the-money European put option on Eagletron stock?

b. What is the value today of a one-year European put option on Eagletron stock with a strike price of $20?

c. Suppose the put options in parts (a) and (b) could either be exercised immediately, or in one year. What would their values be in this case?

a. Pu = 0, Pd = 5, delta = (0 – 5)/(20 – 5) = -1/3, B = (5 – 5(-1/3))/1.25 = 5.33

P = –1/3(10) + 5.33 = $2.00

b. The payoffs are Pu = 0, Pd = 15. Because these payoffs are three times the payoffs in (a), the put must be worth 3 × $2 = $6.

c. We can exercise the put immediately and get its intrinsic value. In (a), intrinsic value = 0, so not relevant, value is still $2

In (b) intrinsic value = 20 – 10 = $10, so it is better to exercise now => value is $10 (not $6).

21-8. What is the highest possible value for the delta of a call option? What is the lowest possible value? (*Hint*: See Figure 21.1.)

Delta <= 1, Delta >= 0

21-9. Hema Corp. is an all equity firm with a current market value of $1000 million (i.e., $1 billion), and will be worth $900 million or $1400 million in one year. The risk-free interest rate is 5%. Suppose Hema Corp. issues zero-coupon, one-year debt with a face value of $1050 million, and uses the proceeds to pay a special dividend to shareholders. Assuming perfect capital markets, use the binomial model to answer the following:

a. What are the payoffs of the firm's debt in one year?

b. What is the value today of the debt today?

c. What is the yield on the debt?

d. Using Modigliani-Miller, what is the value of Hema's equity before the dividend is paid? What is the value of equity just after the dividend is paid?

e. Show that the ex-dividend value of Hema's equity is consistent with the binomial model. What is the Δ of the equity, when viewed as a call option on the firm's assets?

a. Either 1050 (if the firm does well) or 900 (if the firm does poorly and defaults).

b. We can use the binomial model: delta = (1050 – 900)/(1400 – 900) = 0.3, B = (900 – 900(.3))/(1.05) = 600, Debt value = 0.3(1000)+600 = 900.

c. 1050/900 = 16.67%

d. MM: initial value should not change = $1000. Subtract dividend of $900 (debt value) to determine ex-div value = $100.

e. Equity payoffs are 1400 – 1050 = 350 or 0.

Delta = (350-0)/(1400-900) = 0.70

B = (0 – 900(.7))/1.05 = -600

Equity Value = .7(1000)-600 = 100

21-10. Consider the setting of Problem 9. Suppose that in the event Hema Corp. defaults, $90 million of its value will be lost to bankruptcy costs. Assume there are no other market imperfections.

a. What is the present value of these bankruptcy costs, and what is their delta with respect to the firm's assets?

b. In this case, what is the value and yield of Hema's debt?

c. In this case, what is the value of Hema's equity before the dividend is paid? What is the value of equity just after the dividend is paid?

a. Bankruptcy costs are 0 or 90.

Delta = (0 – 90)/(1400 – 900) = –0.18

B = (90 – 900(–.18))/1.05 = 240

BC value = –0.18(1000) + 240 = $60 million

b. Debt value = $900 less BC = 900 – 60 = $840

Yield = 1050/840 – 1 = 25%

c. On announcement, equity value declines by BC = $1000 – 60 = $940. Subtract dividend of $840 (debt value) to determine ex-div value = $100 (Note this ex-div value is the same as in Problem 9 because equity holders have the same final payoffs.)

21-11. Roslin Robotics stock has a volatility of 30% and a current stock price of $60 per share. Roslin pays no dividends. The risk-free interest is 5%. Determine the Black-Scholes value of a one-year, at-the-money call option on Roslin stock.

BS value = $8.50

21-12. Rebecca is interested in purchasing a European call on a hot new stock, Up, Inc. The call has a strike price of $100 and expires in 90 days. The current price of Up stock is $120, and the stock has a standard deviation of 40% per year. The risk-free interest rate is 6.18% per year.

a. Using the Black-Scholes formula, compute the price of the call.

b. Use put-call parity to compute the price of the put with the same strike and expiration date.

a. Using the Black-Sholes formula:

$$\text{PV(K)} = 100/(1.0638)^{\frac{90}{365}} = 98.487,\ d_1 = \frac{\ln\left(\frac{120}{98.487}\right)}{0.4\sqrt{90/365}} + \frac{0.4\sqrt{90/365}}{2} = 1.094$$

$$= 1.09167$$

$$d_2 = 1.094 - 0.4\sqrt{90/365} = 0.895$$

$$C = S \times N(d_1) - PV(K)N(d_2) = 120 \times 0.863 - 98.487 \times 0.815 = \$23.29$$

b. Using put-call parity:

$$P = C + PV(K) - S = 23.29 + 98.487 - 120 = \$1.78$$

21-13. Using the data in Table 21.1, compare the price on July 24, 2009, of the following options on JetBlue stock to the price predicted by the Black-Scholes formula. Assume that the standard deviation of JetBlue stock is 65% per year and that the short-term risk-free rate of interest is 1% per year.

a. December 2009 call option with a $5 strike price

b. December 2009 put option with a $6 strike price

c. March 2010 put option with a $7 strike price

The January contract expires on the third Friday of January (20th); there are 45 days left until expiration.

$PV(K) = 11/(1+0.0438)^{45/365} = 10.942$,

$$d_1 = \frac{\ln(\frac{S_t}{PV(K)})}{\sigma\sqrt{T}} + \frac{\sigma\sqrt{T}}{2} = \frac{\ln(\frac{12.585}{10.942})}{0.25\sqrt{45/365}} + \frac{0.25\sqrt{45/365}}{2} = 1.638$$

$$d_2 = d_1 - \sigma\sqrt{T} = 1.638 - 0.25\sqrt{45/365} = 1.550$$

Substituting d_1 and d_2 into the Black-Scholes formula gives:

$$C_t(S_t, K, T, \sigma, r) = S_t\ N(d_1) - PV(K)N(d_2)$$
$$= 12.585 \times 0.949 - 10.942 \times 0.939 = 1.67.$$

This value is between the bid and ask prices of $1.65 and $1.75.

a. BS price = $0.85

b. BS price = $1.45

c. BS price = $2.42

21-14. Using the market data in Figure 20.10 and a risk-free rate of 1% per annum, calculate the implied volatility of Google stock in July 2009, using the 320 January 2011 call option.

The bid and ask prices of the call are $133.90 and 135.90, the time to expiration is approximately 1.53 years (July 13, 2009 to Jan 21, 2011 = 18 + 153 +365 + 21 = 557 days), and the price of the stock is $422.27.

With PV(K) = $320/(1+0.01)^{1.53} = 315.18$,

$$d_1 = \frac{\ln\left(\frac{422.27}{315.18}\right)}{\sigma\sqrt{1.53}} + \frac{\sigma\sqrt{1.53}}{2}, \quad d_2 = d_1 - \sigma\sqrt{1.53}.$$

The Black-Scholes formula, Eq. 21.7, implies: $C = 422.27 \times N(d_1) - 315.18 \times N(d_2)$.

You can verify that C is between the bid and ask prices for the call option when σ = 38%.(You can find the σ by guessing or using a calculator or spreadsheet program.) Thus, the implied volatility for Google derived from this call option is about 38.3%.

.

21-15. Using the implied volatility you calculated in Problem 14, and the information in that problem, use the Black-Scholes option pricing formula to calculate the value of the 340 January 2011 call option.

Implied volatility is 38.5% from Problem 21.9. The strike price = 340, current stock price is 405.85, and the risk-free rate is 4.5%, with a time to maturity of 2.12 years.

The Black-Scholes formula gives:

$$d_1 = \frac{\ln(\frac{405.85}{309.71})}{0.385\sqrt{2.12}} + \frac{0.385\sqrt{2.12}}{2} = 0.763, \quad d_2 = 0.763 - 0.385\sqrt{2.12} = 0.202.$$

Therefore,

$$C = S \times N(d_1) - PV(K)N(d_2) = 405.85 \times 0.777 - 309.71 \times 0.580 = \$135.71$$

$P = C + PV(K) - S = 135.71 + 309.71 - 405.85 = \$39.57.$

Note that the call price is within the range of the quotes provided in Table 20.5.

BS value using 38.5% vol = $122.53

21-16. Plot the value of a two-year European put option with a strike price of $20 on World Wide Plants as a function of the stock price. Recall that World Wide Plants has a constant dividend yield of 5% per year and that its volatility is 20% per year. The two-year risk-free rate of interest is 4%. Explain why there is a region where the option trades for less than its intrinsic value.

The price of the put is given by the standard Black-Scholes equation for puts, but with the stock price replaced everywhere with $S/(1+q)^T = S/(1+0.05)^2 = S/1.1025$. Given PV(K) = 20/1.04² = 18.491. Therefore,

$$d_1 = \frac{\ln(\frac{S^x}{PV(K)})}{\sigma\sqrt{T}} + \frac{\sigma\sqrt{T}}{2} = \frac{\ln(\frac{S/1.1025}{18.491})}{0.2\sqrt{2}} + 0.1\sqrt{2}$$

$$d_2 = d_1 - \sigma\sqrt{T} = \frac{\ln(\frac{S/1.1025}{18.491})}{0.2\sqrt{2}} - 0.1\sqrt{2}$$

so, the value of the put option given current stock price S is

$$P(S) = PV(K)\,(1 - N(d_2)) - \left(S^x\right)(1 - N(d_1))$$

$$= 18.491 \times \left(1 - N\left(\frac{\ln(\frac{S/1.1025}{18.491})}{0.2\sqrt{2}} - 0.1\sqrt{2}\right)\right) - S/1.1025 \times \left(1 - N\left(\frac{\ln(\frac{S/1.1025}{18.491})}{0.2\sqrt{2}} + 0.1\sqrt{2}\right)\right).$$

Plotting this function (the curved line below) gives:

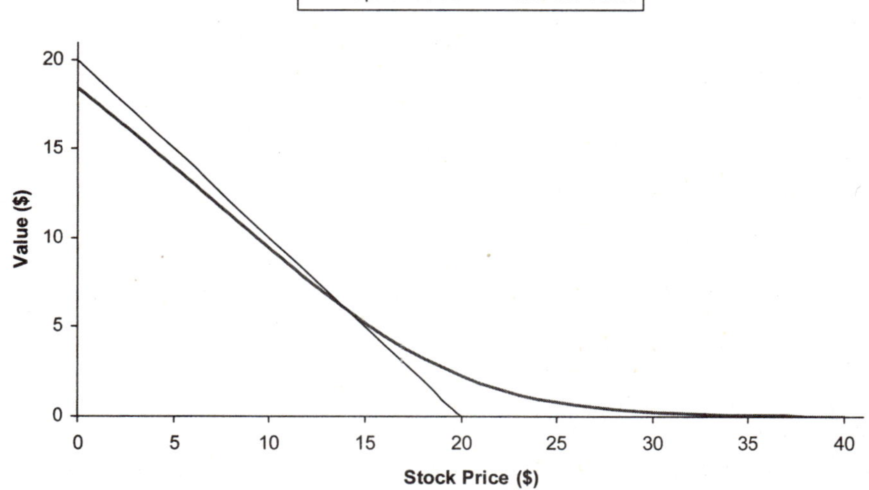

Notice that when the put is deep in the money it is worth less than its intrinsic value. In this case the time value is negative because the size of the discount on a two year zero-coupon bond is larger than the value of the dividends and the call option, implying a negative time value for the option.

21-17. Consider the at-the-money call option on Roslin Robotics evaluated in Problem 11. Suppose the call option is not available for trade in the market. You would like to replicate a long position in 1000 call options.

a. What portfolio should you hold today?

b. Suppose you purchase the portfolio in part (a). If Roslin stock goes up in value to $62 per share today, what is the value of this portfolio now? If the call option were available for trade, what would be the difference in value between the call option and the portfolio (expressed as percent of the value of the call)?

c. After the stock price changein part (b), how should you adjust your portfolio to continue to replicate the options?

a. Delta = N(d1) = N(0.312634) = 0.6227, so purchase 623 shares.

B = –28.859, so borrow $28,859.

Cost = 622.27 × 60 – 28859 = $8,504

b. Portfolio = 622.27 × 62 – 28859 = 9749

Call = 9790

Difference = (9749 – 9790)/9790 = –0.42%

c. Delta = .663

Increase shares to 663.

Borrow additional (663 – 623) × 62 = $2526.

21-18. Consider again the at-the-money call option on Roslin Robotics evaluated in Problem 11. What is the impact on the value of this call option of each of the following changes (evaluated separately)?

a. The stock price increases by $1 to $61.

b. The volatility of the stock goes up by 1% to 31%.

c. Interest rates go up by 1% to 6%.

d. One month elapses, with no other change.

e. The firm announces a $1 dividend, paid immediately.

Original BS price = $8.50

a. BS price = $9.14

b. BS price = $8.73

c. BS price = $8.78

d. BS price = $8.09

e. Ex-div stock price = $59, BS price = $7.89

21-19. Harbin Manufacturing has 10 million shares outstanding with a current share price of $20 per share. In one year, the share price is equally likely to be $30 or $18. The risk-free interest rate is 5%.

a. What is the expected return on Harbin stock?

b. What is the risk neutral probability that Harbin's stock price will increase?

a. .5(30+18)/20 – 1 = 20%

b. 25%

21-20. Using the information on Harbin Manufacturing in Problem 19, answer the following:

a. **Using the risk neutral probabilities, what is the value of a one-year call option on Harbin stock with a strike price of $25?**

b. **What is the expected return of the call option?**

c. **Using the risk neutral probabilities, what is the value of a one-year put option on Harbin stock with a strike price of $25?**

d. **What is the expected return of the put option?**

a. 25% × (30-25)/1.05 = $1.19

b. 50% × (5)/1.19 – 1 = 110%

c. 75% × (25 – 18)/1.05 = $5

d. 50% × (7)/5 – 1 = -30%

21-21. Using the information in Problem 1, calculate the risk-neutral probabilities. Then use them to price the option.

The risk neutral probabilities can be calculated using:

$$\rho = \frac{(1+r_f)S - S_d}{S_u - S_d} = \frac{(1.06)25 - 20}{30 - 20} = 0.65.$$

Using these probabilities the price of the option is

$$\frac{5(0.65)+0(0.35)}{1.06} = \$3.066.$$

21-22. Using the information in Problem 3, calculate the risk-neutral probabilities. Then use them to price the option.

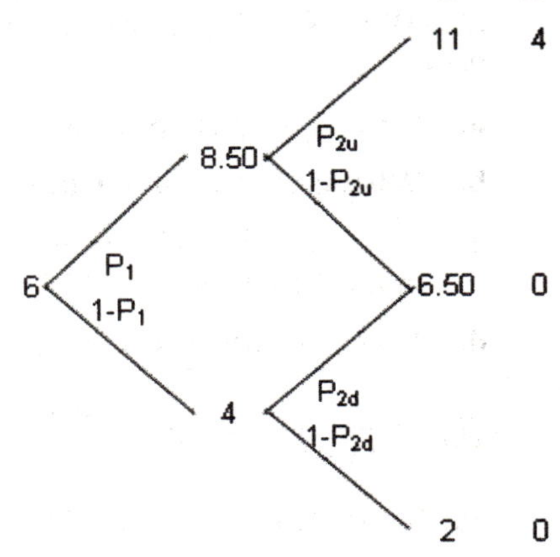

The risk neutral probabilities are

$$p_1 = \frac{(1.03)6 - 4}{8.5 - 4} = 48.44\%$$

$$p_{2u} = \frac{(1.03)8.5 - 6.5}{11 - 6.5} = 50.11\%$$

$$p_{2d} = \frac{(1.03)4 - 2}{6.5 - 2} = 47.11\%.$$

The value of the call is therefore:

$$\frac{1}{1.03^2}\left(4p_1p_{2u} + 0\left(p_1\left(1-p_{2u}\right)+\left(1-p_1\right)\left(p_{2d}\right)\right)+0\left(1-p_1\right)\left(1-p_{2d}\right)\right)$$

$$= \frac{4(0.4844)(0.5011)}{1.03^2} = \$0.9153.$$

21-23. Explain the difference between the risk-neutral and actual probabilities. In which states is one higher than the other? Why?

Actual probabilities are the probabilities with which an event will happen. Risk-neutral probabilities are the probabilities of an event happening *in a world where investors are risk-neutral.* Thus, risk-neutral probabilities are a construction and do not reflect reality. Assuming that investors are risk-averse, risk-neutral probabilities are lower in good states and larger in bad states. This has to be the case because if investors were risk-neutral, then the expected returns are the risk-free rate, whereas risk-averse demand higher returns. And given the same payoffs, a higher expected return implies good states are more likely.

21-24. Explain why risk-neutral probabilities can be used to price derivative securities in a world where investors are risk averse.

Risk neutral probabilities can be used to price derivative securities because the pricing of derivatives only depends on the characteristics of the underlying asset. By construction, the value of the underlying asset can be calculated using risk-neutral probabilities and therefore the value of the call will depend on these probabilities. Risk-neutral probabilities are the easiest probabilities to work with, given that they simplify the calculations, and that is why we use them.

21-25. Calculate the beta of the January 2010 \$9 call option on JetBlue listed in Table 21.1. Assume that the volatility of JetBlue is 65% per year and its beta is 0.85. The short-term risk-free rate of interest is 1% per year. What is the option's leverage ratio?

$$\beta_{call} = \frac{\Delta S}{\Delta S + B}\beta_S = \frac{N(d_1)S}{C}\beta_S$$

Call option: 175 days to maturity, S = 5.035, K = 9, σ = 65%,
$r_f = 1\% \Rightarrow N(d_1) = 0.146, \quad C = \$0.141.$

$$\beta_{call} = \frac{0.146 \times 5.035}{0.141} \times 0.85 = 4.4, \text{ and } \textit{Leverage ratio} = \frac{N(d_1)S}{C} = 5.2$$

21-26. Consider the March 2010 \$5 put option on JetBlue listed in Table 21.1. Assume that the volatility of JetBlue is 65% per year and its beta is 0.85. The short-term risk-free rate of interest is 1% per year.

a. What is the put option's leverage ratio?

b. What is the beta of the put option?

c. If the expected risk premium of the market is 6%, what is the expected return of the put option based on the CAPM?

d. Given its expected return, why would an investor buy a put option?

$$\beta_{put} = \frac{\Delta S}{\Delta S + B}\beta_S = \frac{-(1 - N(d_1)S}{P}\beta_S$$

Put option: 238 days to maturity, S = 5.035, K=5, σ=65%, $r_f = 1\% \Rightarrow N(d_1) = 0.613, \quad P = \$1.002$

a. $$\textit{Leverage ratio} = \frac{-(1 - N(d_1))S}{P} = -1.9$$

b. $$\beta_{put} = \frac{-(1 - .613) \times 5.035}{1.002} \times 0.85 = -1.65$$

c. $$E(R) = r_f + \beta_{put}\left(E\left(R_{Mkt}\right) - r_f\right) = 0.01 + (-1.65)(0.06) = -0.089$$

d. An investor would buy a put option given a negative expected return to act as a hedge against losses. The negative beta implies the return will move inverse to the market. Giving good returns when times are bad (when positive returns are the most valuable).

21-27. Return to Example 20.10, in which Google was contemplating issuing zero-coupon debt due in 18 months with a face value of \$96 billion, and using the proceeds to pay a special dividend. Google currently has a market value of \$135.1 billion and the risk-free rate is 1%. Using the market data in Figure 20.10, answer the following:

a. If Google's current equity beta is 1.45, estimate Google's equity beta after the debt is issued.

b. Estimate the beta of the new debt.

$$\beta_E = \Delta \frac{A}{E} \beta_U = \Delta(1 + \frac{D}{E})\beta_U$$

a. We want the β_E following the debt issuance:

$$\beta_E = \left(\Delta(1 + \frac{D}{E}) \right) \beta_U = \left(N(d_1)(1 + \frac{D}{E}) \right) \beta_U$$

We have: S = 135.1, K = 96, r = 1%, T = 1.5 years, $\sigma_{implied}$ = 38.6% from problem 21.14

$\Rightarrow N(d_1) = 0.839, \;\; C = 47.37.$

So Google's equity beta would be $0.839 \times (1 + \frac{135.1 - 47.37}{47.37}) \times 1.45 = 3.47.$

b. $\beta_D = (1 - \Delta)\frac{A}{D}\beta_U = (1 - \Delta)\left(1 + \frac{E}{D}\right)\beta_U$

$$\beta_D = \left((1 - \Delta)(1 + \frac{D}{E}) \right) \beta_U = \left((1 - N(d_1))(1 + \frac{D}{E}) \right) \beta_U$$

So Google's debt beta would be $(1 - 0.839) \times \left(1 + \frac{135.1 - 47.37}{47.37}\right) \times 1.45 = 0.67.$

21-28. You would like to know the unlevered beta of Schwartz Industries (SI). SI's value of outstanding equity is \$400 million, and you have estimated its beta to be 1.2. SI has four-year zero-coupon debt outstanding with a face value of \$100 million that currently trades for \$75 million. SI pays no dividends and reinvests all of its earnings. The four-year risk-free rate of interest is currently 5.13%. Use the Black-Scholes formula to estimate the unlevered beta of the firm.

The equity can be interpreted as a four-year call option on the firm's assets with a strike price of \$100 million. The current market value of assets is 400 + 75 = \$475 million.

Using the Black-Scholes formula, we can get the implied volatility of assets: Call option value = 400, K = 100, S = 475, T = 4, r = 0.0513 $\Rightarrow \sigma = 60.6\%$.

Using the volatility:

$$\Delta = N(d_1) = N\left[\frac{\ln(\frac{475}{100/(1+0.0513)^4})}{0.606\sqrt{4}} + \frac{0.606\sqrt{4}}{2} \right] = 0.980$$

$$\beta_U = \frac{\beta_E}{\Delta(1+\frac{D}{E})} = \frac{1.2}{0.980\times(1+\frac{75}{400})} = 1.03$$

a: D = 900/1.09^5 = 585. S = D + E = 585 + 20 × 25 = 1085, rf = 5%, K = 900, T = 5

σ Vol = 35%

b: B_d D/B_e E = (1-delta)/delta = (1-.827)/.827 = 0.209

c: Asset value could fall to 1008, and with volatility of 45%, equity call option is worth 500. Thus, NPV could be 1008 – 1085 = –77 million, and equity holders still gain!

21-29. The J. Miles Corp. has 25 million shares outstanding with a share price of \$20 per share. Miles also has outstanding zero-coupon debt with a 5-year maturity, a face value of \$900 million, and a yield to maturity of 9%. The risk-free interest rate is 5%.

a. What is the implied volatility of Miles' assets?

b. What is the minimum profitability index required for equity holders to gain by funding a new investment that does not change the volatility of the Miles' assets?

c. Suppose Miles is considering investing cash on hand in a new investment that will increase the volatility of its assets by 10%. What is the minimum NPV such that this investment will increase the value of Miles' shares?

a: Miles' equity can be viewed as a call option on Miles' assets with a strike price of 900, five years to maturity, and a market value of \$20/share × 25 million shares = \$500 million. The market value of Miles' debt is D = 900/1.09^5 = 585. Using Black-Scholes with parameters S = D+E = 585 + 500 = 1085, rf = 5%, K = 900, T = 5, we find an implied volatility of Mile's assets of 35%.

b: We can use Black-Scholes to calculate the delta of the equity call option in (a) to be Δ = 0.827. Then, the profitability index must exceed (see Example 21.11 and also Eq. 16.2) $\beta_d D/(\beta_e E) = (1 - \Delta)/\Delta$ = (1 – .827)/.827 = 0.209. (To understand this, note that a \$1 investment by equity holders with and NPV of \$0.209 will increase the value of the assets by \$1.209, and so increase the value of equity by approximately 0.827 × 1.209 = \$1.)

c: Asset value could fall to 1009, and with volatility of 45%, equity call option has value just over 500.

Thus, NPV could be 1009 – 1085 = – 76 million, and equity holders still gain!

Chapter 22
Real Options

22-1. Your company is planning on opening an office in Japan. Profits depend on how fast the economy in Japan recovers from its current recession. There is a 50% chance of recovery this year. You are trying to decide whether to open the office now or in a year. Construct the decision tree that shows the choices you have to open the office either today or one year from now.

Decision Tree

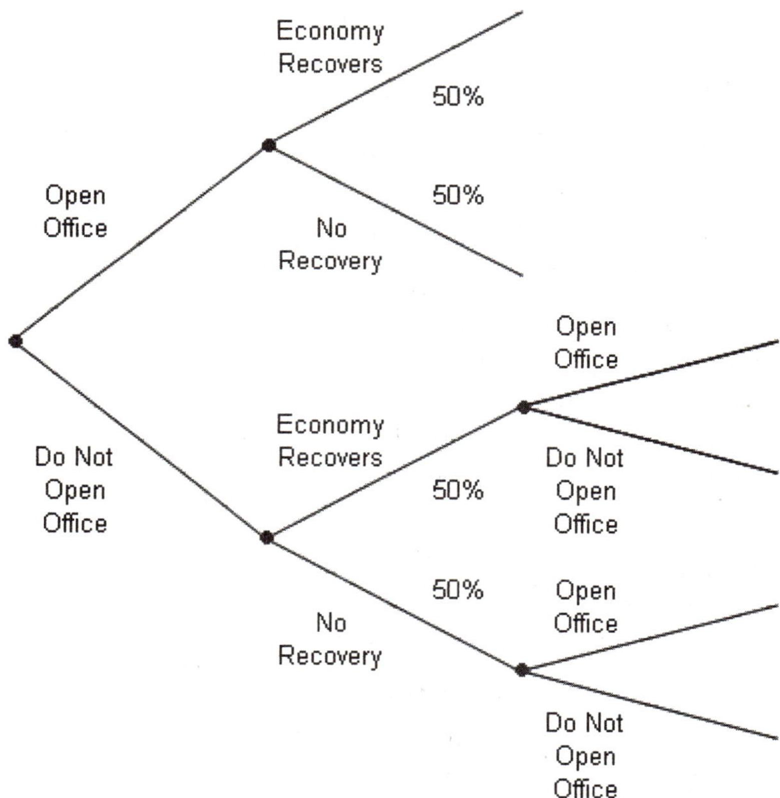

22-2. **You are trying to decide whether to make an investment of $500 million in a new technology to produce Everlasting Gobstoppers. There is a 60% chance that the market for these candies will produce profits of $100 million annually, a 20% chance the market will produce profits of $50 million, and a 20% chance that there will be no profits. The size of the market will become clear one year from now. Currently, the cost of capital of the project is 11% per year. There is a 20% chance that the cost of capital will drop to 9% in a year and stay at that level forever, and an 80% chance that it will stay at 11% forever. Movements in the cost of capital are unrelated to the size of the candy market. Construct the decision tree that shows the choices you have to make the investment either today or one year from now.**

Decision Tree

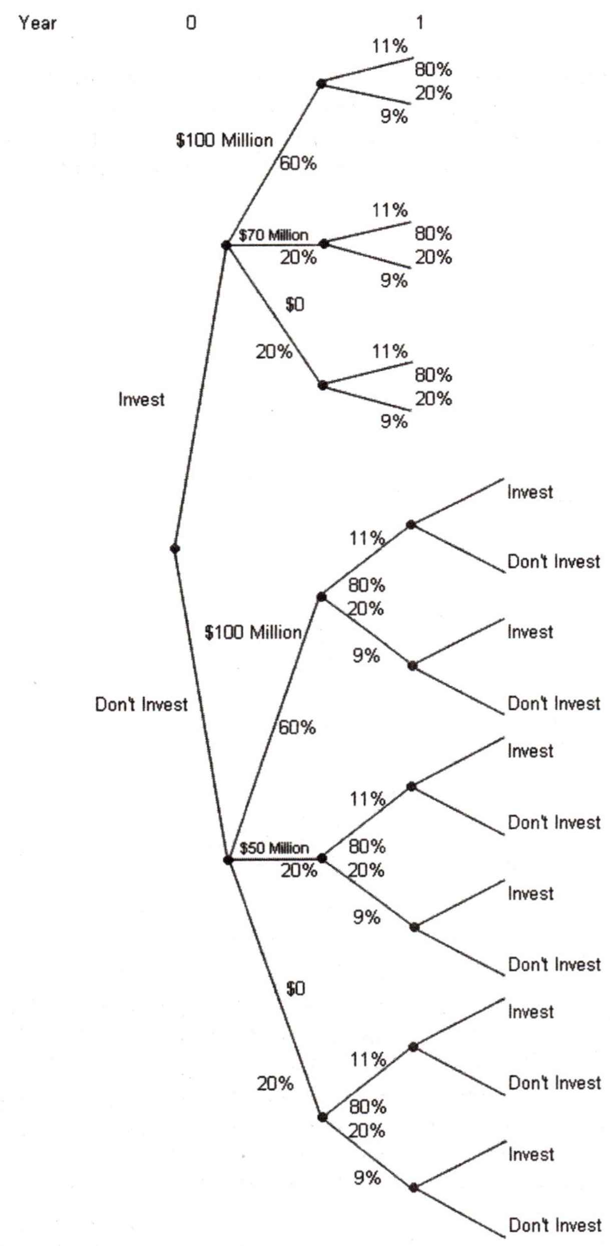

22-3. Using the information in Problem 2, rework the problem assuming you find out the size of the Everlasting Gobstopper market one year *after* you make the investment. That is, if you do not make the investment, you do not find out the size of the market. Construct the decision tree that shows the choices you have under these circumstances.

Decision Tree

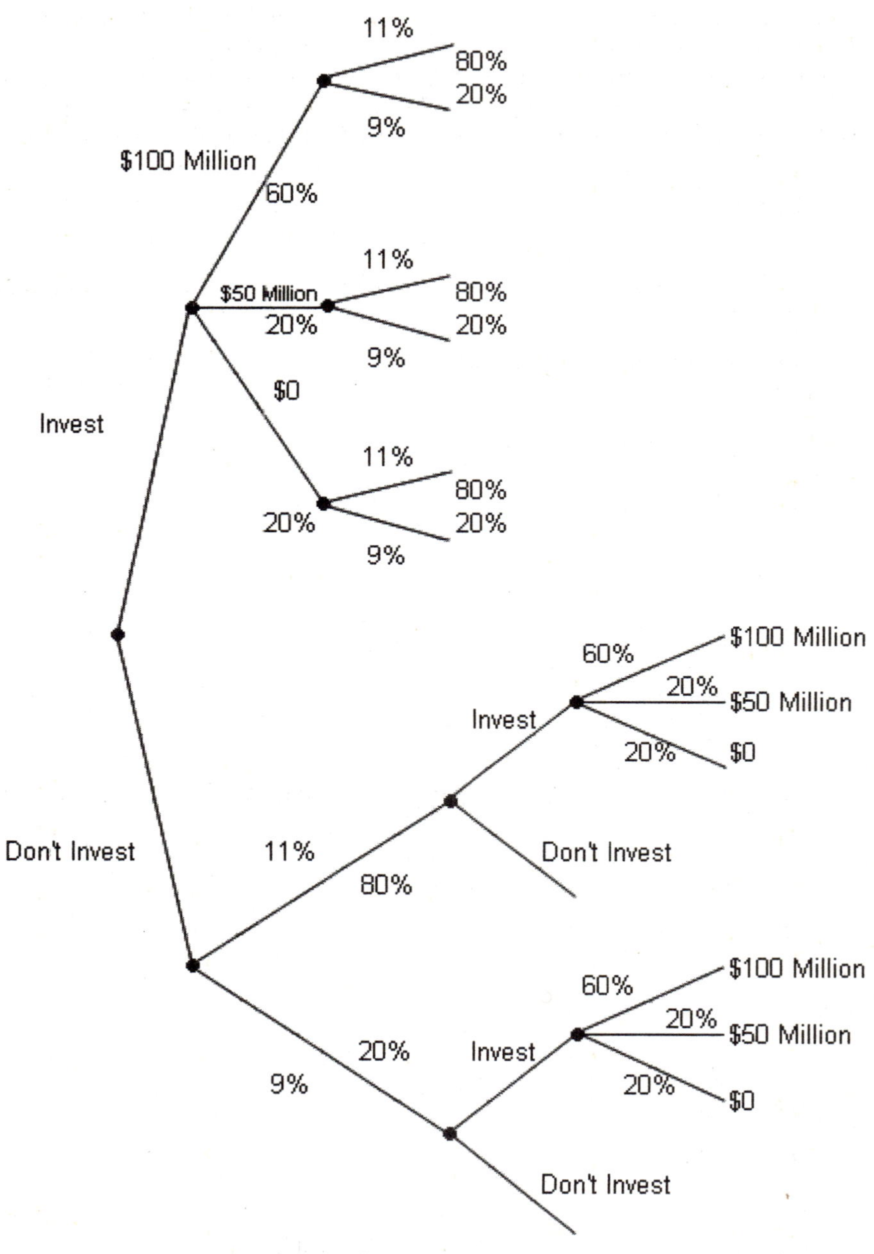

22-4. Describe the benefits and costs of delaying an investment opportunity.

By delaying, you delay the benefits of taking on the project and your competitors might take advantage of this delay. However, by delaying, uncertainty can be resolved, so you can become better informed and make better decisions.

22-5. You are a financial analyst at Global Conglomerate and are considering entering the shoe business. You believe that you have a very narrow window for entering this market. Because of Christmas demand, the time is right today and you believe that exactly a year from now would also be a good opportunity. Other than these two windows, you do not think another opportunity will exist to break into this business. It will cost you $35 million to enter the market. Because other shoe manufacturers exist and are public companies, you can construct a perfectly comparable company. Hence, you have decided to use the Black-Scholes formula to decide when and if you should enter the shoe business. Your analysis implies that the current value of an operating shoe company is $40 million. However, the flow of customers is uncertain, so the value of the company is volatile—your analysis indicates that the volatility is 25% per year. Fifteen percent of the value of the company is attributable to the value of the free cash flows (cash available to you to spend how you wish) expected in the first year. If the one-year risk-free rate of interest is 4%:

a. **Should Global enter this business and, if so, when?**

b. **How will the decision change if the current value of a shoe company is $36 million instead of $40 million?**

c. **Plot the value of your investment opportunity as a function of the current value of a shoe company.**

a. $S^x = S - PV(Div) = 40(1 - 0.15) = 40(0.85)$

$PV(K) = 35 / (1.04) = 33.6538$

$T = 1$

$\sigma = 0.25$

$$d_1 = \frac{\ln(S^x / PV(K)}{\sigma\sqrt{K}} + \frac{\sigma\sqrt{T}}{2} = 0.1659$$

$$d_2 = -0.0841$$

$$C = S^x N(d_1) - PV(K)N(d_2) = \$3.54$$

So the value of waiting is $3.54 million. The value of investing today is $40 – $35 = $5 million.

So they should enter the business now.

b. $S^x = S - PV(Div) = 36(1. - 15) = 36(0.85)$

$PV(K) = 35 / (1.04) = 33.6538$

$T = 1$

$\sigma = 0.25$

$$d_1 = \frac{\ln(S^x / PV(K)}{\sigma\sqrt{K}} + \frac{\sigma\sqrt{T}}{2} = 0.2555$$

$$d_2 = -0.5055$$

$$C = S^x N(d_1) - PV(K)N(d_2) = \$1.90$$

So the value of waiting is $1.90 million. The value of investing today is $36 – $35 = $1 million.

So they should not enter the business now.

c.

Decision Tree

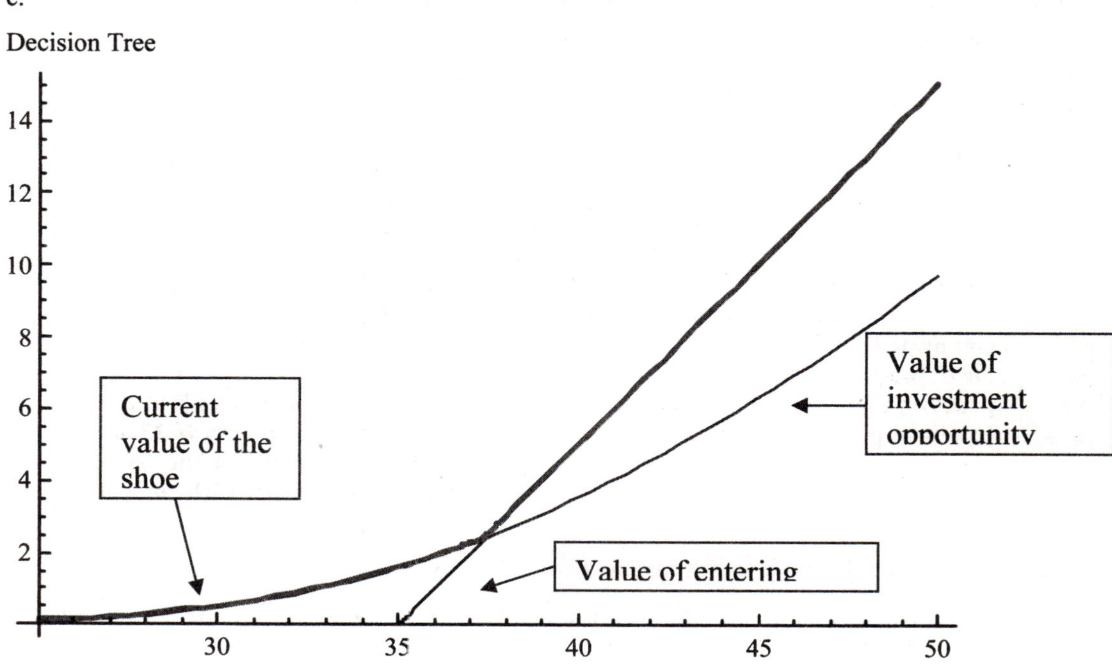

22-6. **It is the beginning of September and you have been offered the following deal to go heli-skiing. If you pick the first week in January and pay for your vacation now, you can get a week of heli-skiing for $2500. However, if you cannot ski because the helicopters cannot fly due to bad weather, there is no snow, or you get sick, you do not get a refund. There is a 40% probability that you will not be able to ski. If you wait until the last minute and go only if you know that the conditions are perfect and you are healthy, the vacation will cost $4000. You estimate that the pleasure you get from heli-skiing is worth $6000 per week to you (if you had to pay any more than that, you would choose not to go). If your cost of capital is 8% per year, should you book ahead or wait?**

Decision Tree

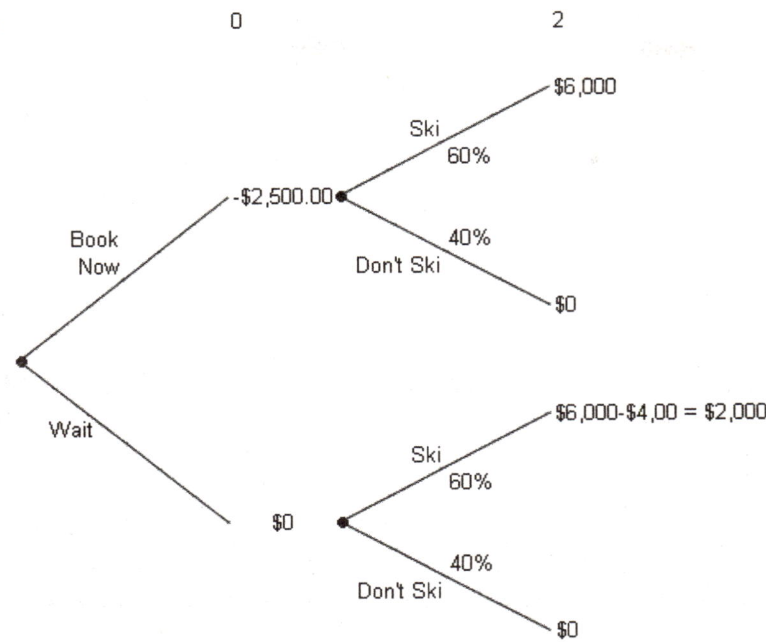

If you book now, your expected benefit from skiing in 4 months is:

$6,000(0.60) + 0(0.40) = \$3,600$

The NPV of booking today is therefore:

$$NPV = \frac{3,600}{1.08^{\frac{4}{12}}} - 2,500 = \$1,008.82$$

If you wait to book the expected benefit in 4 months is:

$2,000(0.60) + 0(0.4)0 = \$1,200$

The PV of this today is

$$\frac{\$1,200}{1.08^{\frac{4}{12}}} = \$1,169.61$$

So you should wait.

22-7. A professor in the Computer Science department at United States Institute of Technology has just patented a new search engine technology and would like to sell it to you, an interested venture capitalist. The patent has a 17-year life. The technology will take a year to implement (there are no cash flows in the first year) and has an up-front cost of $100 million. You believe this technology will be able to capture 1% of the Internet search market, and currently this market generates profits of $1 billion per year. Over the next five years, the risk-neutral probability that profits will grow at 10% per year is 20% and the risk-neutral probability that profits will grow at 5% per year is 80%. This growth rate will become clear one year from now (after the first year of growth). After five years, profits are expected to decline 2% annually. No profits are expected after the patent runs out. Assume that all risk-free interest rates are constant (regardless of the term) at 10% per year.

a. Calculate the NPV of undertaking the investment today.

b. Calculate the NPV of waiting a year to make the investment decision.

c. What is your optimal investment strategy?

a. Decision Tree

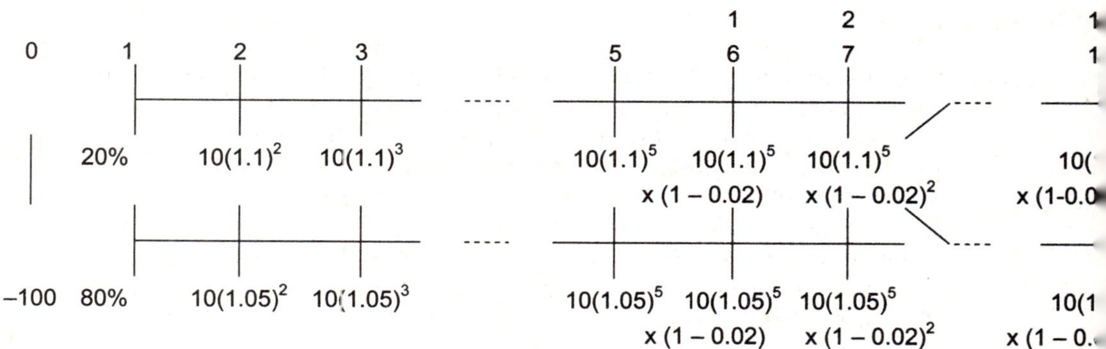

If the high growth rate state occurs, then the NPV is:

$$NPV_{high} = 4(10) + \frac{1}{(1.1)^5}\left(\frac{10(1.1)^5(1-0.02)}{0.1+0.02}\right)\left(1-\left(\frac{0.98}{1.1}\right)^{12}\right) - 100$$
$$= \$1,247,147.$$

Note: Since the first four cash flows grow out of the same rate as the discount rate, their present value is just the sum of the cash flows.

If the low growth rate state occurs, then the NPV is:

$$NPV_{low} = \frac{1}{1.1}\left(\frac{10(1.05)^2}{0.1-0.05}\left(1-\left(\frac{1.05}{1.1}\right)^4\right)\right) + \frac{1}{(1.1)^5}\left(\frac{10(1.05)^5(1-0.02)}{0.1+0.02}\right)\left(1-\left(\frac{0.98}{1.1}\right)^{12}\right) - 100$$
$$= -17.428 \text{ million.}$$

So the expected value is:

$$\text{NPV} = 1.25(0.20) + -17.428(0.80)$$
$$= -13.6927 \text{ million.}$$

b. Decision Tree

If the high growth rate state occurs, then the NPV at time 1 is:

$$\text{NPV}_{\text{high}} = 3(10)(1.1) + \frac{1}{(1.1)^4}\left(\frac{10(1.1)^5(1-0.02)}{0.1+0.02}\right)\left(1-\left(\frac{0.98}{1.1}\right)^{12}\right) - 100$$
$$= 0.372 \text{ million.}$$

Note: Since the first three cash flows grow at the same rate as the discount rate, their present value is just the sum of the cash flows, so the value at time 1 is just the PV compounded.

If the low growth rate state occurs, then the NPV at time 1 is:

$$NPV_{low} = \frac{1}{1.1}\left(\frac{10(1.05)^3}{0.1-0.05}\left(1-\left(\frac{1.05}{1.1}\right)^3\right)\right) + \frac{1}{(1.1)^4}\left(\frac{10(1.05)^5(1-0.02)}{0.1+0.02}\right)\left(1-\left(\frac{0.98}{1.1}\right)^{12}\right) - 100$$
$$= -19.19 \text{ million.}$$

So investment will only occur in the high growth state. The value today of this is:

$$NPV_0 = (0.2)\left(\frac{0.372}{1.1}\right) = \$67.6 \text{ million}$$

c. Since the NPV of investing today is negative, you should wait and only invest if the high state occurs.

22-8. The management of Southern Express Corporation is considering investing 10% of all future earnings in growth. The company has a single growth opportunity that it can take either now or in one period. Although the managers do not know the return on investment with certainty, they know it is equally likely to be either 10% or 14% per year. In one period, they will find out which state will occur. Currently the firm pays out all earnings as a dividend of $10 million; if it does not make the investment, dividends are expected to remain at this level forever. If Southern Express undertakes the investment, the new dividend will reflect the realized return on investment and will grow at the realized rate forever. Assuming the opportunity cost of capital is 10.1%, what is the value of the company just before the current dividend is paid (the cum-dividend value)?

Notice that if the firm makes the investment, the current dividend will be 10(1 – 0.1) = $9 million. It will have two possible growth rates in one period. If the return on investment turns out to be 14%, then the growth rate will be g = retention ratio × return on new investment = 0.1 × 0.14 = 1.4%. If the return on new investment is 10%, then the growth rate will be $g = 0.1 \times 0.1 = 1\%$. Assume the firm decides to wait to find out what the return on investment will be before making a decision. In this case, we need to decide whether to make the investment decision at time 1. If we make the investment and the return on investment is 10%, so the growth rate is 1% (the *low growth* state), the timeline will be as shown.

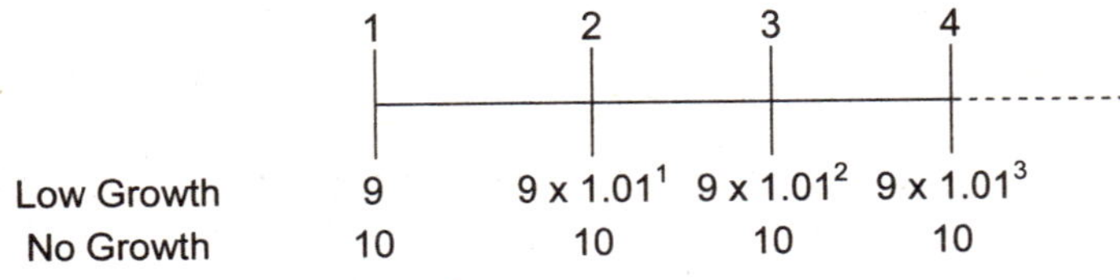

From the timeline we can see that the value of the firm at time 1 (before the dividend is paid) if the firm decides to invest and grow is:

$$P^l_{invest} = 9 + \frac{9(1.01)}{.101 - 0.01} = 108.89.$$

When the firm chooses not to invest, the value of the firm is:

$$P_{noinvest} = 10 + \frac{10}{.101} = 109.01.$$

Clearly, the firm is better off not investing, so its value in this state is $109.01 million. (One way to see this immediately is to note that in this state the return on investment is less than the opportunity cost of capital.)

The return on investment is 14%, so the growth rate is 1.4% (the *high growth* state); the same logic shows that if the investment is undertaken, the value of the firm is:

$$P^h_{invest} = 9 + \frac{9(1.014)}{.101 - 0.014} = 113.897.$$

This value exceeds $109.01, the value if the investment is not undertaken, so the firm should undertake the investment. (Here the return on investment exceeds the opportunity cost of capital.)

What is the value of this firm today? To solve this problem, first write down the decision tree:

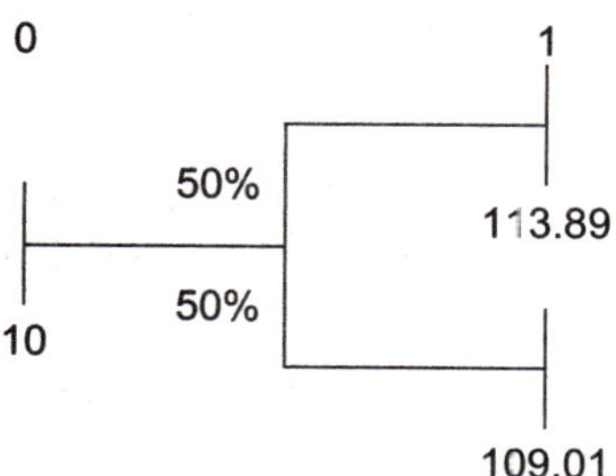

Since each state is equally likely, the expected value of the firm in one period is 113.897 (0.5) + 109.01 (0.5). Computing the present value and adding today's dividend (remember, we are computing the value before the dividend is paid) gives the firm value today of:

$$P = \frac{\frac{1}{2}(109.01 + 113.897)}{1.101} + 10 = 111.229.$$

Consider what would have happened if instead of waiting one period to make the investment decision, Southern's managers decided to make the decision today, i.e., at time 0 on the time line. In this case, the decision tree looks like this:

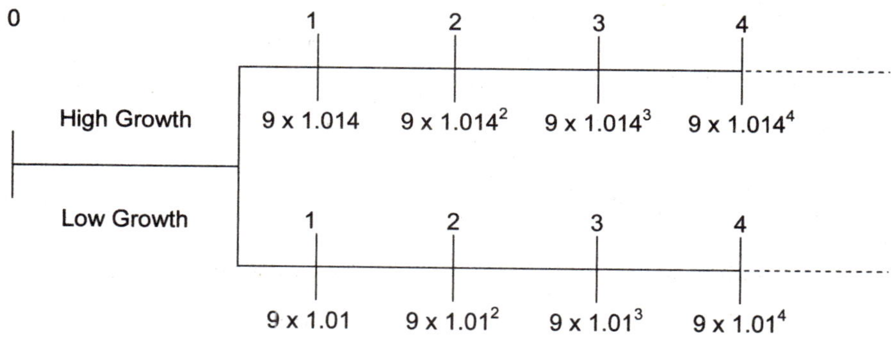

We can derive the value of the firm using the same logic as above. The present value today (time 0) of the future dividends if the growth rate turns out to be high is:

$$P^h_{invest} = \frac{9(1.014)}{0.101 - 0.014} = 104.897.$$

When the growth rate is low, the present value of future dividends at time 0 is:

$$P^l_{invest} = \frac{9(1.01)}{0.101 - 0.01} = 99.89.$$

The value of the firm today is the present value of the expected future dividends plus the dividend today. Since both states are equally likely, we have:

$$P_{invest} = 9 + \tfrac{1}{2}(99.89) + \tfrac{1}{2}(104.897) = 111.39.$$

Note that this value is *higher* than the value of the firm if management waits and makes the decision at time 1 when the return on investment becomes certain. So managers should give up the option to wait and invest today. Hence the value of the company is $111.39 million.

22-9. What decision should you make in Problem 2 if the one-year cost of capital is 15.44% and the profits last forever?

Decision Tree

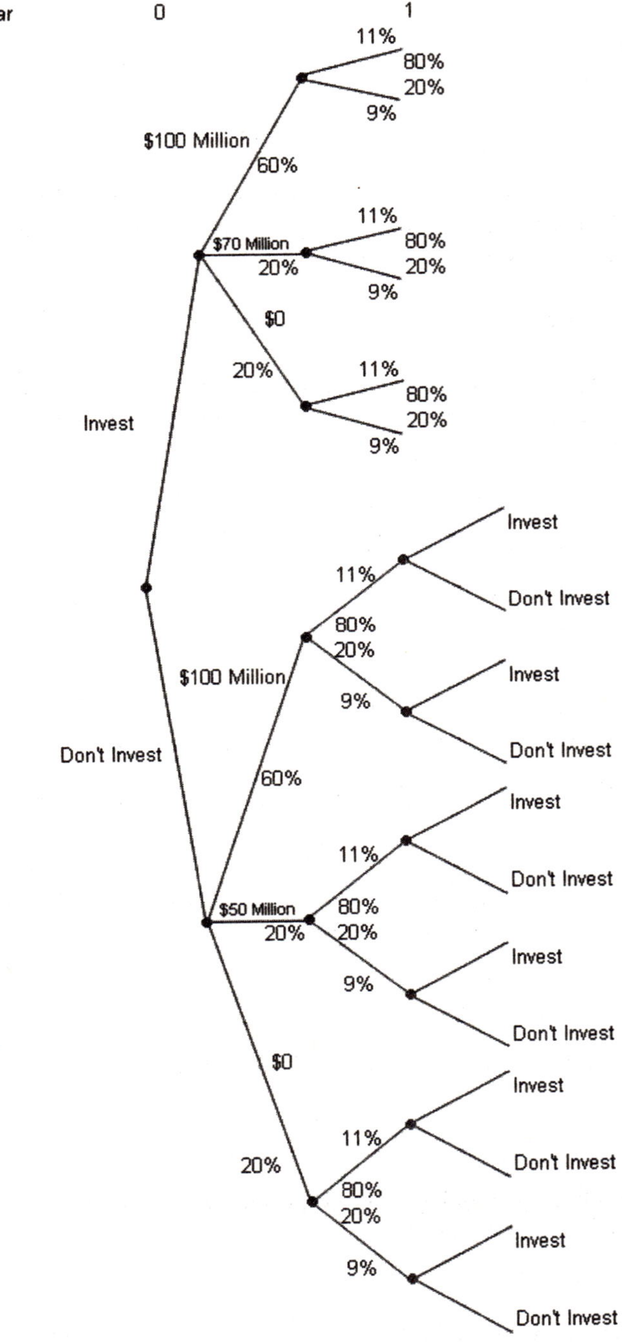

First let's calculate the NPV of investing in 3 possible states:

1. $100 Million State:

   Timeline:

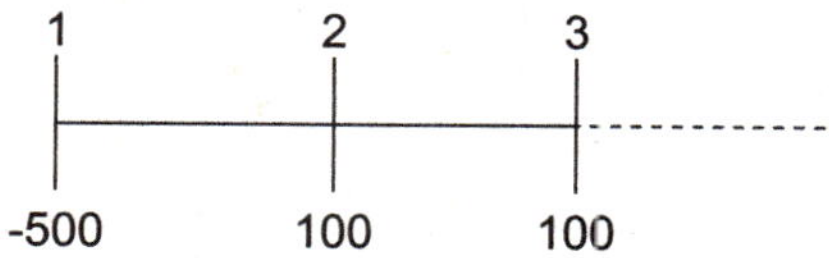

$$\text{NPV}(\text{r}) = \frac{100}{r} - 500$$
$$\text{NPV}(11\%) = \$409 \text{ million}$$
$$\text{NPV}(9\%) = 611.11 \text{ million}$$

   So the expected value if this state occurs is

$$\begin{aligned}\text{EV}_{100} &= 409(0.8) + 611.11(0.2)\\ &= 450.\end{aligned}$$

2. $50 Million State:

   Timeline:

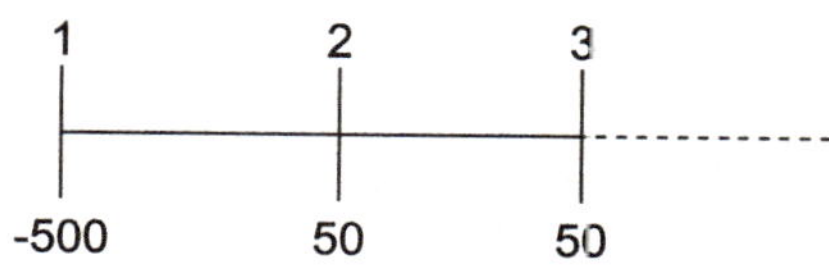

$$\text{NPV}(\text{r}) = \frac{100}{\text{r}} - 500$$
$$\text{NPV}(11\%) = -45.45$$
$$\text{NPV}(9\%) = 55.56$$

$$\begin{aligned}\text{EV}_{100} &= 55.56(0.2)\\ &= 11.11\end{aligned}$$

3. NPV is zero in the worst state, since profits are zero so the project will not be undertaken.

   So the present value at time 0 of the expected value at time 1 is:

$$\frac{0.6 \times 450 + 0.2 \times 11.11}{1.1544} = \$235.54 \text{ million.}$$

   If the investment is made at time 0, then the NPV is the PV of the expected cash flows minus the initial investment. The expected cash flows are:

   $0.6 \times 100 + 0.2 \times 50 = 70$ per year.

Timeline:

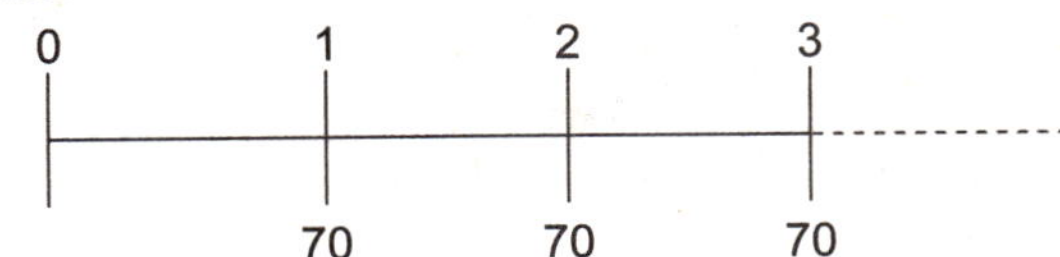

$$NPV = \frac{70}{0.11} - 500 = \$136.36 \text{ million}$$

Alternatively, you can calculate the value of the project one year from now and discount that to get the same answer:

$$NPV = 0.2 \times \left(\frac{70}{0.09} \times \frac{1}{1.1544} + \frac{70}{1.1544} - 500 \right) + 0.8 \times \left(\frac{70}{1.1} \times \frac{1}{1.1544} + \frac{70}{1.1544} - 500 \right)$$
$$= 136.39 \text{ million.}$$

So you are better off waiting.

22-10. Your R&D division has just synthesized a material that will superconduct electricity at room temperature; you have given the go-ahead to try to produce this material commercially. It will take five years to find out whether the material is commercially viable, and you estimate that the probability of success is 25%. Development will cost $10 million per year, paid at the beginning of each year. If development is successful and you decide to produce the material, the factory will be built immediately. It will cost $1 billion to put in place, and will generate profits of $100 million at the end of every year in perpetuity. Assume that the current five-year risk-free interest rate is 10% per year, and the yield on a perpetual risk-free bond will be 12%, 10%, 8%, or 5% in five years. Assume that the risk-neutral probability of each possible rate is the same. What is the value today of this project?

Decision Tree

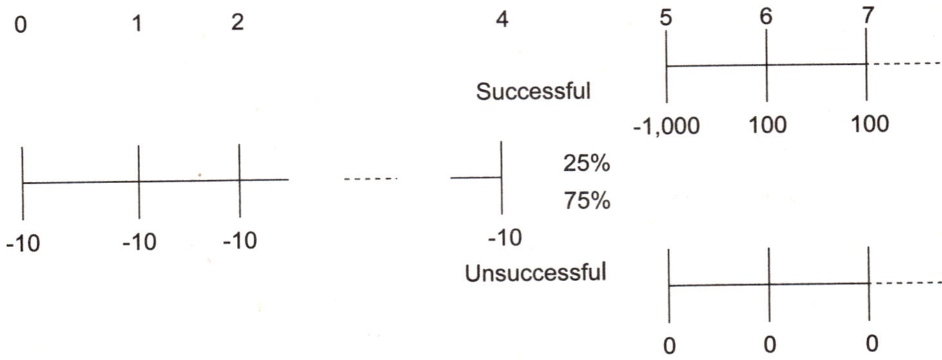

If development is successful, then the NPV (at time 5) of producing the wire is:

$$\text{NPV}_5(\text{r}) = \frac{100}{\text{r}} - 1{,}000.$$

This is negative for $r > 10\%$, so the wire will only be produced if the rates are 8% or 5%:

$$\text{NPV}_5(0.08) = \frac{100}{0.08} - 1{,}000 = 250$$
$$\text{NPV}_5(0.05) = 1{,}000.$$

So the expected value of the growth opportunity at time 5 if development is successful is:

$$\begin{aligned}EV_S &= 250(0.25)+1{,}000(0.25)\\ &= 312.5.\end{aligned}$$

There is a 25% chance of success so the expected value at time 5 of the investment opportunity is:

$$EV = 312.5 \times 0.25 = \$78.125.$$

The NPV of the development opportunity at time 0 is therefore

$$\begin{aligned}NPV &= -10 - \frac{10}{0.1}\left(1-\left(\frac{1}{1.1}\right)^4\right)+\frac{78.125}{(1.1)^5}\\ &= \$6.811 \text{ million.}\end{aligned}$$

22-11. You are an analyst working for Goldman Sachs, and you are trying to value the growth potential of a large, established company, Big Industries. Big Industries has a thriving R&D division that has consistently turned out successful products. You estimate that, on average, the R&D division generates two new product proposals every three years, so that there is a 66% chance that a project will be proposed every year. Typically, the investment opportunities the R&D division produces require an initial investment of $10 million and yield profits of $1 million per year that grow at one of three possible growth rates in perpetuity: 3%, 0%, and −3%. All three growth rates are equally likely for any given project. These opportunities are always "take it or leave it" opportunities: If they are not undertaken immediately, they disappear forever. Assume that the cost of capital will always remain at 12% per year. What is the present value of all future growth opportunities Big Industries will produce?

Take a project that arrives in year n. The timeline is as follows.

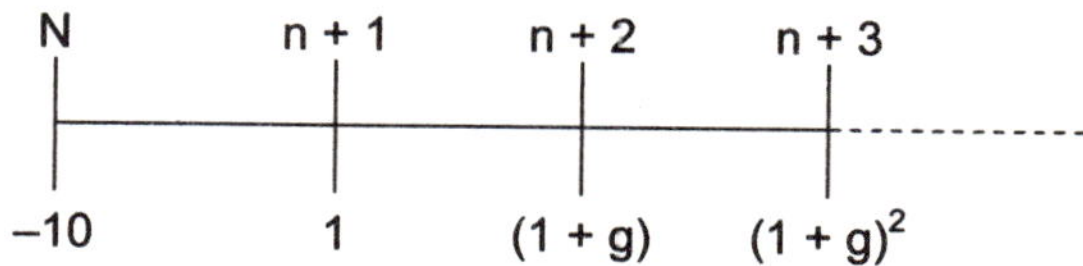

The NPV of this investment opportunity is:

$$NPV_n(g) = \frac{1}{0.12-g} - 10.$$

Now:

$$NPV_n(g=3\%) = \frac{1}{0.12-0.03} - 10 = \$1.11 \text{ million}$$

$$NPV_n(g=0\%) = \frac{1}{0.12-0} - 10 = -\$1.67 \text{ million}$$

$$NPV_n(g=-3\%) = \frac{1}{0.12+0.03} - 10 = -\$3.33 \text{ million}$$

Therefore, only the projects with positive growth rates will be taken on. Thus, the expected value of any given investment opportunity is

$$EV_n = 1.11 \times \frac{1}{3} = \$370{,}370.$$

The probability that a project will arrive in any given year is 2/3, and so the expected value of the growth opportunity that will arrive in year n is:

$$G_n = 370{,}370 \times \frac{2}{3} = \$246{,}914.$$

Putting this on a timeline:

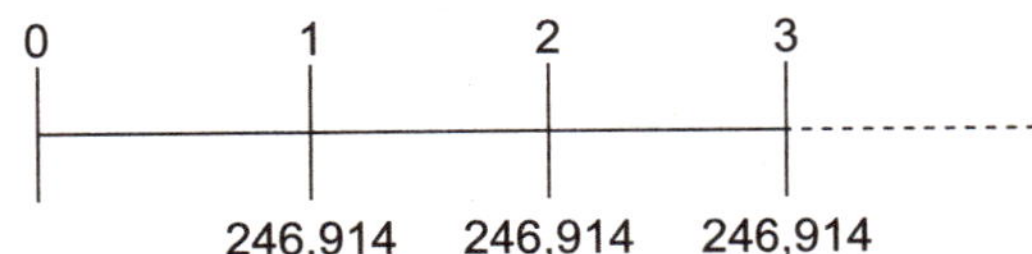

So the PV of all these opportunities today is:

$$PV = \frac{246{,}914}{0.12} = \$2.058 \text{ million.}$$

22-12. Repeat Problem 11, but this time assume that all the probabilities are risk-neutral probabilities, which means the cost of capital is always the risk-free rate and risk-free rates are as follows: The current interest rate for a risk-free perpetuity is 8%; in one year, there is a 64.375% chance that all risk-free interest rates will be 10% and stay there forever, and a 35.625% chance that they will be 6% and stay there forever. The current one-year risk-free rate is 7%.

Take a project that arrives in year n. The timeline is as follows.

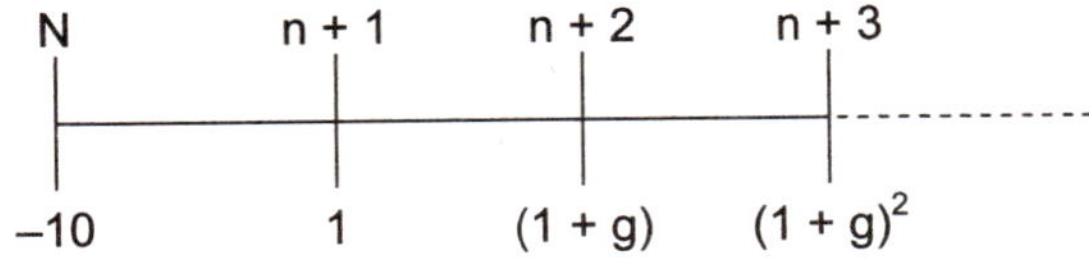

The NPV of this investment opportunity is:

$$\text{NPV}_n(g,r) = \frac{1}{r-g} - 10.$$

If the risk free rate is 10%:

$$\text{NPV}(3\%,10\%) = \frac{1}{0.1-0.03} - 10 = \$4.286 \text{ million}$$

$$\text{NPV}(0\%,10\%) = \frac{1}{0.1} - 10 = 0$$

$$\text{NPV}(-3\%,10\%) = \frac{1}{0.1+0.03} - 10 = -\$2.308 \text{ million.}$$

Therefore, only the projects with positive rates will be taken on. Thus, the expected value of any given investment opportunity is:

$$EV_n = 4.286 \times \frac{1}{3} = \$1.4286 \text{ million.}$$

The probability that a project will arrive in any given year is 2/3, so the expected value of the growth opportunity that will arrive in year n is:

$$G_n = 1.4286 \times \frac{2}{3} = \$952{,}381.$$

Putting this on a timeline:

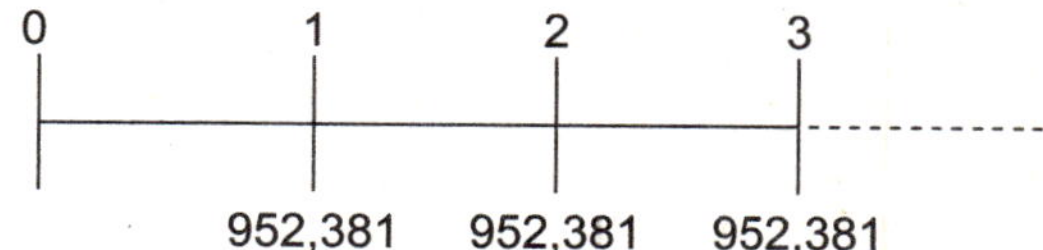

So the PV at time 1 of all these opportunities is:

$$\begin{aligned} PV &= 952{,}381 + \frac{952{,}381}{0.1} \\ &= \$10.4762 \text{ million.} \end{aligned}$$

Now, if the risk free rate is 6%:

$$\text{NPV}(3\%, 6\%) = \frac{1}{0.06 - 0.03} - 10 = 23.333$$

$$\text{NPV}(0\%, 6\%) = \frac{1}{0.06} - 10 = 6.667$$

$$\text{NPV}(-3\%, 6\%) = \frac{1}{0.06 + 0.03} - 10 = 1.111.$$

Therefore, regardless of the growth rate, all projects will be taken on. Thus, the expected value of any given investment opportunity is:

$$EV_n = 23.33 \times \frac{1}{3} + 6.67 \times \frac{1}{3} + 1.111 \times \frac{1}{3} = \$10.37 \text{ million.}$$

The probability that a project will arrive in any given year is 2/3, and so the expected value of the growth opportunity that will arrive in year n is

$$G_n = 10.37 \times \frac{2}{3} = \$6.844 \text{ million.}$$

Putting this on a timeline:

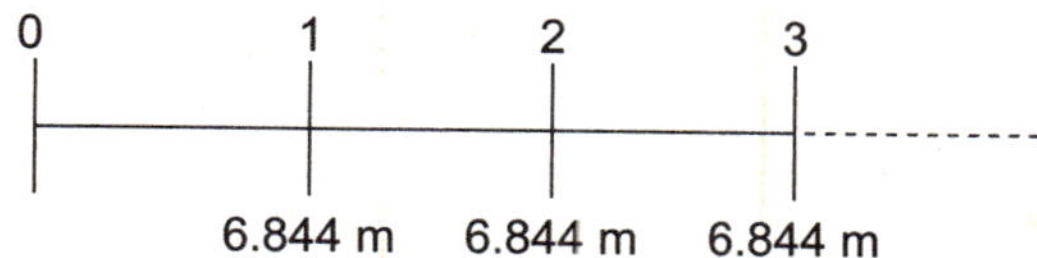

So the PV at time 1 of all these opportunities is:

$$PV = 6.844 + \frac{6.844}{0.06} = \$120.91 \text{ million.}$$

There is a 64.375% chance of rates going to 10% and a 35.625% chance of rates going to 6%. Putting this on a decision tree

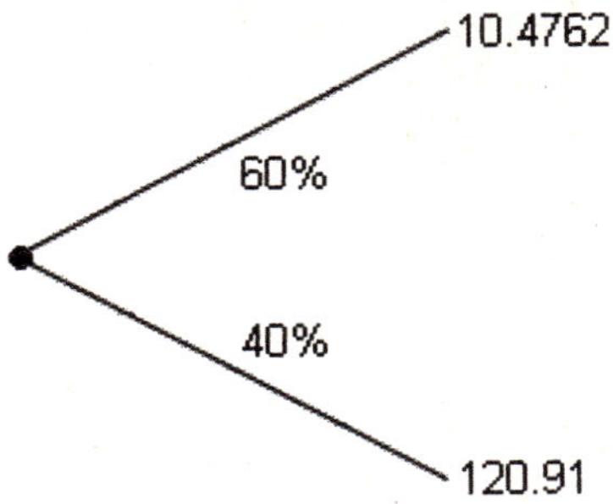

So the expected value is:

$10.4762 \times 0.64375 + 120.91 \times 0.35625 = 49.82.$

Computing the PV gives the answer:

$$\frac{49.82}{1.07} = \$46.56 \text{ million.}$$

22-13. You own a small networking startup. You have just received an offer to buy your firm from a large, publicly traded firm, JCH Systems. Under the terms of the offer, you will receive 1 million shares of JCH. JCH stock currently trades for $25 per share. You can sell the shares of JCH that you will receive in the market at any time. But as part of the offer, JCH also agrees that at the end of the next year, it will buy the shares back from you for $25 per share if you desire. Suppose the current one-year risk-free rate is 6.18%, the volatility of JCH stock is 30%, and JCH does not pay dividends.

a. Is this offer worth more than $25 million? Explain.

b. What is the value of the offer?

a. The offer is worth more than $25 million because of the put option.

b. The value of the offer is the current value of the shares plus the value of the put option.

To calculate the value of the put:

$S = 25$

$PV(K) = 25 / (1.0618)$

$T = 1$

$\sigma = 0.30$

$$d_1 = \frac{\ln(S / PV(K)}{\sigma\sqrt{K}} + \frac{\sigma\sqrt{T}}{2} = 0.3499$$

$d_2 = 0.04989$

$P = PV(K)(1 - N(d_2) - S(1 - N(d_2)) = 2.224$

So, the value of the offer is 25 + 2.224 = $27.224 million.

(Note that the actual value will be slightly higher because this uses the value of a European put.)

22-14. You own a wholesale plumbing supply store. The store currently generates revenues of $1 million per year. Next year, revenues will either decrease by 10% or increase by 5%, with equal probability, and then stay at that level as long as you operate the store. You own the store outright. Other costs run $900,000 per year. There are no costs for shutting down; in that case, you can always sell the store for $500,000. What is the business worth today if the cost of capital is fixed at 10%?

Decision Tree

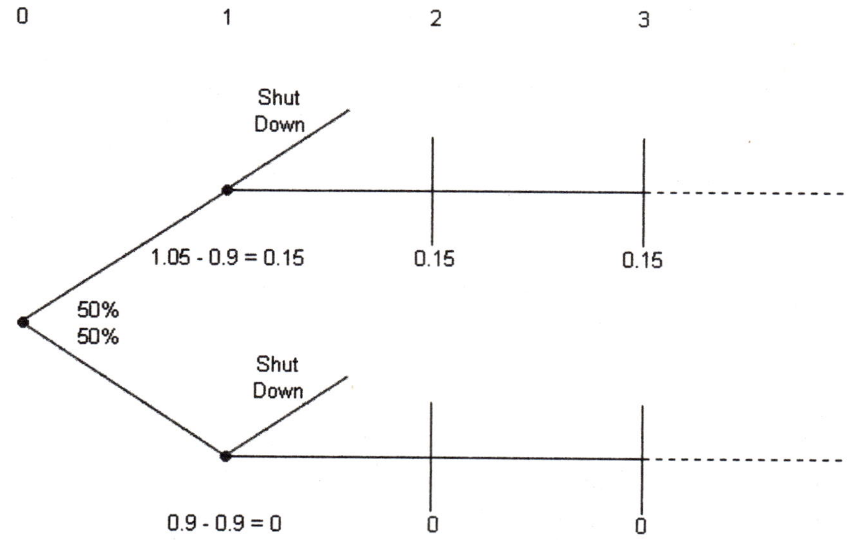

The value of the store is the maximum of the PV of all future profits and $500,000, the value of selling the store.

If the revenues decrease, then future profits are zero so the store should be shut down. Hence the value in this state is $500,000.

If the revenues increase, then the PV of future profits at time 1 are:

$$(1.05-0.9)+\frac{1.05-0.9}{0.1}=0.15+\frac{0.15}{0.1}=\$1.65 \text{ million.}$$

So it is optimal to keep the store running. Putting this on a decision tree:

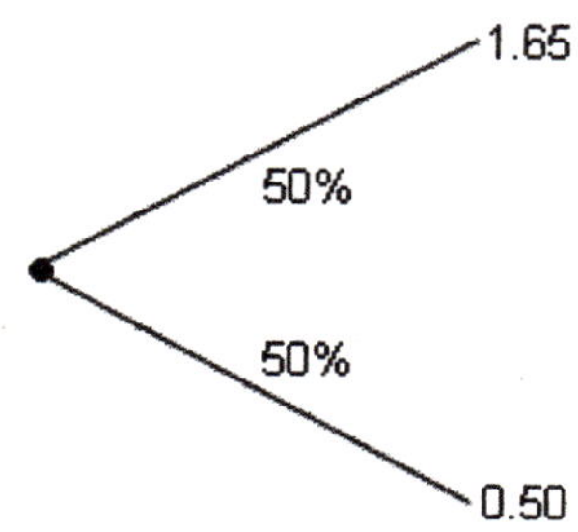

So the PV of the time 1 expected value is:

$$\frac{1.65\frac{1}{2}+0.5\frac{1}{2}}{1.1}=\$977,273.$$

Since this is greater than $500,000, the value of the store is $977,273 with the option to abandon.

22-15. You own a copper mine. The price of copper is currently $1.50 per pound. The mine produces 1 million pounds of copper per year and costs $2 million per year to operate. It has enough copper to operate for 100 years. Shutting the mine down would entail bringing the land up to EPA standards and is expected to cost $5 million. Reopening the mine once it is shut down would be an impossibility given current environmental standards. The price of copper has an equal (and independent) probability of going up or down by 25% each year for the next two years and then will stay at that level forever. Calculate the NPV of continuing to operate the mine if the cost of capital is fixed at 15%. Is it optimal to abandon the mine or keep it operating?

Decision Tree:

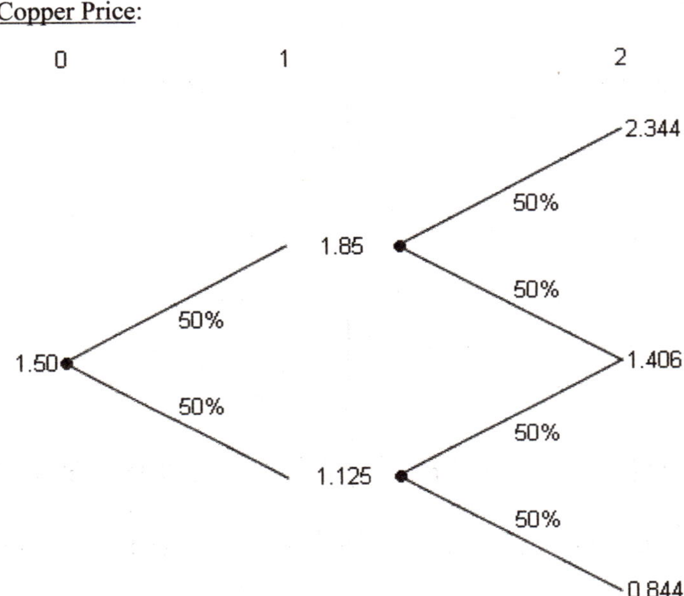

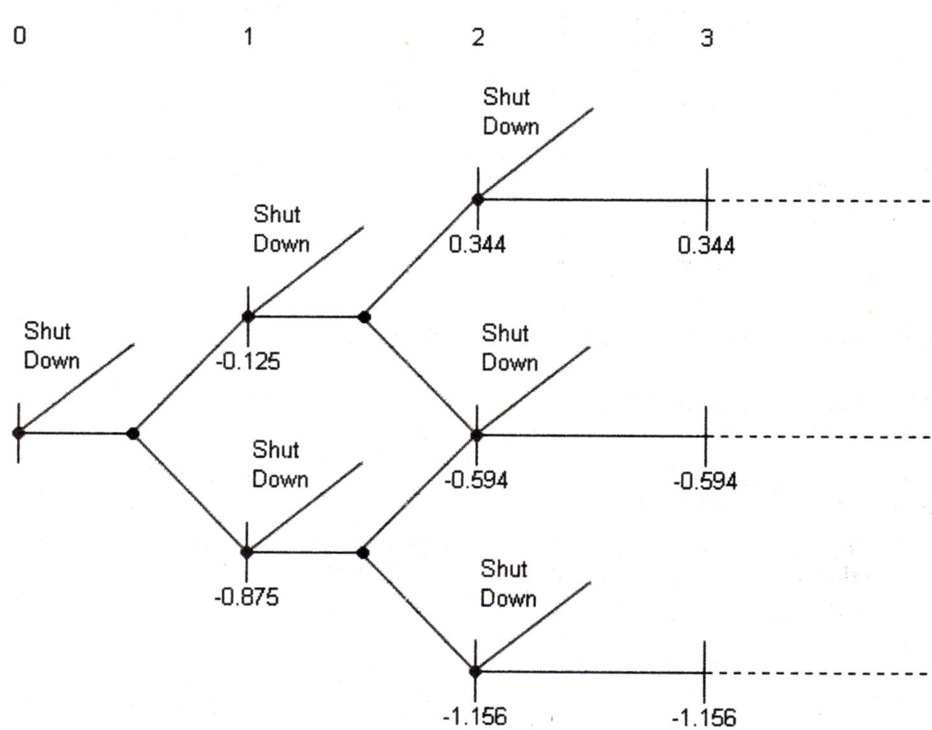

First, determine whether the mine is operating or shut down in each possible state at time 2.

When the copper price is \$2.344, the mine's profits are \$0.344 million/year for 98 years and then it will cost \$5 million to shut the mine down. The PV at time 2 of these cash flows is:

$$PV_{2,0.344} = \frac{0.344}{0.15}\left(1 - \frac{1}{(1.15)^{98}}\right) - \frac{5}{(1.15)^{98}} = \$2.293 \text{ million.}$$

Since it will cost \$5 million to shut the mine down, it is better to leave it operating.

Similarly, when the copper price is \$1.406,

$$PV_{1.406} = \frac{-0.594}{015}\left(1 - \frac{1}{(1.15)^{9.8}}\right) - \frac{5}{(1.15)^{98}} = -3.96 \text{ million.}$$

Again, since the value is greater than –\$5 million, it is better to operate the mine.

Finally, when the copper price is \$0.844:

$$PV_{0.844} = \frac{-1.156}{0.15}\left(1 - \frac{1}{(1.15)^{98}}\right) - \frac{5}{(1.15)^{98}} = -\$7.7 \text{ million.}$$

Since it is smaller than –\$5 million, the mine should be shut down.

Next, calculate the value of the mine if it is operating at time 1 when the copper price is \$1.85. Putting the value of the mine plus the cash flow at time 2 on a decision tree:

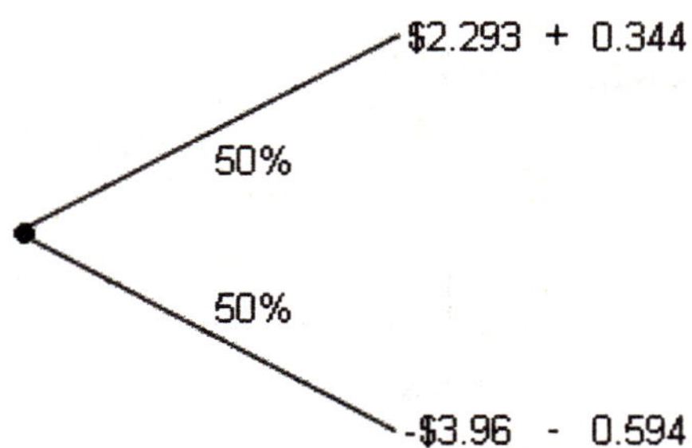

The present value at time 1 of the expected value at time 2 is

$$\frac{(2.293+0.344)\frac{1}{2}+(-3.96-0.594)\frac{1}{2}}{1.15}=-\$0.8337 \text{ million.}$$

So it is optimal to run the mine in this state.

Next, calculate the value of the mine if it is operating at time 1 when the copper price is $1.125. Putting the value of the mine plus the cash flow at time 2 on a decision tree:

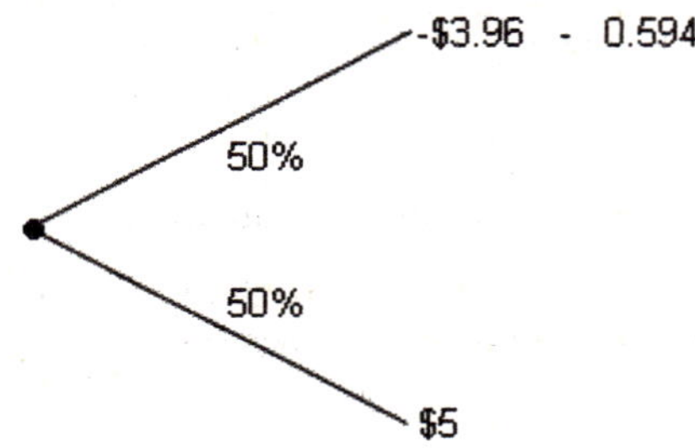

The present value at time 1 of the expected value at time 2 is

$$\frac{-5\times\frac{1}{2}+(-3.96-1.594)\frac{1}{2}}{1.15}=-\$4.154 \text{ million.}$$

So it is optimal to run the mine in this state.

Finally, we calculate the value of the value of the mine at time 0 if it is operating.

Putting the value of the mine plus the cash flow at time 1 on a decision tree:

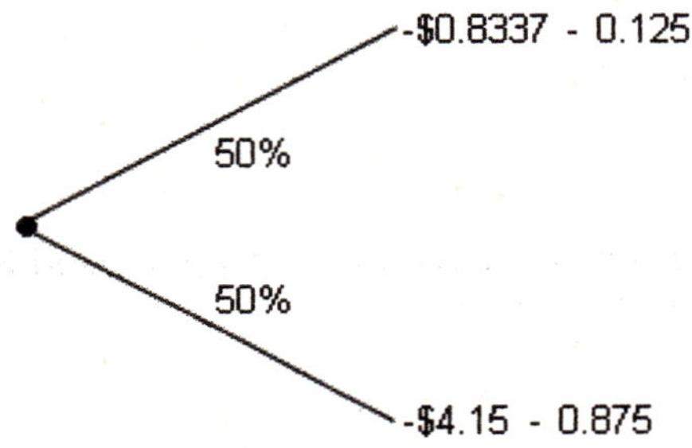

The present value at time 0 of the expected value at time 1 is:

$$\frac{(-0.8337-0.125)\frac{1}{2}+(-4.154-0.875)\frac{1}{2}}{1.15}=-\$2.603\text{ million.}$$

So the mine is worth –$2.603 million. Even though it is worth a negative amount because in most states it will lose money for the next 98 years, it is not optimal to shut down the mine at time 0 because the costs of shutting down are even greater.

22-16. An original silver dollar from the late eighteenth century consists of approximately 24 grams of silver. At a price of $.019 per gram ($6 per troy ounce), the silver content of the coin is currently worth about $4.50. Assume that these coins are in plentiful supply and are not collector's items, so they have no numismatic value. If the current price of silver is $0.19 per gram, will the price of the coin be greater than, less than, or equal to $4.50? Justify your answer.

The silver dollar is actually a real option because you always have the option to use it as a dollar coin. Although at the current price of silver this does not make sense, if the price of silver dropped below 4.1¢/gram ($1.28/troy ounce) the value of the silver in the coin would drop below $1. The coin can always be used a dollar coin, so its price cannot fall below a dollar (by the Law of One Price). Since the price of 24 grams of silver can drop below $1, the coin must be worth more than 24 grams of silver or $4.50. So the coin must be worth $4.50.

22-17. What implicit assumption is made when managers use the equivalent annual benefit method to decide between two projects with different lives that use the same resource?

The equivalent annual cost method implicitly assumes that, at the end of the life of the shorter length project, you can replace the shorter length project on the original terms.

22-18. You own a cab company and are evaluating two options to replace your fleet. Either you can take out a five-year lease on the replacement cabs for $500 per month per cab, or you can purchase the cabs outright for $30,000, in which case the cabs will last eight years. You must return the cabs to the leasing company at the end of the lease. The leasing company is responsible for all maintenance costs, but if you purchase the cabs, you will buy a maintenance contract that will cost $100 per month for the life of each cab. Each cab will generate revenues of $1000 per month. Assume the cost of capital is fixed at 12%.

a. Calculate the NPV per cab of both possibilities: purchasing the cabs or leasing them.

b. Calculate the equivalent monthly annual benefit of both opportunities.

c. If you are leasing a cab, you have the opportunity to buy the used cab after five years. Assume that in five years a five-year-old cab will cost either $10,000 or $16,000 with equal likelihood, will have maintenance costs of $500 per month, and will last three more years. Which option should you take?

a. Timeline:

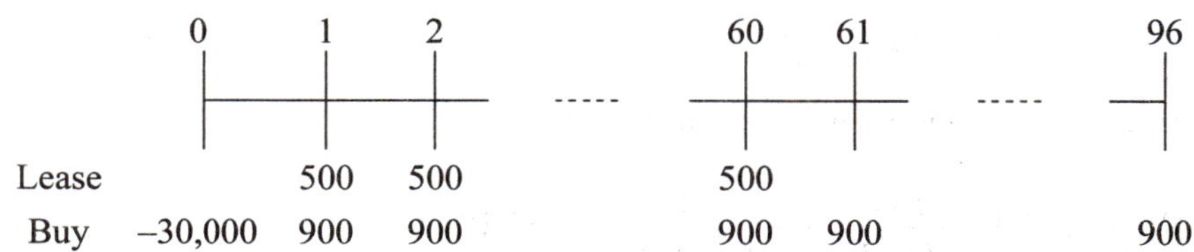

Converting the cost of capital to a monthly discount rate gives:

$(1.12)^{\frac{1}{12}} - 1 = .00949$, so the monthly discount rate is 0.949%.

$$\text{NPV}_{\text{Lease}} = \frac{500}{0.00949}\left(1 - \frac{1}{(1.00949)^{60}}\right)$$
$$= \$22,794$$

$$\text{NPV}_{\text{Buy}} = -30,000 + \frac{900}{0.00949}\left(1 - \frac{1}{(1.00949)^{96}}\right)$$
$$= \$26,541$$

b. Timeline:

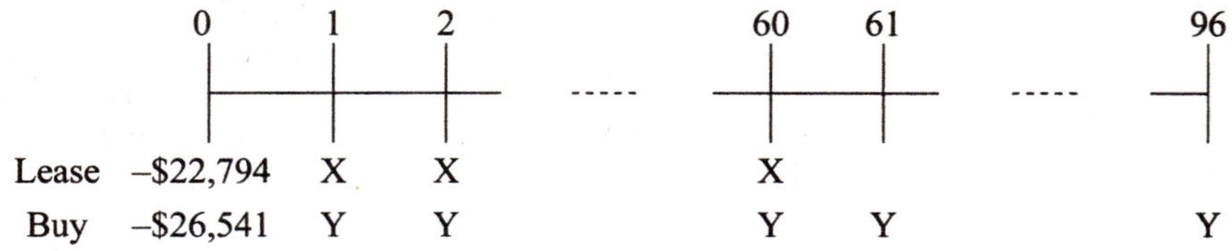

Solving for the EAB of leasing:

$$22,794 = \frac{X}{0.00949}\left(1 - \frac{1}{(1.00949)^{60}}\right) \Rightarrow X = \$500.$$

Solving for the EAB of buying:

$$26,541 = \frac{Y}{0.00949}\left(1 - \frac{1}{(1.00949)^{60}}\right) \Rightarrow Y = \$422.$$

c. Decision Tree

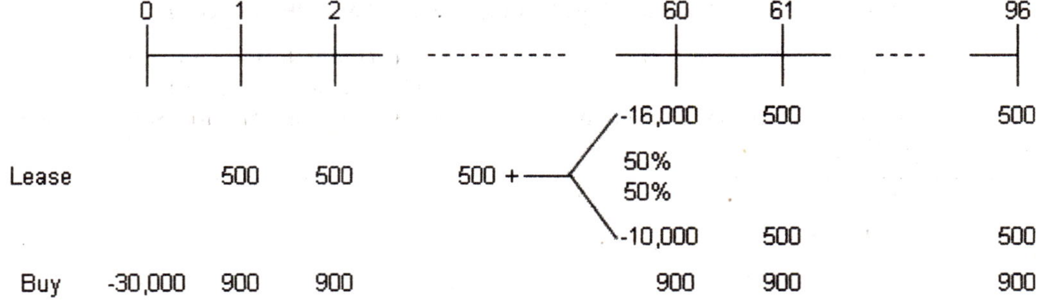

In month 60, the NPV of buying a cab is either

$$\text{NPV} = -10,000 + \frac{500}{0.00949}\left(1 - \frac{1}{(1.00949)^{36}}\right) = \$5,188.$$

Or

$$NPV = -16,000 + \frac{500}{0.00949}\left(1 - \frac{1}{(1.00949)^{36}}\right) = -\$813.$$

The expected value of replacing the cabs in year 5 is:

$$EV = 5188(0.5) = \$2,594.$$

The value today of this:

$$PV = \frac{2,594}{(1.00949)^{60}} = \$1,472.$$

Adding this to the NPV of leasing from part a gives:

$$NPV_{Lease} = 1,472 + 22,794 = \$24,266.$$

Since the NPV of buying as not changed

$$NPV_{Buy} = \$26,541.$$

So you should *buy* the cab.

22-19. You own a piece of raw land in an up-and-coming area in Gotham City. The costs to construct a building increase disproportionately with the size of the building. A building of q square feet costs 0.1 × q^2 to build. After you construct a building on the lot, it will last forever but you are committed to it: You cannot put another building on the lot. Buildings currently rent at \$100 per square foot per month. Rents in this area are expected to increase in five years. There is a 50% chance that they will rise to \$200 per square foot per month and stay there forever, and a 50% chance that they will stay at \$100 per square foot per month forever. The cost of capital is fixed at 12% per year.

a. **Should you construct a building on the lot right away? If so, how large should the building be?**

b. **If you choose to delay the decision, how large a building will you construct in each possible state in five years?**

a. Converting the cost of capital to a monthly discount rate gives:

$$(1.12)^{\frac{1}{12}} - 1 = .00949.$$

So 12% per year is equivalent to 0.949% per month. If rents rise then a building of size q will be worth:

$$\frac{200q}{0.00949}.$$

This building will cost $0.1q^2$ to build, so the NPV is:

$$\frac{200q}{0.00949} - 0.1q^2.$$

To find the maximum value of this function, take the derivative and set the results equal to zero:

$$\frac{200}{0.00949} - 0.2q = 0.$$

Solving for q gives:

q = 105,387 sq. ft.

Doing the same thing in the state with $100/sq. ft. rents gives:

q = 52,694.

b. If you wait then the NPV of building in 200 sq. ft. state is

$$\frac{200q}{0.00949} - 0.1q^2 = \frac{200 \times 105{,}387}{0.00949} - 0.1(105{,}387)^2 = \$1.11 \text{ billion.}$$

Repeating for the $100 sq ft state gives $278 million.

So the PV of this today is:

$$PV = \frac{1{,}110(0.5) + 278(0.5)}{(1.00949)^{60}} = \$394 \text{ million.}$$

If we build today the expected cash flows are:

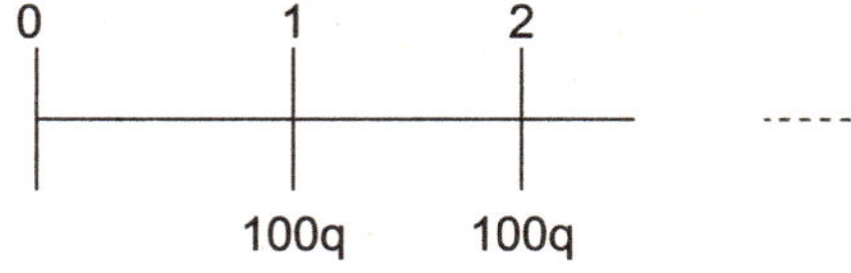

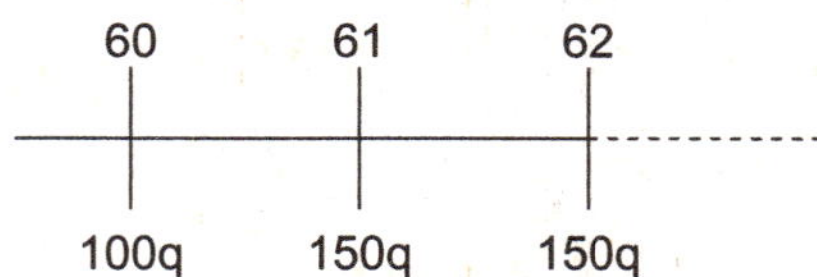

$$NPV = \frac{100q}{0.00949}\left(1 - \frac{1}{(1.00949)^{60}}\right) + \frac{150q}{0.00949}\left(\frac{1}{1.00949}\right)^{60} - 0.1q^2.$$

Taking the derivative, setting the result equal to zero and solving for q gives the optimal size to the building today:

$$\frac{100}{0.00949}\left(1 - \frac{1}{(1.00949)^{60}}\right) + \frac{150}{0.00949}\left(\frac{1}{1.00949}\right)^{60} - 0.2q = 0.$$

q = 67,644 sq. ft.

So the NPV is:

NPV = $458 million.

So we should build a building of 67,644 sq. ft. today.

22-20. Genenco is developing a new drug that will slow the aging process. In order to succeed, two breakthroughs are needed, one to increase the potency of the drug, and the second to eliminate toxic side effects. Research to improve the drug's potency is expected to require an upfront investment of $10 million and take 2 years; the drug has a 5% chance of success. Reducing the drug's toxicity will require a $30 million up-front investment, take 4 years, and has a 20% chance of success. If both efforts are successful, Genenco can sell the patent for the drug to a major drug company for $2 billion. All risk is idiosyncratic, and the risk-free rate is 6%.

a. What is the NPV of launching both research efforts simultaneously?

b. What is the optimal order to stage the investments?

c. What is the NPV with the optimal staging?

a. $-10 - 30 + .05 \times 20 \times 2000/1.06^4 = -24$ million

b. Potency : $(1 - .05/1.06^2)/10 = 0.096$

Toxicity: $(1 - .20/1.06^4)/30 = 0.028$

So, work on potency, then toxicity—higher risk and smaller investment.

c. If potency works, then the NPV of continuing is

$(-30 + .2\ 2000/1.06^4)$

So the NPV of starting is

$-10 + 0.05$ (NPV of starting toxicity)$/1.06^2$

$= -10 + 0.05\ (-30 + .2\ 2000/1.06^4)/1.06^2 = \$2.76$ million.

22-21. Your engineers are developing a new product to launch next year that will require both software and hardware innovations. The software team requests a budget of $5 million and forecasts an 80% chance of success. The hardware team requests a $10 million budget and forecasts a 50% chance of success. Both teams will need 6 months to work on the product, and the risk-free interest rate is 4% APR with semiannual compounding.

a. Which team should work on the project first?

b. Suppose that before anyone has worked on the project, the hardware team comes back and revises their proposal, changing the estimated chance of success to 75% based on new information. Will this affect your decision in (a)?

a. Software: $(1 - .80/1.02)/5 = 0.043$

Hardware: $(1 - .50/1.02)/10 = 0.051$

>> Hardware should go first

b. Hardware: $(1 - .75/1.02)/10 = 0.026$

>> Yes, software should go first now.

22-22. Your firm is thinking of expanding. If you invest today, the expansion will generate $10 million in FCF at the end of the year, and will have a continuation value of either $150 million (if the economy improves) or $50 million (if the economy does not improve). If you wait until next year to invest, you will lose the opportunity to make $10 million in FCF, but you will know the continuation value of the investment in the following year (that is, in a year from now, you will know what the investment continuation value will be in the following year). Suppose the risk-free rate is 5%, and the risk-neutral probability that the economy improves is 45%. Assume the cost of expanding is the same this year or next year.

a. If the cost of expanding is $80 million, should you do so today, or wait until next year to decide?

b. At what cost of expanding would there be no difference between expanding now and waiting? To what profitability index does this correspond?

a. $V0 = (.45 \times (150) + .55 \times (50) + 10)/1.05 = 100$

NPV(expand) = $100 - 80 = 20$

NPV(wait) = $.45 \times (150-80)/1.05 = 30$

So, optimal to wait.

b. NPV(expand) = $100 - C =$

NPV(wait) = $.45 \times (150 - C)/1.05$

So, $C = 62.5$

Prof Index = NPV/C = $(100 - 62.5)/62.5 = 0.6$

22-23. Assume that the project in Example 22.5 pays an annual cash flow of $100,000 (instead of $90,000).

a. What is the NPV of investing today?

b. What is the NPV of waiting and investing tomorrow?

c. Verify that the hurdle rate rule of thumb gives the correct time to invest in this case.

a. 100k/.054 – 1m = 851.852k

b. NPV(up) = 0, NPV(down) = 100k/.05 – 1m = 1m

PV = 0.9 × 1m/1.08 = $833,333k

c. Hurdle rate rule: NPV = 100k/.09 – 1m = 111.11k > 0, so invest now, correct.

22-24. Assume that the project in Example 22.5 pays an annual cash flow of $80,000 (instead of $90,000).

a. What is the NPV of investing today?

b. What is the NPV of waiting and investing tomorrow?

c. Verify that the hurdle rate rule of thumb gives the correct time to invest in this case.

a. 80k/.054 – 1m = 481.48k

b. Npv(down) = 80k/.05 – 1m = 600k

PV = .9 × 600/1.08 = 500k

c. 80/.09 – 1m = –111k, so wait, correct

Chapter 23
Raising Equity Capital

23-1. What are some of the alternative sources from which private companies can raise equity capital?

Private companies can raise equity capital from angel investors, venture capitalists, institutional investors, or corporate investors.

23-2. What are the advantages and the disadvantages to a private company of raising money from a corporate investor?

Advantages of raising money from a corporate investor are that the large corporate partner may provide benefits such as capital, expertise, or access to distribution channels. The corporate partner may become an important customer or supplier for the startup firm, and the willingness of an established company to invest may be an important endorsement of the new company.

The disadvantages are that not all corporate investments are successful. The corporate partner may gain access to proprietary technology, or eventually even become a competitor. Once a young firm has aligned itself with one corporate partner, the competitors of this partner may be unwilling to do business with the startup.

23-3. Starware Software was founded last year to develop software for gaming applications. Initially, the founder invested \$800,000 and received 8 million shares of stock. Starware now needs to raise a second round of capital, and it has identified an interested venture capitalist. This venture capitalist will invest \$1 million and wants to own 20% of the company after the investment is completed.

a. How many shares must the venture capitalist receive to end up with 20% of the company? What is the implied price per share of this funding round?

b. What will the value of the whole firm be after this investment (the post-money valuation)?

a. After the funding round, the founder's 8 million shares will represent 80% ownership of the firm. To solve for the new total number of shares (TOTAL):

$8,000,000 = .80 \times \text{TOTAL}$

So TOTAL = 10,000,000 shares. If the new total is 10 million shares, and the venture capitalist will end up with 20%, then the venture capitalist must buy 2 million shares. Given the investment of \$1 million for 2 million shares, the implied price per share is \$0.50.

b. After this investment, there will be 10 million shares outstanding, with a price of \$0.50 per share, so the post-money valuation is \$5 million.

23-4. **Suppose venture capital firm GSB partners raised $100 of committed capital. Each year over the 10-year life of the fund, 2% of this committed capital will be used to pay GSB's management fee. As is typical in the venture capital industry, GSB will only invest $80 million (committed capital less lifetime management fees). A the end of 10 years, the investments made by the fund are worth $400 million. GSB also charges 20% carried interest on the profits of the fund (net of management fees).**

a. Assuming the $80 million in invested capital is invested immediately and all proceeds were received at the end of 10 years, what is the IRR of the investments GSB partners made? That is, compute IRR ignoring all management fees.

b. Of course, as an investor, or limited partner, you are more interested in your own IRR, that is the IRR including all fees paid. Assuming that investors gave GSB partners the full $100 million up front, what is the IRR for GSB's limited partners (that is, the IRR net of *all* fees paid).

a. IRR solves NPV(Total invested) $= \dfrac{400}{(1+r)^{10}} - 80 = 0$

So $r = \left(\dfrac{400}{80}\right)^{1/10} - 1 = 17.46\%$

b.

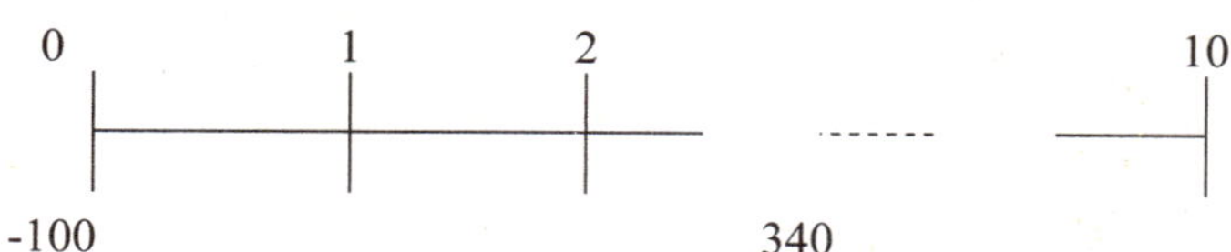

$100 million invested

Profit = 400 – 100 = 300

Carried interest = 20% × 300 = $60 million

LP payoff = 400 – 60 = 340

So IRR $= \left(\dfrac{340}{100}\right)^{1/10} - 1 = 13.02\%$ solves

23-5. **Three years ago, you founded your own company. You invested $100,000 of your money and received 5 million shares of Series A preferred stock. Since then, your company has been through three additional rounds of financing.**

Round	Price ($)	Number of Shares
Series B	0.50	1,000,000
Series C	2.00	500,000
Series D	4.00	500,000

a. What is the pre-money valuation for the Series D funding round?

b. What is the post-money valuation for the Series D funding round?

c. **Assuming that you own only the Series A preferred stock (and that each share of all series of preferred stock is convertible into one share of common stock), what percentage of the firm do you own after the last funding round?**

a. Before the Series D funding round, there are (5,000,000 + 1,000,000 + 500,000 = 6,500,000) shares outstanding. Given a Series D funding price of $4.00 per share, the pre-money valuation is (6,500,000) × $4.00/share = $26 million.

b. After the funding round, there will be (6,500,000 + 500,000 = 7,000,000) shares outstanding, so the post-money valuation is (7,000,000) × $4.00/share = $28,000,000.

c. You will own 5,000,000 / 7,000,000 = 71.4% of the firm after the last funding round.

23-6. What are the main advantages and disadvantages of going public?

The two main advantages of going public are liquidity and access to capital. One of the major disadvantages of an IPO is that once a company becomes a public company, it must satisfy all of the requirements of being a public company such as SEC filings and listing requirements of the securities exchanges.

23-7. Do underwriters face the most risk from a best-efforts IPO, a firm commitment IPO, or an auction IPO? Why?

Underwriters face the most risk from a firm commitment IPO. With this method, they guarantee that they will sell all of the stock at the offer price. If the entire issue does not sell at the IPO price, the remaining shares must be sold at a lower price and the underwriter must take the loss.

With a best-efforts IPO, the underwriter does not guarantee that the stock will be sold, but instead tries to sell the stock for the best possible price. In an auction IPO, the underwriters let the market determine the price by auctioning off the company.

23-8. Roundtree Software is going public using an auction IPO. The firm has received the following bids:

Price ($)	Number of Shares
14.00	100,000
13.80	200,000
13.60	500,000
13.40	1,000,000
13.20	1,200,000
13.00	800,000
12.80	400,000

Assuming Roundtree would like to sell 1.8 million shares in its IPO, what will the winning auction offer price be?

First, compute the cumulative total number of shares demanded at or above any given price:

Price	Cumulative Demand
14.00	100,000
13.80	300,000
13.60	800,000
13.40	1,800,000
13.20	3,000,000
13.00	3,800,000
12.80	4,200,000

The winning price should be $13.40, because investors have placed orders for a total of 1.8 million shares at a price of $13.40 or higher.

23-9. Three years ago, you founded Outdoor Recreation, Inc., a retailer specializing in the sale of equipment and clothing for recreational activities such as camping, skiing, and hiking. So far, your company has gone through three funding rounds:

Round	Date	Investor	Shares	Share Price ($)
Series A	Feb. 2002	You	500,000	1.00
Series B	Aug. 2003	Angels	1,000,000	2.00
Series C	Sept. 2004	Venture capital	2,000,000	3.50

Currently, it is 2007 and you need to raise additional capital to expand your business. You have decided to take your firm public through an IPO. You would like to issue an additional 6.5 million new shares through this IPO. Assuming that your firm successfully completes its IPO, you forecast that 2007 net income will be $7.5 million.

a. Your investment banker advises you that the prices of other recent IPOs have been set such that the P/E ratios based on 2007 forecasted earnings average 20.0. Assuming that your IPO is set at a price that implies a similar multiple, what will your IPO price per share be?

b. What percentage of the firm will you own after the IPO?

a. With a P/E ratio of 20.0x, and 2005 earnings of $7.5 million, the total value of the firm at the IPO should be:

$$\frac{P}{7.5} = 20.0x \Rightarrow P = \$150 \text{ million.}$$

There are currently (500,000 + 1,000,000 + 2,000,000) = 3,500,000 shares outstanding (before the IPO). At the IPO, the firm will issue an additional 6.5 million shares, so there will be 10 million shares outstanding immediately after the IPO. With a total market value of $150 million, each share should be worth $150 / 10 = $15 per share.

b. After the IPO, you will own 500,000 of the 10 million shares outstanding, or 5% of the firm.

23-10. What is IPO underpricing? If you decide to try to buy shares in every IPO, will you necessarily make money from the underpricing?

Underpricing refers to the fact that, on average, underwriters pick the IPO issue price so that the average first-day return is positive. If you followed a strategy of placing an order for a fixed number of shares on every IPO, your order will be completely filled when the stock price goes down, but you will be rationed when it goes up. In effect you only get substantial amounts of stock when you do not want it. The winners' curse is substantial enough so that the strategy of investing in every IPO does not yield above market returns.

23-11. Margoles Publishing recently completed its IPO. The stock was offered at a price of $14 per share. On the first day of trading, the stock closed at $19 per share. What was the initial return on Margoles? Who benefited from this underpricing? Who lost, and why?

The initial return on Margoles Publishing stock is ($19.00 – $14.00) / ($14.00) = 35.7%.

Who gains from the price increase? Investors who were able to buy at the IPO price of $14/share see an immediate return of 35.7% on their investment. Owners of the other shares outstanding that were not sold as part of the IPO see the value of their shares increase. To the extent that the investors who were able to obtain shares in the IPO have other relationships with the investment banks, the investment banks may benefit indirectly from the deal through their future business with these customers.

Who loses from the price increase? The original shareholders lose, because they sold stock for $14.00 per share when the market was willing to pay $19.00 per share.

23-12. Chen Brothers, Inc., sold 4 million shares in its IPO, at a price of $18.50 per share. Management negotiated a fee (the underwriting spread) of 7% on this transaction. What was the dollar cost of this fee?

The total dollar value of the IPO was ($18.50) × (4 million) = $74 million. The spread equaled (0.07) × ($74 million) or $5.18 million.

23-13. Your firm has 10 million shares outstanding, and you are about to issue 5 million new shares in an IPO. The IPO price has been set at $20 per share, and the underwriting spread is 7%. The IPO is a big success with investors, and the share price rises to $50 the first day of trading.

a. How much did your firm raise from the IPO?

b. What is the market value of the firm after the IPO?

c. Assume that the post IPO value of your firm is its fair market value. Suppose your firm could have issued shares directly to investors at their fair market value, in a perfect market with no underwriting spread and no underpricing. What would the share price have been in this case, if you raise the same amount as in part (a)?

d. Comparing part (b) and part (c), what is the total cost to the firm's original investors due to market imperfections from the IPO?

a. 5m × (20 – 7% × 20) = $93 million

b. 15m × 50 = $750 million

c. Market value of firm assets absent new cash raised = 750 – 93 = $657 million.

$657m/(10m original shares) = $65.70 per share

Check: 93m/65.70 = 1.4155m new shares,

$750/11.4155 = $65.7

d. (65.7 – 50) × 10m = $157 million

23-14. You have an arrangement with your broker to request 1000 shares of all available IPOs. Suppose that 10% of the time, the IPO is "very successful" and appreciates by 100% on the first day, 80% of the time it is "successful" and appreciates by 10%, and 10% of the time it "fails" and falls by 15%.

a. By what amount does the average IPO appreciate the first day; that is, what is the average IPO underpricing?

b. Suppose you expect to receive 50 shares when the IPO is very successful, 200 shares when it is successful, and 1000 shares when it fails. Assume the average IPO price is $15. What is your expected one-day return on your IPO investments?

a. .10(100%) + .80(10%) + .10(–15%) = 16.5%

b. Average investment = .10(50 × 15) + .80(200 × 15) + .10(1000 × 15) = $3975

Ave gain = .10(50 × 15 × 100%) + .80(200 × 15 × 10%)+.10(1000 × 15 × –15%) = $90

Return = 90/3975 = 2.3%

23-15. On January 20, Metropolitan, Inc., sold 8 million shares of stock in an SEO. The current market price of Metropolitan at the time was $42.50 per share. Of the 8 million shares sold, 5 million shares were primary shares being sold by the company, and the remaining 3 million shares were being sold by the venture capital investors. Assume the underwriter charges 5% of the gross proceeds as an underwriting fee (which is shared proportionately between primary and secondary shares).

a. How much money did Metropolitan raise?

b. How much money did the venture capitalists receive?

a. The company sold 5 million shares at $42.50 per share, so it raised ($42.50) × (5,000,000) = $212.5 million. After underwriting fees, it will keep 212.50 × (1 – 0.05) = $201.875 million.

b. The venture capitalists raised ($42.50) × (3,000,000) = $127.5 million. After underwriting fees, they will keep 127.5 × (1 – 0.05) = $121.125 million.

So, in total, the SEO was worth $201.875 + $121.125 = ($42.50) × (8,000,000) × 0.95 = $323 million.

23-16. What are the advantages to a company of selling stock in an SEO using a cash offer? What are the advantages of a rights offer?

A cash offer is when a company offers the new shares to investors at large. A rights offer is when the new shares are offered only to existing shareholders. Rights offers protect existing shareholders from underpricing. However, with a rights offer, only existing shareholders are offered stock to purchase. Demand may be lower, because existing shareholders are only a subset of all possible investors, and because they may not want to increase the percentage weight of this stock in their portfolios. If demand is lower, firms may receive a lower price from rights offers.

23-17. MacKenzie Corporation currently has 10 million shares of stock outstanding at a price of $40 per share. The company would like to raise money and has announced a rights issue. Every existing shareholder will be sent one right per share of stock that he or she owns. The company plans to require five rights to purchase one share at a price of $40 per share.

a. Assuming the rights issue is successful, how much money will it raise?

b. What will the share price be after the rights issue? (Assume perfect capital markets.)

Suppose instead that the firm changes the plan so that *each* right gives the holder the right to purchase one share at $8 per share.

c. How much money will the new plan raise?

d. What will the share price be after the rights issue?

e. Which plan is better for the firm's shareholders? Which is more likely to raise the full amount of capital?

a. 10m shares/5 × 40 = $80 million

b. 12m total shares, Value = $400 million + 80 million in new capital = $480

Share price = 480/12 = $40

c. 10m × $8 = $80 million

d. $480/20 = $24 per share

e. Shareholders are the same either way. In the first case, each share is worth $40, and exercising the right has 0 npv, so the total value of a share is $40.

In the second case, the share is worth $24, but the right is worth (24 – 8) = $16, so the total value from owning a share is $24 + $16 = $40 per share.

However, the second plan is much more likely to be fully subscribed, because exercising the right is a good deal. In the first case, shareholders are indifferent between exercising and not exercising.

Chapter 24
Debt Financing

24-1. Explain some of the differences between a public debt offering and a private debt offering.

In a public debt offering, a prospectus is created with details of the offering and a formal contract between the bond issuer and the trust company is signed. The trust company makes sure the terms of the contract are enforced. In a private offering there is no need for a prospectus or a formal contract. Instead a promissory note can be enough. Moreover, the contract in a private placement does not have to be standard.

24-2. Why do bonds with lower seniority have higher yields than equivalent bonds with higher seniority?

Requiring coupon payments protects the bondholders from waiting a long time in case the debtor defaults. Without coupon payments default only happens when the bond matures, but by then the corporation might have depleted all of its assets. In contrast, with coupon payments the debtor would be in default the moment it misses one of the coupon payments, and the bondholders can then force the firm into bankruptcy. At this stage, they might be able to get a larger fraction of the value of the original debt than if they waited until maturity.

24-3. Explain the difference between a secured corporate and an unsecured corporate bond.

A secured corporate bond gives the bondholder the right over particular assets that serve as collateral in case of default. An unsecured corporate bond does not offer such protection to the bondholder. Thus, with an unsecured corporate bond the bondholders are residual claimants in the case of bankruptcy after the secured assets have been given to the corresponding bondholders.

24-4. What is the difference between a foreign bond and a Eurobond?

A foreign bond is a bond issued by a foreign company in a local market. Eurobonds, on the other hand, are bonds denominated in a different currency of the country in which they are issued.

24-5. Describe the kinds of securities the U.S. government uses to finance the federal debt.

The U.S. government use treasury bills, note, bonds, and TIPS. Treasury bills are pure discount bonds with maturities of one year or less. Treasury notes are coupon bonds with semi-annual coupon payments with maturities between 1 and 10 years. Treasury bonds are semi-annual coupon bonds with maturities longer than 10 years. Finally, TIPS are bonds with coupon payments that adjust with the rate of inflation. The final payment is protected against deflation since the value of the final payment is the maximum between the face value and the inflation adjusted face value.

24-6. On January 15, 2010, the U.S. Treasury issued a five-year inflation-indexed note with a coupon of 3%. On the date of issue, the consumer price index (CPI) was 250. By January 15, 2015, the CPI had increased to 300. What principal and coupon payment was made on January 15, 2015?

The CPI index appreciated by:

$$\frac{300}{250} = 1.2.$$

Consequently, the principal amount of the bond increased by this amount; that is, the original face value of $1,000 increased to $1,2000.

Since the bond pays semi-annual coupons, the coupon payment is:

$$1.2 \times \left(\frac{0.03}{2}\right) \times \$1,000 = \$18.$$

24-7. On January 15, 2020, the U.S. Treasury issued a 10-year inflation-indexed note with a coupon of 6%. On the date of issue, the CPI was 400. By January 15, 2030, the CPI had decreased to 300. What principal and coupon payment was made on January 15, 2030?

The CPI index depreciated by

$$\frac{300}{400} = 0.75.$$

Consequently, the principal amount of the bond decreased by this amount; that is, the original face value $1,000 decreased to $750.

Since the bond pays semi-annual coupons, the coupon payment is:

$$0.75 \times \left(\frac{0.06}{2}\right) \times \$1,000 = \$22.5.$$

However, the final payment of the maturity (i.e. the principal) is protected against deflation. So since $750 is less than the original face value of $1,000, the original mount is repaid, i.e. $1,000.

24-8. Describe what prepayment risk in a GNMA is.

Holders of the GNMA securities face payment risk because homeowners have the option to prepay their debt whenever they decide to do so. In particular, they will prepay if interest rates fall and they can obtain new debt at a lower interest rate. This is precisely when the holders of GNMA securities would like to *avoid* payments, since they can only reinvest at a lower interest rate.

24-9. What is the distinguishing feature of how municipal bonds are taxed?

The distinguishing feature is that income from municipal bonds is not taxed at the federal level.

24-10. Explain why bond issuers might voluntarily choose to put restrictive covenants into a new bond issue.

Bond issuers benefit from placing restricting covenants because by doing so they can obtain a lower interest rate.

24-11. General Electric has just issued a callable 10-year, 6% coupon bond with annual coupon payments. The bond can be called at par in one year or anytime thereafter on a coupon payment date. It has a price of $102. What is the bond's yield to maturity and yield to call?

Timeline:

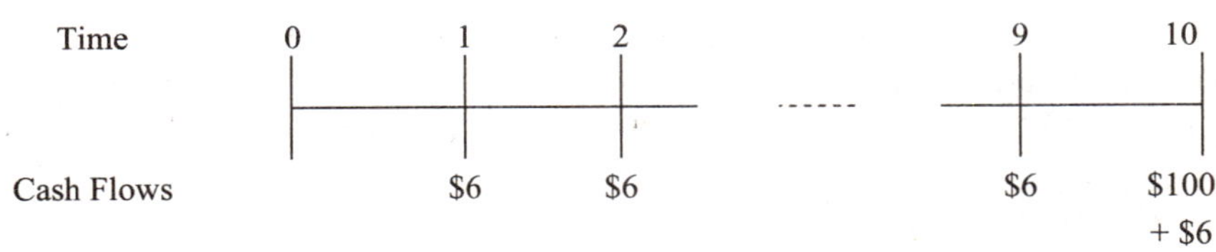

The present value formula to e solved is:

$$102 = \frac{6}{\text{YTM}}\left(1 - \frac{1}{(1+\text{YTM})^{10}}\right) + \frac{100}{(1+\text{YTM})^{10}}$$

Using the annuity calculator:

YTM = 5.73%

<u>YTC:</u>

Timeline:

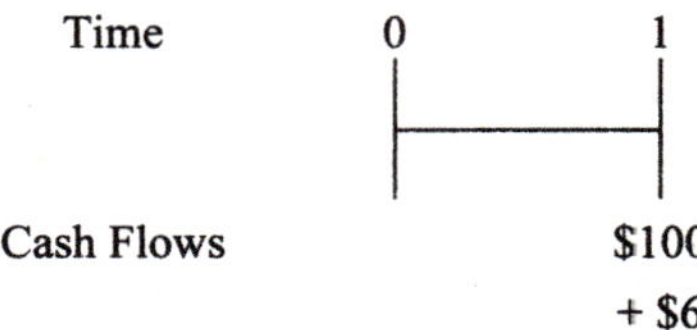

The present value formula to be solved is:

$$102 = \frac{106}{1+\text{YTC}}$$

$$\Rightarrow \text{YTC} = \frac{106}{102} - 1 = 3.92\%.$$

24-12. Boeing Corporation has just issued a callable (at par) three-year, 5% coupon bond with semiannual coupon payments. The bond can be called at par in two years or anytime thereafter on a coupon payment date. It has a price of $99. What is the bond's yield to maturity and yield to call?

Timeline:

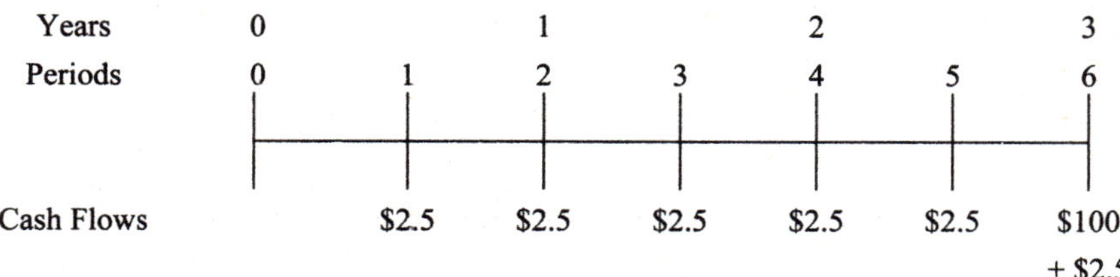

The present value formula to be solved is:

$$99 = \frac{2.5}{i}\left(1 - \frac{1}{(1+i)^6}\right) + \frac{100}{(1+i)^6}.$$

Using the annuity calculator:

$i = 2.68\%$.

So since YTM are quoted as APR's:

$\text{YTM} = \text{i} \times 2 = 2.68\% \times 2 = 5.36\%.$

YTC:

Timeline:

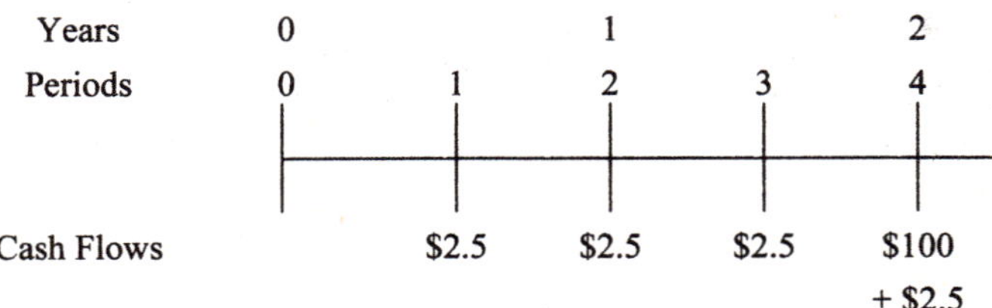

The present value formula to be solved is:

$$99 = \frac{2.5}{\text{i}}\left(1 - \frac{1}{(1+\text{i})^4}\right) + \frac{100}{(1+\text{i})^4}.$$

Using the annuity calculator:

$\text{i} = 2.77\%.$

Since YTM (and therefore YTC) are quoted as APR's:

$$\begin{aligned}\text{YTC} &= \text{i} \times 2 \\ &= 5.54\%.\end{aligned}$$

24-13. Explain why the yield on a convertible bond is lower than the yield on an otherwise identical bond without a conversion feature.

The option to convert the bond into stock is valuable, hence its price will be higher and its yield lower.

24-14. You own a bond with a face value of $10,000 and a conversion ratio of 450. What is the conversion price?

The conversion price is the face value of the bond divided by the conversion ratio. In this case:

$$\text{P} = \frac{\text{Face value}}{\text{Conversion ratio}} = \frac{\$10{,}000}{450}$$

$\text{P} = \$22.22.$

Chapter 25
Leasing

25-1. Suppose an H1200 supercomputer has a cost of $200,000 and will have a residual market value of $60,000 in five years. The risk-free interest rate is 5% APR with monthly compounding.

a. What is the risk-free monthly lease rate for a five-year lease in a perfect market?

b. What would be the monthly payment for a five-year $200,000 risk-free loan to purchase the H1200?

a. From Eq. 25.1, for a five-year (60 month) lease,

PV(Lease payments) = 200,000 – 60,000/(1 + .05/12)^{60} = $153,248.

Because the first lease payment is paid upfront, and the remaining 59 payments are paid as an annuity:

$$153,248 = L\left(1+\frac{1}{.05/12}\left(1-\frac{1}{(1+.05/12)^{59}}\right)\right)$$

Therefore, L = $2,880.

b. From Eq. 25.2, (see also Example 25.2)

$$200,000 = M\frac{1}{.05/12}\left(1-\frac{1}{(1+.05/12)^{60}}\right)$$

Therefore, M = $3,774.

25-2. Suppose the risk-free interest rate is 5% APR with monthly compounding. If a $2 million MRI machine can be leased for seven years for $22,000 per month, what residual value must the lessor recover to break even in a perfect market with no risk?

From Eq. 25.1, PV(Residual Value) = Purchase Price – PV(Lease Payments)

$$= \$2 \text{ million - } 22,000\left(1+\frac{1}{.05/12}\left(1-\frac{1}{(1+.05/12)^{83}}\right)\right)$$

= $436,974.

The future residual value in 84 months is therefore:

Residual Value = $436,974 × (1+.05/12)^{84} = $619,645.

25-3. Consider a five-year lease for a $400,000 bottling machine, with a residual market value of $150,000 at the end of the five years. If the risk-free interest rate is 6% APR with monthly compounding, compute the monthly lease payment in a perfect market for the following leases:

a. A fair market value lease

b. A $1.00 out lease

c. A fixed price lease with an $80,000 final price

a. From Eq. 25.1, for a five-year (60 month) lease with a monthly interest rate of 6%/12 = 0.5%,

PV(Lease payments) = 400,000 – 150,000/(1.005)^{60} = $288,794.

Because the first lease payment is paid upfront, and the remaining 59 payments are paid as an annuity:

$$288,794 = L\left(1 + \frac{1}{.005}\left(1 - \frac{1}{1.005^{59}}\right)\right).$$

Therefore, L = $5555.

b. In this case, the lessor will only receive $1 at the conclusion of the lease. Therefore, the present value of the lease payments should be $400,000:

$$400,000 = L\left(1 + \frac{1}{.005}\left(1 - \frac{1}{1.005^{59}}\right)\right).$$

Therefore, L = $7695.

c. In this case the lessor will receive $80,000 at the conclusion of the lease. Thus,

PV(Lease payments) = 400,000 – 80,000/(1.005)^{60} = $340,690.

Because the first lease payment is paid upfront, and the remaining 59 payments are paid as an annuity:

$$340,690 = L\left(1 + \frac{1}{.005}\left(1 - \frac{1}{1.005^{59}}\right)\right).$$

Therefore, L = $6554.

25-4. Acme Distribution currently has the following items on its balance sheet:

Assets		Liabilities	
Cash	20	Debt	70
Property, Plant, and Equipment	175	Equity	125

How will Acme's balance sheet change if it enters into an $80 million capital lease for new warehouses? What will its book debt-equity ratio be? How will Acme's balance sheet and debt-equity ratio change if the lease is an operating lease?

(See Example 25.4) Capital Lease: property added to balance sheet, lease added to debt –

Assets		Liabilities	
Cash	20	Debt	150
Prop., Plant, Equip.	255	Equity	125

Book D/E = 150 / 120 = 1.25

Operating Lease: no change to balance sheet. Book D/E = 70/125 = 0.56

25-5. Your firm is considering leasing a $50,000 copier. The copier has an estimated economic life of eight years. Suppose the appropriate discount rate is 9% APR with monthly compounding.

Classify each lease below as a capital lease or operating lease, and explain why:

a. **A four-year fair market value lease with payments of $1150 per month**

b. **A six-year fair market value lease with payments of $790 per month**

c. **A five-year fair market value lease with payments of $925 per month**

d. **A five-year fair market value lease with payments of $1000 per month and an option to cancel after three years with a $9000 cancellation penalty**

a. A four-year fair market value lease with payments of $1,150 per month.

$$\text{PV(Lease Payments)} = 1150 \times \left(1 + \frac{1}{.09/12}\left(1 - \frac{1}{(1+.09/12)^{47}}\right)\right) = \$46,559.$$

This is 46,559/50,000 = 93% of the purchase price. Because it exceeds 90% of the purchase price, this is a capital lease.

b. A six-year fair market value lease with payments of $790 per month.

The lease term is 75% or more of the economic life of the asset (75% × 8 years = 6 years), and so this is a capital lease.

c. A five-year fair market value lease with payments of $925 per month.

$$\text{PV(Lease Payments)} = 925 \times \left(1 + \frac{1}{.09/12}\left(1 - \frac{1}{(1+.09/12)^{59}}\right)\right) = \$44,895.$$

This is 44,895/50,000 = 89.8% of the purchase price. Because it is less than 90% of the purchase price, and the term is less than 6 years, and it is a fair market value lease, this is an operating lease.

d. A five-year fair market value lease with payments of $1000 per month and an option to cancel after three years with a $9000 cancellation penalty.

Without the cancellation option, the PV of the lease payments would exceed 90% of the purchase price.

With the cancellation option,

PV(Min. Lease Pmts) =

$$1000 \times \left(1 + \frac{1}{.09/12}\left(1 - \frac{1}{(1+.09/12)^{35}}\right)\right) + \frac{9000}{(1+.09/12)^{36}} = \$38,560.$$

As this is less than 90% of the purchase price, the lease qualifies as an operating lease.

25-6. Craxton Engineering will either purchase or lease a new $756,000 fabricator. If purchased, the fabricator will be depreciated on a straight-line basis over seven years. Craxton can lease the fabricator for $130,000 per year for seven years. Craxton's tax rate is 35%. (Assume the fabricator has no residual value at the end of the seven years.)

a. **What are the free cash flow consequences of buying the fabricator if the lease is a true tax lease?**

b. **What are the free cash flow consequences of leasing the fabricator if the lease is a true tax lease?**

c. **What are the incremental free cash flows of leasing versus buying?**

a. FCF_0 = Capital Expenditure = $756,000

$FCF_{1\text{-}7}$ = Depreciation tax shield = 35% × 756,000/7 = $37,800

b. $FCF_{0\text{-}6}$ = After-tax lease payment = 130,000 × (1 – 35%) = $84,500

c. FCF_0 = –84,500 – (–756,000) = $671,500

$FCF_{1\text{-}6}$ = –84,500 – (37,800) = $122,300

FCF_7 = 0 – (37,800) = $37,800

25-7. Riverton Mining plans to purchase or lease $220,000 worth of excavation equipment. If purchased, the equipment will be depreciated on a straight-line basis over five years, after which it will be worthless. If leased, the annual lease payments will be $55,000 per year for five years. Assume Riverton's borrowing cost is 8%, its tax rate is 35%, and the lease qualifies as a true tax lease.

a. If Riverton purchases the equipment, what is the amount of the lease-equivalent loan?

b. Is Riverton better off leasing the equipment or financing the purchase using the lease equivalent loan?

c. What is the effective after-tax lease borrowing rate? How does this compare to Riverton's actual after-tax borrowing rate?

a. If Riverton buys the equipment, it will pay $220,000 upfront and have depreciation expenses of 220,000 / 5 = $44,000 per year, generating a depreciation tax shield of 35% × 44,000 = $15,400 per year for years 1–5.

If it leases, the after-tax lease payments are $55,000 × (1 – .35) = $35,750. Thus, the FCF of leasing versus buying is –35,750 – (–220,000) = 184,250 in year 0, –35,750 – (15,400) = –51,150 in years 1–4, and 0 – (15,400) = –15,400 in year 5.

The initial amount of the lease equivalent loan is the PV of the incremental free cash flows in years 1–5 at Riverton's after-tax borrowing rate of 8%(1 – .35) = 5.2%:

$$\text{Loan Amt} = \frac{-51{,}150}{1.052} + \frac{-51{,}150}{1.052^2} + \frac{-51{,}150}{1.052^3} + \frac{-51{,}150}{1.052^4} + \frac{-15{,}400}{1.052^5}\sqrt{2}$$
$$= -192{,}488.$$

That is, leasing leads to the same future cash flows as buying the equipment and borrowing $192,488 initially.

b. If Riverton leases, it pays $35,750 after-tax as an initial lease payment. If it buys using the lease equivalent loan, it pays 220,000 – 192,488 = $27,512 upfront. Because the future liabilities are the same, buying with the lease equivalent loan is cheaper by 35,750 – 27,512 = $8,238 today. Thus, the lease is not attractive.

c. We compute the effective after-tax lease borrowing rate as the IRR of the incremental FCF calculated in (a): 184,250; –51,150; –51,150; –51,150; –51,150; –15,400.

Using Excel, we find the IRR is 7.0%, which is higher than Riverton's actual after-tax borrowing rate of 8% × (1 – .35) = 5.2%. Thus, the lease is not attractive.

25-8. Suppose Clorox can lease a new computer data processing system for $975,000 per year for five years. Alternatively, it can purchase the system for $4.25 million. Assume Clorox has a borrowing cost of 7% and a tax rate of 35%, and the system will be obsolete at the end of five years.

a. If Clorox will depreciate the computer equipment on a straight-line basis over the next five years, and if the lease qualifies as a true tax lease, is it better to lease or finance the purchase of the equipment?

b. Suppose that if Clorox buys the equipment, it will use accelerated depreciation for tax purposes. Specifically, suppose it can expense 20% of the purchase price immediately and

can take depreciation deductions equal to 32%, 19.2%, 11.52%, 11.52%, and 5.76% of the purchase price over the next five years. Compare leasing with purchase in this case.

a. If Clorox buys the equipment, it will pay $4.25 million upfront and have depreciation expenses of 4.25 / 5 = $850,000 per year, generating a depreciation tax shield of 35% × 850,000 = $297,500 per year for years 1–5.

If it leases, the after-tax lease payments are $975,000 × (1 – .35) = $633,750. Thus, the FCF of leasing versus buying is –633,750 – (–4,250,000) = 3,616,250 in year 0, –633,750 – (297,500) = –931,250 in years 1-4, and 0 – (297,500) = –297,500 in year 5. We can determine the gain from leasing by discounting the incremental cash flows at Clorox's after-tax borrowing rate of 7% (1 – .35) = 4.55%:

$$\text{NPV(Lease-Buy)} = 3{,}616{,}250 - \frac{931{,}250}{1.0455} - \frac{931{,}250}{1.0455^2} - \frac{931{,}250}{1.0455^3} - \frac{931{,}250}{1.0455^4} - \frac{297{,}500}{1.0455^5}$$
$$= \$41{,}112.$$

Under these assumptions, the lease is more attractive than financing a purchase of the computer.

b. The depreciation tax shield if Clorox buys is now 35% × ($4.25 million × 20%) = $297,500 in year 0. Therefore, the incremental FCF from leasing is 633,750 – (–4,250,000) – 297,500 = $3,318,750 in year 0. In year 1, the depreciation tax shield is 35% × ($4.25 million × 32%) = $476,000, and the incremental cash flow is –633,750 – (476,000) = –1,109,750. We can continue in this way each year as shown in the spreadsheet below:

	A	B	C	D	E	F	G	H	I
41			**Year**	**0**	**1**	**2**	**3**	**4**	**5**
42	**Buy:**								
43	1	Capital Expenditures		(4,250,000)	-	-	-	-	-
46	2	Depreciation tax shield at 35%		297,500	476,000	285,600	171,360	171,360	85,680
47	3	**Free Cash Flow (Buy)**		(3,952,500)	476,000	285,600	171,360	171,360	85,680
48	**Lease:**								
49	4	Lease payments		(975,000)	(975,000)	(975,000)	(975,000)	(975,000)	-
50	5	Income tax savings at 35%		341,250	341,250	341,250	341,250	341,250	-
51	6	**Free Cash Flow (Lease)**		(633,750)	(633,750)	(633,750)	(633,750)	(633,750)	-
52	**Lease vs. Buy:**								
53	7	**Lease - Buy**		**3,318,750**	**(1,109,750)**	**(919,350)**	**(805,110)**	**(805,110)**	**(85,680)**
56			NPV I	(30,712)					

Therefore:

$$\text{NPV(Lease-Buy)} = 3{,}318{,}750 - \frac{1{,}109{,}750}{1.0455} - \frac{919{,}350}{1.0455^2} - \frac{805{,}110}{1.0455^3} - \frac{805{,}110}{1.0455^4} - \frac{85{,}680}{1.0455^5}$$
$$= -\$30{,}712$$

and so the lease is no longer attractive.

25-9. **Suppose Procter and Gamble (P&G) is considering purchasing $15 million in new manufacturing equipment. If it purchases the equipment, it will depreciate it on a straight-line basis over the five years, after which the equipment will be worthless. It will also be responsible for maintenance expenses of $1 million per year. Alternatively, it can lease the equipment for $4.2 million per year for the five years, in which case the lessor will provide necessary maintenance. Assume P&G's tax rate is 35% and its borrowing cost is 7%.**

a. **What is the NPV associated with leasing the equipment versus financing it with the lease equivalent loan?**

b. **What is the break-even lease rate—that is, what lease amount could P&G pay each year and be indifferent between leasing and financing a purchase?**

a. If P&G buys the equipment, it will pay $15 million upfront, and have depreciation expenses of 15 / 5 = $3 million per year, generating a depreciation tax shield of 35% × 3 = $1.05 million per year for years 1–5. It will also have after tax maintenance expenses of \$1 million × (1 – .35) = 0.65 million. Thus, the FCF from buying is 1.05 – .65 = \$0.4 million in years 1–5.

If it leases, the after-tax lease payments are \$4.2 million × (1 – .35) = \$2.73 million. Thus, the FCF of leasing versus buying is –2.73 – (–15) = 12.27 million in year 0, –2.73 – (0.4) = –3.13 million in years 1–4, and 0 – (0.4) = –0.4 million in year 5. We can determine the gain from leasing by discounting the incremental cash flows at P&G's after-tax borrowing rate of 7%(1 – .35) = 4.55%:

$$\text{NPV(Lease-Buy)} = 12.27 - \frac{3.13}{1.0455} - \frac{3.13}{1.0455^2} - \frac{3.13}{1.0455^3} - \frac{3.13}{1.0455^4} - \frac{0.4}{1.0455^5}$$
$$= \$733{,}955.$$

Under these assumptions, the lease is more attractive than financing a purchase of the computer.

b. We can increase the after-tax lease payments by an amount with present value equal to the NPV in (a). Thus,

$$733{,}955 = (\text{Increase in L}) \times (1 - 0.35) \times \left(1 + \frac{1}{.0455}\left(1 - \frac{1}{1.0455^4}\right)\right)$$

so that $\text{Increase in L} = 246{,}363$. Therefore, the break-even lease rate is 4.2 + 0.246363 = \$4.446363 million per year, as verified in the following spreadsheet:

	Year	0	1	2	3	4	5
Buy							
1	Capital Expenditures	(15,000,000)	—	—	—	—	—
2	After-tax maintenance cost	—	(650,000)	(650,000)	(650,000)	(650,000)	(650,000)
3	Depreciation tax shield at 35%	—	1,050,000	1,050,000	1,050,000	1,050,000	1,050,000
4	**Free Cash Flow (Buy)**	(15,000,000)	400,000	400,000	400,000	400,000	400,000
Lease							
5	Lease Payments	(4,446,363)	(4,446,363)	(4,446,363)	(4,446,363)	(4,446,363)	—
6	Income tax savings at 35%	1,556,227	1,556,227	1,556,227	1,556,227	1,556,227	—
7	**Free Cash Flow (Lease)**	(2,890,136)	(2,890,136)	(2,890,136)	(2,890,136)	(2,890,136)	—
Lease vs. Buy							
8	**Lease-Buy**	**12,109,864**	**(3,290,136)**	**(3,290,136)**	**(3,290,136)**	**(3,290,136)**	**(400,000)**
	NPV(Lease-Buy)	(0)					

25-10. Suppose Netflix is considering the purchase of computer servers and network infrastructure to facilitate its move into video-on-demand services. In total, it will purchase \$48 million in new equipment. This equipment will qualify for accelerated depreciation: 20% can be expensed immediately, followed by 32%, 19.2%, 11.52%, 11.52%, and 5.76% over the next five years. However, because of the firm's substantial loss carryforwards, Netflix estimates its marginal tax rate to be 10% over the next five years, so it will get very little tax benefit from the depreciation expenses. Thus, Netflix considers leasing the equipment instead. Suppose Netflix and the lessor face the same 8% borrowing rate, but the lessor has a 35% tax rate. For the purpose of this question, assume the equipment is worthless after five years, the lease term is five years, and the lease qualifies as a true tax lease.

a. **What is the lease rate for which the lessor will break even?**

b. **What is the gain to Netflix with this lease rate?**

c. **What is the source of the gain in this transaction?**

a. The break-even lease rate for the lessor is 11,080,000 as shown in the spreadsheet:

LESSOR	tcb	35%	5.2%				
	Year	**0**	**1**	**2**	**3**	**4**	**5**
Buy							
1 Capital Expenditures		(48,000)	—	—	—	—	—
2 Depreciation tax shield at 35%		3,360	5,376	3,226	1,935	1,935	968
3 **Free Cash Flow (Buy)**		(44,640)	5,376	3,226	1,935	1,935	968
Lease							
4 Lease Payments		11,080	11,080	11,080	11,080	11,080	—
5 Income tax at 35%		(3,878)	(3,878)	(3,878)	(3,878)	(3,878)	—
6 **Free Cash Flow (Lease)**		7,202	7,202	7,202	7,202	7,202	—
Lessor Free Cash Flow							
7 **Buy & Lease**		**(37,438)**	**12,578**	**10,428**	**9,137**	**9,137**	**968**
NPV(Buy & Lease)		0					

To compute this amount, first we compute the FCF from buying the machine. The depreciation tax shield is 0.35 × ($48m × 0.20) = $3.36 million in year 0, 0.35 × ($48m × 0.32) = $5.376 million in year 1, etc, as shown in line 2. The NPV of the FCF from buying the machine (line 3) is:

$$\text{NPV(Buy)} = -44.64 + \frac{5.376}{1.052} + \frac{3.226}{1.052^2} + \frac{1.935}{1.052^3} + \frac{1.935}{1.052^4} + \frac{0.968}{1.052^5}$$
$$= -32.622.$$

Therefore, to break-even, the PV of the after-tax lease payments must equal $32.622 million:

$$32.622 = \text{L} \times (1 - 0.35) \times \left(1 + \frac{1}{.052}\left(1 - \frac{1}{1.052^4}\right)\right)$$

and so L = 11.080 million.

b. At a lease rate of $11.080 and a tax rate of 10%, Netflix has a gain of $0.145 million.

	A	B	C	D	E	F	G	H	I
38			rD	8%					
39	**LESSEE**		tca	10%	7.200%				
40									
41			**Year**	**0**	**1**	**2**	**3**	**4**	**5**
42	**Buy:**								
43	1	Capital Expenditures		(48,000)	-	-	-	-	-
46	2	Depreciation tax shield at 10%		960	1,536	922	553	553	276
47	3	**Free Cash Flow (Buy)**		(47,040)	1,536	922	553	553	276
48	**Lease:**								
49	4	Lease payments		(11,080)	(11,080)	(11,080)	(11,080)	(11,080)	-
50	5	Income tax savings at 10%		1,108	1,108	1,108	1,108	1,108	-
51	6	**Free Cash Flow (Lease)**		(9,972)	(9,972)	(9,972)	(9,972)	(9,972)	-
52	**Lease vs. Buy:**								
53	7	**Lease - Buy**		**37,068**	**(11,508)**	**(10,894)**	**(10,525)**	**(10,525)**	**(276)**
56		NPV(Lease-Buy)		145					

c. The source of the gain is the difference in tax rates between the two parties. Because the depreciation tax shield is more accelerated than the lease payments, there is a gain from shifting the depreciation tax shields to the party with the higher tax rate.

Chapter 26

Working Capital Management

26-1. Answer the following:

a. What is the difference between a firm's cash cycle and its operating cycle?

b. How will a firm's cash cycle be affected if a firm increases its inventory, all else being equal?

c. How will a firm's cash cycle be affected if a firm begins to take the discounts offered by its suppliers, all else being equal?

a. A firm's cash cycle is the average length of time from when a firm pays cash for its inventory to when it receives cash from the sale of that inventory (or the end product that the firm produced with the inventory). It is calculated as the average number of days between the purchase of the initial inventory and the sale of the end product plus the average number of days it takes the firm's customers to pay cash for the inventory they purchase minus the average number of days the firm takes to pay its suppliers for the inventory. A firm's operating cycle is the average length of time between when a firm purchases its inventory and when the firm receives cash from the sale of the inventory. It is calculated as the average number of days between the purchase of the initial inventory and the sale of the end product plus the average number of days it takes the firm's customers to pay for the inventory they purchase. If a firm were to pay cash for its inventory, rather than buying the inventory on credit, the cash cycle and the operating cycle of the firm would be identical. In most cases, however, firms buy their inventory on credit, so the cash cycle is shorter than the operating cycle of the firm.

b. If a firm increases its inventory, its inventory days will increase, all else equal. This will, therefore, increase the cash cycle of the firm.

c. If a firm begins to take discounts offered by its suppliers, its accounts payable days will decrease. All else equal, this will cause the cash cycle of the firm to increase.

26-2. Does an increase in a firm's cash cycle necessarily mean that a firm is managing its cash poorly?

No. An increase in a firm's cash cycle does not necessarily mean that the firm is managing its cash poorly. The increase may be due to a conscious management decision. For example, a firm may decide to increase its inventory in order if it has been experiencing excessive stock-outs. All else equal, this would result in an increase in its cash cycle. Or a firm may decide to loosen its credit policy in order to attract customers from its competitors. This would result in an increase in accounts receivable days, and all else equal, result in an increase in the firm's cash cycle. And if a firm chooses to take the discounts offered by its suppliers, the accounts payable days will decrease, leading to an increase in the firm's cash cycle.

26-3. Aberdeen Outboard Motors is contemplating building a new plant. The company anticipates that the plant will require an initial investment of $2 million in net working capital today. The plant will last 10 years, at which point the full investment in net working capital will be recovered. Given an annual discount rate of 6%, what is the net present value of this working capital investment?

Ignoring revenues and other expenses associated with the new plant, the NPV of the $2 million investment in net working capital is simply the present value of the $2 million that the firm will recoup at the end of ten years minus the initial $2 million investment.

$$\text{NPV} = -\$2{,}000{,}000 + \frac{\$2{,}000{,}000}{(1.06)^{10}} = -\$883{,}210$$

26-4. The Greek Connection had sales of $32 million in 2009, and a cost of goods sold of $20 million. A simplified balance sheet for the firm appears below:

THE GREEK CONNECTION
Balance Sheet
As of December 31, 2009
($ thousands)

Assets		Liabilities and Equity	
Cash	$ 2,000	Accounts payable	$ 1,500
Accounts receivable	3,950	Notes payable	1,000
Inventory	1,300	Accruals	1,220
Total current assets	$ 7,250	Total current liabilities	$ 3,720
		Long-term debt	3,000
		Total liabilities	$ 6,720
Net plant, property, and equipment	$ 8,500	Common equity	9,030
Total assets	$ 15,750	Total liabilities and equity	$ 15,750

a. **Calculate The Greek Connection's net working capital in 2009.**

b. **Calculate the cash conversion cycle of The Greek Connection in 2009.**

c. **The industry average accounts receivable days is 30 days. What would the cash conversion cycle for The Greek Connection have been in 2009 had it matched the industry average for accounts receivable days?**

a. Net working capital is current assets minus current liabilities. Using this definition, The Greek Connection's net working capital is $7,250 – $3,720 = $3,530. Some analysts calculate the net operating working capital instead, which is the non-interest earning current assets minus the non-interest bearing current liabilities. In this case, the notes payable would not be included in the calculation since they are assumed to be interest bearing. Net operating working capital for The Greek Connection is $7,250 – ($1,500 + $1,220) = $4,530.

b. The cash conversion cycle (CCC) is equal to the inventory days plus the accounts receivable days minus the accounts payable days. The Greek Connection's cash conversion cycle for 2004 was 41.4 days.

$$\text{CCC} = \frac{\text{inventory}}{\text{average daily COGS}} + \frac{\text{accounts receivable}}{\text{average daily sales}} - \frac{\text{accounts payable}}{\text{average daily COGS}}$$

$$\text{CCC}_{2004} = \frac{\$1{,}300}{\frac{\$20{,}000}{365}} + \frac{\$3{,}950}{\frac{\$32{,}000}{365}} - \frac{\$1{,}500}{\frac{\$20{,}000}{365}}$$

$$= 23.7 \text{ days} + 45.1 \text{ days} - 27.4 \text{ days} = 41.4 \text{ days}$$

c. If The Greek Connection accounts receivable days had been 30 days, its cash conversion cycle would have been only 26.3 days:

CCC = 23.7 days + 30 days – 27.4 days = 26.3 days

26-5. Assume the credit terms offered to your firm by your suppliers are 3/5, Net 30. Calculate the cost of the trade credit if your firm does not take the discount and pays on day 30.

In this instance, the customer will have the use of $97 for an additional 25 days (30 – 5) if he chooses not to take the discount. It will cost him $3 to do so since he must pay $100 for the goods if he pays after the 5-day discount period. Thus, the interest rate per period is:

$$\frac{\$3}{\$97} = 0.0309 = 3.09\%.$$

The number of 25-day periods in a year is 365/25 = 14.6 periods. So the effective annual cost of the trade credit is:

$$\text{EAR} = (1.0309)^{14.6} - 1 = 55.94\%.$$

26-6. Your supplier offers terms of 1/10, Net 45. What is the effective annual cost of trade credit if you choose to forgo the discount and pay on day 45?

If you were to pay within the 10-day discount period, you would pay $99 for $100 worth of goods. If you wait until day 45, you will owe $100. Thus, you are paying $1 in interest for a 35-day (45 – 10) loan. The interest rate per period is:

$$\frac{\$1}{\$99} = 0.0101 = 1.01\%.$$

The number of 35-day periods in a year is 365 / 35 = 10.43 periods. So the effective annual cost of the trade credit is:

$$\text{EAR} = (1.0101)^{10.43} - 1 = 11.05\%.$$

26-7. The Fast Reader Company supplies bulletin board services to numerous hotel chains nationwide. The owner of the firm is investigating the benefit of employing a billing firm to do her billing and collections. Because the billing firm specializes in these services, collection float will be reduced by 20 days. Average daily collections are $1200, and the owner can earn 8% annually (expressed as an APR with monthly compounding) on her investments. If the billing firm charges $250 per month, should the owner employ the billing firm?

The benefit of outsourcing the billing and collection to the other firm is equal to what Fast Reader can earn on the funds that are freed up. Since average daily collections are $1,200 and float will be reduced by 20 days, Fast Reader will have an additional $24,000 ($1,200 x 20). (Think about this as follows. Immediately after hiring the billing firm, its collection float drops by 20 days, so all collections due within the next 20 days are immediately available.) The billing firm charges $250 per month. At an 8% annual rate, the monthly discount rate is 1.081 / 12 – 1 = 6.43%, so the present value of these charges in perpetuity is 250/0.0643 = $38,856. Thus, the costs ($38,856) exceed the benefits ($24,000), and Fast Reader should not employ the billing firm.

26-8. The Saban Corporation is trying to decide whether to switch to a bank that will accommodate electronic funds transfers from Saban's customers. Saban's financial manager believes the new system would decrease its collection float by as much as five days. The new bank would require a compensating balance of $30,000, whereas its present bank has no compensating balance requirement. Saban's average daily collections are $10,000, and it can earn 8% on its short-term investments. Should Saban make the switch? (Assume the compensating balance at the new bank will be deposited in a non-interest-earning account.)

The electronic funds transfer system will free up $50,000 (= 5 × $10,000) (Think about this as follows. Immediately after switching banks its collections due within the next five days are immediately available.) On the other hand, Saban will have to pay a cost because it has to hold $30,000 in a non-interest earning account, which means it has essentially given up these funds. Because the benefits ($50,000) are larger than the costs ($30,000) it should switch banks.

26-9. What are the three steps involved in establishing a credit policy?

The three steps involved in establishing a credit policy are:

(1) Establish credit standards. In this step, the firm must decide how much credit risk it is willing to accept.

(2) Establish credit terms. Here, the firm decides on the length of time before payment must be made and whether or not it will offer a discount. If a discount is to be offered, the amount of the discount and the length of the discount period must also be established.

(3) Establish a collection policy. In this step, the firm must decide how it will handle late payers.

26-10. The Manana Corporation had sales of $60 million this year. Its accounts receivable balance averaged $2 million. How long, on average, does it take the firm to collect on its sales?

If we assume all the sales were made on credit, the average length of time it takes Manana to collect on its sales is 12.2 days:

$$\text{Accounts receivable days} = \frac{\text{Accounts receivable}}{\text{Average daily sales}} = \frac{\$2,000,000}{\frac{\$60,000,000}{365}} = 12.2 \text{ days.}$$

26-11. The Mighty Power Tool Company has the following accounts on its books:

Customer	Amount Owed ($)	Age (days)
ABC	50,000	35
DEF	35,000	5
GHI	15,000	10
KLM	75,000	22
NOP	42,000	40
QRS	18,000	12
TUV	82,000	53
WXY	36,000	90

The firm extends credit on terms of 1/15, Net 30. Develop an aging schedule using 15-day increments through 60 days, and then indicate any accounts that have been outstanding for more than 60 days.

Mighty Power Tool Company Aging Schedule

Days Outstanding	Amount Owed	Percent of Accounts Receivable
0-15	$ 68,000	19.3%
16–30	$ 75,000	21.2%
31–45	$ 92,000	26.1%
46–60	$ 82,000	23.2%
over 60	$ 36,000	10.2%
	$353,000	100.0%

26-12. What is meant by "stretching the accounts payable"?

"Stretching the accounts payable" refers to a customer's not paying by the payment date specified.

26-13. Simple Simon's Bakery purchases supplies on terms of 1/10, Net 25. If Simple Simon's chooses to take the discount offered, it must obtain a bank loan to meet its short-term financing needs. A local bank has quoted Simple Simon's owner an interest rate of 12% on borrowed funds. Should Simple Simon's enter the loan agreement with the bank and begin taking the discount?

If Simple Simon's takes the discount, it must pay $99 in 10 days for every $100 of purchases. If it elects not to take the discount, it will owe the full $100 in 25 days. The interest rate on the loan is:

$$\frac{\$1}{\$99} = 1.01\%.$$

The loan period is 15 days (= 25 – 10). The effective annual cost of the trade credit is:

$$\text{EAR} = (1.0101)^{365/15} - 1 = 27.7\%.$$

Since the bank loan is only 12%, Simple Simon should borrow the funds from the bank in order to take advantage of the discount.

26-14. Your firm purchases goods from its supplier on terms of 3/15, Net 40.

a. What is the effective annual cost to your firm if it chooses not to take the discount and makes its payment on day 40?

b. What is the effective annual cost to your firm if it chooses not to take the discount and makes its payment on day 50?

a. Your firm is paying $3 to borrow $97 for 25 days (= 40 – 15). The interest rate per period is:

$$\frac{\$3}{\$97} = 0.0309 = 3.09\%.$$

The effective annual rate is $(1.0309)^{365/25} - 1 = 55.9\%$.

b. In this case, your firm is stretching its accounts payable. You are still paying $3 to borrow $97, so the interest rate per period is 3.09%. However, the loan period is now 35 days (= 50 – 15). The effective annual rate is reduced to 37.4% because your firm has use of the money for a longer period of time:

$$\text{EAR} = (1.0309)^{365/35} - 1 = 37.4\%.$$

26-15. Use the financial statements supplied below for International Motor Corporation (IMC) to answer the following questions.

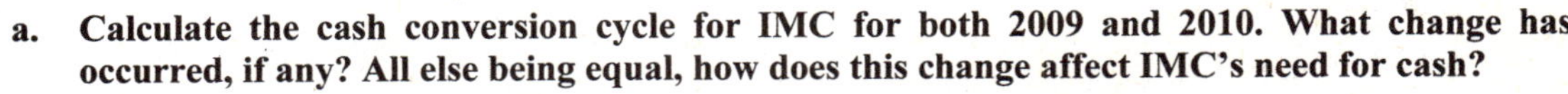

a. Calculate the cash conversion cycle for IMC for both 2009 and 2010. What change has occurred, if any? All else being equal, how does this change affect IMC's need for cash?

b. IMC's suppliers offer terms of Net 30. Does it appear that IMC is doing a good job of managing its accounts payable?

INTERNATIONAL MOTOR CORPORATION
Income Statement (in millions)
for the Years Ending December 31

	2009	2010
Sales	$ 60,000	$ 75,000
Cost of goods sold	52,000	61,000
Gross profit	$ 8,000	$ 14,000
Selling and general and administrative expenses	6,000	8,000
Operating profit	$ 2,000	$ 6,000
Interest expense	1,400	1,300
Earnings before tax	$ 600	$ 4,700
Taxes	300	2,350
Earnings after tax	$ 300	$ 2,350

INTERNATIONAL MOTOR CORPORATION
Balance Sheet (in millions)
as of December 31

	2009	2010		2009	2010
Assets			**Liabilities**		
Cash	$ 3,080	$ 6,100	Accounts payable	$ 3,600	$ 4,600
Accounts receivable	2,800	6,900	Notes payable	1,180	1,250
Inventory	6,200	6,600	Accruals	5,600	6,211
Total current assets	$ 12,080	$ 19,600	Total current liabilities	$ 10,380	$ 12,061
Net plant, property, and equipment	$ 23,087	$ 20,098	Long-term debt	$ 6,500	$ 7,000
Total assets	$ 35,167	$ 39,698	Total liabilities	$ 16,880	$ 19,061
			Equity		
			Common stock	$ 2,735	$ 2,735
			Retained earnings	$ 15,552	$ 17,902
			Total equity	$ 18,287	$ 20,637
			Total liabilities and equity	$ 35,167	$ 39,698

a. The cash conversion cycle (CCC) is equal to the inventory days plus the accounts receivable days minus the accounts payable days. IMC's cash conversion cycle for 2003 was 35.2 days, and for 2004, it was 45.6 days.

$$CCC = \frac{\text{inventory}}{\text{average daily COGS}} + \frac{\text{accounts receivable}}{\text{average daily sales}} - \frac{\text{accounts payable}}{\text{average daily COGS}}$$

$$CCC_{2003} = \frac{\$6,200}{\frac{\$52,000}{365}} + \frac{\$2,800}{\frac{\$60,000}{365}} - \frac{\$3,600}{\frac{\$52,000}{365}}$$

$$= 43.5 \text{ days} + 17.0 \text{ days} - 25.3 \text{ days} = 35.2 \text{ days}$$

$$CCC_{2004} = \frac{\$6,600}{\frac{\$61,000}{365}} + \frac{\$6,900}{\frac{\$75,000}{365}} - \frac{\$4,600}{\frac{\$61,000}{365}}$$

$$= 39.5 \text{ days} + 33.6 \text{ days} - 27.5 \text{ days} = 45.6 \text{ days}$$

IMC's cash conversion cycle has lengthened in 2004, due to an increase in its accounts receivable days. The number of days goods are held in inventory has decreased, and IMC is taking longer to pay its suppliers, both of which would decrease the cash conversion cycle all else equal. These changes were not enough to offset the increase in the amount of time it is taking IMC's customers to pay for purchases made on credit. The lengthening of the cash conversion cycle means that IMC will require more cash.

b. If IMC's suppliers are offering terms of net 30, IMC should consider waiting longer to pay for its purchases. In 2003, it paid nearly five days earlier than necessary, and in 2004, it paid 2.5 days earlier. IMC could, therefore, have kept the money working for it longer because there was no discount offered for early payment. The early payment may give IMC a preferred position with its suppliers, however, which may have benefits that are not presented here. IMC's decision on whether to extend its accounts payable days would have to take these benefits into consideration.

26-16. Ohio Valley Homecare Suppliers, Inc. (OVHS), had $20 million in sales in 2009. Its cost of goods sold was $8 million, and its average inventory balance was $2,000,000.

a. Calculate the average number of inventory days outstanding for OVHS.

b. The average days of inventory in the industry is 73 days. By how much would OVHS reduce its investment in inventory if it could improve its inventory days to meet the industry average?

a. The inventory days ratio is equal to the inventory divided by average daily cost of goods sold. This was 91.25 days for Ohio Valley Homecare Suppliers in 2004:

$$\text{inventory days} = \frac{\$2{,}000{,}000}{\frac{\$8{,}000{,}000}{365}} = 91.25 \text{ days.}$$

The inventory turnover ratio for Ohio Valley Homecare Supplies was four times in 2004:

$$\text{inventory turnover} = \frac{\text{cost of goods sold}}{\text{inventory}} = \frac{\$8{,}000{,}000}{\$2{,}000{,}000} = 4\text{X}.$$

b. OVHS could increase its inventory turnover to five times by reducing its inventory to $1,600,000:

$$5 = \frac{\$8{,}000{,}000}{\text{inventory}} \Rightarrow \text{inventory} = \$1{,}600{,}000.$$

This means OVHS could reduce its investment in inventory by $400,000 (= $2,000,000 – $1,600,000).

26-17. Which of the following short-term securities would you expect to offer the highest before-tax return: Treasury bills, certificates of deposit, short-term tax exempts, or commercial paper? Why?

Commercial paper. Treasury bills and certificates of deposit are considered to be free of default risk, so they offer lower returns than a security that has default risk associated with it. Short-term tax exempts have default risk, but the interest on these instruments is free from federal taxation; thus, they offer a lower yield than a similarly risky, fully taxable security. Commercial paper exposes the investor to default risk and the interest earned is fully taxable. It would, therefore, have to offer the investor a higher before-tax return than the other instruments.

Chapter 27
Short-Term Financial Planning

27-1. Which of the following companies are likely to have high short-term financing needs? Why?

a. A clothing retailer

b. A professional sports team

c. An electric utility

d. A company that operates toll roads

e. A restaurant chain

The professional sports team is likely to have very high short-term financing needs because of the seasonality of its revenue stream. Several months before the season actually begins for the team, it may have large cash flow requirements—equipment, tickets, advertising, etc.—that it will need to finance since the bulk of its cash inflows will occur during the season.

The clothing retailer may have high short-term financing needs because of the seasonality of its business. Sales are often highest in the fall and spring, so the retailer may need short-term financing in order to purchase inventory prior to the high seasons. It may need even more short-term financing due to a negative cash flow shock. For example, if the store's buyer misjudged the fashion trends and overbought a particular style that the store was unable to sell, the store might experience a large net cash outflow for that season. In that case, it may require more short-term financing than normal in order to purchase inventory for the upcoming season.

27-2. Sailboats Etc. is a retail company specializing in sailboats and other sailing-related equipment. The following table contains financial forecasts as well as current (month 0) working capital levels. During which months are the firm's seasonal working capital needs the greatest? When does it have surplus cash?

	Month						
($000)	**0**	**1**	**2**	**3**	**4**	**5**	**6**
Net Income		$10	$12	$15	$25	$30	$18
Depreciation		2	3	3	4	5	4
Capital Expenditures		1	0	0	1	0	0
Levels of Working Capital							
Accounts Receivable	$2	3	4	5	7	10	6
Inventory	3	2	4	5	5	4	2
Accounts Payable	2	2	2	2	2	2	2

To determine Sailboats seasonal working capital needs, we calculate the changes in net working capital for the firm.

Changes in working capital	Month					
	1	2	3	4	5	6
Accounts receivable	$1	$1	$1	$2	$3	–$4
Inventory	–$1	$2	$1	0	–$1	–$2
Accounts payable	0	0	0	0	0	0
Change in net working capital	$0	$3	$2	$2	$2	–$6

From the table it can be seen that Sailboat's working capital needs are highest in Month 2 because its investments in accounts receivable and in inventory increased the most in that month.

Sailboats, Etc. has a surplus cash position in every month as shown below:

	Month					
($000)	1	2	3	4	5	6
Net income	$10	$12	$15	$25	$30	$18
plus depreciation	2	3	3	4	5	4
minus changes in net working capital	0	3	2	2	2	–6
Cash flow from operations	$12	$12	$16	$27	$33	$28
minus capital expenditures	1	0	0	1	0	0
Change in cash	$11	$12	$16	$26	$33	$28

27-3. What is the difference between permanent working capital and temporary working capital?

Permanent working capital is the amount that a firm has to keep invested in its short-term assets in order to support its operations. For example, a toy retailer may need to keep a minimum amount invested in inventory at all times. Temporary working capital, on the other hand, is the result of seasonal fluctuations and/or unanticipated cash flow shocks. The toy retailer, for example, may need to have more invested in inventory just prior to its peak season. Temporary working capital is the difference between the actual level of investment in short-term assets and the permanent working capital investment.

27-4. Quarterly working capital levels for your firm for the next year are included in the following table. What are the permanent working capital needs of your company? What are the temporary needs?

	Quarter			
($000)	**1**	**2**	**3**	**4**
Cash	$100	$100	$100	$100
Accounts Receivable	200	100	100	600
Inventory	200	500	900	50
Accounts Payable	100	100	100	100

The net working capital for each quarter is calculated below:

	Quarter			
($000)	1	2	3	4
Cash	$100	$100	$ 100	$100
Accounts receivable	$200	$100	$ 100	$600
Inventory	$200	$500	$ 900	$ 50
Accounts payable	$100	$100	$ 100	$100
Net working capital	$400	$600	$1,000	$650

The minimum level of net working capital—$400,000 in Quarter 1—represents the firm's permanent working capital. The difference between the higher net working capital levels in each quarter and the permanent working capital needs represents the firm's temporary working capital needs. Thus the firm has temporary working capital needs of $200,000 in Quarter 2, $600,000 in Quarter 3, and $250,000 in Quarter 4.

27-5. Why might a company choose to finance permanent working capital with short-term debt?

Financing permanent working capital with short-term debt is an aggressive financing policy and is considered risky. Although under a normal term structure, the interest rates on short-term debt are lower than those on long-term debt, the firm faces the risk that it will have to pay more when it needs to refinance the debt in the future. This increased risk will be reflected in a higher cost of equity for the firm. Nevertheless, a firm may decide to use short-term debt to finance permanent working capital if it believes that one or more market imperfections exist. For example, short-term debt is less sensitive to a firm's credit quality than is long-term debt and so will be less affected by management's actions or information. Thus, short-term debt may have lower agency and lemons costs than long-term debt. Management may also believe it has superior knowledge regarding the future cash flows for the firm, which is not yet reflected in the firm's credit rating. If management believes its ability to produce future cash flows will have a positive impact on its credit rating in the future, management may elect to use lower-cost, short-term debt to finance its permanent working capital for the time being with the expectation that it will refinance it with long-term debt in the near future when the market has recognized the firm's improved future prospects and rewarded it with a higher credit rating, which can result in a lower cost of long-term debt to the firm.

27-6. The Hand-to-Mouth Company needs a $10,000 loan for the next 30 days. It is trying to decide which of three alternatives to use:

***Alternative A*: Forgo the discount on its trade credit agreement that offers terms of 2/10, Net 30.**

***Alternative B*: Borrow the money from Bank A, which has offered to lend the firm $10,000 for 30 days at an APR of 12%. The bank will require a (no-interest) compensating balance of 5% of the face value of the loan and will charge a $100 loan origination fee, which means Hand-to-Mouth must borrow even more than the $10,000.**

***Alternative C*: Borrow the money from Bank B, which has offered to lend the firm $10,000 for 30 days at an APR of 15%. The loan has a 1% loan origination fee.**

Which alternative is the cheapest source of financing for Hand-to-Mouth?

Alternative A: The effective annual cost of the trade credit is 44.6%, calculated as follows:

$$\text{Interest rate per period} = \frac{\$2}{\$98} = 2.041\%.$$

The loan period is 20 (= 30 – 10) periods, and there are 18.25 periods in a year (365 / 20 = 18.25).

$\text{EAR} = 1.02041^{18.25} - 1 = 44.6\%$

Alternative B: Hand-to-Mouth will need to borrow \$10,100 just to cover its loan origination fee. Beyond that, it needs to have enough to meet the compensating balance requirement. So the total amount that Hand-to-Mouth must borrow is \$10,632:

$$\text{Amount needed} = \frac{\$10{,}100}{1-0.05} = \$10{,}632.$$

At a 12% APR, the interest expense for the 30-day loan will be 0.01(\$10,632) = \$106.32.

Since the loan origination fee is simply additional interest, the total interest on the 30-day loan is \$106.32 + \$100 = \$206.32. The firm's usable proceeds from the loan is \$10,000. So the interest rate per period is 2.063% $\left(=\dfrac{\$206.32}{\$10{,}000}\right)$.

The effective annual rate of alternative B is $(1.02063)^{365/30} - 1 = 28.2\%$.

Alternative C: Hand-to-Mouth will need to borrow \$10,100 in order to cover the loan origination fee. An APR of 15% translates to an interest rate of 1.25% $\left(=\dfrac{15\%}{12}\right)$ for 30 days. The interest expense for one month is 0.0125 × \$10,100 = \$126.25. This with the loan origination fee makes the total interest charge \$226.25 for the 30-day loan. This amounts to 2.263% for 30 days: $\dfrac{\$226.25}{\$10{,}000}$.

The effective annual rate is $(1.02263)^{365/30} - 1 = 31.3\%$.

Thus in Alternative A, the cost of trade credit is the most expensive at an effective annual rate of 44.6%.

27-7. Consider two loans with a 1-year maturity and identical face values: an 8% loan with a 1% loan origination fee and an 8% loan with a 5% (no-interest) compensating balance requirement. Which loan would have the higher effective annual rate? Why?

The loan with the 1% loan origination fee would cost the most since the loan origination fee is just another form of interest, so on a \$1,000 loan, the borrower is paying \$90 in interest and will have the use of only \$990 for the period, making the effective annual cost of the loan over 9% (\$90/\$990 = 9.1%). The compensating balance requirement of 5% on a \$1,000 loan reduces the usable proceeds of the firm by 5% to \$950, but the interest rate is still 8%, so the effective annual cost of that arrangement is 8.4% $\left(=\dfrac{\$80}{\$950}\right)$. The effective annual rate is not increased by a full percentage.

27-8. What is the difference between evergreen credit and a revolving line of credit?

The major difference between a revolving line of credit and evergreen credit is the commitment period. A revolving line of credit is a committed line of credit that involves a solid commitment from the bank for a period that is longer than the typical one-year term of a regular line of credit. The revolving line of credit is usually good for two or three years before it must be renegotiated. Evergreen credit is a revolving line of credit that has *no* fixed maturity.

27-9. Which of the following one-year \$1000 bank loans offers the lowest effective annual rate?

a. A loan with an APR of 6%, compounded monthly

b. A loan with an APR of 6%, compounded annually, that also has a compensating balance requirement of 10% (on which no interest is paid)

c. A loan with an APR of 6%, compounded annually, that has a 1% loan origination fee

The effective annual rates of each of the alternatives are calculated as follows.

a. Since the APR is 6%, the monthly rate is 6%/12 = 0.5%. This translates to an effective annual rate of $(1.005)^{12} - 1 = 6.2\%$.

b. The compensating balance is $1,000 × 0.10 = $100. Therefore, the borrower will have use of only $900 of the $1,000. The interest is 0.06 × $1,000 = $60. The interest rate per period is $60 / $900 = 6.7%. Since this alternative assumes annual compounding, the effective annual rate is 6.7% as well.

c. The interest expense is 0.06 × $1,000, and the loan origination fee is 0.01 × $1,000 = $10. The loan origination fee reduces the usable proceeds of the loan to $990 because it is paid at the beginning of the loan. The interest rate per period is $70 / $990 = 7.1%. Since the loan is compounded annually in this case, 7.1% is the effective annual rate.

Thus, alternative (a) offers the lowest effective annual cost.

27-10. The Needy Corporation borrowed $10,000 from Bank Ease. According to the terms of the loan, Needy must pay the bank $400 in interest every three months for the three-year life of the loan, with the principal to be repaid at the maturity of the loan. What effective annual rate is Needy paying?

In this problem, Needy must pay $400 every three months to have the use of $10,000. Thus, the interest rate per period is $400 / $10,000 = 4%. Since there are four three-month periods in a year, the effective annual rate is $(1.04)^4 - 1 \approx 17\%$.

27-11. The Treadwater Bank wants to raise $1 million using three-month commercial paper. The net proceeds to the bank will be $985,000. What is the effective annual rate of this financing for Treadwater?

Treadwater is paying $15,000 (= $1,000,000 – $985,000) to use $985,000 for three months, so the three-month interest rate is $15,000/$985,000 = 1.523%. There are four three-month periods in a year, making the effective annual rate $(1.01523)^4 - 1 = 6.2\%$.

27-12. Magna Corporation has an issue of commercial paper with a face value of $1,000,000 and a maturity of six months. Magna received net proceeds of $973,710 when it sold the paper. What is the effective annual rate of the paper to Magna?

Magna is paying $26,290 (= $1,000,000 – $973,710) to use $973,710 for six months. The six-month interest rate is $26,290 / $973,710 = 2.7%. There are two six-month periods in one year, so the effective annual rate is $(1.027)^2 - 1 = 5.5\%$.

27-13. What is the difference between direct paper and dealer paper?

Direct paper is a method by which a firm sells its commercial paper directly to investors. Dealer paper refers to the sale of commercial paper through dealers. The dealers get a fee for their services, thus reducing the proceeds that the issuing firm receives (and increasing the effective cost to the firm).

27-14. The Signet Corporation has issued four-month commercial paper with a $6 million face value. The firm netted $5,870,850 on the sale. What effective annual rate is Signet paying for these funds?

Signet's interest expense on this loan is $129,150 (= $6,000,000 – $5,870,850), and the usable proceeds are $5,870,850. The interest rate for the four-month period is $129,150 / $5,870,850 = 2.2%. The effective annual rate is $(1.022)^3 - 1 = 6.7\%$.

27-15. What is the difference between pledging accounts receivable to secure a loan and factoring accounts receivable?

When accounts receivable are pledged, the borrowing firm is simply using its accounts receivable as collateral for a loan. The lender reviews the invoices for the credit sales of the borrower and determines which accounts are acceptable collateral. The lender will then lend some percentage of the dollar amount of the accepted invoices. If one or more of the borrowing firm's customers fail to pay, the firm is still responsible to the lender for the money it has borrowed. In a factoring arrangement, the accounts receivable are sold to the lender (i.e., factor), and the firm's customers typically make their payments directly to the lender. The lender agrees to pay the borrowing firm the amount due from the firm's customers at the end of the firm's payment period, but the firm may borrow a certain percentage of the face value of its receivables in order to receive the money in advance. The factoring arrangement may be "with recourse," which means that if any of the borrowing firm's customers defaults on its bills, the factor can require the borrowing firm to make the payment. It may also be "without recourse," in which case the lender bears the risk that one or more customers will default on their bills. The borrowing firm is not responsible for the payments.

27-16. The Ohio Valley Steel Corporation has borrowed $5 million for one month at a stated annual rate of 9%, using inventory stored in a field warehouse as collateral. The warehouser charges a $5000 fee, payable at the end of the month. What is the effective annual rate of this loan?

The monthly interest rate is 9% / 12 = 0.75%, so Ohio Valley Steel must pay 0.0075 × $5,000,000 = $37,500 in interest on the loan. Combining this with the $5,000 warehouser fee makes the monthly cost of the loan $42,500. Since the fee is paid at the end of the month, Ohio Valley Steel has use of the full $5,000,000 for the month. The interest rate per period is $42,500 / $5,000,000 = 0.85%. There are 12 months in a year, so the effective annual rate is $(1.0085)^{12} - 1 = 10.7\%$.

27-17. Discuss the three different arrangements under which a firm may use inventory to secure a loan.

The three different methods under which inventory is used as collateral for a loan are floating liens, trust receipts, and warehouse arrangements.

With a floating lien (also called a "general lien" or a "blanket lien"), all of the borrower's inventory serves as collateral for a loan. The value of the collateral declines as the firm sells its inventory. In times of financial distress, a firm may decide to sell its inventory without making payments on the loan and may not have enough money to replenish the inventory it has sold. The loan is then under-collateralized. This is the riskiest arrangement from the lender's standpoint, and the loan will carry a higher interest rate than if one of the other two methods is used. Additionally, the lender will lend a much smaller percentage of the inventory value under this arrangement.

In a trust receipt (or floor planning) arrangement, specific inventory items are identified as collateral for the loan. As the specified inventory is sold, the firm uses the cash received to repay the loan. The lender will send someone to the borrower's premises periodically to ensure that none of the specified inventory has been sold without a repayment made.

In a warehouse arrangement, the inventory serving as collateral is stored in a warehouse. One type of warehouse is a public warehouse, which is a business that exists for the sole purpose of tracking the flow of the inventory. The inventory is delivered to the public warehouse by the borrowing firm, and the lender extends a loan based on the value of that inventory. When the borrowing firm needs the inventory to sell, it must return to the warehouse to retrieve it after receiving permission from the lender to do so. This arrangement is the least risky from the standpoint of the lender since it allows the lender to maintain the tightest control over the inventory, but it is only feasible for some types of inventory. This method would not be usable for inventory that is subject to spoilage or that is bulky and difficult to transport. In this latter case, a field warehouse might be a good alternative. A field warehouse is established on the borrower's premises, but it is separated from the borrower's main plant. It is operated by a third party. This type of arrangement is more convenient for the borrower, but it still gives the lender the added security of having the inventory that serves as collateral tracked by a third party.

27-18. The Rasputin Brewery is considering using a public warehouse loan as part of its short-term financing. The firm will require a loan of $500,000. Interest on the loan will be 10% (APR, annual compounding) to be paid at the end of the year. The warehouse charges 1% of the face value of the loan, payable at the beginning of the year. What is the effective annual rate of this warehousing arrangement?

Rasputin's interest expense is 0.10($500,000) = $50,000. The warehouse fee is 0.01($500,000) = $5,000. Because the warehouse fee must be paid at the beginning of the year, Rasputin's usable proceeds from the loan are only $495,000 (= $500,000 – $5,000). The effective annual rate is $55,000 / $495,000 = 11.1%.

Chapter 28
Mergers and Acquisitions

28-1. **What are the two primary mechanisms under which ownership and control of a public corporation can change?**

Either another corporation or group of individuals can acquire the target firm, or the target firm can merge with another firm.

28-2. **Why do you think mergers cluster in time, causing merger waves?**

There are many competing theories as to why this is so. They generally fall into two camps: either stock market valuations drive merger activity or industry shocks accompanying economic expansions drive merger activity. It is clear that merger activity is much greater during economic expansions than during contractions and that merger activity strongly correlates with bull markets. Thus, there must be something about economic expansions in general and higher stock market valuations in particular that grease the wheels of the merger process. However, unless you are willing to believe that the majority of managers simply buy other companies because they can, without regard to economic reasoning, this can't be the whole story. There must be real economic impetus to the activity. Many of the same technological and economic conditions that lead to bull markets also motivate managers to reshuffle assets through merger and acquisitions. Thus, it takes a combination of forces usually only present during strong economic expansions to drive peaks in merger activity.

28-3. **What are some reasons why a horizontal merger might create value for shareholders?**

Horizontal mergers are more likely to create value for acquiring shareholders. Horizontal mergers combine two firms in the same industry. This provides for greater potential synergies in eliminating redundant functions within the two firms and potentially increased pricing power with both vendors and customers.

28-4. **Why do you think shareholders from target companies enjoy an average gain when acquired, while acquiring shareholders on average often do not gain anything?**

The acquiring firm has to compete against other firms, thus reducing the gains it can obtain from the transaction. Target shareholders benefit from this competition, as they obtain higher bids for the company.

28-5. **If you are planning an acquisition that is motivated by trying to acquire expertise, you are basically seeking to gain intellectual capital. What concerns would you have in structuring the deal and the post-merger integration that would be different from the concerns you would have when buying physical capital?**

In cases where you are buying a lot of intangible assets, especially human capital, you have to be particularly worried about how you are going to create incentives for the target's employees to stay-on. Retention bonuses are common for key employees in these types of acquisitions. It is also hard to be successful with a hostile acquisition when retention of target employees is critical. Keeping uncertainty low and moving quickly during the integration phase are both critical to acquisitions of expertise.

28-6. Do you agree that the European Union should be able to block mergers between two U.S.-based firms? Why or why not?

The argument can go either way on this. Some of the critical factors to consider are: What is the social good created by antitrust regulation? Do European regulators have a right to regulate firms doing business in Europe, regardless of where those firms are headquartered? What would be the alternatives?

28-7. How do the carryforward and carryback provisions of the U.S. tax code affect the benefits of merging to capture operating losses?

Carryforward and carryback provisions generally reduce the attractiveness of tax losses as a motivation to merger. Since the tax loss motivation is based on the ability of a larger firm to capture the tax deduction from the losses of the target, it requires that the target not be able to capture the value of that deduction itself. Carryforward and carryback provisions give the target more opportunities to capture the deduction either through recapture of previously paid taxes or by applying the deduction in the future when the company returns to profitability.

28-8. Diversification is good for shareholders. So why shouldn't managers acquire firms in different industries to diversify a company?

Yes, diversification is good for shareholders, and they can do it efficiently themselves by purchasing shares in different companies. There is no need for managers to do this for them by creating a conglomerate through purchasing other companies at a premium over market prices. Given the premium paid in an acquisition and the differing preferences of shareholders, it cannot be efficient for managers to diversify the company rather than leaving it to shareholders to diversify their portfolio.

28-9. Your company has earnings per share of \$4. It has 1 million shares outstanding, each of which has a price of \$40. You are thinking of buying TargetCo, which has earnings per share of \$2, 1 million shares outstanding, and a price per share of \$25. You will pay for TargetCo by issuing new shares. There are no expected synergies from the transaction.

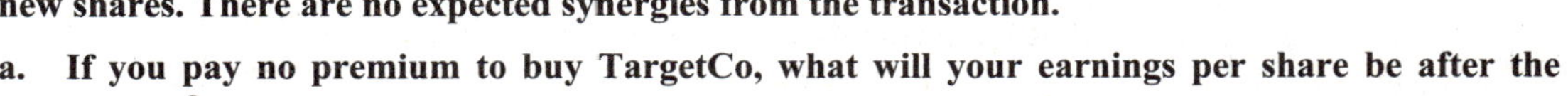

a. **If you pay no premium to buy TargetCo, what will your earnings per share be after the merger?**

b. **Suppose you offer an exchange ratio such that, at current pre-announcement share prices for both firms, the offer represents a 20% premium to buy TargetCo, what will your earnings per share be after the merger?**

c. **What explains the change in earnings per share in part (a)? Are your shareholders any better or worse off?**

d. **What will your price-earnings ratio be after the merger (if you pay no premium)? How does this compare to your P/E ratio before the merger? How does this compare to TargetCo's premerger P/E ratio?**

a. TargetCo's shares are worth \$25, and your shares are worth \$40. You will have to issue 25/40 (= 5/8) shares per share of TargetCo to buy it. That means that in aggregate, you have to issue (5/8) × 1 million = 625,000 new shares. After the merger, you will have a total of 1,625,000 shares outstanding (the original 1 million plus the 625,000 new shares). Your total earnings will be \$6 million. This comes from the \$4 per share × 1 million shares = \$4 million you were earning before the merger and the \$2 per share × 1 million shares = \$2 million that TargetCo was earning. Thus, your new EPS will be \$6 million/1.625 million shares = \$3.69.

b. A 20% premium means that you will have to pay \$30 per share to buy TargetCo (= \$25 × 1.20). Thus, you will have to issue \$30/\$40 = 0.75 of your shares per share of TargetCo, or a total of 750,000 new shares. With total earnings of \$6 million and total shares outstanding after the merger of 1,750,000, you will have EPS of \$6 million/1.75 million shares = \$3.43.

c. In part (a), the change in the EPS simply came from combining the two companies, one of which was earning \$4 per share and the other was earning \$2 per share. However, you will notice that even though TargetCo has half your EPS, it is trading for more than half your value. That is possible if TargetCo's earnings are less risky or if they are expected to grow more in the future. Thus, although your shareholders end-up with lower EPS after the transaction, they have paid a fair price, exchanging their $4 per share before the transaction for either lower, but safer EPS after the transaction, or lower EPS that are expected to grow more in the future. Either way, focusing on EPS alone cannot tell you whether shareholders are better or worse off.

d. If you simply combine the two companies without any indicated synergies, then the total value of the company will be $40 million + $25 million = $65 million. You will have earnings totaling $6 million, so your P/E ratio is $65 / $6 = 10.83. Your P/E ratio before the merger was $40/$4 = 10, and TargetCo's was $25/$2 = 12.5. You can see that by buying TargetCo for its market price and creating no synergies, the transaction simply ends-up with a company whose P/E ratio is between the P/E ratios of the two companies going into the transaction. Again, simply focusing on metrics like P/E does not tell you whether you are better or worse off. (Your P/E went-up from 10 to 10.83, but your shareholders are no better or worse off.)

28-10. If companies in the same industry as TargetCo (from Problem 9) are trading at multiples of 14 times earnings, what would be one estimate of an appropriate premium for TargetCo?

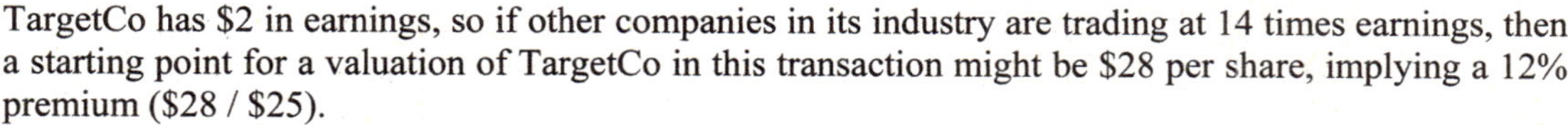

TargetCo has $2 in earnings, so if other companies in its industry are trading at 14 times earnings, then a starting point for a valuation of TargetCo in this transaction might be $28 per share, implying a 12% premium ($28 / $25).

28-11. You are invested in GreenFrame, Inc. The CEO owns 3% of GreenFrame and is considering an acquisition. If the acquisition destroys $50 million of GreenFrame's value, but the present value of the CEO's compensation increases by $5 million, will he be better or worse off?

The CEO will be better off. His portion of the $50 million loss in firm value is 3%, or $1.5 million. If his compensation increases by $5 million, even for only one year, he will be better off by $3.5 million.

28-12. Loki, Inc., and Thor, Inc., have entered into a stock swap merger agreement whereby Loki will pay a 40% premium over Thor's premerger price. If Thor's premerger price per share was $40 and Loki's was $50, what exchange ratio will Loki need to offer?

The premium is 40%, so the compensation to Thor shareholders must be 1.4(40) or $56. Loki's shares are worth $50, so it will need to offer $56/$50 = 1.12 shares of Loki for every share of Thor.

28-13. The NFF Corporation has announced plans to acquire LE Corporation. NFF is trading for $35 per share and LE is trading for $25 per share, implying a premerger value of LE of approximately $4 billion. If the projected synergies are $1 billion, what is the maximum exchange ratio NFF could offer in a stock swap and still generate a positive NPV?

First, calculate the number of shares of LE:

$$\text{Number of shares} = \frac{\$4,000,000,000}{\$25} = 1,600,000,000.$$

Including synergies, LE will be worth S4 billion + $1 billion = $5 billion, or $31.25 per share (= $5 billion / 1.6 billion).

Hence the maximum exchange ratio that NFF can offer is:

$$\text{Exchange ratio} = \frac{\$31.25}{\$35} = 0.893.$$

Thus, NFF can offer a maximum exchange ratio of 0.893 of its share in exchange of each share of LE.

28-14. Let's reconsider part (b) of Problem 9. The actual premium that your company will pay for TargetCo will not be 20%, because on the announcement the target price will go up and your price will go down to reflect the fact that you are willing to pay a premium for TargetCo. Assume that the takeover will occur with certainty and all market participants know this on the announcement of the takeover.

a. What is the price per share of the combined corporation immediately after the merger is completed?

b. What is the price of your company immediately after the announcement?

c. What is the price of TargetCo immediately after the announcement?

d. What is the actual premium your company will pay?

a. Since 0.75 million new shares will be issued, the share price will be (40 + 25)/1.75 = $37.143

b. Same as the price after the merger, $37.143.

c. Since TargetCo shareholders will receive 0.75 × 37.143 = 27.86 million, and there are 1 million shareholders the share price will be $27.86.

d. 27.86/25 – 1 = 11.43%

28-15. ABC has 1 million shares outstanding, each of which has a price of $20. It has made a takeover offer of XYZ Corporation which has 1 million shares outstanding, and a price per share of $2.50. Assume that the takeover will occur with certainty and all market participants know this. Furthermore, there are no synergies to merging the two firms.

a. Assume ABC made a cash offer to purchase XYZ for $3 million. What happens to the price of ABC and XYZ on the announcement? What premium over the current market price does this offer represent?

b. Assume ABC makes a stock offer with an exchange ratio of 0.15. What happens to the price of ABC and XYZ this time? What premium over the current market price does this offer represent?

c. At current market prices, both offers are offers to purchase XYZ for $3 million. Does that mean that your answers to parts (a) and (b) must be identical? Explain.

a. Price of XYZ = $3. Premium = 20%

Price of ABC = 20 – premium × 2.5= $19.50

b. ABC price = price of combine entity = 22.50/1.15 = $19.5652.

XYZ price = amount shareholders will receive = 0.15 × $19.5652 = $2.9345

Premium = 2.9345/2.5 = 17.4% premium

c. No, the premium in the stock offer is lower because market prices change to reflect the fact that ABC shareholders are giving XYZ shareholders money because they are paying a premium. The part (b) announcement means XYZ stock goes up and ABC stock goes down, which lowers the premium relative to the cash offer.

28-16. BAD Company's stock price is $20, and the firm has 2 million shares outstanding. You believe you can increase the company's value if you buy it and replace the management. Assume that BAD has a poison pill with a 20% trigger. If it is triggered, all BAD's shareholders—other than the acquirer—will be able to buy one new share in BAD for each share they own at a 50% discount. Assume that the price remains at $20 while you are acquiring your shares. If BAD's management decides to resist your buyout attempt, and you cross the 20% threshold of ownership:

a. How many new shares will be issued and at what price?

b. What will happen to your percentage ownership of BAD?

c. What will happen to the price of your shares of BAD?

d. Do you lose or gain from triggering the poison pill? If you lose, where does the loss go (who benefits)? If you gain, from where does the gain come (who loses)?

a. If you trigger the poison pill, then you own 20% of the company, or 400,000 shares (= 20% × 2,000,000 shares). When you trigger the poison pill, every other shareholder will buy a new share for every share they hold, so 1,600,000 shares (= 2,000,000 – 400,000) will be issued. These shares will be issued at $10, which is 50% of the price immediately before triggering the poison pill (which we assume stays constant at $20).

b. After the new 1,600,000 shares are issued, there will be a total of 3,600,000 shares (= 2,000,000 + 1,600,000). You will own 400,000 of them, so your participation will be 11.11% (= 400,000/ 3,600,000).

c. When the poison pill is triggered, the market value of the firm will increase to $56 million [= ($20 × 2,000,000) + ($10 × 1,600,000)]. The new stock price will be $15.56 (= $56 million/3,600,000).

d. You lose from triggering the poison pill (you bought shares at $20 that are now worth $15.56). Every other shareholder in the target firm gains (they end with $31.12 (= $15.56 × 2) worth of shares for which they only paid $30 (= $20 + $10).

28-17. How does a toehold help overcome the free rider problem?

Since the acquirer gains the full amount of the value improvement on the shares acquired as a toehold, a toehold provides an incentive to undertake the acquisition, even if the acquirer must pay a price equal to the with-improvement value for the rest of the shares.

28-18. You work for a leveraged buyout firm and are evaluating a potential buyout of UnderWater Company. UnderWater's stock price is $20, and it has 2 million shares outstanding. You believe that if you buy the company and replace its management, its value will increase by 40%. You are planning on doing a leveraged buyout of UnderWater, and will offer $25 per share for control of the company.

a. Assuming you get 50% control, what will happen to the price of non-tendered shares?

b. Given the answer in part (a), will shareholders tender their shares, not tender their shares, or be indifferent?

c. What will your gain from the transaction be?

a. The value should reflect the expected improvement that you will make by replacing the management, so the value of the company will be $40 million plus 40% = $56 million. If you buy 50% of the shares for $25 apiece, you will buy 1 million shares, paying $25 million. However, you will borrow this money, pledging the shares as collateral and then assign the loan to the company once you have control. This means that the new value of the equity will be $56 million – $25 million in debt = $31 million. With 2 million shares outstanding, the price of the equity will drop to $15.50.

b. Since the price of the shares will drop from $20 to $15.50 after the tender offer, everyone will want to tender their shares for $25.

c. Assuming that everyone tenders their shares and you buy them all at $25 apiece, you will pay $50 million to acquire the company and it will be worth $56 million. You will own 100% of the equity, which will be $56 million – $50 million loan to buy the shares = $6 million.

Chapter 29
Corporate Governance

29-1. What inherent characteristic of corporations creates the need for a system of checks on manager behavior?

The corporation allows for the separation of management and ownership. Thus, those who control the operations of the corporation and how its money is spent are not the same who have invested in the corporation. This creates a clear conflict of interest and this conflict between the investors and managers creates the need for investors to devise a system of checks on managers—the system of corporate governance.

29-2. What are some examples of agency problems?

Examples of agency problems are excessive perquisite consumption (more company jets/company jet travel than needed, nicer office than necessary, etc.). Others are value-destroying acquisitions that nonetheless increase the pecuniary or non-pecuniary benefits to the CEO on net.

29-3. What are the advantages and disadvantages of the corporate organizational structure?

The corporate organizational form allows those who have the capital to fund an enterprise to be different from those who have the expertise to manage the enterprise. This critical separation allows a wide class of investors to share the risk of the enterprise. However, as mentioned in the answer to question 1, this separation comes at a cost—the managers will act in their own best interests, not in the best interests of the shareholders who own the firm.

29-4. What is the role of the board of directors in corporate governance?

The board of directors is the primary internal control mechanism and the first line of defense to prevent fraud, agency conflicts, and mismanagement. The board is empowered to hire and fire managers, set compensation contracts, approve major investment decisions, etc.

29-5. How does a board become captured by a CEO?

Over time, a long-standing CEO can maneuver the nomination process so that his or her associates and friends are nominated to the board. Additionally, board members representing customers, suppliers, or others who have the potential for business relationships with the firm will sometimes compromise their fiduciary duty in order to keep the management of the firm happy. This desire to keep the CEO happy or a reluctance to challenge him or her interferes with the board's primary function of monitoring the management.

29-6. What role do security analysts play in monitoring?

By knowing a company and its industry as well as possible, they are in a position to uncover irregularities. They also participate in earnings calls with the CEO and CFO, asking difficult and probing questions.

29-7. How are lenders part of corporate governance?

Lenders are exposed to the firm as creditors and so are motivated to carefully monitor the firm. They often include covenants in their loans that require the company to maintain certain profitability and liquidity levels. Breaking these covenants can be a warning sign of deeper trouble.

29-8. What is a whistleblower?

Whistleblowers can be anyone but are typically employees who uncover outright wrongdoing and "blow the whistle," on the fraud by reporting it to the authorities.

29-9. What are the advantages and disadvantages of increasing the options granted to CEOs?

The advantages are that, since options increase in value when the firm's stock price increases, the CEO's wealth and incentives will be more closely tied to the shareholders' wealth. The disadvantage is that option grants can increase a CEO's incentives to game the system by timing the release of information to fit the option granting schedule or to artificially smooth earnings.

29-10. Is it necessarily true that increasing managerial ownership stakes will improve firm performance?

No. There are two counter arguments here. First, as Demsetz and Lehn (1985) argue, there is no reason to expect a simple relation between ownership and performance. There are many dimensions to the corporate governance system and a one-size-fits-all approach is too simplistic; the correct ownership level for one firm may not be the correct level for another. Second, some studies have shown a non-linear relationship between firm valuation and ownership—specifically that increasing ownership is good at first, but that in a certain range, managers can use their ownership level to partially block efforts to constrain them, even though they still own a minority of the shares. In this "entrenching" range, increasing ownership could reduce performance.

29-11. How can proxy contests be used to overcome a captured board?

Proxy contests are simply contested elections for directors. In a proxy contest, two competing slates of directors rather than just one slate are proposed by the company. If a board has become captured or unresponsive to shareholder demands, shareholders can put their own slate of new directors up for election. If the dissident slate wins, then shareholders will have succeeded in placing new directors, presumably not beholden to the CEO, on the board.

29-12. What is a say-on-pay vote?

A say-on-pay vote is a non-binding vote whereby the shareholders indicate whether they approve of an executive's pay package or not.

29-13. What are a board's options when confronted with dissident shareholders?

When confronted with a dissident shareholder, a board can:

- Ignore the shareholder, which will result in either the shareholder going away or launching a proxy fight, in which case the board will need to expend resources in an attempt to convince shareholders not to side with the dissident; or
- Negotiate with the dissident shareholder to come to a solution on which the board and the shareholder can agree.

29-14. What is the essential trade-off faced by government in designing regulation of public firms?

The government should be trying to maximize societal welfare. Thus, in designing regulation, it must trade off the effects of direct and indirect enforcement, compliance and other costs associated with regulation against the aggregate benefits that accrue to shareholders and the economy as a whole.

29-15. Many of the provisions of the Sarbanes-Oxley Act of 2002 were aimed at auditors. How does this affect corporate governance?

Auditors are important to corporate governance. Auditors ensure that the financial picture of the firm presented to outside investors is clear and accurate. Part of the role of auditors is to detect financial fraud before it threatens the viability of the firm. Sarbanes-Oxley included measures designed to reduce conflicts of interest among auditors and to increase the penalties for fraud.

29-16. What are the costs and benefits of prohibiting insider trading?

Trading is how prices come to reflect all material information about a company's prospects. By restricting a set of investors from trading, we decrease the efficiency of the prices because it will take longer for the prices to reflect that private information. We rely on efficient prices to make sure that capital is allocated to its best use. While that is a cost of prohibiting insider trading, there is also a benefit. In order for a capital market to fulfill its function, uninformed investors must be willing to invest their money—providing liquidity and lowering the cost of capital. If investors thought that the stock market was just a fools' game where they lost to insiders, they would be unwilling to invest or would price their expected loss into their required return. This increases the cost of capital for companies and slows economic growth.

29-17. How do the laws on insider trading differ for merger- versus non-merger-related trading?

The laws are much stricter for merger-related trading. Anyone who has information about a pending merger is restricted from trading. Non-merger restrictions depend on the source of the material non-public information. If the source violated a fiduciary duty to the shareholders, then the trading is prohibited.

29-18. Are the rights of shareholders better protected in the United States or in France?

They are better protected in the United States. The U.S. legal system is based on British common law, which offers considerably more protection to minority shareholders than French civil law does.

29-19. How can a controlling family use a pyramidal control structure to benefit itself at the expense of other shareholders?

Because pyramidal structures allow a controlling family to control firms in which they have little actual cash flow rights, the family can use their control to move profits away from firms where they get a small percentage of the cash flows to firms in which they can claim a larger fraction of the cash flows. For example, they can have one firm sell to another at a reduced price.

Chapter 30

Risk Management

30-1. The William Companies (WMB) owns and operates natural gas pipelines that deliver 12% of the natural gas consumed in the United States. WMB is concerned that a major hurricane could disrupt its Gulfstream pipeline, which runs 691 miles through the Gulf of Mexico. In the event of a disruption, the firm anticipates a loss of profits of $65 million. Suppose the likelihood of a disruption is 3% per year, and the beta associated with such a loss is −0.25. If the risk-free interest rate is 5% and the expected return of the market is 10%, what is the actuarially fair insurance premium?

From the SML, the required return for a beta of –0.25 is $r_L = 5\% - 0.25(10\% - 5\%) = 3.75\%$. From Eq. 30.1:

$$\text{Premium} = \frac{3\% \times \$65 \text{ million}}{1.0375} = \$1.88 \text{ millon.}$$

30-2. Genentech's main facility is located in South San Francisco. Suppose that Genentech would experience a direct loss of $450 million in the event of a major earthquake that disrupted its operations. The chance of such an earthquake is 2% per year, with a beta of −0.5.

a. If the risk-free interest rate is 5% and the expected return of the market is 10%, what is the actuarially fair insurance premium required to cover Genentech's loss?

b. Suppose the insurance company raises the premium by an additional 15% over the amount calculated in part (a) to cover its administrative and overhead costs. What amount of financial distress or issuance costs would Genentech have to suffer if it were not insured to justify purchasing the insurance?

a. From the SML, the required return for a beta of -0.5 is $r_L = 5\% - 0.5(10\% - 5\%) = 2.5\%$. From Eq. 30.1:

$$\text{Premium} = \frac{2\% \times \$450 \text{ million}}{1.025} = \$8.78 \text{ millon.}$$

b. With 15% overhead costs, the insurance premium will be $8.78 × (1.15) = $10.098 million. Buying insurance is positive NPV for Genentech if it experiences distress or issuance costs equal to 15% of the amount of the loss. That is, it must experience distress or issuance costs of 15% × 450 = $67.5 million in the event of a loss. In that case:

$$\text{NPV(buy insurance)} = -10.098 + \frac{2\% \times \$(450 + 67.5) \text{ million}}{1.025} = 0.$$

30-3. Your firm imports manufactured goods from China. You are worried that U.S.–China trade negotiations could break down next year, leading to a moratorium on imports. In the event of a moratorium, your firm expects its operating profits to decline substantially and its marginal tax rate to fall from its current level of 40% to 10%.

An insurance firm has agreed to write a trade insurance policy that will pay \$500,000 in the event of an import moratorium. The chance of a moratorium is estimated to be 10%, with a beta of −1.5. Suppose the risk-free interest rate is 5% and the expected return of the market is 10%.

a. What is the actuarially fair premium for this insurance?

b. What is the NPV of purchasing this insurance for your firm? What is the source of this gain?

a. From the SML, the required return for a beta of −1.5 is $r_L = 5\% - 1.5(10\% - 5\%) = -2.5\%$. From Eq. 30.1:

$$\text{Premium} = \frac{10\% \times \$500{,}000}{1 - 0.025} = \$51{,}282.$$

b. If we consider after-tax cash flows:

$$\text{NPV} = -51{,}282 \times (1 - 0.40) + \frac{10\% \times \$500{,}000 \times (1 - 0.10)}{1 - 0.025} = \$15{,}385.$$

The gain arises because the firm pays for the insurance when its tax rate is high, but receives the insurance payment when its tax rate is low.

30-4. Your firm faces a 9% chance of a potential loss of \$10 million next year. If your firm implements new policies, it can reduce the chance of this loss to 4%, but these new policies have an upfront cost of \$100,000. Suppose the beta of the loss is 0, and the risk-free interest rate is 5%.

a. If the firm is uninsured, what is the NPV of implementing the new policies?

b. If the firm is fully insured, what is the NPV of implementing the new policies?

c. Given your answer to part (b), what is the actuarially fair cost of full insurance?

d. What is the minimum-size deductible that would leave your firm with an incentive to implement the new policies?

e. What is the actuarially fair price of an insurance policy with the deductible in part (d)?

a. New policies reduce the chance of loss by 9% – 4% = 5%, for an expected savings of 5% × \$10 million = \$500,000. Therefore, the NPV is

NPV = – 100,000 + 500,000/1.05 = \$376,190.

b. If the firm is fully insured, then it will not experience a loss. Thus, there is no benefit to the firm from the new policies. Therefore, NPV = –100,000.

c. If the firm insures fully, it will not have an incentive to implement the new safety policies. Therefore, the insurance company will expected a 9% chance of loss. Therefore, the actuarially fair premium would be

Premium = 9% × \$10 million/1.05 = \$857,143.

d. If the insurance policy has a deductible, then the firm will benefit from the new policies because it will avoid a loss, and therefore avoid paying the deductible, 5% of the time. Let D be the amount of the deductible. Then the NPV of the new policies is NPV = –100,000 + 5%(D)/1.05.

Setting the NPV to 0 and solving for D we get D = \$2.1 million.

e. With a deductible of 2.1 million, the insurance company can expect the firm to implement the new policies. Therefore, it can expect a 4% chance of loss. In the event of a loss, the insurance will pay (10 – 2.1) = \$7.9 million. Therefore:

Premium = 4% × \$7.9 million/1.05 = \$300,952.

Aside: With this policy, the firm will pay \$300,952 for insurance, \$100,000 to implement the new policies, and 4% × \$2.1 million = \$84,000 in expected deductibles. Thus, the firm will pay

\$300,952 + 100,000 + 84,000 = \$484,952 in total, which is much less than the amount it would pay for full insurance in (c).

30-5. BHP Billiton is the world's largest mining firm. BHP expects to produce 2 billion pounds of copper next year, with a production cost of \$0.90 per pound.

a. What will be BHP's operating profit from copper next year if the price of copper is \$1.25, \$1.50, or \$1.75 per pound, and the firm plans to sell all of its copper next year at the going price?

b. What will be BHP's operating profit from copper next year if the firm enters into a contract to supply copper to end users at an average price of \$1.45 per pound?

c. What will be BHP's operating profit from copper next year if copper prices are described as in part (a), and the firm enters into supply contracts as in part (b) for only 50% of its total output?

d. Describe situations for which each of the strategies in parts (a), (b), and (c) might be optimal.

a. Operating profit = 2 billion pounds × (Price per pound – \$0.90/lb). Thus:

Price (\$/lb)	1.25	1.50	1.75
Operating Profit (\$ billion)	0.70	1.20	1.70

b. In this case, they will sell for the contract price of \$1.45/lb, no matter what the spot price of copper is next year:

Contract price (\$/lb)	1.45
Operating Profit (\$ billion)	1.10

That is, Oper Profit = 2 × (1.45 – 0.90) = \$1.10 billion.

c. In this case, Operating Profit = 1 × (1.45 – 0.90) + 1×(Price – 0.90). Therefore:

Contract price (\$/lb)	1.45		
Contract Amount	1.00 billion pounds		
Spot Price (\$/lb)	1.25	1.50	1.75
Operating Profit (\$ billion)	0.90	1.15	1.40

d. Strategy (a) could be optimal if the firm is sufficiently profitable that it will not be distressed even if the copper price next year is low. Equity holders will in this case bear the risk of copper price fluctuations, and there is no gain from hedging the risk. It could also be optimal if the firm is currently in or near financial distress. Then by not hedging, the firm increases its risk. Equity holders can benefit if the price of copper is high, but debt holders suffer if the price is low. (Recall the discussion in Chapter 16 regarding equity holders incentive to increase risk when the firm is in or near financial distress.)

Strategy (b) could be optimal if the firm is not in distress now, but would be if the price of copper next year is low and it does not hedge. Then, by locking in the price it will receive at \$1.45/lb, the firm can avoid financial distress costs next year.

Strategy (c) could be optimal if the firm would risk distress with operating profits of \$0.7 billion from copper but would not with operating profits of \$0.9 billion. In that case, the firm can partially hedge and avoid any risk of financial distress.

30-6. Your utility company will need to buy 100,000 barrels of oil in 10 days time, and it is worried about fuel costs. Suppose you go long 100 oil futures contracts, each for 1000 barrels of oil, at the current futures price of $60 per barrel. Suppose futures prices change each day as follows:

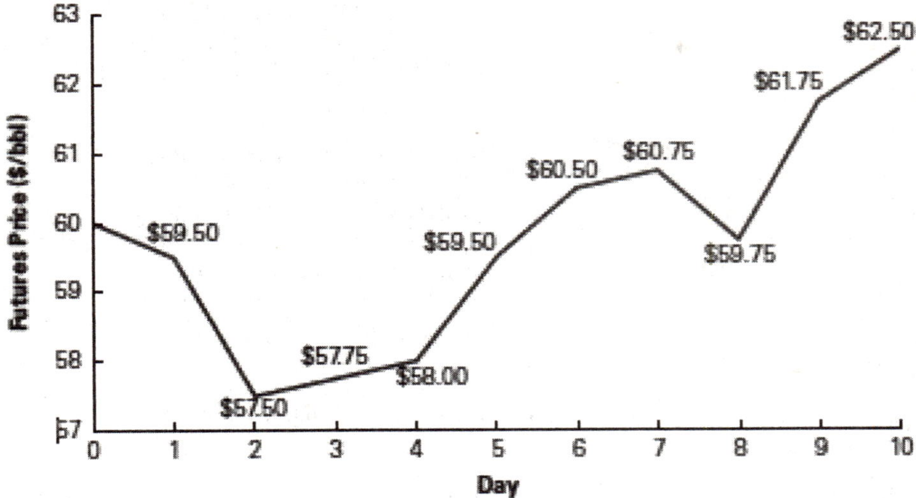

a. What is the mark-to-market profit or loss (in dollars) that you will have on each date?

b. What is your total profit or loss after 10 days? Have you been protected against a rise in oil prices?

c. What is the largest cumulative loss you will experience over the 10-day period? In what case might this be a problem?

a. You have gone long 100 × 1000 = 100,000 barrels of oil. Therefore, the mark-to-market profit or loss will equal 100,000 times the change in the futures price each day.

Day	Price	Price Change	Profit/Loss
0	$ 60.00		
1	$ 59.50	($0.50)	($50,000)
2	$ 57.50	($2.00)	($200,000)
3	$ 57.75	$0.25	$25,000
4	$ 58.00	$0.25	$25,000
5	$ 59.50	$1.50	$150,000
6	$ 60.50	$1.00	$100,000
7	$ 60.75	$0.25	$25,000
8	$ 59.75	($1.00)	($100,000)
9	$ 61.75	$2.00	$200,000
10	$ 62.50	$0.75	$75,000

b. Summing the daily profit/loss amounts, the total is a gain of $250,000. This gain offsets your increase in cost from the overall $2.50 increase in oil prices over the 10 days, which increases your total cost of oil by 100,000 × $2.50 = $250,000.

c. After the second day, you have lost a total of $250,000. This loss could be a problem if you do not have sufficient resources to cover the loss. In that case, your position would have been liquidated on day 2, and you would have been stuck with the loss *and* had to pay the higher cost of oil on day 10.

30-7. Suppose Starbucks consumes 100 million pounds of coffee beans per year. As the price of coffee rises, Starbucks expects to pass along 60% of the cost to its customers through higher prices per cup of coffee. To hedge its profits from fluctuations in coffee prices, Starbucks should lock in the price of how many pounds of coffee beans using supply contracts?

If the price of coffee goes up by \$0.01 per pound, Starbucks' cost of coffee will go up by \$0.01 × 100 million = \$1 million. But because it can charge higher prices, its revenues will go up by 60% × \$1 million = \$0.6 million. To hedge this risk, Starbucks should lock in the price for 40 million pounds of coffee, so that it will only suffer an increase in cost for the remaining 60 million pounds of coffee.

30-8. Your start-up company has negotiated a contract to provide a database installation for a manufacturing company in Poland. That firm has agreed to pay you \$100,000 in three months time when the installation will occur. However, it insists on paying in Polish zloty (PLN). You don't want to lose the deal (the company is your first client!), but are worried about the exchange rate risk. In particular, you are worried the zloty could depreciate relative to the dollar. You contact Fortis Bank in Poland to see if you can lock in an exchange rate for the zloty in advance.

a. You find the following table posted on the bank's Web site, showing zloty per dollar, per euro, and per British pound:

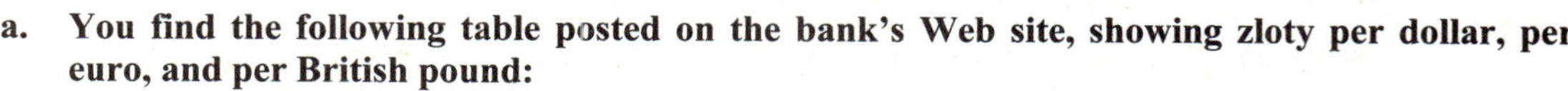

	1 week	2 weeks	1 month	2 months	3 months
			USD		
purchase	3.1433	3.1429	3.1419	3.1390	3.1361
sale	3.1764	3.1761	3.1755	3.1735	3.1712
			EUR		
purchase	3.7804	3.7814	3.7836	3.7871	3.7906
sale	3.8214	3.8226	3.8254	3.8298	3.8342
			GBP		
purchase	5.5131	5.5131	5.5112	5.5078	5.5048
sale	5.5750	5.5750	5.5735	5.5705	5.5681

What exchange rate could you lock in for the zloty in three months? How many zloty should you demand in the contract to receive \$100,000?

b. Given the bank forward rates in part (a), were short-term interest rates higher or lower in Poland than in the United States at the time? How did Polish rates compare to euro or pound rates? Explain.

a. Check out the Web site for Fortis Bank (www.fortisbank.com.pl). In the upper left of the page you can choose "English" from the menu, and then "currency exch." There you will be able to find exchange rates for currency forward contracts. Find the rates that applied on Mar 3, 2006 at 4:15pm. What exchange rate could you lock-in for zloty in three months? How many zloty should you demand in the contract in order to receive \$100,000?

Here is the table from the Web site, showing zloty per $, per euro, and per British pound:

	1 week	2 weeks	1 month	2 months	3 months
USD					
purchase	3.1433	3.1429	3.1419	3.1390	3.1361
sale	3.1764	3.1761	3.1755	3.1735	3.1712
EUR					
purchase	3.7804	3.7814	3.7836	3.7871	3.7906
sale	3.8214	3.8226	3.8254	3.8298	3.8342
GBP					
purchase	5.5131	5.5131	5.5112	5.5078	5.5048
sale	5.5750	5.5750	5.5735	5.5705	5.5681

Thus, you could lock in an exchange rate of 3.1712 zloty per U.S. dollar in three months time through a forward contract with the bank. (Note that when converting zloty to $, you pay the higher rate.) In order to receive $100,000, you would therefore need to write the contract for $100{,}000 \times 3.1712 = 317{,}120$ zloty.

b. The forward rates show that fewer zloty per $ are needed for longer maturities. From Eq 30.3, in terms of zloty per $,

$$F_T = S \times \frac{(1 + r_z)^T}{(1 + r_\$)^T}.$$

Thus, the zloty interest rate is below the $ interest rate.

In general, from Eq. 30.2, we can tell which rate is higher by seeing if the forward rate is above or below the spot rate. From the table, the forward rates appear to be lower for the British pound, so the pound interest rate was higher at the time of these quotes (March 2006). The euro forward rates are higher than the spot rates, however, suggesting that Polish interest rates were higher than those for the euro.

30-9. You are a broker for frozen seafood products for Choyce Products. You just signed a deal with a Belgian distributor. Under the terms of the contract, in one year you will deliver 4000 kilograms of frozen king crab for 100,000 euros. Your cost for obtaining the king crab is $110,000. All cash flows occur in exactly one year.

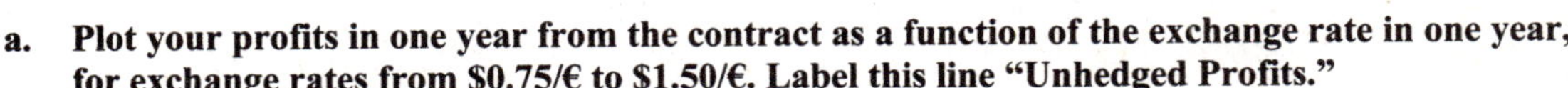

a. Plot your profits in one year from the contract as a function of the exchange rate in one year, for exchange rates from $0.75/€ to $1.50/€. Label this line "Unhedged Profits."

b. Suppose the one-year forward exchange rate is $1.25/€. Suppose you enter into a forward contract to sell the euros you will receive at this rate. In the figure from part (a), plot your combined profits from the crab contract and the forward contract as a function of the exchange rate in one year. Label this line "Forward Hedge."

c. Suppose that instead of using a forward contract, you consider using options. A one-year call option to buy euros at a strike price of $1.25/€ is trading for $0.10/€. Similarly a one year put option to sell euros at a strike price of $1.25/€ is trading for $0.10/€. To hedge the risk of your profits, should you buy or sell the call or the put?

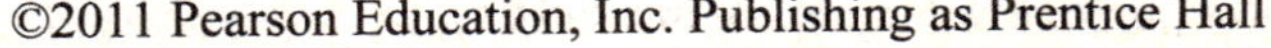

d. In the figure from parts (a) and (b), plot your "all in" profits using the option hedge (combined profits of crab contract, option contract, and option price) as a function of the exchange rate in one year. Label this line "Option Hedge." (*Note* : You can ignore the effect of interest on the option price.)

e. Suppose that by the end of the year, a trade war erupts, leading to a European embargo on U.S. food products. As a result, your deal is cancelled, and you don't receive the euros or incur the costs of procuring the crab. However, you still have the profits (or losses) associated with your forward or options contract. In a new figure, plot the profits associated with the forward hedge and the options hedge (labeling each line). When there is a risk of cancellation, which type of hedge has the least downside risk? Explain briefly.

a. Unhedged profit = (100,000 euros) × (S_1 \$/euro) – 110,000. See figure below.

b. Forward Hedged profit = (100,000 euros) × (1.25 \$/euro) – 110,000 = \$15,000. See figure below.

c. You want to sell euros in exchange for dollars. Thus, buying put options will protect the price at which you can sell euros.

d. Buying put options for 100,000 euros costs 100,000 × \$0.10 = \$10,000.

The put allows you to sell the euros for a minimum of \$1.25/euro. Therefore,

All-in Option hedged profit

= (100,000 euros) × (max[1.25,S_1] \$/euro) – 110,000 – 10,000

= max[\$5,000, (100,000 euros) × (S_1 \$/euro) – 120,000].

See figure below.

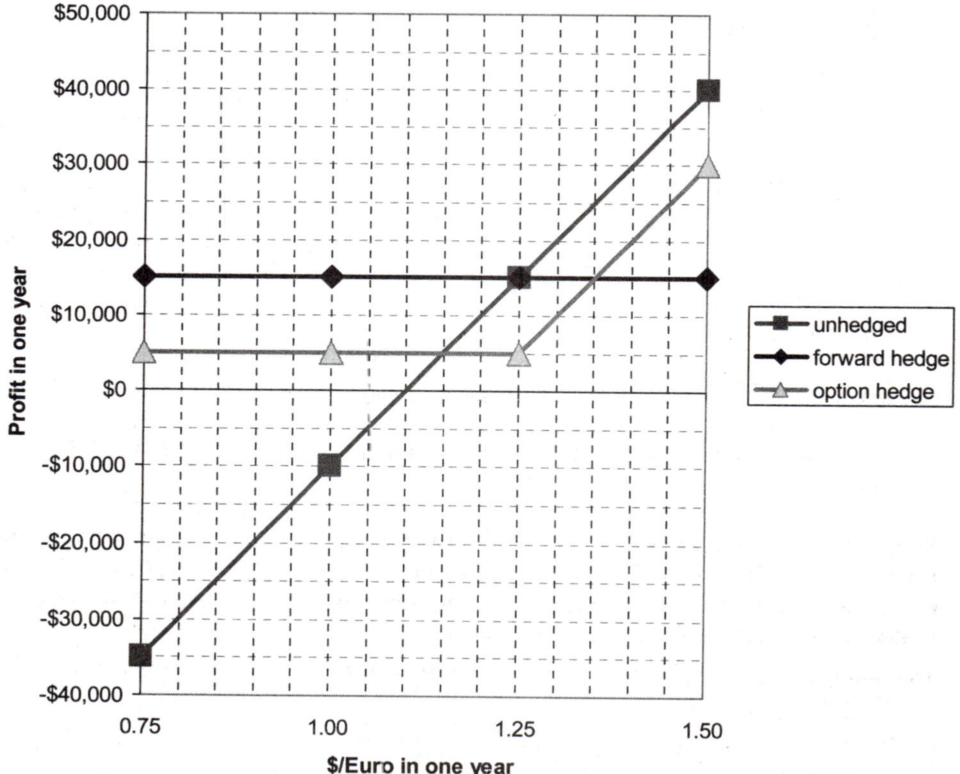

e. For the forward hedge, you receive a payoff from the forward if the value of the euro declines. If the euro appreciates, you have a loss on your forward position. The profit is:

(100,000 euros) × (1.25 – S_1 \$/euro).

If the euro appreciates significantly, the loss from the forward hedge can be very large. (See figure below.)

For the option hedge, you receive a payoff from the put if the value of the euro declines. If the euro appreciates, the put is worthless (and are out the original purchase price of the puts). The profit is:

max[0, (100,000 euros)×(1.25 – S_1 \$/euro)] – 10,000.

With the puts, the maximum loss is their initial cost of \$10,000. (See figure below.)

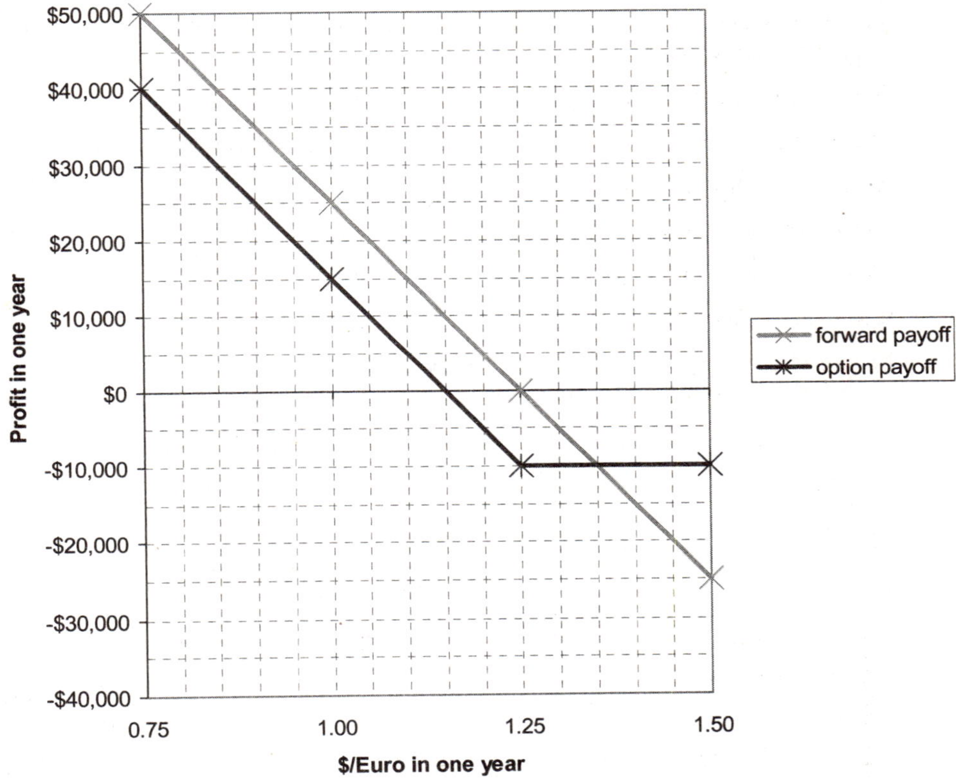

From the picture, an advantage of hedging with options is the limited downside risk in the event of cancellation.

30-10. Suppose the current exchange rate is \$1.80/£, the interest rate in the United States is 5.25%, the interest rate in the United Kingdom is 4%, and the volatility of the \$/£ exchange rate is 10%. Use the Black-Scholes formula to determine the price of a six-month European call option on the British pound with a strike price of \$1.80/£.

The inputs are S = spot exchange rate = 1.80, K = strike price = 1.80, T = 0.5, $r_\$ = 5.25\%$, $r_£ = 4.0\%$, σ = volatility = 10%. From Eq. 30.3,

$F_T = S(1 + r_\$)^T / (1 + r_£)^T = 1.80(1.0525)^{0.5} / (1.04)^{0.5} = \$1.8108/£$.

Therefore, from Eq. 30.5

$$d_1 = \frac{\ln(1.8108/1.80)}{10\%\sqrt{0.5}} + \frac{10\%\sqrt{0.5}}{2} = 0.120\text{, and } d_2 = d_1 - 10\%\sqrt{0.5} = 0.049$$

and so $N(d_1) = 0.548$ and $N(d_1) = 0.520$.

From Eq. 30.4, $C = (1.80 / (1.04)^{0.5}) \times (0.548) - (1.80/(1.0525)^{0.5}) \times (0.520) = \$0.0549$

Thus, the call option price is $0.0549/£.

30-11. Assume each of the following securities has the same yield-to-maturity: a five-year, zero-coupon bond; a nine-year, zero-coupon bond; a five-year annuity; and a nine-year annuity. Rank these securities from lowest to highest duration.

The duration of a security is equal to the weighted-average maturity of its cash flows (Eq. 30.6). Thus, the duration of a five-year zero coupon bond is five years, and the duration of the nine-year zero-coupon bond is nine years (see Ex 30.11).

We cannot determine the durations of the annuities exactly without knowing the current interest rate. But because the cash flows of an annuity are equal and at regular intervals, the duration of an annuity must be less than its average maturity (because weighting by present values will put less weight on later cash flows). Thus, the five-year annuity has a duration of less than (1 + 2 + 3 + 4 + 5) / 5 = 3 years, and the nine-year annuity has a duration of less than (1 + 2 + 3 + 4 + 5 + 6 + 7 + 8 + 9) / 9 = 5 years. The ranking is therefore:

five-year annuity, nine-year annuity, five-year zero, nine-year zero.

30-12. You have been hired as a risk manager for Acorn Savings and Loan. Currently, Acorn's balance sheet is as follows (in millions of dollars):

Assets		Liabilities	
Cash Reserves	50	Checking and Savings	80
Auto Loans	100	Certificates of Deposit	100
Mortgages	150	Long-Term Financing	100
Total Assets	300	Total Liabilities	280
		Owner's Equity	20
		Total Liabilities and Equity	300

When you analyze the duration of loans, find that the duration of the auto loans is two years, while the mortgages have a duration of seven years. Both the cash reserves and the checking and savings accounts have a zero duration. The CDs have a duration of two years and the long-term financing has a 10-year duration.

a. **What is the duration of Acorn's equity?**

b. **Suppose Acorn experiences a rash of mortgage prepayments, reducing the size of the mortgage portfolio from $150 million to $100 million, and increasing cash reserves to $100 million. What is the duration of Acorn's equity now? If interest rates are currently 4% but fall to 3%, estimate the approximate change in the value of Acorn's equity.**

c. **Suppose that after the prepayments in part (b), but before a change in interest rates, Acorn considers managing its risk by selling mortgages and/or buying 10-year Treasury STRIPS (zero-coupon bonds). How many should the firm buy or sell to eliminate its current interest rate risk?**

a. From Eq. 30.8,

$$\text{Asset Duration} = \frac{50}{300}(0\text{yrs}) + \frac{100}{300}(2\text{yrs}) + \frac{150}{300}(7\text{yrs}) = 4.17\text{yrs}$$

$$\text{Liability Duration} = \frac{80}{280}(0\text{yrs}) + \frac{100}{280}(2\text{yrs}) + \frac{100}{280}(10\text{yrs}) = 4.29\text{yrs}$$

From Eq. 30.9,

$$\text{Equity Duration} = \frac{300}{20}(4.17\text{yrs}) - \frac{280}{20}(4.29\text{yrs}) = 2.49\text{yrs}$$

b. $$\text{Asset Duration} = \frac{100}{300}(0\text{yrs}) + \frac{100}{300}(2\text{yrs}) + \frac{100}{300}(7\text{yrs}) = 3.0\text{yrs}$$

$$\text{Equity Duration} = \frac{300}{20}(3.0\text{yrs}) - \frac{280}{20}(4.29\text{yrs}) = -15.0\text{yrs}$$

Therefore, if interest rates drop by 1%, we would expect the value of Acorn's equity to drop by about 15% (or more precisely from Eq. 30.7, 15%/1.04, which equals 14.4%).

c. Acorn would like to increase the duration of its assets, so it should use cash to buy long-term bonds. Because 10-year STRIPS (zero-coupon bonds) have a 10-year duration, we can use Eq. 30.10:

$$\text{Amount} = \frac{\overbrace{(15\text{yrs})}^{\text{change in equity duration}} \times \overbrace{20}^{\text{equity value}}}{\underbrace{10\text{yrs}}_{\text{duration of STRIPS (vs. cash)}}} = 30$$

That is, we should buy $30 million worth of 10-year STRIPS.

30-13. The Citrix Fund has invested in a portfolio of government bonds that has a current market value of $44.8 million. The duration of this portfolio of bonds is 13.5 years. The fund has borrowed to purchase these bonds, and the current value of its liabilities (i.e., the current value of the bonds it has issued) is $39.2 million. The duration of these liabilities is four years. The equity in the Citrix Fund (or its net worth) is obviously $5.6 million. The market-value balance sheet below summarizes this information:

Assets		**Liabilities (Debt) and Equity**	
Portfolio of Government Bonds (duration = 13.5)	$44,800,000	Short- and Long-Term Debt (duration = 4.0)	$39,200,000
		Equity	$5,600,000
Total	$44,800,000	Total	$44,800,000

Assume that the current yield curve is flat at 5.5%. You have been hired by the board of directors to evaluate the risk of this fund.

a. Consider the effect of a surprise increase in interest rates, such that the yields rise by 50 basis points (i.e., the yield curve is now flat at 6%). What would happen to the value of the assets in the Citrix Fund? What would happen to the value of the liabilities? What can you conclude about the change in the value of the equity under these conditions?

b. What is the initial duration of the Citrix Fund (i.e., the duration of the equity)?

c. As a result of your analysis, the board of directors fires the current manager of the fund. You are hired and given the objective of minimizing the fund's exposure to interest rate

fluctuations. You are instructed to do so by liquidating a portion of the fund's assets and reinvesting the proceeds in short-term Treasury bills and notes with an average duration of two years. How many dollars do you need to liquidate and reinvest to minimize the fund's interest rate sensitivity?

d. **Rather than immunizing the fund using the strategy in part (c), you consider using a swap contract. If the duration of a 10-year, fixed-coupon bond is seven years, what is the notational amount of the swap you should enter into? Should you receive or pay the fixed rate portion of the swap?**

a. The duration of the assets is 13.5 years. To estimate the effect of a parallel interest-rate of 0.5%, we use the duration formula:

$$\%\text{change} = -\text{Duration} \times \frac{\varepsilon}{1+r} = -13.5 \times \frac{0.50\%}{1.055} = -6.40\%,$$

or a drop in value of 6.40% × \$44.8 million = \$2.87 million.

Similarly, for the liabilities:

$$\%\text{change} = -\text{Duration} \times \frac{\varepsilon}{1+r} = -4.0 \times \frac{0.50\%}{1.055} = -1.90\%,$$

or a drop in value of 1.90% × \$39.2 million = \$0.74 million.

As a result, the value of equity will decline by about 2.87 – 0.74 = \$2.13 million (a loss of 38% of its value!).

b. From Eq. 30.9:

$$\text{Equity Duration} = \frac{44.8}{5.6}(13.5\text{yrs}) - \frac{39.2}{5.6}(4.0\text{yrs}) = 80\text{yrs}$$

This explains the extreme sensitivity of the equity value to changes in interest rates.

c. Liquidating a portion of the assets and investing in T-bills and notes will reduce the duration of these assets by 13.5 – 2 = 11.5 years. From Eq. 30.10:

$$\text{Amount} = \frac{\overbrace{(80\text{yrs})}^{\text{change in equity duration}} \times \overbrace{5.6}^{\text{equity value}}}{\underbrace{11.5\text{yrs}}_{\text{change in asset duration}}} = \$38.96 \text{ million.}$$

That is, we should liquidate \$38.96 million of the fund's assets.

d. We can also reduce the duration of the fund by entering into a swap contract in which Citrix will receive a floating rate and pay a fixed rate. This swap will increase in value when interest rates rise, offsetting the decline in the value of the rest of the fund. To determine the size of the swap, we proceed as in Ex. 30.14:

$$\text{Amount} = \frac{\overbrace{(80\text{yrs})}^{\text{change in equity duration}} \times \overbrace{5.6}^{\text{equity value}}}{\underbrace{(7.0 - 0.5)\text{yrs}}_{\text{difference in duration of fixed and floating rate 10-yr bond}}} = \$68.92 \text{ million.}$$

That is, we should enter a swap with a notional value of \$68.92 million.

30-14. Your firm needs to raise $100 million in funds. You can borrow short term at a spread of 1% over LIBOR. Alternatively, you can issue 10-year, fixed-rate bonds at a spread of 2.50% over 10-year Treasuries, which currently yield 7.60%. Current 10-year interest rate swaps are quoted at LIBOR versus the 8% fixed rate.

Management believes that the firm is currently "underrated" and that its credit rating is likely to improve in the next year or two. Nevertheless, the managers are not comfortable with the interest rate risk associated with using short-term debt.

a. Suggest a strategy for borrowing the $100 million. What is your effective borrowing rate?

b. Suppose the firm's credit rating does improve three years later. It can now borrow at a spread of 0.50% over Treasuries, which now yield 9.10% for a seven-year maturity. Also, seven-year interest rate swaps are quoted at LIBOR versus 9.50%. How would you lock in your new credit quality for the next seven years? What is your effective borrowing rate now?

a. Borrow $100m short term and paying LIBOR + 1.0%. Then enter a $100m notional swap to receive LIBOR and pay 8.0% fixed. Effective borrowing rate is (LIBOR + 1.0%) – LIBOR + 8.0% = 9.0%.

(Note: borrowing long-term would have cost 7.6% + 2.5% = 10.1%.)

b. Refinance $100m short-term loan with long-term loan at 9.10% + 0.50% = 9.60%. Unwind swap by entering new swap to pay LIBOR and receive 9.50%. Effective borrowing cost now:

9.60% + (–LIBOR + 8.0%) + (LIBOR – 9.50%) = 8.10%.

(Note: This rate is equal to the original long-term rate, less the 2% decline in the firm's credit spread. The firm gets the benefit of its improved credit quality without being exposed to the increase in interest rates that occurred.)

Chapter 31

International Corporate Finance

31-1. You are a U.S. investor who is trying to calculate the present value of a €5 million cash inflow that will occur one year in the future. The spot exchange rate is S = $1.25/€ and the forward rate is F_1 = $1.215/€. You estimate that the appropriate dollar discount rate for this cash flow is 4% and the appropriate euro discount rate is 7%.

a. What is the present value of the €5 million cash inflow computed by first discounting the euro and then converting it into dollars?

b. What is the present value of the €5 million cash inflow computed by first converting the cash flow into dollars and then discounting?

c. What can you conclude about whether these markets are internationally integrated, based on your answers to parts (a) and (b)?

a. $€5/(1.07) \times 1.25 = \$5.84112$ million

b. $(€5 \times 1.214953)/1.04 = \$5.84112$ million

c. Yes, the markets are internationally integrated because the answers to (a) and (b) are identical.

31-2. Mia Caruso Enterprises, a U.S. manufacturer of children's toys, has made a sale in Cyprus and is expecting a C£4 million cash inflow in one year. (The currency of Cyprus is the Cypriot pound, C£. Cyprus is a member of the European Union, but has not yet adopted the euro.) The current spot rate is S = $1.80/C£ and the one-year forward rate is F_1 = $1.8857/C£.

a. What is the present value of Mia Caruso's C£4 million inflow computed by first discounting the cash flow at the appropriate Cypriot pound discount rate of 5%, and then converting the result into dollars?

b. What is the present value of Mia Caruso's C£4 million inflow computed by first converting the cash flow into dollars, and then discounting at the appropriate dollar discount rate of 10%?

c. What can you conclude about whether these markets are internationally integrated, based on your answers to parts (a) and (b)?

a. $C£4/(1.05) \times 1.80 = \$6.8571$ million

b. $C£4/(1.10) \times 1.885 = \$6.8545$ million

c. No, the markets are not internationally integrated because the answers to (a) and (b) are not the same.

31-3. **Etemadi Amalgamated, a U.S. manufacturing firm, is considering a new project in the euro area. You are in Etemadi's corporate finance department and are responsible for deciding whether to undertake the project. The expected free cash flows, in euros, are shown here:**

Year	Free Cash Flow (€ millions)
0	−15
1	9
2	10
3	11
4	12

You know that the spot exchange rate is S = $1.15/€. In addition, the risk-free interest rate on dollars is 4% and the risk-free interest rate on euros is 6%.

Assume that these markets are internationally integrated and the uncertainty in the free cash flows is not correlated with uncertainty in the exchange rate. You determine that the dollar WACC for these cash flows is 8.5%. What is the dollar present value of the project? Should Etemadi Amalgamated undertake the project?

First, calculate the forward rates:

$$F_1 = (\$1.15/€)\frac{(1.04)}{(1.06)} = \$1.1283/€$$

$$F_2 = (\$1.15/€)\frac{(1.04)^2}{(1.06)^2} = \$1.1070/€$$

$$F_3 = (\$1.15/€)\frac{(1.04)^3}{(1.06)^3} = \$1.0861/€$$

$$F_4 = (\$1.15/€)\frac{(1.04)^4}{(1.06)^4} = \$1.0656/€$$

Next, convert euro cash flows into dollars:

Year	Euro Cash Flow	Exchange Rate	Dollar Cash Flow
0	−15	1.1500	−17.250
1	9	1.1283	10.155
2	10	1.1070	11.070
3	11	1.0861	11.947
4	12	1.0656	12.788

Finally, the net present value is:

$$\text{NPV} = -17.250 + \frac{10.154}{1.085} + \frac{11.070}{1.085^2} + \frac{11.947}{1.085^3} + \frac{12.788}{1.085^4} = \$20.094 \text{ million.}$$

Etemadi Amalgamated should undertake the project because the net present value is positive.

31-4. Etemadi Amalgamated, the U.S. manufacturing company in Problem 3, is still considering a new project in the euro area. All information presented in Problem 3 is still accurate, except the spot rate is now S = \$0.85/€, about 26% lower. What is the new present value of the project in dollars? Should Etemadi Amalgamated undertake the project?

With the 26% drop in the spot rate, the forward rates need to be recalculated:

$$F_1 = (\$0.85/€)\frac{(1.04)}{(1.06)} = \$0.83396/€$$

$$F_2 = (\$0.85/€)\frac{(1.04)^2}{(1.06)^2} = \$0.81823/€$$

$$F_3 = (\$0.85/€)\frac{(1.04)^3}{(1.06)^3} = \$0.80279/€$$

$$F_4 = (\$0.85/€)\frac{(1.04)^4}{(1.06)^4} = \$0.78764/€$$

Next, euro cash flows are reconverted into dollars:

Year	Euro Cash Flow	Exchange Rate	Dollar Cash Flow
0	–15	0.85000	–12.750
1	9	0.83396	7.506
2	10	0.81823	8.182
3	11	0.80279	8.831
4	12	0.78764	9.452

Finally, the net present value is:

$$NPV = -12.750 + \frac{7.505}{1.085} + \frac{8.182}{1.085^2} + \frac{8.831}{1.085^3} + \frac{9.452}{1.085^4} = \$14.852 \text{ million.}$$

Etemadi Amalgamated should still undertake the project because the net present value is positive. Note that this is 26% lower than the answer in 31-5, which is consistent with the 26% drop in the spot exchange rate.

31-5. You work for a U.S. firm, and your boss has asked you to estimate the cost of capital for countries using the euro. You know that S = \$1.20/€ and F_1 = \$1.157/€. Suppose the dollar WACC for your company is known to be 8%. If these markets are internationally integrated, estimate the euro cost of capital for a project with free cash flows that are uncorrelated with spot exchange rates. Assume the firm pays the same tax rate no matter where the cash flows are earned.

The Law of One Price tells us: $\left(1 + r_€^*\right) = \frac{S}{F}\left(1 + r_\$^*\right)$.

As a result, we have: $r_€^* = \frac{S}{F}\left(1 + r_\$^*\right) - 1 = \frac{1.2}{1.157} \times \left(1 + 0.08\right) - 1 = 12.014\%$.

31-6. Maryland Light, a U.S. light fixtures manufacturer, is considering an investment in Japan. The dollar cost of equity for Maryland Light is 11%. You are in the corporate treasury department, and you need to know the comparable cost of equity in Japanese yen for a project with free cash flows that are uncorrelated with spot exchange rates. The risk-free interest rates on dollars and

yen are $r_\$ = 5\%$ and $r_¥ = 1\%$, respectively. Maryland Light is willing to assume that capital markets are internationally integrated. What is the yen cost of equity?

Using the formula for the Internationalization of the Cost of Capital, we have: $1 + r_¥^* = \frac{1 + r_¥}{1 + r_\$}(1 + r_\$^*)$.

As a result, we obtain:

$$r_¥^* = \frac{1 + r_¥}{1 + r_\$}(1 + r_\$^*) - 1 = \frac{1 + 0.01}{1 + 0.05} \times (1 + 0.11) - 1 = 6.771\%.$$

31-7. The dollar cost of debt for Coval Consulting, a U.S. research firm, is 7.5%. The firm faces a tax rate of 30% on all income, no matter where it is earned. Managers in the firm need to know its yen cost of debt because they are considering launching a new bond issue in Tokyo to raise money for a new investment there. The risk-free interest rates on dollars and yen are $r_\$ = 5\%$ and $r_¥ = 1\%$, respectively. Coval Consulting is willing to assume that capital markets are internationally integrated and that its free cash flows are uncorrelated with the yen-dollar spot rate. What is Coval Consulting's after-tax cost of debt in yen? (*Hint* : Start by finding the after-tax cost of debt in dollars and then find the yen equivalent.)

The after-tax cost of debt in dollars is (0.075)(1 – 0.30) = 0.0525 or 5.25%.

Using the formula for the Internationalization of the Cost of Capital, we have: $1 + r_¥^* = \frac{1 + r_¥}{1 + r_\$}(1 + r_\$^*)$.

As a result, we obtain:

$$r_¥^* = \frac{1 + r_¥}{1 + r_\$}(1 + r_\$^*) - 1 = \frac{1 + 0.01}{1 + 0.05} \times (1 + 0.0525) - 1 = 1.24\%.$$

31-8. Manzetti Foods, a U.S. food processing and distribution company, is considering an investment in the euro area. You are in Manzetti's corporate finance department and are responsible for deciding whether to undertake the project. The expected free cash flows, in euros, are uncorrelated to the spot exchange rate and are shown here:

Year	Free Cash Flow (€ millions)
0	–25
1	12
2	14
3	15
4	15

The new project has similar dollar risk to Manzetti's other projects. The company knows that its overall dollar WACC is 9.5%, so it feels comfortable using this WACC for the project. The risk-free interest rate on dollars is 4.5% and the risk-free interest rate on euros is 7%.

a. Manzetti is willing to assume that capital markets in the United States and the euro area are internationally integrated. What is the company's euro WACC?

b. What is the present value of the project in euros?

a. Using the formula for the Internationalization of the Cost of Capital, we have:

$$1 + r_€^* = \frac{1 + r_€}{1 + r_\$}(1 + r_\$^*).$$

As a result, we obtain:

$$r_{€}^{*} = \frac{1+r_{€}}{1+r_{\$}}(1+r_{\$}^{*}) - 1 = \frac{1+0.07}{1+0.045} \times (1+0.095) - 1 = 12.12\% .$$

b. $\text{NPV} = -25 + \frac{12}{1.1212} + \frac{14}{1.1212^2} + \frac{15}{1.1212^3} + \frac{15}{1.1212^4} = €16.975 \text{ million.}$

31-9. Tailor Johnson, a U.S. maker of fine menswear, has a subsidiary in Ethiopia. This year, the subsidiary reported and repatriated earnings before interest and taxes (EBIT) of 100 million Ethiopian birrs. The current exchange rate is 8 birr/\$ or *S*1 = \$0.125/birr. The Ethiopian tax rate on this activity is 25%. U.S. tax law requires Tailor Johnson to pay taxes on the Ethiopian earnings at the same rate as profits earned in the United States, which is currently 45%. However, the United States gives a full tax credit for foreign taxes paid up to the amount of the U.S. tax liability. What is Tailor Johnson's U.S. tax liability on its Ethiopian subsidiary?

With earnings of 100 million birrs and the Ethiopian tax rate of 25%, the tax paid in Ethiopia is 25 million birrs. With an exchange rate of 0.125/birr, the earnings amount to \$12.5 million and the Ethiopian taxes amount to \$3.125 million. With a tax rate of 45%, the U.S. tax on Tailor Johnson's Ethiopian income would be $0.45 \times 12.5 = \$5.625$ million. However, Tailor Johnson is able to claim a tax credit of \$3.125, for a net tax liability of 5.625 – 3.125 = \$2.5 million.

31-10. Tailor Johnson, the menswear company with a subsidiary in Ethiopia described in Problem 9, is considering the tax benefits resulting from deferring repatriation of the earnings from the subsidiary. Under U.S. tax law, the U.S. tax liability is not incurred until the profits are brought back home. Tailor Johnson reasonably expects to defer repatriation for 10 years, at which point the birr earnings will be converted into dollars at the prevailing spot rate, S_{10}, and the tax credit for Ethiopian taxes paid will still be converted at the exchange rate S_1 = \$0.125/birr. Tailor Johnson's after-tax cost of debt is 5%.

a. Suppose the exchange rate in 10 years is identical to this year's exchange rate, so S_{10} = \$0.125/birr. What is the present value of deferring the U.S. tax liability on Tailor Johnson's Ethiopian earnings for 10 years?

b. How will the exchange rate in 10 years affect the actual amount of the U.S. tax liability? Write an equation for the U.S. tax liability as a function of the exchange rate *S*10.

a. From question 31-9, the tax liability is \$2.5 million. Deferred for 10 years, using the after-tax cost of debt at 5%, the present value is $2.5/1.05^{10} = \$1.53$ million. Hence, the value of deferral is 2.5 – 1.53 = \$0.97 million.

b. The earnings will need to be converted at the future exchange rate, S_{10}, although the tax credit will still be calculated at $S_1 = \$0.125/\text{birr}$. Hence, the U.S. tax liability will be $(0.45)(S_{10})(100) - 3.125$.

31-11. Peripatetic Enterprises, a U.S. import-export trading firm, is considering its international tax situation. U.S. tax law requires U.S. corporations to pay taxes on their foreign earnings at the same rate as profits earned in the United States; this rate is currently 45%. However, a full tax credit is given for the foreign taxes paid up to the amount of the U.S. tax liability. Peripatetic has major operations in Poland, where the tax rate is 20%, and in Sweden, where the tax rate is 60%. The profits, which are fully and immediately repatriated, and foreign taxes paid for the current year are shown here:

	Poland	Sweden
Earnings before interest and taxes (EBIT)	\$80 million	\$100 million
Host country taxes paid	\$16 million	\$60 million
Earnings before interest after taxes	\$64 million	\$40 million

a. **What is the U.S. tax liability on the earnings from the Polish subsidiary assuming the Swedish subsidiary did not exist?**

b. **What is the U.S. tax liability on the earnings from the Swedish subsidiary assuming the Polish subsidiary did not exist?**

c. **Under U.S. tax law, Peripatetic is able to pool the earnings from its operations in Poland and Sweden when computing its U.S. tax liability on foreign earnings. Total EBIT is thus \$180 million and the total host country taxes paid is \$76 million. What is the total U.S. tax liability on foreign earnings? Show how this relates to the answers in parts (a) and (b).**

a. The net U.S. tax liability, after claiming the credit for taxes paid in Poland, is $(0.45)(80) - 16 = \$20$ million.

b. The net U.S. tax liability, after claiming the credit for taxes paid in Sweden, is $(0.45)(100) - 60 = -\$15$ million. However, the use of the tax credit is limited to the U.S. tax liability, so the liability is actually zero. This is an excess tax credit of \$15 million that is lost.

c. Pooling the Polish and Swedish subsidiaries, the net U.S. tax liability is: $(0.45)(180) - 76 = \$5$ million. By pooling, Peripatetic Enterprises is able to use the \$15 million excess tax credit from earnings in Sweden to offset \$15 million of the \$20 million net tax liability from earnings in Poland, leaving a net U.S. tax liability of \$5 million.

31-12. Suppose the interest on Russian government bonds is 7.5%, and the current exchange rate is 28 rubles per dollar. If the forward exchange rate is 28.5 rubles per dollar, and the current U.S. risk-free interest rate is 4.5%, what is the implied credit spread for Russian government bonds?

From Eq 30.3 (covered interest parity), the forward and spot ruble/\$ exchange rates satisfy:

$$F = S \times \frac{1 + r_R}{1 + r_\$}$$

where r_R and $r_\$$ are risk-free interest rates in rubles and dollars respectively. With this equation we can use the spot and forward exchange rates, and the risk-free \$ interest rate, to solve for the risk-free ruble interest rate:

$$28.5 = 28 \times \frac{1 + r_R}{1.045}, \text{ which implies } r_R = 28.5 \times \frac{1.045}{28} - 1 = 6.37\%.$$

Therefore, the implied risk-free ruble interest rate is 6.37%, implying that Russian government bonds have an implied credit spread of 7.5% – 6.37% = 1.13% to compensate investors for the possibility of the Russian government defaulting.

(See example 31.3 for a similar problem. Note also that an investor can obtain a risk-free investment in rubles by exchange rubles for \$ at the spot rate of 28 rubles/\$, investing in U.S. Treasuries at 4.5%, and locking in a forward exchange rate of 28.5 rubles/\$ to convert the proceeds back to rubles. The rate r_R computed above is the effective return from this transaction.)

31-13. Assume that in the original Ityesi example in Table 31.1, all sales actually occur in the United States and are projected to be $60 million per year for four years. Keeping other costs the same, calculate the NPV of the investment opportunity.

The solution to this problem is in the following Excel spreadsheet:

	0	1	2	3	4
Sales in UK		0	0	0	0
Cost of Sales		-15.625	-15.625	-15.625	-15.625
Gross Profit		-15.625	-15.625	-15.625	-15.625
Operating Expenses	-4.167	-5.625	-5.625	-5.625	-5.625
Depreciation		-3.75	-3.75	-3.75	-3.75
EBIT	-4.167	-25	-25	-25	-25
Less: Taxes	1.667	-5	-5	-5	-5
Plus: Depreciation		3.75	3.75	3.75	3.75
Less: Capital Expenditures	-15				
FCF (£ millions)	**-17.500**	**-26.250**	**-26.250**	**-26.250**	**-26.250**
Forward Exchange Rate	1.6000	1.5551	1.5115	1.4692	1.4280
FCF ($ millions)	**-28.000**	**-40.822**	**-39.678**	**-38.565**	**-37.484**
Sales in the US		60	60	60	60
CF ($ millions)	-28.000	19.178	20.322	21.435	22.516
WACC	6.80%				
NPV ($ millions)	**42.6749**